WRIGHT ON EXHIBIT

WRIGHT ON EXHIBIT

Frank Lloyd Wright's Architectural Exhibitions

KATHRYN SMITH

Princeton University Press
Princeton and Oxford

Wright on Exhibit features extensive images from the Frank Lloyd Wright Foundation Archives (Museum of Modern Art, New York / Avery Architectural and Fine Arts Library, Columbia University, New York). The author and publisher express their gratitude to all three organizations for the use of these images.

To Randy

Published by Princeton University Press, 41 William Street, Princeton, New Jersey 08540
In the United Kingdom: Princeton University Press, 6 Oxford Street, Woodstock, Oxfordshire OX20 1TR

press.princeton.edu

Jacket illustrations (*front*): Frank Lloyd Wright installing *Sixty Years of Living Architecture*, Solomon R. Guggenheim Museum, New York, 1953. © 2017 Pedro E. Guerrero Archives. (*back*) Frank Lloyd Wright exhibition, Chicago Architectural Club, Art Institute of Chicago, 1907. Photograph by Henry Fuermann and Sons (FLWFA, 0700.0004).

Frontispiece: Frank Lloyd Wright with Price Tower model, *Sixty Years of Living Architecture*, Solomon R. Guggenheim Museum, New York, 1953. Photograph by Pedro E. Guerrero. (© 2017 Pedro E. Guerrero Archives)

Page x: Frank Lloyd Wright looking at the Wingspread, Herbert Johnson House, model at the Hillside Drafting Studio, Taliesin, with models—*foreground to background*: Suntop Homes, SC Johnson Administration Building, Jester House—for the 1940 MoMA retrospective. (Courtesy SC Johnson Foundation)

Library of Congress Cataloging-in-Publication Data

Names: Smith, Kathryn, 1945- author.
Title: Wright on exhibit : Frank Lloyd Wright's architectural exhibitions / Kathryn Smith.
Description: Princeton : Princeton University Press, 2017. | Includes bibliographical references and index.
Identifiers: LCCN 2016025182 | ISBN 9780691167220 (hardcover : alk. paper)
Subjects: LCSH: Wright, Frank Lloyd, 1867–1959—Criticism and interpretation. | Wright, Frank Lloyd, 1867–1959—Exhibitions.
Classification: LCC NA737.W7 S434 2017 | DDC 720.92—dc23
LC record available at https://lccn.loc.gov/2016025182

British Library Cataloging-in-Publication Data is available

Designed by Rita Jules and Anjali Pala, Miko McGinty Inc.

This book has been composed in Equity Text and Akkurat

Printed on acid-free paper. ∞

Printed in China

10 9 8 7 6 5 4 3 2 1

Contents

Acknowledgments

This book was researched and written over the course of a decade and draws on a lifetime in the study of Frank Lloyd Wright in the United States, Europe, and Japan. The idea of *Wright on Exhibit* came about after the bulk of the Frank Lloyd Wright correspondence from the Archives at the Frank Lloyd Wright Foundation, Taliesin West, was duplicated on microfiche and put on deposit at the Getty Research Institute, Los Angeles. I had long known that one of the biggest mysteries of Wright's career was the unpublished catalog for his 1940–41 career retrospective, *Frank Lloyd Wright: American Architect*, at the Museum of Modern Art. Robert L. Sweeney had cited several of the essays—which had appeared in journals in the 1940s—in his *Frank Lloyd Wright: An Annotated Bibliography* (1976). However, the complete contents of the catalog were still unknown as was the reason the publication never appeared.

I began research in the correspondence files, and two events followed soon thereafter. The first was the opportunity to present my preliminary findings at the Frank Lloyd Wright Building Conservancy conference at White Plains, New York, in 2002. Some months later, Peter Reed, then curator in MoMA's Department of Architecture and Design, invited me to write the principal essay, "The Show to End All Shows: Frank Lloyd Wright and the Museum of Modern Art, 1940," for *Studies in Modern Art* 8 (2004), part of a publication on the 1940–41 exhibition that the Modern had been planning for some time. My aim was to provide an account of the exhibition and the unpublished catalog as well as to analyze Wright's relationship to his critics, the architectural profession, and the museum in the years leading up to his career retrospective. MoMA generously opened their archives to me; I benefited immeasurably from the scholarship and expertise of John Elderfield, Reed, and William Kaizen, and I am grateful to the museum for the opportunity to publish in their series, *Studies in Modern Art*, from which parts of this book have been based. The MoMA publication has become the definitive account of a pivotal event in Wright's exhibition history.

As a result of these experiences, I was encouraged to expand the topic to include all of Wright's architectural exhibitions (as distinct from the exhibitions he curated and designed on Asian art) during his lifetime. Although the major ones were known, I had no idea how many I would eventually discover. In the ensuing years, I have incurred debts to people, archives, libraries, and private collections too numerous to mention.

This book would not exist without the cooperation of the Frank Lloyd Wright Foundation. From my first trip to examine drawings in the archives in March 1975, Bruce Brooks Pfeiffer, director, gave unstintingly of his time and knowledge. I especially wish to express gratitude to Margo Stipe, Oskar Muñoz, and Indira Berndtson, who lent their valuable assistance to me on innumerable occasions. It is impossible to overstate the magnitude of their contributions to this book.

Research for this study was made possible by a National Endowment for the Humanities Fellowship. The American Heritage Center, University of Wyoming, facilitated my research with a travel grant to Laramie. The Frank Lloyd Wright Building Conservancy on two occasions provided me with a public forum to present my preliminary findings.

For his encouragement and support from the early stages of research to the beginning of the publication process, I am indebted to Neil Levine. It is a pleasure to acknowledge his assistance at points of critical juncture, which made this book far better. For continuous support on almost a weekly basis, I would like to thank Thomas S. Hines, with whom I shared triumphs and frustrations. His encouragement was important at every turning point. I conducted an oral history, "Taliesin Drawings," in March 1987 of the late John H. Howe, Wright's chief draftsman between 1932 and 1959. I am grateful to him and to his wife, Lu, for their cooperation and hospitality during that interview. I owe a great deal to David Michael Hertz, who steered me in the right direction when I needed it the most.

My research was carried out in a number of institutions. I wish especially to thank Wim de Wit and the staff of the Getty Research Institute, Los Angeles—Susan Flanigan, Jay Gam, Ross Garcia, Mahsa Hatam, Mark Henderson, Christian Huemer, Karen Lanzoni, Jane Mandel, Sally McKay, Alexa Sekyra, Charlie Rossow, and Ted Walbye. I would also like to express special gratitude to Barry Bergdoll of the Museum of Modern Art and the archivists, Michelle Elligott and Michelle Harvey, and Thomas Grischkowski, MoMA Archives, Photographic Archives; Paul Galloway, Architecture and Design Study Center, MoMA; Ellen Moody, and Reiko Sunami Kopelson. I am indebted to Erica Stoller (Esto) for her gracious assistance with photographs by Ezra Stoller.

I am also grateful to the following institutions, which provided access to and assistance with visual resources: Avery Architectural and Fine Arts Library, Columbia University, New York (Janet Parks, Margaret Smithglass, Nicole L. Richard, Jason Escalante); American Heritage Center, University of Wyoming, Laramie (Leslie Shores, Mark A. Greene, Rick Ewig, Ginny Kilander, John R. Waggener, Hailey Kaylene Woodall); Archives of American Art, Smithsonian Institution, Washington, DC (Elizabeth Willson Christopher, Wendy Hurlock Baker, Darcy Tell); Ryerson and Burnham Libraries, Art Institute of Chicago (Mary Woolever, Serena Washington); Pedro E. Guerrero Archives (Dixie Guerrero); Wisconsin State Historical Society, Madison (Andy Kraushaar, Jack Holzhueter, David Benjamin, Lisa Marine); Fondazione Centro Studi Di Licia e Carlo Ludivico Ragghianti, Lucca, Italy (Valentina Del Frate); Rare Book and Manuscript Library, Butler Library, Columbia University (Jennifer B. Lee); Metropolitan Museum of Art Archives, New York (James Moske); Chicago History Museum (Dana Lamparello, Lesley Martin, Angela Hoover); Carnegie Library of Pittsburgh (Gilbert Pietzrak); Marin County Civic Center (Laurie Thompson, Carol Acquaviva); University of Wisconsin–Milwaukee Libraries, Archives / Milwaukee Area Research Center, Wisconsin Historical Society; Special Collections Research Center, University of Chicago Library (Daniel Meyer, Barbara Gilbert, Christine Colburn); Boston Public Library; SC Johnson Foundation (Board of Trustees, Terri Boesel, Barbara Suprak, Helen Lukas); DeGolyer Library, Southern Methodist University, Dallas (Anne E. Peterson, Terre Heydari, Katie Dziminski); Huntington Library (Brian Moeller); Library of Congress (Kelly Dyson); Pennsylvania State University Libraries (James P. Quigley Jr., Alexandra Bainbridge, Tim Babcock); Leavenworth Photography (Roger Boettcher); Wellesley College Archives (Laura Reiner); Greenbelt Museum, Greenbelt, Maryland (Megan Searing Young); Prince George's County Memorial Library System, Greenbelt, Maryland (Elizabeth Wilkins); Art Resource Inc. (Liz Kurtulik Mercuri, Ann Miniutti); Archivio Foto Locchi, Florence, Italy (Erika Ghilardi); Getty Images (Martha McClintock); Guggenheim Museum (Kim Bush).

Many individuals aided greatly with both the text and illustrations. To Filippo Fici, whose name appears frequently in the notes, I extend my gratitude for his aid with and insights into Wright's associations with Italy. For generously sharing their knowledge, I would like to thank Robert Wojtowicz, Helen Searing, Pierluigi Serraino, Bill Hasbrouck, Ernst J. Wasmuth and his niece, Christiane Starck, Mosette Broderick, M. J. Hamilton, Jan Novie, Kai Gutschow, William J. Schwarz, George Nichols, Doris Berger, David Jameson, John Geiger, Phil Feddersen, Casie Kesterman, Susan Morgan, Ferruccio Canali, Valentina La Salvia, and Paul Turner. Donald Kalec provided unique color images of Wright's models from his personal collection. Invaluable help was given in Japan by Atsuko Tanaka, Karen Severns, and Koichi Mori. Randolph Henning, William Blair Scott, and Douglas Steiner generously provided fine copy digital images from their collections. Eric O'Malley gave generously of his expertise and performed miracles with the mysteries of the digital world. And to Z.C.M.O., who remained in the background, but whose presence was always felt.

Special thanks to Princeton University Press, particularly to Michelle Komie, executive editor, for her encouragement and guidance. Throughout the editorial process, Terri O'Prey provided essential help when it was needed most. Steven Sears was skillful with the digital images. Gratitude is also owed to Dawn Hall for an excellent job of copyediting. Miko McGinty made an artful blend of text and images in her splendid book design.

My greatest debt is to my husband, Randall H. Kennon. This book is dedicated to him.

WRIGHT ON EXHIBIT

Chicago Architectural Club, 1894–1914

When Frank Lloyd Wright (1867–1959), not quite twenty, left Wisconsin in 1887 to make his way as an architect, he was fortunate that the closest major city was Chicago, still in the midst of a building boom brought on by the devastating 1871 conflagration that destroyed the heart of the pre–Civil War city (figure 1.1). Amid the teeming activity of the downtown Loop, Wright soon identified the most progressive architectural firms, those applying industrial construction techniques to the problems of new building typologies. On the brink of what was then the most creative period of commercial design in the world, he was lucky in 1888 to find employment with two professionals about to make history: Dankmar Adler and Louis Sullivan.

By his choice of Chicago, Wright was thrust into the most crucial debate of late nineteenth-century architecture: whether the social and technical consequences of the Industrial Revolution would lead in the field of architecture to the rejection of historic styles—in other words, "eclecticism"—in favor of a new design methodology. As Adler declared in 1886, "How great is the privilege granted us, in being part, not of a Renaissance, but of a naissance in architecture. For there is surely being born into our world a new style, the style of America, the style of the civilization of the nineteenth century, developed by its wants, its conditions and limitations."[1]

It now seems destined that Wright, who had voluntarily left the university before graduation, would spend his formative years, 1888–93, under the tutelage of Sullivan. While steel frame office buildings were being transformed by his "Lieber Meister" into vertical towers, the raging argument of the day remained whether European styles should continue to be imposed on American conditions. Sullivan interpreted the argument in literary terms, borrowing from his heroes: Ralph Waldo Emerson and Walt Whitman. "Before we can have an indigenous architecture, the American architect must himself become indigenous," Sullivan explained in 1899. "How this is to be done is very easy to explain, but rather difficult of performance; for it is equivalent to asking him to become a poet, in the sense that he must absorb into his heart and brain his own country and his own people."[2]

At the center of Sullivan's ideology was democracy, which he spelled with a capital "D," acknowledging that "what we call Democracy or The New Way, is but the ancient primordial urge within us of integrity or oneness." Referring back to "Nature," the "urge" as an "organic law" was the "essential nature of Democracy. For Democracy and the oneness of all things are one."[3] Yet Sullivan believed that neither the true indigenous American architecture nor Democracy, the two inextricably linked, had yet been achieved. To accomplish these ends required an immense effort because, "Should anything come fresher from the soil of a richly cultivated nature, should anything be more natural, more spontaneous, in its unfolding plan, should anything, can anything come straighter from the life of the people, straighter from the heart, the brain, of the artist than a truly fine building?"[4] Calling the architecture all around him "hideous," and the cause of both "shame" and "humiliation," he now declared "the beauteous art of architecture, as a once living presence in the heart of man," now "dead and gone." But "if there is to be a new art, there must be a new birth." Sullivan's conclusion made in 1897, only four years after Wright left the firm, stated that the realization of a truly indigenous American architecture, grounded in the organic

1.1 Frank Lloyd Wright, ca. 1895. (FLWFA, 6002.003)

laws of Nature, that itself would realize Democracy, "awaits only the coming of a great, an intense, personality:—a man of passion:—with a great and beautiful architecture in his heart."[5]

These ideas resonated with many in the Chicago architectural community in the 1880s and 1890s, especially the younger generation. The battleground came with the founding of a new organization that brought together both experienced professionals and novices. Within it, Wright would find comrades of like mind, a showcase for his accomplishments, and a training ground for publicly presenting his work, and of this last, he would hold to its lessons for the remainder of his life.

CHICAGO ARCHITECTURAL CLUB

The Chicago Architectural Club (the Chicago Architectural Sketch Club at its origin in 1885 until the name change in 1895) began as an educational venture. The club scheduled lectures, design competitions, social activities, and their main public event—an annual exhibition—so that draftsmen could improve their skills by exposure to the senior men. Although such clubs existed in other major American cities—for instance, Boston and Philadelphia—in the late nineteenth century unique regional circumstances crafted a creative synergy in Chicago.[6] Chicago as the growing commercial center of the Midwest was meeting the demand for tall towers, which maximized the potential profit of land, and, at the same time, kept construction costs low. Access to new materials such as steel and plate glass and inventions such as the elevator revolutionized the design of office buildings, hotels, and department stores. Architectural firms such as Adler and Sullivan, Burnham and Root, Holabird and Roche, and William Le Baron Jenny were leaders in engineering techniques and design solutions for modern building types. After direct experience with the new architecture, when the younger generation matured and left the large firms to start their own practices they carried with them doubts about the authority of historical styles. Lively debate and theoretical discussions were characteristic of these progressives, who became active members of the club, ultimately rising to influential positions. By the time Wright entered his first exhibition in 1894, Robert C. Spencer, Richard E. Schmidt, Hugh M. G. Garden, George Dean, and Dwight H. Perkins were all active in club affairs.

In the earliest years (1895–99), the club's activities were devoted to its membership, in other words, architects and draftsmen, but with the new century, the general public was drawn increasingly to the annual exhibition, which was held at the Art Institute of Chicago, the city's major art museum and school of fine arts. Coverage, including announcements and reviews, expanded from professional publications such as *Inland Architect*, the *Brickbuilder*, and *American Architect and Building News* to the numerous daily newspapers including the *Tribune*, *Examiner*, *Evening Post*, *Inter-Ocean*, *Chronicle*, and *Times Herald*.[7] In 1899, a consortium of clubs from major cities such as Chicago, Saint Louis, Boston, Pittsburgh, and Detroit among others agreed on a nonconflicting schedule that would allow local members to send their work on a circuit of out-of-town venues. Thus architects gained wider exposure for their built and unbuilt work, which otherwise was known only to a few.

The debate over a new direction for American architecture continued with lectures and papers by members throughout the twenty years Wright followed club affairs. The dominant position was that of the established generation, who adhered to historical revival styles and held to the doctrines of the École des Beaux-Arts. The slogan "Progress before Precedent" was put forward as the objective of the Architectural League of America in June 1899.[8] While on the surface, the argument revolved around the choice between following a design methodology that arose out of the requirements and materials of the job versus passively applying a historic style copied from ancient models, for the most thoughtful of the Chicago architects, it was far more complicated. For instance, both Sullivan and Wright rejected the motto for different reasons. Wright would give his clearest rebuttal in the March 1908 *Architectural Record* under the slogan, "In the Cause of Architecture."

Architectural discourse in Chicago became more heated in the decades leading up to World War I. Club politics were played out behind the scenes, and in some years the progressives gained ascendancy, and in other years they were driven out of influential positions and remained on the sidelines. The extent of Wright's participation in club exhibitions was directly tied to these political swings of power, which is why his most important Chicago Architectural Club shows were in 1900, 1902, and 1907, all years the progressives were in control.[9]

In the early years of the twentieth century, no single architect had more exposure or critical attention under the auspices of the Chicago Architectural Club than Frank Lloyd Wright. In the two decades between 1894 and 1914, Wright participated in eight exhibitions with the club, experiences that would mold him for the rest of his career. This was ironic, as he never joined the organization, remaining always an outsider.[10] His success in acquiring the private display spaces and personalized publications he desired was derived from his cultivation of friendships with powerful members who made the important decisions about who would exhibit and under what circumstances. Through these associations he attained a privileged status that became a double-edged sword. It allowed him to gain almost total control over how his work was displayed, but it also ultimately led to harsh personal attacks and retribution against himself and his allies from other club members.

Wright was extremely fortunate that one of his closest friends, Robert Clossen Spencer Jr. (1865–1953), was very active in the politics of the club. Wright, no doubt, found Spencer compatible because they had a common background. Spencer, two years older than Wright, was also born in Wisconsin; he attended the university at Madison and graduated with a degree in engineering. Preparing for a career in design, he left Wisconsin to spend two years in the architectural program at Massachusetts Institute of Technology. Then, while still in the Boston area, he worked for a few years in established firms; first with Wheelwright and Haven and then the successor firm to Henry Hobson Richardson: Shepley, Rutan, and Coolidge. In contrast to Wright, who served his apprenticeship with Sullivan, Spencer followed a more conservative path and toured Europe for two years after being awarded the prestigious Rotch scholarship. On his return, Spencer entered the Chicago office of Shepley, Rutan, and Coolidge to take direct charge of the interior design and decoration of the Chicago Public Library (1892). In 1895, he opened his independent practice, moving into the Schiller Building near Wright.[11]

A pivotal moment in the development of modern architecture occurred in May 1897, when Wright, Spencer, and Myron Hunt joined Perkins in his office at 1107 Steinway Hall. From this location, alliances were forged and experimental work undertaken. Both H. Allen Brooks and Wilbert Hasbrouck, historians of this period, describe the outgrowth of this group sometimes as the "Eighteen," as Wright later called it, or more loosely as a luncheon club, but both agree that the artistic fervor decidedly affected the direction of the Chicago Architectural Club.[12]

By this time, Wright was making clearly defined breakthroughs in planning and in the organization of elevations, especially in his residential work. Connections he made through Steinway Hall would propel him into prominence after 1900 by achieving preferred treatment in the club exhibitions. By 1903, due to Wright's artistic leadership and commanding personality, the center of creative breakthroughs would shift from Steinway Hall to his Oak Park Studio (opened in 1898).

1894–99

In retrospect, it would seem obvious that Wright's exhibitions at the Chicago Architectural Club, parallel in time with the achievements of the Oak Park Studio years, would stand out as milestones in his career. But it is doubtful that he would have achieved even a fraction of his prominence without the support of his close-knit group of colleagues. It was during the five years between 1894 and 1899 that a certain commonality existed among the progressives; at the same time, year by year, Wright gradually began to differentiate himself from the others in the experimental nature of his design and in the ambitious character of his personality.

Wright wasted no time in exhibiting his work, submitting his first items in May 1894, just one year after starting his independent practice. Since 1893 had been a year of economic recession,

1.2 Frank Lloyd Wright, Milwaukee Library and Museum competition entry, 1893. Ink on paper, 23⅜ × 45⅝ in. (FLWFA, 9306.002)

his amount of work was slight. Perhaps the most surprising revelation is that the first one of his own drawings that Wright ever exhibited was his submission to the Milwaukee Public Library and Museum competition, held October 3, 1893, to January 5, 1894: a symmetrical composition that was a study in the classical orders (figure 1.2). The building, resting on a high base, was divided into five parts with a pair of colonnades flanking a central pedimented entrance topped with a dome.

Of the six items Wright exhibited that year, five were houses drawn in watercolor by Ernest Albert (1857–1946).[13] Albert was thirty-seven, ten years older than Wright, when the architect chose him as one of his first renderers. Born in New York, he moved to Chicago to provide color schemes and ornamental designs for many buildings at the 1893 World's Columbian Exposition. A locally recognized painter and scenic artist, he probably met Wright while working on stage design for the Auditorium Building. Their association deepened through a mutual interest in the pictorial depiction of landscape and when he became one of a group of painters, which included Charles Corwin, William Wendt, and Charles Francis Browne, whose artwork Wright collected and displayed in his Oak Park home in the 1890s. In fact, Wright's involvement may have extended to venturing out with his friends to create his own plein air drawings and photographs of plant life. After his return to New York, Albert began devoting himself to his primary interest, landscape painting.[14]

In the first decade of his practice, Wright chose watercolor as the medium for his perspectives, which allowed for equal treatment of the building and its surroundings—almost always, landscape—using identical colors and tonal values. Although he employed different renderers, this painterly approach was consistent throughout the 1890s, until a more graphic style, influenced by the two-dimensionality of Japanese woodblock prints, began to be adopted in the early 1900s.

Unfortunately, it is not possible to identify which houses Wright exhibited in 1894, as the only available information appears on the exhibition checklist where each item is simply listed as "Water Color—Residence." The one exception is the Dutch Colonial design for the executed Frederick Bagley House (1894; Hinsdale, Illinois) because it was reproduced in the catalog (figure 1.3).[15] Almost no renderings exist from 1893 in the Frank Lloyd Wright Archives, but it is likely that the William H. Winslow House (1893–94; River Forest, Illinois) was displayed (figure 1.4).

In the years ahead, how and when Wright exhibited with the club was directly related to the fortunes of his allies. It was not until 1900 that the progressives, principally Spencer and Perkins, assumed important leadership roles. Up to that time, Wright's participation was slight, exhibiting one item per year in 1895 and 1898, and none between 1896 and 1897.[16]

1.3 Frederick Bagley House, Hinsdale, Illinois, 1894. Ernest Albert, delineator. Watercolor on paper, dimensions unknown. (Chicago Architectural Sketch Club Collection, Ryerson and Burnham Archives, The Art Institute of Chicago. Digital File # casc.1894_08)

1900–1902

By 1900, it is clear that several things began to coalesce simultaneously. First, Wright had reached a new level of maturity as a designer, and with it had come an ambition for recognition; this, coupled with the support of powerful club members, led to a series of unparalleled exhibitions and publications. From this date forward, Wright would establish a personal approach to presenting his work that he would adhere to for the remainder of his career.

Wright exhibited at both the 1900 and 1902 Chicago Architectural Club annuals, but it is the sequence of events between 1900 and 1902 taken together that point to a permanent pattern in the years ahead. First, he chose to exhibit his work in the largest quantity possible in a separate space of his own, creating what amounted to a one-man show; second, to further showcase his designs he wanted them published, and that publication should be lavishly illustrated and elegantly designed by himself, with the highest quality printing and reproduction; third, to be better understood, a separate publication expressing his philosophy should be available; and last, a writer from his inner circle should evaluate his work sympathetically in an article or book with even more high quality illustrations. This is exactly what happened between 1900 and 1902, and the series of events was repeated again between 1907 and 1911. These dates distinguish the two major phases of Wright's first twenty years of practice: the experimental and the mature periods.

By 1900, despite the economic depression of the 1890s, Wright had passed through an exploration stage to a breakthrough of design invention that encompassed residential and commercial buildings and decorative arts such as furniture, art glass, and vases. In collaboration with Spencer, he set about creating an appropriate showcase. No doubt through his professional contacts in Boston where he had lived for many years, Spencer was able to successfully propose an extensively illustrated critical summary, "The Work of Frank Lloyd Wright," for the June issue of the well-respected journal, *Architectural Review*.[17] This article was clearly in process when plans were forming for the Thirteenth Annual club exhibition.[18] Timing was opportune as Spencer was also first vice president of the club, as well as on the Executive, Hanging, and Publicity Committees.[19] When the exhibition opened on March 20, 1900, it contained the largest selection of Wright items ever to be on public view.

On display in a club gallery at the Art Institute of Chicago were six photographs, four renderings (called "sketches" on the checklist), and a perspective, for a total of eleven items. With Perkins as editor of the exhibition catalog, Wright was accorded an unprecedented ten-page section illustrating five photographs, six renderings, and eight plans, for a total of nineteen illustrations (figure 1.5). But when Spencer's article appeared three and one half months later, it was generously illustrated with ninety-seven illustrations (figure 1.6). Because of the close relationship between Wright and Spencer, it is probable that Wright suggested the illustrations, or he chose them himself.[20] In order to deduce Wright's intentions in his first major survey of his independent work, it is necessary to judge all three components together: the *Review* article, the exhibition, and the section of the club catalog.

Spencer was the inevitable choice as author of the first article to assess Wright's nineteenth-century accomplishments. He was an experienced architectural writer, a Wright champion, and a modern in his preferences and philosophy. His main argument concerns Wright's place as second only to Sullivan as a leader of a "living, national architecture" in opposition to practitioners of the "outward forms of the various styles and periods ... 'adapted,' plagiarized or caricatured according to the caliber and taste of the individual designer." In so doing, he analyzed several buildings in detail—Nathan Moore House (1895; Oak Park, Illinois), Wright Studio (1897–98; Oak Park, Illinois), William H. Winslow House, and Abraham Lincoln Center (1898–1905; Chicago)—but also provided cogent analysis of architectural issues. For instance, anticipating a debate that would preoccupy Wright in the 1940s, Spencer declared, "While it is true that in a building form should follow function, the proposition is true only in its larger sense, in the sense in which it is exemplified in nature, who always seeks to clothe the

1.4 William H. Winslow House, River Forest, Illinois, 1893–94. Ernest Albert, delineator?
Watercolor on paper, 12 × 32⅝ in. (FLWFA, 9305.013)

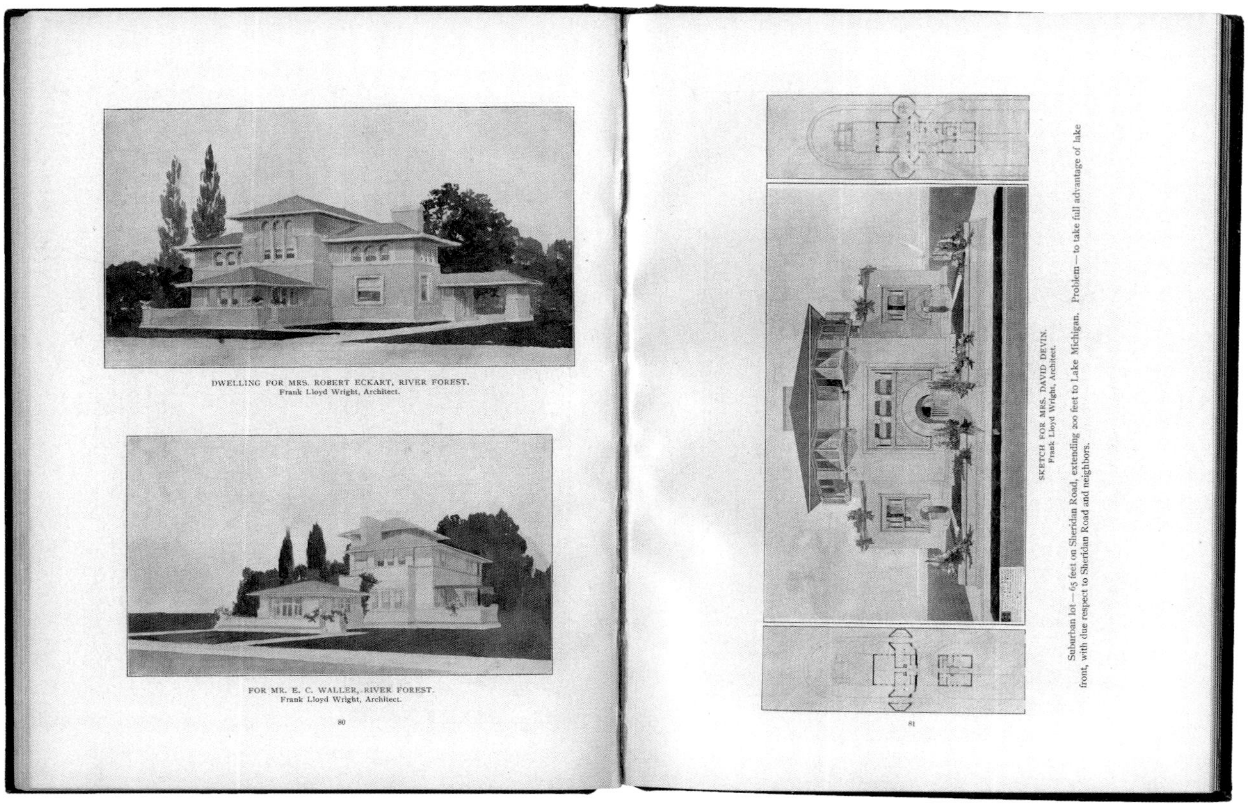

1.5 *Annual of the Chicago Architectural Club Being the Book of the Thirteenth Annual Exhibition 1900* (Chicago: Art Institute, 1900), Frank Lloyd Wright section, 1900. (Courtesy Randolph C. Henning with permission.) The two illustrations on the left are mistitled. The *top* illustration is the E. C. Waller House; the *lower* one, Mrs. Robert Eckhart, his daughter.

working mechanism of her organisms beneath a protective covering none the less fair or beautiful because fitted to its purpose. The sticklers for naked cast-iron in façades of modern construction would do well to contrast the plumaged bird with the plucked and naked specimen, and that in turn with the bony skeleton."[21] While in later years Wright would edit the text of some of his commentators, it is certain that Spencer's opinions remained uncensored because he enumerated Wright's main influences—Sullivan, Friedrich Froebel, Nature, and Japanese architecture. In later years, Wright would argue to have some of these topics excised from essays about his work.

Although Spencer's text has a distinct organizational structure, the illustrations were not presented either chronologically or thematically. Wright's predilection was always to exhibit as much material as possible, unless constraints such as limited space were a factor. Thus the *Review* article provides a penetrating insight into how he viewed his first seven years of practice. Wright chose not to display any work done with Adler and Sullivan as an employee or outside of his contract, the so-called bootlegged houses such as the Robert G. Emmond (1892; La Grange, Illinois), Warren McArthur (1892; Chicago), or George Blossom (1892; Chicago) Houses. The exceptions to this rule are the Henry N. Cooper House (1887/1890–95; La Grange, Illinois) and the Dr. Allison W. Harlan House (1892; Chicago), both of which Wright held in high esteem throughout his entire life. In fact, many decades later, Wright made a strong stand to have the little known Harlan House exhibited in his last career retrospective in Florence, Italy.

While he singled out his daring design for his Oak Park Studio, the accomplished Isidore Heller House (1897; Chicago), and the prophetic Winslow House and Stable for full-page plates, they were side by side with the Tudor-style Nathan Moore House. It appears, at this early date, that Wright did not intend to edit his work to emphasize its modernity, as he also published the H. C. Goodrich (1896; Oak Park, Illinois), H. P. Young (1895; Oak Park, Illinois), and Chauncey Williams (1895; River Forest,

THE ARCHITECTURAL REVIEW. 65

scroll beneath the fruitful tree typify the elements of an architect's work. The solemn secretary birds have their meaning to the designer who in these caps has enjoyed taking a quiet fling at the reactionary spirits who dominate the "Arts and Crafts" movement. With their broad backs and hoary heads bent low, their forms crouched into rigid masses, the two hoary figures which flank the porch were well named by the sculptor, Richard Bock, who created them, "The Boulder," as typifying the struggle of the oppressed and shackled soul to break its bonds and find self expression. Seen upon a summer day, embowered with trees, generous the stone urns which flank the steps overflowing with flowers and dripping masses of foliage, the façade of this architect's workshop, is one of his most successful creations. It is to be hoped that this experiment in separating the creative and executive activities of an architect, giving to the former a quiet, congenial and helpful setting, will continue to prove as satisfactory in every way as it has since it was undertaken.

About two miles west of Oak Park in the suburb of River Forest, there are several examples of Mr. Wright's work, one of which, the Winslow House, is more than worth a pilgrimage to see. In fact, it is the broadest, the most characteristic and the most completely satisfying thing that he has done. This opportunity came to him in the third year of his independent practice and is the only site beautiful in itself that has yet come into his hands. Upon the chosen site Nature has been at work for years building the wonderful elm which, with its spreading arms and feathery sprays, was destined to shade this house, and the character of the house was somewhat determined by the circumstance of this tree. The sympathy that has been firmly established between them is felt by the cultivated and uncultivated. The street façade, as will be seen in the photograph, is simple with a breadth of treatment that carries the exquisite refinement of its detail with perfect dignity. Within the grounds to the rear we are afforded a more intimate knowledge of the conditions of life within and the scheme becomes less reticent and is more picturesque without sacrificing the quiet formality of the whole. The impression conveyed by the exterior is the impression conveyed by the elm. A certain simple power of an organic nature that seems to have as much right to its place and is as much a part of the site as the tree. The analogy begins there and continues, for the details of the house are as much in their place and as consistent in themselves and in relation to each other, as the whole house is to its surroundings. A "layman" has said that his first view of this house gave him the same thrill that he felt when listening for the first time to an orchestra. The stable in the rear, with its background of tall trees, one of which shoots upward through the eaves, is a classic little gem in keeping with the house, and contains the printing shop of the Auvergne Press, where Mr. Winslow and

1.6 Robert C. Spencer Jr., "The Work of Frank Lloyd Wright," *Architectural Review*, June 1900, 65 (Kathryn Smith collection). The illustrations on this page are primarily devoted to Wright's house and studio (1889–98), with the exception of the Bagley House, *top center*.

1.7 C. A. McAfee House, Kenilworth, Illinois, 1894. Robert C. Spencer Jr., delineator. Watercolor and watercolor wash on art paper, 10 × 29 in. (FLWFA, 9407.01). *Legend*: "Designed June 5, 1894 for C. A. McAfee, Kenilworth, Frank Lloyd Wright Architect." This drawing was reproduced in the 1900 CAC Annual, Wright section, 79.

Illinois) Houses. Nor did he seek to distance himself from Sullivan's influence as both the Heller and Joseph and Helen Husser (1899; Chicago) Houses were well represented. This was the first, and only, instance where the largely forgotten Orrin Goan House (1894; La Grange, Illinois) was published (by a perspective and an inset plan). The article presented Wright as a residential architect, as the first seven of the twelve pages were devoted to houses. However, larger structures were included. The Francis Apartments (1895; Chicago) and Francisco Terrace (1895; Chicago) were well illustrated. The exceptional Mendota Boathouse (1893; Madison, Wisconsin) had two photographs and a split plan. Oddly, the somewhat awkward Cheltenham Beach Resort (1899; Chicago) was featured, while the more accomplished Wolf Lake Amusement Park (1895; Chicago) was not. The problematic design for the Abraham Lincoln Center, a commission from his uncle, Jenkin Lloyd Jones, appears, but the daring design of the executed Romeo and Juliet Windmill (1896; Spring Green, Wisconsin), for his aunts, Jane and Ellen, was excluded. Although the text was exemplary—although idolatrous—especially for such an early date, the size of the illustrations, which, in most cases were the size of postage stamps, was extremely disappointing to Wright. By 1910, he would say he was sick of "over reduction."[22]

From this vast richness of material, Wright chose only six works to exhibit at the Art Institute. Of course, he was thinking of the audience in both cases. The *Architectural Review* was a national publication primarily directed at other architects and designers, while the Chicago exhibition was open to the general public—potential clients—as well as the local design community. As a result, he opened the show with five photographs of his recently completed Oak Park Studio, four color renderings of residential projects in idealized settings, and the unexecuted Lincoln Center. The fact that Wright chose all unbuilt houses—C. A. McAfee (1894; Kenilworth, Illinois; figure 1.7), Mrs. David Devin (1896; Chicago), E. C. Waller (1898; River Forest, Illinois), and Mrs. Robert Eckhart (1899; River Forest, Illinois; figure 1.8)—all rendered in a similar style indicates that he was presenting work that was for hire. Thus the show announced that he was open for business as a residential architect of exquisite sensibility, while the *Review* presented an important new American architect of great originality.

In addition to exhibitions, Wright used public lectures to advance his avant-garde program; he gave one of his most important theoretical statements, "The Art and Craft of the Machine," at Hull House on March 6, 1901, which was subsequently printed in the club catalog that year.[23] With this paper he presented an impassioned plea for the use of the machine in elevating the quality of architecture as long as it was used as a tool by artist-architects and not as an end in itself. This lecture became in the decades ahead one of Wright's most influential manifestos, yet, at the same time, it was misunderstood by the next generation of European architects, who first hailed him as a prophet and then castigated him for rejecting his own first principles with his 1920s designs.

1.8 Mrs. Robert Eckhart House, River Forest, Illinois, 1899. Watercolor on paper, 10 × 18⅛ in. (FLWFA, 9805.008).
E. C. Waller commissioned this house for his daughter. It was reproduced in the 1900 CAC Annual, but mistitled as E. C. Waller House, 80. See figure 1.5.

1902

The timing of the March 1902 Fifteenth Annual could not have been better. By that date, Wright had made his revolutionary conceptual breakthrough with two distinct plan types for residences and public buildings that he would refine for the rest of the decade: the "open plan" Prairie House and the binuclear plan for churches and schools. On an artistic level, the 1902 exhibition was groundbreaking for Wright. He was fortunate that the key members of the "Eighteen" were totally in control from the top down: Spencer was serving as president and as a member of the jury alongside Schmidt and Dean, who also was editor of the catalog.[24] He was also fortunate that these rival architects recognized the quality of his work, and breaking with club precedent accorded him privileges never given to others.

First, he was allocated a separate gallery at the Art Institute and the freedom to design the installation. Second, he was allowed more items than anyone else, sixty-four in total: Wright expanded his exhibition technique beyond simulacra—drawings and photographs—to include furniture and decorative arts such as lamps, bowls, vases, and lighting, which made up at least half of his display.[25] In addition, the catalog, which was monopolized by the progressives, contained a fourteen-page section devoted to the Oak Park architect, titled in his own graphic style "The Work of Frank Lloyd Wright," certainly selected and designed by Wright, which amounted to a small monograph in and of itself (figures 1.9–10).[26]

The 1902 annual also marked the first public exhibition of Wright's collaboration with the first of his most important architectural photographers: Henry Fuermann, whose firm

1.9 Chicago Architectural Club Annual, 1902, title page. (Scott Architectural Archive)

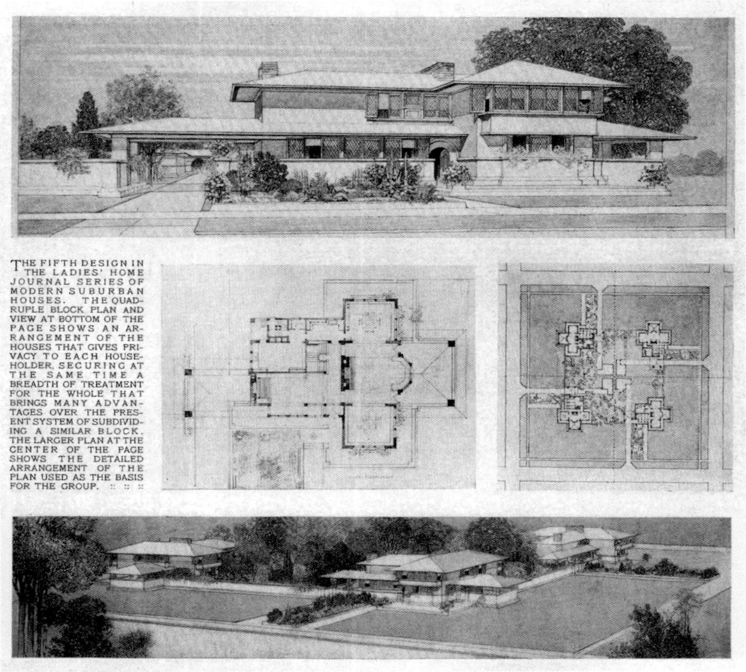

1.10 Chicago Architectural Club Annual, 1902, page one. (Scott Architectural Archive)

photographed much of Wright's built work between 1902 and 1914. Born in Watertown, Wisconsin, northeast of Madison, Fuermann (1861–1949) opened his business in Chicago in early 1902 under the company name, Fuermann and Williams. Over time, he brought in his two eldest children, Clarence and Leon, and changed the name to Henry Fuermann and Sons; Henry and Clarence have been credited with extensively photographing the work of Wright and of Adler and Sullivan before World War I. Fuermann photographs are known for their exquisite tonal values and clarity of detail due to the fact that prints were made from large-format glass negatives. Wright apparently prized the work of both photographers, Henry and Clarence, as he employed them continuously up to and including 1914, some of the few collaborators who stayed with him after his move to Wisconsin in 1911.[27]

In conformance with his aesthetic ideal of Gesamtkunstwerk (total work of art), Wright designed the gallery as an extension of his architectural studio. The color scheme (soft brown and gray) and decorative details were coordinated with the furniture and craft objects on display. The walls were covered in brown burlap banded with strips of natural wood to harmonize with the drawing frames. Desks and tables (fabricated by John Ayers, mainly for the B. Harley Bradley [1900; Kankakee, Illinois] and Warren Hickox [1900; Kankakee, Illinois] Houses) draped with brown leather covers were placed around the gallery; they served as surfaces to display tall slender copper vases and bronze repoussé bowls (made by James A. Miller) filled with arrangements of delicate dry branches and milkweed pods.

Wright took advantage of the generous amount of space he had been given by displaying a good selection—about 40 percent—of nineteenth-century work. He devoted the most prominent place to the Winslow House and Stable and the Husser House, shown alongside the McAfee, Heller (figure 1.11), and Frank Thomas (1901; Oak Park, Illinois, figure 1.12) Houses. But the most groundbreaking aspects of the show were the drawings and photographs devoted to the Bradley and Hickox Houses shown in context with displays of houses and the plan for a Prairie Town, which appeared in the February and July 1901 *Ladies' Home Journal* (figures 1.13–16). Also in the same gallery were drawings or photographs illustrating the Oak Park Studio (figure 1.17) and the Hillside Home School (1901–3; Spring Green, Wisconsin). The spatial discoveries in this group of buildings were revolutionary and secured Wright's reputation as a modern architect.

1.11 Isidore Heller House, Chicago, Illinois, 1897.
Watercolor and graphite pencil on tracing paper mounted to heavy art paper, 12¼ × 30 in. (FLWFA, 9606.007)

1.12 Frank Thomas House, Oak Park, Illinois, 1901.
Ink and watercolor on tracing paper, 7⅞ × 21⅞ in. Drummond, Long, or Mahony, delineator. (FLWFA, 0106.001)

1.13 B. Harley Bradley House, Kankakee, Illinois, 1900. Photograph by Henry Fuermann and Sons. (FLWFA, 0002.0056). Wright reproduced this photograph in his 1902 catalog.

1.14 B. Harley Bradley House, Kankakee, Illinois, 1900. Photograph by Henry Fuermann and Sons. (FLWFA, 0002.0009). This photograph is almost identical to the one illustrated in the 1902 CAC catalog.

1.15 Warren Hickox House, Kankakee, Illinois, 1900. Photograph by Henry Fuermann and Sons. (FLWFA, 0004.0014).
This photograph is almost identical to the one illustrated in the 1902 catalog.

1.16 “A Home in a Prairie Town,” for *Ladies’ Home Journal*, 1900.
India ink, graphite pencil, watercolor, and white tempera on gray art paper, 14½ × 25 in. Marion Mahony and others, delineator. (FLWFA, 0007.001).
This drawing was simplified for an illustration in the 1902 annual, see figure 1.10.

1.17 Frank Lloyd Wright and others, Frank Lloyd Wright Studio, Oak Park, Illinois, 1897–98. Sepia ink on paper, 6 × 19½ in. (FLWFA, 9506.001)

At this period of Wright's career, the spatial plan of the Prairie House was more important than structural innovation. By analyzing the functional components of the single family dwelling, he went from what he called "the general to the particular." For instance, he categorized the public spaces (living, dining, and library) as primary and the service spaces (entry, kitchen, pantry, servants' quarters) as secondary. Using axial organization and a square grid system as ordering devices, he gave modern expression to the classical principle of hierarchy of spaces.

A major conceptual breakthrough that he made early on was the realization that mechanized heating made it no longer necessary to close rooms off from each other to conserve heat. This discovery led to the open plan in public spaces—for instance, where the living room opened to the dining room on a diagonal—while maintaining compartmentalized rooms for services. With the hearth no longer used as the major source of heat, Wright was free to use it as a freestanding vertical plane in space.

The other major advance represented by the Prairie House was the rejection of the wall as the traditional solid barrier between inside and outside. Rather, with the Bradley House, for example, he broke the wall down into a series of elements such as piers, flat planes, and window bands—all geometrically organized by dark wood strips. The wall was now defined as an enclosure of space. Windows were no longer holes punched through a mass, but a light screen filtering sunlight into the interior. The movement outward toward the landscape was amplified by the addition of porches, terraces, flower boxes, and planter urns.

It is clear that by 1901, Wright had derived inspiration from nature, absorbing his studies of the Midwest prairies, woods, and ponds. One of his greatest sources was from the land itself, including all aspects of the natural world: wildflowers, leaves, and grasses. The turning point came when he began to incorporate specific characteristics into his architectural language. The straight line of the horizon became the low sheltering roof, trees and flowers were abstracted as geometric patterns in the art glass windows, and leaves contributed their autumnal palette to the plaster surfaces.

While Wright could feel confident in the recognition of his peers—although it is not clear how deeply Spencer, Dean, and Perkins understood how radical Wright's spatial experiments were—the reviews in the popular press were decidedly mixed. The *Chicago Post* neither recognized nor understood the innovations in the houses or public buildings, but focused on the more accessible decorative arts, politely noting that, "All about are object lessons in good taste." The furniture was lauded for being "designed along lines of beauty and restfulness" and "made to last a generation."[28] While the anonymous reviewer for the *American Architect* took a different tack, classifying Wright's designs with the "less important work of the younger men ... who strive for the semi-grotesque, the catchy. Their compositions lack the best principles of honest design." Sounding a very caustic note, the reviewer questioned, "Why in an architectural exhibit, the chief one in Chicago for the year, why should Mr. Wright's tables and chairs, and his teazles and milkweeds and pine branches cover so much space?"[29]

The reviewer was decidedly sympathetic with the more conservative branch of architecture, but even more damning, he raised a moral issue. "From the standpoint of professional ethics," he queried, "it seems questionable whether such a pronounced personal exhibit should have its place in a general architectural exhibition, as it certainly smacks of advertising more than anything else."[30] The accusation of favoritism hung over the club exhibitions until 1914—the last of Wright's participation—and created a backlash against the progressives for the next five years.[31] More important, by 1902, Wright's preferences for exhibiting were fully formed; he would not compromise in the decades ahead without first waging a strategy of intimidation to the shock and dismay of others.

The conservatives gained ascendency in 1903 and, as a result, Wright spent the next few years estranged from the club. After the outrage of 1902, the club adopted a rule prohibiting "special exhibits by individuals," a policy that was unacceptable to Wright.[32] But these would be years of creative ferment and great productivity. While drawings Wright hung in future exhibitions rarely came solely from his own hand, something far more significant was on display as Barry Byrne, employed in the Oak Park Studio from 1902 to 1909, recalled, "In the period I have indicated he transformed himself from the more superficial precision of the draftsman type into a master architect whose occupation was no longer mere delineation, but whose concern was that immeasurably greater thing, the large-scale manipulation of spaces and masses into a vital, intrinsic architecture. In that transformation the relatively lesser person, the careful pictorial draftsman, diminished in importance and skill ... by 1908 ... Wright as draftsman had almost ceased to exist and that more vital being, Wright as architect, was operating in full possession of his extraordinary creative power."[33]

1.18 Frank Lloyd Wright, ca. 1908. (FLWFA, 6002.0002)

1907–11

Although there were four years of stalemate, there was a positive outcome. By 1907, when sympathetic members, principally Irving K. Pond and Howard van Doren Shaw (along with Alfred H. Granger), were appointed as the Jury of Admission, Wright had good reason to mount a solo exhibition (figure 1.18).[34] He had produced work that would establish his reputation in Chicago and beyond for the remainder of his life. He had no illustrated section of the catalog that year, but as events unfolded during the aftermath of the exhibition, he was motivated to create some of his most enduring publications.

Following an already established pattern, Wright designed his installation at the 1907 annual to create a dynamic rather than static space. Within the rectangular room, he used three-dimensional objects—large-scale pedestals holding aloft white plaster models; sparkling, colorful art glass panels; and metal office furniture where glazed ceramic vases, bronze lamps, and piles of black-and-white photographs rested—to create a spatial experience where the viewer strolled from one area to the other, never taking in the entire exhibition at one glance. The walls were covered with framed drawings, arranged salon style, hanging from a picture rail by colored silk cords; the cords themselves establishing a linear decorative pattern across the gallery walls (figure 1.19). One reviewer took special note, commenting at the time, "The quiet color of the walls, the restfulness of the small molding decoration, the framing of prints unite with objects of decoration and furniture to stimulate more than passing interest."[35]

Installation photographs by Fuermann, which Wright commissioned, communicate the overall effect, which was like walking into his Oak Park Studio. Within the center of the gallery, he created a triangular configuration of three freestanding pedestals or furniture groupings. In one corner was the model of Unity Temple (1905–8; Oak Park, Illinois); diagonally opposite on a higher pedestal the Lincoln Center model, flanked by a Teco "Triplicate" vase and his most extraordinary work in glass, a door panel from the Susan Lawrence Dana House (1902–4; Springfield, Illinois) (figures 1.20–21); on the opposite diagonal was a furniture grouping: a metal desk with built-in seat and an office chair, both from the Larkin Company Administration Building (1902–6; Buffalo, New York) (figure 1.22).[36] The Larkin furniture was surrounded on two sides by a partition and pedestal with the Larkin model held aloft, creating a room within a room. The overall effect was of an exhibition of exquisite drawings punctuated with the bold form of three-dimensional models. The photographs were presented casually for the visitor to examine by hand.

With the exception of a few outstanding works shown in 1902, which were prototypes of what was to evolve—the *Ladies' Home Journal* houses and Quadruple Plan, Lincoln Center, and early Prairie Houses—the buildings were a survey of work undertaken or completed since his last exhibition. The catalog listed thirty-eight buildings and projects. In retrospect, except for the last masterpieces completed after his departure for Europe, all the great works were there: the full elaboration of the Prairie House and the two experimental public buildings (figure 1.23).

The 1907 exhibition was particularly noteworthy for the quality of perspectives—drawings made for either publication or for presentation to clients, who were not adept at reading plans and elevations—most of which were executed by Marion Mahony. Although Wright had hired other renderers, such as Charles Corwin, Louis Rasmussen, and Birch Burdette Long among others, in the past, Mahony, who had started work for Wright at Steinway Hall in 1895, developed a highly refined individual style that enhanced Wright's designs for his clients and the public. Using the medium of india ink or sepia ink alone or

1.19 Frank Lloyc Wright exhibition, Chicago Architectural Club, Art Institute of Chicago, 1907.
Photograph by Henry Fuermann and Sons. (FLWFA, 0700.0006).
Left, metal office furniture from the Larkin Administration Building; *top right*, Metzger House drawing.

1.20 Frank Lloyd Wright exhibition, Chicago Architectural Club, Art Institute of Chicago, 1907.
Photograph by Henry Fuermann and Sons. (FLWFA, 0700.0004). *Left*, Larkin Administration Building model with a maquette of a column for Unity Temple; *middle*, Abraham Lincoln Center model; *right*, partial view of Unity Temple model.

1.21 Frank Lloyd Wright exhibition, Chicago Architectural Club, Art Institute of Chicago, 1907.
Photograph by Henry Fuermann and Sons. (FLWFA, 0700.0005). *Left*, art glass door panel from the Susan Lawrence Dana House; *middle*, Abraham Lincoln Center model; *right*, Teco "Triplicate" vase.

1.22 Frank Lloyd Wright exhibition, Chicago Architectural Club, Art Institute of Chicago, 1907.
Photograph by Henry Fuermann and Sons. (FLWFA, 0403.0068).
Left, Larkin Administration Building model; *middle*, Larkin Administration Building metal office furniture;
right, Edwin Cheney House perspective.

1.23 Unity Temple, Oak Park, Illinois, 1905–8. Marion Mahony, delineator.
Sepia ink and watercolor on off-white art paper, 11½ × 25⅛ in. (FLWFA, 0611.003)

1.24 K. C. De Rhodes House, South Bend, Indiana, 1906. Marion Mahony, delineator. Sepia ink, pencil, and watercolor wash on off-white paper, 18¾ × 25¾ in. (FLWFA, 0602.001). Mahony's initials appear within the drawing at *lower left*; Wright inscribed marginalia in pencil at *lower right*, "Drawn by Mahony—After FLlW and Hiroshige," at a later date.

Opposite top: 1.25 Edwin Cheney House, Oak Park, Illinois, 1903–4. Marion Mahony, delineator. India and sepia ink, graphite pencil on off-white tracing paper, 12¼ × 29½ in. (FLWFA, 0401.017). This drawing can be seen in figure 1.22 at the *right*.

Opposite bottom: 1.26 C. Thaxter Shaw House, Montreal, Canada, 1906. Marion Mahony, delineator. Sepia ink on paper, 19 5/6 × 27½ in. (FLWFA, 0617.001). At *lower right* within the drawing: C. Thaxter Shaw Dwelling, Westmount, Montreal.

with watercolor wash, Mahony was skilled at delineating the building within an ideal landscape setting that evoked Japanese art in general, and woodblock printmakers such as Ando Hiroshige—Wright's favorite artist, whose work he collected in quantity—specifically (figure 1.24). While Wright collaborated on the genesis of these perspectives, Mahony seems to have been given latitude in carrying the drawing to completion. These drawings differ from the earlier use of watercolor alone—the painterly approach—where the building and its surroundings blend together; the new technique focused on architecture as subject.[37] Among the houses shown were the Victor Metzger (1902; Sault Ste. Marie, Michigan), Dana, Edwin Cheney (1903–4; Oak Park, Illinois; figure 1.25), Darwin D. Martin (1903–5; Buffalo, New York), C. Thaxter Shaw (1906; Montreal, Canada; figure 1.26), and Avery Coonley Houses (1906–9; Riverside, Illinois), his most complete works where the budget was generous.

For large-scale work, Wright seemed well aware of his achievement in creating two monumental buildings, both of which represented innovations in planning and materials—the Larkin Building and Unity Temple—as the placement of the models, fabricated by the Chicago sculptor, Albert Van den Berghen, made them visible from any point in the gallery.[38] The Yahara Boathouse (1905; Lake Mendota, Madison, Wisconsin), exhibited as U. of W. (University of Wisconsin) Boathouse, was not singled out for special attention, nor would it be published a year later in the *Architectural Record*. It would take several decades before Wright came to understand its importance for modern architecture; that would be a lesson learned from Europe. It certainly was characteristic of Wright at the Chicago Architectural Club exhibitions to concentrate on recent work, but, for the 1907 event, Wright seemed to understand precisely that this grouping of buildings represented an unprecedented achievement in his career. It was one of the six most important exhibitions in his sixty-six years of practice.

This was only partially understood in the popular press. While some newspapers were generous in their praise, recognizing the Oak Park architect as a great innovator in his field, others were less perceptive. The *Chicago Record Herald* described him as "an original genius," who had attracted "a considerable following, so that he is actually one of those rare architects who

Cheney 1904

MR. C. THAXTER SHAW -
DWELLING - WESTMOUNT - MONTREAL -

1.27 Harriet Monroe. Photograph by Foltz. (University of Chicago Photographic Archive, apf1-00894. Special Collections Research Center, University of Chicago Library)

have the honor of founding a school." The anonymous writer clearly admired the residential designs, pointing out "[the] long, low roof, casement windows, banded under the broad eaves, or otherwise arranged as an adornment; much unbroken wall space, and frequent use of garden or terrace walls to give the house privacy."[39] The *Chicago Post* also was laudatory: "Mr. Wright's model of Unity Church, Oak Park, which is constructed in concrete," the reviewer opined, "and the numerous drawings and plans make the collection housed in this gallery an exhibition of considerable merit."[40]

But 1907 was remarkable for another reason, Wright faced his first objective art critic: the formidable Harriet Monroe (1860–1936; figure 1.27). The sister-in-law of John Root, the talented design partner of Daniel Burnham before his untimely death in 1891, Monroe aspired to be a published poet but often supported herself with intermittent jobs as a journalist. Although she traveled widely (two trips to Europe, 1890 and 1897; western United States, 1898; Europe and Asia, 1910), she made her reputation in her hometown, Chicago, as a writer for the *Examiner* and the *Tribune*. Her enduring reputation rests on her founding of *Poetry: A Magazine of Verse*, which first opened its pages to new serious poets in 1912, thereby bringing the modern idiom of T. S. Eliot, Ezra Pound, Carl Sandburg, and Wallace Stevens among many others to a wider audience.

Wright's encounter with Monroe was extremely important, not the least for what it reveals about how he would handle adverse criticism in the decades ahead, but also, because her reaction motivated him to write his manifesto, "In the Cause of Architecture," published the following year. Monroe, who devoted an entire column to Wright's exhibition, was charmed by his houses, which she wrote, "seem to grow out of the ground as naturally as the trees, and to express our hospitable suburban American life, a life of indoors and outdoors, as spontaneously as certain Italian villas express the more pompous and splendid life of those old gorgeous centuries. Especially graceful in the grouping of lines and masses are the dwellings of Avery Coonley at Riverside, of Elizabeth Stone at Glencoe, of T. P. Hardy of Racine, and of V. H. Metzger away up on a rocky hill at Sault St. Marie" (figure 1.28). However, she disliked his public buildings, which were "so unusual, at times even bizarre," looking "like fantastic blockhouses, full of corners and angles and squat, square columns, massive and weighty, without grace or ease nor monumental beauty." She summed him up by explaining that he believed "the three Greek orders have done their utmost in the service of man, until in modern hands their true meaning is distorted and lost. Therefore, he thinks it is time to discard them and all their renaissance derivatives, and begin afresh from the beginning."[41]

Wright lost little time in sitting down and thinking through a very long, well-composed response that ran to fourteen paragraphs. After putting her in her place as a "critic," accusing her indirectly of "I-may-not-know-what-Art-is-but-I-know-what-I-like," he went on to the essence of his argument. Using words that would almost be repeated word for word in the 1908 *Architectural Record*, he explained: "it is the very spirit that gave life to the old forms that this work courts. That it is the true inspiration that made of the time honored precedent in its own time a living thing that it craves. Venerable traditional forms are held by this work still too sacred to be paraded as a meretricious mask for the indecencies and iniquities of the market place! Long ago, yes, ages ago, from Nature came inspiration to the Architect and back to Nature with the principles deduced from these dead forms or formulae we will go again for inspiration. I know we shall find it for the Gods still live."[42] He continued, "Concerning our friend, the 'squat'—we

1.28 Victor Metzger House, Sault Ste. Marie, Michigan, 1902. Birch Burdette Long, delineator? India ink and watercolor on tan tracing paper, 9½ × 38½ in. (FLWFA, 0209.002)

happen to be living on the prairie. The prairie has a beauty of its own. A building on the prairie should recognize the features of its quiet level and accentuate them harmoniously. It should be quiet, broad, inclusive. . . . Hence, broad sheltering eaves over determined masses, gentle roofs, spreading base and outreaching walls. What is publicly set forth in this little collection could hardly be American Architecture. No—not yet."[43]

Monroe complained, "You responded by calling me names. Thus unhappily the argument was cut off where it began. And I am with much regret that it seems impossible to pursue it."[44] Wright's immediate retort was unexpected in the circumstances, but characteristic nonetheless. Offering his apology, he concluded with, "Anyhow, Whistler had his 'Arry',—now have I not my 'Arriet'? Hers and henceforth hers only, Frank Lloyd Wright."[45] As charmingly as the correspondence came to a close, the argument had not ended; in the months ahead, Wright made plans to publish an even longer well-thought-out response.

The importance of the 1907 exhibition can hardly be overestimated. It was Wright's most well designed mounting of his most distinguished work of the first fifteen years of his career. It brought him face to face with an objective critic, whose challenge motivated him to write the clearest expression of his design principles to date. When he opened his essay, "In the Cause of Architecture," the following year with the sentence, "Radical though it be, the work here illustrated is dedicated to a cause conservative in the best sense of the word," surely Monroe's review was in the back of his mind.[46]

1908

The 1907 exhibition was not accompanied by a publication of Wright's work, so it seems that Monroe's critical opinions motivated him to rectify that absence. While the editors of *Architectural Record* were already aware of him because he had been positively reviewed in the July 1905 issue, the March 1908 article, which illustrated thirty-four buildings and projects, served as the de facto catalog of the 1907 club exhibition with 50 percent of its contents illustrated.[47] The graphic layout divided Wright's article into two distinct parts: the text and a portfolio of black-and-white illustrations, predominantly of built work, but also perspectives, plans, one model, and one work of sculpture. It is significant that the text ends with an illustration of the 1907 exhibition (figure 1.29).

The Larkin Building was prominently featured, introducing the illustrated section with eleven exterior and interior photos. The long explanatory caption ended with the sentence, "Therefore the work may have the same claim to consideration as a 'work of art' as an ocean liner, a locomotive or a battleship."[48] It would be another fifteen years before Le Corbusier published a similar statement. What followed was a portfolio of fifty-six photographs, primarily by Fuermann and Sons, of executed Prairie Houses, exterior and interior views, and one of Unity Temple. At publication, it was Wright's best illustrated and clearest exposition of his accomplishments in architecture to date.

1.29 Frank Lloyd Wright exhibition, Chicago Architectural Club, Art Institute of Chicago, 1907. Photograph by Henry Fuermann and Sons. This photograph was reproduced as the last illustration in "In the Cause of Architecture," *Architectural Record* 1908. (FLWFA, 0700.0001)

ERNST WASMUTH VERLAG, BERLIN, 1908–11

Although the 1908 text of "In the Cause of Architecture" is now regarded as a seminal work in Wright literature, the illustrations were poorly printed and the architect was justifiably disappointed. In the same year, Wright received a letter from the Berlin publishing firm Ernst Wasmuth Verlag, soliciting his cooperation in the publication of a book of photographs of his executed work. Ernst Wasmuth (1845–1897) founded the eponymous firm in 1872, and was joined by his younger brother, Emil (1848–1894), in 1875. At the time, photographic reproduction, especially color lithography and collotype, was dramatically changing art publishing in Germany; in 1884, the firm expanded into a multistoried building—containing offices, photography and graphic design studios, storage, and later, exhibition space for architectural drawings—where the brothers produced an impressive range of books on the history of the arts and architecture.[49]

The next major chapter in the history of the firm began when Emil's widow, Antonie, inherited the business at the death of her brother-in-law, Ernst, in 1897. While she raised her five children, Otto Dorn (18??–1926), a Berlin bookseller, appointed managing director, continued the growth of the company.[50] Dorn assumed authority at an auspicious time when German architects and architectural students were demanding more exposure to "modern" architecture.[51] Under Dorn's leadership between 1898 and 1913, the firm was incorporated in 1903, four major architecture magazines flourished, and milestone books and folios were published.[52]

In 1897, Bruno Möhring, along with Ernst Splinder, began to edit the monthly titled *Berliner Architekturwelt: Zeitschrift für Baukunst, Malerei, Plastik und Kunstgewerbe* (*Berlin Architecture World: Magazine for Architecture, Painting, Sculpture, and Arts and Crafts*), under the auspices of the Association of Berlin Architects. As a supplement to that journal, in 1901 the publisher conceived small books known as *sonderheft* (special issue), titled *Berliner Kunstlerhefte* (*Berlin Artist Books*), inexpensive monographs on the work of individual artists or designers offered at a discount price to existing subscribers.[53]

In the same year, the firm began publication of two additional periodicals, the lavish and expensive annual, *Architektur des XX. Jahrhunderts: Zeitschrift für moderne Baukunst* (*20th Century Architecture: Journal of Modern Architecture*) and *Charakteristische Details von ausgeführten Bauwerken* (*Characteristic Details of Executed Buildings*).[54] These publications, ventures that focused on contemporary architecture, were edited by Hugo Licht (1841–1923), an architect, who began working with the Wasmuth brothers in 1877, editing architectural books (figure 1.30).[55] Licht influenced the development of modern German architecture through these two periodicals by publishing new building types such as office buildings, stores, and factories as valid works of architecture and by presenting German architects to an international audience.[56] By 1907 or early 1908, following the popular success of the sale of *sonderhefte* to *Berliner Architekturwelt* subscribers, a similar series was created as a supplement to the annual *Architektur des XX. Jahrhunderts*. The books, varying in length from fifty to one hundred pages, devoted to the executed work of one architect from selected cities or regions of Germany, consisted of black-and-white photographs and some plans, with a brief introductory text by the art historian Max Creutz (1876–1932), the director of the Museum of Applied Arts in Cologne.[57] The first issue, devoted to the work of Friedrich von Thiersch (1852–1921), who taught for forty years at the Technische Hochschule in Munich, did not look forward, but rather backward toward the nineteenth century as he practiced in the neo-Romanesque style. Despite this conservative start, the timing of the Wasmuth firm's letter to Wright indicates that he was among the first architects chosen for the series.[58]

1.30 Hugo Licht, 1900. Photograph by Hermann Walter. (Stadtgeschichtliches Museum, Leipzig. Wikimedia Commons)

For both personal and professional reasons, Wright contemplated going to Berlin, but he needed to postpone the trip due to new commissions.[59] Wright was at this time deeply in love with

Mamah Borthwick Cheney, who had been an Oak Park residential client along with her husband, Edwin, in 1903. He and Mamah proposed to marry, but Wright's wife, Catherine, arguing for a one-year wait, refused to grant him a divorce. In the meantime, Wasmuth Verlag moved ahead with plans for the first of the *Architektur des XX. Jahrhunderts sonderhefte*. It is tempting to think that Licht personally selected Wright due to the power and authority he held over *Architektur des XX. Jahrhunderts*, but there is no evidence to support this conclusion.[60] In his autobiography, Wright speculated that it was Kuno Francke, a professor of German history and literature at Harvard University, a visitor to his Oak Park Studio, who had recommended him.[61] The architectural historian Anthony Alofsin has speculated that it was Bruno Möhring, who had been in the Midwest in 1904 attending the Louisiana Purchase Exposition held in Saint Louis.[62] On the other hand, Creutz is another possibility as he had been in the Midwest also for the exposition.[63] Whether it was Licht, Möhring, Francke, Creutz, or some other individual or a combination of several people, it is likely that the March 1908 *Architectural Record* played a role. It would have been concrete evidence that there were a sufficient number of photographs of executed buildings to fill a book of fifty to one hundred pages.[64] In the year that elapsed before Wright's departure for Europe in September 1909, two new *Architeketur des XX. Jahrhunderts sonderhefte*, numbers 2 and 3, both with introductions by Creutz, appeared. They were *Carl Moritz—Cöln, Wohnhauser und Villen* (*Carl Moritz—Cologne, Apartment Houses and Villas*) and *Joseph M. Olbrich—Dusseldorf, Warenhaus Tietz in Dusseldorf* (*Joseph M. Olbrich—Dusseldorf, Tietz Department Store, Dusseldorf*).

The latter volume had additional meaning because Olbrich had died on August 8, 1908, while the Berlin firm was in the midst of publishing a lavish portfolio, *Architektur von Olbrich*, in installments: no. 1 (1901), no. 2 (1904). The Olbrich folios, which were designed by the Austrian architect himself, were superb examples of fine art bookmaking. They consisted of large format loose monochromatic and color plates illustrating buildings as well as applied arts and furniture. The separate sheets were contained within folders printed with a decorative design and the title, series number, and name and address of the publisher on the cover in hand-lettered type. Each plate was stamped with a chop designed by Olbrich with the title of the book and the name and address of the publisher within a square.[65]

When Wright first stepped into the Wasmuth offices in early November 1909, it is clear that he would have been shown *sonderhefte* one, two, and three of *XX. Jahrhunderts* and the two Olbrich folios, almost certainly by Otto Dorn.[66] A few months later, Wright explained to the English designer Charles R. Ashbee the details of his initial contact with the German publishing house, "[Wasmuth Verlag] had written me in America for material for a Sonderheft [Special Issue] to appear in a regular series now in publication. This material to consist wholly of photographs of actual work and plans. . . . This work was their enterprise. . . . The article . . . was to have been written by some German in Cologne whom I do not know." Wright also declared that he owned "outright" a larger work of "about 100 plates" because he believed it would be "profitable and there is no cleaner way for an architect to find his money than in the sale of his own works in this way."[67] Wright's account, which is contemporary with events as they occurred, points to the fact that it was he who had proposed the lavish two-volume portfolio, *Ausgeführte Bauten und Entwürfe von Frank Lloyd Wright (Executed Buildings and Studies by Frank Lloyd Wright),* as his own "enterprise," to Wasmuth Verlag. One that he conceived and designed, specified as to paper, inks, and binding, and that he financed and owned outright as his own publishing venture for sale in the United States. There is no record of how Wright became inspired to create this ambitious art book, but consistent with his personality, it is probable that he came to the idea in Berlin after reviewing the large-format Olbrich folios with which it bares a very close comparison. In fact, Wright said so as much himself in 1911 when he described his two folios as "the finest publication of an Architect's work in any country—not excepting the work of the Austrian Architect, Olbrich."[68] During the month of November 1909, no doubt, Wright worked out the details of the large-format folios with Dorn.[69]

What he intended to create was a handmade fine art book, recalling the days when he worked with his client, William Winslow, at the Auvergne Press.[70] In order to produce a unified publication, every image—perspectives, plans, and details—had to be redrawn and then transferred to large lithographic stones, a medium that had been used since the mid-nineteenth century for printing books and magazines, but was also employed by European painter-printmakers such as Edgar Degas.

Wright also wanted very fine and varied papers, so he chose cream and gray wove papers and tissue paper for the plans. Drawing on his knowledge of Japanese art, the inks he chose were extremely unusual: sepia and gray for the image, and occasionally gold, with white and blue as accents; bronze powder; and gold ink was used for the title page of the German text enclosure. The line drawings, characteristic of the Oak Park Studio during the

1900s—a synthesis of the style of both Wright and Marion Mahony—were very delicate.[71] According to the November 24, 1909, contract with the publisher, Wright was obligated to remain in Europe until the drawings were complete and he had approved the printer's proof for each plate.[72] By July, Wright was surveying the last steps in the process and making plans to depart Italy in early September 1910.[73]

The *sonderhefte* of *Architektur des XX. Jahrhunderts* continued in publication until 1914, on the eve of the outbreak of World War I; throughout the history of the series, Wasmuth Verlag chose only German or Austrian subjects, Wright was the only exception.[74] He also was the most avant-garde, except for Olbrich; the other architects were primarily working in the conservative historical styles. He also was probably the most difficult. Wright's number was originally scheduled as the fourth issue in 1909 directly after Olbrich's monograph on the Tietz department store. However, by 1910, Wright became more ambitious, wanting to include photographs of work still being completed in America such as the Frederick C. Robie House (1908–10; Chicago). The additional photographs did not arrive in Europe until June, thus causing Wasmuth Verlag to postpone the Wright *sonderheft* until 1911.[75] The publisher moved another issue up to number 4.[76] The change in schedule threw Wasmuth Verlag off completely for issues 5 and 6, so the firm took two books previously published in 1905 and 1906 and offered them to the subscribers.[77]

In October 1910, Wright returned to Chicago after approving all the proofs of the one hundred plates for the two-volume portfolio and the layout of the photographic special issue. He had rejected Creutz and solicited Ashbee to write the introduction: "Frank Lloyd Wright, A Study and Appreciation." After a few months back in the United States, Wright, who had originally been motivated to cooperate with the Berlin publisher because of his disappointment with the poor quality reproductions of the 1908 *Architectural Record*, had serious misgivings about the quality of the special issue with 4,000 copies printed. He decided to reject it in person in Berlin, which gave him the opportunity to redesign the entire book. Ashbee's essay was translated into German for the European and American edition, the latter censored by Wright. Wright objected to some of Ashbee's analysis, especially the allegation that he imitated Japanese art. Not for the last time in his life, Wright edited another man's work by deleting passages that he felt were erroneous or offensive.[78]

Wright signed a new contract with Wasmuth Verlag in February 1911, and in March the publisher advertised the *sonderheft* for sale in the pages of *Berliner Architekturwelt*.[79] The announcement called for a September 1911 release and described the book as 113 pages with 163 illustrations, but when the book appeared the illustrations were reduced to 148.[80] The only known review is of the European *sonderheft*, which appeared eight months later in *Kunst and Kunstler* by Walter Curt Behrendt.[81]

As for the American edition of the *sonderheft*, this is where we see Wright at his characteristic best. It is 141 pages with 193 illustrations. He had created a larger, better quality book with forty-five more photos (30 percent more than offered) and twenty-eight more pages (25 percent more). With all the delays and time spent by Wright to improve the Wasmuth Verlag publications, it was not until well into 1912 that they went on sale. But what had started with his 1907 Chicago Architectural Club exhibition had culminated with permanent landmarks to his first twenty years of architecture.

While all three German publications are now rare collector's items, at the time, they were conceived for a variety of audiences. Wasmuth Verlag intended to sell the Wright *sonderheft* to European subscribers of their more expensive annual publication, *XX. Jahrhunderts*. Wright, it appears, had both pragmatic and idealistic motives for publishing his own work. On the one hand, he professed to believe the sales would bring in much needed revenue: it was a business venture.[82] On the other hand, he directed the work at "the young man in architecture" with the purpose of engaging in architectural discourse, raising consciousness, reforming society, and realizing an authentic American architecture. An unsigned January 1913 letter from Wright's Chicago office (probably by Harry F. Robinson, his assistant) explained, "Mr. Wright's intention . . . [was] to sell the Monograph for $50.00 . . . and the 'Sonderheft' . . . was to be [a complimentary] part of the Monograph set. This idea, however, he gave up as he felt after paying a commission to the book sellers that the price made necessary thereby was too great for the 'younger men' and decided to sell the book from the office here and make the 'Sonderheft' a separate issue."[83] To carry out the idealistic plan, Wright chose to take out advertising with the major trade publications such as *Architectural Record*, *Western Architect*, and the *Brickbuilder*; to work to secure reviews in the same periodicals; and to reduce the price of the monograph to $32 on an installment plan of $4 down and four payments of $7 per month (figure 1.31).[84] He sold the *sonderheft* separately for $3.50.[85] It is difficult to say how successful Wright was at operating a mail order business; surviving correspondence suggests meager returns: a 1912 office report lists seven sales.[86]

102 THE ARCHITECTURAL RECORD.

"Ausgeführte Bauten und Entwürfe von Frank Lloyd Wright"

Two portfolios 17½" x 25½" in size; of lithographed plates showing plans, elevations, and perspectives of seventy buildings by this architect. Published by Ernst Wasmuth, of Berlin.
Special arrangements have been made for selling this work direct to the purchaser. Write for descriptive circular to

FRANK LLOYD WRIGHT, 605 Orchestra Hall, Chicago

CRUSHED TRAP ROCK

The Hardest, Toughest, Cleanest, Best

CONCRETE MATERIAL

It does not *calcine* under fire.
Dampness does not affect it.
It does not "pull out" or "sluff off."

It sells as *cheap* as *inferior* rocks or gravels.
Why not insist upon the *best?*
Why not **specify** Trap Rock in concrete?

Write for list of retail dealers who deliver Trap Rock direct to job in N. Y. City and vicinity.

THE NEW YORK TRAP ROCK CO.
17 Battery Place, New York City

A Mineral-Wool Lined House

As shown in these sections, is **warm in winter, cool in summer,** and is thoroughly **Deafened.** The lining is vermin proof. **Mineral Wool** checks the spread of **Fire** and keeps out the dampness.

Sample and Circular Free

U. S. MINERAL WOOL COMPANY
90 West Street NEW YORK

1.31 Advertisement for *Frank Lloyd Wright Ausgeführe Bauten und Entwürfe*, *Architectural Record*, March 1913, backmatter.

THE MYSTERIOUS BERLIN EXHIBITION, 1910

Much has been written about a comprehensive Wright exhibition held in Berlin in 1910.[87] Of course, if such an event had occurred it would have been of extraordinary importance for the development of modern European architecture and for Wright himself. It is almost certain that it never took place in any way that exhibitions are generally understood; in other words, as an advertised formal display open to the public.[88] By 1910, Wright had developed a very strong attitude about how his work would be presented to others. As long as he was in Europe, which he was, he would not only have been present, he would have chosen the drawings, designed the installation, and hung it himself. He also would have fully informed his intimates at the time and written about it later in his memoirs. This he never did.

In 1911, when Wright reappeared in Chicago with two impressive European publications immortalizing his Oak Park practice, he was perceived very differently than he had been before he had left. He was not famous. Rather, he was infamous. He was now tarred with the domestic scandal that resulted from his wife's refusal to give him a divorce, forcing him to live with Mamah Borthwick out of wedlock. In 1911, the estrangement took on another aspect when Wright and Borthwick, both back in the Midwest, moved out of Chicago, building a new home and studio, Taliesin, adjacent to Wright's ancestral lands in southern Wisconsin.

1913–14

By his return to Chicago in 1911, Wright had broken his close ties with his former allies in the Chicago Architectural Club; his last show being in 1907. The club had been grappling with accusations of favoritism as a result of Wright's demands for a private gallery to hang a one-man show. He was not ready to exhibit again until 1913, but when he did, he faced an entirely different climate than he had enjoyed at the height of his accomplishments between 1902 and 1907. Local circumstances, both positive and negative, influenced not only how he was critically received, but also how he responded. With the closing of the Oak Park Studio in 1909, his former employees and contemporaries had opened their own practices; obtained commissions, large and small; and entered competitions. Architects such as Walter Burley Griffin, William Drummond, and the firms of Purcell, Feick, and Elmslie and Spencer and Powers were engaged all over the Midwest building churches, schools, and houses. In addition, in 1912, Griffin had won the competition to design the federal capitol for Canberra, Australia, garnering international publicity. At the same time, although he was still alive, Sullivan's career was on the wane, but his place in history was on the ascendant. All this was occurring while Wright was seeking not only to reestablish his prominence but also to find an appreciative and paying public for his German publications.

He began tentatively by entering a modest selection of work—Hotel Madison (1911; Madison, Wisconsin), Lake Geneva Hotel (1911; Lake Geneva, Illinois), and the Sherman Booth (1911–12; Glencoe, Illinois) and Edward Schroeder (1911; Milwaukee, Wisconsin) Houses—in the Twenty-Sixth Annual Chicago Architectural Club exhibition, which opened May 6,

1913.[89] The critical reception was almost nonexistent. Monroe gave him one sentence—although this time it was positive—remarking on "the one or two fine things marked by horizontal lines."[90] The first public inkling of the dismissive attitude was in a review by Griffin's brother-in-law, Roy A. Lippincott, in the June *Architectural Record*. The wide-ranging article found praise for both eastern and midwestern architects, but rejected Wright's entries as "typical of his peculiar genius."[91]

But a few months later the *Chicago Tribune* article, "'Rebels' of West Shatter Styles of Architecture," under the byline of staff writer Henry M. Hyde, clearly attracted Wright's attention.[92] Hyde asserted that there was a "New School Ascendant" where, for the first time, there was an "art indigenous to the American soil being developed. For the first time a new form, a new style, free from the traditions of historic schools, has begun to win recognition." Proclaiming Sullivan the "master," the principles he laid down were "form should follow function," and "progress should go before precedent." Although Wright was listed as "among the leading members," he was not singled out, but was lumped into a list that included Griffin, and firms such as Perkins, Fellows, and Hamilton and Tallmadge and Watson. Hyde then continued by declaring that Wright was "the most extreme member of the school," and that he was accused of sacrificing "the practical to the picturesque." He then went on to devote four concluding paragraphs to enumerating the elements of the new school, echoing Wright's 1908 "In the Cause" manifesto. Wright must have been seething when he read the last line: "their work is attracting more attention and causing more comment than any other architectural development in America." Ironically, a similar argument was emerging in Europe with the writings of the Dutchman, H. P. Berlage, who had visited America in 1911; although, in this case, Wright was the center of the discussion.[93] Wright's characteristic reaction to this type of press coverage was to immediately pick up his pen and write a rebuttal. In combination with a generous display of his recent drawings and models, he believed he could set the record straight. This is the background to the last exhibition Wright would mount at the Chicago Architectural Club, falling twenty years from the date of his first.

1914

By 1913, Wright had become adept at publications. With his 1907 show, he had to wait a full year before his well-illustrated article appeared in *Architectural Record*, the delay blunting the public effect. He turned again to the *Record*, where Michael A. Mikkelsen, who would prove a strong ally in difficult times, was just taking over as editor from Herbert Croly. What he proposed was highly unusual: first, the essay had no illustrations; it was not devoted to any past or current work; nor did it present an elucidation of design principles. Rather, it was a tirade with accusations of insincerity, imitation, and plagiarism directed at Henry Hyde and those Wright labeled "my disciples and pupils."[94]

It opened with a warning, "Style, therefore, will be the man. Let his forms alone." His tone was maudlin, bitter, and self-serving, but it put forth an argument for distinctions that Wright would hold fast for decades to come, especially when he resurrected the argument against proponents of the "International Style" from the 1930s into the 1950s. Having been formed during the era of the dominance of historical styles—Gothic Revival, Italianate, neo-Classicism—he made a clear distinction between a style that could be learned and imitated by copying visual characteristics or rules and his own definition of style. "Style is a by-product of the process and comes of the man or of the mind in the process," he wrote. "The style of the thing, therefore, will be the man—it is his. *Let his forms alone.* To adopt a 'style' as a motive is to put the cart before the horse and get nowhere beyond the 'Styles'—never to reach *Style*." According to the exhibition checklist, copies of the essay, "In the Cause of Architecture—Second Paper," were available for free at his display in advance of its publication in May 1914.

The arrangements leading up to opening night were unusual. The exhibition was sponsored by three different organizations—Chicago Architectural Club, the Illinois Chapter of the American Institute of Architects, and the Chicago Architects Business Association—Wright was not a member of any of the three. His work was not submitted to the jury, but George Maher explained that there was a shortage of exhibits in 1914. "Mr. Wright was invited to participate," Maher added, "as he has before. We were very glad to get him to take a room." Maher continued, "He wouldn't need to submit his work to a jury. Everybody knows his type of work."[95]

The *Chicago American* opened its pages on the day of the preview, April 9, 1914, with the headline, "Architects Quit Big Exhibit." The staff writer, Florence Patton, identified the "storm-center" as Frank Lloyd Wright. J. F. Surrman, chairman of the Chicago Architectural Club, went on record by stating, "Mr. Wright has been especially granted three walls ... not only on account of the merit of his work, but on account of the interest attached to his private life." With further questioning Surrman added, "Yes, he's just as interesting to the public one way as

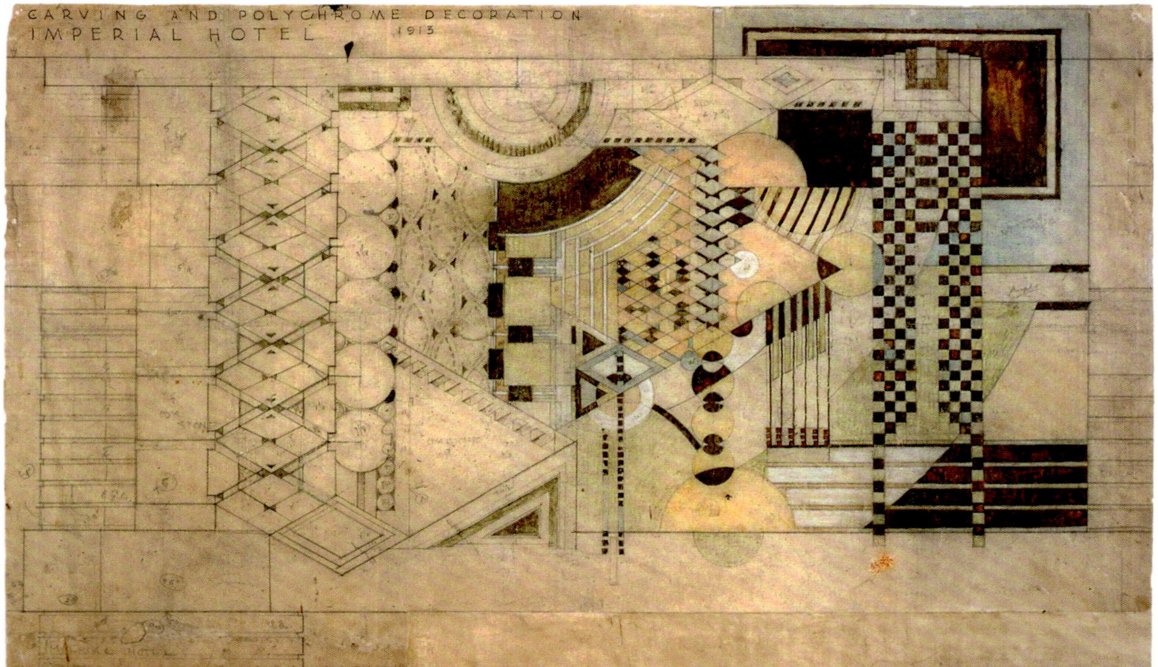

1.32 Sherman M. Booth House, Glencoe, Illinois, 1911–12. Graphite pencil, color pencil, and watercolor on off-white tracing paper, 20⅜ × 27⅞ in. (FLWFA, 1118.001). This drawing can be seen in figure 1.37 at *right*.

1.33 Imperial Hotel, Tokyo, Japan, stone carving and polychrome decoration for north parlor fireplace, 1913–23. Graphite pencil, cclor pencil, and gold ink on tracing paper, 21⅞ × 35¾ in. (FLWFA, 1509.005)

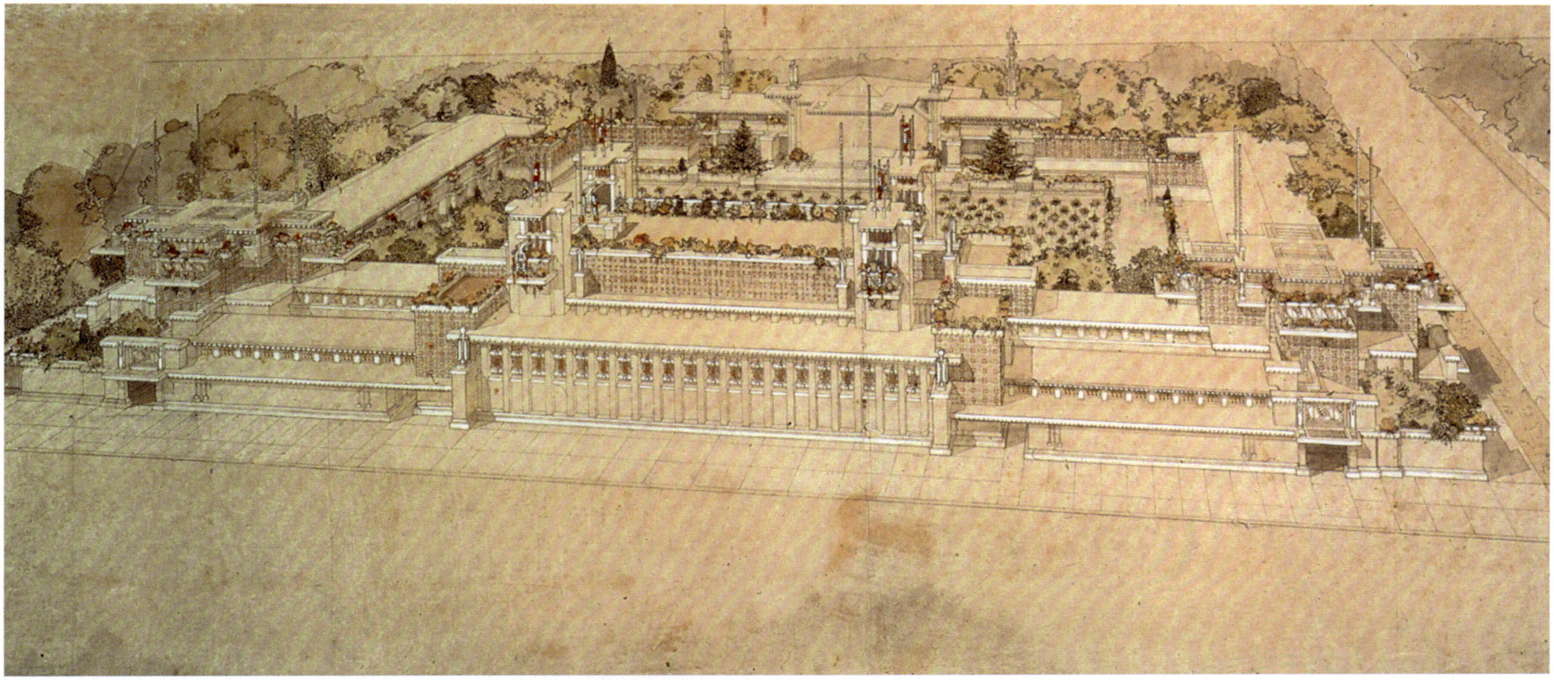

1.34 Midway Gardens, Chicago, Illinois, 1913–14. Ink, color inks, color pencil, and watercolor on off-white tracing paper, 16⅝ × 40⅛ in. (FLWFA, 1401.004). This drawing can be seen in partial view in figure 1.38 at *left*.

another and will draw a big crowd." The following day, the *American* printed that Wright was accused of "buying his way" into the exhibit with a $500 donation, but that allegation was denied by all parties involved. Wright was equally of the same mind as his defenders. The newspaper quoted him as responding, "Let them talk. Let them say what they will. Let them resurrect all the old scandal of the past three years. What do I care. I have three walls for my work. I am erecting the Imperial Hotel at Tokyo and I am doing other big work in the world—both the scandal and what I am doing artistically will bring us greater crowds. Let them talk, let them talk."[96]

As it turns out, it may have been his first exhibition with an official title, *Work of Frank Lloyd Wright: Exhibit Confined to Work Done since Spring of 1911*.[97] And with that, he surely was making a self-conscious attempt to regain his authority after his return from Europe. Unlike previous years, the display contained public buildings and houses equally, with several commissions located outside the United States (Japan and Canada), more than thirty-one items altogether, as some buildings were represented by perspectives, plans, and details; also included were photographs, furniture, and art glass (Coonley Playhouse windows); toys by himself and his sons, Lloyd and John; and Japanese print stands. He put emphasis on his largest or most impressive public buildings by showing plaster models of The Call Building (1912–13; San Francisco, California), Midway Gardens (1913–14; Chicago), and the Coonley Playhouse (1913–14; Riverside, Illinois), but he also exhibited hotels, a library, a post office, and a bank.[98] While many of the residences did not depart from the forms of the Prairie Houses, distinct new directions were evident in the designs for the Sherman Booth House (1911–12; Glencoe, Illinois), Midway Gardens, and the Imperial Hotel (1913–23; Tokyo; figures 1.32–34). He drew on the same principles for installation design as he had in 1907; however, in 1914, the pieces appeared more hastily assembled and mounted. Two models dominated the space; The Call tower was placed on a high pedestal, emphasizing its "tallness," while the Midway Gardens was decidedly low, horizontal, and spread out, occupying the center of the room (figure 1.35). On a diagonal were pieces devoted to children—a model of the Coonley Playhouse opposite a puppet theater that Wright had designed for his youngest child, Robert Llewellyn, then eleven (figure 1.36). On the walls, some perspectives were quietly framed with slender wood frames,

1.35 *The Work of Frank Lloyd Wright*, Chicago Architectural Club, Art Institute of Chicago, 1914. Photograph by Henry Fuermann and Sons. (FLWFA, 1500.001).
Left to right: Midway Gardens model, aerial perspective of the Imperial Hotel, art glass window from Coonley Playhouse,
The Call Building model no. 1, Midway Gardens sculpture maquette.

1.36 *The Work of Frank Lloyd Wright*, Chicago Architectural Club, Art Institute of Chicago, 1914. Photograph by Henry Fuermann and Sons. (FLWFA, 1500.0008).
Background, left to right: Midway Gardens sculpture maquettes, Japanese print stands, Imperial Hotel drawings, The Call Building model no. 1.
Foreground: Fuermann and Sons photographs and Midway Gardens model.

while most were simply pinned on the wall as in a studio. In the center of the room was a table, where the Wasmuth Verlag folios were open to the plates (figure 1.37). Compared with the 1907 mounting, the 1914 exhibition had somewhat of a haphazard feeling; on a table, black-and-white photographs of Taliesin by Fuermann and Sons can be seen scattered about (figure 1.38).

The uproar over the issue of favoritism dominated the newspaper reports, and the only thoughtful review was again by Monroe. During the years 1910–14, when Wright was undergoing a transformation, partly brought on by foreign travel, Monroe was acquiring a new level of sophistication herself. In 1910, she traveled around the world, making extended stays in China and Japan (including Nara, Kobe, Nikko, Kyoto, and Tokyo). On her return, she began planning her avant-garde magazine, *Poetry: A Magazine of Verse*, which under the watchful eye of the irascible Ezra Pound first appeared in October 1912.[99] By 1914, Monroe was in the forefront of the modern poetry movement by being the first to publish Imagist poems written on the Continent.

Monroe's review, "The Orient an Influence on the Architecture of Wright," on April 12 in the *Chicago Tribune*, sparked an exchange between the architect and critic that indicated a rapprochement. After alluding to the now commonly recognized resemblance between Wright's forms and the Japanese, she went beyond the familiar arguments by calling attention to his more recent work. "Perhaps the most complete opportunity which Mr. Wright has had as yet to express his ideas," Monroe explained, "will be the Midway concert gardens ... of which a model is shown." She expressed an opinion that revealed an understanding that had alluded Wright in the popular press when she stated, "Here the general public will have its first opportunity at a fair judgment of this artist, who is devoting his professional career to an effort to give us an authentic and indigenous architecture. Hitherto the public has known too little about his work."[100] This prompted a warm note the next day in which Wright revealed, "I believe that stripped of all this factional professional enmity—the qualities in any artist's endeavor stand truly revealed in course of time—a belief in the immortality of the soul assures me of this."[101]

With letters crossing in the mails—her note is lost—he again took up the correspondence on April 20. In this important letter, he made a gesture that would be more commonplace in the years ahead, especially in the 1930s and 1940s. Sensing a sympathetic tone in Monroe's review, he chose not to challenge her on her claims of Japanese influence, but instead reached out to her in a more substantial way. "The *Record* of New York wants to give a number to the work included in the exhibit to be published soon and something might be done there and then." He explained, "They will want a critical article—something that touches the thing where it lives and explains it with some degree of sympathy—for what it is. ... Would you care to undertake it!"[102]

Wright's proposition to Monroe indicated he was intending to pick up where he had left off before his move to Taliesin. He was intent on his strategy of linking public exhibitions with personally arranged publications in an effort to move his career and his idealistic goal of creating a genuine American architecture forward. However, only four months later, this momentum would literally stop dead in its tracks. In an event that would affect Wright for many years into the future, Mamah, her two children, and four others were killed by a deranged servant, who then proceeded to burn the living quarters of Taliesin to the ground. As Wright recalled, "The entire portion of the edition [of the Wasmuth Verlag folios] meant for America was consumed in the fire destroying the first Taliesin."[103] He had spent two years in their preparation and production, created the drawings and text as a manifesto to his first twenty years of architecture, and for almost two years had strategized to sell them to the next generation of American architects without much success. Certainly, Wright was hoping that this publication would bring him the respect and stature Olbrich commanded in Europe. Unfortunately, this was not to take place in the United States.

In the year of Wright's last exhibition with the Chicago Architectural Club, he was forty-seven years old (life expectancy for an American man was fifty-two years). No one could have predicted that he would live another forty-five years and would have to adapt to changing social values and new European architectural importations. During these early decades, his approach and attitude toward exhibiting were formed in Chicago, but his shows in the future would take place primarily on the East Coast and in Europe. Although he was showing with a group of working professionals, the setting of the Art Institute of Chicago was influential; he soon separated himself from the others and, in the role of artist-architect, took over a private gallery for himself. For the 1907 and 1914 exhibitions, he hired Fuermann and Sons to photograph them (an event unique in club history).

The original purpose of the club was draftsmanship, and Wright adopted a method of exclusively showing drawings and a few models, which were primarily made for public display rather than as design study models, thereby integrating exhibition production into his artistic practice. As his body of built work grew, he displayed black-and-white photographs, primarily by Fuermann and Sons, and placed them in loose piles on tables for closer examination. He believed at this time that delicate line and

1.37 *The Work of Frank Lloyd Wright*, Chicago Architectural Club, Art Institute of Chicago, 1914.
Photograph by Henry Fuermann and Sons. (FLWFA, 1500.0017). *Left to right*: Midway Gardens sculpture maquettes, The Call Building model no. 1.
Foreground: Wasmuth Verlag folios and Fuermann and Sons photographs adjacent to Midway Gardens model. *Right*: Coonley Playhouse model.

1.38 *The Work of Frank Lloyd Wright*, Chicago Architectural Club, Art Institute of Chicago, 1914. Photograph by Henry Fuermann and Sons. (FLWFA, 1500.0012). *Left to right*: Japanese print stands, Imperial Hotel drawings. *Foreground*: Fuermann and Sons photographs of Taliesin.

watercolor drawings should not be hung next to photographs. One represented the architect's ideal, the other a product of construction. From this time forward, he included his own publications set about the gallery for the public and other architects to study; the literary a complement to the architectural.

The audience for his exhibitions changed as he matured from a young aspirant to an accomplished designer and public persona. While his displays could be experienced on several levels, in the early years, 1894–1902, the club drew directly from its membership and a body of related artisans, while by 1907, the general public was in attendance as can be deduced from the considerable coverage in the local press. After 1911, there was a dramatic shift: Wright became an antihero, a perception caused by the public scandal associated with his private life, the self-conscious bohemian manner of his dress and appearance, and his outspoken interviews with inquiring newspaper reporters. By 1914, people came more out of morbid curiosity than aesthetic appreciation.

In keeping with the spirit of the Chicago Architectural Club, Wright viewed his exhibitions and their supplementary publications and lectures as educational, directed to "the young man in architecture" specifically and the American people in general. Due to the privileges accorded him by his allies in the club, he had a direct relationship with the general public, eliminating any mediation by a jury or curator; visitors were invited in as if stepping into his architectural studio.

On an ideological level, Wright was a product of his time and milieu; he had adopted the nineteenth-century belief of Ralph Waldo Emerson, Horatio Greenough, and Walt Whitman that America should develop an original culture—literary and aesthetic—and permanently reject European models and historic styles. Wright believed, like Whitman and Sullivan, that a genuine American architecture was not an end itself, but a means to an end: nothing less than the realization of a true democracy, not in the political definition of the term, but as a state of consciousness that would result in intellectual and spiritual freedom and the development of self-determination. His work could be experienced on many levels, but, intellectually, the primary one for Wright was as the realization of an original, and authentic, American architecture. When confronted with his critics, he was continually disappointed to find that his buildings alone did not serve the didactic influence he intended. Exhibitions either began or ended with literary expositions of his philosophy, which required careful reading. Yet this in itself was a very difficult task as Wright gave familiar words—democracy, nature, and organic—new meanings that were rarely self-evident; rather, they were Platonic ideals, thus his frequent use of the abstractions: Democracy, Nature, and Organic. Wright's point of view was optimistic, his agenda utopian. Remarkably, it remained so throughout his career, though his pedagogy would be subject to severe tests.[104]

What followed after the Taliesin tragedy was a geographic and social break from the Midwest that would continue well into the late 1920s. Commissions arose that took Wright west to the Pacific rim: Asia, and the California coast. While on this journey, also an intellectual odyssey, Wright would remove himself by thousands of miles from the industrial heartland of the United States and settle in Japan: the land of Buddhist temples, landscaped water gardens, antique woodblock prints, and painted screens highlighted with gold leaf. He immersed himself in this culture, which held spiritual significance for him, for more than a decade while the next generation of architects in Germany, Holland, and France were moving forward with the idea of an architecture based on rationalism and machine production. When this exile and spirit journey came to an end and he finally returned home to Taliesin in Wisconsin, his career was in a decline. One of his first thoughts for reviving it: an exhibition at the Art Institute of Chicago.

For the remainder of his career, Wright would not waiver from his pattern of accompanying his public exhibitions with an explanation of his ideology, either in print or, often, in a lecture. However, each circumstance would present new opportunities and challenges. He would face opposition and competing agendas, especially from established art museums; critics and historians were regarded with suspicion or animosity until they were converted to his point of view. Minor exhibitions took place as a matter of routine, but major exhibitions invariably led to last-minute dramas of operatic proportions.

CHAPTER 2

The Work of Frank Lloyd Wright, 1893–1930 and *Modern Architecture: International Exhibition*, Museum of Modern Art, 1932

The founding of the Museum of Modern Art in 1929 prompted a major turning point in Wright's career (figure 2.1). For just over twenty years—from 1932 until the final break in 1953—Wright would be accorded a major retrospective, numerous one-building exhibitions, and would become a fixture of the museum's Circulating Exhibitions Department, while also being included in several architectural surveys. For most of those two decades, MoMA's press releases, sent to hundreds of newspapers, journals, and museums around the country, would authoritatively proclaim him "America's greatest architect." But this national recognition followed fifteen years of relative isolation when Wright spent most of that period in Japan or the American West: California and Arizona. While he had no exhibitions originating in or in cooperation with his studio during these years, a new generation of architects, critics, and historians came of age that would change how Wright was perceived and affect how he presented himself.

After the tragedy at Taliesin in 1914, Wright spent most of his time in Japan on construction of the Imperial Hotel or on the design of a theatrical community for the oil heiress Aline Barnsdall (1917–23; Hollywood). Wright's prolonged stays in Tokyo from 1916 until 1922, where he lived for what amounted to four and one-half years, had a profound impact on his aesthetic. For several decades he had immersed himself in Japonism—Western interest in Japan as a cultural ideal—and he had, through his experience as a writer, curator, and dealer, become one of the foremost Chicago authorities on Japanese woodblock prints.

As his passion for Japanese art grew, he was drawn to the preindustrial culture of the nation before it opened itself to the West in the mid-nineteenth century. As his collection of six-panel screen paintings and lacquerware grew, he developed a particular affinity for the late sixteenth- through the seventeenth-century Momoyama period, which embraced both an opulent gold-embellished decorative style and the counteraesthetic of *wabi sabi*, a rustic simplicity of weathered unpretentious objects. He believed that "life in old Japan must have been a perpetual communion with the divine heart of Nature." His perception, although romanticized, was nevertheless based on close contact with "a people who have made of their land and the buildings upon it, of their gardens, their manners and garb, their utensils, adornments, and their very gods, a single consistent whole, inspired by a living sympathy with Nature as spontaneous as it was inevitable."[1]

On his permanent return to the United States from Asia in 1922, he was immediately greeted with proof that his reputation in Europe was in decline when he read his first copy of *Wendingen*, the architectural journal of the Amsterdam architectural organization Architectura et Amicitia, founded in 1918 under the editorship of Hendricus T. Wijdeveld (1885–1987).[2] Although an article by one of his first champions, H. P. Berlage, was largely

2.1 Frank Lloyd Wright in the Taliesin Studio, ca. 1924. Partial view of the The Call Building model no. 1 in the background. (FLWFA, 6004.0017)

laudatory, acknowledging that Wright "holds a place among the greatest architects of these times," the praise was tempered by the fact that Berlage's admiration for America was based on the priority the United States placed on commercial "machine production," which was not apparent in Wright's designs. "I find it difficult to see Wright," Berlage admitted, "otherwise than as a romanticist and [difficult] to see him as his very antipode, that is, as an 'industrial architect,' as many like to see him—as he likes to see himself."[3]

Berlage's reservations were indicative of a major shift in attitude that had occurred in Europe in the years before and after World War I. The Dutch and German avant-garde had been searching for architectural models for modern life brought on by the use of machine methods in construction, the changing needs of society, and the economic consequences of capitalism and mass production. Drawn to the "scientific management" theories of Frederick W. Taylor and the success of Henry Ford's automobile assembly line, America, more in European rhetoric than in reality, became the ideal of an industrialized twentieth-century social order. It was this preoccupation with *Amerikanismus*—European interest in the United States as a cultural ideal—that had originally brought Wright of the Oak Park Studio to the attention of Wasmuth Verlag. It was Wright of "The Art and Craft of the Machine" that fascinated most of the European postwar architects.

During the 1920s, German architects were moving closer to embracing a machine aesthetic; for example, a turning point occurred in 1923 when Walter Gropius called for "art and technology: a new unity" as the primary goal of his revolutionary design school, the Bauhaus. From the mid- to late 1920s, intellectual debate intensified as journals and magazines proliferated and illustrated books on "modern architecture" became commonplace. *Die Form* (1922/25) and *l'Esprit Nouveau* (1920) joined *De Stijl* (1917) and *Wendingen* (1918). While Le Corbusier's *Vers Une Architecture* (*Toward an Architecture*; 1923) had the most lasting impact, Walter Gropius's *Internationale Architektur* (*International Architecture*; 1925), Adolf Behne's *Der Moderne Zweckbau* (*The Modern Functional Building*; 1926), Gustav Platz's *Die Baukunst der Neuesten Zeit* (*Building Art of the Latest Period*; 1927), Behrendt's *Der Sieg des neuen Baustils* (*The Victory of the New Building Style*; 1927) and Bruno Taut's *Die neue Baukunst in Europa und Amerika* (*Modern Architecture*; 1929) were only the most influential of numerous books being produced, mainly in Germany. In fact, the Harvard undergraduate Philip Johnson (1906–2005), on holiday in Berlin in the summer 1929, informed his mother that he had "bought fifty books on contemporary architecture."[4]

2.2 Erich Mendelsohn, ca. 1925.
(Wikimedia Commons)

It is within this context that two circles of influential individuals formed that would substantially affect the revival of Wright's career in the early 1930s. The first circle consisted of Wijdeveld in Holland, Lewis Mumford in America, and Erich Mendelsohn and Behrendt in Germany. The second circle was all American: Henry-Russell Hitchcock, Alfred H. Barr Jr., and Johnson.

World War I and its aftermath had disrupted the momentum of architectural discourse in Europe. However, it took only a few years for Wijdeveld, a passionate Wright advocate, to assemble a group of supporters to contribute to a series of issues of *Wendingen* devoted to the Midwest architect. One of the first of these was Mendelsohn (1887–1953), the German Jewish architect with whom the Dutchman had formed a close friendship as early as 1922 (figure 2.2). Antagonism toward the industrial city took Mendelsohn to the United States in 1924, where he focused his camera on the concrete canyons of Manhattan, toured the industrial northeast, including the Larkin Building, and saw the masterworks of Chicago architecture with Barry Byrne, a former draftsman in Wright's Oak Park Studio. Moreover, with an introduction from Wijdeveld, he spent a two-day visit with Wright at Taliesin. "[Wright's architecture] is imagination of an unheard-of richness," Mendelsohn declared, "space, relationship with nature, details, materials, color—with masterly discipline. That is genius."[5] He was drawn to Wright's theories immediately, and this impression was reinforced by meeting Lewis Mumford (1895–1990), the New York intellectual critic, who had recently authored *Sticks and Stones* (1924), a penetrating analysis of American architecture (figure 2.3). On his return voyage home, Mendelsohn profited by reading Mumford, and in turn, recommended him to Wijdeveld, who soon requested an essay, "The

2.3 Lewis Mumford. (FLWFA, 6702.0004)

2.4 Walter Curt Behrendt. (Courtesy Kai Gutschow)

Social Background of Frank Lloyd Wright," for the Wright issue of *Wendingen*.

The year 1925 was significant with the appearance of the first reappraisals by Wijdeveld, Mendelsohn, and Mumford in the Wright issues of *Wendingen*. The circle of support widened that year when Mumford met Behrendt (1884–1945), a German civil servant, editor, and polemicist, at a special meeting of a planning conference in New Jersey (figure 2.4).[6] Behrendt had been closely identified with progressive architectural ideas throughout his career, joining the Deutsche Werkbund in 1912, editing *Die Form* from 1925 to 1927, and writing one of the most authoritative monographs on a new unified "industrial style" of architecture, *Der Sieg des neuen Baustils* (*Victory of the New Building Style*; 1927). His recognition of Wright preceded that of his contemporaries when in the only European review of *Frank Lloyd Wright—Chicago*, appearing in 1913, he concluded, "It seems ... as if something significant is to be expected from the new continent, initiating a new development and regeneration in architecture."[7]

Mumford and Behrendt formed a close bond almost immediately over their shared view that while technological advances were necessary, they should not be made at the expense of a humane built environment, one made possible by a new modern building vernacular.[8] To spread their polemic, Behrendt solicited articles from Mumford for *Die Form* and was responsible for having *Sticks and Stones* published in German.

While Wijdeveld was generally understood to be Wright's champion in Holland, Mumford gradually came to assume that role in America. Partly influenced by Mendelsohn's accounts of his Chicago visit, Mumford decided in 1927 to investigate the city himself with Bryne as his guide. In his groundbreaking article, "New York vs. Chicago in Architecture," published in the November 1927 issue of *Architecture*, he declared Chicago the historical frontrunner in architectural innovation, an idea he would develop further in a series of articles in the late 1920s, culminating in *The Brown Decades* (1931), where he established the triumvirate of Henry Hobson Richardson, Louis H. Sullivan, and Wright as the progenitors of European "modernism." "On Richardson's solid foundations, [Sullivan] laid the cornerstone of the new organic architecture," Mumford declared. "Sullivan was the link between two greater masters, Richardson and Frank Lloyd Wright; and with the development of Wright's architecture the last stage in the transition was made: modern architecture in America was born."[9] Mumford's early articles confirming his position as the preeminent American architecture critic drew the attention of Henry-Russell Hitchcock (1903–1987), a graduate student at Harvard University. In 1927, they embarked on a correspondence that would profoundly influence both Wright's career and the acceptance of "modern architecture" in the United States in the decade ahead.

While Wright's life in the last half of the 1920s was dominated by domestic chaos, financial bankruptcy, and exile from his home, Taliesin, in retrospect, he remembered it this way: "I should have closed my architectural career about 1925 and retired peacefully to my family and farm. But I had been too uniformly engaged in all these children of my mind ~~and heart~~ to do that. By way of patient persistent effort these brain children became actual buildings."[10] As this statement, written at the time of his 1940 MoMA retrospective, reveals, 1925 was a significant year in Wright's life. With his "patient persistent effort," he explored a number of opportunities—lecturing, writing a memoir, and opening a design school—to revive his career.

Trying to pick up the thread of his practice in the Midwest where he left off in 1914, he predictably turned to the idea of an exhibition at the Art Institute of Chicago. An air of mystery surrounds this proposed show. Wright mentioned it in a letter to Wijdeveld on January 7, 1925, when he announced, "[The drawings] will be needed here early in February for an exhibition at the Chicago Art Institute which may continue among European countries."[11] The Thirty-Eighth Annual Exhibition of the Chicago Architectural Club opened on February 4, 1925, for a month in the basement of the Art Institute, but the *Daily News* reviewer noted with regret that there was "nothing [in the exhibition] by Frank Lloyd Wright."[12] However, it is likely that he refused to join a group show and held out for a one-man exhibition in the museum, which would have been under the authority of Robert Harshe. Harshe served as director and chief curator of painting and sculpture from 1921 until his death in 1938, and during his tenure he was responsible for expanding the museum building and enlarging the collection with major donations. Wright complained a few years later, "Harshe . . . and the old guard would not consider architecture a fine art but as a profession and might be stupid enough to take the stand that a professional man should flock with his profession and show when they show, how and as."[13] It had been now more than a decade since the fifty-seven-year-old Wright had last exhibited with the Architectural Club. He no longer enjoyed the unconditional support of his former colleagues: Spencer, Perkins, and Dean. To start anew as he had in 1894, he had to seek opportunities elsewhere; fortunately, New York became more welcoming.

2.5 Raymond Hood. (Avery Architectural and Fine Arts Library, Columbia University, New York)

THE ARCHITECTURAL LEAGUE AND PRINCETON UNIVERSITY, 1930

By 1930, the beginning of the Great Depression, Wright was planning an around-the-world tour of drawings, models, and photographs of his work from 1893 to 1930. Although Wright selected the material, designed the installation, and executed all the logistics himself, the initiative for the exhibition came to him without his intervention. The invitation came indirectly in a letter from A. Lawrence Kocher (1885–1969), managing editor of *Architectural Record*, who had overseen fourteen articles by Wright—originally commissioned in 1926 by the magazine's editor, M. A. Mikkelsen—with the title, "In the Cause of Architecture," which ran from May 1927 to December 1928. These essays, which put Wright's name forward in the architectural trades after a long absence, set forth major points of his theory while also illustrating little known work of the 1920s. From the beginning, Wright reserved the right to publish the essays in book form; this idea evolved in 1929 with Kocher and Douglas Haskell, who served as associate editor briefly between 1929 and 1930, into a monograph, *Creative Matter in the Nature of Materials*, with new photography and, at Wright's suggestion, an introduction by Mumford. In this connection, Haskell, though Kocher did not accompany him, visited Taliesin sometime in mid-September.[14]

Shortly thereafter, in a letter dated September 27, 1929, Kocher announced that at a recent "luncheon at the Architectural League with Mr. Raymond Hood, Mr. Ralph Walker, and Mr. Ely Kahn, it was suggested that there be several exhibitions on current architecture. One of the exhibits would feature your work."[15] The passages that followed must have delighted Wright as he could not have received a better offer if he had planned it himself. "I was asked to discover whether you would agree to such an exhibition," Kocher continued, "also whether it would be possible for you to come to New York at the time of the exhibit." Obviously speaking for the Architectural League, Kocher concluded, "The well-selected photographs and drawings would be well hung and the exhibit would be sent to various museums and important architectural clubs throughout the country. I told Hood that I would confer with you regarding the prospect which we all greatly desire." Two points in Kocher's letter are of particular interest; first, that Wright's was to be one exhibition out of several that were being solicited, and second that, from the outset, the league wanted a traveling show.

In 1929, the Architectural League of New York was two years short of its fiftieth anniversary. Among its prominent members, in addition to Hood, Kahn, and Walker, were Joseph Urban, Harvey Wiley Corbett, James Gamble Rogers, Hugh Ferris, and Lee Lawrie. Hood—whose past major achievements included the Chicago Tribune Building (1922–25; Chicago), the American Radiator Building (1924; New York), and the Daily News Building (1929; New York)—as president was the major instigator of programs (figure 2.5). At the time of the invitation to Wright, Hood (1881–1934) was about to embark on one of his most lucrative ventures, Rockefeller Center (1930–39; New York).[16]

As Kocher's letter made clear, the invitation to Wright originated with a group well known in Manhattan as the "Three Little Napoleons of Architecture," lunch regulars at the dining room of the league headquarters on East Fortieth Street a few blocks south of Grand Central Station. In 1927, the league had moved into their newly renovated spaces, conveniently located around the corner from the Architects Building on Park Avenue where many of the members had offices. The new building was fitted out with a gallery and a "ground-floor grill" adjacent to a "lockered-lined room" with "a place for the members to store their 'prohibited' liquor."[17] During one of these gatherings, the group concluded that in addition to their annual exhibition, the league would inaugurate "a series of one-man shows to present to the profession and to the general public a cross-section of the work of living American architects, painters and sculptors." The intention was to "depict the processes of thought and work of individuals or firms who are making distinct contributions to modern American architecture and art design." The first one-man show in February 1930 was given over to Lawrie, an architectural sculptor who collaborated with Ralph Adams Cram, Bertram Goodhue, and James Gamble Rogers.[18] Although the connection between Wright and the league, a conservative body of architects steeped in Beaux-Arts tradition, seems hard to explain, there is a link that drew him close. The key figure was Joseph Urban (1872–1933), an Austrian émigré architect and scenic designer whose close contemporaries had been Olbrich, Josef Hoffmann, and Kolomon Moser, all of whom Wright admired (figure 2.6). In 1915, Urban moved to New York where he began set designs for Broadway revues and the Metropolitan Opera; later returning to architecture, his most important building was the New School for Social Research (1930; New York), a modernist work reflecting European influence. How Wright originally met Urban, whom he described as being "responsible for more lyrical beauty in our world of decoration than anyone I know" is not documented, but their relationship was so well established by 1927 that Urban generously provided financial aid to Wright during his bankruptcy.[19] Urban may have decided that he wanted to help Wright with action as well as cash. It is probable that it was with his support and encouragement in August 1928 that Wright became an honorary member of the American Union of Decorative Artists and Craftsmen (AUDAC), headquartered in the French Building on Fifth Avenue at Forty-Fifth Street. Not surprisingly, the two organizations overlapped, with Hood, Kahn, and Corbett members of both, with Kahn and Corbett serving on important AUDAC committees.[20] As it turns out, Hood was Urban's best friend and a Friday regular, along with Kahn and Walker, at "the 'Four-Hour Lunch Club' that met at Mori's Restaurant," a Greenwich Village landmark dating to 1884.[21]

At the time of the invitation, Wright had begun work on designs for a multistoried apartment building, St. Mark's-in-the-Bouwerie Tower (1927–31; New York), which took him to Manhattan periodically. He was in New York City on October 11, ten days after Kocher's letter, where he was the principal speaker at an AUDAC luncheon.[22] It is likely that he accepted the invitation in person at this time and discussed details. Unfortunately, Wright's appearance in Manhattan coincided with an article in *Time* titled "Genius, Inc.," which reported on his insolvency, characterizing him as "a very original, great and influential architect," who was also "erotic and impulsive."[23]

2.6 Joseph Urban with theatrical set models, New York. (Rare Book and Manuscript Library, courtesy of University Archives, Columbia University, New York)

Wright must have started work on organizing materials and designing the exhibition in a traveling format almost immediately. With the contract for a luxurious resort hotel in the Arizona desert in hand in September 1928, he had begun to hire more draftsmen. By fall 1929, they included Henry Klumb, Donald Walker, Vladimír Karfík, Rudolph Mock, Takehiro Okami, and George Cronin. Wright organized the retrospective to accomplish three major goals: to prove that he had a vital and creative career in the years 1910–30, in other words, to refute what he considered a "postmortem" by his critics; to assert that his latest work employed new materials and ideas such as standardization; and to prove that the principles of the more recent European movement, in other words, "modern architecture," originated with his own work starting as early as 1903. In order to make a demonstrable impact, Wright set his ambitions high for a traveling exhibition in the depths of the Depression that had neither institutional sponsorship nor funding. By the time the material began to circulate in America in 1930, he described it as "600 photos, 1000 drawings, and four models" designed in a demountable installation for a top-lit room, thirty by fifty feet.[24]

In the midst of model making and printing photographs, Wright must have been very pleased to receive a letter from E. Baldwin Smith, acting chair of the Department of Art and Archaeology, Princeton University, dated February 3, 1930. Smith extended an invitation to Wright on behalf of the School of Architecture, a division of his department, to give "eight lectures on Modern Architecture in America and Europe, with emphasis as you see fit upon both the theory and the practice" during the spring from May 5 to May 16.[25] There were several intriguing aspects to Smith's offer that would have caught Wright's attention. In the first place, that the series—known as the Kahn Lectures for the benefactor, Otto Kahn—was primarily directed at "art students and architects," his favorite audience; second, there was a stated desire to "get the University to publish the course lectures as a book or monograph," an opportunity for his first architecture book in the United States; and last, although perhaps not least, the speaker's fee was $750. It is certain that he would accept this offer, but, because he was in the midst of preparations for his first exhibition in sixteen years added to the fact that Princeton was approximately fifty miles from Manhattan (limiting shipping costs), this was an obvious opportunity for another venue.

Wright wasted no time countering Smith's offer. On February 8, he expressed interest by explaining that because he would "be busy in New York about the time you mention tempts me to try" to "sustain interest" in a "series of eight lectures." Then adopting a clever self-serving metaphor, he queried, "But why eight lectures? In six days the world was made, on the seventh the work was visible and the maker no doubt viewing it,—let us assume with 'the modest assurance of con[s]cious worth!![']" Then he proposed "an exhibition I could appropriately arrange, of my own recent work illustrating the ideas and principles involved in the 'course,' ... The plans, photographs and drawings arranged as an exhibition wherever you elected, could remain at Princeton for a week or so after the series ends and be more to the point perhaps than anything that has been done, or could be said."[26] Fortunately, Smith was completely amenable to Wright's suggestions: "Your argument for six days and six lectures, with an exhibition at the end, completely satisfies me."[27] The only detail undetermined was the choice of specific dates.

From that point on, the exhibition at Princeton took precedence over New York. Bowing to the academic calendar and Smith's requirements, Wright set the dates of May 6 to May 14 for his lectures in New Jersey with the exhibition opening May 12; the schedule for the Architectural League was fixed for two weeks from May 29 to June 12, with the preview to coincide with a testimonial dinner planned for the night of May 28.[28] By the end of April, Wright and his draftsmen were working at a feverish pace to assemble the "several hundred photographs to extra-illustrate the plans and drawings" and manufacture the "self-contained unit for travel from place to place," but they were unable to complete the four models planned for the show.[29] Wright queried Smith about the possibility of a postponement because "we only have one [model] to begin with, the most important one, St. Mark's on the Bouwerie."[30] When Smith could not accommodate the request, Wright wired back, "All right, we will work nights and be ready." He explained, "The exhibition to be set up [as] a self-contained unit at the beginning of the second week."[31]

In his first attempt at organizing a traveling show, Wright established a pattern he would follow in the future. He assigned one of his draftsmen (in this case, Donald Walker) to accompany the exhibition material—to facilitate shipping and installation—throughout the tour; he preferred to give his talks without slides, relying on the exhibition to illustrate his ideas (although, in this instance, Smith insisted on slides). Wright delivered his first four lectures from Tuesday, May 6, through Friday, May 9; on the weekend, the exhibition arrived and was ready for hanging. The opening took place on Monday, May 12, and was followed by the remaining two lectures from May 13 to 14. The next night, he was in Manhattan debating Walker ("just back from Germany") on modern architecture at the Architectural League to a capacity audience. On Friday, May 16, he was still in New York, lunching with Henry H. Saylor, editor of *Architecture* magazine; Mumford; Haskell; and Urban.[32] The exhibition closed on Thursday, May 22, and was packed, shipped, and delivered to the league gallery by Monday, May 26, when Wright arrived to supervise the installation. A special feature of the event at the Architectural League was an "approach and setting" designed by Wright's dear friend, Urban (figure 2.7).[33]

Wright's lectures, the original impetus for the events at Princeton University, were published in 1931 as *Modern*

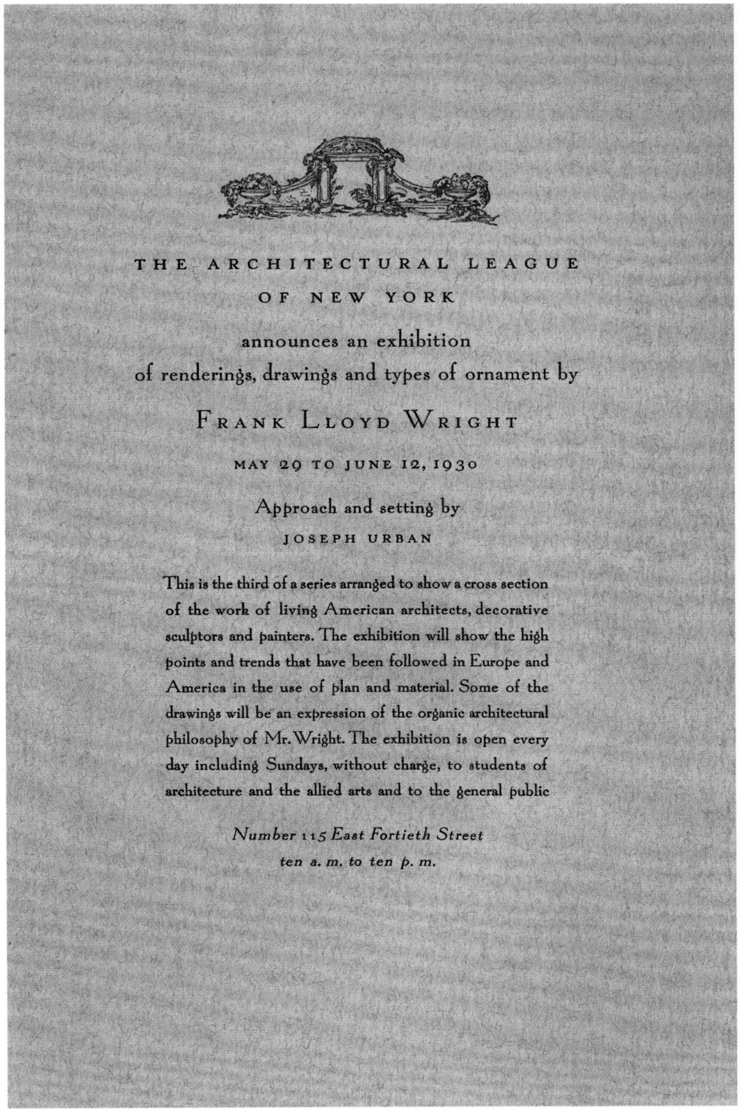

THE ARCHITECTURAL LEAGUE
OF NEW YORK
announces an exhibition
of renderings, drawings and types of ornament by
FRANK LLOYD WRIGHT
MAY 29 TO JUNE 12, 1930
Approach and setting by
JOSEPH URBAN

This is the third of a series arranged to show a cross section of the work of living American architects, decorative sculptors and painters. The exhibition will show the high points and trends that have been followed in Europe and America in the use of plan and material. Some of the drawings will be an expression of the organic architectural philosophy of Mr. Wright. The exhibition is open every day including Sundays, without charge, to students of architecture and the allied arts and to the general public

Number 115 East Fortieth Street
ten a. m. to ten p. m.

2.7 Announcement, Frank Lloyd Wright exhibition, Architectural League of New York, May 29 to June 12, 1930. (Kathryn Smith collection)

Architecture, Being the Kahn Lectures for 1930.[34] It was appropriate that, as in 1908 when his essay "In the Cause of Architecture" followed as a companion to the major 1907 Chicago Architectural Club exhibition, his first published architecture book in the United States should appear along with his first major career retrospective. While Wright was primarily engaged in proselytizing about modern architecture as a duality—positioning his ideology against that of the younger generation of European architects, especially Le Corbusier—the *Lectures* book was also notable for the amount of space devoted to Japanese aesthetics. "All phases of art expression in the Momoyama period were organic," Wright explained. "There was no great and no small art. . . . Here, as a saving grace in one civilization on earth, feeling for significance, simplicity in art was born, becoming soon an ideal naturally attained by organic means." In the decades ahead, Wright's affinity for and understanding of Japanese art of the sixteenth through nineteenth centuries—architecture, fine arts, and crafts—would distinguish and separate him from the leaders of "Machine Age" modernism.

While the Princeton University event was set in academia, the league exhibition, Wright's first in New York City, was very different. Although the lectures were the highlight in New Jersey, at the Architectural League the emphasis was on a testimonial dinner in his honor. In retrospect, the event was incongruous and can only be explained as an effort inspired and encouraged by Urban in all good conscience to bolster his friend's prospects and spirits. There were at least seven dinner speakers (excluding Hood, who was the moderator), of whom only two actually knew Wright: Mumford and Paul T. Frankl (1886–1958), a Viennese architect who made his American reputation as an Art Deco furniture designer. The others were Walker; Corbett; Kahn; Eugene Schoen, a New York architect who specialized in furniture and textile designs; and Bruce Bliven, editor of *The New Republic*. With the exception of Mumford, Frankl, and Bliven, the speakers were all a close group, who practiced in the prevailing "skyscraper set-back" style; in fact, Hood, Corbett, and Schoen were all associated on the design of Rockefeller Center, and Hood, Corbett, and Walker were on the Planning Commission for the "Century of Progress Exposition," to be held in Chicago in 1933.

It is necessary to piece together various accounts to gain an idea of what transpired at the dinner. Saylor, writing in *Architecture*, described it as "very large and vociferous," although with "a distinct note of sadness . . . due to the extreme tardiness of recognition on the part of his brother practitioners."[35] Saylor reported that Wright admitted "for the past twenty years he has been a lonely man, and now suddenly finds that he has been, and is, surrounded by friends." To Hood, Wright was complimentary, stating, "I am so glad to have found comradeship in my own profession at last—with you at the head of the procession."[36] "That hard-boiled New York outfit," he confided to his son, Lloyd Wright, "simply plastered me [with compliments], sincerely, I believe."[37]

But the most forthright exchange occurred between Wright and Mumford. When Wright wrote that "The [speakers] were meant to be 'high, wide and handsome' and somewhat were, but you said the thing to be said, as you usually do," Mumford cut through the flattery to the crux of the matter.[38] "The memory of that dinner makes me grit my teeth and cuss," Mumford responded. "Those boys all meant to do the right thing, I have no doubt: they knew that they owed you a debt, too: at bottom, they realized that they were honoring themselves for posterity by holding a banquet in your honor. . . . They respect you and envy you because you have had a different kind of success: but they were as unable to express the first as they were impotent to conceal the second."[39]

The exhibition and attendant events at Princeton University and the Architectural League, especially the latter, had the intended effect: a rehabilitation of Wright's public image. In addition to the routine press notices, the three giants of print journalism, *New Yorker*, the *New York Times Magazine*, and *Time*, all devoted a story to the resurgence of the man Alexander Woollcott called the "Father of Modern Architecture." Woollcott, who had been a personal friend of Wright since 1925, closed his July 1930 *New Yorker* profile, "The Prodigal Father," with the remark, "if . . . I were suffered to apply the word 'genius' to only one living American, I would have to save it up for Frank Lloyd Wright."[40] *Time*, which had covered his bankruptcy only the year before, concluded, "Comment at and on his Manhattan show must have persuaded Architect Wright that he had lived to see his own time."[41] A common thread throughout the articles was the reference to the recognition Wright had received in Europe and Japan. The *New York Times* reviewer, H. I. Brock, quoting Ely Kahn, who reported he was told on his visit to Germany, " 'Go back,' the Germans said, 'across the Atlantic and get the stuff from the man who gave it to us.' " And of Hood, Brock wrote that he was "among those who credit Frank Lloyd Wright with [the] most influence toward enfranchising and reforming the art of architecture to meet the needs of modern life."[42]

While the New York architectural establishment embraced him in the spring of 1930, the inclusion would be brief and feel hollow by the end of the year. The cause was the decision of Hood and Corbett as the architectural organizers of the 1933 Chicago World's Columbian Exposition, titled the "Century of Progress," to exclude him from participation on the grounds that his individualism would never allow him to collaborate with a committee. While Wright made no public accusations, the issue became a New York "cause célèbre" by the beginning of 1931 due to articles by Haskell in *Nation* and Mumford in *New Republic*. Mumford had written, "The omission of [Wright] . . . is serious. 'Hamlet' without the Price of Denmark could not be a more comical performance."[43] The uproar, pitting Wright directly against Hood, culminated on February 26 at an AUDAC meeting at Town Hall where Mumford, Haskell, and Woollcott vociferously stood up for Wright, after which Hood was allowed time for rebuttal. Wright claimed that the fair "would be nothing more than a continuation of eclecticism." "You cannot take classic motives, wash them behind the ears, and make modernism of them," he was quoted as saying.[44] Walter Kilham and others "from [Hood's] office were so mad we could spit, not at Frank Lloyd Wright, but the speakers of the evening whose 'rapiers' were not only sharpened and polished, but long enough to reach the back seats."[45] In the end, the evening proved an unfortunate affair with bitterness enough on both sides.

AMERICAN TOUR, 1930–31

As the exhibition drew to a close in New York, the question of circulation to other venues came to the forefront. Wright must have been deflated to learn that Boston, the first location seriously considered, was unavailable till fall. Since he preferred to send the exhibition to schools of architecture, the timing was not right: the universities were closing for the summer. Hood wrote Wright that either William Emerson of Massachusetts Institute of Technology or Henry Shepley of the firm Coolidge, Shepley, Bulfinch, and Abbott (successor firm to H. H. Richardson) would contact him later in the summer about a showing in the fall. Hood continued, "I dropped a line to Meeks, Bosworth, and Laird, the heads of the Department of Architecture in Yale, Cornell and Princeton, suggesting that they might tie up at the same time."[46] Although Wright may have felt let down by the league's weak efforts in promoting a traveling show, he could feel some vindication when he was informed that genuine interest had been expressed by two architects, Earl Reed and Pierre Blouke, who wanted to bring the exhibition to Chicago.

By the time the show closed in New York and was shipped back to Wisconsin, Wright was working intensely to shift public perception away from his personal life to his work. With the idea of keeping the show "out in the field for some years to come," he was seriously promoting tours from coast to coast and across Europe: Berlin, Vienna, Prague, Munich, Frankfurt, and Paris.[47] In what would have been a truly daring move, he inquired of his former draftsman, Kameki Tsuchiura, about the possibility of sending the exhibition to Japan.[48] In 1931, at the age of sixty-four, he felt compelled to explain the motive behind his extraordinary campaign: "During the depression . . . I have been able to accept invitations to conferences, formal dinners and lectures ... which may serve to deepen the impression ... that I am out of the field and now singing for my supper around the world. ... When I am no longer a 'practicing' architect, it will be only because of circumstances beyond my control."[49]

While he only had hopes for the East Coast colleges, he already had two firm commitments in the Midwest. On May 29, the Madison Art Association, which was affiliated with the University of Wisconsin, put in a request for October.[50] Plans were also moving ahead successfully for the Art Institute of Chicago. "After all I suppose this show belongs more to Chicago than any other individual city," Wright confided to Reed, formerly of Dwight Perkins's office, "and certainly there is a warmer feeling in relation to the big old town in my heart than for any other." With memories of his last Chicago show in mind (which he incorrectly dated to 1907 instead of 1914), he cautioned, "it might become a basis for a cause 'celebre' and some amusement for the country at large."[51]

By September, Wright had doubled the size of the exhibition with the addition of three models and so many additional drawings the loan fees increased from $50 to $500. As a result, Yale University withdrew due to cost and similarly prospects for the other eastern colleges.[52] By this time, Wright's attention was focused on the Midwest.

ART INSTITUTE OF CHICAGO, 1930

When the exhibition opened at the Art Institute of Chicago on September 25, it was the realization of a goal to which Wright had aspired for five years. With the help of Reed, who was chairman of the Education Committee of the Chicago chapter of the American Institute of Architects (AIA), pressure had been put on Harshe to accord Wright a one-man show in the museum. In fact, one of Wright's associates, Charles Morgan, stated that Harshe had done an about-face, explaining that from the director's viewpoint, "there was nothing that they could possibly do that would honor you sufficiently, but that they would like to do everything possible."[53] Harshe was as good as his word. Not only was the exhibition open to the public for almost two and a half weeks, but Wright also was invited to give the Scammon Lectures established "primarily for students" at the bequest of Maria Sheldon Scammon, an amateur painter, who founded the Chicago Society of Decorative Arts in 1877. At her death in 1901, funds were placed in trust for speakers on the "history, theory and practice of the fine arts." Wright's lectures—"The New Architecture" and "In the Realm of Ideas"—took place on October 1 and 2, and were open free to the public.[54]

Both the lectures and the exhibition were overwhelmingly successful. On October 1, an audience of one thousand people overflowed the auditorium and spilled over into a second hall where the sound was piped in.[55] Newspaper coverage was enthusiastic, with a notice or story appearing almost every day for a week with rotogravure sections on the weekend.[56] A reviewer, Marguerite B. Williams, for the *Chicago Daily News*, reported that there "was an air of excitement" in the gallery "as men gathered around tables of plans and books and perused the epigrams taken from Mr. Wright's Princeton lectures.[57]

The content of *The Work of Frank Lloyd Wright, 1893–1930*, according to the architect, doubled in size over the summer 1930.[58] Wright hired the Oak Park photographer, Gilman Lane, to document the Chicago installation.[59] Wright explained in October 1930 that the exhibition contained six hundred photographs, one thousand drawings, and four models: St. Mark's Tower, Richard Lloyd Jones House (1928–31: Tulsa, Oklahoma), Standardized Overhead Gas Station (1928), and the Blue Sky Mausoleum for Darwin Martin (1925–29; Buffalo).[60] Tables were also used to display portfolios of drawings and copies of the *Wendingen*. Despite the title, the documentation reveals that Wright conceived of this exhibition in much the same way as his earlier Chicago shows. In other words, generally speaking, there was major emphasis on works undertaken from the last exhibition in 1914 up to 1930.

During the 1930 American tour, visitors were able to study a wide range of drawing techniques from different periods in Wright's career. There were representative examples from the Oak Park Studio of the watercolor and ink renderings that were so characteristic of the Chicago Architectural Club exhibitions. But drawings made in his Studio (in Los Angeles and Wisconsin) after his permanent return from Japan in 1922 were an important departure and one that would have lasting significance. Wright adopted a 2H Castell pencil and Koh-I-Noor color wax pencils from Czechoslovakia as tools, his head draftsman after 1932, John H. Howe, explained, because the watercolor technique was "etched in granite" and Wright wanted materials that were "flexible, that could be changed by erasure." "The eraser is more important than the pencil," Howe remembered Wright explaining, "because Wright created by elimination."[61] Drawings from California for the Lake Tahoe Summer Colony (1923–24; Emerald Bay, California) and the textile block houses, superb examples of the new media, also introduced another innovation, the perspective of the building with the ground plan projected below

2.8 Shore Cabin, Lake Tahoe Summer Colony, Emerald Bay, California, 1923–24. Kameki Tsuchiura, delineator. Pencil, color pencil on tracing paper, 18¾ × 15¾ in. (FLWFA, 2205.003)

(figures 2.8–9). Many of these drawings were delineated by his Japanese draftsman, Kameki Tsuchiura, who was instructed in this technique by William E. Smith, a Canadian architect, who had been in the Studio since 1918.[62] While this style of perspective was not continued after 1924, the use of color pencils and the addition of a legend, which included a red square, initialed by Wright indicating his approval of the completed drawing became the Studio standard until his death in 1959 (figure 2.10).[63] In addition to the color pencil drawings, other media were occasionally employed in the studio in the decades ahead: pastel (figure 2.11), watercolor (figure 2.12), ink wash, and tempera.

As much as Wright's tonal color renderings were representative of his association of architecture and landscape, they were difficult to reproduce satisfactorily in publications, and they did not communicate the symbolism of Machine Age modernism. With a European avant-garde audience in mind, Klumb, assisted by Okami and Mock, redrew six buildings designed before 1910—Winslow House, Larkin Building, Yahara Boathouse, Unity Temple (figure 2.13), Robie House, and Richard Bock House (1906; Maywood, Illinois)—as large-format, bold black-and-white perspectives.[64] This skillful editing of such a large corpus of work down to a handful of abstract images was Wright's attempt to demonstrate that as "the father of modern architecture" he had anticipated the radical forms of European modernism by decades.

2.9 Charles Ennis House, Los Angeles, California, 1924–25. Ink, pencil, color pencil on tracing paper, 20¼ × 39 in. (FLWFA, 2401.003)

2.10 National Life Insurance Company Building, Chicago, Illinois, 1924–25. Pencil, color pencil, and ink on paper, 49½ × 41½ in. (FLWFA, 2404.041). (Collection Seymour H. Persky)

2.11 Ralph and Wellington Cudney House, San-Marcos-in-the-Desert Resort, Chandler, Arizona, 1929. Graphite pencil, color pencil, and pastel on white tracing paper, 17 × 27 in. (FLWFA, 2706.007)

2.12 San Marcos-in-the-Desert Resort, Chandler, Arizona, 1928–29. Lloyd Wright, delineator. Graphite pencil and watercolor on art paper, 25 × 65 in. (FLWFA, 2704.048)

The exhibition covered a wide range of themes and building types: prefabrication and standardization as seen in the American System-Built Houses (1915–17) and the textile block system; large-scale commercial buildings such as Midway Gardens, the Imperial Hotel, and San-Marcos-in-the-Desert Resort (1928–29; Chandler, Arizona); and skyscrapers including The Call Building, National Life Insurance (1924–25; Chicago), and St. Mark's Tower. But these ideas were probably not discernable to the vast majority of visitors due to the style of the installation (figure 2.14). Wright did not favor traditional salon-style hanging, nor did he adopt the installation methods of the European avant-garde such as the Bauhaus teachers or Mies van der Rohe; rather, the overall effect was yet again evocative of his architectural studio. As a result, except for the models, there were few text labels to identify the work; while some projects were hung together on wall panels—the perspectives for the Lake Tahoe Summer Colony, for instance—other work was mixed together, such as full-scale drawings for Imperial Hotel ornament and *Liberty* magazine covers (1926–27; figure 2.15).

He preferred to show drawings and photographs separately, unmatted, to avoid the "danger of killing drawings by photographs."[65] To accommodate this preference, Wright designed a unique system of freestanding boxes: on the long sides, large boards set at an angle created "easel panels" for the drawings; on the short ends were "swinging slabs" for photographs (figure 2.16). His presentation style was not uniform; some drawings were matted, others mounted on boards, others simply pinned to the panels. The most immediate impression was one of quantity; every surface was covered from edge to edge (figure 2.17).

A few years later, he stated his exhibition philosophy as follows: "There are many reasons why I shall never exhibit a detached piece or two of my work. In the first place the ideal of an organic architecture, which I represent as distinguished from my contemporaries, can only be seen where several buildings

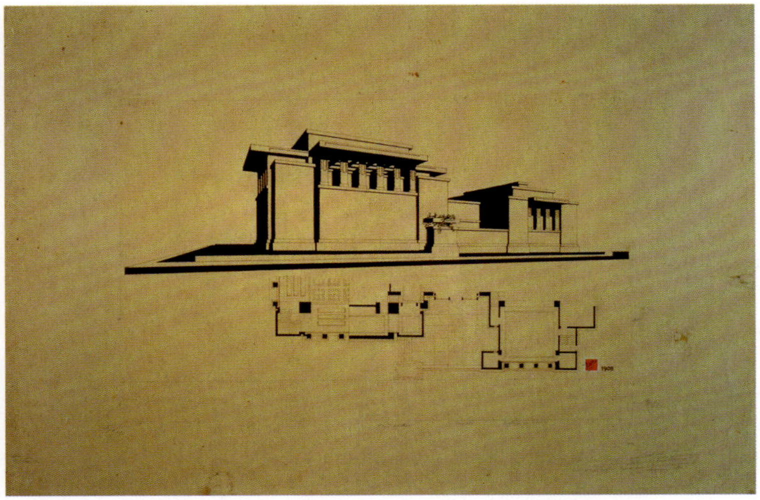

2.13 Unity Temple, Oak Park, Illinois, 1905–8.
Heinrich Klumb and Takehiro Okami, delineators (redrawn 1929).
Pencil and ink on paper, 23 × 36 in. (FLWFA, 0611.007)

2.14 *The Work of Frank Lloyd Wright, 1893–1930*, Art Institute of Chicago, September 25–October 12, 1930. Photograph by Gilman Lane. (FLWFA, 3000.0005). *Left*: St. Mark's Tower model in front of Larkin Administration Building perspective; *middle rear*: Darwin D. Martin Blue Sky Mausoleum; *foreground*: Richard Lloyd Jones model.

2.15 *The Work of Frank Lloyd Wright, 1893–1930*, Art Institute of Chicago, September 25–October 12, 1930. Photograph by Gilman Lane. (FLWAF, 3000.0003). *Foreground*: *Liberty* magazine cover design, “Toy Balloons”; Richard Lloyd Jones House perspective, Imperial Hotel ornamental panel; *above*, Imperial Hotel ornamental grill. *Right*: Skyscraper Vase, St. Mark’s Tower model.

2.16 *The Work of Frank Lloyd Wright, 1893–1930*, Art Institute of Chicago, September 25–October 12, 1930. Photograph by Gilman Lane. (FLWFA, 3000.0006). *Foreground*: Wasmuth Verlag folios and *Wendingen* on tables; *left to right*: St. Mark's Tower model, National Life Insurance, and San Marcos-in-the-Desert Resort perspectives; *right*: Ennis House perspective, Rosenwald School perspective, Barnsdall Kindergarten drawings.

2.17 *The Work of Frank Lloyd Wright, 1893–1930*, Art Institute of Chicago, September 25–October 12, 1930. Photograph by Gilman Lane. (FLWFA, 3000.0020). Models *left to right*: Richard Lloyd Jones House, St. Mark's Tower.

have adequate representation. Photographs do not serve nor do merely drawings. Only the drawings, some photographs and a three-dimensional model can convey adequately any one of the buildings I expected to contribute. And several buildings differing in type would be necessary to bring out the general value of the ideal present in all."[66]

Wright's intention was clearly to show that for the previous fifteen years, despite the implication of headlines in the popular press, he had been intensely active as an architect. Although the majority of the work remained unbuilt, especially in California and Arizona, the exhibition proved that he had moved beyond the single-family house to large-scale commissions, including monumental buildings. While the drawings revealed, on close inspection, that Wright had been pursuing a fecund direction in planning and structural innovation since his last public presentation in Chicago, most observers would probably have been struck by the exotic locations: from Japan to the Hollywood Hills to the arid mountains of the Arizona desert. The newspapers, on the other hand, exploited the daring use of industrial materials, writing of "glass houses" and "glass apartment buildings." The *Christian Science Monitor* reported: "Mr. Wright sees glorious possibilities for the transforming of cities from what he calls 'sodden imitations of medieval strongholds' to lovely shimmering realms of light as a result of the use of glass."[67] Compared to the initial humiliation he had experienced with the Chicago Architectural Club in 1914, his return to the Art Institute was something of a redemption (figure 2.18). In other words, Chicago had redeemed itself in Wright's eyes. With that said, it would be the last Wright exhibition in Chicago in his lifetime, with the exception of Museum of Modern Art circulating shows.

2.18 Frank Lloyd Wright with Richard Lloyd Jones House model and perspective, Art Institute of Chicago, ca. September 24–25, 1930. (Courtesy Douglas M. Steiner, Edmonds, Washington)

During the run in Chicago, Wright contemplated his next step. While he conveyed to the press that the exhibition was going back to the East Coast and then on to Europe, these plans appear to have had no foundation. Rather, he had to settle for a tour through Wisconsin and then down the West Coast. By this time, the exhibition was a package, which included one or two lectures by the architect. From Chicago, it was seen at the State Historical Library at Madison, October 15–25, 1930, through the efforts of Franz Aust and Walter Agard under the sponsorship of the Madison Art Association.

Charlotte Partridge, director of the Layton Art Gallery in Milwaukee, had been an Oak Park neighbor of the Wright family, where her mother had been a friend of the architect's first wife, Catherine. She requested the exhibition in October and after weeks of negotiations over fees and dates, it was ultimately shown November 20 to December 8, where Wright again became "a cause célèbre and an amusement to the country."[68] The newspapers exploited the architect's attack on the neo-Classic Milwaukee County Courthouse then nearing completion. With quips like, "That sort of thing no longer exists for the best and highest minds; it is dead, and the structure grins there like a death mask," and, "In the new courthouse you are spending millions to advertise to the future that Milwaukee in your day was neither a scholar nor a gentleman," Wright garnered headlines.[69] The uproar continued during the entire run of the show, which—either in spite of it or because of it—ended with large attendance figures for both the lectures and the exhibition.

WEST COAST TOUR, 1930

The Great Depression was sorely affecting Wright's opportunities for booking his exhibition: the fees were too high for the colleges and universities that he preferred. Luckily, another acquaintance wrote him unexpectedly while the show was still at the Art Institute. Walter R. B. Willcox (1869–1947), who started his architectural career in Chicago in the 1880s, moved to the Northwest in 1907, first to Seattle, and finally to Eugene, Oregon, in 1922. As head of the Department of Architecture at the University of Oregon, he was the prime mover in bringing the exhibition and Wright to Eugene, March 6–10, with a lecture on March 7, and then on to the Henry Gallery, University of Washington, Seattle, March 11–15, with a lecture March 12.[70] This was one of the few confirmed instances in which a Wright exhibition led to a potential commission. Through Willcox's efforts Wright was introduced to George Putnam, owner and editor of the *Capital Journal* newspaper in Salem, Oregon. After some discussion and payment of a retainer, Wright turned to designing one of his most prophetic buildings—a glass enclosed two-story volume supported with fifty-six interior columns—that anticipated the SC Johnson Administration Building. Unfortunately for a number of reasons including financial problems, Putnam declined to move forward.[71]

EUROPEAN TOUR 1931

By the end of the year, Wright was working on two fronts: to expand the schedule beyond the Pacific Northwest to include California and to make the European tour a reality. He turned to Los Angeles: to his son, Lloyd, a local architect, as the major organizer, but he also sought help from his former clients, Aline Barnsdall and Alice Millard, and from Pauline Schindler, the former wife of R. M. Schindler, who had supervised the Hollyhock House (1919–21; Hollywood) construction between 1920 and 1921.[72] Chicago installation photographs were sent to each venue to promote the show.[73]

By mid-1930, the long-term effects of the Depression were becoming permanent. Wright's prospects for Arizona and Manhattan were fading. He now was engaged in activities that had previously been merely adjuncts: lecturing, organizing exhibitions, writing articles and books. He felt triumphant when all three came together at the same time. With the absence of commissions, Wright turned to curating his built and unbuilt work by creating what amounted to a catalogue raisonné. From mid-1929 to mid-1930 he assigned Okami to compile a list, including clients' names, locations, and dates.[74] This became the basis for a catalog he intended to publish to accompany the European tour, and later, was made available to MoMA for their scholarly research.

Since his exhibition was without institutional support and absent of any funding, Wright's efforts to send the exhibition abroad involved a tremendous amount of risk taking. While the show was still in Chicago, he started a letter-writing campaign to dedicated European admirers and decided to send an emissary to Germany to handle the details in person. He first wrote to Wijdeveld to interest him in bringing it to Holland and then "to Berlin, Munich, Vienna, Prague, and Paris before coming home."[75] A month later, with thoughts of Germany in the forefront of his mind, he wrote simultaneously to Mendelsohn and Heinrich de Fries (1887–1938) of Düsseldorf, an architectural critic who had edited *Frank Lloyd Wright: Aus dem Lebenswerke eines Architekten* in 1926.[76] With that gesture, he, knowingly or unknowingly, pitted the two Germans against each other in a competition to bring the exhibition to Berlin. This came out into the open shortly after Heinrich Klumb arrived in Germany on Christmas Eve.

According to Klumb's detailed reports to his master, the issues uppermost in the assistant's mind were to place the exhibition in prime locations—Berlin, Amsterdam, Hamburg, Mannheim, Stuttgart, Zürich, Vienna, Leipzig, Paris, Brussels, London, Stockholm, and Prague—and to work out shared expenses, making the entire enterprise economically feasible for each venue. The first obstacle Klumb encountered was de Fries's insistence that he be exclusively in charge because "he considers the exhibition . . . a personal matter without regarding anybody else and without thinking of expenses." Obviously shocked, Klumb added: "He says you should pay for [it]!"[77] Although de Fries went directly ahead and secured the Prussian Academy of Arts, the situation soon degenerated when he not only pressed ahead to the exclusion of Wijdeveld, but wrote him a nasty letter as well.

Klumb began to shuttle back and forth between Holland and Germany over the issue of which city would host the exhibition first.[78] The matter came to a head in early March when Klumb received a letter from officials at the academy that they no longer could work with de Fries. Out of this, the close friends, Wijdeveld and Mendelsohn, took over the tour management, and logistics were resolved directly with Alexander Amersdorfer, secretary to the president of the academy, Max Liebermann, the distinguished painter-printmaker. It was agreed "the circuit throughout Europa will be managed from Amsterdam through Mr. Wijdeveld."[79]

AMSTERDAM 1931

As plans for an opening in Amsterdam on May 5 were moving ahead, Wijdeveld in his boundless enthusiasm did not take heed of the shift in Europe's critical assessment of Wright's work. Twenty years had elapsed since the Wasmuth Verlag publications and six since Wijdeveld had produced the *Wendingen*. Not only had attitudes changed within Holland, but also Wright had produced a body of new work that departed in form and character from the period 1893–1909. In 1918 Oud could state that "[Wright's] masses slide back and forth and left and right; there are plastic effects in all directions. This movement ... opens up entirely new aesthetic possibilities for architecture."[80] By 1925, after the "puritanical asceticism" and "mental abstinence" of the new De Stijl movement, led by Theo van Doesburg, became ascendant in Holland, Oud declared that Wright's formal qualities were having a "pernicious" effect "on this side of the Atlantic." He cautioned, since the American "proved to be an artist rather than a prophet ... we must place less importance on Wright's influence on European architecture."[81]

The organization, design, and manufacture of the European exhibition took place at Taliesin under Wright's direction during the winter hiatus, January–February 1931. Wright continued to use the panel system, but he remounted matted drawings on double thicknesses of Prestwood, some for slanted "easels" to be attached on both sides of four freestanding large boxes and others intended for the walls. Stands were designed for the traveling models; a new one, San Marcos Water Gardens (1929; Chandler, Arizona), was finished in February, making a total of five for the tour.[82]

Wijdeveld, who had boundless passion for Wright's work, seemed even more motivated by the opportunity of opening Wright's first European exhibition in Amsterdam. His initial thought, he told Wright, was to "publish a second book [similar to the *Wendingen*] with your latest work" and "with an introduction by myself, an article ... by yourself ... and articles by the best modern architects in Europe and America." In essence, in what amounted to a proposal for a collected "Life Work," Wijdeveld suggested over time to add "a third and fourth book to combine gradually all your work in a way worthy to it."[83] Wijdeveld was dedicated to this idea and brought it up again several months later, assuring Wright that he had consulted with the original publisher, C. A. Mees, who was favorable. Although Wijdeveld continued to work on the new volume in the months ahead, requesting from Wright "*construction*-drawings-*plans-details* of the *St. Marks Tower* [and] *Arizona hotel*," nothing ever came of it.[84] At the time, Wright was in the middle of a number of book projects, including *Creative Matter in the Nature of Materials*, which had much in common in design and content with the 1925 *Wendingen*.[85]

Instead, Wright created text and design for a European multilingual exhibition catalog; although unpublished, it was the first comprehensive attempt Wright had made to organize his work chronologically in printed form since the Wasmuth Verlag publications.[86] Unlike the exhibition panel system, which was not organized chronologically or by project, the catalog contains 125 selected buildings or projects from 1891 to 1930 in chronological order with text in English, French, and German. Each entry, where appropriate, gives the project or building name, location, and date, followed by a short description, ostensibly by Wright. For example, the Larkin Building text reads: "Brick. Stone washes. Building sealed. Fresh air intake at corners, combined with stairways. Artificially ventilated. Natural light. First negation of the ornamental building of the nineteenth century. Magnesite used for floors over mat of 'Excelsior' (wood fibre) drenched in magnesite. All interior trim magnesite castings. Entire furnishing and filing-systems of steel, baked finish, and magnesite. First metal furniture made in U.S.A." As well as documenting his most important buildings and singling out those greatly admired in Europe, he also begins to confront history by addressing the question of who was the originator of the forms and theories of modern architecture. It is a pattern he continued for the remainder of his career.

By early April, Wright sent the "dummy" to Amsterdam, apologizing to Wijdeveld for "trespassing again on your time and skill," but adding that he believed it could "be done cheaper and better in Holland with your direction."[87] He agreed with Wijdeveld that the text in three languages should be printed in different colors—English in black, French in red, German in blue—with the "Introduction ... printed on [a] separate leaflet attached to the text sheet."[88] With the opening set for less than a month away, time was pressing. While Wijdeveld replied that two thousand copies of the catalog for Wright's use in America could be produced for $500, and the American architect agreed to the terms if payment could be deferred to midsummer, nothing came of the proposal.[89]

While these negotiations were taking place, Wright hoped to ship the crates to Europe around April 15 on the Holland America Line. Wijdeveld was continuously moving forward on several fronts. He was writing "in four languages" to many foreign countries, but he believed that hard times was the explanation why "[Prague]-Paris-Vienna-Breslau or Rome didn't go

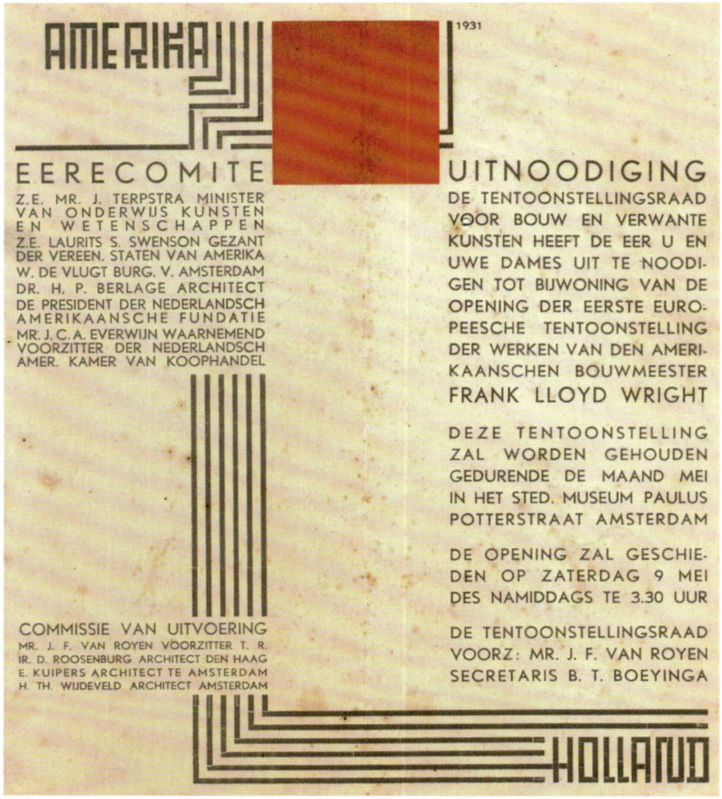

2.19 Hendricus Theodorus Wijdeveld, *Amerika-Holland*, invitation to *The Work of Frank Lloyd Wright, 1893–1930*, Stedelijk Museum, Amsterdam, 1931. Lithograph in color. (FLWFA, 1047.006). *Left*: Honorary Committee list and Executive Commission list; *right*: "Exhibition Board for Architecture and Allied Arts invites you and your wives to the opening of the first European exhibition of the work of Frank Lloyd Wright May 9 at 3:30 p.m."

in for my proposals. The latest news from Zürich (where Werner Moser tried his best) is in a way of accepting;—but *sure* is only *Antwerp* for September and *Rotterdam* for December."[90]

Within Holland, he was acquiring the support of notable government and cultural figures to form various committees for the Frank Lloyd Wright exhibition, the America-Holland initiative. The Honorary Committee was made up of J. Terpstra, Dutch minister of education, arts, and sciences; Laurits S. Swenson, the United States ambassador; J.C.A. Everwijn, Netherlands-American Chamber of Commerce; Willem de Vlugt, the mayor of Amsterdam; and Berlage representing the Netherlands-American Foundation. An Exhibition Committee of designers, charged with duties, consisted of Jean François van Royen, printer and typographer, president; B. T. Boeyinga, secretary; Dirk Roosenburg; E. Kuipers; and Wijdeveld (figure 2.19).

When the crates were opened at the Stedelijk Museum, Klumb discovered "all the drawings were blistered and others badly scratched" (figure 2.20). This necessitated removing all of them from their mounts and once done, revealed "a better possibility of arranging the whole, more fit for the room we had." "People are critical," Klumb warned Wright, "in fact very critical in looking at your work and even at the way of showing it. The smallest error we would make in arranging and presenting it would have done much harm."[91] To this end, Wijdeveld decided to redesign much of the installation. First, he ordered "a load of triplex boards (Oregon pine 60 × 200 in. in size)" to cover the walls making "a surface of the most beautiful texture" to hang the drawings. In the center of the room were the easels—mounted only with "delicate" colored drawings on Japanese paper—trimmed by two feet to allow more room for the pedestals (figure 2.21). Atmosphere was created by plants and Dutch "flowers of different colors in glass bowls" set on tables and the floor. Wijdeveld designed an entrance with slabs of Oregon pine in staggered rows mounted with the exhibition poster (figures 2.22–23).[92]

The opening was a grand occasion with a note of embarrassment. Notables from the committees were present; Ambassador Swenson was scheduled to officially open the exhibition to the public. The sixty-six-year-old Swenson was a career diplomat; although he was born in Minnesota, he spent most of his adult life in Europe representing the United States in various northern countries. It is reputed that he had no knowledge of Wright, although Wijdeveld supplied him with information in advance, including a copy of the Princeton lectures. The Dutch took center stage: Van Royen "mentioned the great value which [Wright's work] has given to the world . . . although eminent Americans of Politic[s], Industry and Finance did not even know about it." Wijdeveld spoke "a stream of joyful words. Nobody dared to breathe." Swenson, according to Klumb, "talked about the colors of the flag," and "declared the exhibition formally open."[93]

While the grand ambitions were never realized, Wijdeveld did use his influence to prepare the way for an impressive Dutch reception. First, he designed a poster and an invitation that was very much in character with the style of the 1925 *Wendingen* that Wright admired. With his move during the late 1920s to *Bouwkundig Weekblad*, it was this journal that covered the exhibition. A month before the opening, Wijdeveld contributed more than ten illustrated pages on Wright: an introduction, "Architect Frank Lloyd Wright in Europe: An Exhibition of His Work in Amsterdam," and Dutch translations of three Wright articles, "The Architect and the Machine," "The New World," and "Technique and

2.20 Installing *The Work of Frank Lloyd Wright, 1893–1930*, Stedelijk Museum, Amsterdam, May 1931. (FLWFA, 3100.0015). Page from the scrapbook Wijdeveld made for Wright. *Center*: H.Th. Wijdeveld handling drawings; *right*: Heinrich Klumb with St. Mark's Tower model.

2.21 *The Work of Frank Lloyd Wright, 1893–1930*, Stedelijk Museum, Amsterdam, May 1931. (FLWFA, 3100.0001). Page from scrapbook Wijdeveld made for Wright. *Left to right*: Darwin D. Martin Blue Sky Mausoleum model; Doheny Ranch, Lake Tahoe Summer Colony, Freeman House drawings; *rear*, Standardized Overhead Gas Station and St. Mark's Tower models.

2.22 Entrance, *The Work of Frank Lloyd Wright, 1893–1931*, Stedelijk Museum, Amsterdam, May 1931. (FLWFA, 3100.0002). Poster designed by H.Th. Wijdeveld.

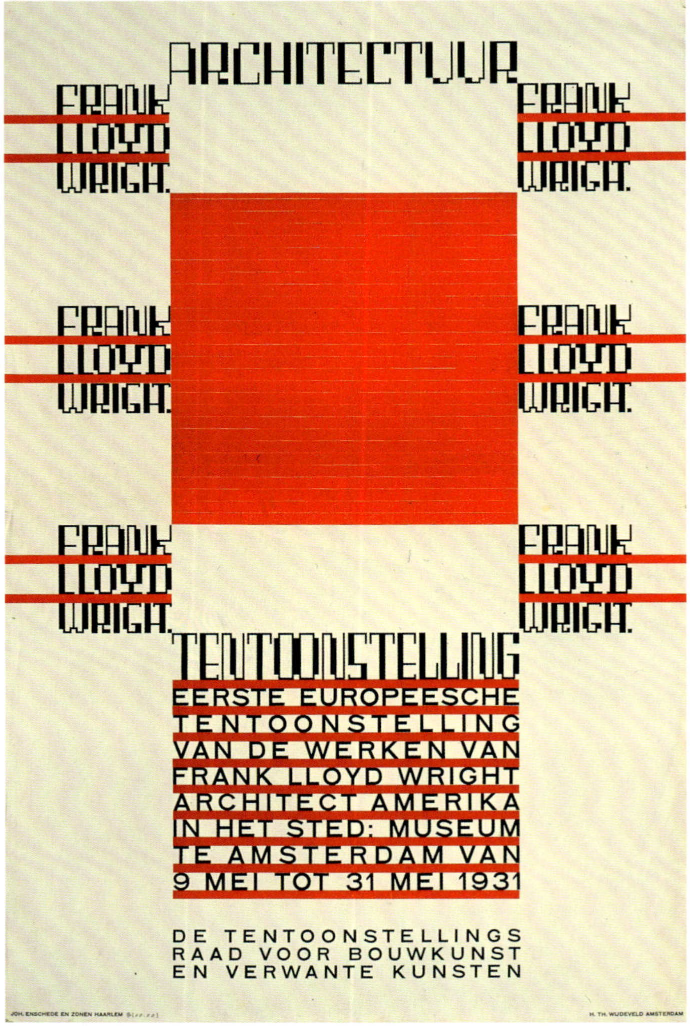

2.23 Hendricus Theodorus Wijdeveld, "Architectuur—Frank Lloyd Wright Exhibition" poster, 1931. Lithograph in color, 30½ × 19¼ in. (FLWFA, 3100.001). *Text*: "First European exhibition of the work of Frank Lloyd Wright, Architect, America, in the Sted. Museum in Amsterdam, May 9 to May 31, 1931."

Imagination." The articles were illustrated with drawings, photographs of models, and a few photographs of built work spanning the period from 1922 to 1929, essentially new work that had not been previously published in Holland. Wijdeveld's text was rhapsodic and, for some, such adulation was open to criticism. He declared: "[Wright] became King in the land of imagination, winning new dominions by his riches and his donations. Thus he gained Holland, and through our country the whole of Europe. We now have the task of supporting him to conquer the last bulwark; his native country. Let us therefore receive him as a king and honour his work as a possession of permanent value. Can we, architects, fancy a more beautiful blossoming of Spring than just this year, now that Wright through his work, is coming to visit us in May."[94]

A notice announcing the European tour appeared on May 9, and a rather bland, but positive review, by the second-generation Amsterdam school architect, Jan Boterenbrood, appeared on May 23 in the same journal. Wijdeveld's influence can be seen in the other notable article by W. J. de Gruyter, who concluded after some qualification that "Frank Lloyd Wright is a giant among architects of our day; indeed, 'one of the gods upon earth.' "[95]

Considering the difficulties Wright and Wijdeveld had to surmount to realize the American architect's first European exhibition, the Amsterdam show was a success, if not an ideological breakthrough. In a revealing confession marked with eccentric punctuation, Wijdeveld could be speaking for individuals in the past and those still in the decades ahead who did make and who would make great personal sacrifices to realize Wright's exhibitions. "I made the exhibition of your work at Amsterdam (and through Europe) ... please, believe me, ... not for you, ... not for the sake of one man only, whom (certainly) I admire, ... but for the growth of an *Idea*, ... which might be now an *Ideal*, but which will one day be *Reality*: 'The happiness of mankind' 'The coming of a new Culture' " (Wijdeveld's punctuation).[96]

BERLIN 1931

Critical reception in Holland was mild compared to the newspaper and journal coverage Wright would receive in Germany where the impact of landmark events such as the opening of both the Gropius-designed Bauhaus (1926) in Dessau and the Deutscher Werkbund's Weissenhof Siedlung (Weissenhof housing exposition) in Stuttgart (1927), which showcased buildings by Mies, Oud, and Le Corbusier, all in a unified style, indicated an aesthetic shift. While at the same time, architectural discourse, especially in Berlin, was intense and complex, involving philosophical and political positions toward modern life and institutions, and, only rarely, particulars of style. Within this context, discussion of Wright's contributions would swing from the extreme of uncritical acceptance by the expressionists to disillusionment from the functionalists to outright hostility by the Communists. He was a lightning rod for controversy.

Wright's favorable reputation in Germany rested generally on two aspects: his theory, first, and his executed buildings, second. The critics focused on his essay, "The Art and Craft of the Machine," and the 1908 "In the Cause of Architecture" as manifestos of the new Machine Age, and with this background regarded the Larkin Building and the Robie House as his most important works. But by 1931, Wright's projects and buildings in Japan, California, and Arizona were known through their publication by de Fries in *Frank Lloyd Wright: Aus dem Lebenswerke eines Architekten* and in an article, "Neue Pläne von Frank Lloyd Wright" (New Plans), that appeared along with excerpts from his Princeton lectures in *Die Form* (July 1930).[97] Siegfried Scharfe, an art historian who had visited Taliesin in fall 1928 while he was a visiting professor at the University of Wisconsin, Madison, provided more exposure. Scharfe authored two articles about Wright and published translations of three of his *Architectural Record* articles: "Sheet Metal" (August 1929), "Concrete" (January 1930), and "Glass" (March 1930), in the prestigious *Wasmuths Monatshefte*.[98]

In fact, within the pages of the same journal the Wright debate continued. Mendelsohn took a stand championing him as "A great artist we revere. A great man we love."[99] Yet the American had come under negative scrutiny from Werner Hegemann, a city planner, who served as the journal editor from 1925 to 1933. Hegemann, familiar with the United States from studying there at various times in the early years of the twentieth century, was a conservative who admired McKim, Mead, and White and held the 1893 Chicago World's Columbian Exposition in the highest esteem as a model of planning. He dismissed Wright as an "exoticist" due to influences he identified, unfortunately with some confusion, as Chinese and Japanese. He declared that "eighteenth century decorators with Chinoiserie" absorbed Oriental ideas more positively than Wright with his "American Prairie Style."[100]

It was against this backdrop that the Amsterdam exhibition closed on May 31 and was shipped to Germany, where it opened at the Preussische Akademie der Künste in Berlin on June 17. In his inaugural address, which appeared the same day in the newspaper *Berliner Tageblatt*, Mendelsohn dwelt on the fact that America "does not visualize the significance of [Wright's] work" because it is "still short sighted in architectural matters." He offered as proof the fact that Wright was not included in the 1933 Chicago World's Fair "by a clique that mistakes Manhattan for Attica and Architecture for an Art Dictionary." However, the majority of his remarks were a call to arms: "the world must unite toward a new goal, a common world idea that, being beyond the day's reality, will rejuvenate its imagination." He claimed that what was needed was "the living spirit of personal intuition" of "great artists." "One of these is Frank Lloyd Wright," he declared.[101]

Wright, distracted by his desperate financial straits back in Wisconsin, was probably unaware that the German Building Exposition, which had opened on May 9, was being held concurrently in eight exhibition halls at the seventeen-acre Berlin Fair Grounds on Reischskanzlerplatz. The Exposition is best known as the location of the Deutscher Werkbund's exhibition, *Die Wohnung unserer Zeit* (The Dwelling of Our Time), a collection of full-scale mock-ups of different types of housing units; for instance, one-room flats, apartment hotels, single-family houses designed by Gropius, Marcel Breuer, and Hugo Häring among others. The spare and elegant installation by Mies and Lilly Reich elevated exhibition design to a modern art form in its own right. As a centerpiece, Mies designed an Exhibition House, which demonstrated the powerful, spatial De Stijl innovations of interwoven planes and volumes. Philip Johnson, in Berlin at work on an exhibition for MoMA that summer, was so powerfully moved by this work that he wrote a review for the *New York Times*. He concluded that the Exhibition House "conveyed the feeling of openness that, perhaps more than anything else, is the prime characteristic of modern architecture."[102]

While Amsterdam was significant as the location of Wright's first exhibition in Europe, the showing in Berlin was the most important event during the entire two-year tour and one of the six most important exhibitions during his lifetime (figure 2.24). Due to the

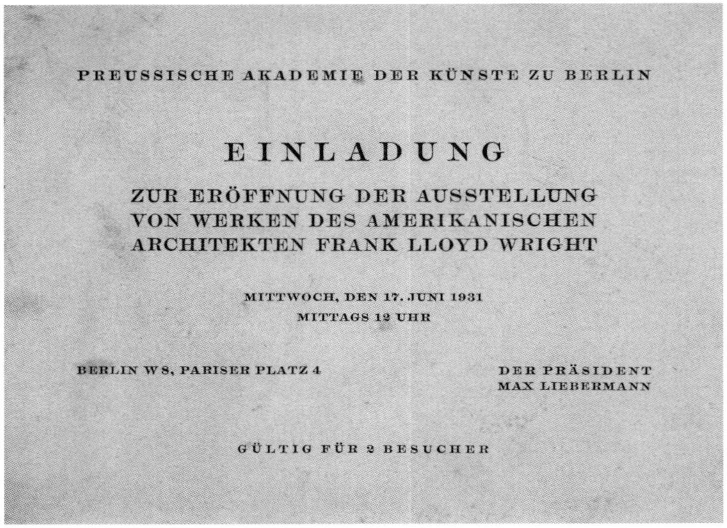
PREUSSISCHE AKADEMIE DER KÜNSTE ZU BERLIN

EINLADUNG

ZUR ERÖFFNUNG DER AUSSTELLUNG
VON WERKEN DES AMERIKANISCHEN
ARCHITEKTEN FRANK LLOYD WRIGHT

MITTWOCH, DEN 17. JUNI 1931
MITTAGS 12 UHR

BERLIN W 8, PARISER PLATZ 4

DER PRÄSIDENT
MAX LIEBERMANN

GÜLTIG FÜR 2 BESUCHER

2.24 Invitation, *The Work of Frank Lloyd Wright, 1893 to 1930*, Prussian Academy of Art, Berlin, June 1931. (FLWFA, 1047.008). *Text*: "Invitation to the opening of the exhibition of the work of American architect, Frank Lloyd Wright, Wednesday, June 17, 1931, lunchtime, 12 o'clock."

German reaction and Wright's response, it dramatically set the tone for his confrontation with European modernism over the next two decades. As far as can be determined, the content was the same as in Holland; while the installation was more sober, it still retained the Wright-designed panel and box system (figure 2.25). Controversy occupied the pages of newspapers such as *Deutsche Bauzeitung*, *Württemberger Zeitung*, and *Frankfurter Zeitung* as well as journals such as *Die Form*. With notable exceptions, reviews reflected the political or ideological biases of the authors.

For instance, Adolph Donath, an art historian and editor of *Der Kunstwandler*, writing in *Berliner Tageblatt*, praised works—Unity Temple and the Larkin Building—that were associated with Wright as a precursor to the Neue Bauen, but also admired 1920s projects such as San-Marcos-in-the-Desert Resort and the Doheny Ranch Development (1923; Los Angeles) where architecture "becomes landscape design."[103]

This was not the case with the acerbic "Greatness and Decline of a Pioneer of Modern Architecture" by Dresden City Museum director Paul F. Schmidt, in the journal, *Baukunst*. Schmidt spent one page of his two-page review fondly recalling the works of 1894–1909 that were favorites of the German functionalists—office buildings and Prairie Houses—before he began his attack on the 1920s projects, objecting on aesthetic and societal grounds. Rejecting the "misinterpreted Japonism, ancient Mexican Inca motifs and the unbearable brutalities of rustic stone," Schmidt primarily was offended by Wright's "American in the negative sense of the word" commissions: "luxury hotels in the middle of the desert with expensive room rates [San-Marcos-in-the-Desert Resort], an automobile outlook with no purpose except enjoying the view [Gordon Strong Automobile Objective and Planetarium], triangular vacation houses [Lake Tahoe Summer Colony], and ornamented gas stations [Standardized Overhead Gas Station]." He then soundly dismissed Wright, stating: "America and its Babbitts [the main character of Sinclair Lewis's 1922 satirical novel of bourgeois life, *Babbitt*] have taken over this man completely, a man, that has been a big hope and a role model for our architects."[104]

Perhaps the most important review, especially for future consequences, was by Behrendt, published on June 30 in the newspaper, *Frankfurter Zeitung Handelsblatt*, which did not dwell on polemics, but rather probed to the essence of Wright's aesthetic breakthroughs. He immediately set the tone by stating that while "this exhibit is long overdue," "it will not show in clarity the real contribution of Wright. The new contribution is not in the formal details, it is in morphogenesis where structural thinking takes place." Unlike other critics, Behrendt began first by analyzing Wright's plans, where he saw "the rooms are arranged around the chimney like a flower arranges itself around the stem." He continued: "Starting out almost from the middle of its power center, those rooms reach into the garden and landscape where they open themselves to light and views on all sides." Moving to the elevations, he explained, "Like a plant, the building can be observed from all sides in their full grace and you can only experience all the views by walking around it." Also distinguishing himself from almost all critics, Behrendt singled out Taliesin as Wright's "most mature work where he pushed it to extremes. In its organic structure and its intimate connection with nature, I use words [Giorgio] Vasari used for Raphael's Villa Farnesina [1506–10]: *non murato, ma veramente nato* [not built, but born]."

Yet as the author of *The Victory of the New Building Style*, Behrendt returned to the question of "new forms for a new building style," finding that since Wright had "erased all historical references," solved "structural problems of the new materials . . . in a functional way with artistic expression," he had set a good precedent. However, the critic held distinct reservations about Wright's imagination, "the strongest side of his multi-faceted talent," which was nevertheless "his weakest part" because it caused him to "desert his own theory." Yet Behrendt ended by damning Wright even more when he closed with: "In [his use of

2.25 *The Work of Frank Lloyd Wright, 1893–1930*, Prussian Academy of Art, Berlin, June 1931. (FLWFA, 3100.0032). *Foreground* drawings, *left to right*: Larkin Administration Building; Unity Temple; Winslow and Richard Bock Houses; Larkin Administration Building, Robie House, Yahara Boathouse; Larkin Administration Building. *Center*: St. Mark's Tower model.

ornament], you see clearly how he is part of his generation." In other words, Behrendt implied Wright's relevance was for the past rather than the future.[105] Reports of the German reaction got back to Wright fairly quickly in some form—either through clippings sent by Klumb or letters now lost—which caused him to characteristically see that the meaning of his architecture could not be understood without a critical text.[106] Within a few weeks he composed a rebuttal, "To My Critics in the Land of the Danube and Rhine," which he sent to the *Frankfurter Zeitung* with copies to Wijdeveld, Mendelsohn, and Klumb. In this essay, Wright devoted the majority of his remarks to a rejection of the European style of architecture based on "forms for our Machine-age," which have become "something, by, for and in themselves." Instead, he offered a message that had been very consistent throughout his career, although now more strident. Ignoring the historical context of Europe after a devastating world war and the political, social, and economic upheaval it had caused, he spoke instead in timeless poetic abstractions. "As Artists it is our office not only to overcome the machine by intelligent use of that engine," he wrote, "but by means of it, used as a new tool, to gratify the natural thirst of the human soul for beauty." In place of a universal design methodology based on "emulation," he spoke of a "greater individuality by way of greater imagination because of greater resources and the demands of a deepening sense of life."[107] At this point in his confrontation with European modernism, he simply felt misunderstood, but very soon, he would believe that he was under direct attack with the purpose of "eliminating him from the game."

With the publication in Germany of Wright's rebuttal the controversy widened and deepened, with some commentators coming to his defense. Principal among these was an editorial in the September issue of *Die Form*, "Frank Lloyd Wright und die Kritik" (Frank Lloyd Wright and the Critic), by Wilhelm Lotz. Lotz took as his premise, Wright or Corbusier?, a question he attributed to Behrendt and to which the editor answered: Why choose? "Both are great individuals, both are great architectural poets," Lotz explained. "Is it not very wrong to judge architecture by its form or appearance?" Lotz calmly continued. "Is it not more important for the observer or critic to try to ascertain the intellectual content and to understand the form? If we look at Wright this way, we will suddenly feel much closer to him and we will see him as absolutely modern."[108] Nevertheless, the use of the Wright-Corbusier duality as a means of discussing opposing principles of modern architecture continued into 1932.[109] There was one other very important commentator who saw Wright's exhibition in Berlin: Philip Johnson visited it on July 11, the day before it closed. He was in the midst of gathering European material—models and photographs—for the Museum of Modern Art's first architectural exhibition, scheduled for 1932. Johnson had already invited Wright to participate, but this was his first encounter with a survey of his work in original drawings, models, and photographs, as he had never been to Taliesin. He met Klumb, who was acting as guide, and there was an exchange of information about the MoMA exhibition. Johnson was highly critical of what he saw, confessing to Alfred H. Barr Jr., "you should see what papa Wright is going to give us unless he gets busy. It will give you nightmares."[110] Johnson, as a great admirer of Mies and Lily Reich, with the memory of "The Dwelling of Our Time" fresh in his mind, found Wright's installation design "frightful."[111]

EUROPEAN TOUR: STUTTGART, ANTWERP, BRUSSELS, ROTTERDAM, 1931

When the exhibition closed in Berlin on July 12, arrangements were already in place to exhibit at Staatliche Beratungsstelle für das Baugewerbe in Stuttgart, July 22 to August16, but there were no other venues confirmed.[112] Wright, in desperate financial straits, cabled Klumb to return to Taliesin with the exhibition.[113] Over the next few months, negotiations for various venues continued, and by the end of July Wright agreed to two locations in Belgium: Kunst van Heden in Antwerp, September 12–28, and the Palais des Beaux-Arts in Brussels, October 3–11; although there was some mention of sending the exhibition to Zürich if Werner Moser would oversee the details. This proposal fell through.[114]

Wijdeveld handled most of the arrangements for the European tour outside Germany, which sometimes entailed giving a lecture or leading a conference, as took place in Antwerp.[115] As the exhibition was closing in Brussels, Wijdeveld, who was in separate discussions with Wright about assuming a role in what shortly became the Taliesin Fellowship, was making plans to travel to Wisconsin. Before he departed, the exhibition was destined for the Academie van Beeldende Kunsten en Technische Wetenschappen in Rotterdam as its last stop. It was on view during December 1931 and closed with a lecture by Wijdeveld on January 1, 1932.

Wright surely heard glowing details of the tour from Wijdeveld when he met him in person in New York on his return from a trip to Brazil.[116] It must have been at this time that Wijdeveld presented Wright with a handmade scrapbook containing photographs and plans drawn by Klumb of each venue on the tour (excluding Rotterdam), along with clippings from newspapers and journals.[117] Fortunately, the crates arrived back at Taliesin on January 20, 1932, as Wright was facing a deadline for an American exhibition. The location was the Museum of Modern Art.

MUSEUM OF MODERN ART, 1929–30

Just as the 1929 stock market crash adversely affected Wright's career, the founding of the Museum of Modern Art at about the same time would prove, over time, one of the most fortuitous events in his professional resurgence. Although there were important earlier efforts to present European radical art to the American public, MoMA, especially with the appointment of Alfred H. Barr Jr. (1902–1981) as its first director, institutionalized what previously had been mainly the province of artists, collectors, and dealers.

Barr, who had spent a year in Europe from 1927 to 1928 gaining direct knowledge of avant-garde movements in Germany, Holland, and Russia, was particularly influenced by two revolutionary design schools: the German Bauhaus and the Russian VKHUTEMAS. What impressed the young Barr, then only twenty-five years old, was that modernism in Dessau and Moscow was not limited to painting and sculpture, but included architecture, photography, film, industrial design, stage design, and typography, and that correspondences among the arts were more important than their differences based on national identity. This experience, together with his training under two distinguished art historians, Charles Rufus Morey, a medievalist at Princeton University, who pioneered a methodology of the categorization of styles, and Paul J. Sachs, a promulgator of the formalist aesthetic as the underpinning of connoisseurship at Harvard University, made Barr the perfect choice for the new museum.

One of Barr's earliest contacts was the brilliant historian and critic Henry-Russell Hitchcock, who had graduated from Harvard University in 1924, where he cultivated his ambition to become an architect (figure 2.26). After studying for a year at the School of Architecture, he then spent 1924–25 in Europe; on his return, however, he chose to pursue the field of architectural history. In 1926, Hitchcock reached a turning point with his "digesting" of Le Corbusier's *Vers Une Architecture* in the original French edition; by this time, his focus had decidedly shifted to the new European architecture, which he saw in person in summer 1927.[118] In the years leading up to the founding of MoMA, Hitchcock published

2.26 Henry-Russell Hitchcock.
(Private collection used with permission)

2.27 Philip Johnson, January 18, 1933.
Photograph by Carl Van Vechten. (Library of Congress, Prints and Photographs Division, Carl Van Vechten Collection [LC-USZ62–127825])

articles and book reviews in *Hound and Horn*, *House Beautiful*, *Cahiers d'Art*, *The Arts*, and *Architectural Record*, culminating with his first major book, *Modern Architecture: Romanticism and Reintegration* (1929), where he stated, "it is enough to call the architecture of the New Pioneers the international style of Le Corbusier, Oud and Gropius, of Lurçat, Rietveld and Miës van der Rohe, which is enrolling more and more the younger architects in Europe and many as well in America about to begin their building career."[119] This statement would serve as the underlying thesis of MoMA's exhibition, *Modern Architecture: International Exhibition*, which would be organized in 1930 and 1931.

While Barr had the vision and Hitchcock the intellect, it would take the ambition and personal fortune of another Harvard student, Philip Johnson, to realize the architecture component of the Modern: first, the inaugural exhibition, and shortly after, the founding of the Department of Architecture (figure 2.27). While Johnson, majoring in classics and philosophy, pursued an undergraduate curriculum during the academic year, his practical education occurred on prolonged stays in Europe—primarily with Berlin as his base—in the summers of 1929, 1930, and 1931. His first unofficial tutor was Barr, whom he had met in June 1929. They immediately fell into intense conversations regarding European modern architecture, which prompted Barr to provide Johnson with a study list of buildings to see and architects to meet in the summer months. Johnson's trip took on even greater purpose when he encountered John McAndrew, an architect and Harvard graduate, at a European museum. The two joined forces and drove through Holland and Germany in a Packard Johnson had shipped over from the United States, visiting the Dessau Bauhaus, the Weissenhof Siedlung in Stuttgart, and works by Oud and Mendelsohn. By September 1929, Johnson and McAndrew decided "to make a book, a fact-picture book, with a minimum of metaphysics and aesthetics in it," but with "good pictures."[120] From this earliest date, Johnson's intentions were primarily visual and aimed at a general audience, rather than specialists.

During the fall and winter season of 1929/30, there was a significant shift in Johnson's extracurricular activity. As Barr was drawn into his demanding duties as museum director, Hitchcock replaced him as Johnson's informal tutor and, in the summer of 1930, became his travel companion, after he agreed to rewrite his book, *Modern Architecture: Romanticism and Reintegration*, "in a more popular way paying careful attention to the buildings illustrated" and "incorporate about 150 full page half tones."[121] At this stage of the project, the intention was to produce a beautifully illustrated book on the modern style (excluding expressionism and functionalism) of European architecture to be published in German for a general audience. In other words, they planned to enter the European marketplace and compete with Behrendt's *Victory of the New Building Style* and Platz's *Die Baukunst Der Neuesten Zeit*, especially the latter, which both Hitchcock and Johnson knew so well it appears to have been used as a model. Johnson's role was "to stand over Russell while he writes, to have the last word on what photos go in, and worst, to collect the photos from dilatory architects."[122]

However, even as Hitchcock was making progress on the text, they discovered that "no one wants another book on modern architecture here in Germany" and "picture books are too many." "In vain do we explain," Johnson lamented, "that there has been no book covering the whole style and nothing but the style, and that with our opportunities of travel we can have a much better complete showing."[123] By the end of the summer, Hitchcock and Johnson had not given up on their book, with the working title *Also doch ein Baustil* (*Nevertheless, an Architectural Style*), with progress made on the text and illustrations, yet they were sailing home after reaching a dead end with German publishers.

MODERN ARCHITECTURE: INTERNATIONAL EXHIBITION, 1932

Just after *Modern Architecture: International Exhibition* closed in April 1932, Johnson explained to Oud that, "Frank Lloyd Wright was included [in the show] only from courtesy and in recognition of his past contributions."[124] This remark seems overly brash coming from a twenty-six-year-old recent college graduate about the only modern architect of international stature the United States had yet produced, but a review of the first phase of curatorial development from October 1930 until April 1931, the month Johnson wrote a preliminary letter of invitation to the Wisconsin architect, puts his statement in context.

On their return to America, Johnson and Hitchcock were seriously reevaluating their project. By that time, Barr was now in his second year as MoMA's director, Johnson was on the Junior Advisory Board, and Hitchcock was almost a de facto member of the curatorial staff. While Hitchcock was busy with the academic year at Wesleyan University, Barr and Johnson were living in the same building on Fifty-Second Street in Manhattan.[125] When conversation turned to the wealth of material that had been gathered on modern European architecture it was inevitable that the subject would lead to a MoMA exhibition; only resolution of the details and logistics remained. There appear to have been two major stumbling blocks: there was no American component, as the total focus from the beginning had been entirely European and, as the Depression deepened, the financing had to be secured outside the museum's operating budget.

Of the first obstacle, there is no definitive explanation of how the curators arrived at the solution.[126] To this point, Elizabeth Mock, MoMA's curator of architecture, revealed in *Built in USA: 1932–1944*, "Turning the pages of the [1932] catalog, one is amazed by the curious assortment of American work which was included. It can now be disclosed that the Museum's trustees gave their support to the enterprise only on condition that an exact balance be preserved between the number of American and foreign architects featured in the exhibition."[127] Except for this admission by a MoMA curator, who was surely privy to internal communication and whose statement appeared in a MoMA publication, there is no further direct evidence in available primary documents. However, there is considerable circumstantial evidence. First, up to fall 1930, neither Barr nor Johnson expressed interest in American architecture, and while Hitchcock had written about Wright, he dismissed him as a "New Traditionalist" in the same company as Henry Hobson Richardson and Louis Sullivan, both of whom were dead.[128] Second, all the research done by Johnson and Hitchcock for the exhibition had been in Europe, obviously the focus of their interests. And more important, when the exhibition opened there were two separate publications: the book, *The International Style: Architecture since 1922* and the MoMA catalog, *Modern Architecture: International Exhibition*, which bear similarities, but are distinctly different in very significant ways. The book was the illustrated art historical tract that Johnson and Hitchcock originally intended to publish in German, but that finally came out in English under the imprint of the New York publisher W. W. Norton.[129] The catalog, on the other hand, was an educational tool prepared by the museum with the compromises required. Le Corbusier, Gropius, and Oud were unarguably first choices of all involved, Mies was added with the encouragement of Johnson. From that point on, four American individuals or firms were required to balance the four Europeans; the result in the first proposal of December 1930: Raymond Hood, Norman Bel Geddes (replaced by Richard Neutra by March 1931), Howe and Lescaze, and the Bowman Brothers. As Mock implied, it is hard to believe that Hitchcock and Johnson considered Hood and the Bowman Brothers the equal of Le Corbusier and Mies.[130] With the roster of architects balanced with four Europeans and four Americans, the question remained: What to do about Wright? Johnson explained at the time of the initial planning, "Mr. Hitchcock says Wright is a special case."[131] He did not fit the co-curators' criteria, yet Hitchcock chose to include him. Beginning with Johnson's first proposal to A. Conger Goodyear, president of the Board of Trustees, in December 1930, he was listed as an equal among the other eight participants. From the time of this important decision and continuing through the eighteen-month-long development of the MoMA architecture show right up to the opening, Wright held an ambiguous place, which ultimately led to ideological conflicts, organizational crises, and, unexpectedly, a strategic advantage.

From the outset, the co-curators were deeply involved with the European leaders professionally and personally; they needed to devote additional time to acquaint themselves with the four American representatives, but they had little or no contact with Wright. He was truly "a special case," and as a result, prior to the opening, there is no evidence that Hitchcock had any contact with him, in person or in correspondence, and Johnson only conducted basic formalities necessary for organizing the exhibition and catalog material.

When Goodyear gave preliminary approval to Johnson's proposal in December 1930, it was on condition that the decision would remain confidential, except for an inner circle of interested parties, until secured financing was in place. On January 3, Johnson revealed to Mumford that he was the exhibition director by stating, "May I give you a little premature information with the request that you keep it for the time being secret. ... Since we haven't the money yet, [the plan] is rather nebulous."[132] While Johnson and his father were primary donors, the idea of circulating the exhibition to museums was also raised as a potential source of revenue. An ambitious itinerary included a global tour from England throughout western Europe—Germany, Austria, Switzerland, France, Italy, Spain, Belgium, Holland, Poland, Sweden—and on to Japan.[133] This quickly proved unfeasible and attention was soon directed to venues on the East Coast and the Midwest. By late March, Johnson prepared to contact Wright, who had been kept entirely in the dark about the exhibition until Mumford gave him a brief alert.[134]

Hitchcock later described *Modern Architecture: International Exhibition* not as "a history of the subject but rather, at least for the United States, an event *in* its history."[135] For Wright, it generated perhaps the most highly charged public controversy in his exhibition history and set the tone for the twenty-year relationship between the architect and the museum. The ten-month period of planning, correspondence, and face-to-face meetings between Johnson and Wright was characterized by bad timing, confusion, nonchalance, and a general lack of clear communication, which meant that the real work did not begin until two months before the opening. This lost time can partly be explained by the fact that Wright was deeply involved in fighting for the resurrection of his career on several fronts at once while staving off foreclosure on his Wisconsin house and studio, and Johnson was preoccupied with organizing the European component of the show while simply going through the motions with the Midwest architect, which, in effect, kept him at both a personal and geographic distance (figure 2.28).

2.28 Frank Lloyd Wright, 1930. Photograph by Price Studios. (FLWFA, 6004.0043)

Johnson's first letter to Wright, typed on his personal letterhead, was dated April 1, 1931. He opened by stating that he knew Mumford "has written [you] ... about the Architectural Exhibition which we are planning to hold at the Museum of Modern Art." Johnson added that he was sending "a pamphlet under separate cover, which further explains the nature of the Show. You will note there the composition of the Committee appointed to direct the project." The main point of the letter was "an invitation to be represented by a model." Johnson further stated that after Wright informed him what type of model he chose to submit, "a formal invitation" would be forthcoming followed by a discussion of the "details of the execution." He closed by explaining that he would "be in Chicago soon and at that time I should like to come and see you."[136]

2.29 Frederick C. Robie House, Chicago, Illinois, 1908–10. Photograph by Henry Fuermann and Sons. (FLWFA, 0908.0024). MoMA exhibited this photograph, which was coincidently Wright's preferred image of the Robie House. The Victorian-era house to the rear was airbrushed out so the Robie House was seen in an ideal setting.

In this letter, Wright was given only the vaguest notion of the constitution of the show. Johnson referred to "the Architectural Exhibition," but the phrases "modern architecture" and "International Style" were never used, neither did he name any of the other architects chosen to submit a model, only describing them as "the most prominent architects of the world." And his reference to the "pamphlet," which was titled *Built to Live In*, an illustrated explication of "modern architecture" and the museum's need to hold an exhibition as "by far the best way of presenting effectively to the public every aspect of the new movement," was not much help either. Johnson wrote it in March as a fund-raising tool, and there is no evidence in the Wright correspondence that he ever received a copy. But even if he had, it would not have told him who the other exhibitors were to be. Although the illustrations were more illuminating than the text on that score—1920s buildings by Mies, Hood, Neutra, Gropius, Oud, and Le Corbusier were prominently featured—nowhere were these architects named as participating in the exhibition. However, the inference was clearly there. Even more ominous was the fact that Wright was illustrated by an exterior of the 1908 Frederick C. Robie House, the one house that European critics unanimously favored as a precursor to modernism, yet, none of Wright's work of the 1920s was reproduced (figure 2.29). As to Johnson's trip to Chicago, he was flying in to see the Bowman Brothers without any precise knowledge of where Taliesin was, and he had no time to investigate, as he needed to return to New York quickly.

When Wright responded almost immediately on April 3, he took advantage of the opportunity to boast of his exhibition that was about to set sail for Holland. Misrepresenting the facts, he declared, "Six European Governments have invited the exhibition and undertaken all expense of transport and showing in the principal cities of Europe. . . . This leaves me flat for material for any other exhibit until next September." He did not close the door, however, inviting Johnson to "come up anyway" to Taliesin so the two could meet.[137]

Turning over ongoing work to Alan R. Blackburn Jr., his secretary at the Modern, and preparing to depart for the summer months in Europe, Johnson explained to Wright on May 22 that his Chicago trip in mid-May had not allowed him to visit Taliesin due to time and distance. Speaking now with more of a sense of specific purpose, Johnson stated, "Would you let me know . . . if you could do something original for us that would represent your latest ideas in, let us say, a country house?" Johnson closed, "I do hope you can do a special model for our Show since it will be so important a factor in whether we can send the Show to Europe afterwards. But if you cannot, perhaps we could use one of the models which are on tour. The Exhibition will not open until February, 1932 and we shall have time to talk of this later but I want to get some idea of what the Show will be before everything has to be done in the last minute rush."[138] Even though Johnson was not convinced of Wright's rightful place in the exhibition, he concealed his doubts behind a professional demeanor.

Johnson had set a deadline of December 1 to obtain everything needed for the exhibition and catalog, but it was not until that date that the two began to work in earnest. The surviving correspondence and other documentation explain these missteps and lost time. The first issue was travel. Johnson left the country on May 29 and did not return to New York until mid-September. He spent most of his time with the principals in Germany—Gropius and Mies—as well as Oud in Holland. Wright sailed for Brazil on September 19, where he stayed with his wife at the luxurious Copacabana Palace Hotel at the invitation of the Pan-American Union of Architects as a judge for the Columbus Memorial Lighthouse competition. Although he expected to return on October 26, he was delayed one week and did not disembark in New York until November 6.[139] Although nothing is known of what transpired, Wright and Johnson did meet face to face in New York; they had lunch a day or two before Wright's September departure, and Johnson attended one of the Wisconsin architect's lectures, "Modern Architecture in South America," on November 13 at the New School for Social Research.

While the principals were traveling, each had designated an assistant to carry on in their absence. This was not effective either. Before leaving for Rio, Wright told Johnson while in New York that "there were two models [a house and a theater] . . . being prepared . . . and [Klumb] would be in charge for him." Johnson, who had met Klumb in Berlin at the Academie der Künste, wrote to him at Taliesin on October 5, "Of the two projects on which you are working I prefer that of the house. As Mr. Wright described it, it would be better than the theatre for publicity purposes."[140] When several of his letters went unanswered, Johnson became frustrated. Klumb did not receive the letters, however, as he was still in Europe.

The year 1931 was a very desperate one for Wright as his debts increased and foreclosure on Taliesin again appeared imminent. The Depression had not caused his dire financial predicament; it had only worsened it. He had seized on the idea of publishing his *Architectural Record* articles as a book, *Creative Matter in the Nature of Materials*, and was promoting it first with Kocher at the *Record* and then with the New York publisher Charles Scribner's Sons, without much satisfaction. Throughout the year he counted on future royalties from his memoir, ultimately titled *An Autobiography*, which appeared under the imprint of Longman, Green in 1932, to be a life savior. He was subsequently disappointed by the meager financial payoff.

He was simultaneously working feverishly on establishing a school at Taliesin. He had long sought to bring Wijdeveld on as director. On his return from Brazil, he met the Dutchman in company with Klumb in New York and escorted him to Taliesin, where they spent days in long conversations about founding a fellowship. With all these irons in the fire, he was intent on keeping his work continuously on exhibition, believing surely that the press coverage would keep his professional name in the public eye. From Wright's perspective, Johnson and the Modern, neither of which at that time had any reputation as influences on architecture, represented just another opportunity to show his work. His Studio was continuously making models, four in 1930 and three in 1931; there were few paid jobs to execute. Against this backdrop, Johnson was, as Wright confided to Mumford, no more than "a feature of the little group Hitchcock is pushing and hangs his hopes on—now emulating the Corbusier. It is not a very talented group, I believe . . . but no doubt helpful if they don't get things too far their way."[141]

Despite a few urgent letters to Taliesin, Johnson did not get responses until after Wijdeveld returned to Europe on December 6. With real deadlines looming, the MoMA curator moved aggressively on issues involving both the exhibition and catalog. In addition to one model and a building plan, Johnson had decided to use six large-format black-and-white photographs to illustrate each architect's works. Wright, of course, differed from the others in that his career spanned almost forty years and comprised over 180 buildings. The plan for the catalog focused on sound scholarship and propaganda efforts. On the first score, Johnson was compiling data for an accurate catalogue raisonné and bibliography for each architect or firm, and on the latter score, requesting certain former clients to join a list of "Patrons to the Exhibition" to give credence to the extent of modern architecture. "We feel that it is good for publicity to have the names of these people on the catalogue as patrons of the Exhibition in order that the general public may realize that it has solid backing," Johnson explained to Wright.[142]

The museum's goal to create a "definitive" list of Wright's buildings was the first institutional effort at this level of scholarship.[143] Johnson explained to the architect on December 4 that, "I consider this of great importance for the Exhibition as an answer to the criticisms that have been leveled against you especially by Mr. Raymond Hood who claims you are no longer a practicing architect."[144] Wright took the lists created by Okami in 1930, revised them, and added explanatory text at the beginning and end.[145] With the February 9 opening looming, from mid-December until mid-January there was a flurry of letters, telegrams, and packages sent back and forth between New York and Taliesin. By early January, Wright began to take the lead: he offered Johnson three models—House on the Mesa (1931–32; Denver), the New Theater (1931; Woodstock, New York), and the Standardized Overhead Gas Station—with the suggestion that after January 20 (when his European exhibition returned from Holland), he could also send St. Mark's Tower, the Richard Lloyd Jones House, and the Blue Sky Mausoleum. Johnson was reading an advance copy of *An Autobiography* to finalize the biography and compile the bibliography, and he found discrepancies in dates. To his queries, Wright, who consistently misdated many of his works, especially before 1930, sent this priceless remark, "Dear Philip, I am anything but a calendar, so thanks for the hunch as to dates. It is hard for me to get them straight."[146] The architect, who always included books in his own exhibitions, followed up by sending a seventy-five-pound crate of forty of his most important publications—mainly European, but rare Japanese works as well—insured for $1,000.[147] "Some of it is included for the entertainment of yourself and your friends," the architect wrote. "You may return whatever you don't see fit to use."[148]

As time drew closer to the opening, Wright found himself directly in the middle of the discourse on American architecture, one that had been intensifying throughout the late 1920s. Johnson had set his sights on discrediting both "eclecticism" and Art Deco. And due to the decision on the part of MoMA's trustees, the "International Style" exhibition was forced to demonstrate, as Johnson declared, "the widespread nature of the movement in our country."[149] While Wright could fully support Johnson on the first score, he was wholeheartedly opposed to him on the latter point.

Once Wright concentrated on the subject in late January and early February, he railed against MoMA's "propaganda," which appeared to be a snide attack on the museum, but he was borrowing the word from Johnson, who began to use it in his letters in the last months of 1931.[150] Some of Johnson's efforts came at the direction of the museum's Publicity Department, which had mapped out a public relations campaign including press releases, but efforts went beyond that to solicitation of articles or reviews from the exhibition participants for advance placement in newspapers and magazines.[151] The two articles Johnson sought from Wright pitted him against his closest American rival: Hood.

First, Johnson asked Wright to rebut an article, "Poets in Steel," by John Cushman Fistere from the December 1931 issue of *Vanity Fair*. Fistere set out to list in order of importance ten American architects who would still be remembered in the twenty-first century. The author, who ranked Wright as number one, nevertheless, dealt the sixty-four-year-old midwesterner this blow: "Mr. Wright has developed a martyr complex, which permits him to tell his fellow architects that he has been a 'lonesome man for thirty years'—thirty years being the period from the time he announced his theories of structural beauty and horizontal housing until Mr. Lewis Mumford discovered him after returning from a trip abroad." If this sarcastic remark was not bad enough, Fistere went even further with the statement, "many believe that Mr. Wright is more genius than architect, and who justify their opinion by pointing ... to the still more significant fact that he has designed comparatively few buildings to support his manifold theories."[152] To make matters worse, Fistere, while ranking Hood number two, praised him while damning Wright. "Hood already has three buildings to his credit to support the claims of his friends that he, and not Wright, is the first architect of the country."[153] Wright's unpublished retort, "Fistere's Poets," was a rambling bemused essay, which included among other literary devices, an imaginary dialogue between Hood and his press agent.

MoMA's Publicity Department's second request to Wright was to review the latest book, *Raymond Hood*, from a series titled "Contemporary American Architects" published by a division of McGraw-Hill.[154] While his article on Hood was thoughtful and carefully written, it was primarily a play on one theme, Hood was a "high-power salesman" who gained his success through the clever use of "advertising" rather than by his "imagination and ability to create." Wright explained, "He stands for most of what I have openly fought against all my life. Have I fought the flu-flu bird (he flies backward because he doesn't care where he is going, just so he can see where he has been), to find the cuckoo on the nest?"[155] Ultimately, neither of these essays was published.

By January 18, Johnson had not received Wright's model, and his anxiety was building when he received an ominous telegram: "Photographs of models forwarded today special delivery. Models soon complete, but learn today have misapprehended character of exhibition. Will see you in New York before long concerning this. Want to cooperate as far as principles will go, but no further."[156] It still remains a mystery how Wright found out the full details of the MoMA exhibition on a Monday in rural Wisconsin when the information had eluded him for nine and a half months. The only plausible explanation is that when the Modern issued a press release the day before announcing the exhibition and its national tour, Wright had gotten wind of it by telephone from an ally.[157]

Wright wasted no time following up with an even more startling telegram later in the day: "My way has been too long and too lonely to make my belated bow to my people as a modern architect in company with a self-advertising amateur and a high powered salesman. No bitterness and sorry but kindly and finally drop me out of your promotion."[158] Johnson would have been only partially baffled by this message as he already had a good idea what Wright thought of Hood, but he did not know of Wright's ambiguous opinion of Richard Neutra. While he personally liked Hood (the high-powered salesman), Wright dismissed him as a commercial architect merely copying the fashionable style of the day. As for Neutra (the self-advertising amateur), with only one major building to his credit, he established his reputation, not by designing, Wright believed, but by lecturing, publishing, and joining professional organizations. Wright was insulted to be in the company of these men and, still more, to be regarded as their inferior.

Luckily for MoMA, Wright's action the next day was two pronged: first, he wrote Johnson; then, he wrote Mumford. The young, inexperienced curator must have been astonished when Wright took his own words—"publicity" and "propaganda"—recast them in sarcastic terms and used them in his argument against the purpose of the exhibition. "I am going to step aside and let the procession go by with its bandwagon," Wright declared. "If you had made the character of the show a little clearer to me in the beginning, we might have saved some waste and expense.... But meantime the scramble of the propagandist 'international' for the band-wagon must have taken place and the procession must be well on its way, without me." While he expressed respect and admiration for Le Corbusier, Mies, and Otto Haesler, he singled out Hood and Neutra as the offenders. "I am sick and tired of the pretense of men who will elect a style, old or new, and get a building badly built ... and then publicize it as a notable achievement. This hits not one man only but a type of which you have chosen a willing and busy exponent in Neutra."[159] Wright's letter to Mumford was primarily an explanation of his objections to Neutra along with a startling announcement. Wright had had direct and personal confrontations with European modernism when Schindler and Neutra worked in his Taliesin Studio in the 1910s and 1920s, respectively.

Wright's most recent unpleasant encounter with both Neutra and Schindler was over the first independent architecture exhibition of his work after the hiatus of 1915–29. Preempting the Modern by two years, Schindler's former wife, Pauline, took advantage of her close ties with the Los Angeles architectural avant-garde to organize a traveling exhibition, *Contemporary Creative Architecture of California*, which was shown at the University of California, Los Angeles, April 21–29, 1930. While her concentration was on Schindler, Neutra, Jock D. Peters, John Weber, Kem Weber, and J. R. Davidson, Pauline, who had lived at Taliesin in the summer 1920, telegraphed Wright to obtain material related to his Los Angeles houses.[160] He agreed to be included, but demurred on sending anything due to his prior commitment to the Princeton University show that spring.[161]

Pauline was undaunted, calling on Brett Weston to photograph Hollyhock House and the textile block houses. Wright's version of the conflict, as told to Mumford, was exaggerated: "I thought very little of the matter until they opened a show under the ballyhoo 'Exhibition of work of Three Architects of International renown.' "[162] Wright, who found out about the roster of architects the day of the opening, fired off a telegram to Pauline, "Kindly remove from exhibit all reference to me or my work. Object to association without authorization."[163] This episode and a few other slights annoyed Wright, but his main objection to Neutra was the fact that he believed he had appropriated Le Corbusier's style, which he believed was just another form of eclecticism. Wright's astonishing reaction to all these events, as he told Mumford, was to "arrange a show—contra—in New York to follow this 'foreign' one.' "[164] Although he compiled his own list of worthy architects, eventually Wright must have realized what a drain on his time and money such an exhibition would entail, and he quietly dropped it.

Mumford found himself in the unenviable position of persuading Wright to stay in the show as a strategic advantage. "Your absence from Modern Museum's architecture show would be calamity. Please reconsider your refusal. I have no concern whatever on behalf of museum but am interested in your own place and influence. We need you and cannot do without you. Your withdrawal will be used by that low rascal Hood to his own glory and advantage. As for company there is no more honorable position than to be crucified between two thieves. Please wire your okay."[165] His skillfully worded telegram had the intended effect. Without argument, Wright telegraphed immediately, "All right, Lewis, your sincere friendship trusted. I will stay in the New York show. The two exceptions I made were chiefly important because showing up the show as the usual politics and propaganda."[166] The next morning, he telegraphed Johnson, "All right, Philip, sorry. Three models going forward in few days," which set off the next round of confusion.[167] Wright offered three models, and then shipped two to New York—the House on the Mesa and the Standardized Overhead Gas Station—when Johnson only wanted the house.[168] Another exchange of tense letters followed this final step before the opening.

The postmortem conducted by Wright and Mumford revealed, unsurprisingly, that they shared the same motivation: to prove that Wright was the most important living American architect. Mumford believed that Wright's inclusion "would influence people who might otherwise think that the barren and imitative as well as dishonest Hood was an exponent of modern architecture." He emphatically stated that, "The withdrawal would have been a real blow to architecture: for the show is scheduled to spend three years on the road, touring the country, and Hood's publicity gang would have made it appear that he was the only American architect worthy of being represented: they would probably have gone the length of hinting, as that rascal [Fistere] did in the *Vanity Fair* article, that you had nothing to show." Mumford further revealed that rather than acting as an intermediary between the Modern and Wright, he had kept the curators at arm's length with the exception of "casual conversation" with Hitchcock. As for Johnson, Mumford thought him a "queer fish," but the "only person around with the time and money" to organize an exhibition of such magnitude. On the brighter side, he revealed to Wright that Johnson had been eager to give him "a full representation" and Hitchcock "is much nearer to you than you imagine."[169] Wright, on the other hand, was so focused on organizing another American tour of his 1930–31 exhibition, returning from Holland that week, that he underestimated the power of the Modern and its commitment to the European avant-garde. He believed that there would be "no great harm" in his "capitulation to the New York show" as long as he "came back quickly" with "a show of [his] own starting in New York and going elsewhere as seems desirable." In what appears to be naive ignorance of the New York museum world, he suggested to Mumford that MoMA would be a good location for his own personal exhibition and he asked him to contact Mrs. Harry Payne Whitney for him![170] Of course, Mrs. Whitney was busy creating the Whitney Museum of American Art.

When *Modern Architecture: International Exhibition* opened on February 9, 1932, it was a watershed event in Wright's exhibition history. At age sixty-four, it was the first major exhibition of his work that he had not curated himself.[171] While it is generally believed by many Wright commentators to have been one of the worst episodes in his professional life, that view obscures the tremendous value his association with the Modern brought him, both in the short and long term. With the exclusion of several severely dismissive comments by Hitchcock and Barr, MoMA's representation of Wright was the single most important effort up to that date to present him, not as a proponent of the "International Style" certainly, but as a modern architect by European standards, and using methods such as strict curatorial discipline, innovative installation design, and serious scholarship, the portrayal carried the weight of authority. The 1932 exhibition was one of the six most important exhibitions during Wright's lifetime. It is well known that Johnson as exhibition director took responsibility for the format and design of the installation while Hitchcock devoted himself to writing most of the texts of the two publications.[172] Yet beyond this generalization, lacking primary evidence, it is difficult to pinpoint the extent of the collaboration between the two curators and to determine how much advice Barr gave. With that said, the exhibition checklist was more important in portraying Wright in a positive light than the publication.

Johnson's installation style was the opposite of Wright's. Johnson was a minimalist, while Wright preferred copious numbers of drawings and photographs. Johnson selected only six photographs for each architect. His choice of four photographs, all houses dated before 1929—Isabel Roberts (1908; River Forest, Illinois; figure 2.30), Frederick C. Robie, Taliesin (1911–59; Spring Green, Wisconsin; figure 2.31), and Alice Millard (1923–24; Pasadena, California; figure 2.32)—followed Hitchcock's dictates exactly, as they were drawn from illustrations in his two books, *Frank Lloyd Wright* (1928; *Cahiers d'Art*) and *Modern Architecture: Romanticism and Re-Integration* (1929); the only exception was Taliesin—Johnson preferred an image from *Wendingen*. The one new building, previously unpublished by Hitchcock, was the Richard Lloyd Jones House (figure 2.33). Johnson's intentions were to portray Wright as a residential

2.30 Isabel Roberts House, River Forest, Illinois, 1908. (FLWFA, 0808.0001). MoMA exhibited this photograph.

architect who not only theorized, but also constructed, since Johnson admitted, "It is much better propaganda to exhibit buildings which have already been built."[173]

The chronological sequence from 1908 to 1932 as shown in the photographs and model established the theme of Wright as a practitioner of the Machine Age of modernism, but this would not have been apparent to museum visitors on a conscious level, with only brief exhibition labels to aid their understanding, and no catalog text in front of them. The first three works displayed—the Roberts and Robie Houses and Taliesin—were clustered between 1908 and 1911, the late period of the Prairie House, reflecting a deliberate editing of Wright's career by excluding all earlier work associated with Sullivan's stylistic influence, especially his use of ornament. The selection of the Robie House was especially revealing as it had been exclusively favored over other Prairie Houses by the European modernists for more than a decade due to what they perceived of as its industrial construction system and urban setting, and from this point forward, MoMA's continuous promotion established it as the canonical Prairie House, despite, as Hitchcock noted in the catalog, "The Coonley House of 1908 Wright himself particularly prefers."[174]

2.31 Taliesin II, 1915–25. Photograph by Henry Fuermann and Sons. (FLWFA, 1403.00280001). MoMA exhibited this photograph.

2.32 Alice Millard House, La Miniatura, Pasadena, California, 1923–4. (FLWFA, 2302.0006). MoMA exhibited this photograph.

2.33 Richard Lloyd Jones House, Tulsa, Oklahoma, 1928–31. (FLWFA, 2902.040), MoMA exhibited this photograph.

While half the photographs were devoted to presenting Wright as a precursor to modernism, the other half focused on the 1920s—the same time frame as the "International Style"—showcasing his use of industrial techniques such as prefabrication and standardization in his textile-block houses. In this case, Johnson chose two buildings that bore the closest resemblance to Wright's younger rivals: the Millard House reminiscent of Le Corbusier's Citrohan House (1920) and the Lloyd Jones House reminiscent of Mies's Concrete Country House (1923). By making this leap in time, Johnson avoided the problematic work of the teens—Midway Gardens, Imperial Hotel, and the Hollyhock House—all works that the European functionalists condemned for their exotic references, excessive ornamentation, and mass.

Throughout the curatorial development of the exhibition, there was little or no coordination between Johnson and Wright over content, yet, remarkably, the model that Wright appears to have made specifically for the Modern, the House on the Mesa, was a brilliant tour de force that continued and reinforced themes Johnson emphasized (figure 2.34). What seems on the surface as a disadvantage for Wright—Johnson's lack of attention, especially in comparison to his close contact with three of the major European architects: Mies, Oud, and Gropius—was actually a benefit resulting in a strategic advantage for the American. Johnson had no input on Wright's creation of House on the Mesa except his initial suggestion of "a country house."[175] Thus Wright was free to choose the location, program, size, and scale—and most important, the fact that it was an entirely new unbuilt design—all without consultation with the Modern.

When the exhibition was installed, surprisingly, Wright was placed in the major, and largest, gallery beside the leaders of the "International Style," Le Corbusier, Mies, and Oud, contrary to the curator's ranking of him and to the exclusion of Gropius, who was relegated to the more cramped middle gallery next to the unknown Bowman Brothers (figure 2.35). Again, any museum visitor who had not read the catalog would have walked away with the impression that Wright was the equal of the Europeans. No official explanation has ever been given for this decision. However, it is possible that Wright's model may have been a factor. All four models in the major gallery were of luxurious houses, and Wright's was the largest at 7 feet 8 inches by 3 feet 10 inches, so grouping by building type and given the need for additional space for House

2.34 House on the Mesa, Denver, Colorado, 1931–32. (Sophia Wittenberg Mumford Papers, Ms. Collection 958, Kislak Center for Special Collections, Rare Books and Manuscripts, University of Pennsylvania. Photograph reproduced courtesy of the Estate of Lewis and Sophia Mumford)

on the Mesa, it was logical that Wright would have been placed where he was.[176] But of the four models, Wright's was the only one that pointed in a new direction, one that anticipated some of his most significant work in the second half of the 1930s, while the other three—Mies's Tugendhat House (1928–30; Brno, Czech Republic), Le Corbusier's Villa Savoye (1929–31; Poissy, France), and Oud's Homer Johnson House (1930–31; Pinehurst, North Carolina)—illustrated a style that reached its apogee in the late 1920s and that had evolved beyond it even before the exhibition opened.[177]

Considering Wright's sporadic bursts of attention in preparing for the MoMA exhibition, it is remarkable how completely his model fit both the museum's requirements and his own. For one of the few times in his career, he departed from his principle of designing only on commission. His project was inspired by the circumstances of a wealthy couple, George and Jean Cranmer, whom he had met on a speaking engagement in Denver, Colorado, in December 1930. Quite large—actually a sprawling mansion—and experimental in materials and structure, for Wright part of the significance of House on the Mesa rested on its location. For the midwesterner, who had spent much of the 1920s in the open country of California and Arizona, the choice of a Colorado mesa was a retort to the submissions from Germany, France, and especially New York. For only in the West, where nature was redemptive, could a genuinely American architecture, in Wright's view—the only true modern architecture—be created.

A variant of the zoned residence that originated with the unbuilt Harold McCormick House (1907–8; Lake Forest, Illinois), and realized the following year in the Coonley House, the MoMA project was sited on a large parcel of wooded land bordering a lake. The house exemplified an evolution of the textile-block system with reinforced concrete slab roofs, plain blocks, and large expanses of glass curtain walls creating "machine-age luxury that would compare favorably in character and integrity with the luxury of the Greeks and Goths, within the limits of an expenditure of some $125,000."[178] While comparisons can be made with the Los Angeles textile-block houses of the early 1920s, the House on the Mesa was lighter, more rectilinear than these earlier examples.

From a formal and technical standpoint House on the Mesa was designed to strike a chord with Wright's detractors. And it did. Hitchcock declared in the catalog entry, "No European architect has been bolder in the use of cantilevering in domestic architecture or more drastic in the introduction of glass walls."

2.35 Frank Lloyd Wright exhibit, *Modern Architecture: International Exhibition*, Museum of Modern Art, New York, February 10–March 23, 1932. Designed by Philip Johnson. Photograph by George H. Van Anda. (The Museum of Modern Art, New York, NY, U.S.A. Digital Image © The Museum of Modern Art/ Licensed by SCALA/Art Resource, NY)

He further acknowledged that Wright's use of the textile-block system "combined with the cantilevered slab roof on isolated supports" produced "an architecture as weightless and non-massive as that of Le Corbusier." While at the same time, Hitchcock concluded that the House on the Mesa did not amount to a rejection of the Midwest architect's past ideals, but, rather, it summed up "a lifetime of experience with the designing of American houses and converges with the line of development of the modern house in Europe."[179]

Another factor that contributed to Wright's integration into the exhibition was Johnson's installation technique.[180] His entire ethos was based on strict discipline applied to the type, size, and number of images chosen for display. With the exception of the Bowman Brothers (who only had projects to their name), all of the architects were represented by uniform-sized, enlarged black-and-white photographs of built work, limited to between five and nine images, hung in a single row just below eye level. "So I spent my time making the photographs as big as I could for the rooms that we had," Johnson explained later. He continued, "I had the photographs especially photographed and especially turned back over the outside, folding over to the back of the photograph, so as not to have frames. This was the first time that had been done. . . . The photographs float then. That was Alfred Barr's or my idea."[181] As a result of the uniformity of the display, the visitor experienced Wright's section and that of Le Corbusier as equivalent—a distinction that would have been far different if Wright's delicate color pencil perspectives had hung near Le Corbusier's strong black-and-white elevations. By what has become MoMA's signature installation design, the museum neutralized the ideological differences between Wright and the Europeans.[182]

While the exhibition was conceived as propaganda aimed at the American public, the catalog was primarily a work of traditional art history, based on the methodology of connoisseurship as it had been taught at Harvard in the 1920s. While the publication served several purposes, there were three distinct parts that pertained to Wright: brief remarks by Barr in the foreword, the Wright essay by Hitchcock, and supplements (a bibliography, a brief biographical outline, and a list of work). Barr had no interest other than the "International Style"; as a result, he had no reason to evaluate Wright's work on its own terms. The Modern's director saw Wright as "one of the Style's most important sources" based on his influence on Oud, Gropius, and Mies. While he was more than a "pioneer ancestor," his "romantic principle of individualism" remained "a challenge to the classical austerity of the style of his best younger contemporaries." Clearly, Barr found no place for Wright in the canon.[183]

Hitchcock, who shared Barr's agenda, nevertheless struck a better balance. His essay, which was the first attempt to summarize Wright's career for an American audience since Robert Spencer in the June 1900 *Architectural Review*, must have convinced Wright of the historian's capabilities as much as it infuriated him. Wright had first taken note of Hitchcock in 1928 almost immediately after the critic had published two essays describing him as a past master: one that appeared in French in *Cahiers d'Art* and the other in *Architectural Record*.[184] In response, Wright wrote Hitchcock a letter that in characteristic fashion began with criticism, but was accompanied by a gift of the Wasmuth Verlag folios and an invitation to visit Taliesin.[185]

But Wright became considerably more incensed after the appearance of *Modern Architecture: Romanticism and Reintegration*—a foreshadowing of the historian's MoMA essay—in 1929. Hitchcock's assessment, spread over five pages, ending with the backhanded compliment, "he is, without qualification ... the greatest American architect of the first quarter of the twentieth century," so drew Wright's ire that he strategized to review the book.[186] Kocher of the *Architectural Record* rebuffed him in favor of Mumford, but suggested he send in a "Letter to the Editor."[187] The result, the unpublished "Poor Little American Architecture," employed rapier wit to attack Hitchcock on a far more personal than ideological level, which is probably why he ultimately decided to withdraw it. However, when he turned his attention to "our own American ideal," the prose became more powerful and eloquent. He repeated his theme of an "American Architecture" of "something deeper," conceiving "culture as more a part of the nature of the thing cultivated and so likely to live in future where all else has had to die in the past."[188]

He ended with a daring prognostication, which provides tremendous insight into how his early confrontation with Hitchcock became a turning point in his sixty-five-year career. "As for myself, this Hitchcock concession of twenty-five years—a quarter of a century—bores me. And I warn Henry right here and now that, having a good start, not only do I fully intend to be the greatest architect who has yet lived but fully intend to be the greatest architect who will ever live. Yes, I intend to be the greatest architect of all time. And I do hereunto affix 'the red square' and sign my name to this warning."[189] On point of fact, Hitchcock remained ignorant of this threat until 1941 because it was not made public until the article was anthologized by Frederick Gutheim in *Frank Lloyd Wright on Architecture: Selected Writings, 1894–1940*. The MoMA catalog was a compromised publication, which was the result of the competing agendas of all those within the museum. Originally, it was intended by its principal authors, Hitchcock and Johnson, as the definitive popular presentation of the "International Style" as they had observed it in Europe in the late 1920s. But the museum's presumed imposition of an American component shifted the focus awkwardly. Hitchcock and Johnson resolved this problem—and ignored Wright—by simultaneously publishing their original book, *The International Style: Architecture since 1922*, with a New York trade publisher, W. W. Norton. As a result, the subject of the museum catalog was widened to modern architecture, a much broader subject that was flexible enough to include Wright. Hitchcock had to do some intellectual juggling because in his mind the "International Style" was the one and only true modern architecture. In his Wright essay, while he condemned the elder architect to the past, he also was the first person to judge his whole career according to the precepts of modern architecture. Up to that point in time, Wright had been the main person to exhibit or publish his work; the architect did little editing except to bring the record up to date. Hitchcock, on the other hand, applied his critical eye. The result was Wright as a modern architect by the standards of Europe.

While Hitchcock's Wright essay incorporated portions of his past articles, the availability of new Wright material gave his text added dimension. He gained access to *An Autobiography* prior to publication in spring 1932 and thus was able to give the first account of the architect's childhood and early influences. Wright's youth spent in Madison and his Chicago apprenticeship were regarded as meaningful, the first because it was "purely Middle Western and authentically intellectual," the latter because many clients were "ready to encourage experiment even if loans were hard to obtain." Hitchcock skipped over the work of the 1890s rather quickly and settled on "Prairie Architecture," which "sprang suddenly into being at the hand of a man ... blissfully ignorant of all architecture except that of Sullivan." While he claimed that Wright had accomplished something equal to "the architects of the fifteenth century," Hitchcock found much to criticize, as "there are many legitimate objections to these houses." The ceilings were "unduly low," the windows "rather narrow," and the interiors "rather dark." Hitchcock ended this section by concluding that "Prairie Architecture" climaxed with the Robie House and Taliesin.[190] Considering the great esteem the Larkin Administration Building received in Europe beginning before World War I, it and Unity Temple, two of Wright's greatest achievements with Machine Age techniques, it is curious they were glossed over in a few sentences. In those years,

Hitchcock later admitted, "I treated Wright purely historically, putting all emphasis, like the Europeans, on the work of the Prairie years and its international influence. Thus I ranked him as a forerunner—or worse, as he never tired of telling me later, ... as an 'old romantic.' "[191]

Hitchcock's next section, which covered the period 1910–20, was devoted to three problematic buildings: Midway Gardens, the Imperial Hotel, and Hollyhock House. The historian's analysis was ambiguous: Midway Gardens "represented an expansion of Wright's architecture in a decorative direction," while the Imperial Hotel was "a technical triumph" that "established Wright's claim to rank as a scientific builder with the best American engineers," yet the Barnsdall House, characterized by an "exuberance of inappropriate ornament," unfortunately continued the phase begun with Midway Gardens.[192] Hitchcock's division of Wright's career up to the end of World War I into the advanced achievements of 1900–1910 and the retrogressive works of the war years remained the accepted view, often repeated, until the end of the architect's life.

In the last section devoted to the 1920s, Hitchcock's method shifted to holding up Wright's designs directly to standards of "International Style" buildings of the same time period. He praised the "concrete block system" due to its similarity to "the preoccupation of the younger architects in Europe with concrete skeleton construction"; although he declared Wright's use "sybaritic" when compared to the asceticism of the Europeans. He also singled out the Lloyd Jones House for its extensive use of glass, concluding that, "No leading architect of Europe would build quite such a house, yet few could fail to accept its relevance in the new world of form." And since in his most recent work Wright had followed the Europeans into "steel construction and the skyscraper," mentioning St. Mark's-in-the-Bouwerie Tower specifically, "Wright's post-War designs have been more radical technically if less restrained in decoration."[193]

Despite the fact that Hitchcock believed "[Wright] has advanced parallel" with his "juniors" and that the "distance between him and even Le Corbusier ... grows ever less," the historian's final judgment was devastating. Two sentences especially would have jumped out at Wright as a call to arms. The first was, "American architecture need not develop entirely in the footsteps of her great individual genius." Marginalizing Wright in the United States when he was taking his "belated bow to [his] people as a modern architect" was unthinkable. But then to declare "The day of the lone pioneer is past. ... Throughout the world there are others beside Wright to lead the way toward the future," was tantamount to declaring Wright a failure at his lifelong crusade of reform and enlightenment.[194] From that moment on, Wright became ever more dedicated to first proving Hitchcock wrong and then winning him over. He began to apply the same strategy he had used with Monroe and Mumford. Eventually, it worked. In six years, Wright would have a solo exhibition at the Modern, and three years later Hitchcock would accept the Midwest architect's invitation to author the first American monograph of his work.

While Wright became even more furious at both Johnson and MoMA in the weeks after the opening, his attitude toward Hitchcock was challenging, but respectful. In a remark to Johnson, he even lumped him in with Mumford and Catherine Bauer, as those "who have grown in appreciation by study of my work."[195] Which is why when he wrote to the historian on February 26 to correct sixteen itemized errors in fact and interpretation in the catalog essay, he closed by noting that they saw "too little of each other" and suggested that, "Some day we may remedy that if the 'bump' of principle doesn't break us."[196]

A generally overlooked aspect of the museum catalog, but one that went far to lift the architect's reputation considerably, was the selected bibliography, the biographical outline, and the abbreviated catalogue raisonné. With the application of high scholarly standards and Wright's cooperation in providing an advance copy of *An Autobiography* and his updated list of work, the museum became the first to authoritatively document Wright's productive career. With a published list of mainly buildings and a few projects six and one-half pages long, Wright could now easily defend himself against any accusation that he "built few buildings." Despite the severely critical remarks of Barr and Hitchcock, MoMA did much to advance Wright's career in 1932, though ideological differences would continue to adversely affect the relationship between the architect and the Modern until his death.

After all the months of planning and preparation, ironically, neither Johnson nor Wright attended the opening on February 9; the curator was hospitalized with exhaustion and the Wisconsin architect could not afford the train fare. He received his first impressions from "Architecture Styled 'International,' " a large illustrated article by the critic Henry Irving Brock in the *New York Times Magazine* on February 7. Shooting off a letter to Johnson, he complained that the article was "the silliest exposition I've seen of the 'hide and horns.' " Now that "the enemies of an organic architecture" were "where they belong—out in front," Wright reminded Johnson that he had "agreed to stay only for the New York show." "Be a good sport, Philip," he implored, "and help me out as gracefully as possible."[197] Johnson replied in a diplomatic manner, "Won't you please, before making your decision, come and see for yourself how your exhibit is received and whether or not you are getting a proper reception from the public."[198] This statement enraged Wright even more. "Good God, my boy—your letter is humiliating. Do you really believe it is my 'credit due' that disturbs me and moves me?" While declaring that "There is a radical divergence between the international propaganda and the ideal of architecture I have fought for all my life," Wright was willing to "cooperate" rather than "fight." He would stay with the show if the museum made his essay, "Of Thee I Sing," available to the public.[199] This settled the matter until the show closed in New York on March 23.

Wright's pleas to be removed entirely from the exhibition or, at least, have the House on the Mesa model returned for repair, continued throughout the tour; first, Johnson rebuffed him, then when the architect would not back down, the matter was turned over to MoMA's lawyers. The Modern argued that the American tour was sold on the basis that all material would be shown at each venue. Although Wright stood up for "principle," in the end, from a realistic point of view, he benefited greatly from the museum's refusal to release him. He received two years of exposure throughout the East Coast, the Midwest, and as far west as Los Angeles, mainly in art museums, his preferred venues; this was fortunate as his persistent efforts to generate one-man shows in New York and abroad were unsuccessful.

The Modern accelerated a discourse about the future of American architecture that had been taking place in the *New York Times*, several trade magazines such as *Architectural Record*, and by 1932, increasingly in the pages of *Shelter: A Magazine of Modern Architecture* (formerly *T-Square*) when Johnson, Barr, Hitchcock, and George Howe became associate editors. They devoted the entire April issue to a symposium organized by Barr at the museum on February 19 to discuss the MoMA exhibition. Not only did they refuse to restrict the pages to the speakers (Hood, Howe, and Hitchcock), they also invited rebuttal from well-known critics of the "International Style." Johnson obtained Wright's permission to include his essay "Of Thee I Sing," which, to the architect's dismay, was published along with other critiques by Arthur T. North, William Adams Delano, Chester Aldrich, and Kurt Lönberg-Holm.[200]

While the exhibition was still at its second stop on the tour, Wright was shocked and horrified when he saw the issue for the first time. "*Definitely* close me *out* at the close of the Philadelphia show," he ordered Johnson.[201] Wright was so livid that his prose sunk to a new level. His attacks on the MoMA curators were particularly shocking. "Sincerity is one of [Hitchcock's] limitations I am bound to respect. Evidently he had a good time making his collection and classifying it. If classifying were classic—Russell is a classic. But I fear he is an ass." He reserved even more flagrant remarks for Johnson. "In short, Philip my King, a strange undignified crowd you are, altogether, all pissing through the same quill or pissing on each other. I am heartily ashamed to be caught with flap open in the circumstances. But I am caught in this crowd as I was caught in the show."[202]

On the brink of a permanent break with Wright, Hitchcock and Johnson reacted independently. Hitchcock's two-page letter, dated April 22, was the stronger of the two, and for that reason he may have refrained from mailing it. The historian accused Wright of "unanswerable vulgarity" and declared "that there is no further reason for attempting to remain on working terms with you." He continued: "If you represent the right path and we the wrong—which is conceivable—you should be delighted that the bad influences that we are supposed to be maliciously propagandizing through this Show are counteracted by the presence of your own work. ... If we were tacticians it would have been to our advantage to have excluded you long ago." Hitchcock's conclusion was pointed, "you can comfort yourself with the consolation ... that Michelangelo was impossible to get on with—and posterity has forgiven him. In so far as we are posterity doubtless we already forgive you." But Hitchcock could not refrain from adding, "I regret now that we have ever begun to know you personally. But knowing you, I realize we would not otherwise have had dealings with you at all."[203]

With a few more days to cool off, Johnson replied with a more matter-of-fact approach. After spending several paragraphs in a patient explanation of how *Shelter* was put together, he continued on April 25, "there have been many misunderstandings on both sides, and as I know I myself am not clear as to what mistakes I have made in interpreting your point of view, I wish we could meet somewhere and talk the whole situation over." In an earlier meeting in New York around March 30, Johnson had mentioned his intention to drive through the Midwest with Hitchcock in the summer to research an upcoming exhibition on Chicago architecture (probably on the occasion of the opening of the *Modern Architecture* show there on June 8). Wright invited them both as guests to Taliesin. With this in mind, Johnson closed with, "I still hope that we can have a good visit when I come West this spring."[204] Wright responded, "Any feeling I have in this whole matter is directly personal to no one."[205]

While Johnson appeared conciliatory toward Wright to his face, undoubtedly he harbored far more antagonistic feelings, as one revealing exchange with Blackburn suggests. In discussing "Of Thee I Sing" he explained, "My idea would be to ... have on the cover just the title and Frank Lloyd Wright's name. This would detract considerably from the importance which ... Wright attributes to this essay. Also we might sell the reprints for five cents a piece, which would certainly keep people from reading it."[206] Ironically, Johnson had written only a couple of months before, "the best architects so seldom receive official recognition. In America, since the days of Sullivan at least, contempt for the great amounts almost to tradition."[207] When tempers cooled, it was fairly obvious to all concerned that America's most important modern architect and its major modern art museum could not part company. In this spirit, the two curators were entertained at Taliesin for the weekend in late June where they also met Olgivanna Wright.[208] Hitchcock and Johnson were in Chicago researching commercial structures and viewing Wright houses for the first time for the MoMA exhibition, *Early Modern Architecture: Chicago, 1870–1910*, which was on view from January 18 to February 23, 1933.[209]

When Johnson readily admitted to Oud in 1930 that his goal was "making propaganda" in America, he added, "We shall not approach the theme from the historical side but in terms of problems of style. Naturally the critical analysis will be purely aesthetic, to the great disappointment of our German 'sach-lich' friends, who think of nothing but sociology."[210] In other words, the MoMA exhibition and two attendant publications cleansed European modern architecture of its sociopolitical content when it was presented in the United States. What resulted was the myth of modern architecture, which had a didactic influence on several generations of American architects. While this significant fact was largely overlooked at the time, Wright made it the main emphasis of his essay, "Of Thee I Sing," which due to its lack of clarity blunted its effectiveness at discrediting what he considered the "opposition."

A case in point is the title, which is oblique and confusing. Most readers probably would have associated it with the New York Broadway play, "Of Thee I Sing," with music and lyrics by George and Ira Gershwin, which opened on December 26, 1931, and ran throughout 1932. However, this entertaining political satire has little resonance with Wright's argument. Rather, it is almost certain that the title was drawn from the 1831 national hymn, "America, My Country 'Tis of Thee," reminding readers of the lyrics, "sweet land of liberty, of thee I sing." For Wright, the subject was the threat the "International Style" posed to "our own ideal of democracy." Wright reiterated his now-familiar argument that modern architecture had originated with his own work around 1907, that the "International Style" was a fraudulent copy, and that the European importation was indistinguishable from a communist agenda. "For a free democracy to accept a communistic tenet of this breed," Wright declared, "disguised as aesthetic formula for architecture is a confession of failure I do not believe we [Americans], as a people, are ready to make."[211]

Throughout his essay, he used the metaphor of impotence to describe the unnamed MoMA organizers. Declaring himself against *Geist der Kleinlichkeit* (the narrow minded), he summarized the beliefs of what he called the European "neuter," with the use of a quote, "The Western soul is dead; Western intelligence, though keen, is therefore sterile and can realize an impression but not expression of life except as life may be recognized as some intellectual formula."[212] "But I think such a confession of genital impotence," he continued, "while valid enough where this cliché is concerned, [is] a senility that healthy youth North, South, East, or West is bound to ridicule and repudiate."[213] These statements become much clearer when traced to their source: a letter Mumford wrote to Wright in 1928. In it Mumford explains Hitchcock as a member of "the post-war generation," and like Le Corbusier and "some Germans of the same guild, his esthetic ideas are biased by an inadequate sociology: he fancies that the age of art is over, and (like Spengler) he thinks the architecture of the future will be engineering or nothing. This view is an expression of impotence." Mumford elaborated, "Your work is necessarily a challenge to these men, as health & vigor is a challenge to the invalid ... your work is a step beyond this, with fuller mastery of the materials & freer expression ... you are still 30 years ahead of Corbusier."[214]

Behind "Of Thee I Sing" is Wright's understanding of Oswald Spengler's landmark two-volume work, *The Decline of the West* (1918–23), in which the philosopher theorized that all cultures evolve over time until they reach the stage of civilization just prior to their collapse. For the West, this period had been reached just before World War I. Wright countered this pessimistic view with his optimistic belief that "centuries forward men will look back and recognize the work of the democratic life of the twentieth century as a great, not a dead style."[215] Paraphrasing Mumford, Wright equated himself with the "living, breathing, healthy, young organism" that was "a great architecture for a great life." His parting words were to Hitchcock, "Our pioneer days are not over."[216]

In an unlikely turn of events, by the end of 1932, the circumstances of the MoMA exhibition were repeated, but this time, in distinct opposition to his earlier position, Philip Johnson became

Wright's champion. Now as chairman of MoMA's Department of Architecture, Johnson became the organizer for American participation in *V Esposizione triennale internazionale delle arti decorative e industriali moderne e dell'architettura moderna* (*Fifth Triennale: International Exhibition of Modern Decorative and Industrial Arts, and Modern Architecture*) in Milan in 1933, to be held in a new building, the Palazzo dell'Arte, designed by Giovanni Muzio, in the Parco Sempione.[217] The Italian plan for the international architecture component of the exposition was to include national exhibits and twelve individual galleries devoted to "architectural greats," which included Auguste Perret, Konstantin Melnikov, André Lurçat, Joseph Hoffmann, Willem Dudok, Walter Gropius, Mies van der Rohe, Erich Mendelsohn, Adolph Loos, Le Corbusier, Antonio Sant'Elia, and Wright.[218] Johnson, acting as the American liaison to Giulio Barella, the director, produced an American survey comprised of three categories: (1) skyscrapers, (2) industrial buildings, (3) various structures including bridges, houses, and an automobile factory.[219] However, the MoMA chairman reserved singular praise for Wright, advising the Italian committee that he "would be the only American architect really to merit full representation."[220] In the Italian catalog, Johnson, in an apparent reversal of his dismissive attitude of 1931, singled Wright out as a "true pioneer," who, owing to the American inclination to look to historic European styles as models for domestic and public buildings, was ignored as a prophet in his own country.[221] It appears that when faced with presenting modern American architecture to Europe, Johnson found perceptions were quite different than he had faced when presenting modern European architecture to America. In both cases, Wright was in a pivotal position that Johnson could not ignore.

It seems clear that Wright warranted the Italian attention even without Johnson's endorsement; as a result, he received an official invitation from the Management Committee of Carlo A. Felice, Giò Ponti, Mario Sironi, and Barella before the year was out. "We consider the Wright exhibition very important," Barella wrote, "and recognize fully the value of this American Architect and this is proved by the fact that, not only we have included him in the 12 architects of the entire world who will enjoy the privilege of a personal exhibition, but also by the fact that we would have been willing to spend, in order to have his material, the not small sum of $200."[222] Alice Garrett, wife of the American ambassador to Italy, John W. Garrett, was brought in as a diplomatic contact in the United States, and she and her husband hosted Wright at their mansion, Evergreen House, in Baltimore in November.[223]

Wright's stay with the Garretts inspired him with such enthusiasm that he decided to personally install his one-man show of models, drawings, and photographs in Milan.[224] Wright's ideas for his exhibition were ambitious and, considering the worldwide Depression, astounding. First, he began work on two new models—Prefabricated Farm Unit for Walter V. Davidson (3 feet 9 inches × 4 feet 3 inches) and San-Marcos-in-the-Desert Resort (11 feet × 4 feet)—which he planned to show alongside the House on the Mesa, St. Marks Tower, and the San Marcos Water Gardens cabins (1929).[225] With paid round-trip transportation between Taliesin and Milan assured, but additional details sketchy, Wright envisioned a tour that was unprecedented in his career. It was planned to last 340 days and follow a global itinerary: Milan (three weeks); Cairo (two weeks); Bombay (two weeks); Delhi (one week); Lucknow, India (one week); Benares, India (one week); Calcutta (one week); Singapore (two weeks); Shanghai (two weeks); Tokyo (two weeks); Moscow (three weeks); Leningrad (two weeks); Stockholm (one week); Copenhagen (one week); and London (two weeks).[226]

As the deadline for shipment to Italy drew closer, Wright requested a plan of the space allotted to him so that he could design the installation.[227] When he discovered that he would exhibit with eleven other architects, and by his calculations, determined his space too small, he withdrew. "I have never been interested in general exhibitions of this nature myself, and with one exception, have never joined one, preferring to exhibit by myself."[228] With the disappointment of the Triennale, plans for the world tour were abandoned: it would be twenty years before Wright considered such an ambitious undertaking again.

In the end, when Wright withdrew, the Italians stepped in and the Commissione Ordinatrice compiled a list of public and residential buildings, which were displayed in black-and-white photographs.[229] Predictably, outstanding works of the Oak Park Studio years, including Unity Temple, the Larkin Building, and the Evans, Coonley, and Robie Houses, were included, but so was work from 1911 to 1925 such as Taliesin, Midway Gardens, the Imperial Hotel, Hollyhock House, and the Strong Automobile Objective.[230] As a result, midyear 1933, Wright was exhibited side by side with a selection of international modern architects on two continents—in Milan and in the MoMA US tour—again, receiving more respect in Europe than in America.

Exhibitions were almost as important for Wright as clients; in fact, in the 1930s, the two were inextricably linked. In 1925, when he was formulating a plan to reestablish himself in the Midwest after a prolonged absence, his first thought was to arrange a public display of his work. Yet the exhibitions of 1930–32 differed greatly from those of 1893 to 1914. His platform was now much wider; his ambitions were national and international. Taking the two tours together, his work was seen in nineteen cities in ten states and three European countries in three years. While the intended audience for his circulating 1930–31 retrospective was architects—students and practicing—and the general public, the MoMA exhibition drew educated and sophisticated museumgoers and critics, who were, ostensibly, equally interested in Paul Cézanne and Vincent van Gogh as in architecture.

Widespread exposure and high attendance led to greater coverage in the popular and professional press. The increasing use of the press release, especially by the Museum of Modern Art, broadened the impact as news stories not only appeared in the host locations but were also picked up by the wire services and circulated to cities and towns throughout the United States. This dissemination coupled with feature stories by the popular magazines, *Time* and the *New Yorker*, made Frank Lloyd Wright a household name as an architect.

Just as he was reestablishing his reputation, his confrontation with Philip Johnson and Henry-Russell Hitchcock in 1932 was a distinct turning point. Up to that time, Wright had never cooperated with anyone who acted as an intermediary between himself and the public. Aside from his allies Robert C. Spencer and Charles R. Ashbee, whom he either influenced or censored, Wright had always been the hero of his own work. The Midwest architect was thrown off guard by Johnson, who rose to instant prominence by introducing the leading European architects of the modern movement to the United States, where they were virtually unknown. The *Modern Architecture* exhibition made the twenty-six-year-old Johnson a star in the architecture and museum world, a role he retained until his death in 2005, with the exception of the mid- to late 1930s when he gravitated into fascist politics. During that interval, Johnson withdrew from architectural discourse, but he reappeared at the Modern after World War II, where he and Wright took up their earlier positions as architectural combatants.

As Wright approached the age at which most people retire or die, he surveyed his entire career from a historical perspective, judging his achievements against the standards of the European modern movement. After reviewing his drawings and compiling a catalogue raisonné, he began to evaluate his past work from the point of view of his European critics, placing emphasis on industrial materials of concrete and steel, methods of standardization, and typologies of the capitalist city. The Larkin Building, which he described as the "first negation of the ornamental building of the nineteenth century," was singled out for special consideration, along with Unity Temple, for its monolithic concrete construction. The Call Building, his first skyscraper design, which he described as "to be run in concrete same as grain elevator is constructed" and misdated 1910, became one of his most favored works; it remained so well into the early 1950s when it was finally supplanted by the Price Tower, his first constructed skyscraper. At this moment Wright began to realize the importance of the University of Wisconsin Boathouse (Yahara Boathouse) after Mies used it as inspiration for the Barcelona Pavilion (1929; Barcelona).[231]

During the years 1930–32, Wright's exhibitions had taken him out of the familiar confines of Chicago and exposed him to a broad range of competing architects and critics, movements and manifestos, claiming supremacy over him as the new architecture for the twentieth century. He was thrown completely off guard, convinced as he had been for decades that his philosophy and designs, what he increasingly called "Organic Architecture," was the one and only true response to conditions of the modern age, one that only an American from the West could create. While he acknowledged that competition existed with Beaux-Arts eclecticism, then more recently with Art Deco commercialism, the challenge posed by MoMA's "International Style" was far more threatening. Many of its tenets overlapped his own—an architecture that remained an art, completely redefining itself through new materials and planning for modern life—but, at the same time, its machine aesthetic and its associations with socialism and communism were anathema to him. His first serious confrontation with this greater challenge was in Berlin in 1931, but it had now tentatively crossed the Atlantic and was poised to take America.

Aside from the ideological clashes among Wright, Hitchcock, and Johnson, the most lasting effect of the Modern's 1932 exhibition occurred when Wright sensed competition from the European avant-garde when he saw the show in Chicago and after study of both the catalog and the book. Maintaining his commitment as a practicing architect and swearing to Hitchcock that he would be the greatest architect that ever lived, he made a shift in the mid-1930s to design in a more abstract idiom. Wright reinvented himself: this was the most important and lasting consequence of the 1930–32 exhibitions. In his confrontation with European modernism, without abandoning his polemic, formally he chose synthesis over opposition.

CHAPTER 3

Broadacre City, 1935

For Wright, the Great Depression was a frustrating continuation of the severe hardships he had faced in the late 1920s when his personal bankruptcy forced him to forfeit Taliesin (figure 3.1). In the challenging years after the 1929 stock market crash, he tried to maintain financial stability by lecturing, writing, exhibiting, and promoting some of his more commercial designs, such as his unbuilt high-rise apartment building, St. Mark's Tower, for New York City. By 1932, these efforts did little more than keep Taliesin just short of foreclosure. Finally, he struck on a solution of lasting significance. He founded a school—more community than academy—called the Taliesin Fellowship.

Nationally, at about the same time in early 1933, Franklin Delano Roosevelt as the newly elected president packed his first one hundred days of office with legislation for "Relief, Recovery, and Reform." Subsequent programs of the New Deal sought to fund jobs through the Federal Emergency Relief Administration (1934) and the Civilian Conservation Corps (1933–42), stimulate home buying by insuring mortgages through the Federal Housing Administration (1934), and ease the housing crisis by planning and building "greenbelt towns" through the Resettlement Administration (1935–36).

Wright remained unable to benefit from any of these official national relief efforts. Rather, he was energized by adding a large drafting room and dormitory to the Hillside Home School for the Taliesin apprentices, designing a playhouse to charge for screening films and cartoons for neighboring farmers, and creating a cultural life that was enriched by chamber music groups; poetry readings; and the writing, designing, and printing of *Taliesin*, an in-house magazine. The "culture" he created on his expansive farmland, he believed, was distinct from, and superior to, the alien "civilization" he encountered in American cities. The rebirth of the agrarian lands of his pioneer ancestors as a "model community" combined with a newfound resolve to engage in the international discourse about modern architecture and urbanism stimulated his imagination in new directions. The result was nothing short of an ingenious plan, Broadacre City, to resettle the entire population of the United States from coast to coast. In so doing, he set his sights on besting his competition: the American rage for Colonial Williamsburg, the European commitment to the "existenzminimum" housing factory workers in Siedlungen, and the Roosevelt administration's proposals for "subsistence homesteads."

INDUSTRIAL ARTS EXPOSITION, NEW YORK, 1935

Up to 1935, Broadacre City was known only through the written word. Wright's first major essay on the subject, "Broadacre City: An Architect's Vision," appeared in the March 1932 *New York Times Magazine* almost as a direct challenge to Le Corbusier, whose own article, "A Noted Architect Dissects Our Cities," was published in the same newspaper just over two months previously.[1] Wright expanded his argument in *The Disappearing City* (released in September), which had limited distribution as the publisher, William Farquhar Payson, went out of business in 1935.[2] In the intervening three years, Wright had never felt it necessary to create perspective drawings—unlike Le Corbusier—conveying

3.1 Frank Lloyd Wright with Taliesin Fellows at the Taliesin Studio, 1935. (FLWFA, 6601.0025). *Left to right*: Eugene Masselink, Benjamin Dombar, Edgar Tafel, and John H. Howe.

what his ideal city would look like. Broadacre City was known through text only until he received an offer from the National Alliance of Art and Industry to exhibit at New York's Rockefeller Center.

The Rockefeller-funded National Alliance of Art and Industry (NAAI) was founded with the avowed purpose of bringing "before the public the outstanding accomplishments of American industry . . . showing how these industrial projects improve living conditions . . . and encouraging experiment and the use of new materials in industrial production . . . to demonstrate that beauty and utility are now determining factors in the minds of all types of consumers."[3] They held the first industrial design exhibit at the Art Center, 65 East Fifty-Sixth Street, June to September 1932.[4] In 1934, the annual exhibition was moved to the newly completed RCA Building at 30 Rockefeller Plaza. The NAAI held a well-received exhibition of commercial photography, September 18–October 6, 1934, which included works by Margaret Bourke-White among others.

At that time, the Executive Committee consisted of Ben Nash, a highly successful authority on using marketing techniques to redesign packaging of consumer goods; Rodney Wilcox Jones, a major manufacturer of knit underwear; and Harvey Wiley Corbett, one of the architects of Rockefeller Center. The director of the alliance was Alon Bement, an artist and art educator, who had trained under the American painter Arthur Wesley Dow, and who later introduced Dow's techniques to his own student, Georgia O'Keeffe.

The Executive Committee appointed thirty-year-old Thomas J. Maloney manager of the 1935 Industrial Arts Exposition scheduled for April. Born in Milwaukee, he came to the East Coast to enroll in the Naval Academy, but soon dropped out, and after several jobs, including assistant advertising manager of New Jersey Zinc Company, formed his own New York agency in 1934, T. J. Maloney Inc., which would grow within a year to a staff of ten. His wide-ranging interests included photography, with which he made a lasting reputation as the editor and publisher of the groundbreaking *U.S. Camera Annuals*, 1935–69. In the 1940s, he advised the Modern on their Department of Photography, where he was successful in recommending his good friend, Edward Steichen, as director.[5]

Maloney was familiar with Wright through Karl E. Jensen (1907–19??), whom he had probably known in Manhattan when Jensen worked at *Architectural Record* just before he joined Wright's Studio in 1930.[6] Maloney had been corresponding with Wright and occasionally visiting Taliesin when he was in Chicago on business beginning as early as 1933. By the fall 1934, Jensen left Wright's employ to work for Walter V. Davidson; he moved back to New York where he immediately got in touch with Maloney. While he sought work for himself, he also was voluntarily on the lookout for opportunities to bring income to Taliesin. Wright and Jensen had parted ways over Jensen's inability to integrate himself with the Fellowship, but he and Wright continued to correspond as each struggled to survive the Depression.

In 1934 Maloney was given full authority, under the direction of Nash, for the organization of the exposition labeled "A Preview of Prosperity, a complete presentation of the coming achievements in Housing, Home Appliances, Transportation and Design," to be held "with Rockefeller-backing" at the Forum galleries on the ground floor of the RCA Building.[7] He began work with a handicap due to the public boycott over past years of the event by leading American industrial designers—Donald Desky, Henry Dreyfus, Walter D. Teague, Russell Wright, Norman Bel Geddes, and Raymond Loewy—and with the loss of Rockefeller financing, although Maloney eventually was able to "persuade Nelson Rockefeller to aid us."[8] Prominent industrial designers announced they were boycotting the 1935 exposition because "the Alliance neither stimulates better design, represents the artist, nor improves the relationship between the designer and industry."[9]

The major goal of the management was to sell 20,000 square feet of space at $5 per square foot to manufacturing corporations and the automobile industry, such as Singer Sewing Machine, International Nickel, Ford, and Bakelite Corporation. "Another phase of this show," Maloney explained, is "Features and Publicity," which he believed was just as important as sales. For this part of the job, he was looking for nationally recognized names that would draw attention to the event in an effort to bring the public in at 25 cents per person.[10]

The second half of 1934 would be an auspicious turning point for Wright, one made partially possible by the close association between Jensen and Maloney. The chain of events began when Edgar J. Kaufmann Sr., a rich Pittsburgh department store owner and civic leader, started looking for a modern architect (figure 3.2). Kaufmann's first letter to Wright, dated August 16, began: "I would greatly appreciate hearing from you, or your secretary, whether or not you ever visit Pittsburgh or New York City. I have a very interesting matter I should like to discuss with you at any time you should come East."[11] Unfortunately, Wright had neither the money nor the inclination to travel to the East Coast on such a vague notion; he had been duped too many times by speculators since the onset of the Depression. Yet he did take advantage of Jensen's presence in New York and his willingness to be of help. He asked his former secretary to investigate the

3.2 Edgar J. Kaufmann Sr., in his office designed by Frank Lloyd Wright, Pittsburgh, Pennsylvania, after 1937. (FLWFA, 6702.0001)

situation for him. Sometime in the first two weeks of September, Kaufmann invited Jensen to his home as an overnight guest. Jensen learned that Kaufmann had two propositions in mind, both Pittsburgh civic projects—a planetarium to be funded by Kaufmann and bridges and tunnels financed under the Civil Works Administration, part of Roosevelt's New Deal. "In either direction, or both," Jensen informed Wright, "I am hopeful it will mean work."[12] Wright's reaction was to send Kaufmann a polite but noncommittal letter stating that he felt sure "something along the line you suggest can be worked out between us."[13]

But Wright was not the only person Jensen told about seeing Kaufmann; he was talking regularly to Maloney, who was always on the lookout for more opportunities for "Features and Publicity." By the time Jensen had his second meeting with Kaufmann at the Central Park Casino about a week to ten days later, events had moved very fast. In addition to the two civic projects for Pittsburgh, the department store president explained that he wanted a new executive office and revealed that his son was seriously interested in joining the Taliesin Fellowship. In fact, Edgar Jr. had already paid a visit to Taliesin and was "impressed." By that time, Jensen and Maloney had decided to incorporate Wright into the April exposition. They first suggested that Wright join a jury of impressive names including Mumford, Edsel Ford, Lessing Rosenwald, Nelson Rockefeller, and Walter Chrysler among others. Jensen mentioned, "I had Maloney include [Kaufmann] because he will be flattered by the company." The first mention of an exhibition appeared almost as an afterthought when Jensen jotted in the margin, "P.S. Models of 'The Farm,' 'Two zone houses' and 'planetarium' would be swell exhibits from you?"[14]

An insight into how profoundly the Depression had negatively affected Wright's outlook can be gauged by his response to Jensen's letters. He was suspicious that anything positive would come from Kaufmann's proposals and angry at Jensen for his actions as a "go-between." "I have very little faith in any 'prospect' at this time," he declared. "That has pretty well [been] taken out of me." Then he added, "But never mind, anything at this juncture is gratefully received. Beggars never were choosers although I've found them more fussy about what they got than those who had everything. The present beneficiaries of relief show up human nature in a ghastly light. I don't want to join in their characteristic. I'll play the game with Kaufmann."[15]

For the month of October, the standoff continued with Kaufmann still pressing Wright to come east, but that attitude shifted by mid-month when Edgar Jr. arrived at Taliesin to join the Fellowship. In the meantime, Maloney was unable to make any further offers to Wright until he spoke about money with the "backers" of the exposition.[16] By November 3, Wright was becoming more forthright with Kaufmann, admitting, "To tell the truth I have never much hope of a great result where officialdom and the committee meeting prevail. But here's hoping."[17] At the same moment, Jensen had come up with a proposition, though on a smaller scale, that had more probability for immediate success. "I have suggested to Tom Maloney that no more appropriate exhibit for the Industrial Arts show . . . would be possible," Jensen explained on November 8, "than a model of 'the broadacre city' as you would visualize the pattern. Surrounding it would be large-scale photographs showing old city-patterns and congestion. The suggestion seems to have taken hold and I will have their final word in a few days. It was my hope that you would take on this model-job and turn it over to the Fellowship as an interesting object-lesson for them to do." While the idea had potential, the financial details were vague. "I was told $300 was available for such a purpose but [I] asked for $1000 as barely covering the cost of making the model." If the money from the National Alliance came through, Jensen asked Wright for a finder's fee of 25 percent or $250 "as a means to get on my feet." But he concluded, "If you think [my requests] are unjustified I will of course do what I can just the same."[18]

In the next week, Maloney explained two versions of Jensen's plans for a Broadacre City exhibition to both Wright (by letter) and Kaufmann (in person in Pittsburgh). With Kaufmann, Maloney illustrated his presentation with photostats of Jensen's sketches without informing Jensen that he was even making the trip.[19] Maloney revealed that Jensen got the idea for the exhibit while lecturing him on decentralization. The first concept was to present four stages of urban development:

1. Babylon
2. A well planned modern city
3. One of the worst American cities, possibly Boston or Pittsburgh
4. Your Broad Acre City

But in his letter to Wright, Maloney explained, "We then felt that perhaps just showing the Broad Acre city would be much better, using large photo-murals to typify the others." Maloney suggested "a striking model layout to cover an area of about ten feet square," and he explained to the architect that he could "get a minimum of $500 and a maximum of $1000 to help toward the building of it." Maloney never specified the source of the financing. Perhaps he had in mind the "Rockefeller funding" that he had secured.[20]

While it does not appear that Maloney discussed any of the financial details with Kaufmann at that early stage, they both favored the large model scheme and concluded that it should travel. Kaufmann wanted the first stop after New York to be his department store.[21] Kaufmann was drawn in even more when Maloney requested that he sponsor the major design prize for the exposition, ultimately called "the Kaufmann Medal."[22] Wright responded enthusiastically to Maloney, "Your project is a grand one," and then he immediately launched into negotiations over concept and money. He preferred the scheme of a model, but wanted "twelve square [feet] in four parts for handling." "Such a thing to be credible and creditable means an awful lot of intelligent work. ... We could illustrate in detail most of the units like the tall building, the automobile objective, the theatre—the gas station—the luxurious machine age house—the little farms unit—the acre subsistence homestead—etc, etc by models we already have." He accepted the figure of $1000, but declared, "If you guarantee this we will *go*, because God knows it will be of immense importance to our country at this time."[23] When Wright used the word "go," he meant it both literally and figuratively. He already had initiated steps to take the Fellowship to Arizona for the winter where he planned to look for land to build on.[24]

A myth has grown up around Kaufmann's visit to Taliesin on November 18, 1934, implying that Kaufmann was there solely to visit his son and that he knew nothing about Broadacre City or the planned exhibition at the RCA Building until that Sunday evening. The event, as Edgar Tafel, a Taliesin apprentice who was present, described it, began with Wright expanding on "his theory for the salvation of America—his vision of the future city based on the automobile," when he added "that if he could, he would create an exhibit of models and drawings of Broadacres and send the message all over the United States. E. J. asked, 'What would it take to produce such an exhibit?' Mr. Wright replied without hesitation, '$1000.' EJ: 'Mr. Wright, you can start tomorrow.' "[25] While it is likely that Wright and Kaufmann discussed the New York exposition in private earlier in the day—Wright acknowledged later that he had "understood Kaufmann [was] cooperating [with] Maloney"—it is true he spontaneously pledged $1,000 on the spot.[26] In fact, both Jensen and Maloney were thrown so far off guard when they heard about the offer a few days later, they had to report to Wright that the National Alliance now "regarded the matter settled."[27] Maloney diplomatically explained the situation to Kaufmann a week later, "You have a way of doing things in a big and decisive manner. ... The financing of the model for Broad Acre City did not present a great problem because I had the directors lined up to do it, but you have taken care of it."[28]

The month of December would be a roller coaster for all involved. Wright's mood improved significantly when he asked Kaufmann for a $500 advance on the model construction, and a check promptly arrived in the mail. He immediately agreed to come to Pittsburgh in a week.[29] But that was Friday's morning mail. Shortly after, he received a plan layout of his allotted space at the RCA Building that was "in a back alley between two posts and in behind a couple of automobiles ... when we need a space about 45′0″ × 45′0″ to show the scheme as a whole with any forceful effect."[30] He shot off three letters in succession to Jensen, Maloney, and Kaufmann with basically the same message, "Count us out of the show. ... But we will make one of our work some other way. I think I can find the way. ... I am not interested in a motor vehicle and transportation exhibition."[31]

First thing Monday morning, Maloney wrote to Wright that the space he was given was "the focal point of the entire show," but he was willing to entertain other options. "You can readily see that with true artistry," he explained, "your idea of 45′ × 45′ would mean over 2,000 [square] ft. ... twice as much space as any exhibitor is allowed ... those 2,000 [square] ft. ... [are] actually costing us $10,000 to show [the model]." At this point, Jensen walked into Maloney's office with news: Wright was coming to New York for the weekend. Maloney jotted in the margin, "Can't

3.3 Broadacre City model in fabrication at La Hacienda, Chandler, Arizona, 1935. (FLWFA, 3402.0084). At the *right*: Frank Lloyd Wright, wearing a beret, adjusting the model.

you go up to Radio City and look over the space with Karl and see just what the space is like?"[32]

The New York visit was only a side trip following his visit to Pittsburgh Tuesday and Wednesday December 18–19, 1934. After those two days in Pennsylvania, Wright came away with more than a minor commission for an executive office remodeling and the invitation to design what would become the most famous modern house of the twentieth century, he had discovered the man who would replace Darwin D. Martin, his most dedicated art patron for the first half of his career. Martin died exactly one year later to the day of Wright's visit to the site of Fallingwater, Kaufmann's future country house. After that change in his fortunes, all went well in Manhattan, as Wright reported to Kaufmann the day after Christmas: "The exhibition space turned out swell when I met those boys face to face. We have the center of the stage and enough of it—all friendly."[33]

The contrast in atmosphere between where the Broadacre City exhibition was fabricated and where it debuted could not have been greater. Between late January and early April, Wright, along with his family and about twenty-five apprentices, set up plywood sheets in the open air of the courtyard of the La Hacienda Hotel in the middle of the Arizona desert outside Phoenix where the four sections of the model were assembled by hand (figure 3.3). Tafel described it as "voluntary exile from 'civilization' and 'the Public' in the interest of both."[34] The first week of April, the demountable parts were driven by truck to Rockefeller Center and set up under Wright's supervision for the grand opening, scheduled for 8:15 p.m. on April 15.

That night, Maloney demonstrated what a New York ad man could accomplish. The *New York Times* reported: "By pressing a gold telegraph key in the Oval Office of the White House . . . President Roosevelt started an electric impulse that set off 120 flash bulbs in the Forum of Rockefeller Center, turned on fifty floodlights, started a siren, dropped an American flag, and turned on the current on an electric organ." Following this "opening ceremony," Corbett presided over remarks by Fiorello La Guardia, mayor of New York; James A. Moffett, Federal Housing Administrator (speaking from Washington, DC, "relayed by a beam of light"); and Clinton L. Bardo, president of the National Association of Manufacturers.[35]

3.4 Broadacre City model, 1935. (FLWFA, 3402.0089)

3.5 Frank Lloyd Wright installing *Broadacre City* exhibition, Industrial Arts Exposition, Rockefeller Center, New York, before April 15, 1935. Photograph by Keystone View Company. (Scott Architectural Archive)

Wright's participation on opening night did not go as smoothly. He was scheduled as the final speaker, but the radio broadcast was cut off before he was introduced. Maloney blamed Corbett. Wright's talk, "Broadacres—A Dream of the City of the Future," was eventually rescheduled for April 30, but that also failed. Instead of Wright, who was back in Wisconsin, Tafel went on the air reluctantly. Wright concluded, the "situation [is] so strange."[36] By this time, disillusionment with the National Alliance was widespread; Maloney was leading the critics.[37] It was widely acknowledged that "the latest orange drink, corn plaster, automobile polish, life insurance, Encyclopedia Britannica, etc." was not industrial art.[38] Douglas Haskell in the *Nation* made the point that, "Most of the worst stuff was simply so much paid space, like advertisements in a magazine."[39]

Despite the missteps by the National Alliance and the blatantly commercial, if not tawdry, nature of the exposition, Wright's contribution was the singular success it was intended to be: attendance was recorded at 40,000 visitors.[40] His exhibition was widely reported in New York City and nationally, featured in trade journals such as *Architectural Record* and *American Architect*, and reviewed in specialty magazines as disparate as the *New Yorker* and the *New Masses*. The didactic nature of the display was evident in the innovative installation design: its strong graphic style utilizing oversize text panels conveyed Wright's ideas in terse, but poetic, aphorisms. Despite the books and articles Wright would publish and the interviews and lectures he would give about decentralization in the decades ahead, the general understanding of his thesis rests on the immediate visual power of the Broadacre City model (figure 3.4).

The opportunity at Rockefeller Center was the first occasion Wright had to take full charge of his own exhibition, as had been his lifelong habit, since the 1931 European tour and his frustrating 1932 experience with Johnson at the Modern: once again, he stepped forward in front of the public without the intermediary of a jury or curator. With time and money short, there were limitations on the material Wright could display. He readily pointed out that it could only be done because he had seven detailed models

3.6 *Broadacre City* exhibition, Industrial Arts Exposition, Rockefeller Center, New York, April 15 to May 15, 1935. Photograph by F. S. Lincoln. (Reproduced with the kind permission of the Special Collections Library, the Pennsylvania State University Libraries). *Left to right*, *foreground*: House on the Mesa (partial view), St. Mark's Tower, Broadacre City model. *Background*, *left to right*: Garages, Top-Turn Intersection, San Marcos Water Gardens cabins, Standardized Overhead Gas Station, Malcolm Willey House I (rear view), New Theater, Colonial Equivalent, one- and two-car houses.

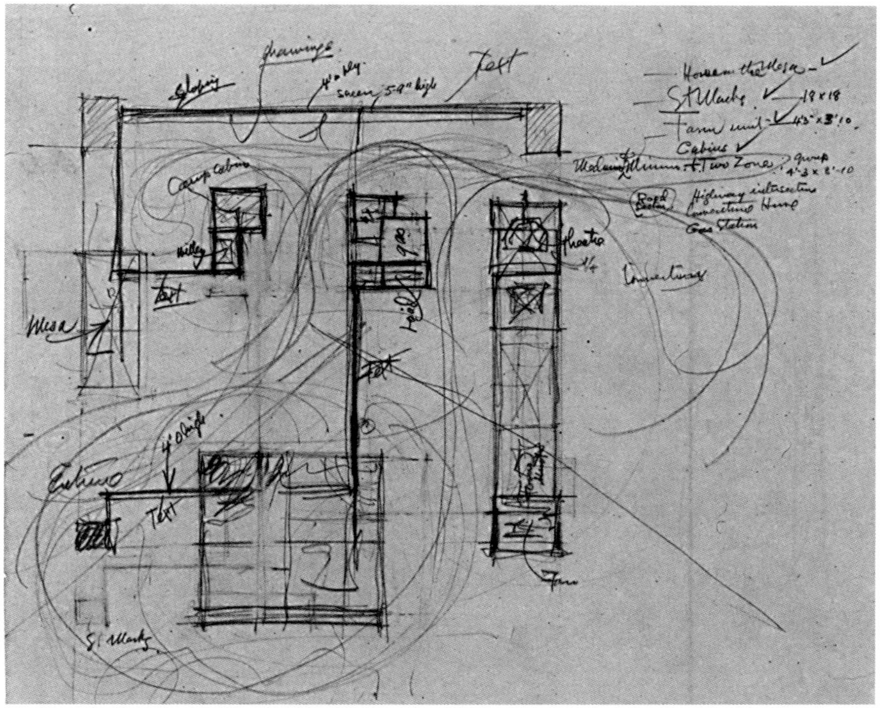

3.7 Frank Lloyd Wright, *Broadacre City* exhibition plan, preliminary drawing, 1935. Pencil on tracing paper, 30 × 15 in. (FLWFA, 3406.0004)

already on hand: St. Mark's Tower, San Marcos Water Gardens, Standardized Overhead Gas Station, New Theater, House on the Mesa, Colonial Equivalent, and Prefabricated Farm Unit for Walter V. Davidson (1932; Buffalo, New York). Although four of these had been exhibited in New York in 1931 and one in 1932, all the models in the exhibition were of unbuilt work with no reference to specific clients or sites, giving them an abstract quality that fit with the theme of being "everywhere and nowhere."

There are two photographs that depict the 1935 exhibition as it was presented in New York: one taken by the Keystone View Company during the installation; the other, of the completed display by New York architectural photographer, Fay S. Lincoln (figures 3.5–6). On the floor of the Forum, spaced between two pillars and set six feet back from a rear wall, in an area roughly 45 feet by 45 feet, Wright designed a layout of freestanding plywood panels and model stands in a group of three interlocking L-configurations abutting one slanted panel for plans and elevations and a long table for smaller models (figure 3.7). On the back wall, he attached matted, color pencil presentation drawings of houses designed for the Lake Tahoe Summer Colony (figure 3.8). The installation formed a self-contained unit with an entrance.

The exhibition had no official title, but a panel at the entrance introduced the principal theme: DECENTRALIZATION INTEGRATION. While the installation had a defined circulation pattern, it was neither arranged chronologically nor by building type. Once within, at the square void in the center, the models and text panels were visible within a 360-degree radius, varying in height, with models generally lower, except for St. Mark's Tower, and text at eye level. Themes were presented in two ways: (1) text with titles such as OUT OF THE GROUND INTO THE LIGHT and A NEW ARCHITECTURE and (2) a plan of the Broadacre City model, with text and slogans, titled A NEW FREEDOM FOR LIVING IN AMERICA (figure 3.9). In a departure from previous exhibition designs, or from future ones as well, large blocks of text arranged so they would be readable from a distance served the polemical nature of the display.[41]

Upon entering the *Broadacre City* exhibit, the visitor had two text panels in immediate view, one to the right and one directly ahead.[42] The introductory panel read: OUT OF THE GROUND INTO THE LIGHT / A NEW WAY FOR MAN BY WAY OF FAIR USE OF THE MACHINE AND SOCIAL CO/ORDINATION ■ LAND DISTRIBUTED BY THE STATE TO BE HELD ONLY BY USE AND

3.8 Cabin Lodge, Lake Tahoe Summer Colony, Emerald Bay, California, 1923–24. Kameki Tsuchiura, delineator. Graphite pencil and color pencil on tracing paper, 21¾ × 15 in. (FLWFA, 2205.001)

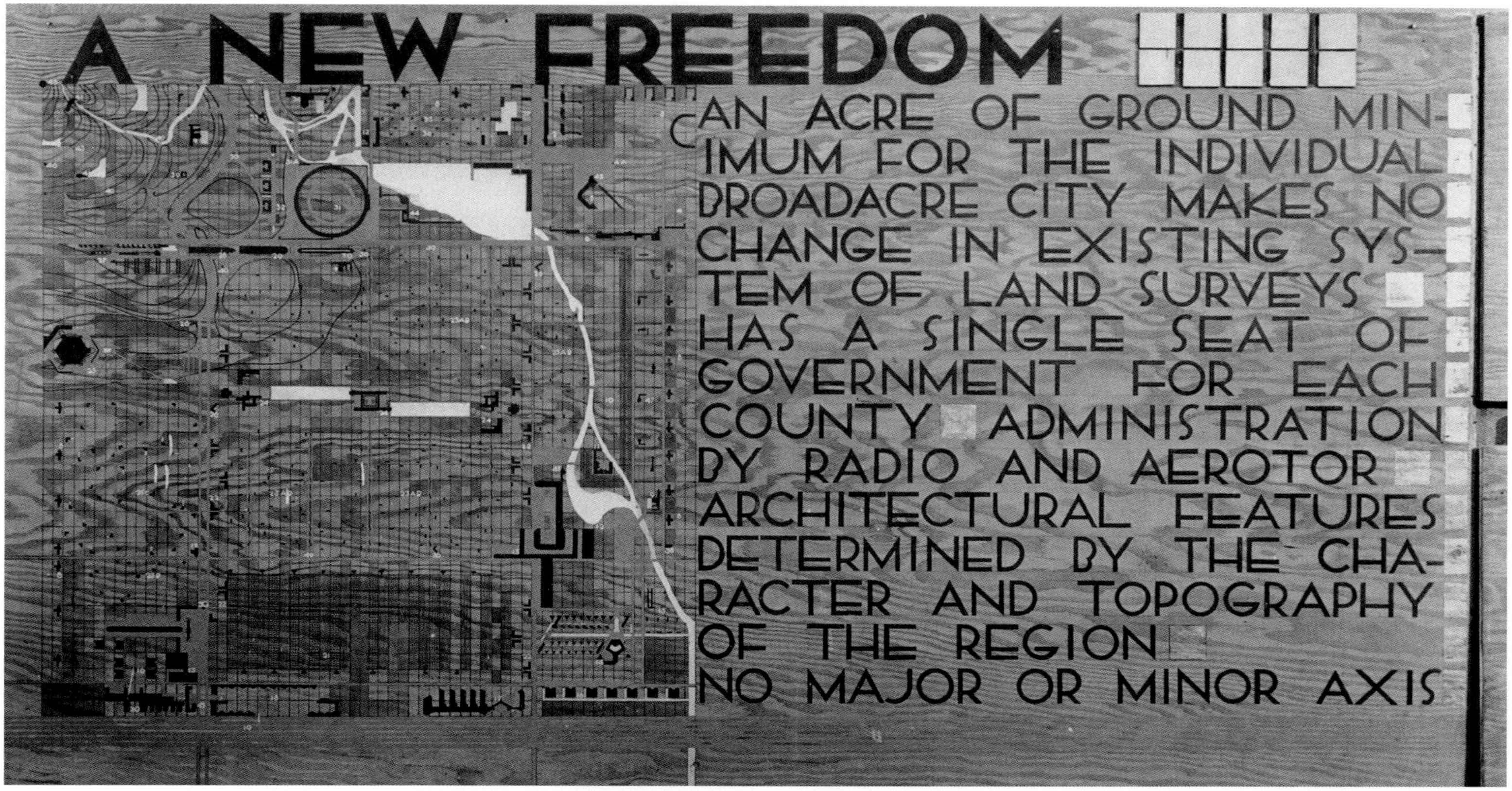

3.9 A NEW FREEDOM panel. Paint on plywood, 48 × 78¼ in. (FLWFA, 3402.0009). The word "For" was covered over by square ornamental blocks when the panel was used as a single panel at a later date.

IM/PROVEMENTS ■ NO REALTORS EXCEPT THE STATE ■ THE COUNTY THE AGENT OF THE / STATE ■ THE ARCHITECT THE AGENT OF THE COUNTY.

The first panel on the right as the visitor turned to enter read: BROADACRE CITY / MODEL MADE BY THE TALIESIN FELLOWSHIP FRANK LLOYD WRIGHT ARCHITECT. The direction for viewing the exhibition began with what Wright called "collateral models" first and concluded with the Broadacre City model. The first work the visitor saw was the House on the Mesa, which Wright called the "machine-age luxury house," on a diagonal with the San Marcos Water Gardens and a new model, the Top-Turn Intersection (figures 3.10–11, also see figure B.26). Directly ahead, as a title over the house plans and elevations, was a slogan in bold sans serif font: THE FUTURE IS EVERYWHERE AND NOWHERE BROADACRE CITY. The Standardized Overhead Gas Station and the Malcolm Willey House I (1932–33; Minneapolis, Minnesota; figures 3.12–13, also see figure B.16) were

3.10 San Marcos Water Gardens cabins model, Chandler, Arizona, 1929. (FLWFA, 2705.0005)

3.11 Top-Turn Intersection model, 1934–35. (FLWFA, 3402.041).

3.12 Standardized Overhead Gas Station model, 1928, fabricated summer 1930. (Sophia Wittenberg Mumford Papers, Ms. Collection 958, Kislak Center for Special Collections, Rare Books and Manuscripts, University of Pennsylvania. Photograph reproduced courtesy of the Estate of Lewis and Sophia Mumford)

3.13 Malcolm Willey House I model, Minneapolis, Minnesota, 1932–33. (FLWFA, 3204.0003)

grouped together, just below the New Theater. Due to the absence of any other installation photographs, it is not known what appeared on the back of some of the panels, presumably more text, as the models—excluding the Farm Unit and Bridge, which were displayed at the end of the long table—are accounted for in the Lincoln photograph (figures 3.14–15, also see figure B.23). While there was a mixture of old and new models, the whole created a convincing vision of a new automobile-dominated society because the building types chosen—the Standardized Overhead Gas Station and tourist cabins, for instance—conveyed that idea as much as the new house types Wright designed, which he categorized by the size of their garage: the one-car, two-car, and five-car residences.

Some of Wright's collateral models need additional explanation, specifically the single-family residences he made especially for the 1935 show. The photographic record as it was published at the time in *Architectural Record* and *American Architect* indicates that there were four models of detached houses with different roof types: two one-car houses (pitched roofs) and two two-car houses (flat roofs), the latter two the most advanced designs of the four (figure 3.16). One of these, also known as Colonial Equivalent, Wright had been revising over a period of years; it was a variation of the Chandler Block House (1929) and the Conventional House (1932; figure 3.17). The other two-car house was the more advanced aesthetically, anticipating the abstract quality of Fallingwater later that year with flat, unadorned surfaces of horizontal and vertical planes, a cantilevered balcony, and continuous ribbons of factory sash (figure 3.18).[43]

These residential designs have elicited little critical commentary in the Wright literature; in fact, this aspect of Broadacre City has almost become forgotten.[44] At the time, Wright emphasized the use of industrial technology: "Most of them are planned for construction with factory fabricated units that permit varied room arrangements. They would also use prefabricated utility assemblies and all of them would have space for at least one automobile."[45] But the text panel next to these models carried provocative political associations: EACH ACCORDING TO PURPOSE OR NEED VARYING ONLY IN EXTENT AND INDIVIDUALITY.

The narrative of the exhibition culminated in two large explanatory panels placed at right angles to each other titled A NEW FREEDOM FOR LIVING IN AMERICA, embracing the 12-foot square model. The first panel was divided into two parts: a schematic plan of the model next to a block of text, which read (see figure 3.9):

3.14 Prefabricated Farm Unit for Walter V. Davidson model, Buffalo, New York, 1932. (Private Collection)

AN ACRE OF GROUND MINIMUM FOR THE INDIVIDUAL ■ BROADACRE CITY MAKES NO CHANGE IN EXISTING SYSTEM OF LAND SURVEYS ■ HAS A SINGLE SEAT OF GOVERNMENT FOR EACH COUNTY ■ ADMINISTRATION BY RADIO AND AEROTOR ■ ARCHITECTURAL FEATURES DETERMINED BY THE CHARACTER AND TOPOGRAPHY OF THE REGION ■ NO MAJOR OR MINOR AXIS

On the opposite panel, the text read:

NO PRIVATE OWNERSHIP OF PUBLIC NEEDS
NO LANDLORD AND TENANT
NO "HOUSING" ■ NO "SUBSISTENCE" HOMESTEADS
NO TRAFFIC PROBLEM ■ NO BACK AND FORTH HAUL
NO RAILROADS ■ NO STREETCARS
NO GRADE CROSSINGS
NO POLES ■ NO WIRES IN SIGHT
NO DITCHES ALONGSIDE THE ROAD
NO HEADLIGHTS ■ NO LIGHT FIXTURES
NO GLARING CEMENT ROADS OR WALKS
NO TALL BUILDINGS EXCEPT AS ISOLATED IN PARKS
NO ROADSIDE ADVERTISING
NO SLUM ■ NO SCUM
NO PUBLIC OWNERSHIP OF PRIVATE NEEDS
NO MAJOR OR MINOR AXIS

Wright's purpose was primarily polemical, with political overtones, but with no overt political agenda; he considered it the architect's job to "visualize" USONIA, not to create a scheme to "realize" it. From past experience, he knew that to avoid the usual misunderstanding he needed to provide illustrated written material for his audience. *Architectural Record* and *Architectural Forum* were both contacted by Maloney and the public relations firm, Riis and Bonner, hired by NAAI, in advance to do a feature story on Broadacre City. All material—text and photographs—had to be prepared in Arizona to meet the deadline for an April issue.[46] In the end, the *Architectural Record* article, "Broadacre City: A New Community Plan," was published because *Record* received an exclusive.[47] Two Taliesin Fellows, Tafel and Byron "Bob" Mosher, who acted as guides, sold the *Architectural Record* reprint for 10 cents.

Wright's text was a rambling argument that reads more like a sermon than an authoritative essay on land planning. It was, in essence, a prescription for a new America—his Usonia—that was made possible by three major technological trends: the automobile; transcontinental communications, that is, radio, telephone, and telegraph; and prefabrication. He saw these forces already at work in the United States, but he proselytized for the "three inherent rights of any man: (1) His social right to a direct medium of exchange in place of gold as a commodity (2) His social right to his place on the ground ... in the sun and air (3) public ownership of invention and scientific discoveries that concern the life of the people."[48]

Newspaper coverage of Wright's contribution was extensive, positive, and routine, again, primarily the result of a campaign led by Riis and Bonner, but genuine reviews were few. Mumford devoted two paragraphs to it in his *New Yorker* column, "The Sky Line." He lauded Wright for producing "the conception of a whole community," which, while "both a generous dream and a rational plan," "functions as an organic whole." His lone criticism, reflecting Mumford's increasing admiration for European low-cost housing solutions, was the "design of the minimal house." Nevertheless, he concluded, "On the whole, Wright's philosophy of life and his mode of planning have never been shown to better advantage."[49] But the more substantial review appeared privately after Wright admitted, "you puzzle me Lewis. ... I don't know what you can mean by preferring the German tenement and slum solution as preferable to the Broadacre's minimum house and maximum of space." He added, "please explain. Will you? You might teach me something I ought to know."[50] Mumford took him at his word, and confessed, "like all the things I write in the *New Yorker* it touched only the surface." He admitted that their main disagreement could be due to Wright's dogmatism, because "it is silly to lump all the good and bad things that have been done in European housing as a 'slum solution.' For me ... the type of city you have so admirably worked out ... is one of half a dozen potential urban types that we can develop in order to achieve the maximum possibilities of life."[51] In private, Wright conceded that Mumford's review was "Not so helpful. The gist of the thing seems to be pretty generally missed. Too simple and easy I suppose."[52] After ten years of a very close relationship, Wright and Mumford were beginning to drift apart because of their political views; although Mumford up to the beginning of World War II would continue to be recognized as the principal Wright authority.

The major risk that Wright took when agreeing to construct and exhibit his land planning scheme for America was that he

3.15 Multi-Lane Bridge over Highway model. (FLWFA, 3407.0001). Wright's description: "Bridge over great arterial Right of Way, which consists of many lanes of speed traffic above, monorail speed trains in the middle, and truck and traffic on lower side lanes. Within the highway structures are storage facilities for raw material."

3.16 Medium and minimum house models for Broadacre City, 1935. *Left to right*: Colonial Equivalent (two-car house), two one-car houses, and two-car house. (Courtesy Douglas M. Steiner, Edmonds, Washington)

would face such serious criticism that he would have to reconsider his own position. Ironically, this was the case with the left-wing reviewer, Stephen Alexander, of the weekly, *New Masses*. Although Alexander approached his subject with a political bias, his attack was cogent because he recognized both Wright's strengths and weaknesses. "Despite his badly confused notions of the nature of social forces in our society—(only a serious and completely sincere person could have written such a naïve concoction of adolescent idealism and Wellesian it's-all-done-with-push-buttons fiction)," Alexander opined, "Frank Lloyd Wright must be regarded as one of the important forces in progressive American architectural thought." He put it bluntly, "He has simply taken author's license to create a utopia of his own making." While he granted that Wright "has a healthy sense of values as to what constitutes 'an ideal life,'" his approach of "simply drawing up blueprints ... makes the project irrelevant and even ludicrous as a program for American architecture today." Not surprisingly, Alexander concluded that the significance of Broadacre City was that it pointed to "the necessity ... of the creation of a socialist society."[53]

Wright's published reply contains important insights into his intentions. "Thanks, Comrade Alexander: I *have* taken 'architect's license' ... but I am guilty of offering no plan for immediate consumption except as it might suggest a desirable objective to others and the steps are only too obvious. Social forces as well as physical are involved in the changes taking place around us and in Broadacre City I have taken them both (by way of each other) to what seemed to me some logical conclusion. Well, perhaps the act is a bit Wellesian as you say. I have committed the sin of 'dreaming.' As for craft, state-craft is not my craft. As any architect I am interested most in natural causes and effects." He then made a point of setting the record straight politically: "But Broadacres has proposed a life as anti-capitalistic as it is, in this sense, anti-Communistic. It is anti-socialistic, too, so far as current socialism goes." He closed by revealing, "I presume any search for such like Broadacre City would be a kind of 'adolescence.' I wish the whole world were not quite so callous and the people in it not utterly sophisticated. Then, something besides war might be inevitable and natural enough to happen soon."[54]

The New York exhibition had not even opened when Maloney started promoting another scheme to get Wright exposure and possibly money. He decided that the model should serve as the Midwest architect's introduction to the Roosevelt administration with the purpose of securing a job through one of the New Deal agencies. If Wright were hired by the United States government to design sections of the country according to the principles of Broadacre City, it would realize his lifelong goal of shaping the country with an intent of realizing an ideal democracy.

CORCORAN GALLERY OF ART, WASHINGTON, DC, 1935

The visitors to the Broadacre City model in New York were distinctly different from the audience Maloney contemplated for the nation's capital: nothing less than the president of the United States and his key advisors, or at least, his activist wife, First Lady Eleanor Roosevelt. While Wright went along willingly with the Industrial Arts Exposition once he had money in hand, he was skeptical at the outset about showing in Washington with the purpose of obtaining an "official job" with the federal government. But the prospect of being awarded New Deal monies became such a driving force behind the Broadacre tour that the commitment to make Kaufmann's Pittsburgh department store the second venue was soon abandoned. In fact, adjustments and

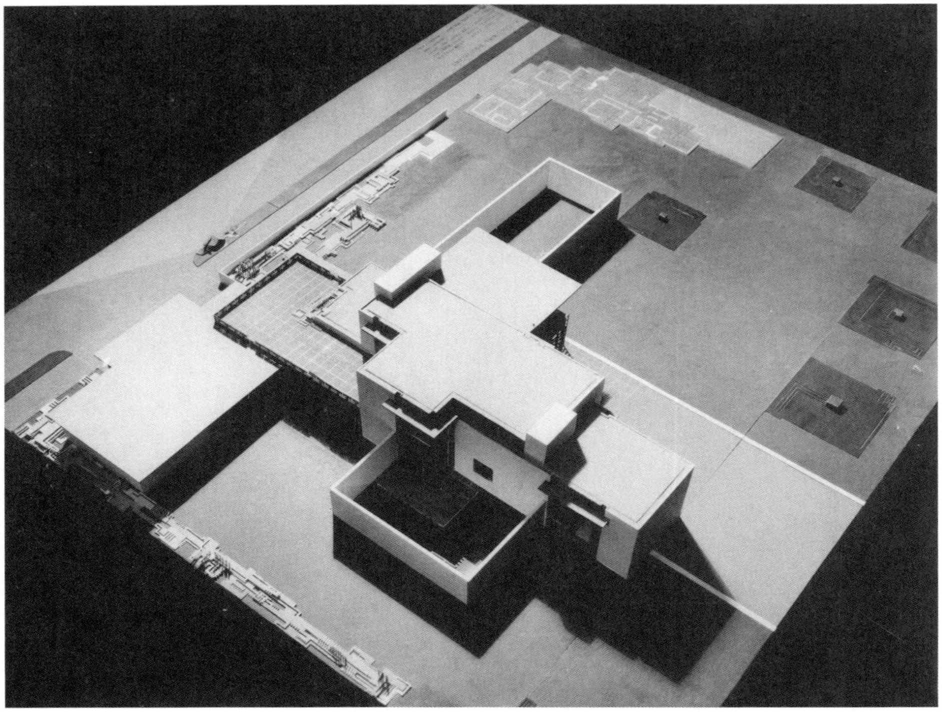

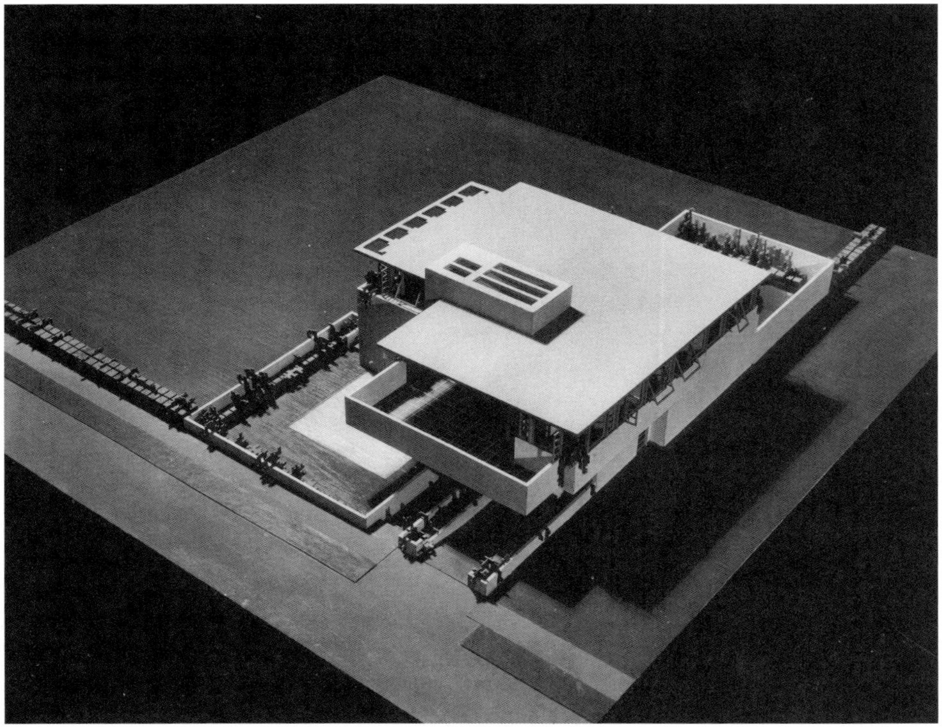

3.17 Colonial Equivalent model. Photo by F. S. Lincoln. (Reproduced with the kind permission of the Special Collections Library, the Pennsylvania State University Libraries)

3.18 Medium House (two-car house) model, 1935. Photograph by F. S. Lincoln. (Reproduced with the kind permission of the Special Collections, Library, the Pennsylvania State University Libraries) postponements to the tour for the summer were periodically being made due to schedule conflicts with government officials.

One aspect of the *Broadacre* exhibition that was sure to resonate with federal architects and planners was the text panels. Unlike the models and drawings illustrating Wright's own work, the text panels were, for the most part, denunciations of contemporary land use, American and European, commercial and idealistic. Here Wright the critic dominated. But these condemnations did prove that he was aware of many of the important reform movements that had emerged after the end of World War I.

World War I had wrought such cataclysmic suffering across society in both America and Europe that architects and planners took on the problem of housing and the reform of unsanitary, overcrowded metropolitan cities. One of the first in the United States to address the challenge was the Regional Planning Association of America (RPAA), created in 1923 by Mumford and his colleagues: Clarence Stein, Henry Wright, and Frederick Bigger, architects; Tracy Augur and Earle Draper, landscape architects; Benton MacKaye, forester and conservationist—with Catherine Bauer joining in 1931.[55] As the leading voice on the subject for a decade, the organization advocated "regional cities," sited at the edge of urban centers but screened from the sprawl by a "greenbelt." The RPAA was best known for two communities: Sunnyside Gardens, Queens, New York, and Radburn, New Jersey, which demonstrated concepts such as the separation of vehicular and pedestrian traffic, housing as superblocks facing inward toward an interior park, and garages on the periphery facing outward toward roads. While the planning ideals of the association were progressive, their architectural preferences were conservative, as they willingly embraced the Colonial Revival style made popular nationally by the restoration of historic Williamsburg, Virginia, in the late 1920s to early 1930s.

Parallel in time with these developments in the United States was the construction of German Siedlungen, government housing projects designed by modern architects in cities such as Stuttgart, Dessau, and especially Römerstadt outside Frankfurt-am-Main. In 1929, CIAM (International Congress of Modern Architecture), the prestigious organization founded by Le Corbusier and Sigfried Giedion, devoted its 1929 meeting to the "existenzminimum" or Minimal Dwelling. By the late 1920s, these forward strides were capturing the attention of progressive Americans, including Mumford, Bauer, and even Philip Johnson. In fact, Mumford under the influence of Behrendt became convinced that these European experiments had more to offer than any other solution for reform. He became a convert. For MoMA's *Modern Architecture* exhibition, Mumford wrote the catalog essay on social housing experiments in America and Europe.

The "emergency" of the Great Depression provided Roosevelt's administration with the opportunity to use the power of the federal government to focus on slum clearance and formulate a national agenda for housing. One of the first proposals was the creation in 1933 of the Division of Subsistence Homesteads within the Department of the Interior, budgeted at $25 million. Subsistence homesteading was described as a program to settle a family on a plot of land where it could grow most of its food and make many of its goods, combined with a part-time job in a factory for cash income. A favorite program of both Franklin and Eleanor Roosevelt, the agency sought to reverse the migration of farmers to the city by building housing in outlying areas with the belief that industry would move to the workers. Sometimes referred to as the realization of the "back-to-the-land" movement, it was subsequently subsumed into the later, more important, Resettlement Administration (RA).

The RA, created on April 30, 1935, under authority of the Emergency Relief Appropriation Act, came under the directorship of the brilliant and idealistic agricultural economist Rexford G. Tugwell (1891–1979), a Columbia University professor and a member of Roosevelt's original "Brain Trust" (figure 3.19). A target of criticism from both the left and the right, Tugwell was seen as a bold radical who criticized the capitalist system, and at the same time had a truly progressive social vision for restoring democracy to America's underclass. Some considered him arrogant, outspoken, and controversial. Tugwell's most daring contribution to the New Deal was his plan for the design and construction of "greenbelt towns," a program he entrusted to his close friend, John S. Lansill, head of the Suburban Resettlement Division. Lansill's mandate, according to the executive order, was to "administer approved projects involving resettlement of destitute or low-income families from rural and urban areas, including the establishment, maintenance, and operation, in such connection, of communities in rural and suburban areas."[56] The Suburban Resettlement Division was controversial throughout its short existence, not the least because of its association with Tugwell, who was considered Roosevelt's most left-wing advisor. By the time of the 1936 election, he was labeled "a visible and personal link . . . between the Comintern in Moscow and the aspiring young reformers in Washington."[57] Organization of the Suburban Division continued through the summer and fall 1935, when the chief of the Planning Section, Thomas Hibben, an engineer, was replaced by Bigger, who had training in architecture and planning. Stein and Catherine Bauer among other respected architects and planners were added as general advisors at this time. In order to deflect criticism and gain access to the allocated monies, which were approved at $68,500,000, but only released by Roosevelt as a first installment of $31,000,000, the agency needed to act quickly on the erection of four proposed towns in Maryland, Ohio, New Jersey, and Wisconsin. As more professionals arrived in Washington, DC, that summer to work on the project, they were caught up in the excitement of realizing the most significant experiment in garden city building the United States had ever contemplated.

Evidently, Maloney was following Roosevelt's New Deal policies closely because his timing was opportune. Just five days before legislation was officially passed creating the Resettlement Administration, he and Tafel went to Washington, DC, where Maloney had set up meetings in advance. His goal was to arrange a suitable place for the exhibition. They were almost immediately put in touch with Tugwell, who "had heard about the exhibit" and volunteered to "do his best for a fair showing." But even greater progress was made when they spent over an hour with Lansill, who, having seen the model in New York two days before the opening, became interested in hiring Wright to "do some work for the government." Plans were made to hold the exhibition in the lobby of the Department of Commerce for six days beginning May 19. However, even more encouraging was Lansill's confidential assurance that "he would like to see [Wright] do one of the rural rehabilitation projects in the area near Milwaukee." Lansill added that he wanted the Wisconsin architect to "come to Washington at the time the model is on exhibition," because he believed that "the President would be keenly interested and that everyone of importance in Washington would certainly see it." When the showing in Pittsburgh was postponed until June 1, Kaufmann agreed that the opportunity with the federal government was "more important at this time than anything else."[58]

Once steps were set in motion for Washington, DC, Wright became restive. He believed that the Department of Commerce looked "a bit undignified" and something like "A sideshow in a vestibule." He queried, "Can't we go into the Corcoran Art Gallery?" As to the government job, he was "not inclined to take it too seriously." But added, "Were there something tangible in prospect I might come down." Moreover, he appeared annoyed that the exhibition was taking equipment and manpower away from Taliesin, where they were needed for ongoing work on roads and the dam. "Can't we pull out there shortly after the first without raising animosity too high?"[59]

For the rest of the summer, the *Broadacre City* tour was at the mercy of delays and postponements by the Resettlement

3.19 Rexford G. Tugwell (in white) with aides, *left to right*: John O. Walker, John L. Lansill, and Frank Schmidt, at Greenbelt, Maryland, July 1936. (Library of Congress, Prints and Photographs Division, FSA/OWI Collection [reproduction number LC-DIG-fsa-8b31370])

Administration.[60] As a result, when the Industrial Arts Exposition closed in New York on May 15, Wright recalled all the material back to Wisconsin and arrangements were made to show it at the State Historical Society in Madison for a week, June 7–14.[61] At last, Wright was able to use the new medium of radio as he had intended in New York by delivering the radio script over local stations WHA and WIBA.[62] Edgar Kaufmann Sr. had taken a back seat, but earlier a sense of urgency entered his communication. "It is imperative that we hear from you immediately," Kaufmann telegraphed Wright on May 28, "as our arrangements have gone pretty far. Wire or telegraph [at] our expense."[63]

On June 18, the *Broadacre City* exhibition opened at Kaufmann's Department Store for ten days as part of "New Homes for Old," advertised as a "thrilling Home Show"—sponsored by the Federal Housing Administration—where it was possible to find "everything you need to know about *Home Modernization*."[64] As a foreshadowing of future events in Washington, the Pittsburgh venue demonstrated what happened when

Wright entered the political arena. Even though he did not appear for the opening, he was soon embroiled in a controversy that involved the FHA and Pittsburgh's mayor.

The situation had begun innocently when a week before the opening the Pittsburgh FHA district director informed Wright by mail that they were sponsoring the exhibition, and and as a result he was requesting a public explanation of what the Broadacre City model "means to Pittsburgh and whether it conveys or seeks to convey any particular message to the Pittsburgh district."[65] Although Wright was taken off guard, as he explained, "I did not know that the Federal Housing Administration was sponsoring our exhibit but I am glad to know it," he expressed his new enthusiasm for radio by suggesting "a hook-up ... at Madison ... our University station."[66] When this option proved too expensive, Wright wrote an article, "Broadacres to Pittsburgh," for the local newspaper.[67] It began, "I know little of Allegheny County, but what I've seen of it shows it very different from county sections typified by Broadacre City." He lamented the lost opportunities of the city's river and hills, and concluded that, "Pittsburgh, in common with all cities, becomes more and more a slum as it becomes less and less livable. And no doubt eventually—as new machines and processes are invented—the city will become wholly obsolete—as a factory may become obsolete overnight."[68]

Controversy arose almost immediately when Pittsburgh's mayor, William Nissley McNair, was quoted as saying, "[Broadacre City is] all right but you could never put Democrats in there. What if they'd want to get drunk or visit somebody's wife? This thing is Utopia. I'll bet they even tell you how many babies to have in each house. I just sent a gang of drunks to the workhouse. Put that bunch in Wright's village and it wouldn't be two weeks before they'd wreck it. This town is built for a lot of social workers."[69]

The FHA immediately took a defensive position, urging Wright to issue a rebuttal: "Such a statement [by you] could command better newspaper play than a local denial—which might get no notice at all."[70] Wright's remarks were published on the eve of his visit to Pittsburgh to close the exhibition with a radio broadcast.[71] He explained that, "Broadacres proceeds from generals to particulars upon the basis that neither land nor money nor creative ideas of public value can be speculative commodities to be traded in or held over against the common good. If that means 'Socialism,' then God help the mayor of Pittsburgh. And God won't." He quipped, "The Mayor knows next to nothing about drunks, babies, or Democracy." Continuing in a combative mood: "'Democrats won't go there,' says Hizzoner [His Honor]. I don't know how any politician is going to go anywhere where he would seriously be required to think about the rights of man. As for the mayor's babies and the mayor's drunks, birth control would be recommended. There would be a place for everyone born there."[72] In what would become a familiar ritual in the years ahead, Wright arrived in the city and was led on a tour with an entourage of reporters taking down his most quotable barbs. "I'm suppose[d] to be an asset to my country," he complained, "and yet, if people want to see me, they must come to a department store. I suppose it's because the department stores are our educational institutions today."[73] In what the local civic leaders must surely have considered an impolite performance, he slung caustic comments at every building and neighborhood with the exception of H. H. Richardson's Allegheny County Courthouse and Jail. In his most unforgettable retort when asked what would improve the city, he responded, "It would be cheaper to abandon it and build another real one. This is a disappearing city; nothing comes out of it."[74]

If Wright had been hired by the federal government to design and construct a new town in his home state, it would have been undeniably the most important job of his career. On his terms, it would have meant nothing less than that America was about to truly realize Democracy. However, the distance between the ideal and the real was very great indeed. Jensen, now in Washington at the Brookings Institution, was trying to coach him on political strategy, more or less, to no avail. Jensen's plan was two-pronged.[75] On the one hand, he wanted Wright to go after state monies through Senator Robert LaFollette Jr. and Congressman Thomas Amlie to provide scholarships for Taliesin Fellows; on the other, he was after federal money for realization of Broadacre City planning concepts. To these ends, Jensen was able to satisfy Wright's desire to exhibit at the Corcoran Gallery of Art by finalizing the details of the schedule and securing the funding from Wright's Prairie House client, Queene Ferry Coonley, and Susan E. Curran, a potential client from 1934.[76] He was also using his contacts in the government to arrange a presentation by Wright to Eleanor Roosevelt and Harry Hopkins, one of the president's closest advisors, who as the Federal Emergency Relief Administration (FERA) director distributed $3 billion between 1933 and 1935.[77] Wright's attitude toward these entreaties wavered between annoyance and naïveté. He revealed, "I wish I knew how the minds up at the top are working."[78] Yet he often suggested that he would be better served if the exhibition was set up at Taliesin where "it would bring ... $50.00 per week in money [charging visitors admission] with no wear and tear nor trouble."[79]

Wright ran into the same problem he had encountered after the Architectural League show in spring 1930: summer was not the best season for last minute arrangements with either museums or important dignitaries, who were likely to be out of the city or traveling. Jensen reported that Mrs. Roosevelt was "off record" until September except for one day, July 29, after the exhibition closed.[80] Once the Corcoran was arranged, Wright was happy to attend the opening on July 3, where he recalled the exhibition was installed "mostly in vain, in the most dignified setting of all at the center of the main gallery on the upper floor."[81] What he meant by "mostly in vain" was, as he lamented, that "Broadacre City was seen there by many eminent Americans, the President and his wife not present."[82]

Eleanor Roosevelt, who had unrivaled influence on the president, was known as a champion of social causes involving women, children, minorities, and the poor, and she took a special interest in the "greenbelt towns." Of the four that were slated for construction, she became the most familiar with Greenbelt, Maryland, because it was located just twelve miles from the Capitol. After construction began on October 10, 1935, she visited the site several times to demonstrate her support.[83] Maloney and Jensen had foundation for their belief that Mrs. Roosevelt could perhaps be the wisest choice as an advocate for Wright's ideas. However, Wright expressed in private on at least two occasions that he felt the cause was futile because he had reason to believe that the Roosevelts were already completely prejudiced against him. He placed the blame for this on the president's first cousin, William Adams Delano, the conservative New York architect, who is best known for Kykuit, the home of John D. Rockefeller Sr. Wright claimed that "Delano sits as a power behind the throne in [an] advisory capacity, and would rather see poison administered to his wife than see organic architecture go ahead. He is one of the Beaux-Arts guard."[84]

Nevertheless, Wright made a personal appeal, not to the president, but to his wife. On July 12, nine days after the opening, he wrote a letter, a little over one page, to "Madame President." He explained: "Were the models in some gallery in Europe I should not have to write a letter to ask my Queen or my King to see it. To them it would be prophetic and so indispensable. I would be better known to them than I am to you because 'no prophet is with honor in his own country'—(you see how modest I am) and so in my own country I ask my madame President (and could I expect my President himself to see it?) to see the work." Although he would not be there, he said that Cornelia Brierly, "a Taliesin Fellowship girl," would be available to provide an explanation. "Perhaps never before with any valid claim to being a work of art," he concluded, "has a cross section of a whole civilization been made visible in every detail."[85] As expected, Wright was informed that Mrs. Roosevelt was traveling and would not return to the White House until after the exhibition closed.[86] However, Wright's letter may have produced some result; Brierly recalled that "Mrs. Roosevelt sent her press secretary, Sigrid Arne, to question me about the ideas proposed by Mr. Wright."[87]

After the exhibition closed, the Resettlement Administration coincidently began moving ahead on the building of Greendale, Wisconsin, just one hundred miles from Taliesin to the east near Milwaukee. According to Lansill's memories, Wright was not hired because "he suggested that the Resettlement Administration scrap its plans, add $70,000,000 to its $30,000,000 allocation and allow [him] to construct 'the finest city in the world.' The great architect further stipulated that there must be no interference with his direction of the project." In an interview thirty years later, Lansill recalled that Wright could not have been serious as his conditions had been unreasonable. Lansill claimed retrospectively that if Wright had been "willing to work within the liberal guidelines," Broadacre City would have been considered. However, he recalled that Wright reacted "with a denunciation of all public and private housing in America and never again communicated with the Suburban Division."[88]

However, the surviving correspondence does not corroborate Lansill's recollection in its details. As plans for Greendale proceeded at the end of 1935, a few of Wright's friends wrote Tugwell, proposing Wisconsin's most famous architect as the best designer for the "greenbelt town." It was Lansill who replied, "Sometime ago we committed ourselves by entrusting the design of each of our Projects to a small group of professional and technical men representing the fields of architecture, community planning, landscape architecture and engineering design instead of selecting one directing head for each Project." He added that it was not a question of "lack of appreciation of Mr. Wright's standing and accomplishments as a distinguished architect."[89] Wright stated after he read Lansill's letter that it "confirmed [his] suspicion that the political aspect of the architectural situation at Washington has been solved by Tugwell and Lansill first. All else is afterward. I sensed that in the air when I was there. They know I am a controversial item in that political respect and they have avoided 'raising the dust.'"[90]

Wright chose not to leave it at that, however. Immediately, he sat down and wrote a letter to Lansill. He noted that, "Since the matter has come up for the record I hope you will go a little further with it." He protested: "Your frank elimination of quality in favor of quantity is no doubt good politics at this time ... and proves only another continuous tax upon the future in order that the greatest number of jobs may be created at the moment." He argued that "your expedient policy can only starve the future to feed the present—where the spirit of man is concerned—or cut it off entirely." In summation, he asked, "So I am wondering just what the thought was that directed you into the course you are pursuing? Would you mind giving a direct answer? I would like to use it in the little magazine 'Taliesin' that we are publishing here."[91] No reply from Lansill exists in the Wright Foundation Archive.

Construction on Greendale, Wisconsin, proceeded from 1936 until 1938, when the first families moved in. Ironically, it is considered the most interesting "greenbelt town" from an aesthetic point of view. This is attributed to the planner, Elbert Peets, who was well known as a coauthor with Werner Hegemann of *The American Vitruvius: An Architect's Handbook of Civic Art* (1922). Peets used Colonial Williamsburg as his model for both town planning and the architectural style of the public buildings.[92]

The Broadacre City model has played a dominant role in influencing popular and scholarly opinion of Wright's planning theories since its construction, exhibition, and publication in 1935. Wright's ideas about decentralization appeared in print before and after the public unveiling of the 12-foot-square model section, but the visual demonstration of the horizontal layout of "little farms, little homes for industry, little factories, little schools, a little university" in a tapestry of highways and roads captured the imagination in a way that his literary work never could.[93] Furthermore, the visual impact of the model enhanced Wright's reputation as a modern theorist and elevated him to a level nearly on a par with Le Corbusier, reconfirming his status as a futurist. The showing in Washington, DC, was one of the six most important exhibitions during his lifetime.

As an exhibition at its various locations, the *Broadacre City* show stands out from his other exhibitions both before and after 1935 in a number of ways. Much to Wright's displeasure, two of the venues were commercial: the Industrial Arts Exposition and Kaufmann's Department Store. While the Pittsburgh store in comparison was rather dignified in its sales campaign, the New York exposition was heavy-handed in using advertising techniques to draw in the general public, first to take their cash and then to sell them cars and radios. While Wright wanted to get his message to the American people, the audience drawn to the Industrial Arts Exposition was more likely to fall into the category of the "mobocracy," a growing segment of the population that Wright disdained. During the opening, a pure spectacle with a circus-like atmosphere—gold telegraph key, flashbulbs, floodlights, siren, American flag, and electric organ—Wright got lost. The one relevant use of a new technology—lecturing on national radio—failed him in New York, but in the future, he adopted it as a means of communicating his theories to the widest possible audience.

As much as Wright felt uncomfortable with the blatant commercialism of the public relations agency, Riis and Bonner, which had promoted his exhibition in New York along with the exposition itself, he profited from the publicity they created. The pronounced goal of PR firms was to sway public opinion in favor of their clients; Wright's purpose in the Broadacre exhibitions was to influence Americans to adopt his radical program for reforming the United States, architecturally and spiritually. Between 1938 and 1948, he again would benefit from public relations techniques when the Modern employed Sarah Newmeyer as director of publicity. Press releases were her specialty.[94]

The most obvious way the *Broadacre City* exhibition was distinct from past shows was in its clear didactic purpose, which was evident in the display: large spatial areas devoted to text panels, which Wright used to advance his avant-garde program of social and political reform. Drawings and models no longer stood on their own; they were supplemented or even dominated by a "book on the wall." Ironically, Wright seemed to adopt public relations techniques himself, since the text was often in the form of slogans, for instance: "The Future Is Everywhere and Nowhere" and "No Slum No Scum." It is hard to judge the effectiveness of his text panels, but he used them again at his 1940–41 MoMA retrospective.

Of all the commissions that Wright's exhibitions could have brought him in his sixty-six-year career, designing and constructing a model town based on Broadacre City in his home state for the American government would have been the pinnacle. If the president of the United States had visited the exhibition in the nation's capital, understood and approved of his planning theories, and bestowed patronage, Wright would have earned the official recognition to which he aspired. While the fabrication of the Broadacre City model was a brilliant tour de force for enhancing Wright's career, the failure to engage the Roosevelt administration was certainly one of his greatest private disappointments.

Museum of Modern Art, 1933–53

Although no one could have predicted it at the time, Wright's structural experiments and spatial planning breakthroughs of the 1910s and 1920s were groundwork for his most productive period, which began in the mid-1930s and continued until his death in 1959 (figure 4.1). A period that would surpass the years 1900–1910 in terms of the construction of masterworks such as the SC Johnson Administration Building and Research Tower (1936–39/1943–50; Racine, Wisconsin), Florida Southern College (begun 1938; Lakeland, Florida), Fallingwater (1934–37; Mill Run, Pennsylvania), and Taliesin West (1938–59; Scottsdale, Arizona). One of the major beneficiaries of this change in Wright's career was the Museum of Modern Art. Writing in 1953, Rene d'Harnoncourt, the director, explained, "The Museum has held fourteen exhibitions [between 1932 and 1953] in which Mr. Wright's work was represented—six of these were devoted exclusively to his work and one was the largest architecture show given at the Museum of Modern Art. Thus the Museum has given him more one man shows than it has given not only to any architect, but to any creative artist."[1] While this statement is impressive as it stands, d'Harnoncourt's claim could have been even greater. During the same time period, the museum's Department of Circulating Exhibitions organized twelve touring shows of Wright's architecture (for sites outside New York City), bringing the total to twenty-six exhibitions that included one or more examples of Wright's work under MoMA's sponsorship.[2] What is even more remarkable about that statistic is the strategy that the museum was compelled to follow to assemble Wright material, particularly after 1940.

Unlike modern painting and sculpture shows—where works could be borrowed from museums, collectors, and dealers—architecture shows required the drawings, photographs, and models architects usually kept as their property after the commission ended. In order to present a Wright exhibition, it was necessary to obtain his cooperation as a lender. This is the procedure the Modern followed for the 1932 modern architecture show and again for his career retrospective held during the 1940/41 winter season. Yet once Wright became a lender, he also gradually began to assume the role of the curator, catalog editor, and installation designer. Obviously, this was an impossible condition that the museum involuntarily endured only once. Avoiding the architect as lender, the Modern mainly turned to working with professional photographers, who shot recently completed buildings on assignment from a trade magazine. After 1940, only one Wright one-man show out of four was initiated solely from within the museum: *Buildings for Johnson's Wax* (1952), curated by Arthur Drexler, who conceived the premise and worked with a professional photographer to execute it. Of the other three, one was derived from a pictorial article originally published by *Fortune*: *Taliesin and Taliesin West* (1947); the second, *A New Country*

4.1 Frank Lloyd Wright with Taliesin Fellows in the Taliesin Studio, November 1937. Photograph by Bill Hedrich. (FLWFA, 6601.0014-H-B). *Architectural Forum* commissioned this photograph for use in the January 1938 Wright issue.

House by Frank Lloyd Wright (1946), was initiated by the client, Gerald Loeb; and the third, *A New Theatre* (1949), traveled from the Wadsworth Atheneum, Hartford. Another important statistic: after 1940 when MoMA decided to shelve the Wright catalog as the result of a conflict with the architect, the museum never produced another publication devoted exclusively to Wright during his lifetime.

Unfortunately, it was not only Wright's temperament that caused tension with the museum, there were distinct ideological differences as well that centered primarily on the direction of modern American architecture. These issues produced even greater conflict in the following decades, because as it turned out the 1932 show was actually more of an anomaly than the norm. Although the exhibition's origins had clearly grown out of Johnson and Hitchcock's intention to publish a study of European developments in modern architecture comparable to Platz's *Die Baukunst Der Neuesten Zeit*, the transformation of the idea into a MoMA exhibition had far-reaching consequences for both the curators and the museum. The Board of Trustees' decision to require an equal emphasis on America forced the co-curators to turn their attention away from Berlin and Paris to Chicago and Taliesin. "Like many Americans of that post-war period," Hitchcock later confessed, "I knew little or nothing of the American cultural achievements of the nineteenth century to which Lewis Mumford had just called attention in his seminal *Brown Decades*."[3]

The result of this reorientation was both immediate and long lasting: the museum began to conceive programs to demonstrate that modern architecture, first and foremost, was an American creation. At the close of the 1932 show, the co-curators began to organize *Early Modern Architecture: Chicago, 1870–1910*—focused on the structural and aesthetic development of the skyscraper—which was mounted in January 1933. As Mumford had earlier pointed out to no avail, the 1932 show needed "a section on the history of modern architecture, so that no one would think it was invented by Norman Bel Geddes and the Bowman Brothers ... the day before yesterday."[4] Terence Riley, former chief curator of MoMA's Department of Architecture and Design, regarded this exhibition as part of Barr's "twofold mission for the young institution," which was "not only to present the best of the art of the day but also to establish a history of modern art that supported contemporary artistic theory ... Henry Hobson Richardson, Louis Sullivan, and Frank Lloyd Wright ... are positioned as the principal protagonists in the aesthetic development of the Chicago school of architecture. ... In fact, the exhibition may even be considered a work-in-progress or as a prologue to the Museum's publication, in 1935, of *Louis Sullivan—Prophet of Modern Architecture* by Hugh Morrison ... and, in 1936, Hitchcock's *The Architecture of Henry Hobson Richardson and His Times*."[5] These initiatives "provided evidence of a distinctly changed attitude on our part," Hitchcock later admitted.[6]

In fact, elevating the stature of American art became a consistent goal of the museum in the years immediately after the *Modern Architecture* exhibition closed. A. Conger Goodyear, who served as board president for the first ten years, explained, "From the opening of the season of 1932–1933 to the fifth anniversary show two years later the exhibitions, almost without exception, were devoted to American art. Alfred Barr ... was given a year's vacation. During his absence we had the good fortune to enlist Holger Cahill as acting director. ... Then began the flood of Americana."[7] Embracing the new technology of radio, the Modern produced a series of seventeen programs and an accompanying book titled *Art in America in Modern Times* in the fall of 1934. Three of the broadcasts, devoted to architecture, were written by Hitchcock, who repeated his belief that Richardson was "the greatest American architect," Sullivan's design was "still the most successful in giving architectural character to the skyscraper," and Wright's "work and influence constitute a new chapter in modern architecture."[8]

The greatest change to the Department of Architecture occurred in December 1934 when Johnson resigned as chairman to pursue his interests in fascist American politics. This left a vacuum of strong leadership until his former traveling companion, John McAndrew (1904–1978), was appointed to the position on September 1, 1937. In the interim, the board chose one of its own, Philip Goodwin, a New York Beaux-Arts architect, as chairman, who proceeded to govern with the aid of a committee consisting of museum stalwarts: Hitchcock; Howe; Johnson; and Joseph Hudnut, dean of the Graduate School of Architecture, Harvard University. Johnson's former secretary, Ernestine M. Fantl, served as curator of architecture and industrial design from 1935 to 1937.[9] "The Architecture Committee plans to provide each year a series of exhibitions which will cover the most significant aspects of contemporary architecture" and "from time to time ... the work of such forerunners of modern architecture who are deserving of revaluation," the museum announced in late 1935. Despite the fact that Wright considered himself a contemporary architect, MoMA's leading authority at the time, Hitchcock, did not. "With no inkling of Wright's productive resurgence that would begin only in the 1930s, I treated Wright purely historically, putting all emphasis, like the Europeans, on the work of the Prairie years and its international influence. Thus I ranked him a forerunner."[10] Just when the Modern had safely relegated Wright to a category that included two other architects, both of whom were dead, his fortunes began to change: he received commissions that would permanently resurrect his position as a leader in contemporary American architecture.

His practice began to pick up clearly by the beginning of 1936 when he had three residences on the boards that represented a clear new direction in his work. The first was a luxurious country house for the Kaufmanns in Pennsylvania, subsequently titled Fallingwater, which when completed defiantly challenged any residence by Le Corbusier or Mies. The other two, for Robert Lusk and Paul Hanna, were prototypes for an affordable system-built residence for the middle class that Wright soon labeled Usonian Houses. By midyear, he would be contacted by Herbert and Katherine Jacobs with the request to design their family home for $5,000. Wright applied all he had learned from the Lusk and Hanna designs to create a quintessential American house for a new client base that he would serve for the next two decades: couples with moderate means, but aspirations for an aesthetic environment. A sure sign that he had regained his national reputation as a practicing architect was securing the commission for a new administration building for the SC Johnson Company of Racine, Wisconsin. This building went into construction in late 1936 and began to attract interest from the trade magazines before it was finished.[11]

In November 1936, Wright was faced with the decision to publish the SC Johnson Administration Building either with *Architectural Record* (where his loyalties lay) or with *Architectural Forum* (which meant beginning a relationship with a new editor, Howard Myers). *Forum* had been brought to him by the faithful Tom Maloney, but, more importantly, it was the choice of the Johnson Company itself. Yet Wright stipulated conditions: "Unable to give exclusive," the architect declared to Maloney, "except where my own story of the building and own drawings illustrating it are concerned."[12] Myers met those conditions, and as the months unfolded, much more. Not since he had persuaded the Chicago Architectural Club to allow him to create his own separate catalog for the 1902 annual, and more famously, to convince Wasmuth Verlag in 1909 to bring out two volumes of hand-drawn lithographs, had Wright seized such an incipient opportunity. In this instance, very little persuasion on Wright's part was necessary.

George Nelson, the well-known industrial designer, was assigned as associate editor to the story and spent several days at Taliesin in the first half of February 1937, where he may have been one of the first journalists to discover Wright's renewed practice. As John Lautner, an apprentice at the time, explained, "Mr. Wright is building five important buildings right now ... has designed at least twenty buildings, not to mention Broadacre City, in the past three years. He is very active: active enough to keep twenty-five boys of 20 to 30 years busy ... the year round."[13] When the information reached the New York office, by May, the *Forum* offered to expand its coverage to include built works such as Fallingwater, the Herbert Jacobs House I (1936–37; Madison, Wisconsin), and "others ... to be completed by the end of the summer." Of even greater interest to Wright than their offer of coverage, however, was their motivation. As Nelson summarized it, "[the collection] would unmistakably call attention to the fact that while the so-called International Style has been taking advantage of every possible bit of publicity, the cause of organic architecture in America is still being vigorously carried on by its first and chief exponent."[14] In Myers, as time would prove, Wright had met his ideal editor, a man who described his "contribution" as "limited largely to applause."[15] Nelson recalled that his boss "loved Mr. Wright because he loved real people and was particularly fond of geniuses: and since the supply of geniuses is limited, he would sort of go off the deep end when he encountered a real one."[16] By July, Myers proposed giving the architect seventy pages, up from the initial sixteen.[17] In the end, the total was 102 pages.

Myers and Wright sat down at Taliesin in late September 1937 to work out details of what became a special issue of *Forum* slated for January 1938. Discussion involved obtaining photography—including hiring Hedrich-Blessing of Chicago to shoot Fallingwater; Taliesin; Wingspread, Herbert Johnson House (1937–39; Racine, Wisconsin)—and design specifications such as a horizontal or vertical format. Myers asserted that "insofar as possible photographs [over drawings] should be used."[18]

In characteristic fashion, Wright took over the entire production, including choice of subjects and photographs, composition of the text, and the graphic design layout. Nelson and Paul Grotz, the art director, converged on Taliesin in November. "Neither Paul nor I realized that we were in for an unforgettable experience," Nelson remembered later. "Paul thought that he was supposed to lay out the magazine and design it, but not so. Somehow Mr. Wright took it away from him, page by page. I thought I was supposed to write it, which turned out to be a complete misconception. Mr. Wright wrote everything."[19]

When the January 1938 *Architectural Forum* appeared, its impact surpassed the influence of the 1930–31 exhibition that toured the United States and Europe. A great deal of the credit for Wright's revived practice, but not all, has generally been attributed to the twelve-page photographic spread on Fallingwater. Yet Wright's intentions were far greater, as clearly stated in his introductory text, "To the Young Man in Architecture—A Challenge," which has survived in manuscript but did not appear in the print edition. In his mind, the magazine contents proved that he was the only source of modern architecture in America. "This *Architectural Forum*," he asserted, "is the first and only record in print of what we have come to call the modern movement, from its inception to its present interpretation." Directing his comments at MoMA and the "machine aesthetic" of the "International Style" without naming either, he explained, "Many of the houses demonstrate the folly of imagining that a true and beautiful house must employ synthetics or steel to be 'modern' or go to the factory to be economical." In another oblique reference, this time to his disappointing experience with the greenbelt towns, he declared, "I would rather solve the small house problem than build anything else I can think of (except the modern theatre). But where is a better small house to come from while government housing itself is only perpetuating the old stupidities." Finally, directing his remarks to the younger generation of aspiring American architects, he closed by stating, "My purpose and hope ... is to promote discussion and rekindle enthusiasm for an honest American architecture."[20]

The 1938 *Forum*, although obviously different in scale and degree from the 1911 Wasmuth Verlag folios, can only be compared to it because both brought together in one publication the architectural and literary, one commenting on the other, creating a whole. Interestingly, one ended the first productive phase of Wright's career while the other ushered in his last productive phase. The special issue was gestated during the same months the architect was making plans to buy land in the wilderness of the Arizona desert for what became the site of his winter home, Taliesin West. Perhaps this new experience in the West is what inspired Wright's prodigious use of quotes from Henry David Thoreau and Walt Whitman scattered throughout his text. They are further clues to his intentions because they tie him to the nineteenth-century poetic movement in his effort to create an original American architecture growing out of the circumstances of the promise of a democracy in nature. In this instance, Wright, through careful editing, made Whitman's words his own.[21] He juxtaposed the iconic photo of Fallingwater with a quote from Whitman's "Song of the Open Road" and "By Blue Ontario's Shore": "I inhale great draughts of space. The east and the west are mine, and the north and the south are mine ... beware the advancing mortal ripening of nature. Beware what precedes the decay of the ruggedness of states and men. Beware civilization."[22]

A NEW HOUSE BY FRANK LLOYD WRIGHT, 1938

While most MoMA Wright exhibitions were planned well in advance, his first one-building show came about spontaneously when Alvar Aalto, the Finnish architect and furniture designer, asked for a postponement of his career survey scheduled for January 1938. It fell to John McAndrew, who came with a variety of credentials preparing him for the job, to fill the gap rather quickly (figure 4.2). McAndrew had studied art history and architecture at Harvard University; he had worked briefly in an architect's office in New York; and he had taught from 1932 to 1937 at Vassar College. Through these associations he knew Hitchcock and Barr and had been the first person Johnson had turned to in 1929 as a collaborator for his proposed book on European modern architecture. Between 1931 and 1932, he worked in the New York photography gallery of his former Harvard classmate, Julien Levy. McAndrew's awareness of Fallingwater did not come from George Nelson, even though he sat on the Architecture Advisory Committee.[23] It came from a relative of the Kaufmann family by marriage.[24] When he visited, he recalled later, Liliane Kaufmann told him he was "the first person from the outside world to see the house."[25] He evidently decided then and there to exhibit Fallingwater when he was shown photographs taken by Luke Swank, a Pittsburgh artist from the Levy Gallery, whom he may have met in 1932.[26]

Even though the house was obviously the most spectacular modern residence McAndrew had ever seen in his life, the show as conceived was rather modest, lacking any Wright drawings. Yet surely the curator immediately discussed the idea with Barr and Hitchcock and was briefed on the difficulties the museum had encountered with Wright in 1932. The Architecture Committee approved the proposal November 19, and McAndrew proceeded to obtain large-format photographs from Swank. Details fell quickly into place and the exhibition was scheduled for January 25 through March 6, 1938.

McAndrew explained to Swank that, "After careful study of the room where the show is to be held, we have decided that fairly large pictures of uniform height [twenty inches] will look the handsomest. ... If you have color shots, we would make a special place to show them, and standard size would not be necessary."[27] Remarkably, Swank was opposed to color views because in a January letter he explained, "Now there is no great amount of color down there, and green is so weak in color."[28] Wright was not consulted about the issue, but he had a definite opinion: "Color [photography] has a significance all its own, and is in a realm all its own. Color is the music of light."[29] Another

4.2 John McAndrew. Photograph by Manlius Villoresi, Rome. (Courtesy the Wellesley College Archives)

McAndrew innovation that would have made the exhibition groundbreaking was to project a construction film that Swank had made, but technical difficulties precluded its use.

Originally, McAndrew's plan was limited to Swank photographs and those he had taken himself; he needed the architect's permission to gain access to the *Forum* material. Wright's apprentice, Edgar Tafel, telegraphed the architect in Scottsdale, where construction was beginning on Taliesin West: "Met Modern Museum's McAndrew through *Forum.* Wanting additional permission to publish ... an elaborate catalog using your *Forum* text and photographs. Time is short, yet I insisted McAndrew get catalog permission from you directly." Then Tafel closed optimistically, "Setup is elegant. McAndrew wants future exhibits and seems sincere much unlike his predecessors, which can help us lots."[30]

McAndrew had also telegraphed Nelson to ask Wright for plans and sections, but toward the end of December he finally took the task on himself.[31] "We would like to issue 2500 copies of a sixteen page picture book of house, and would like to use your text ... as well as plans and some of *Forum* pictures," McAndrew wrote. He added, "Yours would be the only text, all the rest pictures."[32] "All right, John," Wright responded, "Let's see what you can do."[33] With Wright's permission secured, McAndrew moved ahead with Bill Hedrich in Chicago requesting seven prints.[34]

While Luke Swank had an advantage over Bill Hedrich—he had been photographing Fallingwater much longer—Hedrich was more suited to the job as an architectural photographer since Swank had devoted his career to fine art. Swank's main interest had been photography, although he did not turn to it seriously until 1930 at the age of forty. A year later he approached Levy, who put him in a group show at the Brooklyn Museum in March 1932. It was at this time that he may have met McAndrew, who was working in the gallery that year. Levy co-curated with Lincoln Kirstein a major MoMA exhibition the following May, *Murals by American Painters and Photographers*, where Swank was shown alongside Berenice Abbott and Edward Steichen among others. Like these artists, he was a clear exponent of modern photography; he composed his shots by using only the camera as a tool with available light, avoiding darkroom manipulation. His concentration on regional subject matter was evident in his one-man show, *Photographs of the American Scene*, at the Levy Gallery January 28–February 18, 1933.[35]

Swank and Kaufmann Sr. were reported to have been friends for years before Swank began his art career, but probably in the early 1930s the Pittsburgh magnate also acted as his patron. In September 1937, Kaufmann gave the photographer backing for one year by financing a Luke Swank Studio within his department store. So within the time frame of the construction of Fallingwater, it is reasonable to assume that Swank acted as Kaufmann's in-house photographer documenting the building process. At the time, he did not know his work was destined for MoMA, thus his photographs are not characteristic of his style and do not represent his best work.

On the other hand, Ken Hedrich founded his photography studio in downtown Chicago in 1929, with a partner, Henry Blessing, who dropped out after one year; in 1931, his brother, Bill, joined the firm. The brothers received artistic and financial stimulus with the opening of the 1933 "Century of Progress" International Exposition, where their photographs were recognized for their new technique: the use of unconventional perspectives, unusual compositions, and dramatic lighting. By fall 1937, Hedrich-Blessing would have been well known to Howard Myers, who hired Bill to shoot Fallingwater for his high-profile trade magazine.

While it is Hedrich's photos that propelled Fallingwater into instant fame, ironically Wright disliked the iconic view (figure 4.3). "When Frank Lloyd Wright saw the image," Hedrich admitted later, "he initially critiqued it as rather 'acrobatic.' "[36] In fact, in March 1938, when Wright was asked by an English magazine to provide photographs of the house, he referred them to Swank.[37]

4.3 Fallingwater, Mill Run, Pennsylvania, 1934–37. Photograph by Bill Hedrich. (Chicago History Museum, HB-00414-5d3)

A few years later when the architect had completed an addition to Fallingwater, he was moved to write Swank directly. "If I've never written you before thanking you for your fine work in photographing the Kaufmann Guest House: here's to you—quite the finest job of the kind I ever saw. . . . I like pure photographic technique such as yours." He solidified the compliment by offering Swank "an appointment as [his] official photographer of all buildings—Pittsburgh and East."[38] While these remarks clearly reveal that Wright initially rejected the type of photographic interpretation that Hedrich was known for, preferring a more neutral point of view, it begs the question: Why was Hedrich's iconic view featured in a *Forum* double-page spread that was designed by Wright himself? Perhaps in this instance, someone else's opinion held sway.

McAndrew was responsible for the selection of the material and the details of how it was displayed; Wright was preoccupied in Arizona. The title of the exhibition—*A New House on Bear Run, Pennsylvania by Frank Lloyd Wright*—was rather indirect, even oblique, as most museum visitors would not know what "Bear Run" was and would have been unprepared for a house over a waterfall. According to the curator's checklist, there were twenty-three panels consisting of twenty photographs, two panels of plans and elevations, and one credit label. As it turned out, the installation followed the now standard MoMA formula for an architecture show: large-format black-and-white photographs of a uniform size (a method Johnson had introduced in the 1932 *Modern Architecture* show). Although McAndrew wanted to expand the conceptual framework to include a construction film and color views, circumstances prevented their inclusion. The curator had a less rigid definition of the "International Style" than Johnson, and these items would have represented a decided move in a new direction. In his staging, the subjects of his exhibitions and publications, and in his critical discourse, McAndrew had greater sympathy and knowledge of the diversity of contemporary American architecture. With Wright's renewed activity in the late 1930s in residential and commercial architecture, he captured McAndrew's attention.[39]

The twenty-page catalog was a miniature version of the exhibition, only reduced to fourteen black-and-white photographs.[40] Yet the ratio of photographs was the same: Swank predominated with seven, Hedrich was well represented with five, and McAndrew supplemented with two of his own. Since the interior had not yet received the Wright designed furniture, the photographs were limited to exteriors with the exception of a view through the corner of the living room windows to the trees beyond.

Fifteen photographs were devoted to the main idea, which was an idealized 360-degree tour of the building—viewing the house as a modern "sculpture in the round," starting from the entrance bridge and moving in a clockwise direction (figure 4.4). These views presented the house as "object," emphasizing the abstract nature of a composition of solids and voids: contrasting vertical masses anchoring flat horizontal planes floating in space, the transparent bands of glass becoming virtually invisible, all in black and white, providing another element of abstraction (figures 4.5–6). Yet four views were devoted to another theme: Fallingwater within the cycle of nature. These ideas originated with the photographers: Hedrich, who captured a wide view of the building in daylight and lit from within at night (figures 4.7–8); and Swank, who took the same detailed shot of a corner of the house in winter and summer.[41] As important as the show was, it would have been even more remarkable if McAndrew had been able to present Fallingwater in color, departing from rigid adherence to the "International Style," but as it was, the new curator expressed a much broader definition of modern architecture, one that would characterize his MoMA achievements from 1938 to 1940.

The multiple readings of Fallingwater McAndrew provided were evident from the Hedrich photograph chosen for the cover of the catalog, one Wright had used in the *Forum*. McAndrew labeled it "Bear Run with the house in the background" (figure 4.9).[42] Here both Hedrich and McAndrew departed from the European modernist interpretation of architecture as "objecthood" for a more complex understanding of the figure-ground relationship. This photograph, capturing two tiers of falls, would in the years ahead take a backseat to Hedrich's more modernist view, yet it was a more perceptive two-dimensional portrayal of Wright's intentions in creating Fallingwater. While the building differentiates itself from its surroundings and retains its identity as a man-made object, it is perceived as a complement to nature, and as a result, each comments on the other by its presence.

Newspaper and magazine coverage surrounding the MoMA exhibition was extensive, laudatory, and in some cases, effusive, due partly to the MoMA publicity department, but largely to *Time-Life,* the publishing company that owned *Forum*. The MoMA press release titled, "House Built Over Waterfall," described Fallingwater as "spectacularly cantilevered out over a rushing stream" and concluded that "Wright has again demonstrated his powerful romanticism without in any way sacrificing the fundamental principles of modern architecture, in which he has been a world leader for fifty years."[43] *Time* gave Wright a generous cover story, claiming that, "His obvious and arrogant

4.4 Fallingwater, Mill Run, Pennsylvania, 1934–37. Photograph by Bill Hedrich. (Chicago History Museum, HB-04414-5e3)

4.5 Fallingwater, Mill Run, Pennsylvania, 1934–37. Photograph by Luke Swank. (Carnegie Library of Pittsburgh, SW1632b)

4.6 Fallingwater, Mill Run, Pennsylvania, 1934–37. Photograph by Luke Swank. (Carnegie Library of Pittsburgh, SW2218025)

courage has the abstract indestructibility of a triangle."[44] Mumford devoted his *New Yorker* column, "Skyline," to Fallingwater and to one of the first Usonian houses, Malcolm Willey House II (1933–34; Minneapolis, Minnesota).[45] About the Kaufmann House, he concluded, "The perpetual youngness and freshness of [Wright's] mind were never better shown than in his treatment of this extraordinary problem." His estimate of Wright's significance was as yet undiminished as he closed by calling him "the world's greatest living architect." This is a phrase that would be picked up and repeated often, especially in MoMA press releases.

While the Fallingwater show was organized rather quickly, the next exhibition to feature Wright was the result of many years of planning and negotiation. From May 24 until July 31, 1938, at the Galerie Nationale du Jeu de Paume, Paris, the Modern presented *Trois siècles d'art aux États-Unis* (*Three Centuries of American Art*). An encyclopedic survey of American painting, sculpture, architecture, photography, and cinema, the exhibition contained hundreds of artworks, photographs, and models of buildings and other structures, and film screenings from the silent era through the 1930s. The architecture section, organized by McAndrew and his assistant, Elizabeth Bauer Mock, was another major departure for the Modern. While it explored themes such as mechanization and rationalist planning as seen in the development of the skyscraper and in the careers of Richardson, Sullivan, and Wright, it also featured vernacular and industrial structures such as barns, grain elevators, and iron bridges.

As the most comprehensive exposition of American architecture the Modern had ever presented, *Trois siècles d'art aux États-Unis* made the assertion that the current of influence once thought to have flowed from Old World to New had been reversed. In an accompanying essay, "Architecture in the United States," McAndrew, making a direct link between American innovation and European modernism, explained that, "Wright's work was published in Germany in 1910 and 1911, long before it was widely known here. Mies van der Rohe, Gropius, Oud, and other leaders of modern architecture have acknowledged the inspiration they found in his courageous pioneer works. His influence in Holland was such that he could properly be counted one of the founders of the modern Dutch school."[46] Although *Trois siècles* was intended for a French audience, it offers an important insight into a notion shaping subsequent exhibitions at the Modern. American painting and sculpture were considered derivative of European sources, but American architecture, photography, and film were seen as innovative and sui generis. Discussing the general impression of the museum as it was

4.7 Fallingwater, Mill Run, Pennsylvania, 1934–37. Photograph by Bill Hedrich. (Chicago History Museum, HB-04414–5a3)

4.8 Fallingwater, Mill Run, Pennsylvania, 1934–37. Photograph by Bill Hedrich. (Chicago History Museum, HB-04414-5x2)

4.9 Fallingwater, Mill Run, Pennsylvania, 1934–37. Photograph by Bill Hedrich. (Chicago History Museum, HB-04414–5z2). This photograph was used for the cover of the 1938 MoMA exhibition catalog.

equated with "foreign art" in an internal memorandum two years later, Barr described "a tendency on the part of the public to identify art with paintings and sculpture—two fields in which America is not yet, I am afraid, quite the equal of France; but in other fields—the film, architecture and photography, for instance, the United States would seem to be the equal or superior of any other country."[47]

An indirect result of *Trois siècles* was the decision to dedicate an exhibition exclusively to this idea, and by October 1939 the museum had formulated plans for a major show to that effect: *Three Great Americans: Frank Lloyd Wright, Alfred Stieglitz, and D. W. Griffith.*[48]

INSTITUTE OF MODERN ART, BOSTON, 1940

Ironically, the slow gestation of the Wright retrospective from 1935 to 1939 coincided exactly with the resurgence of the architect's built work. Of course, it was impossible for the Modern to predict that over the next two decades Wright would not only produce hundreds of houses, but also the Solomon R. Guggenheim Museum (1943–59; New York), Beth Sholom Synagogue (1953–59; Elkins Park, Pennsylvania), and Marin County Civic Center and Fairgrounds (1957–70; San Rafael, California). When the Architecture Committee definitely proposed the Wright one-man show for fall 1936, it was one week after the opening of Hitchcock's Richardson exhibition. The Wright exhibition was the last step in covering in depth the three American architects the museum considered forerunners of modernism. There were several postponements until 1937, when it was approved for the 1939–40 season to commemorate what the curators justifiably believed to be Wright's seventieth birthday (Wright had used 1869 as his birth year). Yet again, it was delayed another year.[49] By the time MoMA's schedule became formalized it was no longer the only museum planning a large Wright show.

By a stroke of luck, however, the other institution was the Institute of Modern Art, Boston—originally founded in 1935 as the Boston Museum of Modern Art, a branch of MoMA. The Institute had become independent in 1938 (thus the change of name), with one of its founders, James Sachs Plaut (1912–1996), becoming the first director. Close ties still bound the two museums: three important trustees of the Institute had originated with the Modern: Barr; Paul J. Sachs, Plaut's uncle and Barr's mentor at Harvard University and a MoMA trustee; and Jere Abbott, MoMA's first associate director. Plaut had received his undergraduate and graduate degrees from Harvard, another link to Barr and the inner circle of Hitchcock, Johnson, and McAndrew.[50]

Two other founders were also very influential in the operation of the Institute: Nathaniel Saltonstall (1903–1968) and Nelson W. Aldrich (1911–1986), both architects. Saltonstall served as president from 1936 until 1948. Aldrich, whose aunt was Abby Aldrich Rockefeller, one of the three founders of MoMA, had a long and close relationship with the Institute, succeeding Saltonstall as president, serving until 1964. The youth of the three in 1939—Saltonstall was in his early thirties, and Plaut and Aldrich in their late twenties—no doubt, set the tone for the ambitious undertaking.

Due to the harmonious relationship with MoMA, when Plaut approached Wright in May 1939 to obtain his cooperation for "a one-man exhibition" that would open in November or December and circulate thereafter, what could have resulted in conflict became collaboration, with the two institutions sharing costs for some photography and new models.[51] As Plaut concluded, "This is a splendid solution as it will enable us both to get twice as much for nothing or something like that."[52] As it turned out, the Institute's exhibition was postponed; arrangements bogged down in the summer and fall, with both Plaut and Wright out of the country. When correspondence resumed, Plaut first rescheduled the show for January 24–March 3, 1940, and then suggested a meeting.[53] It must have been during his ensuing visit to Taliesin, in the company of Aldrich, September 12–13, that Wright informed him of the pending exhibition at the Modern (figure 4.10). Two weeks later, having returned to Boston, Plaut told Wright: "I told [McAndrew and Barr] that it was our intention to do our exhibition along thematic lines rather than in the retrospective and historical way in which they will undoubtedly do theirs. They both approved of this difference in approach and are very anxious to have the material we use in our exhibition, though it may not be used by them in the same way."[54]

Although the Modern would play the biggest role in presenting architecture exhibitions of Wright's work in the 1940s and early 1950s, the Boston Institute of Modern Art (the Institute of Contemporary Art after 1948) holds the claim to be the first (and last) American institution to independently organize a career survey and publish an accompanying catalog during the architect's lifetime. The Boston show, as Plaut predicted, was a complement to the New York exhibition because it was "by no means comprehensive," but rather "frankly thematic in character" so restricted "to a general development of [Wright's] residential architecture on the arbitrary premise that he is first and last a builder of homes—such successful monuments as the

4.10 Frank Lloyd Wright in Wisconsin, 1937. Photograph by Bill Hedrich. (Chicago History Museum, HB-04414-1i). The Institute of Modern Art, Boston, used this photograph in the catalog for the Frank Lloyd Wright exhibition.

Larkin and Johnson Buildings to the contrary notwithstanding."[55] Nevertheless, both the Larkin Building and the SC Johnson Administration Building were represented (figures 4.11–12).

Plaut organized the Boston show in close association with Aldrich, who also designed the installation, and in consultation with McAndrew. Without any installation photographs or a checklist—registrar lists of materials sent from Boston to New York survive—it is only possible to rough out the outline of the exhibition. Plaut explained to McAndrew that their intention was to produce "along critical rather than documentary lines in an effort to trace the development of Wright's residential architecture and to evaluate each successive step."[56] The concept dictated emphasis on built work over unrealized projects, Prairie Houses and late 1930s houses over the experimental work of the 1910s and 1920s, and large-format black-and-white photographs over delicate colored pencil drawings on tracing paper. The five principal photographs, 40 by 50 inches, featured four houses of 1912 or earlier—the Robert W. Evans (1908; Chicago) and Frederick Robie Houses (see figure 2.29), Coonley House, and Taliesin (figure 4.13)—and Fallingwater, the iconic Hedrich view (see figure 4.3). Large-format photographs illustrated two other Prairie Houses: the Warren Hickox House (see figure 1.15) and Ward W. Willits House (figure 4.14). In fact, it can be said that the exhibition was dedicated to the Prairie House more than any other buildings due to the large display of photographs and numerous photostats of Wasmuth portfolio plates.[57] Models shown were two chosen in consultation with McAndrew and specially commissioned from Wright, the Charles S. Ross (1902; Delavan, Wisconsin) and Herbert Jacobs Houses, in addition to the Stanley Marcus House (1934–36; Dallas, Texas) and the Suntop Homes (1938–39; Ardmore, Pennsylvania) (figures 4.15–16). MoMA sent their model of the Robie House, which the museum had made for the *Trois siècles* exhibition in Paris the previous year.[58] There was also an emphasis on construction and engineering, as the Institute exhibited structural details of the Imperial Hotel, a wall section of the Jacobs House I, a concrete block from Florida Southern College, and photographs of the rubble wall system of Taliesin West.[59]

The critical point of view expressed in the exhibition was clearly influenced by European sources. Aldrich began a conversion away from the Beaux-Arts during his architectural training at Harvard when Gropius and Marcel Breuer arrived in 1937 and became his instructors during his last two years.[60] Plaut and Aldrich edited Wright's forty-five-year career, favoring houses that were fully realized examples of rational planning and structural innovation over radical planning experiments and landscape compositions. The organization fell into three categories the historian Grant C. Manson later described as Wright's "First Golden Age," the "Lean, Lost Years," and the "Second Golden Age."

From the beginning, Plaut wanted Wright to deliver a lecture in Boston to coincide with the opening, which led to an encounter between Wright and Gropius. Wright's lecture at John Hancock Hall was another opportunity for a meeting. As McAndrew confided to Mumford, "You may be glad to know that [Wright] has become reconciled to Gropius and even voluntarily proposed a toast to him at the grandest of the dinner parties."[61] While Wright's reconciliation with Gropius may have been ambivalent at best, his association with Joseph Hudnut (1886–1968),

4.11 Light court, Larkin Company Administration Building, Buffalo, New York, 1902–6. (FLWFA, 0403.0062A). This photograph was paired with one of the SC Johnson Administration Building, Great Workroom, 1936–39, at the 1940 Boston exhibition.

4.12 Great Workroom, SC Johnson Administration Building, Racine, Wisconsin, 1936–39. (FLWFA, 3601.0059). This photograph was exhibited at the 1940 Boston exhibition.

Boston's other conspicuous champion of architectural modernism, he saw as unequivocally disastrous. Hudnut's involvement came about when Plaut was unable to secure Mumford, his first choice for author of a principal essay in the show's publication. Unfortunately for both the Boston and New York exhibitions, Mumford was engaged in a four-volume survey of Western civilization, *The Renewal of Life*. As Plaut told Wright a couple of weeks before the opening, "We tried to get Mumford to do a short preface to the catalogue, but he was too busy with his book, although he was very sympathetic to the idea."[62] Plaut then added, "Dean Hudnut has consented to write about a thousand words for us, and I hope that this will meet with your approval." The organization and content of the sixty-two-page publication were perfectly stated in its title, *Frank Lloyd Wright: A Pictorial Record of Architectural Progress with Notes Selected from the Published Writings of the Architect and a Foreword by Joseph Hudnut, Dean of the Faculty of Design, Harvard University*. The bulk of the booklet consisted of photographs interspersed with quotations from the Princeton lectures, *An Autobiography*, and the 1938 *Forum*.[63]

The two-and-a-half-page foreword is a complex document, but Wright, perhaps understandably, labeled it "the worst introduction I ever had."[64] He was presumably recalling the controversy stirred up in Berlin over his 1931 exhibition. As the former head of Columbia University's architecture school and

4.13 Taliesin I, Spring Green, Wisconsin, 1911–14. Photograph by Henry Fuermann and Sons. (FLWFA, 1104.0010). This photograph was exhibited. Taliesin was one of five residential buildings featured in the 1940 Boston exhibition.

4.14 Ward W. Willits House, Highland Park, Illinois, 1902–3. (FLWFA, 0208.0013–600). This photograph was featured in large format at the 1940 Boston exhibition.

4.15 Herbert Jacobs House I model, Madison, Wisconsin, 1936–37. (FLWFA, 3702.008).
This model, fabricated in November 1939, was commissioned for the 1940 Boston exhibition.

4.16 Suntop Homes model, Ardmore, Pennsylvania, 1938–39. (FLWFA, 3906.0038).
This model was commissioned for the 1940 Boston exhibition.

the dean of the design school at Harvard, Hudnut was in the forefront of the modern architecture scene. He was publicly linked to the European avant-garde, to which he was drawn because it addressed urgent social issues and embraced technology, but he opposed functionalism in favor of a union of aesthetics and construction. Above all, Hudnut believed that modern architecture should directly reflect the experience and circumstances of modern life.[65]

In his foreword he defined Wright as "a poet" rather than "a logician," but admitted that the architect nonetheless fused "intuition and feeling" with "analytical experiment and invention." He admired Wright's "stratified space," which had its origin in function, but dismissed his forms as failing to "develop as inevitable necessities from his inventions." Finally, Hudnut could not come to terms with Wright's view of man and nature, concluding, "The genuine spirit of science, engaged in its eternal struggle with the forces hostile to man, addressed to a collective destiny, building patiently on foundations economically feasible, socially attainable, escapes him entirely; nor can he discover in the new architecture in which this spirit is manifest any quality other than sterility and a pernicious negation." Perhaps most offensive to Wright was the statement, "With all their assertion of modernity [Wright's houses] do not exist in a modern world integral with our time, our way of life."[66]

Hudnut's criticism had a profound impact on the architect, who had only recently bathed in the afterglow of the 1938 *Forum*. Ironically, the close cooperation between the Institute and the Modern, which had proved so fortuitous for the curators, had unintended implications for Wright: he came to view the Boston show, which preceded his MoMA retrospective by nine months, as a dress rehearsal. Although there is no evidence that he objected to the Boston show itself, Hudnut's essay stayed in the forefront of his mind; as he told McAndrew later, "But for the suspicion aroused in me by the Boston experience all might have gone well. But for that I should have trusted you fully."[67] After all the planning and research that went into the MoMA catalog in 1940, it was doomed by the architect's fears of being dismissed by a proponent of the European avant-garde.

THREE GREAT AMERICANS: WRIGHT, STIEGLITZ, AND GRIFFITH

By late October 1939, as plans for the Boston show were being finalized, the program for MoMA's Wright retrospective was taking shape. First, the trustees approved a trio of exhibitions under the title *Three Great Americans: Wright, Stieglitz, and Griffith*.[68] Although the grouping of these artists was meant to convey a greater meaning than three independent presentations would have had—the preeminence of the United States in the arts of architecture, photography, and film—there appears to have been no attempt to coordinate the shows to match any overriding idea. Indeed, McAndrew's concept was developed almost exclusively in concert with the architect.[69] The early exhibition proposal presented a straightforward chronological sequence: 1889–94, 1894–1911, 1911–35, the last years, and Broadacre City. Over the next few months, however, the concept evolved. McAndrew described MoMA's goal as "the first attempt to show the whole range of his architectural career . . . from his earliest designs under Sullivan through his latest work" with the emphasis on his "architectural philosophy rather than simply on the development of his style."[70] The most innovative feature was Wright's suggestion to construct a full-scale Usonian House in the Sculpture Garden behind the museum.[71] The Usonian House was critical in Wright's eyes to an understanding of the spatial experience so essential to his architecture. When bureaucratic difficulties arose over its construction in the months ahead, conflict and disappointment resulted. In 1939, however, these problems were in the future, and McAndrew reviewed the plans for the show with the architect over a two-day stay at Taliesin between October 20 and 26 of that year.[72]

FRANK LLOYD WRIGHT FESTSCHRIFT

With the architect committed to the retrospective, McAndrew turned his attention to the book (figure 4.17). Wright's reputation for sensitivity to criticism probably affected the decision to conceive the publication as a Festschrift, comprising a series of essays of different lengths, "a full chronology of Wright's life and work, [and] a bibliography," researched by Henrietta Callaway, McAndrew's assistant.[73] McAndrew's outline, approved by Barr and Monroe Wheeler, the museum's director of publications, was divided into themes.[74] In the spirit of the publication, there were tributes from living architects—Mies, Harwell Hamilton Harris, and Alvar Aalto—narrowed down from a larger list. As Wright's most famous clients, Edgar Kaufmann Sr., his wife Liliane, and son Edgar Jr. were each asked to write about their experiences with Fallingwater. The thematic sections comprised the topics of Wright's influence on American architecture before 1920 (Talbot Hamlin, architect, historian, and librarian of the Avery Architectural Library, Columbia University, 1934–45), his relationship to

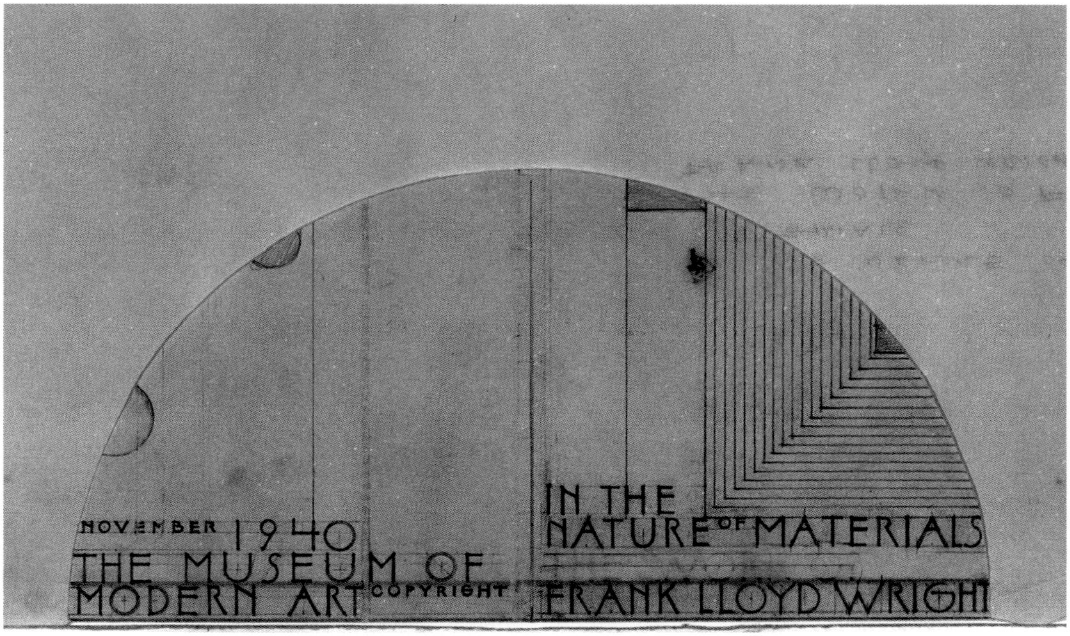

4.17 Catalog cover art for *Frank Lloyd Wright: American Architect*, Museum of Modern Art, New York, 1940. Eugene Masselink, delineator. Pencil on tracing paper, 9 × 21 in. (FLWFA, 4000.002)

the architectural profession in America (Fiske Kimball, architect and historian, well regarded as the director of the Philadelphia Museum of Art), his influence abroad (Hitchcock), his technical innovations (Neutra was the author of *Wie Baut Amerika?*—How America Builds?), and the influence of Japan (Grant C. Manson, whose Harvard University dissertation was later revised and published in 1958 as *Frank Lloyd Wright to 1910: The First Golden Age*). McAndrew's essay has been lost, but evidence indicates he had chosen the topic of Wright and space.[75]

From the outset, McAndrew wanted both Mumford and Behrendt to write principal essays; like Plaut before him, however, he was unable to secure Mumford.[76] At the end of January 1940, while preparing to spend two months in Mexico at work on the mammoth exhibition *Twenty Centuries of Mexican Art*, scheduled to open on May 15 of that year, he wrote to Mumford and Behrendt asking for an essay on a theme of their choice. Unfortunately Behrendt never received his letter due to a change of address, and Mumford, hoping that progress on his book would allow him to participate, waited to reply until McAndrew's return from Mexico, so that the authors' participation remained unresolved for weeks.[77] When Mumford did respond, he explained he was too busy to undertake the project, noting that Behrendt was "in a better position ... for he has actually seen more of Wright's buildings than I have."[78]

Mumford was correct about Behrendt's qualifications, for by 1940 this German critic had written one of the most laudatory and perceptive texts then in print on Wright's work. After immigrating to the United States in 1934 to take a teaching post at Dartmouth College, New Hampshire, Behrendt visited the Midwest to see the architect's buildings. In 1937, when he published a popular textbook on modern architecture, *Modern Building: Its Nature, Problems, and Forms* (in which he extended themes from his earlier *Der Sieg des neuen Baustils*), he added a separate section on Wright. Speaking as a critic and reformer, he made a case for the radical architecture of the European avant-garde, primarily in mass housing, but a central tenet of his book hinged on the influence of America, specifically "that radiant triple star" so familiar to his close friend Mumford: Richardson, Sullivan, and Wright. Interestingly, for his new section on Wright, Behrendt simply expanded the review of the architect's 1931 show in Berlin that he had published in the *Frankfurter Zeitung*. Although he wrote *Modern Building* six years later, and over twenty-five years after the design of the last building he illustrated or referred to in the text, he did not alter his arguments to include Wright's work between 1913 and 1937.[79] As a result, he ignored shifts in the architect's theory and formal development.

Behrendt repeated his earlier premise, "Wright's work is the first creation in the realm of architecture that can be regarded as an independent contribution of the American spirit to European culture."[80] Unlike almost any other writing of the time, this penetrating article went beyond a discussion of style to an analysis of the morphology of Wright's thinking, recognizing that the structural logic of nature was at the root of his architectural compositions. Concentrating on the revolutionary character of Wright's plans, Behrendt wrote, "In the projects in which Wright has achieved the maturity of his style, the rooms are arranged around the nucleus of the chimney part, like leaves of a plant around the stem. Radiating as if from a power center, they reach out into the garden and the landscape, opening themselves to the light and the view on all sides."[81] In one remarkable passage Behrendt also seized on the ephemeral element of light: "Wright treats light as if it were a natural building material. The graduated interplay of light and shade is to him an artistic medium of expression. And similarly, the air is evaluated as an element of form, is drawn into the concept of building.... With this inclusion of the air space in the formation, there is accomplished an intimate connection of the inside with outside, a new feature which from now on becomes the unmistakable characteristic of the modern house."[82] Despite his admiration for Wright, however, Behrendt the reformer was committed to an architecture based on industrial technology rather than on art or tradition. He objected to Wright's use of ornament and laid the blame on the generous budgets provided by wealthy clients. He appreciated Wright in part as a figure from another time: "The nineteenth century ... was in art a period of great personalities.... In architecture probably the last of these ... was Frank Lloyd Wright. His art is founded on the principle of the future, if architecture is again to be a living art. Yet the form in which Wright realizes and represents this general principle is unique: a personal creation, worthy of high esteem, as a product of an exuberant imagination, full of grace and serenity, of gaiety and enjoyment of life, a form of such wealth as we shall not see soon again. The period of individualism, which formed the background of his art, giving the artist a full opportunity to develop his own personality to its utmost potentialities—this happy period is over. It was rudely ended by the World War."[83] With the publication of *Modern Building* in 1937, Behrendt became one of the leading authorities on Wright in America.

In the spring of 1940, however, McAndrew, busy in Mexico, appears not to have informed Wright that he had asked Behrendt to write for the Festschrift. "Work upon the Wright exhibition has been seriously interrupted," the Architecture Committee reported on April 11, "by the Curator's taking charge of the installation of the Mexican exhibition."[84] Activity on the Wright retrospective was almost at a standstill. Eventually, in late May, it was Behrendt himself—while verifying facts—who informed Wright that he was writing an essay for the publication.[85] Immediately reminded of his experience with Hudnut only three months before, and also no doubt visited by lingering memories of the harsh criticism accompanying his 1931 Berlin exhibition, the architect sat down and wrote a warning letter to McAndrew even before replying to Behrendt: "Many felt that the [Boston] show was put on with 'tongue in cheek' owing to the scandalous introduction by Gropius mouthpiece—Hudnut." Wright explained. "Let's veer away from that sort of thing if we are heading into it. Once is enough." After posing the rhetorical question, "Who sits in judgment?" he then pretended to read McAndrew's mind by jotting in the margin, "No, I am not getting a persecution complex—we—the people—are like that—that's all."[86] No response from McAndrew survives in the Wright Foundation or MoMA archives, so it is impossible to determine how he handled Wright's alarm, but with all the responsibilities following the opening of the Mexico exhibition on May 15, McAndrew did not turn his attention back to the Wright show itself until mid-June.

If Wright had had reservations about *Modern Building*, its publication had been outside his control, but a book connected to the first major exhibition of his work in America was a completely different matter. When Wright imagined a book about his architecture, it would have been documentary: heavily illustrated with photographs (ideally in color), plans, and perspectives, and supplied with descriptive text only, interspersed with quotations from his own writing. It is clear that McAndrew never consulted him about the museum's publication, or even informed him of the numerous authors who had been chosen. When the architect learned, after the fact, of Behrendt's involvement, he was as gracious as possible. He wrote a short, straightforward letter answering the writer's queries and closed with, "I am glad that you are writing something. Undoubtedly it should have authority lacking in the perfectly silly foreword by Hudnut in the catalogue of the Boston show at the Museum of Modern Art last winter." In an attempt to influence Behrendt's opinions, he added, "Why not come up and see me sometime?"[87] Wright's persuasive attention had often turned adversaries into allies in the past. Behrendt did not respond to the offer.

Meanwhile, another event was developing that would derail MoMA's plans: the cancellation of the photography component of *Three Great Americans*. Alfred Stieglitz had been reviewing his work for the show with the future curator of the museum's photography department, Beaumont Newhall, when he became disenchanted with MoMA over a perceived slight and canceled his retrospective.[88] With Stieglitz's withdrawal, the original coherence of the three exhibitions was lost. Unfortunately, the pairing of Wright alone with a master of the silent screen took on a different meaning for the architect—the connotation of being viewed as an anachronism or as he put it later, "a kind of 'Americana' extra, illustrated by Griffith's bygone—etc."[89]

FRANK LLOYD WRIGHT: AMERICAN ARCHITECT, 1940–41

Since Wright was providing all the material for his retrospective, he had considerable control from the beginning. Shortly after McAndrew's visit in October 1939, he began preparations for new photography and models. To introduce the innovation of large-format color transparencies, he ordered apprentice Larry Cuneo to begin building a new photography studio at Taliesin.[90]

By December he was seeking funds to support this project, so he asked McAndrew for money; when told the photo budget was $1,250, he requested all of it. McAndrew could not oblige, however, because the money was not available until the next fiscal year, so Wright settled for a smaller advance.[91] Early in 1940, he instructed apprentices to begin construction on the more complicated models, including those for the Herbert Johnson House, Wingspread; the Lloyd Lewis House (1939–41; Libertyville, Illinois; figure 4.18 and figure B.42); the Ralph Jester House (1938–39; Palos Verdes, California; figure 4.19 and figure B.37), and Usonia I (1939; Lansing, Michigan).[92]

As summer turned to fall, with Wright in Wisconsin and McAndrew and Barr in New York (although Wright made occasional trips east and McAndrew went more than once to Taliesin), they were, as things turned out, working at cross-purposes. Wright had an overpowering personality and a past experience of complete control of his own exhibitions, and he wanted a show that presented his philosophy of architecture while promoting his most recent work. He hoped to tap the power and resources of the Modern to produce the most important exhibition of his work *he* had ever mounted—what he began to call "the show to end all shows"—and he brought all his negotiating skill to bear in his dealings with MoMA. The Modern, on the other hand, was seeking to provide a factual background and thematic dimension for one of two Americans, originators of a modern art form that had gone on to influence Europe. Equally important for the museum was its obligation to the public—to organize its presentations so that an educated audience, as well as specialists, would come away enlightened.

4.18 Lloyd Lewis House model, Libertyville, Illinois, 1939–41. (Courtesy Don Kalec)

4.19 Ralph Jester House model, Palos Verdes, California, 1938–39. (Courtesy Don Kalec)

As the weeks moved closer to the scheduled opening day—October 28—events would take a dramatic turn, resulting in bitter disappointment for both Wright and the museum.[93] In early September, Wright began to focus with growing intensity on his agenda for the MoMA exhibition, his attention sparked by receipt of McAndrew's production schedule. Apparently ignoring McAndrew's efforts totally, he sought to take complete control over the program. "Getting lousy with ideas concerning catalogue, show, and exhibition house," Wright telegraphed McAndrew on September 10, "Can you fly up with your catalogue engineer and what material you have and see what we've got." Later the same day he impatiently cabled again: "Want to show you general scheme for catalog and show and house. Drop everything."[94]

McAndrew's quick trip to Taliesin two days later, September 12 and 13, was more ominous than he realized at the time.

4.20 Frank Lloyd Wright looking at Wingspread, Herbert Johnson House, model at the Hillside Drafting Studio, Taliesin, with models—*foreground to background*: Suntop Homes, SC Johnson Administration Building, Jester House—for the 1940 MoMA retrospective. (Courtesy SC Johnson Foundation)

First, Wright unleashed his ideas by giving McAndrew a tantalizing tour of a dozen models and hundreds of unpublished drawings (figure 4.20). Tapping into McAndrew's enthusiasm, he argued that his show should get more space, but McAndrew was compelled to explain that this was impossible, partly because the Griffith retrospective was slotted into several galleries, but also, he confided, because the museum was working on a show known only to a few, *Exhibition X*. Planned by Leslie Cheek, the director of the Baltimore Museum of Art, and Mumford (unbeknownst to Wright), it had originated over the summer at the request of Abby Aldrich Rockefeller. With a program by Mumford and a design by Cheek, the exhibition, later known as *For Us, the Living*, was intended to tell "the American people of the dangers of Hitler's assault on the Free World and of the necessity for the U.S. to prepare itself for the inevitable war."[95] The innovative feature of the installation was to be the construction of an enormous gallery in the Sculpture Garden abutting Fifty-Fourth Street, the same size as the museum itself, usurping the location for Wright's Exhibition Usonian House. The shock of hearing this news gave Wright pause; a few days later he would recall his momentary reaction, which was to consider canceling the show immediately. Telling the architect there was little room for change, McAndrew nevertheless telegraphed Barr requesting more space on the first floor. In the early stages, when three exhibits were still planned, Barr informed John Abbott the "three one man shows would occupy less than the ground and second floors."[96] Before he left, McAndrew handed over at least two of the essays for the book, including Behrendt's. Wright read it within a day.[97]

What he discovered confirmed his worst fears. His aggression rising to the surface, he shot off a blistering telegram warning,

"If the Museum values [Behrendt's] opinion enough to paste it across the face of my exhibition there is going to be no exhibition." The threat sparked a cross fire of telegrams and letters between New York and Wisconsin over the next five days.[98] Unfortunately, McAndrew's response inflamed matters still more; affirming that the museum wanted to continue with the exhibition and book, he added, "we hope with your cooperation and advice." He also suggested that Wright telegraph the text of the essay he disagreed with and the museum "would try to straighten matters out."[99] This attempt to pacify the architect was destructive in the long run, as it implied the museum was inviting Wright to edit Behrendt's writing. Handed this ammunition, Wright lost little time using it. First, he was outraged that the museum considered going ahead with the show over his objections, demanding, "Am I to understand from your telegram that the Museum intends to continue with or without my cooperation."[100] He then turned to Behrendt's essay, editing sentences and rewriting passages, and on September 14 he instructed his secretary to retype the manuscript and mail it to McAndrew.[101] The parts of Behrendt's essay that Wright objected to seem to have taken him back to the summer of 1931 in Berlin, when he faced his harshest critics. As a personal retort, he revised his own text from that confrontation, sending it to McAndrew with the title, "To My Critics." Although well meaning, McAndrew was clearly outmatched.

With a day to think the matter over, Wright shifted his attention from Behrendt to a campaign to obtain more space for his show. Realizing his threat to withdraw, made only a few weeks before the opening, and McAndrew's conciliatory response to it had given him a powerful advantage, he began to soften his tone, but he did not back down. In two letters to McAndrew dated September 15 and 16, Wright laid out his case. He seemed surprised to have heard during the curator's visit about both the Griffith show and *Exhibition X*, presumably he had not been previously informed. He was angry that these exhibitions were siphoning money out of the budget and reducing the amount of space he needed for his show. "When you were here, I thought I could go through with it," Wright explained to McAndrew, "though greatly disappointed to find that what was to be a concentration of the Museum's resources on a complete showing of my work was to be really several shows, encroaching on the spaces we needed to give a show in keeping with our powers and resources. I intended to make it the show to end all other shows of my work." Wright's upset seems justified: not only had McAndrew, after eight months of work, been unable to raise more than a fraction of the funds necessary to build the house in the garden, but also, more to the point, Wright had lost his Exhibition House site to the building required by *Exhibition X*. Without naming names within the museum, Wright appeared to look beyond McAndrew to those responsible for the lack of funds and space.[102] "My only regret is—at the moment—that I seem to desert you at the last moment when you had evidently been having an uphill pull all the way. It is that 'uphill' pull that I am resenting now. That there should still be (at this time) such back drag is quite too much when all is added together. But I hope we shall continue friends, John, just the same." Meanwhile, Wright was carefully structuring his argument so as not to withdraw definitively, as he continued to repeat, "by biding my time the whole matter might be greatly improved."[103]

While Wright was biding his time, McAndrew was consulting Barr. The director told McAndrew that the museum could not censor the essays, but "if Wright did not want a Festschrift on this basis, we have no other alternative than to abandon it—but the decision is *immediate*."[104] McAndrew, under pressure to save a major exhibition that had already been publicized, crafted a letter on September 18 that solved the problem presently confronting him but caused fresh conflict in the future. In an effort to convince the architect to reconsider canceling the exhibition, he addressed two points: one was the publication, the other *Exhibition X*. Unfortunately, what he told Wright about the publication was that the museum had decided to cancel it since there was "no longer time to see an adequate catalogue through the press." He did not refer to the issue of censorship that Barr had raised. In failing to face the issue squarely, McAndrew allowed Wright to believe his objections to Behrendt's essay had nothing to do with the decision to abandon the book. This would become a bitter issue in the coming months, when the architect got a different impression from Barr. "Another surprise (in talking with Barr) was that you thought I had proscribed any catalogue at all," Wright complained to McAndrew after the opening, continuing, "What I really expected (after you said that owing to my objection to gratuitous pre-mortem essays), there was no time to print the literary efforts you had collected with such good intention—to honor me I am sure—was that you would print the catalogue clean as you had already put the work of a real catalogue upon it. I saw at the museum the feeling engendered by my objection to the ornamental part of it and suppose the feeling was, 'well since he won't have the catalogue we wanted, let's see him get along without any.' "[105] Wright either did not or pretended not to understand, that without the essays, which composed the bulk of the text, the only content remaining were the illustrations and the backmatter—an illustrated catalogue raisonné and bibliography.[106]

Next the museum resolved several questions regarding Wright's request for more exhibit space and additional funding. "As to the space—we will give you the ground floor as originally planned (including the whole garden for the house)," McAndrew announced, "and in addition the five bays on the second floor facing the garden." The monies estimated for the Exhibition House—$5,500—had been raised, and a contractor located who would build it at cost. Finally, *Exhibition X* had been canceled owing to questions of funding, clearing the way for Wright's show.[107] McAndrew told Wright, "The Museum wants to have the exhibition very much, and certainly does not want to make 'Americana' of your work, nor to bury you alive as an 'Old Master.' ... May I beg you one last time to reconsider ... I hope you will wire 'yes.' "[108]

McAndrew's letter explaining these points was delayed, and Wright became more agitated. He telegraphed, "If silence assents that Museum intends show over my head would like interview with Museum authorities when I reach N.Y. next week Wednesday."[109] That same day he also wrote another lengthy letter explaining that he needed to protect his future practice, because "anyone reading the Behrendt piece as a preface to a voluntary showing of my work would consider those statements endorsed by me and would be foolish to ever employ me under any circumstances whatsoever."[110] McAndrew reassured by telegram, "No show here without your consent and help. Sorry to have been slow in answering. Letter was mailed yesterday."[111] Wright's next telegram arrived on September 20: "That equivocal catalogue gone. Agony abated. At work again on exhibit."[112] McAndrew was delighted. The result of Wright's confrontation with the Modern was the loss of the publication, but his tactics were successful: he gained the additional space he had been requesting, and, after months of uncertainty, he was assured that the Exhibition House would be built.

What did Wright object to in Behrendt's essay? And why? Much of Behrendt's text was an updated version of the Wright section in his *Modern Building* book, published three years earlier. He did, however, introduce new themes central to his viewpoint: structural experimentation, low-cost housing (Usonian House), and city planning (Broadacre City). Fallingwater is conspicuous by its absence. Despite its recent worldwide publicity and MoMA's one-building exhibition, Behrendt never mentioned it; however, the client was a wealthy merchant and the building a luxurious weekend retreat so he probably rejected it because it did not conform to his social program. To prove Wright "a great genius, one of the greatest architects of all history," Behrendt structured his argument around several themes: the rejection of academic tradition in favor of a rationalist methodology; the transformation of the plan, elevations, and materials of building to adapt to a new social order; and the relentless pursuit of a radical course of structural experimentation. He reserved his critical judgment for the final pages.[113]

On September 19, at the same time that his negotiations with McAndrew were coming to a head, Wright sent Behrendt a version of the essay showing the "presumptuous editorial amendments" that he had sent to the museum five days earlier. Beyond taking minor exception to wordings and subtleties of interpretation, his fundamental disagreements boiled down to three: "You represent me as a reckless experimenter at the expense of my clients to gratify my own passion for mere experiment, and you misquote me and misunderstand my reference to the undesirability of *a* style (as any style whatever)—and finally you assume that I am a hangover from a past distrusted by youth today because of my personal style as a romanticist and therefore destined to disappear in the larger view of art which is impending."[114]

Behrendt had devoted a major section of the essay to the evolution of Wright's use of structural innovations, beginning with the Romeo and Juliet Windmill (1896; Spring Green, Wisconsin) and concentrating especially on the foundation of the Imperial Hotel and the concrete columns of SC Johnson Administration Building. Wright took exception to the following statement: "For the client it is no easy task to work with an architect who is such a passionate experimenter. ... He has to be willing to put up with disappointment, inefficacy, wearisome detours, perhaps even failure. ... A leaking roof matters little, when a new building material is tried out for the first time. The way to experience is through initial mistakes."[115] After a great struggle to emerge from bankruptcy, Wright could ill afford to scare off potential clients with such an opinion.

Behrendt reserved his most serious qualifications for the final three paragraphs, and here Wright edited heavily. Behrendt took issue with the architect on the question of style by explaining, "Although [Wright] seems to believe, concluding from his own statement, that 'any style is offensive now,' as an artist he is apparently so much of an individualist as not to see that, when forcing his personal style upon his clients, he is acting against his belief. ... And for us, today, and particularly in architecture, as correctly stated by Wright himself, any style has become offensive and most of all the personal one."[116] Wright believed that this statement was on principle a complete distortion of his views. His disagreement with Behrendt, and with most architectural reformers of his day, was that they believed it was imperative to find *a* style—a modern style—to replace the historical styles of the past. For Barr, Hitchcock, and Johnson, it had been the "International Style"; for Behrendt, it was a modern vernacular, neither individualistic nor the product of an avant-garde aestheticism but easily adaptable in the creation of humane social environments. By the 1930s Behrendt had come to accept the "International Style" as that anonymous new vernacular. But there was an important distinction in Wright's use of the term that Behrendt misunderstood based on his own preconceptions. Wright, who had come to maturity as an architect in an era dominated by historical styles, categorically rejected the entire concept of style. This is why he wrote in his rebuttal: "Any tyro may emulate any calculated superficial style. While much talk of principle goes with such calculated effort it is definitely a rationalizing after the fact because principles, if involved in this effort at *a* style, do not fructify creation." Then, using capitalization to reinforce his point, he stated, "I say, *a style* is no longer necessary because it cannot be individual and therefore cannot be free. Why let Style die that way again as it has died so many deaths heretofore?"[117]

Behrendt closed his essay by reprising his theme from *Modern Building*, calling Wright "one of the most imposing figures from the past period of individualism who has lived on into our time." Because Wright was "an emotionalist," "the younger generation is inclined to distrust him," and yet, Behrendt concluded, the principle on which his work was based would last even if his forms did not. Infuriated by the last few sentences, Wright crossed out the entire paragraph, and where Behrendt had written, "But even if the form in which he presented his ideas should prove evanescent," the architect inserted the phrase, "and the individual and democratic state be replaced by the totalitarian or communistic or socialistic ideal of architecture." Wright was increasingly of the opinion that the disagreements between himself and proponents of the "International Style" were fundamentally as much about politics as they were about aesthetics.

Behrendt's closing paragraphs went to the heart of the argument Wright had had with European modernism for almost a decade, so it is no wonder that on the day he read the essay, he edited his own manuscript, "To My Critics in the Land of the Danube and the Rhine," eliminating references to the 1931 Berlin dispute, otherwise refining the language, and retitling the piece "To My Critics." He sent it to McAndrew as his contribution to the publication. Wright's use of this text as his rebuttal to Behrendt is both revealing and ironic. First, it suggests that he had internally been propelled back to 1931, so that he associated Behrendt with the Neue Sachlichkeit critics of his Berlin show. Second, it had been Behrendt who had primarily defended him in that instance using some of the very same arguments and even the exact language he would use in his essay for the Modern. With Wright's letter the confrontation ended; Behrendt bowed out gracefully. On October 5, Wright composed a reply that was both blunt and warm at the same time; although clearly angry, he also conveyed his appreciation for Behrendt's long-standing support. "What you wrote was no doubt written in good faith even if mistaken as I believe," he admitted. "In self-defense I have taken the unusual—perhaps unwarranted—liberty of trying to rectify what I know to be mistaken. But, if you are not convinced, and are of the same opinion still—I shall be your friend just the same as before and hope someday we may understand each other better."[118] To this Behrendt graciously replied, "I regret that until now I did not have any opportunity to talk to you at length and to discuss with you the problems of our mutual interest. I know the loss is all on my side." He signed this letter, "In unchanged admiration I am, as ever, Sincerely yours."[119]

In private, though, Behrendt confided his frank reaction to Mumford: "It is a typical outburst of his exalted temperament. You should see the changes in the manuscript which he suggested: pure megalomania."[120] Mumford, who had already begun to sour on Wright over the war in Europe—Mumford was an uncompromising interventionist, Wright an equally ardent pacifist—had read Behrendt's essay in draft. "It is a wise and penetrating and beautifully balanced appreciation," Mumford told his good friend, "and it does honor and justice to its subject, as no other essay that I know has done."[121] "What depths of uncertainty must lie under that shell of success, for Wright to take such steps to protect himself against criticism," Mumford concluded. "He must have more serious weaknesses than one suspected!"[122]

EXHIBITION USONIAN HOUSE, 1940

The cancellation of the catalog in September was an irretrievable loss, even though several of the essays eventually appeared in art journals. Nor was the publication the only disappointment; in early December, McAndrew learned the Exhibition House also had to be aborted (figure 4.21). As the most inventive aspect of the show, Wright intended the Exhibition House to be a full-scale, completely furnished Usonian House similar to the Herbert Jacobs House I.[123] Because the Usonian House was intended as an affordable housing solution for the middle-class American family, numerous innovations in plan, materials, construction, and mechanical systems were introduced to lower building costs.

An L-shaped plan divided the house into public and private zones; one large room with fireplace combined the functions of living room, dining room, and study. While bedrooms were small, they were outfitted with generous storage. To reduce construction costs, kitchen and bathroom were built back to back. Materials were traditional and industrial—brick, machine-milled wood boards (usually cypress or redwood), and glass—left in their unfinished state and natural color both inside and outside.

Modern model houses had been built in Europe since the early 1920s, like the demonstration houses constructed at the Weimar Bauhaus. The tradition had continued with Le Corbusier's Pavillon de l'Esprit Nouveau, constructed for an exposition in Paris in 1925, and had reached a peak in 1927 with the Weissenhof Housing Colony, Stuttgart, designed by a range of modern architects headed by Mies and sponsored by the Deutsche Werkbund. Later the museum would build two modern houses in the Sculpture Garden (Marcel Breuer, 1949; Gregory Ain, 1950), but when Wright suggested the idea, no American museum had incorporated a feature of such popular appeal in an architecture exhibition.[124] As novel as its construction in the garden would have been, even more daring was the agreement to disassemble the house, crate the parts, and send it on tour.

Throughout 1940 the Exhibition House suffered numerous delays and setbacks that McAndrew and Wright, working together, overcame one by one. First were the issues of the construction estimate and McAndrew's fund-raising campaign; then, in order to obtain a building permit and hire a contractor, Wright's Studio was required to produce eleven sheets of working drawings. Despite the fact that the Exhibition House was not directly tied to the show—with a separate schedule, it was planned to open later, but remain on display much longer—as the months passed, Wright grew impatient, bombarding McAndrew with letters and telegrams: "When can we go to work? We are ready now."[125] The permit process was long and difficult, but fortunately, the office of Philip Goodwin (a MoMA trustee) acted as the architect of record, obtaining, with some difficulty, the required variances and approvals from the city of New York.

In trying to reassure Wright during the confrontation over the publication, McAndrew had inadvertently caused a problem by informing the architect he had "the whole garden for the house." Wright naturally took advantage of this opportunity to site the Exhibition House exactly where he wanted it: directly behind the museum building, so that it would be visible and directly accessible from the glass doors at the rear of the lobby (figure 4.22). When McAndrew suggested another location, Wright argued that in any other location, "All perspectives become bad, unity of show disrupted." "House can go where you wish, but it will then have to be demolished January fifteenth," McAndrew responded; "if it can go twenty-five feet to the west it can remain until next September." Wright immediately retorted, "Would rather have the house right for a fortnight than wrong for a year. When may we start we are ready."[126] In the end, however, neither the city building code nor the siting of the house was the stumbling block that prevented its construction. The problem lay

4.21 Frank Lloyd Wright, Exhibition Usonian House, project for the Museum of Modern Art, New York, 1940. Pencil on tracing paper, 30 × 18 in. (FLWFA, 4010.016)

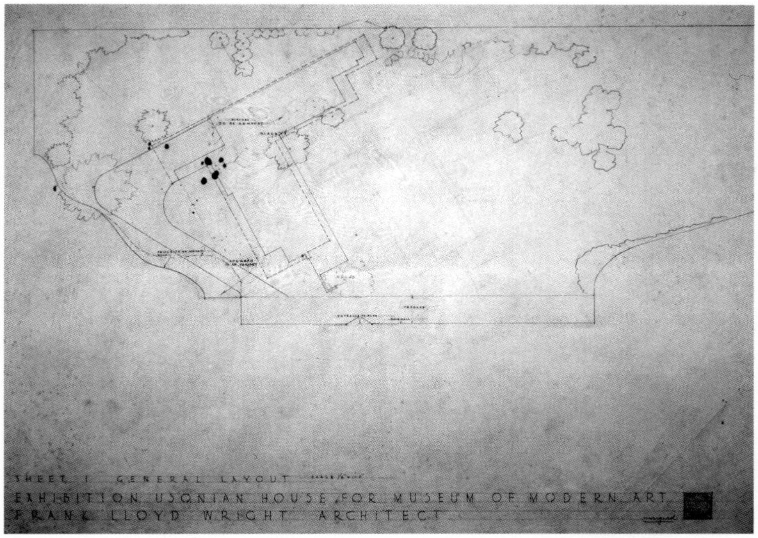

4.22 Site plan, Frank Lloyd Wright, Exhibition Usonian House, the Museum of Modern Art, New York, 1940. Pencil on tracing paper, 26 × 26 in. (FLWFA, 4010.001)

in the legalities of the land ownership behind the museum, a situation of which neither Barr nor McAndrew seems to have been fully cognizant.

The 100-by-400-foot plot actually comprised three distinct areas, all provided to the Modern by John D. Rockefeller Jr. The lot immediately behind the museum, 75 feet wide and 100 feet deep, was deeded to MoMA, but the lots to the west and east of it were at that time leased. Whether land was owned or leased, however, was not the issue; restrictions imposed by Rockefeller precluded the erection of any structures behind the museum, except within a very confined area too small for the Wright house no matter where it stood. McAndrew had thought of the house as an exhibit and not a building; Rockefeller disagreed. The deed and lease restrictions were clear, and Rockefeller rendered his final decision after the show opened. While the issue was strictly legal, Rockefeller also expressed disapproval of Wright's scheme for low-cost housing. "I have myself been much interested in inexpensive, conveniently arranged, well built, modern homes and have spent some time and money in studying and experimenting with the problem," Rockefeller disclosed to John Abbott, MoMA's executive vice president. "From what little I know of the subject," he added, "it does not seem to me that the proposed building is economical either to build, to maintain or to operate."[127] At Abbott's request, McAndrew had argued the case to Rockefeller in a four-page memorandum, but both Rockefeller and the chairman of the board, Stephen C. Clark, were in accord.[128] On December 2, then, McAndrew informed the architect: "We shall have to give up the whole project. This comes hard, as it has been one of my pet schemes for about two years." At this point, the show was scheduled to close in a month, and Wright put up no fight.[129]

By the time of the MoMA retrospective, Wright had become convinced that simulacra were wholly inadequate at communicating his work to the general public. As he explained later, "There's this about architecture: painting you can see, you can get it with your eye; music you can hear; but a building you must *experience*. It's in three dimensions, and no one has ever truly seen a building in a photograph. No one ever will. Even a three-dimensional photograph will give you only a limited sense of that experience."[130] The loss of the Exhibition House was a severe blow for Wright, and in the years ahead he held tenaciously to the idea of building a full-scale Exhibition House despite all the realistic obstacles; in 1953 he was finally successful with his exhibition *Sixty Years of Living Architecture* at the Fifth Avenue site of the future Solomon R. Guggenheim Museum.

THE WORK OF FRANK LLOYD WRIGHT: IN THE NATURE OF MATERIALS, 1940

Plans for the exhibition progressed through the fall in parallel with those for the Exhibition House. McAndrew, following standard museum procedure, composed a program, drew up a work schedule, and issued requests to Wright for the delivery of drawings and models, but once the museum conceded to most of Wright's demands, the architect quickly took over almost total control of the exhibition planning. Indeed, except for the outline he and McAndrew had worked out together, he reverted back to the same methods he employed in 1930–31 and 1935, choosing all the material and designing and installing the exhibition. Aside from his experience in Boston earlier in the year, he had never previously worked with a museum. In an unusual occurrence, the exhibition even opened with two titles, the museum's, *Two Great Americans: Frank Lloyd Wright, American Architect and D. W. Griffith, American Film Master* and Wright's *The Work of Frank Lloyd Wright: In the Nature of Materials.*[131]

As Wright's enthusiasm built up during the fall, he assigned apprentices to the fabrication of more and more models. "As the date for the exhibition grew nearer," Besinger recalled, "much more of everyone's time was required and the pressure and tempo of the work increased."[132] As a result, at Wright's instigation, the opening was postponed from October 28 to November 12. (The

4.23 Frank Lloyd Wright with Wingspread model at the exhibition, *Frank Lloyd Wright, American Architect*, November 13, 1940–January 5, 1941. Photograph by Soichi Sunami. (Museum of Modern Art, New York. Photographic Archive. Museum of Modern Art Archives, New York. Museum of Modern Art, New York, NY, U.S.A. Digital Image © The Museum of Modern Art/Licensed by SCALA/Art Resource, NY)

closing was scheduled for January 5, 1941.)[133] Despite McAndrew's gentle pleadings, Wright respected neither the museum's schedule nor its requests to receive materials in advance; setting his own timetable, the architect arranged to have all the materials in New York just three days before the opening.

"We emptied all the drawings out of the vault in rather strange disarray and put them on a truck," apprentice Victor Cusack remembered. "And I went to New York, but The Museum of Modern Art was not at all prepared, because they wanted to know completely in advance exactly what was going to be shown, how was it going to be mounted and everything else. Mr. Wright wanted to, in his inimitable way, design the exhibition himself. But he felt he could only do that on the site when he had the drawings and he could pick and choose and decide what he wanted to show and what he didn't want to show."[134] When Wright and his wife, Olgivanna, arrived, three intense days commenced of working around the clock. At least one journalist noted that the exhibition bore "the marks of a hurried completion."[135]

With the exception of a few views of Wright posed with models or of models alone, no installation photographs have been found (figure 4.23). One can only speculate on its design and layout from preliminary sketches, Wright's correspondence with the museum, and newspaper accounts. The final outline, written by McAndrew but closely following Wright's ideas, laid out four sections on two floors.[136] On the ground floor the visitor was to move through a gallery titled "Reforming the House," which would explicate Wright's design philosophy and principles of "Organic Architecture." Here models, drawings, and photographs would illustrate the topics "The Human Approach," "Simplification," "The Open Plan," "New Forms," and "Relation to Nature." A sketch for the installation also indicates a small gallery set aside for the projection of a color film, narrated by Wright, documenting the Taliesin Fellowship (figure 4.24). From the ground floor, the visitor was originally to exit through glass doors into the garden for a tour through the Exhibition House, first visible through the glass wall and doors at the rear of the museum's lobby. For Wright this visual relationship was central to his installation: "The house in the court seen through the windows in connection with the plans and models inside the museum was my idea of the show."[137] On the second floor, the visitor would find two sections: "In the Nature of Materials," which focused on the use of both industrial and organic materials, and the 12-by-12-foot model of Broadacre City.

From the sheer number of drawings and photographs on display it is evident that Wright preferred an encyclopedic survey to a narrower scope emphasizing a distinct ideological point of

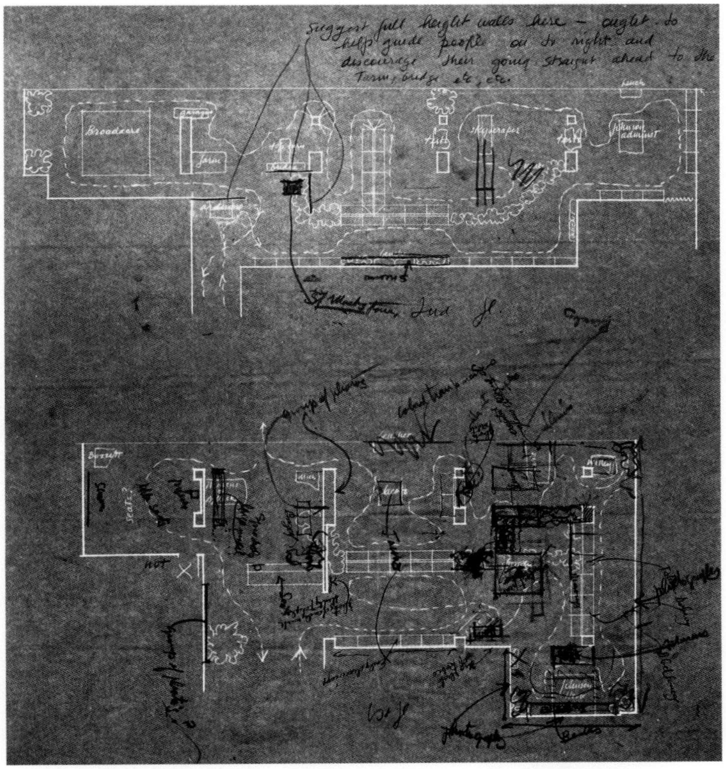

4.24 John McAndrew, installation plan for both floors of *Frank Lloyd Wright: American Architect*, 1940. Blueprint with graphite pencil, 19 × 17 in. (FLWFA, 4000.003)

4.25 The Call Building model no. 2 under construction for *Frank Lloyd Wright: American Architect*, Hillside Fellowship Living Room, Taliesin, summer 1940. Photograph by Pedro E. Guerrero. (© 2017 Pedro E. Guerrero Archives). *Left to right*: Hans Koch with Taliesin Fellows, Marcus Weston, and Blaine Drake.

4.26 Mrs. Thomas Gale House, Oak Park, Illinois, 1909. Sepia ink and white-chalk crayon on brown art paper, section of trees cut out with overlay to paper beneath, 12¾ × 16⅛ in. (FLWFA, 0905.001). At *lower left*: "Mrs T. H. Gale Oak Park 1904," initialed "Fllw," probably at a later date.

4.27 Ward W. Willits House, Highland Park, Illinois, 1902–3. Marion Mahony, delineator. India ink, sepia ink, watercolor, and white tempera on brown art paper, 8½ × 32 in. (FLWFA, 0208.001)

4.28 A. D. German Warehouse, Richland Center, Wisconsin, 1915–20. Lloyd Wright, delineator. India ink, graphite pencil, watercolor, and color pencil on linen, 21½ × 24⅜ in. (FLWFA, 1504.001). *Legend*: "Warehouse for A. D. German Richland Center Wisconsin F. L. Wright Architect."

view. "I wanted ... to give the 'folks' a comprehensive amble through the work of the years for a kind of 'bird's eye view,'" he explained.[138] There was also an emphasis on projects and topics European critics considered "modern." Of the twenty models probably displayed, for instance, only two dated to before 1925: the Robie House, favored by Dutch, German, and Russian critics as Wright's finest and most characteristic work of the Oak Park years, and the San Francisco Call Building, one of his rare essays in that most modern of typologies, the skyscraper. The enormous new wood model he had made of The Call Building extended from a base to within eight inches of the gallery ceiling, towering over the visitor (figure 4.25). In addition to presenting a sheer quantity of material, Wright wanted the show to be a very vivid visual experience. It was rich in color—the models realistic, the perspectives rendered in delicate color pencil. A most important innovation was the use of large-format color transparencies to record the architect's latest structures, such as Taliesin West.

The MoMA retrospective was the first time that a large selection of Wright's original drawings from all eras of his career up to 1940 were displayed, giving the visitor an opportunity to study the various styles of renderings, which broke down into three main categories according to chronology: 1894–1910, 1911–22, and 1923–40. Executing renderings, made for exhibition or presentation to the client, was a collaborative process at Taliesin; Wright dictated the composition to the draftsperson, who laid out the perspective and then usually applied color and detail. Others in the Studio might be brought in to add figures or foliage.[139] During the height of the Oak Park Studio years, watercolor, watercolor wash, and ink were primarily used in a manner associated with Marion Mahony; others were more graphic: india or sepia ink highlighted with color (figures 4.26–27). The period after Wright's 1911 departure from Oak Park to Taliesin until his 1922 return from Japan revealed more variety, from bold use of color to drawings influenced by Asian art, such as Sumi painting (figures 4.28–29). The 1940 exhibition was resplendent with drawings using Koh-I-Noor wax color pencils. The style was more spontaneous than the Oak Park Studio watercolors, as the medium allowed Wright latitude to use free-hand drawing techniques and to apply multiple layers of color blended with a razor blade. One of the masterworks of this technique is the famous perspective of Fallingwater, which was laid out by John H. Howe, Wright's chief draftsperson after 1932, and rendered free hand by Wright with color pencils (figure 4.30).[140] This style of perspective, with some notable exceptions, was used continuously until Wright's death, especially for houses (figure 4.31).

Although all of McAndrew's letters indicate his belief that the museum would supervise the design and installation of the

4.29 Hollyhock House, Aline Barnsdall House, Hollywood, California, 1919–21. Ink and ink wash on paper, 12 × 39 in. (FLWFA, 1705.003)

exhibition, Wright gradually took over all of those functions. First, he asserted that he wanted the drawings and photographs unmatted, and they were to be shown separately because of the "danger of killing the drawings by photographs."[141] The show was to be organized around a series of freestanding screens supporting drawings, with hinged boards on the far ends to mount photographs—a system almost identical to the one Wright had used in his 1930–31 exhibition (figure 4.32). The Taliesin Fellowship made the bases for the models in Wisconsin, although Wright asked the museum to build fifty small plywood stools "so anyone so minded can sit down to the lower perspectives which are invariably enchanting."[142] The finishes and color scheme—unfinished walnut plywood for the screens and model bases and "general wrapping paper tan" paint for the walls—were intended to keep "the show fresh and delicate."[143] One newspaper reported that Masselink "had designed two alphabets, one of two-inch letters and one of one-inch . . . making eight thousand letters of wood and fine veneer cut by members of the fellowship and used in setting up the titles and other legends."[144] Much of the text was to be glued to the bottom edges of the freestanding screens, leading McAndrew to warn Wright that if the public "bend down to read titles four inches from the floor they may get bumped often and intimately."[145] Wright responded with slight modifications.

Text panels presented Wright's ideas on a variety of subjects, including his scathing critique of the Federal Housing Administration. Although visual documentation of these panels is missing, an important one was quoted as saying, "No building in the collection shown here is designed by way of taste. All are founded upon or rooted in principle. What romance and individuality each possesses is by way of principle at work. These buildings are what they are solely because principles understood are comprehensively and conscientiously practiced in conceiving and building them. These buildings have resemblances to each other not because of personal idiosyncrasy but because all have the countenance of principle."[146] Masselink recalled, "We had about twenty beautifully made models and the effect of the softly lit walnut paneled walls and screens covered with drawings and photographs and then suddenly a model brilliantly lit like a solo dancer poised in the center of a carefully arranged space was dramatic and really breath-taking. The last room was devoted only to Broadacre City . . . which was brilliantly lighted with 'sun' of many lights and the walls were left dark."[147] Since the installation had been unprecedented in MoMA's history, beginning with the invitation and continuing with signs affixed to the walls of the galleries, the museum designated the exhibition "arranged by the architect himself" (figure 4.33). Even though the phrase was perfectly accurate, Wright took umbrage by stating, "I was surprised when you dumped the show on me as 'arranged by himself.'"[148] He continually pressed to have the signs removed, and the museum complied.

With these well-thought-out methods, Wright intended to create the "show to end all shows." Why then did the reviewers and critics generally regard it as a failure? The problem was not the content but the installation, which, as in the museum's *Bauhaus: 1919–1928* exhibition of two years earlier, was perceived as unintelligible.[149] Writing in the *New York Times*, Edward Alden Jewell, while conceding that "the installation . . . might be worse,"

4.30 Fallingwater, Edgar J. and Liliane Kaufmann House, Mill Run, Pennsylvania, 1934–37. Frank Lloyd Wright with John H. Howe, delineators. Graphite pencil and color pencil on white tracing paper, 17 × 33 in. (FLWFA, 3602.004)

4.31 John C. Pew House, Madison, Wisconsin, 1938–40. Frank Lloyd Wright and Herbert Fritz Jr., delineators. Graphite pencil and color pencil on tracing paper, 22 × 36 in. (FLWFA, 4012.002). Initialed by Frank Lloyd Wright within red square at *right*.

4.32 Drafting room, Taliesin West, Scottsdale, Arizona. Display racks identical to those used at MoMA in 1940. Photograph by Robert May. (FLWFA, 3803.0863)

FRANK LLOYD WRIGHT

THE PRESIDENT AND TRUSTEES OF THE MUSEUM OF MODERN ART INVITE YOU TO ATTEND THE PRIVATE OPENING OF A COMPREHENSIVE EXHIBITION OF THE WORK OF FRANK LLOYD WRIGHT, ARRANGED BY THE ARCHITECT HIMSELF, ON TUESDAY EVENING, NOVEMBER TWELFTH, 1940, FROM EIGHT-THIRTY TO ELEVEN O'CLOCK AT 11 WEST FIFTY-THIRD STREET, NEW YORK CITY.

THIS INVITATION IS NOT TRANSFERABLE AND WILL ADMIT TWO PERSONS

4.33 Invitation, *Frank Lloyd Wright: American Architect*, Museum of Modern Art, November 12, 1940–January 5, 1941. (Museum of Modern Art. Digital Image © The Museum of Modern Art/Licensed by SCALA/Art Resource, NY)

also complained that "the whole oeuvre is virtually flung at you" with "no simple, systematically marshaled verbal exposition."[150] His colleague, Geoffrey Baker, concluded that the Broadacre City model "was unintelligible without a guide book."[151] Isabel Cooper in *New Masses* admitted Wright was "a great American," but thought the exhibition consisted of "hundreds of uncatalogued items, labeled badly or not at all, with discrepancies of date and exaggerated claims, notably 'firsts' credited to the atelier Wright"; in fact, the designer "simply plumps down contents of files, drafting-table drawers, etc.," and asks the visitor to take "your pick."[152]

The most damning critiques appeared in the art press. Milton Brown wrote in *Parnassus*, "We can only marvel at the scope of his genius, the amazing richness of his invention, and the revolutionary effect of his experiments," but he found the show "a bewildering mélange."[153] Dimitri Tselos in *Art in America* considered "the fragmentary and rather confused exhibition" "a real disappointment" and wished for "drawings and plans touched up, matted, and clearly labeled."[154] Even sympathetic reviewers who were directly or indirectly connected to the museum offered qualified praise or outright criticism. Frederick Gutheim, who had provided citations for the bibliography, found it refreshing after years of viewing "slick drawings and presentations" to encounter "ink stains, dog-eared corners, and thumb prints," giving Wright's drawings "a frank and refreshing authenticity and lack of pretense."[155] Talbot Hamlin, who sat on MoMA's Architecture Committee and had authored an essay in the canceled Festschrift, said in the *Nation*, "Of the exhibition itself as a display it is charitable to say little." Nevertheless he said a lot, chiding Wright "as strangely lacking . . . in any conception of what ordinary museum-going Americans need in the way of explanation and guidance."[156] A consistent complaint echoed by Brown was that "surprisingly enough there is no catalogue."[157] By arrangement with Wright the museum sold copies and subscriptions to a magazine, "Broadacre City: The New Frontier," *Taliesin* 1, no. 1 (October 1940), produced by Wright and the Taliesin Fellowship.[158] This last criticism was a sore point for the museum, motivating Barr to make a public statement. "Mr. Wright, insisting upon 'no prejudgments in advance of the show,' refused to permit the publication of the catalog as planned, although it had been intended as a tribute to him." By this time, Barr was reflecting on Wright's warning—"I am a very difficult man"—made at the beginning of the exhibition planning. "We agree," he declared, "but still believe him to be the greatest living architect."[159]

There was almost no mention of the meaning behind the pairing of Wright and Griffith; the reviewers simply failed to notice it. But the museum issued a press release that was quoted in the *New York Times*: "Actually a curious parallel exists. America's greatest film director and America's greatest architect . . . had an immense influence on European motion pictures and architecture. After the first World War this influence was felt in the country of its origin in the guise of new European trends, even though European architects and motion picture directors openly acknowledged their debt to Wright and Griffith."[160]

The criticisms proliferated despite the best efforts of the museum, which had issued a press release with the title, "Greatest Living Architect Comes to Museum of Modern Art" before the opening.[161] Surely in an effort to secure a favorable review, Sarah Newmeyer, the director of the museum's publicity department, forwarded the document to Mumford along with a personal note.[162] She was obviously unaware of his thoughts on the show, at least as he confided them to Behrendt; the letter itself is lost, but Behrendt replied, "I went to the exhibition . . . which convinced me that my last article was much too tame in its criticism. I heartily agree with everything you say in your last letter about your own experience in the show: badly arranged and bare of all instinct in the selection of material. And his latest work is full of the same formalism and doctrinism which he so loudly and frequently criticized in Le Corbusier's work."[163]

As it turned out, Mumford never published a review, although he appears to have written one. There is no way to determine for certain what transpired, but Wright's behavior during the exhibition's press preview would certainly have incurred his ire. Playing off a story that had dominated the headlines for months—of the Blitz, the massive German air raids on London—Wright chose to present Broadacre City as bombproof. Leading with, "Says an Optimist Could Find a Blessing in the Destruction of European Cities," the *New York Times* quoted the architect as proclaiming, "I would not say that the bombing of Europe is not a blessing because at least it will give the architects there a chance to start all over again." Making a case for the decentralization of his model community, he added, "Concentration of population is murder—whether in peace time or in war."[164] When reminded of the destruction of London buildings designed by Christopher Wren, Wright retorted, "I don't think anyone will miss Wren's work very much."[165] Although these sentiments garnered Wright space in the newspapers, to many they must have appeared insensitive or worse.

By May 1941 Wright's isolationist political views had become so vociferous that Mumford broke off contact with him. They did not speak for ten years.[166] By that time, the New York critic had come to see Wright as "arrogant, violent, despotic, high-handed, and yet with an occasional gleam of self-criticism or an occasional act of self-transcendence that redeems him."[167] Over the years, Mumford did his best to keep some distance in an effort to preserve his objectivity, because the critic realized that "Wright demanded a complete, uncritical acceptance of his outlook and his way of life." He had concluded, "To question his pre-eminence in any sphere was to become a defector."[168] Mumford would never regain the same position with Wright he had held in the 1930s, even after their reconciliation in 1951.

Mumford's silence was one of the great losses of Wright's entire career, given the writer's profound insight into the architect's enduring value—a unique perception for its time, and quite clear in his unpublished review of the MoMA show. Although Mumford briefly mentions the exhibition's inadequacy, he directs most of his remarks to a critique of Wright as an architect and engineer. Taking into account Wright's work of the 1930s, he concedes that Wright is not the leader of a movement for a modern vernacular; instead, he is a formalist. "The human being whose needs he would satisfy," Mumford concludes, "is one who like himself puts architectural logic and esthetic design above every other need in a dwelling place." Yet Mumford rises above polemics to capture one of the most unique characteristics of Wright: a universality far greater than the "International Style": "He was to bring together, by a complete act of spiritual assimilation, the East and the West; he was to create new forms in which the native talents of the West, with its rationality, its skillful engineering, its mechanized energy would be united to the patient handicraft and love of nature that had flowered in the Japanese dwelling ... this union of the orient and occident, which took place long before anyone dreamed of calling the work of Le Corbusier and his imitators the international style, will probably remain one of Wright's outstanding contributions to forms."[169]

IN THE NATURE OF MATERIALS, 1942

As the reviews began to appear in the weeks after the opening, Wright's opinion of the show changed markedly. He was obviously stunned by the criticism that the exhibition was unintelligible, which made him sensitive to the museum's sign reading "Arranged by the architect himself." He also picked up on the comment that the absence of a catalog added to the show's confusion. First, in several letters to McAndrew, he expressed his displeasure, requested that the sign be removed, and refused to allow the exhibition material to continue on as a traveling show. Second, as in the past when he felt disappointed by, what he considered, a lack of understanding by the critics and the American public, he felt the need for an illuminating publication. As it turned out, his decision was more daring than obvious. It would seem that this would have been the perfect time to return to the work he had put in on *Creative Matter in the Nature of Materials*, the one book he had felt most passionately about for almost a decade. It is not known whether it was due to the difficulty and expense of the format or lack of time, nevertheless, Wright appears finally to have abandoned this work for good. For the same number of years, the most well respected and articulate Wright authority had been Mumford. Yet in light of recent events and changed attitudes on the part of both men, this possibility was unfeasible. But in recent years while Mumford had faded into the background, Hitchcock had moved into the foreground.

As late as 1937, Hitchcock had not wavered from his earlier position, as was clearly evident in his article, "The Architectural Future in America," which appeared in the July issue of the London journal *Architectural Review*. While the essay was ostensibly focused on the skyscraper as the American "characteristic form of expression," Hitchcock also discussed "the general bankruptcy of the power of formal creation," referring specifically to "a sense of form wholly of the twentieth century and wholly American, as was Wright's in the days when he was an active architect before the War." While Wright was furious when he read these sentences, certainly he perceived the irony of the situation as he was at that moment composing and laying out the January 1938 *Forum*, which made Hitchcock's conclusion—"The evident lack of a torch bearer in American architecture today is no indication that such a one may not appear within a year or two, as economic recovery increases the volume of modern building and encourages the employment of younger men"—almost prophetic.[170]

Several months after the article's appearance, Hitchcock was taken off guard by what became a public debate. First, two members of the Taliesin Fellowship wrote the historian protest letters that were published in the *Review* charging slander and libel against Wright.[171] In September, the architect followed up with his own more measured response, repeating his now familiar argument that what Hitchcock "observed in the works of Le Corbusier, Ludwig Mies, Oud and some others" preceded "from [his] own work." Yet the thrust of his letter was an accusation: "Our movement in the direction of an organic architecture has suffered a terrible set back from the exploitation of the left wing of which you are a camp follower." He ended with a challenge, "I would like to see you try at least to understand why this is so."[172] The opportunity to "straighten out differences" had arisen rather quickly in spring 1937 when the trustees of Wesleyan University, where Hitchcock was a faculty member, voted to give Wright an honorary master of arts degree. Surprised and delighted at the news, Hitchcock immediately invited Wright and his wife, Olgivanna, to be his houseguests during commencement.[173] The event was postponed until 1938 due to a conflict that arose in Wright's schedule when he decided to travel to Russia.[174] Apparently, the talks went so well Hitchcock entered the inner circle.[175] Like Mumford before him, he was invited to Taliesin; unlike Mumford, Hitchcock accepted. In the summer 1938, he "spent two of the happiest days of [his] life" at Wright's Wisconsin home and studio.[176] By the time of the exhibition opening and dinner, the architect and historian were on cordial terms.[177]

Less than two weeks later, Wright wrote Hitchcock with a tantalizing offer. To make sure the show "could be truly memorialized, properly on record instead of passing out forlornly misunderstood as it is now likely to do," Wright proposed hiring Hitchcock to put photographs "in serial order perhaps under the classification I attempted which was 'in the nature of materials' (grouping buildings under structural headings with some heed paid to chronology) but with not so much critical reviewing as interpretation of the ideas—explaining facts with proper significance." At the same time that Wright was making his intentions for the book clear, he recognized the need to allow the historian some latitude: "The work would be entirely yours and would be as you would have it of course. My function or the relation of any one else in relation to it would be purely as you needed or could use it."[178]

Hitchcock must have foreseen the need for such a publication, since he agreed immediately in an eighteen-page handwritten letter.[179] Several months earlier, in fact, he described his ideal Wright book to McAndrew as "a continuous and coherent critical study ... so that for once ... his work could be all seen and all studied in one volume. There have, I think, been too many tributes to the man and too few serious objective studies. ... However, I imagine that the chances of giving offense are rather great and while he is alive such a study might be dangerous to make."[180]

As the show came to a close, Wright's attention shifted to his publishing venture with Hitchcock, who, because of his close ties with the museum, had open access to the catalogue raisonné of executed buildings and projects previously compiled by Okami and revised by Callaway, and to drawings and photographs exhibited in New York (figure 4.34). As the book took shape through 1941, conflict inevitably arose. With the reprint edition of *In the Nature of Materials* in 1973, Hitchcock provided a succinct and accurate overview of the authorship in the foreword. He admitted he acted "to a degree" as a "ghost" for Wright, noting the copyright was in both their names. He explained, "Mr. Wright personally oversaw the selection and preparation of all the visual material, passed the wording of even the shortest captions, and established all the details of the exceptional design."[181]

In the end, when the book appeared in spring 1942, the reviews were excellent, and Wright seemed to take his cue from them when he wrote Hitchcock: "I am wondering how you like the new book and your role of expositor instead of critic? It seems becoming to you. I agree with your critics—you have 'done a good job.' "[182] In light of their recent encounter, the most gracious review came from Behrendt in the *Yale Review*. He pointed out the text was "subsidiary to the illustrations," making the book more "a catalogue raisonné rather than a critical analysis of Wright's art," but he termed it "long overdue and much wanted in view of the high rank this architect holds." Salvaging one line from his unpublished essay, he closed by reiterating yet again, "In our midst there is living a great genius, one of the greatest architects of all history."[183]

In the years after the close of the Wright retrospective, the turmoil and negative reviews were forgotten. What remained primarily was Hitchcock and Wright's *In the Nature of Materials*, described by the historian in his preface as the "intended," "*ex post facto* catalogue," which became a standard reference for

4.34 Henry-Russell Hitchcock and Frank Lloyd Wright reviewing drawings for *In the Nature of Materials*, Taliesin, 1941. Photograph by Edgar Tafel. (Edgar Tafel architectural records and papers, 1919–2005, Department of Drawings and Archives, Avery Architectural and Fine Arts Library, Columbia University)

almost fifty years. Ironically, its format and method is probably what the Modern would have proposed originally if Wright's temperament had allowed it; up to that time, no book existed that covered Wright's entire career with a complete chronological listing, photographs and plans, and an interpretive text. Hitchcock felt so committed to the publication that he considered bringing it up to date several times, the first was in 1952, and again later after Wright's death in 1959. For a number of reasons, including Wright's mercurial moods, the revision never occurred and the historian was left with the conclusion that the architect's "own sense of history even with regard to his own work was not highly developed."[184]

The Wright retrospective had been played out against great change from within and outside the museum. Europe had become consumed by world war, and it was inevitable that the United States would soon enter on the side of the Allies. This major shift in American politics affected the museum organization by the end of 1941, but real change had already occurred as a result of the museum's growing pains. Goodyear was replaced as chairman of the board by the conservative Stephen C. Clark; Abby Rockefeller moved into the background while her son, Nelson, assumed the newly created position of president, soon to resign for government service in January 1941; and Barr was gradually relieved of more and more of his duties as director.[185] It was at the time of this realignment that McAndrew lost his job. Margaret Scolari Barr recalled that Nelson Rockefeller first issued a warning about McAndrew on January 8, 1941, and finally dismissed him after Alfred H. Barr "failed over the period of six months to convince [Rockefeller] to reverse his decision." "So far as [Alfred] can gather," Margaret Barr reported, "McAndrew has incurred Rockefeller's disapproval as an unreliable staff member" because he was "unreachable in Mexico City."[186]

One significant change with the various departures at the Modern during World War II was that Elizabeth Mock took over as director of the Architecture Department, which brought a major ideological shift, yet one that had been developing under McAndrew.[187] Mock, who graduated from Vassar College in 1932, joined the Taliesin Fellowship in September as a charter member; there she met her first husband, the Swiss architect Rudolph Mock, who had been an apprentice since 1931. The couple left in April 1933 for Switzerland and returned to America in 1937, when Betty was hired at MoMA while her husband worked at the Philadelphia firm of Oscar Stonorov and Louis I. Kahn.[188]

Considering the difficulties the museum encountered during the Wright retrospective, there must have been serious discussions about how Wright would or would not fit in to future museum programming. Obviously, the museum could not ignore him: Wright was an American, professionally active, and continuously in the public eye. The growing availability of photographs—from professional photographers, who were commissioned by trade magazines—limited the need to borrow drawings or models from the architect. The museum took utmost advantage of this circumstance. After 1941, Wright would figure in MoMA exhibitions in three ways: single building exhibitions, surveys of American architecture, and theme shows independently organized by the Circulating Exhibitions Department.

CIRCULATING EXHIBITIONS DEPARTMENT, 1933–52

While the Architecture and Design Department presented Wright's buildings as high art, the twelve exhibitions that included one or more examples of his work prepared exclusively by the museum's Circulating Exhibitions Department between 1939 and 1952 were deliberately aimed at integrating modernism into the daily lives of the general public across the United States. The unprecedented success of the complex program, established in 1933, was due to Elodie Courter (1911–1994), who was appointed secretary in November 1935 and served as director from 1939 until her resignation in 1947.[189] During her tenure, Courter was responsible for presenting Wright with the full weight and authority of the Modern to more people—probably in the hundreds of thousands—than the combined audience for all the monographic or survey exhibitions he appeared in at the museum on Fifty-Third Street. While venues were primarily in the continental United States, occasionally shows circulated internationally; sites varied from museums, universities, and art galleries to department stores and hotel lobbies; tours extended over a few years to as many as seven, with several running simultaneously. The first museum exhibition to tour was *Modern Architecture: International Exhibition* in 1932, but the smaller, less expensive version, *Photographic Exhibition of Modern Architecture*, which traveled to twenty additional venues between 1932 and 1938, is an example of the museum's intentions to reach out to smaller communities.[190]

The majority of the architecture exhibitions were organized either by or with the assistance of another woman: Mock. With the exception of the phenomenally successful *What Is Modern Architecture?* (eighty-six venues, 1938–45), themes addressed the perceived need of the American public—in their homes and neighborhoods—to rationalize their environment according to the precepts and precedents of modern design.[191] In addition to the one-man show, *Houses by Frank Lloyd Wright* (twenty venues, 1946–49), subjects included modern residential design: *If You Want to Build a House* (fifty-one venues, 1946–49)—based on Mock's MoMA book of the same title issued in a print run of 31,000 copies—and the condensed version: *Modern American Houses* (twenty-four venues, 1946–49) and *Modern Houses in America* (twenty-four venues, 1938–41); regionalism: *Regional Building in the United States* (twenty-six venues in two versions, 1941–47); educational building: *Modern Buildings for Schools and Colleges I, II, III* (thirty-six venues, 1947–52); and history: *American Architecture* (fifteen venues, 1942–46).[192] The press release for *Houses by Frank Lloyd Wright* introduced the architect with the claim: "Generally considered the world's greatest living architect, [he] has certainly been the most influential one."[193] Like most of the architecture circulating shows, the exhibition, featuring sixteen Prairie and Usonian Houses, consisted of enlarged photographs, labels, plans, and brief text.

While the purpose of the circulating exhibitions was educational—addressing a broad audience geographically and demographically—in concert with the museum's founding mission in 1929, it is impossible to determine the direct impact the shows had on Wright's career. Based on the popular nature of the exhibitions, clients who came to him in the postwar years may have first been introduced to the Midwest architect's work through the Modern. Far from being elitist, the programs of the Circulating Exhibitions Department were aimed at the general populace.[194]

BUILT IN USA: 1932–1944, 1944

Built in USA: 1932–44 was the architectural component of the museum's fifteenth anniversary exhibition, *Art in Progress*, shown from May 24 to October 15, 1944. The purpose of the exhibition was to present the fifty "finest American architectural works of the last ten years." "Since war conditions will in many cases prevent our first-hand inspection of possibilities," Mock explained, "we shall rely to a great extent in making our selections upon the good advice of interested people all over the country." To this end, three hundred two-page questionnaires were sent out requesting building nominations.[195] The process of selection was addressed by three committees: a newly created Special Advisory Committee of fourteen diverse members including Behrendt, Gutheim, Sigfried Giedion, Howard Myers, Serge Chermayeff, and John Entenza, editor of *California Arts and Architecture*; the existing fifteen-person Architecture Committee including new member Edgar Kaufmann Jr. and Philip Johnson listed as an honorary member; and finally an Executive Committee of Mock, Barr, and Goodwin. Thirty-six buildings were chosen "without any violent differences of opinion," when the Executive Committee, then having the power to expand the list to fifty, stopped with forty-seven buildings. The committee was hampered by one of its own rules: no one architect or firm could be represented by more than three buildings.[196] The Wright buildings chosen were Fallingwater, Taliesin West, and the Alma Goetsch–Kathrine Winckler House (1939–40; Lansing, Michigan; figures 4.35–37). Mock had the task of explaining to Wright that "there was a great struggle within the Committee as to whether the Johnson Wax Office Building should be included rather than a Usonian house." She wrote, "It was finally decided that it would be impossible to omit some reference to your recent work in the field of small houses." She was even more direct when she told him, "In order to make this anything different from a Frank Lloyd Wright exhibition and publication, we shall have to resort to the arbitrary limitation of the number of selections from any one architect's work."[197] She reassured him that "only one other architect is three times included and he only by fortuitous association with other architects."[198] From the outset, Wright was put off by the entire process: he refused to fill out the questionnaire ("I feel about 'the best' work of art as I do about trees. There is no 'best'—only works of art"); he was sarcastic about the rejection of the SC Johnson Administration Building ("The omission is a courageous forward-looking act?"); and he demanded to be withdrawn completely from the New York and traveling exhibition ("I find myself unable to change in such

4.35 Frank Lloyd Wright exhibit, *Built in USA: 1932–1944*, in the series, *Art in Progress: 15th Anniversary Exhibition*, May 24–October 22, 1944. Photograph by Soichi Sunami. (Museum of Modern Art, New York. Photographic Archive. Museum of Modern Art Archives, New York, New York, USA. Digital Image © The Museum of Modern Art/Licensed by SCALA/Art Resource, NY)

4.36 Taliesin West, Scottsdale, Arizona, 1938–59. Photograph by Pedro E. Guerrero. (© 2017 Pedro E. Guerrero Archives). MoMA exhibited this photograph in the 1944 exhibition.

4.37 Alma Goetsch and Kathrine Winckler House, Lansing, Michigan, 1939–40. Photograph by Hi Marple. (Leavenworth Photography, Lansing, Michigan). MoMA exhibited this photograph in the 1944 exhibition.

circumstances as the Museum sets up").[199] It was, clearly, an unfortunate situation as Wright found himself with an unmistakably significant monumental building and was still relegated by the most authoritative international modern art institution to the category of residential architect.

As it turned out, Wright was not the only one who found the exclusion of the SC Johnson Administration Building indefensible. In a sixteen-page black-and-white illustrated spread in the May 1944 *Architectural Forum*, the unsigned editors (Howard Myers and George Nelson were members of the museum's committees) both documented and criticized the exhibition. The two-page editorial found fault with the Modern in two respects: one, the "tendency to pick names rather than buildings," and two, "a habit of looking at architecture the way one looks at painting . . . as a kind of abstraction." They described the three-building rule as "a strait-jacket regulation [that] would never have been adopted had the Museum been as concerned with getting the buildings as it was with including all the proper names." Despite weaknesses, the *Forum* concluded, "*Built in USA* makes a real and important contribution."[200]

Wright's myopia about his perceived rude treatment in the selection process blinded him to Mock's noteworthy catalog essay, which she stated in the acknowledgments, was reviewed (and presumably approved) by Barr. Taking the 1932 *Modern Architecture: International Exhibition* as the touchstone, she presented what can only be described as a revisionist interpretation. She admitted "[the 'International Style'] was directed towards the improvement of the comfort and convenience, health and happiness of society as whole," but she added, "yet there has probably never been an architectural movement more deeply distrusted by the public."[201] Without dismissing the style altogether, she explained that two other factors had emerged since 1932 as equally important: Wright's "renewed creative activity" and "traditional vernacular building." Mock was an active and provocative force at the Modern during the war years, but with peace came a return to the old guard.[202]

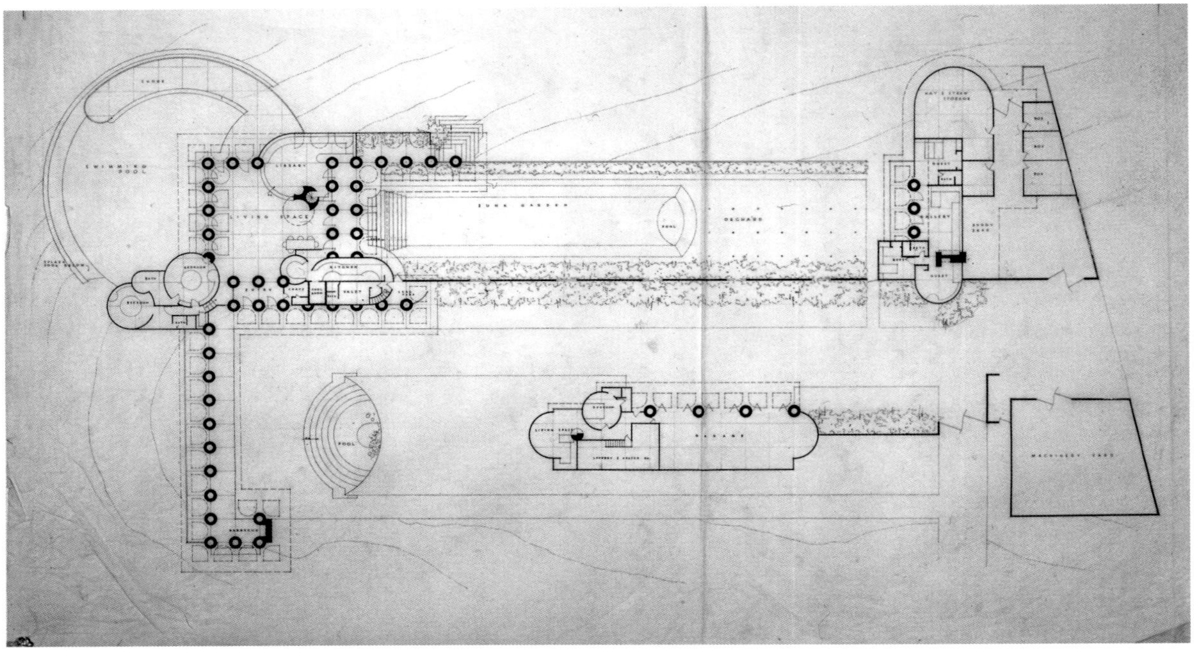

4.38 Pergola House, Gerald Loeb House, plan, Redding, Connecticut, 1944.
Ink on tracing paper, 35½ × 48¾ in. (FLWFA, 4511.040)

Wright's experience with the Department of Architecture and Design in the postwar years was, paradoxically, more significant for what did not take place than what did. The period 1945 to 1954 saw the return of Philip Johnson, the departure of Mock, the arrival of Edgar Kaufmann Jr. (1910–1989), and Johnson's departure yet again. Concurrent with these events, the museum mounted four Wright single-building exhibitions and included him in several theme shows about houses and interiors, but ambitious plans to commemorate what was publicly believed to be his eightieth birthday in 1949 never were realized. Ultimately, when major differences in ideology with the museum, and with Johnson in particular, remained unresolved Wright took his arguments public igniting a war of words for the better part of 1953.

A NEW COUNTRY HOUSE BY FRANK LLOYD WRIGHT: A SCALE MODEL, 1946

The publication and exhibition of Fallingwater in 1938 created a flood of publicity in the print media that made both Wright and his clients, Edgar and Liliane Kaufmann, world famous. One of the unintentional consequences was to inspire other people to follow their lead. It appears that the New York stockbroker Gerald M. Loeb (1899–1974) was one of these. Originally from San Francisco, where he began his career in finance, Loeb moved to New York in 1924, ultimately becoming partner at E. F. Hutton, the brokerage firm. His interests ranged widely from photography to philanthropy, enabling him to develop valuable contacts with people in power throughout New York. Howard Myers of *Forum* introduced him to Wright in November 1940, but he did not commission the architect until 1944.[203] Loeb, who took full advantage of having a Dictaphone and a secretary, wrote Wright voluminous letters that were often answered by one- or two-line replies. He communicated his ecstatic reactions to Wright's ideas and drawings for his windswept site in Redding, Connecticut, in vivid prose. He exclaimed in a letter, inexplicably dated September 32, 1944, "what can we put into a hilltop room that will interest not a few hundred thousand interested in GOOD building but many millions? Sex, when its quotable and mentionable and we want this super quotable and mentionable and picturable, is the first interest. But can you put sex into a house? What can you put into a house that interests TIME, the NY Times, the Manchester Guardian, the Paris Herald not just 'House Beautiful' and the 'American Home'? . . . Here is a challenge."[204] What Wright created was an elaboration of the unbuilt Ralph

Jester House as a weekend retreat for a bachelor who enjoyed entertaining on a grand scale. Loeb responded by spending weeks and months studying and criticizing the plans, urging Wright on with comments such as "This house is not built to please anyone—but to be as near perfect as your genius can make it."[205]

The proposal for a MoMA exhibition grew out of a conversation between Loeb and Mock in early December 1945. Loeb, who had recently created the Sidney S. Loeb Memorial Foundation, had the means to fund a scale model of Wright's design, and Mock believed that it "would be the most beautiful object that we would have shown for a long, long time and I do hope that we can actually pull it off." Wright had explained that he was too busy to make the model so it was mutually agreed that a local model maker, Devon Dennett, would do the job subject to Wright's approval.[206] The plan was flawed from the beginning because the schedule was rushed (originally the model was to be made in thirty days for an opening January 6); it required Wright's approval, yet the work was to be done in New York while he was primarily in Arizona.[207]

When it was soon seen to be an untenable solution, Wright felt pressured to agree to have the Fellowship do the work, but Loeb had financial demands that made the arrangement complicated. He wanted to own the model, but he wanted his tax-exempt foundation to pay for it. Wright required payment, so Loeb agreed to have the Loeb Foundation donate $5,000 to the Modern; MoMA then contracted with the Frank Lloyd Wright Foundation, which meant the museum became the owner. Loeb had an article lined up with *Architectural Forum* through his friend, Myers, which added to the time pressure. As the revised deadline of May 1 for delivery of the 12-by-6-foot model approached, with the opening scheduled for June 11, Wright was annoyed with the entire enterprise. "It was a mistake to push the false deadline at us," Wright complained. "If we could have had the extra six weeks we could have saved a couple of thousand dollars and done an even better job."[208]

Finally, the revised schedule called for the exhibition to be on view from June 19 until September 3; due to the postponement neither the client nor the architect was available to attend the press preview or the opening. The Loeb House was organized as a compound: a two-bedroom main structure connected by a pergola to a three-car garage, caretaker's quarters, and a stable at the end of a walled garden near the entrance. The most dramatic feature was the main living space, a forty-foot-square glass pavilion, containing concrete cylinders—lit only by skylights—for bedrooms, bathrooms, and utility (figure 4.38). The lightness and transparency of the glass walls contrasted with fieldstone

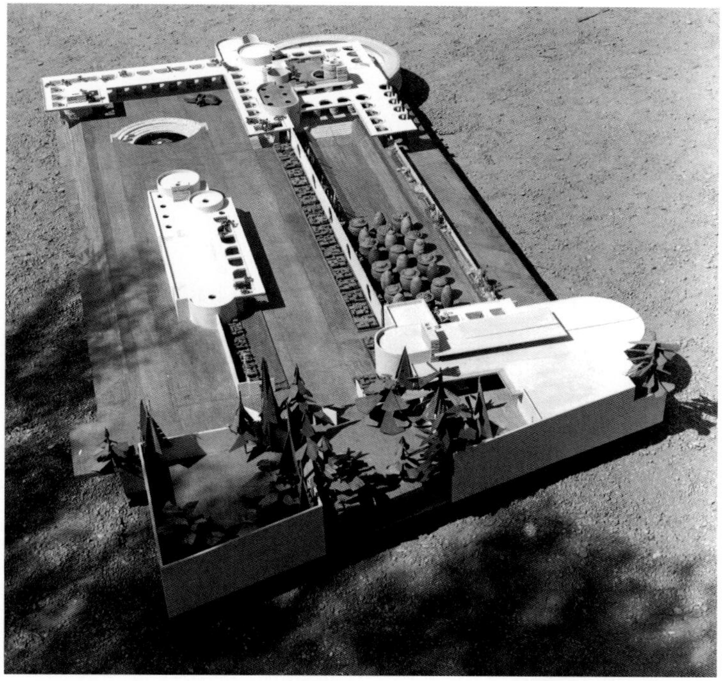

4.39 Pergola House, Gerald Loeb House model, Redding, Connecticut, 1944. Photograph by Ezra Stoller. (© Ezra Stoller/Esto)

columns four feet in diameter that formed a colonnade around the main room.

While newspaper articles were straightforward and even admiring, the Henry Luce–owned publications were stunning in their criticism. "Designed for a barren hilltop, the Loeb house was to be," wrote the anonymous reviewer for *Time*, "as low, flat and full of wrinkles as an unmade Japanese bed." The biggest surprise was the cover story in the June 1946 *Forum*, which declared, "Many who admired the [Guggenheim] Museum ... will detest this house for its massive stonework and prolific mingling of shapes and materials." But the conclusion was even more devastating: "Such criticism ... ignores the fact that it is in this very inconsistency that Wright's genius is rooted. ... As one of Wright's severest critics put it, 'his work—with all of its maddening changes of pace—is, at worst, challenging, at best, sublime.' And the question of which category this particular job belongs in depends on which horn of the over-all dilemma one happens to be impaled." The article was illustrated with eight black-and-white photographs of the model by the architectural photographer Ezra Stoller (figure 4.39 and figure B.49).[209]

The controversy continued in the "Letters" column of the August *Forum*: "A freak building is like a cuckoo clock that recites poetry on the half hour—both are very nice and very expensive, and neither add to the art or science of their development," and "Wright's latest monstrosity is the reason for this outburst" and quite simply, "vulgar display."[210] Loeb put on a brave face explaining to Wright, "If I am disappointed in anything it is in the model rather than what the model represents."[211] It was the architect who was the most irritated. "Concerning the Loeb model," Wright confided to Hilla Rebay, "Howard Myers detests *Look* magazine and not consulting me gave the half finished model a lousy presentation. The model is no way to present a residence. . . . The house is really very simple—an open arbor resting on stone-spools arranged like a crown on the slopes of a hill—like a clambering melon vine. The rooms lie in it like melons and a certain part of the arbor is simply glassed-in between the spools for a Living Room. . . . The whole nestling effect of the dwelling feature is lost entirely in the model as is the hilltop itself."[212] Wright made peace with Myers as he explained that the "Loeb fiasco so well placed and well meant in the *Forum*" was due to those "incriminating photos" by Ezra Stoller. The result Wright predicted was, "that house will never be built. If any one can make head or tail of it—I doubt. I couldn't if I didn't know it."[213] Wright was philosophical about his client: "Poor Loeb! Yes, he is vain but he is in a fervor new to him. He went all out to be a Patron of Fine Art. . . . He is rich and outspoken and mean about money. So they all stone him with his beloved, too much vaunted, model."[214] At the close of the exhibition, Wright requested the return of the model to Taliesin West for completion. The museum amicably agreed; some work was carried out, but Wright retained the model and eventually had it destroyed.[215]

Philip Johnson's return to the museum was a gradual easing in that began shortly after he was mustered out of military service at Fort Belvoir, Virginia, at the end of 1944.[216] It was inevitable that he would supersede Mock, and her departure July 7, 1946, led to his resumption as director of the Department of Architecture in October.[217] He had already reestablished contact with Wright in August 1945 by expressing a desire to "pay his respects" at Taliesin, also reminding him, "I was one of those who went in for 'boxes' which you hate so much, and collaborated with Russell Hitchcock on The International Style." He added a meaningful sentence, which signaled a shift in his attitude from the 1930s: "Since those days, I have grown older and have become myself an architect, so perhaps it is only natural that I should now really appreciate the work of a master."[218] That sentiment set the tone for their relationship for the years ahead. Johnson spent a weekend at Taliesin in September 1945.[219] The rapprochement between the two continued into 1946 as Johnson informed Hitchcock in describing his early studies for his house in New Canaan, which was "turning out half Persius, half Wright. The Wright influence came from a two week stay the master made a month ago." Johnson pointed out, "We got along swell."[220]

Until Johnson's resignation from the Modern in 1954, and even in the years leading up to Wright's death in 1959, there was perhaps no one in the New York architectural world with whom he was closer, especially after Myers died in September 1947, and no one he fought with more vehemently (figure 4.40). "We don't have to see eye to eye to love each other do we?"[221] "I enjoy your intelligent, quiet company so much," Wright explained in 1946. "Seems to quiet me," he added.[222] Two major factors affected their every action: Johnson was gaining recognition as an architect as well as a curator, Wright was encountering numerous obstacles in what would become a sixteen-year campaign to build his masterwork, the Solomon R. Guggenheim Museum in Manhattan.

MAGNUM OPUS AND HOUSE IN THE GARDEN, 1947–49

On Johnson's return, he found that the museum had created a Department of Industrial Design in 1940 with the architect and industrial designer, Eliot Noyes, as director (1939–46). In 1948, Edgar Kaufmann Jr. replaced Noyes in that position. Kaufmann, whose major contribution to the museum had been the successful *Useful Objects Under Five Dollars* exhibition in 1938, found that he and Johnson shared an interest in Wright. In advance of what publicly was considered Wright's eightieth birthday in 1949, Kaufmann and Johnson independently conceived ambitious plans for the Modern to commemorate the event.

In 1947, Kaufmann Jr. met with Monroe Wheeler, the museum's publications director, to work out details to publish all of Wright's buildings and projects in large, color, deluxe format to rival the Wasmuth Verlag folios. Funding was to come from $5,000 donations from Kaufmann Sr., Loeb, Guggenheim, Alden Dow, and Herbert Johnson for a total of $25,000.[223] Kaufmann Jr. had informed Wright of the idea in 1946 and received the architect's enthusiastic encouragement.[224] Along with Kaufmann Sr., Loeb was the first to pledge, and he also agreed to solicit Guggenheim, Dow, and Johnson. With the exception of Dow, who was contemplating a smaller sum, the others declined.[225] Although this idea, what Wright began to call his magnum opus, would continue to be discussed up to the architect's death, especially by Kaufmann Jr., it never found support at the Modern.[226] Wright

4.40 Frank Lloyd Wright and Philip Johnson at Taliesin West, Scottsdale, Arizona, November 1948. Photograph by David Pleydell-Bouverie. (From *Architectural Review*, August 1949)

was remarkably prescient when he predicted in 1947 that such a publication would be "posthumous," and in reference to the museum, he concluded, "not under the present aegis—for which I am truly sorry. The 'Great Book' will probably be published as the others have been—'abroad.'"[227]

At the same time, Johnson informed Wright that he wanted to build a house of his design in the garden. The Midwest architect responded positively to the resurrection of his original 1939 idea—as yet unexecuted by the museum—for the location behind the Fifty-Third Street building, an opportunity made possible by a change in ownership. Although he had kept his plans confidential for months, Johnson told Wright it was "official" in August 1948.[228] To this announcement, Wright responded, "I never build too much on these casual conversations of ours. So I am surprised (and pleased) to know the long proposed 'House in the garden' is still proposed."[229] Johnson had been seeking financial support from "one or two trustees," especially Eliza Bliss Parkinson, and had plans to visit Taliesin West with Mrs. Parkinson for further discussion.[230] By March 1949 Johnson's concept had shifted to a proposal that was more permanent than an exhibition house, as he explained to Wright, "I do not want to build your house just for a season but to remain as a center of architecture for the entire region."[231] He was meeting with "representatives from two western department stores" to discuss "construction of your 19 foot wide house in their cities."[232]

Johnson was motivated to build "a house in the Museum Garden because the public is apathetic towards an exhibition of photographs of architecture," he explained. "A scale model increases their interest, but it is obvious that proportion and enclosed space cannot be shown except at full scale." In his report to the trustees in May 1948, Johnson wrote that the purpose was to demonstrate "how much good living can be purchased for how many dollars." The house was to be competitive as to "cost with any small, singly-built, architect-designed country house," but not with "mass-produced housing" or "prefabricated houses." In what was to be annual event, "a different famous architect of the modern field" would be selected for the task. For the first one in 1949, Marcel Breuer was chosen because "he is ... better equipped than his more famous colleague, Mr. Frank Lloyd Wright, who is not particularly interested in low cost building." To support this project, the five members of the Committee for the House in the Museum Garden, including Johnson and Mrs. Parkinson, each donated $5,000, the others were Goodwin, Goodyear, and Abby Rockefeller's daughter-in-law, Blanchette Rockefeller; the museum allocated $15,000 for overhead.[233]

Johnson kept the plan for the Breuer house confidential from Wright, but it was inevitable that he would find out (figure 4.41). When he read about it in the *New Yorker* in early March 1949, he acted characteristically, inquiring of Johnson, "why the museum prefers to present to the American people these very features and phraseology of my own under the name of one Marcel Breuer."[234] Johnson replied quite cordially, "Mr. Wright do not accuse me of dishonest enthusiasm for your work. I think all my friends and enemies will agree on its sincerity." Although he disagreed that Breuer was imitating the Usonian House, he suggested that if Wright thought so he should take it "as the sincerest form of flattery."[235] After several weeks, Wright responded, "I intended to follow up my explosive rancor with a honeyed word or two of a personal nature but my feeling is not inclined to change concerning the museum. I am through with it. So count me out of the court for life." He closed with a marginal note: "Phil ... how could you allow the museum to buy and *plug with Usonian language* that shanty town version from '33rd Street and the tracks' now in your garden. For Christ's sake—what a travesty."[236]

4.41 Marcel Breuer, House in the Museum Garden, Museum of Modern Art, New York, April 14–October 30, 1949. Photograph by Ezra Stoller. (© Ezra Stoller/Esto)

Despite Johnson's denials, there were several correspondences between the Breuer and Usonian Houses: it was designed "for a hypothetical suburban site approximately one acre in size," planned to be "subdivided into different zones of privacy and activity," constructed with "a standard wood frame" and a "concrete floor slab" containing "radiant heat," the exterior "finished with narrow vertical cypress siding," and "large plate glass areas in fixed frames connect the garden and the interior living area."[237] The program, which was conceived to continue on an annual basis, terminated after the second house by the Los Angeles architect, Gregory Ain, was built in 1950.[238]

The Breuer house was indicative of the major shift that had occurred in American modern architecture after World War II. While the first generation—Mies, Gropius, Neutra, and Breuer—were creating some of their major work, a second generation including Ain, Johnson, Eero Saarinen, I. M. Pei, Paul Rudolph, Harwell Hamilton Harris, Raphael Soriano, William Wurster, and the firm of Skidmore, Owings, and Merrill (SOM) were extending modern architecture domestically and commercially. The field that the Modern needed to address was wide as construction resumed vigorously in the late 1940s and early 1950s. It was within this context that the museum held several one-building Wright exhibitions, some the result of collaborations with others.

TALIESIN AND TALIESIN WEST: THE HOMES OF FRANK LLOYD WRIGHT, 1947

Taliesin and Taliesin West, exhibited from April 15 to June 15, 1947, originated with George Nelson, a *Forum* editor, and an employee of *Time* Inc. He had been advising the Department of Architecture for almost a decade and had worked closely with Wright on several magazine special issues. As an ardent admirer, he explained to Wright, "I used to want to see you and your work get as much favorable publicity as possible in the hope that more people might come to know what good architecture could be. I now think that publicity of any kind has only one use, and that is to provide new opportunities for you to build."[239] Living up to his word, Nelson proposed "a portfolio of pictures of Taliesin and the desert camp [Taliesin West]" in color to appear in the *Time* Inc. business magazine, *Fortune*, to illustrate that "the two most truly luxurious houses in America [are] owned, not by a soft drink tycoon but by an architect and that their luxury stems, not from expensive gadgetry, but from the underlying concept of living and the use of space and materials."[240]

The ten-page article, "Wright's Houses," appeared in the August 1946 *Fortune* as "Genius Americanus," number six in the series "Men of Adventure," with text by Nelson and photographs by Stoller.[241] There were several things wrong with the article, one of which was how it fit in with the magazine content. Wright seemed incongruous following other "Men of Adventure" previously profiled, such as Charles S. Davis, president of Borg-Warner Corporation, the automobile parts manufacturer, and Richard S. Reynolds, inventor of aluminum foil.[242] The biggest problem was the production of the magazine itself. The magazine was not primarily visual except for advertising, and, in the postwar shortages, was printed on various paper types. The illustrations, printed dark and muddy on very poor paper, were disappointing for Nelson, Wright, and Stoller since the originals were "beautiful kodachromes," 8 by 10 transparencies.[243] Stoller—who would become one of Wright's primary photographers in the 1950s, shooting numerous houses but also the SC Johnson Administration Building and Research Tower, the Herbert Johnson House, Florida Southern College, and Price Tower (1952–56; Bartlesville, Oklahoma)—applied his professional technique making the monumental postwar buildings of Mies, Johnson, Rudolph, Saarinen, Pei, and SOM icons of modern architecture.[244] Stoller believed that "there is only one kind of architectural photograph, and that is the one which conveys the architect's idea."[245] Stoller was famous for the amount of time he spent on an assignment consciously studying the building to replicate it in two dimensions, using "the quality of light, the perspective, the viewpoint, the relation to other objects, the instant of exposure, the distortion or lack of it, the color."[246] Stoller was a perfectionist, generally using a large-format camera that created very precise detail and clarity. "I think the reason I managed to hit it off with Mr. Wright," Stoller explained, "is because I got the point of what *he* was trying to do and I worked to that point—and sometimes, even exceeded it a little bit, which you can do."[247]

Color photography in a public display was new in the post-war period and an arrangement between the Modern and *Fortune* allowed sixteen of Stoller's thirty-eight 8 by 10 transparencies to be exhibited in four 4 foot by 4 foot wall-mounted lighting boxes in the Architecture and Design Gallery, and then on exhibit at the *Time-Life* Building for the summer, to be followed by a one-year tour organized by MoMA's Department of Circulating Exhibitions (figures 4.42–43).[248] Johnson asked Wright to provide two new up-to-date plans. It would be the first of a number of MoMA experiments in the ways color and 3-D photography could transform architectural exhibitions.

4.42 Taliesin III, Spring Green, Wisconsin, 1925–59. Photograph by Ezra Stoller. (© Ezra Stoller/Esto). This photograph appeared in the MoMA exhibition.

4.43 Taliesin West, Scottsdale, Arizona, 1938–59. Photograph by Ezra Stoller. (© Ezra Stoller/Esto). This photograph appeared in the MoMA exhibition.

4.44 New Theatre model with, *left to right*: Paton Price, Frank Lloyd Wright, and Henry-Russell Hitchcock, Hartford, Connecticut, 1949. (Rare Book and Manuscript Library, courtesy of University Archives, Columbia University in the City of New York)

4.45 New Theatre model, Hartford, Connecticut, 1948–49. (FLWFA, 4922.0004)

FRANK LLOYD WRIGHT: A NEW THEATRE, 1949

The third one-building show, *Frank Lloyd Wright: A New Theatre*, was on view from April 6 to April 17, 1949. When contacted by Paton Price (1916–82), acting coach and director of the Canton Summer Theatre, to build a theater for a site in Hartford, Connecticut, the architect based his plans on a 1931 unbuilt design for Woodstock, New York. Wright had spent many decades experimenting with the elimination of the traditional proscenium and the above-stage gridiron.[249]

To begin fund-raising, Francis Murphy, publisher of the *Hartford Times*, sponsored a luncheon at the Hartford Club on January 25, 1949, to host important politicians and theater people with Wright as the guest of honor and Hitchcock as the speaker (figure 4.44). Wright collaborated by writing a text for the publication of a brochure. During the planning of the luncheon, Charles Cunningham, director of the Wadsworth Atheneum Museum of Art, successor to Arthur "Chick" Austin, requested the scale model and four color renderings for a showing at the Hartford museum (figures 4.45–46). The exhibition was displayed from January 26 to February 27, when arrangements were made to travel to the Modern for a short period (figure 4.47). The Hartford theater was never built, Wright had to wait until 1958 when a modified version, the Kalita Humphreys Theater, went into construction in Dallas, Texas.

By the late 1940s, residential, commercial, and monumental public building production was increasing at such a rapid pace that the discourse surrounding the validity of modern architecture was resurrected. Lectures and essays were reminiscent of the arguments of the late 1920s and early 1930s, pitting many of the same protagonists against one another: Mumford versus Hitchcock, Wright versus Johnson. While the basis of the arguments was polemical, the intensity of feeling on both sides was often fueled by extraneous events.

Johnson had the opportunity to publicly acknowledge the prophetic nature of the 1932 *Modern Architecture* exhibition by producing two programs bringing the subject up to date after fifteen years: a Mies van der Rohe retrospective (September 16, 1947–January 25, 1948) and a symposium, "What Is Happening to Modern Architecture?" on February 11, 1948. The public museum program was quickly organized after Mumford challenged both Barr and Johnson with his assertion that the "California Bay Region style"—from Bernard Maybeck to William Wurster—was more universal than the "International Style" due to adaptations to regional conditions.[250] After the McAndrew-Mock years of pluralism, a return to polemics set the tone for the next five years.[251]

These two MoMA events did not involve Wright, but he took notice of them; while he did not attend the symposium—although Johnson invited him—he did attend the Mies opening.

4.46 New Theatre for Paton Price and Associates, Hartford, Connecticut, 1948–49.
Ink, colored pencil, and pencil on tracing paper, 19⅜ × 35½ in. (FLWFA, 4922.001)

4.47 *Frank Lloyd Wright: A New Theatre*, April 5–April 17, 1949. Museum of Modern Art, New York. Photograph by Soichi Sunami. (Photographic Archive. Museum of Modern Art, New York, New York, USA. Digital Image © The Museum of Modern Art/Licensed by SCALA/Art Resource, NY)

But what really caught his attention was the exhibition, *Louis H. Sullivan, 1856–1924*, held May 25 to July 25, 1948. Wright was in the completion stage of *Genius and the Mobocracy*, a book about Sullivan, which was excerpted in the June 1949 *Architectural Review*. He objected to the assertion that Sullivan's ideology was the basis for functionalism, which he equated with the "International Style." Taking the argument to the extreme, he opined that the claim was a fascist conspiracy against "Organic Architecture."[252] Johnson quickly rebutted Wright's accusations in an article, "The Frontiersman," in the August issue.[253] Johnson's ambivalent attitude was apparent in the final four pages of the article, where he illustrated an impressive pictorial homage to Taliesin West.

Wright and Johnson had developed a friendship outside the Modern during these years, and the sparring in public had taken its toll. Yet both men were practicing architects, and by the late 1940s each had produced a building that would permanently affect their relationship. On March 18, 1948, Johnson broke ground on a private residence for himself that would eventually become world famous: the Glass House.[254] He moved in and began sharing it publicly on December 31, 1949.[255] Wright took an instant dislike to Johnson's home and began using it to belittle him in private and in public. Without seeing it in person, Wright began to call it "a monkey house at the zoo ... the best place to study human nature."[256] To this Johnson sent a magnanimous letter on private stationery sincerely praising Taliesin West. On a visit in November when Johnson had the opportunity to "study the incredible effects ... the small spaces and the large; the vistas; the right angle turns; the shallow steps down and up. I must say it is a mystery to me, as it is I think to all architects, just exactly with what means you achieve the inexhaustible excitement. It is impossible to describe it; one can only feel it." Johnson told Wright that Taliesin West "was the greatest architectural experience in the western hemisphere."[257]

Wright was apparently moved by this tribute and responded by sending a one-sentence reply: "Our relationship needs house-cleaning."[258] Johnson replied on private stationery: "You are right. May I visit you?"[259] To this, Wright wrote: "I don't like to have your gore on my hands in my own house. But if you are willing to shed it—choose your own time."[260] It is not possible to know what measure of truce was worked out behind closed doors at Taliesin West.

Certainly, Wright had ideological differences with Johnson and felt let down, if not betrayed, by the cancellation—for the second time—of the house in the Sculpture Garden, but the voracity of his attacks in the years ahead can partly be explained by the circumstances surrounding the Guggenheim commission. By 1948, progress had slowed to a standstill as Guggenheim, at eighty-seven years old, was ill, which eventuated in his death on November 3, 1949. What followed was several years of uncertainty as the reorganization of the Guggenheim Foundation took place: rumors were rampant that competing interests wanted the project canceled; the architect dedicated himself relentlessly, even feverishly, to finding allies on the board; plans were revised and revised yet again. In spring 1952, the Guggenheim Foundation applied for a building permit; Wright anticipated that the structural and formal character of the building would be a challenge to New York City regulations. He was correct. By fall, the permit was rejected due to fifteen code violations, and Wright formulated a battle plan to address the Board of Standards and Appeals. In order to realize his dream, ten years in the making, Wright was in a struggle throughout 1953. The court of public opinion had condemned the museum design, while others praised it, including the Modern, which requested a one-building exhibition.[261] The Guggenheim commission was what brought Wright to New York more and more frequently during the late 1940s and steadily throughout the 1950s; he was sensitive, bordering on paranoia, about how his reputation was shaped in that city depending on the progress, or lack of progress, toward construction. In his eyes, it was one factor in whether or not the Guggenheim Museum would be built.[262]

FRANK LLOYD WRIGHT: BUILDINGS FOR JOHNSON'S WAX, 1952

The last one-building Wright exhibition, *Frank Lloyd Wright: Buildings for Johnson's Wax*, held from January 16 to March 16, 1952, was a departure from previous MoMA Wright shows in several respects. First, it was conceived and organized by Arthur Drexler (1925–1987), who had been hired by Johnson as curator in his department in 1951. No doubt in an effort to find more innovative ways to present the spatial qualities of architecture to the general public, Drexler mounted a show of 3-D color slides of the SC Johnson Administration Building and Research Tower (tower completed in 1950). Dubbing the exhibition a "peep show," thirty-eight individual Stereo Realist viewers were set up in a darkened gallery giving museum visitors "a startlingly realistic 'grand tour'" of Wright's structures, including dramatic day and night views. Drexler had worked closely with David White Sales Company in Milwaukee (manufacturers of the new equipment), its engineer, Richard Bills, and a Racine photographer to document the entire corporate complex.[263] The introductory wall panel stated, "Powerful and genuinely monumental, these buildings have also the easy—almost playful—exuberance of detail, and the variety of architectural space, characteristic of Wright's greatest work."[264] Although Wright had difficulty saying anything positive about the Modern at this time, much later, he revealed the impact this exhibition had on him. He stated plainly, "I think the only photograph that can be made of architecture is three-dimensional. This recent stereoscopic photograph. It's the only way you can get that third dimension. In the kind of architecture that I represent, it's that dimension—the depth—that gives it quality and effect. . . . So I've never been much interested in photographs of my work until . . . this third-dimension process came in. . . . Now you can get a photograph of a building that will really give you the experience of being in that building."[265]

Unfortunately, MoMA was never aware of Wright's approval of this technique; this show caused a flurry of anguished letters back and forth between Johnson and Wright. Wright ordered the museum to return or destroy "whatever photographs . . . drawings, models, writings etc." that it was using "without due authorization from me in writing" because the architect had "no desire to be hung out on the line with the wash at any museum anywhere."[266] Johnson explained the concept of the exhibition in a cooperative tone and assured Wright that he would have approval of each image.[267] Wright's reply revealed some self-reflection when he explained: "So the answer is yes. . . . I am sick of having you for an enemy anyway Phil. When someone you've liked much gets into that category the feeling is unwholesome. . . . You once wrote me a note that warmed my heart toward you. The ambiguity of the letter and following events I ascribed to the ambiguity of your position—a practicing architect eligible for a job sitting in judgment upon his competitors in a public place. A hypocrite was bound to that issue, Philip. I guess you have thought it over and came to a decision on your account. The loss of a friend is more and more serious to me as I grow up. I always deplored your loss. Even if you were phony you were agreeable and interesting to me." He closed, "Let's be friendly again."[268] This détente, however, was short-lived. The highlight of the coming 1952/53 winter season was planned as a twentieth anniversary commemoration of the *Modern Architecture* exhibition.

BUILT IN USA: POST-WAR ARCHITECTURE, 1953

For the second *Built in USA* exhibition, held January 20 to March 15, 1953, great care was taken "to make the final selections as representative as possible of current expert opinion." To that end, the museum appointed an Advisory Committee of twelve members including three editors of *Magazine of Building* (formerly *Architectural Forum*), two editors each of *Architectural Record* and *Progressive Architecture*, Entenza of *Arts and Architecture*, Hamlin of Columbia University, Hudnut of Harvard, G. Holmes Perkins of the University of Pennsylvania, and Elizabeth Mock Kassler. All the nominations were submitted to Hitchcock, who, using the criteria of "quality and significance of the moment," made the final choice of forty-three buildings constructed between 1945 and 1952. The installation featured conventional elements such as large photographs, scale models, and text panels, but also innovations such as 3-D color slides and large-scale photomurals (figures 4.48–49). Of the photomurals, the introductory wall panel, 14 feet high by 20 feet wide, was of the SC Johnson Research Tower, and there were four 10-foot-high photomurals of 860–880 Lake Shore Drive (1949–51; Chicago) by Mies, the United Nations Secretariat (1947–52; New York) by Wallace K. Harrison and consultants, Lever House (1950–52; New York) by SOM, and General Motors Technical Center (1949–55; Warren, Michigan) by Saarinen, Saarinen and Associates. A 128-page hardback book with a color photograph of the SC Johnson Research Tower by Stoller as the frontispiece, 189 black-and-white photographs, a preface by Johnson, introduction

4.48 *Built in USA: Post-war Architecture*, January 20–March 15, 1953. Photograph by David E. Scherman. (Museum of Modern Art, New York. Photographic Archive. Museum of Modern Art, New York, New York, USA. Digital Image © The Museum of Modern Art). Enlarged photographs of SC Johnson Research Tower and V. C. Morris Gift Shop.

by Hitchcock, and the principal essay by Drexler was produced by Thames and Hudson in England.

Wright was represented with four works, more than any other architect: the V. C. Morris Gift Shop (1948–49; San Francisco), Herbert Jacobs House II (1943–48; Middleton, Wisconsin), Sol Friedman House (1948; Pleasantville, New York), and the SC Johnson Research Tower (figures 4.50–53). Mies was second with three buildings: 860–880 Lake Shore Drive Apartments, Edith Farnsworth House (1945–51; Plano, Illinois), and the Boiler Plant at Illinois Institute of Technology (1945–50; Chicago). Gropius and Breuer were included along with their former students from the Harvard Graduate School of Design: Edward Larrabee Barnes, Paul Rudolph, and Johnson. Three of the architects were related directly or indirectly to Wright and "Organic Architecture"—his son Lloyd Wright, former Taliesin Fellow Paolo Soleri, and Paul Schweikher (Schweikher and Elting). Although architects trained and practicing in the Northeast predominated, there was evident variety in the California work of Ain, Soriano, Charles (and Ray, uncredited) Eames, Gardner Dailey, and Maynard Lyndon.

Two months in advance of the opening, Wright found out about the show and initiated the usual procedure: He wanted to be removed. Johnson reacted as usual: It was too late; the book was printed. Johnson, nevertheless, pleaded, "Please, please, dear Mr. Wright, do not be too angry. There is no use trying to have a Department of Architecture in the Museum without your good wishes."[269] But with the opening and during the run of the exhibition, matters began to escalate until the debate erupted into the public arena. First, Harrison, a museum trustee and an

4.49 *Built in USA: Post-war Architecture*, January 20–March 15, 1953. Photograph by David E. Scherman. (Museum of Modern Art, New York. Photographic Archive. Museum of Modern Art, New York, New York, USA. Digital Image © The Museum of Modern Art)

4.50 V. C. Morris Gift Shop, San Francisco, California, 1948–49. Photograph by Maynard L. Parker. (Courtesy of the Huntington Library, San Marino, California). This photograph appeared in the 1953 MoMA exhibition.

4.51 Solar Hemicycle, Herbert Jacobs House II, Middleton, Wisconsin, 1943–48. Photograph by Ezra Stoller. (© Ezra Stoller/Esto). This photograph appeared in the 1953 MoMA exhibition.

4.52 Toyhill, Sol Friedman House, Pleasantville, New York, 1948–49. Photograph by Ezra Stoller. (© Ezra Stoller/Esto). This photograph appeared in the 1953 MoMA exhibition.

architect represented in the exhibition, sent a formal letter inviting Wright and his wife "to a dinner to be given in the Museum Penthouse" for "a private preview and to meet some of the other leaders in the field concerned." To this, Wright shot back, "Dear Wally: Too far away. In every sense. But Belthazzer [Balthazar] will be there."[270]

Wright focused on Hitchcock as the key figure behind the exhibition and wrote him a two-page diatribe rehashing familiar arguments: "Where is the brain behind those whiskers? Have just read your specious American Bauhaus rationalizations ... just published by the 'Haus.' There (in the 'Haus') is undoubtedly where you belong. I nominate you for Director." Revealing some bitterness and hurt feelings, he admitted, "I never felt you were quite comfortable with me because you were never sure of what I was all about." And his fears about the future of his Guggenheim Museum commission: "go see the 'corkscrew museum': Bauhaus epithet of the neophyte Drexler to help me build the new Museum? This word for the opus shows how much the Bauhaus really wants to see that building built." He ended with the maudlin, "So, au revoir, Russell ... I have loved thee in my fashion. You are back there again where you belong because on that level you can believe. ... Affection, nevertheless—"[271]

Wright was propelled not only back to 1932, as might be expected, but to 1893 when he believed the classicism of the Chicago World's Columbian Exposition had put an end to "the modern movement then led by Louis Sullivan." Very much in

4.53 SC Johnson Research Tower, Racine, Wisconsin, 1943–50. Photograph by Ezra Stoller. (© Ezra Stoller/Esto). This photograph was reproduced in the 1953 MoMA catalog.

the heat of the moment, he composed a rebuttal, "In the Cause of Architecture: 'The International Style,'" which started out as a rant but was softened through several edits over the next few months. The first version was self-published in February 1953 by the Taliesin Press in an occasional series of broadsides that Wright circulated privately. The essay reprised themes from *Genius and the Mobocracy*, but with pointed barbs at the Modern: "We do not like much of what we see or any of what we read in 'Post-war Architecture.'"[272] As a jab to the academics on the jury, he wrote, "A main point of vantage for 'internationalism,' or any such propaganda for a style that might become the fashion, lies in 'collectivism.' Collectivism as taught in architecture by our schools—schools themselves an eclecticism just below the general level of universal imitation. Collectivism serves either totalitarian or communist but can never serve democracy because it is merely a conditioning, not an enlightening, of the herd instinct."[273] Using inflammatory language of the Cold War era, he began to equate the idea of the "International Style" with Communism. "Communism (factual religion of collectivism), once established," Wright declared, "the sun of creation goes down."[274]

In the past, this is where the discourse would have ended, but what happened next was extraordinary in the annals of Wright's ideological clashes with the Modern: someone of influence agreed with him in public. Not since Mumford in the 1930s or Myers in the 1940s had a person with a platform sympathized with his ideas so unreservedly. In the April issue of *House Beautiful*, editor Elizabeth Gordon wrote in "The Threat to the Next America," in obvious reference to Mies's Farnsworth House and Johnson's Glass House, "The much touted all-glass cube of International Style architecture is perhaps the most unlivable type of home for man since he descended from the tree and entered a cave."[275] In words that echoed Wright's own of years before, she stated, "International Stylists and Bauhaus designers have had beyond a doubt the best publicists in the market place. They promise more and perform less than any school of design in history."[276] Like Wright, Gordon carried the argument one step further into political insinuations. "For if we can be sold on accepting dictators in matters of taste and how our homes are to be ordered, our minds are certainly well prepared to accept dictators in other departments of life." Wright's heart probably warmed to every paragraph of Gordon's illustrated article, which ran to five pages, except she only mentioned him in passing as a precursor, and instead put Edward Wormley, a modernist furniture designer, forward as "the answer to bad modern design."[277]

"Surprised and delighted," Wright telegraphed Gordon. "Did not know you had it in you. From now on at your service. Sending you the latest from my standpoint." The telegram was signed "Godfather."[278] Wright followed up with a letter, which he worked over in several drafts, where he paraphrased Mumford by saying, "Why have you been describing the play of Hamlet with Hamlet left out."[279] This was quickly changed; Wright had acquired a new editor and new magazine as an outlet for his opinions.[280] Gordon immediately accepted his article for *House Beautiful* and proceeded with production. Wright must have been having second thoughts because he now wanted the language toned down: "I must not attack and belittle the architects involved *but attack the promotion behind them* .... If we are to succeed there must appear neither bitterness nor jealousy."[281]

"Frank Lloyd Wright Speaks Up," his original article substantially revised, ran for four pages in the July 1953 issue, but, nevertheless, containing sentences such as "The 'International Style,' an architectural *ism*, at first no more than a 'chic' notion, is becoming, by the efforts of its gulled converts, an evil crusade."[282] Wright continued, "About twenty years ago, in the shadow cast upon modern organic architecture by the then new Museum of Modern Art, the 'International Style' was named ... this confluence of equivocal minds and circumstances now is identifiable as a sinister attempt to repeat the betrayal of American organic architecture in the way the Chicago World's Fair of '93 did it to the modern movement led by Louis Sullivan."[283]

By this time, an abbreviated version of the same essay had appeared in the "Opinion" section of the June issue of *Architectural Record*.[284] At this point, the museum decided to act, although Johnson remained silent publicly. On June 19, MoMA issued a press release that was published in the September *Record* and elsewhere that carried a statement by Rene d'Harnoncourt, who had become director in 1949.[285] Defending charges of an "evil crusade" and "totalitarianism," he called for "factual clarification." After enumerating the number of MoMA exhibitions accorded to Wright, the statement pointed out that in *Post-war Architecture*, "Mr. Wright was given the place of honor which he deserves." With the great tact that was his signature, d'Harnoncourt concluded, "We strongly deny the sinister motives Mr. Wright ascribes to the International Style and we will, of course, continue to present the work of the architects who carry on its tradition together with distinguished work by other architects. By the same token, Mr. Wright's attacks will not diminish our admiration for him as a great artist and builder."[286] This statement coming from a source that Wright knew and respected inspired him to reply to d'Harnoncourt privately.[287]

The architect attributed his explosion to three phrases in the exhibition catalog. First, Hitchcock's sentence, "Twenty years ago, ... Wright's work seemed so differently conceived from that of the Europeans ... that it could be considered *passé*."[288] Johnson in the preface writing, "*Every building* in this book *would look different if it had not been for the International Style*."[289] And Drexler's statement, "But in respect of fantasy no building even approaches the marvelous *concrete corkscrew* Frank Lloyd Wright has planned for New York City's Museum of Non-Objective Art."[290] As Wright explained, "[The book] is written as though modern architecture began with the International Style." While his tone to d'Harnoncourt was respectful, he did insert some colorful jibes, such as "the Museum has been liberal in its use of me as window-dressing for its international impregnation 'a la Bauhaus.' Too blatantly false for me now." But he was simmering with another incontrovertible objection that obviously referred to Johnson, without naming him: "No position of trust should be administered by a self-interested practicing architect, himself building manifest imitations credited to Mies. As I take it, a high-class museum is supposed to impartially hold up to 'them asses' the noblest truth of being available in whatever line—not the petty personal addictions of any individual." Closing with his warmest greeting—Affection—he ended, "My soul is not yet so narrow nor am I so mean that I can not know either gratitude or shame, though the kind of life we are now asked to lead leaves little room for either."[291]

After this confrontation, unlike those of the past, there were lasting consequences. The result of all this proselytizing was that by the end of the year Johnson resigned from the Modern, later crediting Wright's influence with his decision, and within a year he was aiding Mies on the design of the Seagram Building (1954–58; New York) on Park Avenue.[292] Wright's association with the museum, lasting just over twenty years, was at an end, perhaps by mutual consent. But the Midwest architect still had something to prove and he already was formulating a plan to do so. As his relationship with MoMA had been deteriorating over the previous five years, the largest exhibition of his work ever mounted was successfully touring Europe. He had one more destination in mind: he decided to bring it to Manhattan. He was planning a blockbuster. This time he would prove something to MoMA, but not with words, this time it was through construction: a Usonian House built from the ground up and fully furnished on Fifth Avenue.

While Wright believed that MoMA's Department of Architecture and Design was promoting the ideology of the European avant-garde to the exclusion of any other point of view—most especially his own—he was incorrect. Architectural programming at the Modern during the years 1933 to 1953 was pluralistic, reflecting the shifting priorities and circumstances of the museum. The original principals of the 1932 *Modern Architecture* exhibition—Barr, Hitchcock, and Johnson—had diminished influence over time as Barr was demoted, Hitchcock participated depending on his academic schedule, and Johnson moved back and forth between the foreground and the background. The groundwork for the exhibition had taken place during the prosperous years of the late 1920s—the tenets were already codified by 1930—but, the crisis of the Great Depression influenced the mood of the country toward nationalism. Within this context, McAndrew and Mock shifted primary focus away from aestheticizing in an exploration of vernacular architecture, regional identity, social housing, and community planning as important themes in their presentation of modern architecture. Acting as mediators between Wright and the public, their interpretation was less doctrinaire and more inclusive than their predecessors.' Although he never staged a Wright exhibition, Kaufmann Jr., a former Taliesin Fellow, was a significant ally at the Modern, first with his proposal to publish an illustrated Wright catalogue raisonné and then with his popular booklets on modern design aimed at the general public.[293]

Some exhibitions came about as a result of the initiatives of trustees: Goodyear and Goodwin, for example.[294] A long-standing approach in the Department of Architecture after 1934 was the creation of Advisory Committees, which reviewed and approved exhibition proposals, or, in the case of the two American surveys of 1944 and 1953, the work was selected through balloting. While there was an understandable bias toward the Northeast, by the 1940s buildings across America were featured; during the McAndrew-Mock era, regional identity became one of the hallmarks of programming. Alliances with outside sponsors—trade and shelter magazines, such as *Ladies' Home Journal* and *Fortune*—broadened the type of subject matter that was presented. And, of course, the Modern exhibited more of Wright's work than any other architect or designer up to the time of his death. A review of MoMA's exhibitions and publications, including the Circulating Exhibitions Department, for the two decades of 1933–53 reveals that rather than being primarily elitist the Modern was shaping popular taste by its efforts to educate and convert the general public no less than members of the social register and the art world, business and industrial leaders to modernism as design consumers at home and in their communities.[295]

In truth, Wright was more interested—fixated would be a more accurate term—with the "International Style" than almost anyone at the Modern with the exception of Johnson. In the exhibition catalog, *Built in USA: Post-war Architecture*, the term was only mentioned once. In the preface, Johnson wrote: "The International Style which Henry-Russell Hitchcock's book of 1932 heralded has ripened, spread and been absorbed by the wide stream of historical progress. Every building in this book would look different if it had not been for the International Style, yet few buildings today recall the rigorous patterns of those days—the cubic boxes with asymmetric window arrangements so characteristic of the twenties." He concluded, "With the mid-century modern architecture has come of age."[296] By 1953, as both Johnson and Wright had become "media" stars, the competition between the two fueled their debates over ideology.

When MoMA embarked on an architecture component in 1932, modern architecture was the inevitable label. Wright, needing to differentiate himself from competing architects and movements, completely ignored the term but was forced to adopt a label himself. Although Wright wrote continuously about "Organic Architecture," a clear definition eluded him. Variously it was simply equated with his work or that of Sullivan, but in his reference to principles they were so obscure, and sometimes inconsistent, confusion resulted. Wright sensed this in mid-1953 and issued another broadside, "Organic Architecture," listing nine terms in an attempt to clarify his ideas. The first line was "Organic (or intrinsic) architecture is the free architecture of ideal democracy."[297] Except for his own buildings, he never referred to any other work after Sullivan's death as "Organic Architecture." In his debate about the 1953 exhibition, he did not claim either the Wayfarers Chapel (1949–51; Palos Verdes, California) by his son, Lloyd Wright, or the Desert House (1950–51; Cave Creek, Arizona) by his former apprentices, Paolo Soleri and Mark Mills, as examples of "Organic Architecture."

The most cogent argument on the subject came from Hitchcock, "The International Style Twenty Years After," in the August 1951 *Architectural Record*, which Wright either read or with which he was familiar.[298] In an indirect reference to Wright, the historian wrote, "The chaos of eclecticism served to give the very idea of style a bad name in the estimation of the first modern architects of the end of the nineteenth and the beginning of the twentieth century."[299] This was clearly Wright's position. Hitchcock was willing to concede that, "The idea of modern style should remain ... somewhat loose. ... To attempt to dismiss style altogether is culturally ingenuous; it is also Utopian, or more accurately, millennial (in one sense at least, there were no 'styles' in the Garden of Eden!)."[300] Hitchcock's last sentence really was his last word, "The living architecture of the twentieth century may well be called merely 'modern.' "[301]

While the critical discourse on modern architecture was never resolved in Wright's favor, he did benefit immeasurably, as an artist-architect, from display in a museological setting. Exhibitions were a major way people came to know about Wright because his interiors were not included in any museum collections at that time; even after *In the Nature of Materials* was published in 1942, books were few (the 1938 and 1948 issues of *Architectural Forum* were significant, but limited in their readership); and cultural tourism in the United States had yet to become a factor with the public, or even with critics.[302] What is clear is that technology began to offer multiple ways to escape the limitations of simulacra. There was a conscious effort at the Modern to simulate the three-dimensional experience of architecture: every improvement was investigated as technology developed during the post–World War II years. Black-and-white photographs grew in size from 20 square inches up to photomurals 14 by 20 feet; large-format color transparencies were introduced both by Wright in the 1940–41 retrospective and by Stoller in the 1947 *Taliesin and Taliesin West* show; Drexler took the next logical step by experimenting with stereo slides of the SC Johnson Administration Building and Research Tower in 1952. By the late 1940s, photography was more important for Wright exhibitions than drawings, which posed an additional problem. Who now was the hero of Wright's work: the architect as creator or the famous photographer with the instantly recognizable two-dimensional image?[303] The ultimate solution—to build a full-scale building in a museum setting—was adopted by the Modern, but eluded Wright, temporarily.

CHAPTER 5

The Italian Exhibition and *Sixty Years of Living Architecture*, 1948–56

In 1949 when Frank Lloyd Wright learned about a proposal for a career retrospective in Italy, the invitation came at an opportune time (figure 5.1). He was nearing the height of his career and was beginning the end of his relationship with the Museum of Modern Art in New York, which had been the primary venue for his architectural exhibitions since 1932. The broad outline for what became the largest Wright exhibition ever mounted during his lifetime has long been known, but numerous aspects of the origins and preparations have remained unknown.

THE "ITALIAN EXHIBITION," 1948–51

What Wright affectionately called the "Italian exhibition" opened on June 24, 1951, under the sponsorship of the city of Florence and the Studio Italiano di Storia dell'arte (Italian Institute of Art History) at La Strozzina, a gallery housed in a splendid example of Renaissance architecture, the fifteenth-century Palazzo Strozzi, after a preview at Gimbel Brothers Department Store in Philadelphia in January and February. It was extraordinary that the idea of the exhibition originated in Italy due to the political and economic conditions affecting that nation after World War II. Italy was at a crossroads between revolution and restoration; the result of the war was a dramatic reduction in the production of both agricultural and manufactured goods affecting the monetary system, which caused severe hardship throughout the country. With rampant inflation and the devaluation of the currency—the lira—many reforms were difficult to sustain. However, with the advent of the American Marshall Plan in 1948–49, stabilization began to replace the era of struggle and conflict, although the lira would not recover its prewar value for many more years. It was during this postwar period of turmoil that three major political parties became dominant: Socialists, Christian Democrats, and Communists. While the Christian Democrats enjoyed the backing of the Vatican, Italy was home to the largest Communist Party in the Western world.[1] The proposal to hold a Wright exhibition was the idea of Carlo Ludovico Ragghianti (1910–1987), a man of unbounded ambition and extraordinary productivity. Born in Lucca, he was strongly influenced at an early age by his father, a builder and designer, who instilled in him a steadfast opposition to Fascism and an admiration for democracy. He studied literature at the University of Pisa, where he was introduced to the writings of the philosopher Benedetto Croce (1866–1952), and the German theoretician, Konrad Fiedler (1841–1895). As a result of this exposure, Ragghianti developed his philological approach to the visual arts—painting, sculpture, architecture, photography, and film—which he called "figurative prose." After moving to Rome to attend graduate school in art history, he met, among others, Bruno Zevi, the architect, with whom he remained close for the remainder of his life.

During the war years, he was active in the underground movement against the regime of Benito Mussolini, ultimately becoming a founder of the Partito d'Azione (Action Party), which resulted in his direct involvement in the insurrection and liberation of Florence in late summer 1944.[2] In 1945, he served briefly as undersecretary of fine arts at the Education Ministry during

5.1 Frank Lloyd Wright in his Studio in front of the The Call Building model no. 2 made for the 1940 MoMA retrospective, Taliesin, Spring Green, Wisconsin, 1947. Photograph by Pedro E. Guerrero. (© 2017 Pedro E. Guerrero Archives). This photograph was chosen for the introductory photomural for the "Italian exhibition."

the Ferruccio Parri administration, at which time he established an Urban Planning Office, appointing Zevi as director.[3] In the years following the war, Ragghianti took on many roles simultaneously, which was characteristic of his career. He became a tenured faculty member of the Literature and Philosophy Department at the University of Pisa, where he taught medieval and modern art as well as art theory, historiography, film, performing arts, museology, architecture, and urban planning.[4] As a permanent resident of Florence, he became involved in plans for the reconstruction of the city after the destruction by the retreating German army. In this effort, he first collaborated with the architect Edoardo Detti (1913–1984), who later became one of his advisors on exhibitions at the Palazzo Strozzi.[5]

By 1947, Ragghianti, under the auspices of his Italian Institute of Art History, created—in cooperation with the Communist mayor, Mario Fabiani, city of Florence, who served as president—La Strozzina, an artistic and cultural center to stage "an unbroken series of exhibitions of ancient and modern figurative art" at the Palazzo Strozzi. Ragghianti intended from the outset to also feature architecture by making "a series of shows (two or three per year) dedicated to important personalities of international architecture, such as Wright, Le Corbusier, Neutra, Sullivan, Mies van der Rohe, etc." By late 1948, he had chosen Wright as the subject of the first architectural exhibition, roughly slated for February–June 1949, and he turned to Zevi, the foremost Italian authority on the American architect, to collaborate.[6] Ragghianti had conceptualized the exhibition with Zevi in the lead as he explained to him at the beginning: "you shall make the catalogue, you will have the reins, make suggestions, recommend appropriate action. Institute [of Art History] is the promoter, but Zevi the implementer."[7]

Zevi, born in Rome in 1918 of an aristocratic Jewish family, grew up under the dictatorship of Mussolini. While a student at the Faculty of Architecture, University of Rome, he was influenced, as was Ragghianti, by Benedetto Croce's stance against Italian Fascism. From this time until the end of World War II, Zevi's life was consumed by politics, and architecture became a tool in the battle against tyranny. At the time of the enactment of anti-Semitic laws in 1938, Zevi left Italy to become part of the resistance abroad: first, he went to London in 1939 to attend the Architectural Association School, then to the United States where he became a student at the Graduate School of Design (GSD), Harvard University. There he encountered two very strong forces of European modernism: Walter Gropius, the former director of the Bauhaus; and the Swiss critic Sigfried Giedion, whose 1938–39 Charles Eliot Norton lectures were being prepared for publication as the seminal book, *Space, Time, and Architecture: Growth of a New Tradition.*

Zevi disagreed with Giedion's argument on the development of modern architecture, specifically the importance he placed on the Bauhaus, and on Gropius specifically. Rather than relegating Wright to a supporting role, Zevi believed that the American architect's position was paramount. By the time he had completed his master's degree in 1941, Zevi decided to write his own book: *Verso un'architettura organica* (*Toward an Organic Architecture*, 1945). He declared, "I just translated *Space, Time, and Architecture*, making one single modification: I put the chapter on Frank Lloyd Wright after the one on Le Corbusier."[8] Zevi embraced "Organic Architecture" with its emphasis on the dynamic exploration of space, while condemning the "International Style" as a pernicious sterility. Like Wijdeveld before him, Zevi sought to promote Wright throughout Europe as the worthiest alternative to European modernism.

In 1943, Zevi returned to Europe, in company with other Italian partisans—including Alberto Tarchiani, the future ambassador to the United States—where he eventually joined Ragghianti as part of the Partito d'Azione with the goal of establishing a republic following the defeat of Mussolini. One difference between the Fascists and the Nazis after the war was that Fascist architects still remained in positions of power, including in the schools of architecture. After the liberation, Zevi sought to play a role in reconstructing Italy along democratic lines. He began his strategy by founding the Associazione per l'Architettura Organica (APAO: Association for Organic Architecture) and its publishing organ, the magazine *Metron.* In 1945, Zevi met Wright for the first time in New York, where he invited him to become a member of APAO while eliciting his cooperation in publishing a modest monograph of his built works. *Frank Lloyd Wright*, the first postwar Italian book on the American architect, was published in 1947.[9] Zevi shared Ragghianti's ideals, both politically and culturally; he was the obvious choice to help bring Wright to Florence.

With his proposal for a Wright manifestation, Ragghianti inaugurated one of the most ambitious and diplomatically complex international cultural events of the postwar era.[10] At the outset, he realized that due to economic privations and the devaluation of the lira, the city of Florence would only be able to cover the expenses of a catalog and the management and installation of the exhibition; thus, transportation and insurance costs, he strategized, would be borne by the United States government.[11] To this end, contact was made with the American consulate in Florence, specifically with the officer of the United States

Information Service (USIS), Marjorie Ferguson, and with Charles R. Morey, cultural attaché at the American embassy in Rome. As it turned out, it was on Ferguson's initiative that the crucial first steps were made.

What most of the parties involved anticipated, that the Italian exhibition would become an international event at the highest diplomatic level, ultimately became a superhuman struggle on the part of individuals on both sides of the Atlantic that led to a clash of cultures, ultimatums, and misunderstandings that threatened the cancellation of the entire enterprise at the last minute. But from January until April 1949, sincere efforts to seek financial support from private American sponsors and the State Department were pursued with mixed results. Success with the former, failure with the latter.

PRELIMINARY PLANNING, JANUARY–APRIL 1949

Postwar conditions dictated novel and improvisational solutions to international cultural initiatives. Within a matter of months, private individuals, who were close associates of each other, but not in the inner circle of either the Italians or Wright, committed to make the exhibition a reality. It was the expediency of the solution that sabotaged Ragghianti's idealistic goals for his first architectural "manifestation" at the Palazzo Strozzi, but he was compelled by the circumstances to contact the Florentine American consulate, which set the process in motion.

Ferguson, who left Italy for three months in the United States in fall 1948, first contacted Helen Rogers Reid, owner and publisher of the *International Herald Tribune*. Ferguson was probably motivated by the fact that the newspaper employed Frederick Gutheim, Wisconsin-born architect and journalist, who had a long association with Wright beginning in 1928. His most well-known work was *Frank Lloyd Wright on Architecture* (1941), an anthology of the architect's writings. Reid contacted Gutheim in New York almost immediately. Gutheim, with a network of connections in the American architecture community, reached out to his close friend, Oscar Stonorov, who was responsive.[12]

As the Wright exhibition evolved over the planning period and later, it needed an organizer who was multilingual, familiar with major European capitals, experienced with standard American museum and trade publication practices, with a personality that was idealistic, patient, and tolerant of artistic temperament. Although he was ideally qualified, Stonorov would have been one of the last people Wright would have chosen for the job because he was closely associated with first-generation European modern architects. Born in Frankfurt, Germany, in 1905, he had studied at the University of Florence in 1924–25 and under the Swiss architect Karl Moser—whose son, Werner Moser, had been a Wright draftsman in the mid-1920s—at the Eidgenössische Technische Hochschule (ETH) in Zürich, 1925–28. In the late 1920s, he had opportunities to study sculpture with Aristide Maillol and associated himself with two of the founding members of the Congrès International d'Architecture Moderne (CIAM): André Lurçat and Le Corbusier. He worked in Lurçat's Paris studio, and along with Willy Boesiger, edited *Ihr gesamtes Werk von 1910–1929*, the 1930 German edition of the first volume of the complete works of Le Corbusier and Pierre Jeanneret.

After his immigration to America in 1929, he became known as a social activist concerned primarily with public housing, which brought him in contact with national figures such as Catherine Bauer. In this field, he is best known for the Carl Mackley Apartments (A Community Development for Hosiery Workers) in Philadelphia (1931–32), which adapted European ideas, particularly those of Le Corbusier.

The Modern recognized Stonorov in the early years of World War II when he became a partner of George Howe and Louis I. Kahn. He was well known to both Rudolph and Elizabeth Mock, Wright's former apprentices, as Stonorov, Kahn, and Mock had entered the Wheaton College Competition sponsored by MoMA in 1938.[13] As Howe, Stonorov, and Kahn, the firm received special notice from the museum when their housing project, Carver Court, in Coatesville, Pennsylvania, was exhibited in Betty Mock's *Built in USA: 1932–1944*. By this time, Stonorov had become known to two people who would be key figures in the Wright retrospective: Arthur C. Kaufmann, chief executive of Gimbel Brothers Department Store, and Ezra Stoller, the architectural photographer. By the end of the war years, as the partnership was ending, Stonorov was recognized for one of his most significant achievements, the organization of the exhibition *Better Philadelphia*, at Gimbels in 1947. It was the spectacular success of this enterprise, no doubt, that influenced Gutheim's judgment that Stonorov was the best person to plan the Wright retrospective.

In 1944, Stonorov had initiated a proposal to mount an exhibition with the prominent urban planner Edmund N. Bacon, to educate the Philadelphia populace. Kaufmann donated two floors of Gimbels as the venue for the civic endeavor. *Better Philadelphia*, which cost $340,000, was seen by 385,000 people in five weeks from September 8 until October 15, 1947. Often described as second only to Norman Bel Geddes's *Futurama* exhibit at the 1939 New York World's Fair, the Gimbels exhibition used multiple innovative display techniques:

three-dimensional models, a huge aerial photo map, movies, a diorama, murals, wall panels, cartoons, a full-scale model of a street corner, a recorded narrator with sound at each stage of the exhibition, and mechanical gadgets to communicate their complicated message. The centerpiece of the exhibition was a model of Philadelphia, 33 feet by 14 feet, divided into thirteen sections, which cost $50,000. Stoller's extensive photographs of the installation appeared in a twenty-four-page story in *Architectural Forum*.[14]

By the time Stonorov first heard of the Italian exhibition proposal, he and Kaufmann had a good working relationship of two years standing. Kaufmann, the cousin of Edgar Kaufmann Sr., Wright's client for Fallingwater, often supported civic and cultural institutions. He was well known as a benefactor not only in Philadelphia but also nationally.[15] He would have been the obvious first choice when Stonorov needed financial support for an international exhibition. One of the biggest hurdles was solved at the outset: Kaufmann agreed to finance the organization and fabrication, including the services of Stonorov as curator and designer, on the condition that the first showing would be at Gimbels prior to the departure for Florence. However, he added a crucial caveat: his financing did not include transportation and insurance costs outside the United States. This issue remained unresolved by both the Americans and Italians for two years right up to the closing of the Philadelphia exhibition.

Along with this obstacle, another equally vexing stumbling block was the State Department's detached attitude, which baffled and disappointed Kaufmann, Stonorov, and Gutheim but frustrated and nearly paralyzed Ragghianti and his supporters, including Ferguson and Morey. Kaufmann and Stonorov were seeking financial support for the additional costs, but also official recognition on the part of their government. Ragghianti's position was stronger, as he explained to Stonorov on January 12, 1951: the president of the Republic of Italy could not assume his customary role as patron without the president of the United States assuming the same position.[16] He repeated this protocol in March: "The Mayor of Florence as such can have as his equivalent Mr. Kaufmann and the American Committee, which has promoted the exhibition. However, to have the Italian government participate it stands to reason that on the part of the Americans, their government must be represented by people of similar status."[17] Diplomatic channels failed throughout the entire planning process. From the early correspondence, it is clear that both Ragghianti and Kaufmann strongly anticipated that the State Department would willingly accept a role. That assumption was completely wrong, causing bitter disappointment on both sides and ultimately precipitating a crisis at the last moment when the exhibition was ready to be shipped to Florence.[18]

Among the many letters documenting the problem with the State Department is a memorandum dated February 21, 1949, from Gutheim to Helen Reid: "Before Marjorie Ferguson returned to Italy last Thursday she learned [American] Ambassador [James] Dunn [in Rome] had sent a cable to the State Department stating that the Mayor of the city of Florence wished to invite Frank Lloyd Wright to send an exhibition of his work to be shown in the Institute of Art History, and seeking the assistance of the State Department in this project. The Italians were agreeable to paying all expenses that could be paid in lira. Mr. Dunn strongly endorsed the invitation and urged the Department to act on it immediately and favorably."[19] Gutheim then went on to explain why the State Department would not comply. He said he had learned that "the Department should not do anything that might be connected with the arts, in view of past unfavorable publicity in affairs of this sort," adding it should also "avoid placing itself in a position where it might be criticized for favoring any individual architect."[20]

The "Italian exhibition" played out against the backdrop of the Cold War. As several art historians have pointed out, the State Department had a controversial record in promotion of the arts abroad. It was still reeling from the aftermath of the 1946 touring exhibition, *Advancing American Art*, which included works by Arthur Dove, John Marin, Ben Shahn, and Georgia O'Keeffe among others. The collection of paintings, which had been purchased by the State Department, came under attack for their resemblance to "radicalism of the new trends in European art" and as such was regarded as "un-American," leading to suggestions that the artists' political backgrounds warranted investigation. The tour was aborted and the government sold the paintings in 1948. Serge Guilbaut, in his landmark study *How New York Stole the Idea of Modern Art: Abstract Expressionism, Freedom, and the Cold War*, pointed out, "after the failure of the traveling show 'Advancing American Art' in 1946, the administration preferred to bypass Congress by using such government agencies as the United States Information Service (USIS) to finance cultural ventures abroad."[21] Yet the USIS did not step forward with funding either. "The promotion abroad of American art and letters after 1946," the cultural critic Louis Menand explained, "required a delicate form of intrigue between private institutions and government agencies."[22] The standoff continued throughout the entire two and one half years leading up to the opening of the exhibition in Philadelphia. A possible explanation has been given by Tom Braden, head of the International Organizations Division of the

Central Intelligence Agency during this period: "[The State Department] weren't with it, they didn't know how to use what they had, everything they did was third or fourth rate."[23]

If Cold War politics did not assume a foreground role in the Wright "Italian exhibition," they were clearly part of the background. Ragghianti and Zevi had been united throughout the war in their opposition to Mussolini's Fascism, taking a position of prodemocracy, which predisposed them to Wright.[24] There is also some evidence that Kaufmann's immediate willingness to finance the endeavor was due to his opposition to Italian Communism, which posed a threat to the Western allies, especially the United States.[25]

AGREEMENT REACHED IN FLORENCE, MAY 1949

With the question of additional funding from the American or Italian governments unresolved, plans for the exhibition began to stall in spring 1949, but the decision to proceed was made on May 23 when Kaufmann used the opportunity of his annual trip to Europe to meet with Ragghianti, Ferguson, and Fabiani in the mayor's office in Florence. According to a two-page memorandum drafted by Ragghianti, the Italians set forth seven major requirements, which explained how they intended the exhibition to be realized. The major point was the creation of dual national committees: the first would be "honorary," consisting of "heads of both states or by the foreign ministers," the second was "responsible," with Kaufmann at the head of the American committee matched by Fabiani, and the last, charged with the organization, was the executive, the heads of which were unnamed, but eventually became Stonorov and Zevi. The date was reset "between March and May 1950" to coordinate a "congress of the adherents of modern architecture ... to give major scope and an appreciative background to the honor bestowed upon Wright." Kaufmann was to assume costs in the United States while the Italians agreed to cover expenses in Florence, but payment for transportation was left unresolved because the details were still unknown. Lastly, the Italians wanted "the exhibition ... shown in Florence exclusively, and this should also be understood for the rest of Europe."[26]

After seven months of deliberations, matters began to move rapidly. The Italian press was notified immediately, and the story broke the next day in the Roman daily, *Il Globo*.[27] The last person to be informed was Wright. Stonorov met with him in Washington, DC, on May 26, where, after the architect agreed to cooperate, he was informed that requests had already been received for the exhibition to tour European cities.[28] When Ragghianti was notified a few months later that Wright was in favor of touring, he capitulated.[29]

It is probable that Ragghianti had never contemplated that an American outsider would be invited to curate, organize, and design the exhibition. The appointment of Stonorov was unplanned and left the Italians removed from direct involvement with Wright and from the content and form of the exhibition.

Zevi shared Ragghianti's idealistic view of the exhibition, which they both believed should be directed at Italian and European architects, students, scholars, and the public with the purpose of using Wright's work to initiate discourse on contemporary issues of postwar modernism. To this end, Ragghianti and Zevi were in agreement that an international conference, in cooperation with other European associations, with Wright in attendance, should be the centerpiece of the exhibition.[30] Ragghianti pursued this idea with Stonorov after he was informed Wright would travel to Florence. "I am enormously glad that Mr. Wright has the intention to come to Florence. ... As I have written you already, he can have an official invitation from the government, from the city and cultural organizations. I beg you to remember that we have every desire to give this manifestation the greatest background, which includes a congress of architects and students of modern architecture. It should be to Mr. Wright the homage of Italian culture."[31]

Unfortunately, this was another point of the Italian initiative that was never realized. There were several reasons why the international congress did not materialize: CIAM had met in Italy in 1949 and was slated for another country in 1951. On the local level, the architecture faculty of the University of Florence refused to be involved with the plans due to lingering resentments over past conflicts with Ragghianti.[32]

Ragghianti was not the only person who had to accommodate himself to Stonorov. Wright, for only the second time in his life, was willingly turning over control of a major retrospective. Yet his circumstances were entirely different than they had been with John McAndrew in 1940, when he finally pushed him aside at the last minute. In 1949, Wright's practice had burgeoned in the postwar economy and after several fallow decades, he was taking advantage of every commission. In addition to construction of the Unitarian Church (1948–51; Madison, Wisconsin); the SC Johnson Research Tower; the V. C. Morris Gift Shop; and continuous work on the Guggenheim Museum and Florida Southern College; there were five houses in construction, thirteen buildings with completed drawings about to start construction, and twenty-two new buildings (mostly houses) on the drafting boards.[33] As a result of Wright's preoccupation with his practice, the organization of the "Italian exhibition" would depart radically from Wright's previous method: it would be planned and executed by an outsider. However, it appeared that unless he compromised with Kaufmann's sponsorship and accepted Stonorov's position, there would be no "Italian exhibition." In the months and years ahead when misunderstandings arose and communication was lax, Wright's resentment would eventually surface and erupt in explosions of temper.

EXHIBITION PLANNING, JUNE 1949–JANUARY 1951

On Stonorov's first meeting with Wright June 2–4 at Taliesin, he arrived in company with Gutheim. "The old gentleman is quite excited about the Italian show," Stonorov reported to Ferguson, "but not quite so sure about the exhibition at Gimbels because of his apprehension about commercial exploitation." Wright also felt that his foundation was entitled to a $25,000 donation from Kaufmann supporting its efforts in preparing the exhibition material.[34] Stonorov began planning almost immediately, if not on paper, at least in his mind. His first impressions were captured in brief notes jotted down in the pages of his diary: "FLW—The man, The landscape, His life, His looks/Poetry, Sentiment, Structure, Scale/creator-architect, inventor (gadget for living), engineer (steel, concrete). Universality (to remain), sentiment. Houses make love to trees and grow."[35] He elaborated in a letter to the Wrights on June 13: "the exhibition that I have in mind is not an enumeration of the buildings of Frank Lloyd Wright arranged either chronologically or according to subject matter ... [Stonorov ellipsis] The exhibition that I envisage is one of atmosphere. The *quality* of the kind of democratic life that can be created with the work of Frank Lloyd Wright: not in terms of making so many little Wrights, but in terms of the substance of the heritage that is extant." "It must be the authority of esoteric knowledge pervading the presentation of your work," he concluded, "nobility that is unavailable to imitation, but perceivable to instinct—quality of essence, not of degree. Since leaving Taliesin I have, of course, been unable to think of anything else but of how I am going to do it."[36]

Wright agreed to the exhibition on the condition that Stonorov would work directly with him and that all details would meet his approval. Up to the opening in Philadelphia, Stonorov made four trips to confer with Wright; the first three were to Taliesin in Wisconsin and the last was to Taliesin West in Arizona. The first in August 1949 with Kaufmann was a meeting where broad guidelines—"150 panels 4-foot by 8-foot and 8-foot by 8-foot, some 15 large models"—were established.[37] Following this meeting, Stonorov went to Italy for the last two weeks of September to inform Ragghianti, Zevi, Morey, Detti, and Ferguson of the progress to date. In addition to discussing logistics (financing, transportation, committees), Stonorov apparently gave a summary of the exhibition content as it had developed after consultation with Wright. Evidently, early in the planning process, Wright had again proposed the inclusion of an exhibition Usonian House, which would be demountable for travel from Philadelphia to Florence (this component, while accepted, was scaled down when it was installed at Gimbel Brothers Department Store in 1951). The last three trips occurred as progress was being made toward completion. The first, in June 1950, was to refine the general scheme for the exhibition; the second, in November 1950, was to present the design and selection of material; and the last, January 1951, just a couple of weeks before the Philadelphia opening, was to receive Wright's final approval and to make last minute changes and additions.

One of the reasons the Italian exhibition is the most complex of Wright's career is because of the four major principals—Wright, Stonorov, Zevi, and Ragghianti—each, at one time or the other, wanted to be the curator. As it turned out, circumstances dictated that Wright and Stonorov collaborate; while Zevi, no doubt, not wanting to confront Wright or challenge Stonorov, moved to the background, ultimately taking responsibility for publications in Italy. Ragghianti, while occupied with organizing a major Etruscan exhibition parallel with the Wright planning, ultimately came to the conclusion that he was the only person who understood Wright's architecture once he saw the material in Florence. While both Ragghianti and Zevi originally intended to employ a historical and critical methodology to elucidate Wright's modernity emerging from the context of nineteenth-century American historicism, the architect himself imposed his own personal exhibition on Stonorov, emphasizing his architectural innovations, thus contributing to the substantial mythification of his career.[38]

Stonorov's original intentions were captured in a memorandum in which he sketched out a tripartite division for the show.[39] The first of his sections was titled "When Frank Lloyd Wright started his own practice in 1893, the architecture in the United States looked like this." Stonorov wanted to stress: "It was Sullivan who started Wright on his way, therefore show some of the main points of Sullivan's work, which Wright took and developed further." When Stonorov proposed this idea to Wright, he vetoed the major thrust of the inquiry by turning it around;

5.2 "Potpourri," Frank Lloyd Wright, Palazzo Strozzi, Florence, Italy, June 24, 1951. (FLWFA, 6808.0010). *Left to right*: Bruno Zevi, Count Carlo Sforza, Wright.

5.3 "Point of Departure," Frank Lloyd Wright, Ahoy'gebouw, Rotterdam, Holland, July–August 1952. (FLWFA, 1047.041–3a)

instead of showing lines of similarity between his work and Sullivan's, he instead sought to show exactly how his work differed from his Lieber Meister.

The Italians argued against Wright's viewpoint when Stonorov informed them in Rome in September 1949. They responded by repeating a need for "examination in a specific way about the historical part in the Wright exhibition relating to the requirements of the Italian and European public to understand Wright's position in American architecture." "It is agreed," Ragghianti insisted, "that Mr. Wright should be advised of this requirement."[40]

Despite this plea, when exhibited in Florence, this section was reduced to two photomurals: the first, "Potpourri," a photographic montage of the 1893 Chicago World's Columbian Exposition; the second, a photograph of the Guaranty Building (1896; Buffalo, New York), titled "Point of Departure" (figures 5.2–3). Wright prefaced the latter with a statement: "To clear up lines of departure that mark my own work as distinguished from Lieber Meister's, it was thought expedient to show more of the master's work as 'opener' for this exhibition of mine. I objected." In an effort to assert his superiority over Sullivan, he explained, "In any careful study of his work . . . you may see that Lieber Meister cared little or nothing about either the Machine or (outside Terra Cotta) the Nature of Materials." While he acknowledged that the Guaranty Building "became [Sullivan's] greatest contribution to the architecture of the period," he was intent on pointing out that in comparison with his Larkin Building in the same city, "The nature of materials worked into a building by way of the machine was my thesis not his." He concluded by indirectly staking a claim over Le Corbusier as well, when he boasted, "The Larkin Building was the first AFFIRMATIVE PROTESTANT. I wrote beneath its publication in the *Architectural Record* published in 1908—three years after it was designed, 'Here again most of the critic's architecture has been left out. Therefore the work may have the same claim to consideration as a work of art as an ocean liner, a locomotive, or a battleship.' "[41] Wright was staking a claim on his preeminence in the vanguard of Machine Age modernism.

The second section in Stonorov's outline certainly had greater appeal for the architect, "With this background Frank Lloyd Wright laid the cornerstones of modern architecture." However, within this section, Stonorov sought to provide some clarifying interpretation by distilling "the basic theory of his architecture" into "fundamental principles," described as simplicity, style, individuality, and sense of materials and their use. This section never materialized, likely due to the fact that Wright dominated the planning process. As it evolved, Stonorov's last section focused on Wright's buildings and projects, but here again Stonorov put emphasis on interpretation by choosing to exhibit works "so that the things which were new about them, the definite contributions to a new concept of architecture would be emphasized." As it turned out, on this point Wright and Stonorov agreed.

FRANK LLOYD WRIGHT'S OUTLINE

In response to Stonorov's proposal, probably at the first meeting in June 1949, Wright evidently was prompted to rough out a handwritten draft of an outline. His proposal is extremely revealing for a number of reasons, because it is a thematic narrative set within a strictly chronological framework. It also was tripartite with the middle segment causing the architect much confusion over dates and choice of important ideas and buildings. It is fascinating, as it records Wright's first immediate impressions on the subject; considerable editing reveals notable additions and some curious exclusions. And finally, the exhibition as organized bore a closer resemblance to Wright's outline than to anything Stonorov or the Italians proposed.[42]

1889 THE SCENE page 29 *Genius and the Mob* (Gold Coast houses—apartment houses etc, Old Board of Trade, Boyington, Pullman Bldg—S. S. Beman, Palmer House, Potter Palmer Residence)

1893 THE BREAKTHROUGH (Auditorium and Wainwright, The Guarantee [*sic*], Dining Room—Auditorium, Charnley, and Harlan) AND THE DISASTER (Columbian Fair)

1900 THE FOLLOW UP (In the Nature of Materials/Prairie Houses—Willets [*sic*], unit system, Quad, Dana etc.)

1901 THE SPACE CONCEPTS (The Free Plan, ~~Unity Temple, Prairie Houses)~~

1906 THE FIRST NEGATION PROTESTANT (LARKIN BLDG, FLAT ROOFS BUILDINGS, GALE, ETC.)

1910 INFLUENCE UPON EUROPE (Visit Kuno Francke, Wasmuth Publications, Taliesin I)

~~1911~~ 1913 MIDWAY GARDENS, COONLEY KINDERGARTENS, Imperial Hotel, YAHARA BOATHOUSES ETC. Taliesin II

~~1919~~ 1921–1925 NEW MATERIALS Taliesin III, (Concrete Block Construction—L.A. Houses), St. Marks Tower, Automobile Objective, Elizabeth Noble, etc. Kaufman [*sic*] etc.

1925 UNIT SYSTEM, METAL FARM BLDG~~S~~

~~1932 BROADACRE CITY MODELED, STEEL HOUSES, TALIESIN WEST~~

1927–~~1934~~

1927–1930 (STEEL HOUSES) San Marcos in the Desert, Quadruple-Sun Tops, COTTAGES FOR DR. CHANDLER AND HIS CLIENTS

1934 CONCRETE HOUSES, TALIESIN FELLOWSHIP, BROADACRE CITY MODELED, USONIAN HOUSES

1940–1950 Huntington Hartford Sports Club, Pittsburg [*sic*]–Peoples Playground—Point Park—Scheme I and Scheme II, Guggenheim Memorial Museum, Kaufman (sic) Garage—Pittsburg [*sic*], USONIAN HOUSES, Morris Shop, USONIAN AUTOMATIC

He blocked out the first third of his career rather definitively and without hesitation, although he departed in a noteworthy way in some points from widely accepted art historical assessments. The first of the chronological segments covered the context Wright entered when he joined Adler and Sullivan. He referred to the work of William W. Boyington (1818–1898), who designed the Board of Trade Building (1885), and S. S. Beman, architect of the Pullman Building (1884, demolished in 1958). Thinking in terms of his recent book, *Genius and the Mobocracy* (1949), he made references to the eclectic taste for historic styles during the Victorian era, as exemplified in the Potter Palmer Mansion (1882–85) located in the Gold Coast neighborhood along Lake Michigan. This segment was not included in the exhibition as realized.

The next chronological sections continue Wright's mythification of the origins of modern architecture in Sullivan's buildings and his own early work. He singled out Adler and Sullivan's Wainwright Building (1890; Saint Louis, Missouri), Guaranty Building, and the dining room of the Auditorium Building (1887–89; Chicago) to illustrate the theme of achieving an artistic breakthrough, only to be curtailed by the triumph of Beaux-Arts classicism after 1893. The earliest designs Wright chose to highlight were the James Charnley (1891; Chicago) and Dr. Allison Harlan Houses, the only two examples out of the dozen or so designed while still with Adler and Sullivan. While the Charnley House is often cited as a seminal work, the Harlan House has never received equal critical attention (figure 5.4). Even though Stonorov told Wright directly that it was not needed, Wright persisted and it appeared near the entrance to the exhibition. Clearly, Wright believed the Harlan House was the first work that established his independent design ideas.

Wright then departed in method from the first two segments by dealing less with chronology and more with architectural themes. By choosing the dates of 1900, 1901, and 1906 as extremely significant, he placed greater weight on distilling the first principles of his era of experimentation. With some hesitation and even indecision, he finally settled on the ideas of materials, the unit system, the free plan, and flat roof buildings as his major achievements. His intent seemed directed at the European audience to establish proof of his validity as the originator of these concepts—those ideas either claimed by European

5.4 Dr. Allison Harlan House, Chicago, Illinois, 1891–92. (FLWFA, 9204.0014)

architects (such as the free plan of Le Corbusier) or admired by them—well before any European modern architect. So the fact that he chose Ward W. Willits (1902–3; Highland Park, Illinois), Susan Lawrence Dana, the Larkin Building, and Mrs. Thomas Gale House (1909; Oak Park, Illinois) over more widely regarded examples such as the Darwin D. Martin, Avery Coonley, and Robie Houses can be explained by his emphasis, not on the elaboration of an idea, but on the date of the origin of the idea. While the years 1901 and 1906 establish him as the sole originator of modern space and form, by the elimination of most of his buildings and projects of the decade, emphasis is put on an underlying unity of design and a singleness of purpose. The assumption being that the Coonley and Robie Houses were generated after a period of experimentation was drawing to a close by 1906.

Wright did not block out such a clear development for the middle period from 1911 until 1934 presenting problems of theme and chronology; in fact, he jotted down dates and buildings, only to edit them out, grappling with varying viewpoints. He refrained from emphasizing his more conservative and ornamented works while drawing attention to themes that were highly regarded by European modern architects such as new materials of concrete and steel. What is remarkable about this section, aside from the obvious lapses in dates (for instance, placing the Yahara Boathouse after 1913 and Edgar J. Kaufmann Sr. as a client before 1925), is the fact that he never mentions Fallingwater by name at any point in the chronology. Indeed, even Kaufmann Sr. as a client is jotted down almost as an afterthought.

The closing sections are more decisive concerning dates, yet again, it is noteworthy that the year 1936, which is generally acknowledged by critics and historians alike as the turning point in Wright's career—with commissions for Fallingwater, SC Johnson Administration Building, and the Herbert Jacobs House I—does not appear in Wright's outline. The last decade is notable for the flurry of excitement he conveys in the numerous current projects he lists.

Wright's intentions were clearly not concerned with historiography; he was not intent on documenting his own work in a linear chronological narrative. He was first concerned with ideas rather than with a presentation of critically recognized buildings. Indeed, in an unpublished conceptual sketch that Wright made over a floor plan of the Palazzo Strozzi, his attention was on what he called "The Big Idea, space conceives architecture." After devoting the first four rooms to "Early work, 1889" contrasted with the "American scene, 1889," he labeled the fifth room "1906." This is followed up by his exposition of the "Big Idea" in Room 6 as follows:

> The sense of human scale. The human figure as the norm.
> The Abolition of the Box.
> Act I Walls as Screens. Free space.
> Act II The Abolition of the Box. Move support from corner. Walls free (a screen) (cantilever) rethink construction.
> Act III Construction becomes an affair of screensing.
> (No basement. No attic.)
> The abolition of dead space either above or below the living space of the structure.
> Concept: New sense of a building as developing as Architecture from within outward.[43]

The exhibition plan, a collaboration between Stonorov and Wright, was presented to Ragghianti and Zevi in Rome September 26–27, 1949. Zevi, critical of Stonorov's organization of the exhibition because it portrayed Wright as isolated from his historical context, submitted his own outline to Ragghianti a week later.[44] Zevi's major contribution to the Florentine exhibition, which was not used, consisted of five thematic sections: The background behind Wright; the historical development of Wright's architecture; the main works; Wright, the man; Wright's influence, especially in Europe. Zevi's interpretation of the historical context of Wright's early career is significant, as it differed from prevailing interpretations. Zevi wanted to highlight American colonial houses, the Chicago school, the Bay Regional Style, the Charles Greene and Henry Greene brothers in California, and contemporaries of Wright, especially George Elmslie. In this section, he also sought to compare the Rationalism of the Chicago school with that of the European, "so that the visitor can become aware of the linguistic differences between European and American modern architecture." Zevi also stressed that the chronological divisions of Wright's career be treated equally with no weight given to one period over the other.[45] Zevi also suggested to Ragghianti that one of them ("possibly not me, given the many commitments I have this year") should go to Philadelphia to see the show to determine what additional material needed to be added for the comprehension of the Italians.[46]

Along with the failure to hold an international congress, Zevi's withdrawal from the direction of the show was probably the greatest Italian disappointment. A year later, it was clear the Italians would not have any direct input as no one made any attempt to travel to the United States to participate in the exhibition organization. When Ragghianti sensed Zevi's detachment, he felt compelled to scold him, "You have great qualities to organize an excellent thing. For our part, you will receive every possible help, but it is necessary that you do your part."[47]

With the Gimbel's preview set to open in January 1951, Stonorov was moving ahead on several fronts in the fall of 1950. First, he was pressing to receive from Taliesin all the original material in Philadelphia by early December. He was corresponding with Zevi about details for the Italian installation and proposed publications. Most importantly, he was pressing Ragghianti for a firm commitment to pay for the insurance and round-trip transport to Europe. On November 28, 1950, he wrote, "I have taken from your and Mayor Fabiani's letters that everything is settled in regards to transportation and insurance and have shown the letters to [Italian Ambassador] Tarchiani at our luncheon at Washington last month. Please let us not have any more complications in this respect." Lest Ragghianti still did not get the point after almost two years, Stonorov continued, "There is *no possibility* for Mr. Kaufmann to assume the cost of insurance. It has to be clearly understood that with handing over to the representative of the Italian embassy of all the exhibition material at the pier of New York, Mr. Kaufmann's responsibility will have ended."[48] Unfortunately, this did not settle the matter, and a crisis was looming.

However, to lighten the mood by showing his diplomatic side, Stonorov added on the next page, "Mr. Wright is very excited about the show in Florence and I have told him that you and I will see to it that the Piazza della Signoria will be cleared and surrounded by municipal police for the reception of Mr. Wright by the Mayor, and there will be formed a procession from the Signoria to the Palazzo Strozzi, in which will participate architects, dignitaries, abbots, bishops and archbishops and the ghosts of Bramante, Brunelleschi, Michel Angelo and the unfinished projects of Leonardo. There will be silver trumpets and ringing of the bells and a special performance of the Scoppio del Carro [Explosion of the Cart] fuori stagione [out of season]."[49]

WRIGHT THREATENS TO CANCEL THE EXHIBITION

By early December, when all the original material was delivered to Philadelphia, Stonorov's idealism began to get the better of him, precipitating a crisis that threatened to cancel the exhibition. Stonorov had entered into an agreement with Gerald Loeb to have the nine hundred drawings photographed in Philadelphia at Loeb's expense through his charitable organization. The agreement as stated in Loeb's letter to Stonorov, December 21, was to have all the negatives held by the Sidney S. Loeb Memorial Foundation until they could be donated to the University of California, Berkeley, under the supervision of William Wurster. From this nonprofit institution, "enlargements [would be made] available to other sources at cost, etc." "As to the second set," Loeb explained, "I'm quite agreeable for you ... to give those to Mr. Wright and the Fellowship as a Christmas gift or what have you, etc."[50]

Loeb's naïveté was evident when he announced to Stonorov, "As regards Frank Lloyd Wright, I'll write him and send you a copy of the letter telling him what we're doing and have the letter describe the arrangements that I made with you. As you told me yesterday, he's trusting this work to you and I'm sure that all these arrangements will meet with his complete approval."[51] Further, the fact that Loeb was taking charge seems clear when he added, "I'd rather handle, finance and manage the whole thing myself and do it in the way that I think will give these pictures the widest possible eventual distribution at the lowest conceivable cost. Later on, I'll go into the subject of how that might be accomplished with you and Mr. Wurster and I'm writing to him also."[52] The very same day, Loeb wrote Wright in a very amiable manner telling him the news. He informed him that Stonorov was bringing a set of prints as a Christmas gift and then added, "The negatives, however, ought to be kept in some safe vault where they are always available for posterity."[53]

Wright wasted no time in firing off a telegram: "Stop right where you are concerning negatives of my work. Taliesin is their only repository. Will credit your check on your unpaid architect's fee. Astonished by Stonorov's leniency and your gall. Your corkscrew is silly or are you just crazy."[54] By December 1950, Wright harbored resentment toward Loeb for past transgressions. In addition to the MoMA model, which Wright so disliked he eventually had it destroyed, he was smoldering over the fact that Loeb had not built the house he had designed. To make matters worse, *Progressive Architecture* had published in its December issue an addition that had been built on the same property, designed by Harwell Hamilton Harris. And even more insulting, on the last page of the same issue, drawings were reproduced for another addition by Loeb's nephew in the form of a circle that curled into itself, thus forming in Wright's mind the corkscrew shape.

The days leading up to the preview became hectic with telegrams and letters crisscrossing the country. Kaufmann was drawn in, but Stonorov took the brunt of Wright's anger. "Stop where you are with that Loeb steal of the negatives of my drawings," Wright wrote, "Astonished you would let him go so far without reference to me. You or I will repay Loeb or no show."[55] As Loeb finally explained to Wright the idea had originated with Douglas Haskell of *Architectural Forum*, who sought funds to underwrite a photographic record of Wright's drawings. "His idea," Loeb explained, "was that your work should be in a safe place in duplicate for posterity and next, it should be available to students, admirers and disciples who want to get copies."[56] Much to all their amazement, Wright shared none of their concerns about the future. "Posterity has always taken care of itself," Wright stated bluntly, "I am not interested." As to his former client, he added, "As a matter of course, Loeb's self interest stinks of a generosity that costs him none of it."[57]

Things could not have been worse for Stonorov. The crisis came at the moment he was installing the show at Gimbels, reviewing details for the gala preview opening night, pressuring Ragghianti to solve the insurance and transportation problem, fielding requests from Zevi for photographs for a large Wright book to precede the May exhibition, and juggling correspondence with venues in Zürich, Paris, and Munich to set up the next stops on the European tour.

On January 4, he received the following telegram from Wright: "Your idea of generosity purely commercial. Have never consciously released Kaufmanns and Gimbels responsibility to me for either you or any feature of my contribution to the Italian exhibition. Had no idea anything involved outside scope of exhibition nor any such intimation. Come and apologize and pay up."[58] With Stonorov's arrival at Taliesin West by January 11, the storm had passed and calm was restored when the Philadelphia architect issued instructions to turn over all the negatives and two sets of prints (the only ones made) to Wright as his sole property. On January 12, Wright telegraphed Kaufmann, "The Stonorov heart is in the right place but both his head and mine a little muddled. All now nice as a piece of pie at Taliesin Saturday evening. Affection."[59] Although the way was now clear for events to continue unimpeded, the drawing crisis was not forgotten in the months ahead. One set of prints was bound into six volumes, which Wright decided should be included in the exhibition. He began to call the volumes his "Magnum Opus."

In spite of the dramatic build-up, by all accounts the opening of the Gimbels preview went smoothly. Kaufmann, who had obviously looked forward to the occasion with great anticipation, planned an evening for five hundred people, as he explained, "from the fields of science and art, from education in its manifold and varied branches: philosophy, history, music; and not the least from that great art-science, *ARCHITECTURE*."[60] The dinner program contained a list of sponsors, but it consisted of Wright's personal choices, both living and dead, and did not reflect the diplomatic protocol the Italians had requested (figure 5.5). The group in the first category was made up of primarily international figures, who would be or had been instrumental in Wright's European exhibition tours, such as Wijdeveld, Zevi, Auguste Perret, and J.J.P. Oud. Of his apprentices, he acknowledged those

5.5 Dinner in honor of Frank Lloyd Wright, Gimbel Brothers Department Store, Philadelphia, Pennsylvania, January 25, 1951. (FLWFA, 6808.0040). *Left to right*: Unidentified man, Arthur C. Kaufmann, Frank Lloyd Wright, unidentified man.

before 1932: Moser, Klumb, Yen Liang, and Arato Endo. And of the Taliesin Fellowship only Mansinhji Rana. Among Americans, Wright singled out both Edgar Kaufmanns, father and son; Douglas Orr and Ralph Walker, past and present presidents of the American Institute of Architects, respectively. There was a separate listing of people who had supported the Italian exhibition: Reid, Gutheim, and Stonorov along with P. I. Prentice and Douglas Haskell, both of the *Architectural Forum*, which had published a special issue that served as a publication for the exhibition. Rounding out this group was Bernard F. Gimbel and George Howe, two important Philadelphia figures.[61]

CRISIS AT THE DOCK

As the days and weeks elapsed after the Philadelphia opening, the euphoria and goodwill began to fade as the unavoidable realities of sending the exhibition to Italy for the inauguration on May 26 became evident. Kaufmann had stated from the outset that Gimbels would not pay for transportation or insurance; on the other hand, the Italians repeated that they could not commit to a solution until they knew what the costs would be. Stonorov's letters to Ragghianti became more emphatic with each week. On February 14, 1951, he wrote, "Your letter was not very encouraging and thus it seems to me the whole exhibition is in jeopardy." After explaining that an additional sum of $2,000 was being spent on packing crates, he repeated, "Therefore the decision *to have or not to have* an exhibition must be made within one week: which means you will have to cable me immediately upon receipt of this letter."[62]

The situation began to heat up when Wright finally realized that Kaufmann was not going to finance any more expenses after the exhibition left Philadelphia, shifting responsibility to himself. "Neither the Italian Foreign Office," Stonorov reported to Wright on February 22, "nor the City of Florence, has any foreign funds to pay $1614.00 for insurance." That news was coupled with another deep disappointment: the Usonian House mock-up was not going to Europe, again due to costs.[63] Wright's reply to Stonorov reflected his frustration and distress. "There is an old Russian proverb which you might call to the attention of your employer and my benefactor," he began. "When you go the Whole Hog, pay the postage. The back of the Italian show is broken anyway with the promised house down and out. As for me . . . [Wright's ellipsis] send all the stuff to Taliesin and we will start again from there. Send the knock-down of the mock-up full size 'space' along with it. We will pay the extra cost. I suppose the equation is now finished so far as 'A.C.K.' is concerned? Too bad—! All this, of course, if the affair doesn't 'iron out.' " He then jotted in the margin, "I hope it may."[64] He followed up with a telegram to Kaufmann: "Too bad your generosity probably mistaken for commercial exploitation. Kindly send show back to place of origin."[65] In Kaufmann's response to Wright, his distrust came to the surface when he revealed his attitude about the Italians. "My experience with these foreign countries is that they are not beneath accepting anyone's generosity," Kaufmann confided, "especially the Americans'—which, if my memory serves me correctly, they have been receiving over a long period of years, and still have their hand out for more. The trouble simply is that they will not bestir themselves for anybody or anything. Another evidence of their lack of interest in this exhibition in general, is the fact that they sent no one over here to see the show. Wouldn't you think, after the stacks of correspondence which have gone forward and backward, that the least they would have done would be to find enough lira to pay for Professor Ragghianti or someone else to come to the show so as to get the full significance of it." He concluded, "As Oskar undoubtedly told you, he can arrange for private financing of the insurance, but even though we had our hearts set on it, it seems too bad to hand them the exhibition on a silver platter in view of their unenthusiastic and almost disinterested approach."[66]

As February 26 drew near, the closing day of the Philadelphia show, the exhibition proved to be a blockbuster with attendance figures topping 100,000.[67] Buoyed by such good news, Stonorov stepped forward to resolve the crisis. By now, he had spent over two years in planning and preparation and was already in serious discussions with officials in Paris, Zürich, and Munich to stage the exhibition. "I just couldn't let the thing go after the Italians fell down with the insurance," Stonorov explained to Wright, "so I arranged for some of my friends to contribute to your cause and was successful."[68]

But this did not end the crisis; attention was now shifted to the transport from New York to Florence. Everyone resumed their former positions: Wright wanted the exhibition canceled and the entire show returned to Taliesin, Kaufmann reiterated in a calm businesslike tone why his financial support stopped, and Stonorov fielded letters and telegrams back and forth in an effort to resolve the problems.

One month after the Philadelphia show closed, the Americans and the Italians were still talking past each other. Stonorov and Kaufmann were irate that the specific practical information about the transatlantic shipping was not forthcoming, coupled with the indifference they perceived on the part of the Italian ambassador. Stonorov informed Ragghianti that "the behavior of the Italian Embassy was less than helpful and it took all Mr. Kaufmann's and my patience to match our enthusiasm with the Ambassador's coldness and lack of understanding." He then went one step further when he suggested: "some small gesture on the part of the Italian government would be appreciated by all of us, and it seems to me that such a small gesture could be the invitation to Mr. Wright, Mr. Kaufmann, and myself to come to Italy at the expense of the government." He concluded "that it is not Mr. Kaufmann's job to ask for [patronage] of the American government," rather it was "up to the Italian Ambassador in Washington."[69]

In April, Zevi, who was in the United States for other purposes, met with Stonorov and Gutheim, who informed him of the misunderstandings between the Italians and Americans. Progress was made, however, when the crates were finally shipped out on the Italian steamship SS *Saturnia*, on April 28.[70] Kaufmann had been in Europe for several weeks while Stonorov departed for Naples, the port where the ship was scheduled to dock May 9–10, 1951.[71] But events took another unexpected turn when special municipal elections were called by the government, which necessitated postponing the opening until June 16. Both Kaufmann and Stonorov could not change their travel plans, thus insuring that neither one of them would be able to attend the opening ceremonies. However, before Stonorov left Florence, the mayor extended a special invitation to the June 16 inauguration, providing him with suitable housing.[72]

THE SPECTACLE IN ITALY

When the Wright event took place in Florence in June, it compromised Ragghianti's highly idealistic intentions for both the exhibition and the manifestation that surrounded Wright's personal appearance. The opening date, finally set for June 24, had changed three times in just a few months, upsetting the schedule. As a result, President Luigi Einaudi was unable to attend the ceremonies, which left Count Sforza as the highest-ranking dignitary representing the national government. Disappointment also surrounded the fact that President Harry Truman and Dean Acheson, secretary of state, were not on the Honorary Committee. In fact, contrary to protocol, the committees consisted almost entirely of Italians, with a few Americans, the highest rank of which was Ambassador James Clement Dunn.[73]

The last-minute postponements had both fortunate and unfortunate consequences. Stonorov spent almost three weeks in

5.6 "Introduction," Frank Lloyd Wright exhibition, Palazzo Strozzi, Florence, Italy, June 1951. Photograph by Ancillotti and Co., Milan. (From *Edilizia Moderna*, December 1951, Milan). Note plywood and red paint used in the panels.

Florence, certainly in close association with Ragghianti and Detti, installing the exhibition and handling other details in relation to the opening and publications.[74] Wright's early arrival meant he had more time in Italy and European cities such as London, Zürich, and Paris to meet with colleagues and supporters.[75] Due to the last-minute change in schedule, the principals—Stonorov, Wright, Ragghianti, Detti, and Zevi—were all, surprisingly, in Florence, at one time or the other, during the installation. While Stonorov had some power as the designer of the panel system, efforts were underway to undermine him. In late February, Wright wrote Zevi, "I would like you to be arbiter of the installation in Italy—where it was designed to appear."[76] Perhaps to avoid the confrontational role, Zevi did not comply with this dictate.

Since Wright appeared at the Palazzo Strozzi several days early, he had an opportunity to critique the installation. "A few hours after Wright's arrival in Florence, when he visited the exhibition and suggested some little variations," Zevi recalled, "Stonorov told him gently but firmly that nothing would be changed because it had been conceived as Wright's first posthumous exhibition, only the corpse was still alive."[77] Since Stonorov had designed the installation with a "lack of obvious display technique so that the feeling of the message is dominant," Detti had the ability to add elements to complement the details of the Renaissance interior (figure 5.6).[78] Wright observed, "The Florentines picked up the work with enthusiasm. . . . Oskar gave

5.7 Frank Lloyd Wright in Venice, Italy, with Carlo Scarpa at *right*, June 21, 1951. (FLWFA, 6808.0027)

general supervision and seemed much at home with the Italians."[79]

Instead of an international discourse on modern architecture and urbanism in postwar Europe, Wright's experience in Italy was one of pure spectacle. Zevi recalled, "in Florence nobody really cared about Wright, except for a few hundred people who came from all parts of the peninsula. But in Venice the Taliesin master was a popular myth because the school of architecture was composed of people with a passion for him."[80] Due to the change of dates, the festivities began on Thursday, June 21, at the fourteenth-century Palazzo Ducale (Doge's Palace), where he was awarded *honoris causa* (an honorary degree) from the Venetian School of Architecture in the Sala dei Pregadi.[81] In retrospect, Wright described this as the highlight of his trip, as enthusiastic admirers such as Zevi, Giuseppe Samonà (1898–1983), the director of the Istituto Universitario di Architettura (Venice School of Architecture), and, not the least, Carlo Scarpa (1906–1978), and young architecture students surrounded him (figure 5.7).

On Sunday, June 24, "approximately 500 specially invited people witnessed the ceremony in the Sala dei Dugento (Hall of the Two Hundred) of the Palazzo Vecchio," Stonorov recalled, "where Count Carlo Sforza awarded the architect a gold medal of the City of Florence, conferring honorary citizenship" (figure 5.8). And "over 3000 people stormed the Palazzo Strozzi at the opening hour behind gala uniformed Carabinieri as Sforza inaugurated the exhibition among all the medieval splendor that the City Council of Florence could lend it in the Palazzo della Signoria."[82] Wright then led Sforza; Ragghianti and his wife, Licia; Zevi; Detti; Stonorov; Olgivanna and Iovanna, his wife and daughter; and Kathryn Lewis, a client and good friend, on a personalized tour of the exhibition (figures 5.9–11).

Reflecting on what surely was a once-in-a-lifetime experience, Wright turned genuinely sentimental in a thank-you letter to Kaufmann. "It was exactly too bad that you should have missed the festivities opening the Italian show," he wrote. "It was truly warm and splendid. Dramatic. The Italians have taken the show

5.8 Count Carlo Sforza conducting ceremony awarding Wright a gold medal conferring Florentine honorary citizenship, Hall of the Two Hundred, Palazzo Vecchio, June 24, 1951. (FLWFA, 6808.0053). *Front row center, left to right*: Frank Lloyd Wright, Olgivanna Lloyd Wright, Kathryn Lewis, unidentified man, Iovanna Lloyd Wright; Oscar Stonorov is in the *second row* to the *left* of Wright.

5.11 Frank Lloyd Wright with volumes of *Life Work*, Frank Lloyd Wright exhibition, Palazzo Strozzi, June 24, 1951. (© Archivio Foto Locchi Firenze). *On the right*: Carlo Ludovico Ragghianti and Count Carlo Sforza.

5.9 Frank Lloyd Wright exhibition, Palazzo Strozzi, June 24, 1951. (Oscar Stonorov Papers, American Heritage Center, University of Wyoming). *Left to right*: Francesco Ragghianti, Carlo Ludovico Ragghianti, Bruno Zevi, Count Carlo Sforza, and Wright in front of Wilcox House panel.

5.10 Broadacre City model, Frank Lloyd Wright exhibition, Palazzo Strozzi, June 24, 1951. (Oscar Stonorov Papers, American Heritage Center, University of Wyoming). *Left to right*: Olgivanna Lloyd Wright, Frank Lloyd Wright, Bruno Zevi (partial view), Kathryn Lewis, Iovanna Lloyd Wright, Carlo Ludovico Ragghianti, Count Carlo Sforza, Oscar Stonorov, Licia Collobi Ragghianti.

to their hearts (Venice particularly) and it looks as well or better in the many tall rooms of the Strozzi as it did in Philadelphia." Yet he was not ignorant of some of the behind-the-scenes complications. "I now quite understand your desire to get out from under the Italian show," he confided. "There really was a mix-up in Italy. I was charmingly welcomed by a just-defeated communist Florentine 'sindaco' [mayor] and on leaving was bid good-bye in a similar manner by a Christian Democratic 'sindaco.' Everything was politically betwixt and between—up in the air—at the time you were looking for appreciative cooperation." But he graciously added, "You were remembered in the ceremonies."[83]

PALAZZO STROZZI, JUNE 1951

Description of the Florentine installation must be assembled from several sources. Photographs were taken the day of the opening ceremonies, and at the vernissage the night before, but they focus on Wright and his Italian hosts with the displays in the background. Two comprehensive documents match each other almost exactly: *Mostra di Frank Lloyd Wright, Palazzo Strozzi, Catalogo Itinerario, 24 giugno–settembre 1951*, which contains an annotated checklist that can be dated to a week to ten days before

5.12 Frank Lloyd Wright exhibition, Gimbel Brothers Department Store, Philadelphia, Pennsylvania, January–February 1951. (Oscar Stonorov Papers, American Heritage Center, University of Wyoming). *Left to right*: Larkin Administration Building, Coonley Playhouse, Little House II, The Call Building model no. 2, Robie House, Fallingwater, Unity Temple.

the opening, and a Stonorov plan sent to Ragghianti on February 14, 1951.[84]

It is unlikely Ragghianti and Detti would have edited the photomurals and models in light of Wright's presence, yet Ragghianti believed the exhibition as it was delivered was missing essential details. He stayed behind to refine the presentation while the others departed for Venice, as he explained to Zevi on June 20: "These last few days I have had very disappointing experiences, actually really tragic ones, since it is not just two or three people, but the majority who do not understand an absolute iota of Wright, and above all, they are not even faintly informed of the fact that Wright is a sort of Dante Alighieri, one of those geniuses who invents languages. Now, the texts that Stonorov provided for the show are totally useless, actually for their very nature they are even counterproductive, to the extent that I decided to keep them in English as they are and to have us place, instead, labels, a bit Froebelian, but more conducive to make the experts understand and for all the others to get a glimpse of the significance of the architecture of Wright."[85]

The Florentine show was the largest Wright exhibition, and possibly the largest one-man architecture retrospective, ever assembled, at a minimum consisting of nine hundred drawings and sixteen models. Stonorov designed it at the outset to travel to multiple cities; as a result, the panels were based on a four-foot modular system that could easily be made smaller if space were a premium and configured to fit a variety of room sizes and shapes. As the show appeared in Philadelphia, there were twenty-six wall-hung one-sided panels, forty-seven free-standing double-sided panels that could be grouped together, standing in a straight or zigzag line. On the panels were mounted enlarged photographs, original drawings, or blown-up text, as was the case for poetry excerpts (figures 5.12–14).

While Zevi had wanted an exhibition that put equal weight on each chronological period, the available models shifted the emphasis. Of the period before 1939, there were only four: The Call Building (1913), the larger wood model from 1940; St. Mark's Tower (1927–31); Davidson Farm Unit (1932); and Broadacre City (1935). Half dated from the 1940 MoMA retrospective: houses for Malcolm Willey I (1932), Herbert Johnson Wingspread (1937–39), Gregor Affleck (1940), Sidney Bazett (1939), Lloyd Lewis (1939–41), Ralph Jester (1938–39) and the housing developments Usonia I, Lansing, Michigan (1939) and the Suntop Homes, Ardmore, Pennsylvania (1938). The remainder included: Roy E. Peterson House (1941); the New Theatre, Hartford Connecticut (1948–49); Solomon R. Guggenheim Museum, the second model (1947),

5.13 Frank Lloyd Wright exhibition, Gimbel Brothers Department Store, Philadelphia, Pennsylvania, January–February 1951. (Oscar Stonorov Papers, American Heritage Center, University of Wyoming). Guggenheim Museum model no. 2 with torso fragment by Praxitiles and Wingspread photomural in *background*. Stonorov sculpted a head of Wright that he planned to pair with the Guggenheim model, but the bust had been damaged.

5.14 Frank Lloyd Wright exhibition, Gimbel Brothers Department Store, Philadelphia, Pennsylvania, January–February 1951. (Oscar Stonorov Papers, American Heritage Center, University of Wyoming). *Left to right*: New Theatre model (1948–49), Huntington Hartford Sports Club drawings, Lloyd Lewis House model, George Sturges House photographs.

the first model had been destroyed in shipping (figures 5.15–16 and figure B.47). Lastly, Wright made a small cutaway model of the Donald Schaberg House (1950), Okemos, Michigan.[86]

Wright had originally planned to bring the exhibition up to date with new models. From his more recent work he chose the Huntington Hartford Sports Club (1946–48; Los Angeles) and the David Wright House (1950–52; Phoenix, Arizona), which the architect preferred to call "How to Live in the Southwest." The proposal for these two models occurred in 1949 when Wright requested a $25,000 contribution. In the end, Kaufmann struck

5.15 Solomon R. Guggenheim Museum model no. 1, New York, 1945. Cutaway section, on display.
Photograph by Ezra Stoller. (© Ezra Stoller/Esto). In the *background*: Rudolf Bauer, "Pink Circle," 1938, oil, 51 × 61 in.

5.16 Fabrication of Solomon R. Guggenheim Museum model no. 1, 1945, model workshop, Taliesin, Spring Green, Wisconsin (Eric O'Malley/OAD Archives). *Left to right*, Burton Goodrich, John de Koven Hill, Douglas Lockwood, Beatrice Reik, and Lee Kawahara.

5.17 View into living room, Usonian Exhibition House, Frank Lloyd Wright exhibition, Gimbel Brothers Department Store, Philadelphia, Pennsylvania, January–February 1951. (Oscar Stonorov Papers, American Heritage Center, University of Wyoming)

a harder bargain and only donated $5,000, which allowed for refurbishing existing models and the creation of the Hartford model. The David Wright House model was eliminated at the preliminary stage. Wright decided to choose a friend, Max Moffett, as model maker, though living in Dublin, Ireland, who proceeded with fabrication throughout 1950.[87] The Huntington Hartford model was plagued with delays that continued right up to the opening in Italy.[88] In the end, the model was never exhibited at any of the venues, and its final whereabouts is unknown. It appears that Moffett failed to deliver.

Introducing a new exhibition technique, especially for a touring show, Wright called yet again for the construction of a full-scale, fully furnished Usonian House as a three-dimensional demonstration of his principles. His steadfast determination is revealed by this proposal as the Museum of Modern Art had denied him this essential exhibition component three times; first in 1940 as part of his retrospective exhibition, and again in 1949 and 1950 when Johnson had promised him the opportunity only to first give it to Breuer and then Ain.

As it turned out, the Usonian House would again become a subject of controversy. When it was installed in Philadelphia only a portion of a house was built: a living room with fireplace and a small bedroom (figure 5.17).[89] It was planned on a 30/60-degree module with walls of brick and glass French doors opening onto an exterior terrace. Although Wright had designed it to be "demountable," it was not sent to Italy as the cost was considered prohibitive. The installation also introduced sound and color, creating a dynamic visitor experience with seventeen color lantern slides by Stoller projected every two minutes onto a 10-by-12-foot screen, and a ten-minute audio recording played every hour of the architect explaining the concepts of Broadacre City over the model.

Stonorov admitted that he had departed from "a critical scholarly appraisal" in the organization of the exhibition in an attempt to create "a symphonic impression out of the wealth of [Wright's] work." Apparently in opposition to Ragghianti and Zevi, he wanted "a psychological exhibition," improvising "the very feeling, the very atmosphere of all Wright buildings in their curious consonance with each other through time and space" by "the modest use of elements of his architectural grammar in color, texture, juxtaposition of models and photographs in scale—physical or emotional."[90]

The exhibition, which took up eighteen rooms in the Palazzo, followed a linear chronological narrative. The earliest building shown was the James Charnley House (1891) and the latest was a Parking Garage Project (1949), Pittsburgh, commissioned by Edgar Kaufmann Sr. In between, projects and buildings were weighed in a ratio of 27 percent before 1932 and 73 percent after (not including views of Taliesin), even though the former represented forty-one years of work and the latter seventeen. Wright typically favored his most recent work in all of his exhibitions, but it was clear that

5.18 Frank Lloyd Wright exhibition, Ahoy'gebouw, Rotterdam, Holland, July–August 1952. (FLWFA, 1047.041-2a). Photomurals, *left to right*: Taliesin; Walt Whitman, "And Thou, America"; Frank Lloyd Wright at his Taliesin Studio; Taliesin West; "Work Song" by Frank Lloyd Wright.

in Florence after establishing his claim over the origins of modern architecture, he sought to emphasize that as an eighty-four-year-old architect, he was at the height of his powers and success.

Combining Wright's desire for a chronological and thematic narrative with Stonorov's goal to communicate something of Wright's "atmosphere," the visitor entered the galleries and faced the introduction, which consisted of a large portrait of the architect in white shirt and tie leaning over a drafting board with the The Call Building model towering above him (figure 5.18, and see figure 5.1). This photomural was flanked by three images: Taliesin and Taliesin West set in their surrounding landscapes, and Pedro E. Guerrero's image of apprentices in construction at Taliesin West.[91]

Beneath Wright's commanding portrait was a legend, "IN THE REALM OF IDEAS. TO YOU: THIS RECORD OF PATIENT RESEARCH AND GENUINE EXPERIMENT ACCORDING TO EXPERIENCE FAITHFUL TO THE NATURE OF WHATEVER WAS BEING DONE."

Literary associations were inserted in the introductory section with several carefully chosen excerpts from poetry. In addition to the full text of the 1896 "Work Song," there was Wright's favorite passage, "And Thou, America," stanzas five and six from Walt Whitman's "Song of the Universal," published in *Leaves of Grass* (1881–82), and an excerpt from William Wordsworth's dramatic poem *The Excursion* (1814). At the heart of both the Whitman and Wordsworth passages was a theory of Nature, which Wright always capitalized. To Wright and the Romantic poets, Nature meant something more than the outward world. It was Life, Soul, God. Wright looked upon matter as being animated by Spirit, as Wordsworth wrote, "an active principle," which "subsists in all things."[92] The following two rooms, which represented the period from 1900 to 1909, reveal Wright's reappraisal of his formative years as he sought to influence a European perception of his "creation of a new architectural language," as Ragghianti, who preferred to compare the architect with Dante, liked to think of it. His designs for Willits, Hickox, Thomas, Dana, and Ross proved that he had made crucial spatial discoveries before the movement of Cubism. For instance, in the *Catalogo Itinerario*, the Hickox caption stated

5.19 Frank Lloyd Wright exhibition, Ahoy'gebouw, Rotterdam, Holland, July–August 1952. (FLWFA 1047.041-9a). *Left to right*: SC Johnson Administration Building and Research Tower, Lloyd Lewis House model, Herbert Jacobs House I, Taliesin West, V. C. Morris Gift Shop.

that the plan showed the "free plan," which became part of Le Corbusier's theory twenty years later. To round out the display of Prairie Houses, panels containing blown-up photographs, floor plans, and original perspectives of the Dana, Robie, Martin, Coonley, Roberts, and Eugene A. Gilmore (1908; Madison, Wisconsin) Houses were exhibited. The modernity of this epoch was accentuated in several examples by blow-ups of the graphic black-and-white drawings made by Klumb and others for the 1930–31 tour.

There were three significant radical buildings included in these rooms: Yahara Boathouse, the Larkin Building, and the focal point, the towering The Call Building model no. 2. Unity Temple was grouped in the following room along with works that reflected experiments in materials of concrete and steel such as St. Mark's Tower, Midway Gardens, Imperial Hotel, the Barnsdall House, concluding with the early Usonian Houses such as Willey, Jacobs I, and Sidney Bazett. This room culminated with several large photomurals of Hedrich's iconic images of an Italian favorite: Fallingwater.

The next gallery contained the Broadacre City model, which was displayed beneath an elevated platform designed specifically so that the visitor would have a bird's-eye view (see figure 5.10). After the first four rooms, it was clear that Wright's career was being portrayed as a division between the "visionary/experimental" era and realizations of those ideas in built work; as a result, the 1940s was well documented. Along with the Usonian Houses shown at MoMA in 1940, the SC Johnson Administration Building and Research Tower was well represented with numerous large panels (figure 5.19). A darkened room was devoted to a continuous rear projection of large-format color slides by Stoller—Florida Southern College, SC Johnson Administration Building and Research Tower, Jacobs II, Friedman, Walter, and John Pew Houses; Taliesin and Taliesin West—changing every two minutes, on a 10-by-12-foot screen.[93]

The next five galleries took on the character of Wright's exhibitions at the Chicago Architectural Club: a review of his most recent work, 1947–50, in quantity. As well as Usonian Houses such as Herbert Jacobs II; Glen McCord (1948) and Ruth Keith

5.20 Sports Club for Huntington Hartford, Hollywood, California, 1946–48. John H. Howe, delineator. Graphite pencil and color pencil on white tracing paper, 35½ × 52 in. (FLWFA, 4731.020). This drawing appears in the installation view at Gimbel Brothers Department Store.

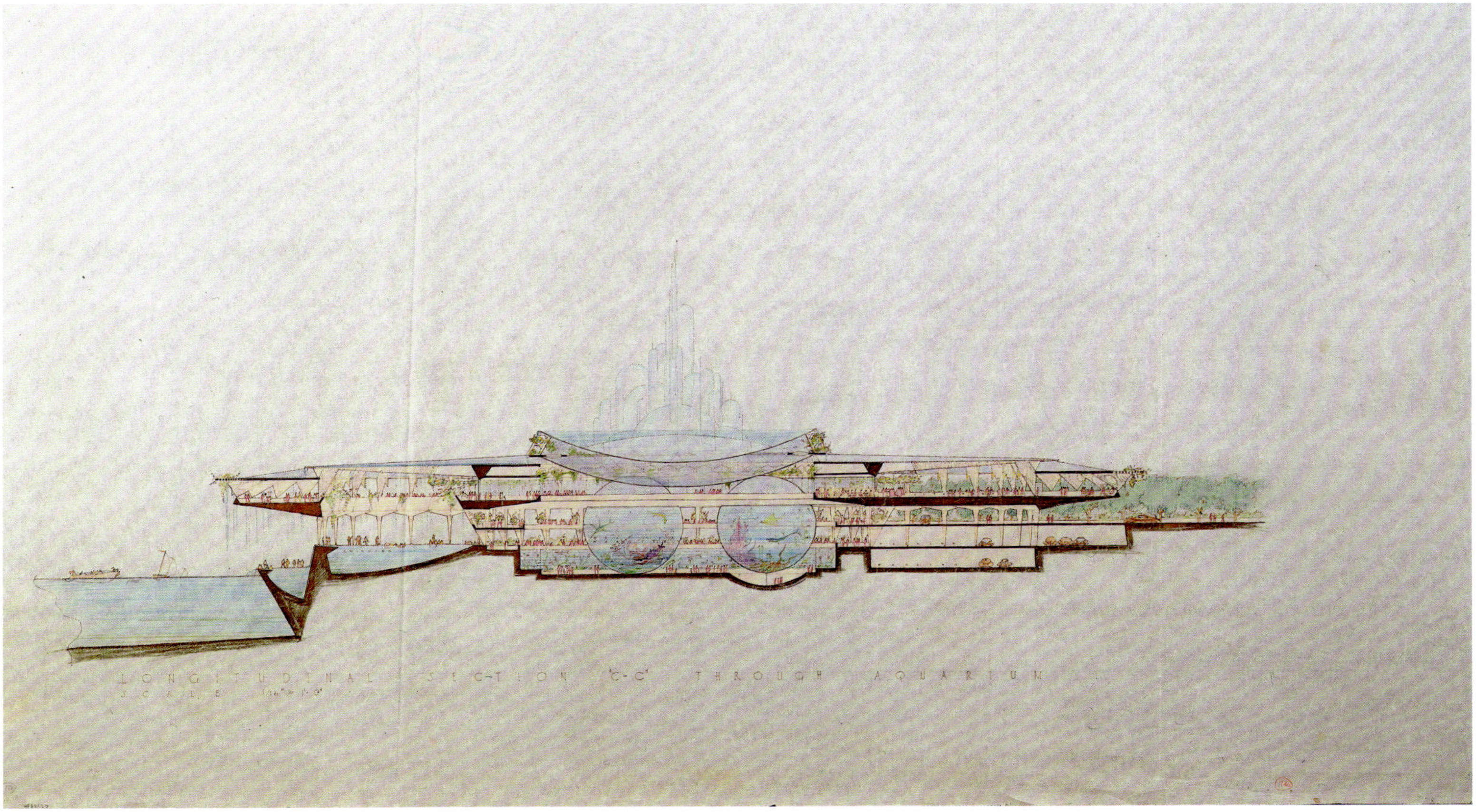

5.21 Pittsburgh Point Park Civic Center, Pittsburgh, Pennsylvania, 1947–48.
Graphite pencil and color pencil on tracing paper, 39 × 88 in. (FLWFA, 4821.027)

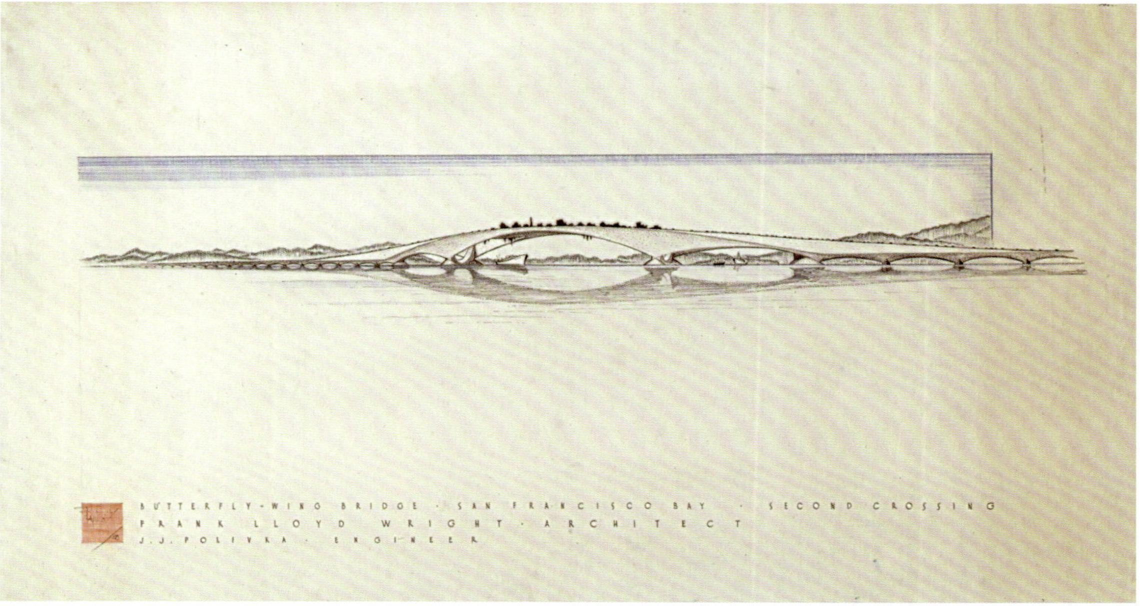

5.22 Rogers Lacy Hotel, Dallas, Texas, 1946–47. Graphite pencil, color pencil, and india ink on Japanese paper; ink and pencil on the verso, color on the recto, 30¾ × 42½ in. (FLWFA, 4606.003-600)

5.23 San Francisco Butterfly Bridge, San Francisco, California, 1949–53. John H. Howe, delineator. Ink, pencil, and color pencil on tracing paper, 23 × 42 in. (FLWFA, 4921.027)

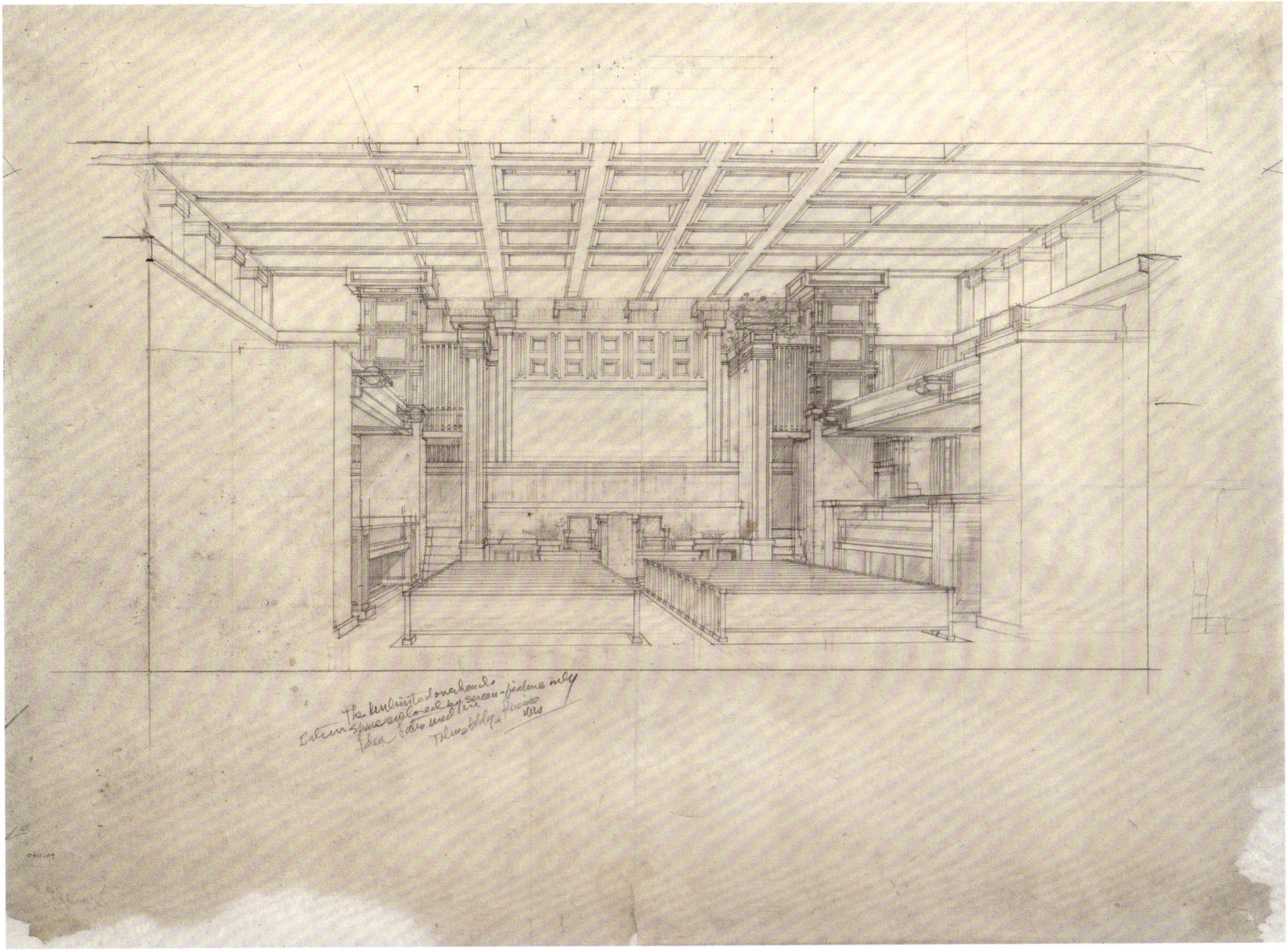

5.24 Unity Temple, Oak Park, Illinois, 1905–8. Pencil on tracing paper, 21 × 27 in. (FLWFA, 06011.009). Wright inscribed at lower left margin (probably in 1940–50s): "The unlimited overhead between space enclosed by screen *illegible* only. Idea later used in Johnson Bldg., Racine, Wis."

(1947), both Arlington, New Jersey; selections were made from Parkwyn Village (1947; Kalamazoo, Michigan) and Usonia II (1948; Pleasantville, New York). Numerous public building projects were also displayed, such as the Hartford projects; Rogers Lacy Hotel (1946–47; Dallas); Pittsburgh Point Park Civic Center (1947–48); the San Francisco Bridge (1949–53); and New Theatre, Hartford, Connecticut (1948–49) (figures 5.20–23).

A special section was reserved for eight double cabinets displaying a selection of sixty drawings, the majority of which were before 1914, including Wolf Lake Amusement Park; Cooper House; Harold McCormick House; Larkin Building; Unity Temple; Wright Studio at Fiesole, Italy; and Midway Gardens (figure 5.24). Major works after 1914 included Fallingwater; Crystal Heights (1939; Washington, DC); and Jacobs House I.[94] The last room, labeled by Stonorov as "Sanctum," was reserved for the model of the Guggenheim Museum, which was elevated on a platform and approached by a staircase, so the visitor was at eye level (figure 5.25 and figure B.50).

5.25 Solomon R. Guggenheim Museum model no. 2, New York, 1943–59. Photograph by Volmar Wentzel. (National Geographic/Getty Images). Wright and Taliesin Fellows in model workshop, Taliesin, Spring Green, Wisconsin, ca. 1956.

PUBLICATIONS

While the Italians had no direct involvement in organizing the exhibition, they did have the opportunity to concentrate on books and catalogs. For both Stonorov and Zevi, producing a major publication on Wright's work was in their thoughts from the beginning. In fact, Stonorov's first idea was that the exhibition should be expanded into "a first class international event" that would require "an important catalog" portraying Wright "the man, the land, his inventions and his already transcontinental presence in the mind of every American."[95] When it came Zevi's turn, he reacted in the same vein. "We would like to publish a true book," Zevi explained, "however, we need two things: a small catalogue just for the visitors, and a big book that should be on sale one month before the opening of the exhibition."[96]

The Italians were again thwarted in their original intentions despite the fact that there was serious discussion about the publications for many months before the opening. In December 1950, Zevi suggested to Ragghianti that they publish Wright's preface to the Wasmuth Verlag folios, which had been written in Fiesole in 1910, and that they create "two special issues" of their own magazines, *La Critica d'Arte* and *Metron*.[97] Ragghianti agreed to the first suggestion, but had objections to Zevi's recommendations for the other publications. "If the Italian architects do not feel the exceptional importance of this manifestation for the development of architectural culture and the architecture of our own country," Ragghianti complained, "they are incompetents and perfectly deserve [Marcello] Piacentini [Fascist architect to Mussolini] and companions." He then added bluntly, "It would be equally idiotic if on this occasion you came out to talk about all the nonsense in '-isms' on the pretext of controversy or negative attitudes, which would be totally out of place, or rather petty and childish."[98]

In the decade that elapsed after the 1940 MoMA catalog was canceled and then replaced by *In the Nature of Materials*, no one else attempted a major publication. *Sixty Years of Living Architecture* never appeared as a title for either the exhibition or any of the publications until Werner Moser used it in 1952, probably at Wright's suggestion, as the title of the book he edited for appearance in Switzerland and Germany, and for the Zürich and Munich catalogs, and it was not used again until Wright mounted the show himself in New York, Los Angeles, and Chicago.[99] Although ambitions for a comprehensive catalog were once again unrealized, the publications for the Italian exhibition were both numerous and, in two cases, autonomous.

In the end, Zevi did produce a double issue of *Metron*, but Ragghianti did not present his theories until December 1951, and it was not until January and July 1954 that he devoted two issues of *La Critica d'Arte* to the American architect.[100] *Metron* came the closest to an independent publication on Wright, yet it too carried subject matter based on the American architect's preferences. For instance, the illustrated section concentrated on his most recent work, 1947–51: houses for Eric V. Brown (1949; Kalamazoo, Michigan), Glenn McCord (1948; Arlington, New Jersey), and Benjamin Adelman (1948; Fox Point, Wisconsin) and large structures such as Valley National Bank (1948; Phoenix, Arizona), San Francisco Bridge (1949–53), Pittsburgh Point Park (1947–49), and SC Johnson Research Tower (1943–50), and also among the large structures, St. Mark's Tower (1927–31), Crystal Heights Hotel (1939), and Herbert Jacobs House II (1943–48).

The most important aspect of Zevi's issue was the inclusion of a very laudatory text, "The Architecture of Frank Lloyd Wright," by Giuseppe Samonà.[101] Samonà's essay is important for several reasons. Firstly, it was the only time an independent work of architectural criticism had been included in a Wright catalog since the Boston Institute of Modern Art published Hudnut's controversial foreword in 1940. Secondly, it was one of the very few critiques that Wright singled out for high praise when he read it in translation, even inspiring him to write an effusive congratulatory letter to the author. "I have for the first time," he declared, "comprehensive insight of the nature of [my] work." The feeling stayed with him for quite some time, as he informed Elizabeth Gordon two years after the fact that "Giancarlo [D]e Carlo, Bruno Zevi, and Samonà are the most important critics in Europe at the present time."[102]

Lastly, Samonà addressed Wright's entire oeuvre, finding a profound philosophical thread that united four periods from the Prairie Houses to later works such as Taliesin West and SC Johnson. Rejecting arguments that analyzed Wright's buildings in terms of mathematical formulas, Samonà concluded that unity could be found in the "concentrated matter expressed as pure mass, unidirectional in tension, eliminating every opposition of energies and allowing space to flow horizontally, infinitely free and laden with plastic power." Recognizing in his later work, such as the Guggenheim Museum, that, "Matter can now come to life in circular or spiral form with absolute logic. These forms are reintroduced into architecture, free of any mechanistic symbolism, in perhaps the most extraordinary and definitive works of Wright's genius."[103]

The other Italian publication was *Catalogo Itinerario*, a twelve-page unillustrated booklet, which is a complex document that from internal evidence was still being written up to a week before the June 24 opening (figure 5.26). Although text that was

Mostra di Frank Lloyd Wright

Firenze — Palazzo Strozzi — 24 giugno - settembre 1951

CATALOGO ITINERARIO

Questa è la mostra dell'opera di Frank Lloyd Wright, architetto.
Perchè è stata organizzata questa mostra?
Perchè l'Italia e l'Europa potessero compiere una esperienza storica di cultura di grande significato.
A sessant'anni di distanza dall'inizio dell'attività del Maestro, noi possiamo qui vedere il nascere, il formarsi, il concretarsi di un nuovo linguaggio. Il linguaggio di un artista, che nell'architettura è diventato, in tanta parte, il linguaggio del nostro tempo.
Noi italiani parliamo ancora, a distanza di secoli, una lingua che alla sua origine è stata la creazione di una personalità, di un poeta: Dante.
Che questo ricordo, famigliare ad ogni italiano, aiuti a comprendere il grande fatto che è rappresentato in questa mostra: la creazione di una lingua.
Questa è la seconda mostra di Frank Lloyd Wright. La prima fu fatta a Berlino nel 1910, e fu la consacrazione dell'architettura moderna. Wright aveva allora quaranta anni.
Questa Mostra di Firenze recapitola altri quaranta anni di continuo, straordinario lavoro, in tutto sessanta anni di attività creativa.
Presentiamo in Palazzo Strozzi oltre duecentocinquanta opere, scelte fra le più che ottocento compiute o progettate dal Maestro.
Gli storici, i critici, gli artisti di tutto il mondo hanno avuto piena coscienza che con Frank Lloyd Wright è nata l'espressione architettonica moderna. Scrive lo storico Siegfried Giedion: « In Europa, fra il 1900 e il 1910, non c'era nulla di equivalente alle creazioni di Wright... ». E Bruno Zevi: « Nulla si sottrae all'originalità degli artisti europei ed americani moderni, col riconoscere che il *fatto* Wright è il precedente da cui si muovono le loro esperienze e le loro espressioni... ».
Ma ascoltiamo direttamente la voce degli artisti, di coloro che sono universalmente riconosciuti come i maggiori architetti del nostro tempo. Ascoltiamo il loro omaggio filiale a Frank Lloyd Wright.
Wright deve la sua gloria all'Europa. Era già apprezzato in Inghilterra, in Olanda e in Germania fra il 1900 e il 1908. Nel 1910 fu pubblicata la prima grande illustrazione delle sue architetture, che influenzò od orientò profondamente i movimenti architettonici europei.
Berlage, il famoso architetto olandese, si recò negli Stati Uniti per vedere le opere di Wright, e definì l'architetto americano « un Maestro senza eguali in Europa ».
Il grande architetto austriaco Adolf Loos, che pure andò in America, dopo la pubblicazione dell'opera di Wright nel 1910 manifestò il proprio tributo alla sua innovazione architettonica.
Nel 1921, Le Corbusier dichiara che senza l'opera di Wright non sarebbe concepibile l'architettura moderna.
Mies van der Rohe così rievoca la mostra di Berlino del 1910: « La vitalità dell'idea architettonica era andata dispersa... La grande mostra e l'esauriente pubblicazione dei lavori di Wright ebbero un significato fondamentale per lo sviluppo europeo... L'opera del grande maestro presentava un mondo architettonico nuovo, di insospettata forza, chiarezza di linguaggio e ricchezza sconcertante di forme. In lui trovavamo finalmente un artista ispirato alla reale sorgente dell'architettura, che con vera originalità innalzava le sue costruzioni alla luce... L'impulso dinamico che emanò dalla sua arte dominò un'intera generazione... ».
Ed Erich Mendelsohn, il grande architetto tedesco, scriveva nel 1925: « L'opera di Wright sta al centro del nostro tempo. Il dominio delle sue idee creative di forma è inesausto. È un grande artista che noi onoriamo; un grande uomo che noi amiamo ».
Oud, il maggiore architetto olandese, riassumeva nel 1924, in un meditato saggio, il valore storico dell'opera di Wright: « La figura di Frank Lloyd Wright emerge così sicuramente sul mondo circostante, da poterla senza dubbio definire una delle maggiori del nostro tempo, senza timore che il futuro possa respingere questo giudizio... L'influenza di questo genio dominò le avanguardie dell'architettura in Olanda, Polonia, Germania, Cecoslovacchia, Francia, Belgio... Le caratteristiche dell'arte di Wright distinguono una notevole percentuale della moderna produzione architettonica europea... ».
Walter Gropius, che nella sua arte prima fu profondamente influenzato dall'opera di Wright, inseriva l'opera del Maestro fra le esperienze considerate fondamentali dalla Bauhaus.
Tralasciamo di dire le testimonianze di Mallet-Stevens, di Doesburg, di Dudok, di Mumford, di Neutra, di Aalto, dei due Moser, per riassumere il significato dell'opera di Wright con le parole di storici e critici dell'architettura come Hitchcock, Malkiel-Jirmounski, Persico e Pevsner: « Lo stile di Wright ha influenzato tutti gli architetti europei... Gli elementi della sua arte sono divenuti quelli dell'architettura moderna... Ma si può e si deve andare oltre: in Wright si può vedere quale alta coscienza etica sostiene questa che è una delle espressioni artistiche più originali e creative di tutti i tempi ».

Messaggio di F. Ll. Wright

Tornando qui, nella vostra grande Patria, segnata dal tempo, sento ora tutta la simpatia di un figlio grato che desidera onorare i grandi artisti che videro il tramonto in Occidente — il Rinascimento Italiano — e credettero che fosse un'aurora.

L'essenza dello spirito creativo italiano che tutti gli artisti amano vivrà sempre, non come « Rinascita », ma come Nascita: un'alba che non dovrà conoscere la notte.

L'arte italiana diverrà ancora forte, tanto più forte quanto più vicina alla terra, « anche se non è ancora il tempo del raccolto ». Sant'Agostino è con noi per guidare i suoi figli ormai svegli verso gli eterni principi che io spero la giovane Italia sia desiderosa di conoscere: una nuova gloria, fondata sull'eterno corso di un sole che potrà talvolta essere meno splendente, ma che non tramonterà mai, perchè alimentato da organica luce, perennemente presente nel cuore umano: un cuore che sa la Bellezza essere Verità.

Alla giovane Italia la mia speranza più forte, il mio augurio che l'Italia sia giovane.

FRANK LLOYD WRIGHT

Firenze, giugno 1951.

Notizia biografica di Frank Lloyd Wright

Frank Lloyd Wright è nato nel 1869.
Lavorò da giovanissimo nello studio degli architetti Adler e Sullivan a Chicago. Le sue prime costruzioni risalgono all'anno 1887. La fase più intensa della sua prima attività è situata fra il 1900 e il 1910: periodo detto delle *Prairie Houses*, case di campagna e ville sparse in tutto il territorio degli Stati Uniti.
Nel 1910 era già famoso in Europa: chiamato in Inghilterra, in Olanda e in Germania, le sue opere vengono studiate ed illustrate nelle maggiori riviste di architettura, e si riconosce in lui (Berlage) « un Maestro senza eguali in Europa ».
Nel 1910 viene in Europa, prepara il materiale per la memorabile mostra di Berlino, e l'editore Wasmuth pubblica in un volume monumentale la sua opera, che determina tutti i movimenti e gli sviluppi dell'architettura moderna: come sarà riconosciuto nelle testimonianze della rivista « Wendingen » (1924) ed in quelle premesse alla seconda grande edizione delle sue opere dai maggiori architetti europei contemporanei, l'olandese Oud, il tedesco Mendelsohn, il francese Mallet-Stevens, l'olandese Berlage, l'austriaco Adolf Loos, il tedesco Gropius, Mies van der Rohe, Dudok, ed altri.
Fra il 1914 ed il 1925 Wright operò prevalentemente in Giappone (1916-22), pure eseguendo molti edifici in America. Dal 1925 al 1935 la sua attività si diradò fortemente.
Dopo tale anno il suo lavoro creativo riprende con straordinaria intensità. È il periodo che prende nome dalla *Casa sulla cascata*, considerata il capolavoro dell'architettura moderna, e dalle Usonian Houses. In esso si inserisce anche l'Edificio della Amministrazione Johnson (1936...), e un'originale creazione di case individuali d'abitazione.
La produzione architettonica di Wright è caratterizzata da una fantasia eccezionale e da risorse d'innovazione non soltanto spaziale, ma anche tecnica ed ingegneresca; si ricordi che le sue invenzioni nell'uso dei materiali superarono ogni scetticismo e negazione dei tecnici della costruzione: l'Albergo Imperiale di Tokio, costruito a terrazze continue appoggiate a piloni, fu uno dei pochi edifici che resisterono al terremoto del 1923; le strutture librate della Casa sulla cascata furono costruite contro il parere degli ingegneri e calcolatori, e così il famoso sistema di colonne a fungo in cemento armato degli Uffici Johnson, che non corrispondeva a nessun calcolo convenzionato.
Wright ha costruito oltre trecento edifici di vario carattere, ed è autore di più che altrettanti progetti. Lo spirito della sua opera è illustrato in molti volumi scritti da Wright, a partire dal 1901, e tutti tradotti nelle varie lingue (in italiano: *Architettura e Democrazia*; *Architettura organica*; in preparazione l'*Autobiografia*, del 1932).
Della vastissima bibliografia sulla sua opera, van-

5.26 *Catalogo Itinerario*. (Kathryn Smith collection). Catalog for the Wright exhibition at the Palazzo Strozzi, 1951.

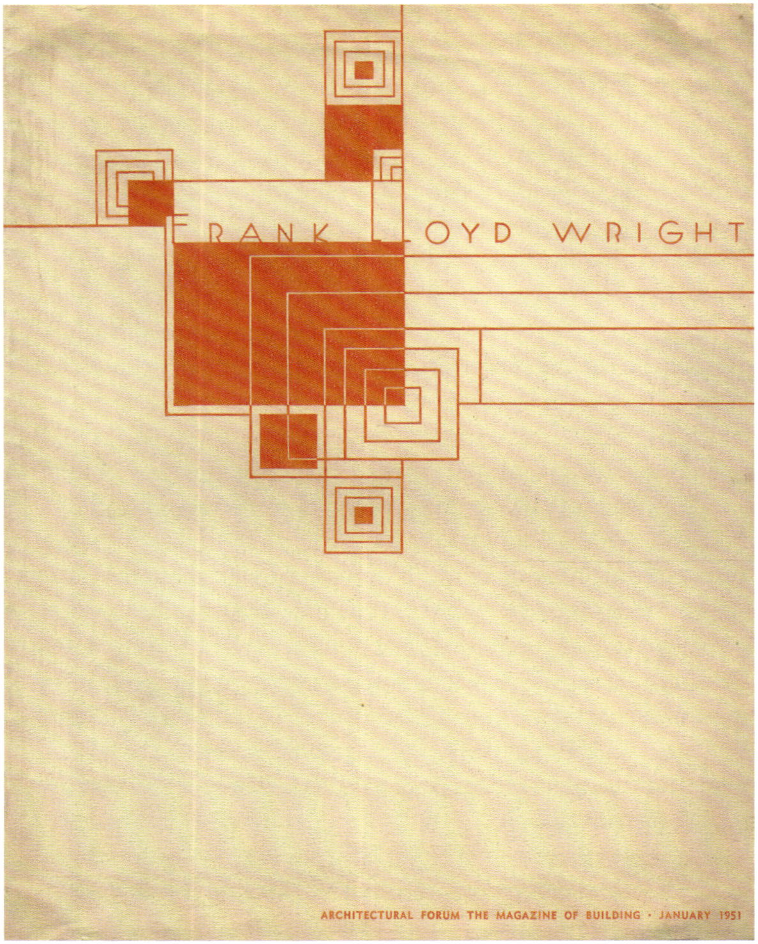

5.27 "Frank Lloyd Wright," offprint, *Architectural Forum*, January 1951. (Kathryn Smith collection). This publication was distributed at the exhibitions in Philadelphia and Florence, Italy.

not credited to either Wright or Stonorov is unsigned, the preface is certainly by Ragghianti. Stonorov was graciously acknowledged as the exhibition organizer, but the only person recognized for participation in the catalog was Ragghianti's wife, Licia. While the catalog was certainly prepared by the Italians, the major text—the checklist with captions—appears to have originated with the work of Stonorov and Wright.

The *Catalogo* contains nine parts, including an unsigned general preface, "Messaggio di F. Ll. Wright" (F. Ll. Wright's Message) dated "Firenze, giugno 1951" (Florence, June 1951); biographical notes; list of academic honors; message from Gimbel Brothers; checklist; acknowledgments; "Wright's writings: To my European collaborators, 1910, and Some Words about Grammar," dated January 16, 1951, Taliesin West; "An Architecture for Democracy"; and "Dialogue on Broadacre City." An addendum listing the Italian Honorary, Technical, and Executive Committees was tipped in as the last page.

Ragghianti's preface is the first example of his personal insight into Wright's architecture. Ragghianti applied his aesthetic theories of "visual language" to Wright's body of work. Unlike other Italian commentators, Ragghianti cast Wright into a wider historical and cultural context. Accepting the idea that he was the originator of modern architecture, Ragghianti went one step further by comparing him to Dante Alighieri (1265–1321), the Florentine poet of the *Divine Comedy*. The Wright exhibition, Ragghianti declared, presented "the birth, the formation, the materializing of a new language." "The language of an artist, that architecture has become," he wrote, "in large part, the language of our time. We still speak Italian, after centuries, and the poet, Dante, was responsible for the origin of that language. This memory will help every Italian family to understand the great fact that is represented in this exhibition: the creation of a language."[104]

One of the most important aspects were the captions, which were planned to appear with the exhibition panels; they were the primary means by which the importance of Wright's architecture was to be communicated to the Italian audience. With the architectural conference aborted and the exhibition arriving prepackaged in crates, it was the only way that Ragghianti had remaining to him to shape the content as he originally planned.

As was characteristic, Wright also contributed his own publications. None were planned for the Gimbel Brothers show—as far as Wright was concerned it was only a preview to Florence—thus all the publications were planned for Italy, but two were distributed in Philadelphia. First and foremost, Douglas Haskell, of *Architectural Forum*, worked closely with Wright and Stoller to create a special January issue that also appeared as a thirty-page offprint with cover for distribution in Philadelphia (figure 5.27).[105] Similar to the Wright 1938 and 1948 *Forum* issues, the magazine was lavishly illustrated with principal photography by Stoller documenting recent houses—Lowell Walter (1948–50), Benjamin Adelman (1948), Herbert Jacobs II (1943–48), John Pew (1938–40), Sol Friedman (1948)—and, as a first, added numerous color pages, at the beginning and end, of the SC Johnson Administration Building and Research Tower and the Annie M. Pfeiffer Chapel at Florida Southern College (1939–41), respectively. The text and layout throughout was primarily by Wright, beginning with a brief preface, "Whatever His Age ... To the Young Man in Architecture," and ending with "A Dialogue [with Buddha]," dated December 15, 1950.

With the exception of the *Forum* offprint, none of Wright's self-publications deal with specifics of his design methodology or descriptions of his buildings. Rather, they constitute arguments putting forth principles of "Organic Architecture," especially as he intended to differentiate them from the modern movement in European architecture. There was a concerted effort to avoid reference to the Prairie period and to emphasize his most recently completed buildings.

Because he was busier than at any other time in his career, he simplified his writing task, for the most part, by editing texts he had already written and reissuing them. The first previously published text Wright chose was the foreword to *When Democracy Builds* (1945). He revised this short text on January 16, 1951, with a new title, "On an Architecture for Democracy," and issued it on the day of the Philadelphia preview as number 15 in the series *Taliesin Square-Paper: A Nonpolitical Voice from Our Democratic Minority*. As such, it was distributed in Philadelphia. It was translated and appeared in the *Catalogo Itinerario*.

The second text, suggested by Zevi, had both theoretical and sentimental value, the introduction to the Wasmuth Verlag folios, which had been partly written during Wright's stay in Fiesole. For the reissue, he retitled the essay *The Sovereignty of the Individual, In the Cause of Architecture*, which was only available in Florence, where it appeared in both English and Italian.[106] In addition to the two texts that put forth the philosophy that informed "Organic Architecture," Wright created a third publication that was in the form of a dialogue about Broadacre City between Stonorov and himself. Obviously, Wright was very concerned that Europeans would understand his planning theories.

Ironically, the book that preoccupied most of the principals—Italian and American—was the one that never appeared. After Loeb released the photostats of Wright's drawings to the architect, he had them bound in six volumes for display in Florence (see figure 5.11). Wright called them his "Magnum Opus," which inspired plans to publish a mammoth edition of his lifework. Apparently, one evening in Florence at the home of Marjorie Ferguson, Zevi and Stonorov approached Wright and his wife, Olgivanna, about producing a monumental publication.[107] The proposal as Zevi itemized it in a memorandum to Stonorov recalled his outline for the Italian exhibition, when he had been thwarted from participation; it called for an extremely ambitious definitive multivolume publication that would put forth the "story of Wright's artistic conception." Zevi sought to integrate Wright's autobiography, collected writings, and all his buildings and projects to illustrate "the first ideas, the first drawings, the reasons for the various steps [from] one drawing to another, the various aspects of the building from many angles." Zevi returned to the idea of providing a historical context when he stated that the first chapter should be devoted to American architecture in the late nineteenth century when Wright began his career. To accomplish this work, he proposed a committee to be headed by Olgivanna Wright with Stonorov as the lead coordinator, Zevi as the general editor, Edgar Kaufmann (certainly Junior) as director of documentation, Kathryn Lewis (or similar person) as a coordinator with two additional people at Taliesin, who would help with the photographs and drawings.[108] As Zevi conceived it, the proposal was unrealistic from the beginning.

Zevi and Stonorov's "Magnum Opus" was the grandest and most ambitious publishing idea ever conceived as a result of one of Wright's exhibitions, materially exceeding both the Wasmuth

Verlag folios and *In the Nature of Materials* in scale and degree. Kaufmann Jr., who had been formulating a similar project since 1947 when he originally proposed it to MoMA, was simultaneously moving forward on a smaller format: *Taliesin Drawings: Recent Architecture of Frank Lloyd Wright Selected from His Drawings*, which was published by Wittenborn, Schultz, Inc., in New York in 1952.[109]

While Wright gave Zevi permission to "go ahead as you wish with the magnum-opus and the translation of the Autobiography" in January 1952, Zevi explained that he was waiting for the American committee to do the preliminary work.[110] Zevi's grand idea never saw fruition; however, Kaufmann Jr. continued to pursue publication ventures with Wright throughout the 1950s. The proposal that came the closest to the "Magnum Opus" was Edgar Kaufmann Sr.'s 1952 offer to "publish 100 houses in a big portfolio," and "at the completion of each single opus presentation he was to give the Foundation $1000 or a total of $150,000 ... for expenses."[111] This proposal still seemed to be current as late as March 1956 when Wright reported to Stonorov that he was engaged in "preparation of a $500.00 per volume of the drawings, details, and designs of my life time. No photographs—starting 1903 and ending 1957."[112] Wright died before seeing the only book he supervised during his lifetime that came close to the ambitions inspired by the Italian exhibition: *Frank Lloyd Wright: Drawings for a Living Architecture* (Bear Run Foundation Inc. and the Edgar J. Kaufmann Charitable Foundation by Horizon Press, New York, 1959), which included Samonà's essay in English translation and reproduced two hundred original sketches and presentation drawings, with seventy-five in color.

CRITICAL REACTION

While the international congress on modern architecture was never realized, the Wright exhibition served as a significant catalyst in postwar Italian discourse about the direction of architecture. The discussion was initiated by Zevi and APAO members, who sought to, first, undermine the influence of Fascist architects, who still occupied most positions of national authority; and second, to prove that "Organic Architecture" was superior to functionalism, which they declared a sterile formula.

The inner circle of anti-Fascist architects included Giancarlo De Carlo (1919–2005), a recent graduate of the Venice School of Architecture, who wrote one of the most favorable reviews, which Ragghianti placed in his journal, *SeleArte*, founded in 1952.[113] Starting with the premise that Wright was superior to the "International Style" because he taught that architecture "is a thing of life, something completely and entirely human," De Carlo defined those qualities the Italians were seeking: "Wright's architecture and Wright's spirit, his profound humanism, his belief in the spiritual power of man, his feeling of the unity of man with nature and the cosmos, his spirituality that recognizes and enhances the intellectual forces in ethical human freedom. This is why his art, as well as [his] architectonic expression, which is among the most original of all time, can also be a warm message to humanity."[114]

Yet outside the circle of APAO, the reception was more guarded and far more critical. Two other highly respected academics, Giusta Nicco Fasola (1901–1960) and Giovanni Michelucci (1891–1990), agreed that Wright's prominence was based on his identification of man with nature, but both dismissed his interpretation as a myth, almost taking on religious overtones.[115] Indeed, unlike Samonà, Fasola did not see Wright's later work as a culmination, but rather as a descent into a formalism bordering on mannerism.

Based on Zevi's underlying premise for the exhibition that Wright represented the best model for a democratic architecture, Broadacre City was of paramount importance. This proved to be one of the most controversial aspects of the Wright event. Critics were even found within the inner circle; surprisingly, Detti was one. "Detti's reaction in front of this masterpiece," Ragghianti recalled some years later, "that is possibly one of the most personal conceptions of the whole 20th century, and that is in a certain sense one of the fundamental expressions of our era, was not one of agreement. Because there was a profoundly utopian aspect that offended his inner being ... he felt no attraction of a utopian nature, of utopistic rationality."[116]

To one of the most astute observers, Ermanno Migliorini (1924–1999), Wright's "utopia" was neither city nor country, but "an abstract illusion" that people fled to as an escape. To augment their poor social life, the "urban fugitives" would need "to keep in touch [by] the telephone, [and] television, to cover the distance [by] the car"; however, for them, there was no need to know more about the world than what these gadgets provided.[117] Another critical commentator was Piero Bottoni (1903–1973), a Communist adherent of the functionalist movement, who decried what he regarded as "an ostentatious display" toward Wright by Zevi and his colleagues. In Zevi's salute to Wright in the first pages of the double issue of *Metron*, he wrote, "We bow before your genius, and defend democracy and individual rights," closing with "GOD BLESS YOU."[118] In reaction, Bottoni, a former member of the magazine's editorial board, protested: "Wright's genius is diminished by the servile hand-kissing, just as [would be the case] of Le Corbusier or Gropius."[119]

After the exhibition closed, Zevi recalled: "There is, perhaps, not a single journal or an illustrated magazine that does not speak of his work; radio dedicated two long programs to the American architect." The result of all this public attention, Zevi admitted, was controversy, itemizing the most repeated criticisms: Wright was a prima donna; he disliked the Italian Renaissance, modern Italian architecture, and "followers," which included the organizers of the exhibition; his houses, while beautiful, were not suitable for Italy so why talk about him when there is no relevancy; and his buildings merge with their environment rather than creating a geometric form against a background. Zevi defended all points on the grounds that Wright was a genius. In this instance, he seemed to have forgotten his early assessment of Wright while still a student at Harvard: "This obscure genius has a deep interest in social problems, but, in their solution, he is overshadowed by his own personality. We regard him, as he probably will be regarded by history, as a genius able to free himself from the conventions of the outside world, but never able to free himself from himself."[120]

ITALIAN AFTERMATH: MILAN, 1951

Unfortunately, as the exhibition closed early in Florence on August 20 after a two-month showing, conflict and anger arose again, an indirect result of Ragghianti's disappointments. His original intentions for the exhibition had included the official patronage of the Italian president (conferring participation of the Republic of Italy) and large attendance figures, especially from the architectural profession and the public outside Florence. "I regret again that circumstances independent of my wishes," Ragghianti confided to Stonorov on August 29, "had not allowed all the success worthy of Mr. Wright."[121] So Ragghianti took everyone by surprise by shipping the show to the Palazzo dell'Arte for display at the Triennale because Milan "is a city of 1½ million people, socially most advanced ... with the greatest interest and activity in modern architecture." "I have the thought in my conscience," Ragghianti confessed, "that it might displease Mr. Wright." He then quickly asked for Wright's permission after the fact.[122] Once the crates were received in Milan, there was no space available and they were sent into storage. At this point the exhibition was uninsured; Wright was both perplexed and furious. Ragghianti had been told in the spring that the Philadelphia exhibition had drawn 100,000 visitors, which must have fed his ambitions, but Stonorov reported that attendance at the Palazzo Strozzi had been 25,000. Ragghianti must have felt disappointment at the low attendance. Yet the attendance was almost identical to the other European venues, with the exception of Paris, which drew 35,000.[123] The Florentine show had been a success, especially in light of the enormous difficulties that had to be overcome. Yet Ragghianti had been left with a feeling of failure.

He had intentions to put his own interpretation into print for the Italian culture, but he needed access to Wright's drawings, so he held back the six volumes of the "Magnum Opus" from the exhibition. The whole affair came to a head on February 2, 1952, when the show, under Werner Moser's supervision, opened in Zürich without them. Stonorov reprimanded Ragghianti, "You only released them after Mr. Moser had to send his son-in-law to fetch them from you. He also reports that you had the volumes taken apart, evidently for some purposes of your own."[124] Stonorov reported to Wright, on February 28, that "the book by Ragghianti and Detti had been advertised."[125] Finally, Wright had to step in and demand an explanation from Ragghianti.[126]

EUROPEAN TOUR, 1952: ZÜRICH, PARIS, MUNICH, AND ROTTERDAM

While the Italians had originally refused to allow the Wright exhibition to travel, at the same time Ragghianti wanted the event to have a profound influence throughout Europe, and it did, but not in the way Ragghianti had intended. He believed the show should be a catalyst for serious debate about the future of modern architecture and its implications for European postwar reconstruction, physically, socially, and politically. Since the exhibition had been organized as a personal exhibition, the results, although impressive, served the purpose primarily of adding to Wright's stature.

The European tour traveled to major museums and cultural centers for seven months from February through August 1952 without permanent governmental or institutional support, primarily through the efforts of Stonorov, who worked out the financial and logistical details with the organizers at each venue. The show opened at Kunsthaus, Zürich, where Wright asked his former draftsman, Werner Moser, to be in charge; then to Paris at the École Nationale Supérieure des Beaux-Arts, under the direction of Darthea Speyer, USIA; to the Haus der Kunst, Munich, organized by Brigitte D'Ortschy and Otto Bartning; ending at the Ahoy'gebouw in Rotterdam, with an installation, at Wright's request, by J.J.P. Oud (figures 5.28–29). Wright agreed to attend the Paris opening—the only European one other than Florence—

5.28 Kunsthaus, *Zürich, Frank Lloyd Wright: Sechzig Jahre lebendige Architektur; Sixty Years of Living Architecture*, poster, 1952. (Private collection)

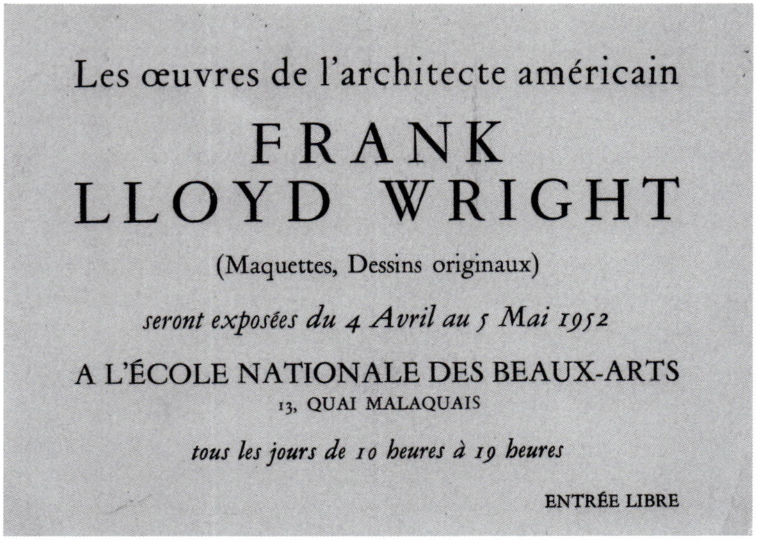

5.29 Announcement, l'École Nationale Supérieure des Beaux-Arts, Paris, April 4–May 5, 1952. (FLWFA)

because Auguste Perret had been his guest at Taliesin in October 1949 and he felt a personal connection as a result.[127] The Paris venue was the only one that received financial support from the State Department; Speyer had succeeded with the American government where all others had failed. Following the close of the exhibition in Rotterdam, Wright chose Mexico City as the next destination to complement his participation in the Eighth Pan American Congress of Architects organized by Carlos Lazo, president of the Sociedad de Arquitectos, that was held at the Colegio Nacional de Arquitectura, Ciudad Universitaria, October 19–26, 1952.[128]

While discussions were still ongoing about publishing a "Magnum Opus," smaller publications appeared in German, French, and Dutch. The largest was a 100-page book in German, *Frank Lloyd Wright: Sechzig Jahre lebendige Architektur; Sixty Years of Living Architecture*, with 157 illustrations in color and black and white, by Werner Moser, that came the closest to a Taliesin product. In addition to two essays by Moser, there were articles by three recent Wright clients—Herbert Jacobs and Paul and Jean Hanna—and an essay on the life of Taliesin students by Peter Steiger among other text material.[129] Each of the four venues published small catalogs containing content that originally appeared in the *Catalogo Itinerario*: a short message from Wright, architect's biography, excerpt from *When Democracy Builds*, Wright-Stonorov dialogue on Broadacre City, selection of black-and-white photographs (with the exception of Paris), and a checklist. The Munich catalog contained a short text by Stonorov, and the Rotterdam catalog contained one by Oud.[130] Following the example of special issues of magazines—*Architectural Forum* and *Metron—Architecture Française*, under the editorship of Louis-George Noviant, published a seventy-page fully illustrated catalog that concentrated mainly on the work after 1936.[131]

While the Italians did not plan the traveling show, it did more to advance Wright's work and theories in Europe than his publications with Wasmuth Verlag in 1911. With very little other than private initiative, 101,000 people visited the exhibitions in Europe in 1952 at a total cost of $35,000, excluding return transport across the Atlantic.[132] After adding the 1951 attendance figures for Philadelphia and Florence, the total comes to approximately 226,000 visitors on two continents. Taking into account local journalism, catalogs, pamphlets, architectural journals, a book, opening night speeches, and radio coverage, it is possible to posit that a quarter of a million people or more were exposed to what started out as the "Italian exhibition." While Ragghianti felt disappointed that the Wright manifestation in Florence had not lived up to his original vision, his initiative produced unprecedented results throughout Western Europe and the United States. The exhibition at the Palazzo Strozzi was one of the six most important shows during Wright's lifetime.

"THE GREATEST SHOW ON EARTH," NEW YORK, 1953

Wright's version of the Italian exhibition, which he titled *Sixty Years of Living Architecture: In the Realm of Ideas*, held in Manhattan in fall 1953, is one of the six most important shows of his career, perhaps the most important. By this time, he had dispensed with Stonorov and had taken total control: setting his own goals, introducing new display techniques, and targeting an audience that encompassed everyone from journalists and museum professionals to the general public. The rewards were great, but the risk significant. The venture ended as an artistic and personal victory, but it came at a high cost, physically and financially.

The proposal to show in New York was mentioned while the exhibition was still in Europe; Wright told Stonorov that he had tired of touring and was trying to decide whether to return the crates to Taliesin or have one last showing at the Metropolitan Museum of Art.[133] His original intention was probably to have a "dignified" American exhibition venue as he had objected to the commercialism of Gimbel Brothers Department Store, but his motivation changed in January 1953 when the Modern mounted *Built in USA*, which had thrown him into a furor.

5.30 Temporary Exhibition Pavilion, Solomon R. Guggenheim Museum, New York, 1953. Pencil on tracing paper, 36 × 77 in. (FLWFA, 5314.001). The Pavilion seen from Fifth Avenue with the existing Guggenheim Museum building to the right.

Taking the exhibition to New York was a strategy to advance his avant-garde program at a time when modern architecture was at a turning point in postwar America. Due to the fact that the modern movement was becoming more widely accepted by the American mainstream—the general public and corporations—it was more hotly debated than ever before. Wright had been increasingly discouraged by and hostile to MoMA ever since the promise of Johnson's return to the museum had been hugely disappointing. Wright now sought to use the Modern's own method—an exhibition and a demonstration house—to "knock the cult clean out," as he boasted to Gordon.[134] The idea had many benefits: he could use his Taliesin Fellowship as a work force to his advantage, design the exhibition himself, and erect a full-scale Usonian House, a goal that had been denied him since he originally proposed it in 1939. The disadvantage was, however, that Wright was responsible for the finances, insurance, and deadlines.

By May 1953, Wright began to take direct action on several fronts. His evolving course of action was to bring what he called "The Greatest Show on Earth" to the future site of the Guggenheim Museum at the corner of Fifth Avenue and Eighty-Ninth Street, receive in-kind contributions from *House Beautiful* in erecting and furnishing the Usonian House, while still trying to secure the Metropolitan Museum as his first choice. In the middle of the month, he met with the director, Francis Henry Taylor, who finally explained that due to remodeling the museum was short on space until early 1954.[135]

So on July 24, the Board of Trustees of the Guggenheim Foundation approved an arrangement where the empty plot (currently being used as a parking lot) would be turned over to Wright for the erection of a temporary building as long as certain conditions were met. "Mr. Wright will arrange to take care of all costs and expenses incident to the exhibit," the board decreed, "and restoring the area to its former condition, in excess of admissions collected and $10,000 contributed by the Foundation." The agreement also came with a boilerplate clause: Wright would "protect the [Guggenheim] Foundation against any and all claims which might arise from the project." Ominously, the agreement carried no reference to the erection of a Usonian House and set the opening date at September 1 at the latest.[136]

With this agreement, Wright initiated the most ambitious installation program of his career: he designed and built two new structures—a 1,700-square-foot fully furnished two-bedroom Usonian House and a temporary pavilion—that housed the

5.31 Temporary Exhibition Pavilion and Usonian Exhibition House, Solomon R. Guggenheim Museum, New York, 1953. Photograph by Pedro E. Guerrero. (© 2017 Pedro E. Guerrero Archives). Eighty-Ninth Street frontage.

largest exhibition of his work to be held in New York during his lifetime. The first Wright buildings constructed in New York were built on the northeast corner of the site with the pavilion fronting Fifth Avenue and the house immediately behind it to the east off Eighty-Ninth Street (figures 5.30–31). For the temporary gallery, he used a pipe scaffolding system, screened with alternate panels of wire glass and Cemesto (cement and asbestos), creating a translucent tent 145 feet long and 50 feet wide (figures 5.32–33).[137] Wright planned to landscape the Fifth Avenue frontage with cedar trees, banked with low junipers, and tall arbor vitae; the interior featured "a triangular planted area with three streams of water flowing over boulders and greenery."[138]

Although for the public, displaying a full-scale house in a museum setting was no longer original, for Wright, it was a personal milestone (figure 5.34). His determination to never relinquish his idea was not due to the need to provide visitors with a novelty or even display something more accessible than simulacra, he strongly believed that his architecture was subject to being misunderstood unless it could be experienced three dimensionally.

The 1953 Exhibition House was smaller than his 1939 MoMA proposal and fit more tightly into the confined space off Eighty-Ninth Street than his siting had been in the MoMA Sculpture Garden (figure 5.35). It was designed as a suburban postwar home for a couple with a young child. Paradoxically, Wright saw himself as the best alternative to two polar opposites: Colonial-style homes and examples from the transplanted European avant-garde such as Mies's Edith Farnsworth House (1953). For the great number of visitors during the months of November and December, their frame of reference was more likely to be the tract houses of Levittown selling for $8,000 or less across the East River on Long Island. Yet Wright had explained the year before that he was aiming for "the upper section of the middle third of society—not from the mobocrats, at the bottom, or the Fascists, or Mr. Big, at the top."[139]

The two-bedroom house was constructed primarily of donated material: Brickcrete (concrete block material), glass, and oak plywood for the floors, walls, and built-in cabinetry, but Wright estimated that it would cost $35,000 to build for a client. The average American was no doubt impressed with the 26-by-32-foot living room, with 12½-foot ceiling, splendidly furnished with custom-made Wright furniture, Japanese screens, and decorative objects from the collection of his daughter, Frances (figure 5.36). At the front door, original works of sculpture, including an Alexander Calder mobile borrowed from the museum's collection, greeted the visitors.[140] Yet the price tag was probably out of reach for most GI families, but, for Wright, he had provided an alternative to the Modern's Breuer and Ain demonstration houses.

During summer and fall 1953, Wright realized that the exhibition could serve another vital purpose: to affect public

5.32 *Sixty Years of Living Architecture*, Solomon R. Guggenheim Museum, New York, 1953. Photograph by Pedro E. Guerrero. (© 2017 Pedro E. Guerrero Archives). Price Tower model in the distant background.

5.33 *Sixty Years of Living Architecture*, Solomon R. Guggenheim Museum, New York, 1953. (FLWFA, 5314.0117). Wingspread model and Guggenheim Museum model no. 2.

5.34 Frank Lloyd Wright, Olgivanna Lloyd Wright, and Taliesin Fellows in the Exhibition Usonian House living room at the opening of *Sixty Years of Living Architecture*, October 22, 1953. Photograph by Pedro E. Guerrero. (© 2017 Pedro E. Guerrero Archives)

opinion through the press, draw high attendance, and inspire positive newspaper reviews in an effort to influence city officials to grant him permission to build the Guggenheim Museum. He was making bimonthly trips to New York in a herculean effort to obtain the building permit because the city had imposed code restrictions covering structural, fire, and emergency evacuation requirements that necessitated substantial redesign. Wright was going through an appeals process while engaged in a campaign to retain the financial and psychological support of his client.

The *New York Times* gave him continuous coverage leading up to the press preview, which had been postponed to October 21, but he took advantage of television to reach a mass audience. In 1953, he appeared on NBC's *Conversations with Elder Men* with Hugh Downs, other guests had been Bertrand Russell, Igor Stravinsky, and Jawaharlal Nehru; the *Today* program with Dave Garroway; and *Omnibus* with Alistair Cooke.[141] Even before the exhibition opened, Wright obtained results. In a September 5 editorial that Wright could have written himself, the *New York Times* opined: "The new museum proposes systems of reinforced concrete construction in which America lags far behind Europe. Its structural calculations, figured in terms of cantilever and continuity rather than post and beam, will hold fertile suggestions for future architecture." Citing the upcoming retrospective as an opportunity for reconsideration, the newspaper concluded, "New York still has no building by America's most renowned architect. Will New York continue to be rigid in its refusal to give him a chance to demonstrate his genius in our town?"[142] Wright's efforts to shape public opinion in his favor had borne results.

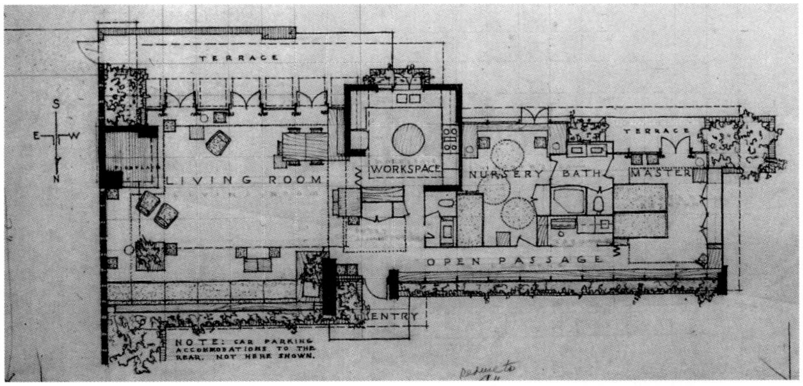

5.35 Frank Lloyd Wright, Exhibition Usonian House plan, *Sixty Years of Living Architecture*, Solomon R. Guggenheim Museum, New York, 1953. Ink on paper, 30 × 40 in. (FLWFA, 5314.021)

5.36 Frank Lloyd Wright, Exhibition Usonian House living room, *Sixty Years of Living Architecture*, Solomon R. Guggenheim Museum, New York, 1953. Photograph by Pedro E. Guerrero. (© 2017 Pedro E. Guerrero Archives)

5.37 Frank Lloyd Wright with Price Tower model, *Sixty Years of Living Architecture*, Solomon R. Guggenheim Museum, New York, 1953. Photograph by Pedro E. Guerrero. (© 2017 Pedro E. Guerrero Archives)

For the first time, Wright now had complete control over the exhibition installation and the demonstration Usonian House. He took advantage of the situation by editing out some of the earlier buildings, but more important, updating the show with work begun or completed from 1952 to 1953. The most significant additions were drawings for the Masieri Memorial (1951/52–55; Venice, Italy); Point View Residences for Edgar Kaufmann Sr. (1951–53; Pittsburgh, Pennsylvania); and the H. C. Price Company Tower. For the Price Tower, a new model took pride of place, another triumph for Wright, who had finally realized the design of St. Mark's Tower in built form (figure 5.37 and see figure B.56). He also produced two softcover catalogs, *Sixty Years of Living Architecture: The Work of Frank Lloyd Wright* (thirty-six pages with fifty black-and-white illustrations) and *The Usonian House, Souvenir of the Exhibition: 60 Years of Living Architecture* (ten pages with ten black-and-white illustrations) (figure 5.38).[143]

In addition to the favorable reports of the *New York Times*—especially stories by the associate art editor and critic Aline B. Louchheim (later Saarinen)—*Time*, *New Republic*, *Art News*, *Architectural Forum*, *Architectural Record*, and *House and Home* all covered the exhibition. Wright laid himself open to the critics, and, with the notable exception of the most important reviewer, this time the press was generous in its, albeit superficial, praise. In a glorious gesture that no doubt brought back memories of the early 1930s, Wright took Mumford on a personal tour of the exhibition. "In seeing his life ... spread before me, with his voice as a persistent undertone," Mumford revealed, "I realized as never before how the insolence of his genius sometimes repelled me." His review, which appeared in two parts in the November 28 and December 12 *New Yorker*, was a tour de force combining a deep familiarity with the length and breadth of Wright's oeuvre with an objective and critical eye. While Mumford admitted that the better he knew the work, "the more I found in its whole span to admire" because "no one else could rival him in sheer fertility of imagination and constructive innovation," while at the same time, "the more I found to question in his unwillingness to admit, as copartners in shaping the design, his individual clients, the contributions of his disciples or rivals, or the communal traditions that support and enhance every work designed to meet the varied needs of life."[144]

Mumford subjected Wright's work to a specific set of criteria: "what [the work] stands for itself, as the unique expression of a powerful and superbly endowed personality, and what it means in relation to the time, the place, the community, the civilization." Of course, the result was a very complex assessment. So while Mumford could state that "having seized upon a certain geometric form ... he will ... apply it to every nook and corner," causing "one's eye vainly [to seek] relief from this almost obsessive reiterativeness," he also concluded that Wright "is the most original architect the United States has produced, and—what is even more important—he is one of the most creative architectural geniuses of all time."[145] Mumford penetrated past fawning praise, for instance, when he stated, "Wright never took seriously the doctrine Sullivan preached, that form must *follow* function," rather, the critic believed "his tendency has been toward demonstrativeness, toward dramatic exaggeration even when he is at work with the purely mechanical elements."

Taking up the argument that Wright had put forward through most of 1953 concerning "the Usonian way of life" versus "foreign importations," Mumford noted that Wright spoke as if the work of Mies and Gropius were "not merely 'inorganic'

5.38 Frank Lloyd Wright, *The Usonian House: Souvenir of the Exhibition: 60 Years of Living Architecture, The Work of Frank Lloyd Wright*, Solomon R. Guggenheim Museum, 1953. (Kathryn Smith collection)

but un-American." But Mumford went further, seizing on a point that transcended architectural jealousy: "His true genius, like the true genius of America, is expressed in neither his rejections of the foreign nor his self-assertions of the merely native but in his generous comprehensions and inclusions, his outgoingness and his receptivity, his unrivaled capacity for synthesis."[146] He amplified this idea by writing, "As for the influence of Japan, his readiness to accept it was an expression of the union of the East and West that began long ago in the minds of Thoreau and Emerson." Following this line of reasoning, he concluded, Wright "unites the great streams of thought flowing from Europe and Asia into America and creates new buildings and structures in which the modern spirit can feel at home with both nature and the machine, in which every homely activity is transmuted into art."[147]

With a clear idea of how Wright would react to his essays, Mumford decided to get in the first word, warning him that "in fear and trembling and admiration and love I dared write the article about your work that no one else, friendly or hostile, has yet dared to write."[148] Of course, Mumford, who feared for the worst, was correct. Wright read the article on a plane flying into New York and dashed off a note while still on board. Invoking his familiar political argument once more, Wright replied, "Now Lewis do you advocate that a man should shun the master and take the slave in order that his own individuality may not suffer eclipse. If so, viva 'Le International'—The communist wins over the Democrat?"[149]

Mumford aside, the exhibition was a critical and popular success. Visitors waiting to enter extended in long lines down Fifth Avenue, while crowds of people, each of whom had paid an admission fee of fifty cents, filled the Pavilion. In the first forty-five days, the Guggenheim Foundation reported a total of 60,000 visitors.[150] The museum was open seven days a week with evening hours until 10:00 p.m. Wednesdays and Saturdays; demand was so great closing day was extended from November 29 to December 13.[151]

Once the euphoria of the opening had passed and the reviews were in, the bills started coming due. There were several unpleasant surprises that differed greatly from the original understandings. The actual cost of the exhibition came to approximately $75,000, exceeding Wright's original estimate by $40,000.[152]

Harry Guggenheim confronted Wright, reminding him of the original terms of the agreement including the fact that income from admissions and publication sales would be credited back to the Guggenheim Foundation. Wright countered by cabling, "Don't believe you mean exhibitor must pay for exhibiting at Museum and if deficit exhibitor pays that also, if so beneficence out, commerce in."[153] As time passed, suppliers threatened to place liens against the Fifth Avenue property. Wright had flown off to San Francisco in a state of exhaustion and was recovering in the warmer climate.[154] By early in 1954, the Guggenheim Foundation began to gradually pay off creditors.[155] As these measures were being carried out, Wright wrote a bitter self-serving letter to the trustees of the Solomon R. Guggenheim Museum in care of Harry Guggenheim. "As for the fool who believed that in refusing the offer of the Metropolitan Museum to provide a dignified setting and conduct the whole exhibition in January with no expense whatever to the fool," he lamented, "well, he (the fool) refused because he intended to remind New York that it really had a Guggenheim Museum and would now show to many thousands of them who did not know, where it was and how, but show them also that that museum meant something more to the people than just pictures on the wall." The letter continued on in the same vein for three single-spaced typed pages. The exhibition had been a success, but it had taken its toll in many more ways than money.[156] Nevertheless, the eighty-four-year-old architect was simultaneously in negotiations to mount the show in Los Angeles, Manila, Tokyo, and New Delhi in 1954. A few months after his indignant letter to Guggenheim, disagreements seemed to evaporate; he rented a suite at the Plaza Hotel as his permanent New York office, which was necessary as construction was anticipated on the museum.[157]

INDO-ASIAN TOUR, 1954: MANILA, TOKYO, NEW DELHI

Throughout 1953, one of the most significant prospects for *Sixty Years of Living Architecture* was a tour across the Pacific Ocean to the Philippines, Japan, and India, which would have provided opportunities for new audiences with entirely different points of reference. The proposal for India had arisen first in 1952 from a friend of Stonorov, Lawrence Meredith Clemson Smith (1902–1975), president of the American Federation of the Arts (AFA), who had been instrumental in contributing AFA funds to send the exhibition to Italy. The problem from the beginning was funding. Burton Cummings, AFA director, approached the Ford Foundation at Smith's suggestion, but did not receive a definite answer; they replied that the proposal would be considered if it were part of a larger American program, and to receive approval, would need to include Japan.[158]

While the exhibition was in Mexico City in October 1952, Jose M. Zaragoza, president of the Philippine Institute of Architects, through the presence of a Philippine delegate invited Wright as guest of honor to the Pan-Asiatic Congress of Architects scheduled for January 1953 in Manila.[159] Wright, in turn, offered his exhibition. Correspondence continued throughout 1952 in an effort to get financial support. The discussions came to a head in April 1953 when a major event occurred that broke the stalemate. No doubt discouraged by the lack of response for governmental or institutional funding, Wright turned again to private donors, securing a commitment from the Kaufmanns for $25,000 through their Charitable Trust to cover transport and insurance. From that point on, Stonorov and the AFA dropped out of the enterprise, and Wright was left as the sole person coordinating with Manila, Tokyo, and New Delhi.[160] Reminiscent of his grandiose 1933 world tour proposal, Wright conceived of the idea of continuing the tour beyond the Philippines, Japan, and India to Russia in an effort to influence the Cold War. He went directly to the United States government with the plan by writing the secretary of state, Dean Acheson, promoting his show as a "true peacemaker" that would be accepted in the Soviet Union because "the Russians greatly respect my name as an architect." There is no evidence the State Department replied.[161]

All parties remained committed to the Indo-Asian tour through 1954, but by August, Wright was compelled to cancel it. In a very confidential letter to Kaufmann Sr., he revealed some of the strain he had endured in recent years. "From excess flying about I have had a severe attack of Manieres Syndrome [*sic*: Meniere's disease]—a kind of seasickness on land that has clung to me for three weeks and still hangs on a little," he disclosed to his patron, "so have not been able to carry on at the old pace." As a result, he added, "Owing to the pressure upon me at this time I have abandoned the project of sending the show to the Orient. This show business is too troublesome and hazardous to models and drawings to continue."[162]

LOS ANGELES, 1954; CHICAGO, 1956

In November, while the exhibition was still on view in New York, Wright received a request from Kenneth Ross, director, Municipal Art Department, City of Los Angeles, to send it to Barnsdall Park, the location of Wright's Hollyhock House for Aline Barnsdall.[163] After delays caused by negotiations over the Indo-Asian tour, the show was finally scheduled for June 2–July 11, 1954, and ultimately was extended to July 25 due to its popularity. Wright followed his own New York example by designing and building a temporary pavilion, 20 feet by 192 feet, sited between the main Hollyhock House building and its garage. The materials of the structure were identical to those used in New York except, due to local codes, the pipe frame was welded, and corrugated plastic replaced the wire glass panels.[164] Wright produced a catalog, *Sixty Years of Living Architecture*, using the New York template, with a new cover and updated front and back pages.[165] While this was the last mounting of the exhibition in its original form, Wright did edit the show considerably for a ninth and final occasion, Frank Lloyd Wright Day declared by Mayor Richard J. Daley, held October 16–18, 1956, at the Hotel Sherman in Chicago, for which he produced another small catalog identical in format to the New York and Los Angeles examples (figure 5.39).[166]

The "Italian exhibition," or in its later form *Sixty Years of Living Architecture*, fell short of its potential to circle the globe—the United States, Europe, Central America, Asia, India, Russia—yet its impact is undeniable. While the original initiators, Ragghianti and Zevi, failed to produce an international architectural congress to influence postwar European reconstruction, they did, inadvertently, introduce Wright's work to something close to 450,000 people—the general public, architects, students, scholars, and journalists—in nine cities on two continents. Popularity led to widespread coverage in the media; in addition to local journalism (newspapers and radio), five specialized journals devoted double issues to Wright's work, amounting to small books for people who may never have attended the exhibition.

Wright's last major one-man retrospective was a milestone also for the introduction of display techniques that advanced understanding beyond simulacra by introducing color, sound, and, most important for Wright, a three-dimensional architectural experience in time: the demonstration Usonian House. The attainment of this component—a reduced version at Philadelphia and a full-scale version in New York—took fourteen years from conceptualization to realization. While the exhibition house had lost the effect of its uniqueness, it was the only means for visitors in an exhibition setting to understand Wright's major contribution to modern architecture: interpenetration of space, horizontally and vertically. Unfortunately, the cramped nature of the plot off Eighty-Ninth Street detracted from Wright's original intentions to create a relationship between the building and its landscape, where light, views, and symbolic associations enriched his design. Yet, the Exhibition Usonian House was successful in conveying one of Wright's chief goals: to present to the American people his design for high-quality housing in a single-family residence.

In the year of the European tour and the New York exhibition, coverage of Wright in periodicals skyrocketed to forty articles in 1952 and sixty in 1953, unequaled until the year of his death, 1959, which generated 101. Yet Wright would never see the publication of what amounted to his life's work—carried out many decades later by Bruce Brooks Pfeiffer, director, Frank Lloyd Wright Archives—which began with *Frank Lloyd Wright: The Complete Works in 12 volumes* (Tokyo: A.D.A. Edita, 1984–88), continued with *Frank Lloyd Wright Collected Writings* in five volumes (New York: Rizzoli International, 1992–95), and culminated with Pfeiffer, *Frank Lloyd Wright: Complete Works, 1885–1959* in three volumes (Cologne: Taschen, 2009–11).

In retrospect, while Ragghianti may be faulted for not realizing his original goals, he did do something that eluded Wright for his entire career: Ragghianti sought recognition and honor for Wright at the highest levels of the United States and Italian governments. While American ambassadors had attended the openings of his exhibitions in utter ignorance of his accomplishments during both the 1931 and 1952 European tours, Ragghianti tirelessly, and futilely, demanded that the president of the United States lend his office as patron to the Florentine manifestation. While this proved a failure, he was successful in honoring the Midwest architect in a government ceremony led by Count Carlo Sforza, the foreign minister, Republic of Italy. It is ironic that Wright was never aware of Ragghianti's diligent pursuit of official recognition by the American government of its most celebrated architect.

5.39 Frank Lloyd Wright press conference, October 16, 1956, *Sixty Years of Living Architecture*, Hotel Sherman, Chicago. Wright is presenting the Mile High skyscraper. (Courtesy Douglas M. Steiner, Edmonds, Washington)

CHAPTER 6

Coda, 1957–59

With the close of the last iteration of *Sixty Years of Living Architecture* in Chicago in 1956, Wright was within months of his ninetieth birthday and was occupied with more commissions than at any other time in his career (figure 6.1). Paradoxically, this was the very reason he could not permanently turn his back on exhibiting: his continuous goal of presenting his most recent work to the public. Although he professed abhorrence of the idea, he soon was thinking of organizing another tour when two opportunities arose that he conflated in his mind, resulting ultimately in confusion, conflict, and misunderstanding for all parties involved. This was the backdrop to the last architectural exhibitions that were planned during Wright's lifetime.

In the mid-1950s, the publicity surrounding the Guggenheim Museum, along with Wright's command of the sound bite in print and on television, raised him to the status of national celebrity. In November 1955, *House Beautiful* devoted an entire issue to his career, and, between 1953 and 1958, Ben Raeburn's Horizon Press brought out six books either written by Wright or compiled from his writings.[1] In August 1954, he opened a New York office in a two-room suite of his own design at the Plaza Hotel, which he and his wife occupied periodically until the end of his life.[2] Asked to identify a living architect, his name was the only one that came readily to the lips of the "man on the street."

Yet it was not just the Guggenheim, which broke ground in August 1956, that gave him increased stature, his practice now encompassed other monumental public buildings with construction beginning on the Kalita Humphreys Theater (1954–59; Dallas, Texas); Annunciation Greek Orthodox Church (1955–61; Wauwatosa, Wisconsin); and the Beth Sholom Synagogue. Design was ongoing on Monona Terrace Civic Center II (1954–57; Madison, Wisconsin); Bramlet Motor Hotel (1956; Memphis, Tennessee); Baghdad Opera House and Cultural Center (1957); and the Christian Science Church (1957; Bolinas, California); all of which remained projects.

The Guggenheim was just one of several major modern buildings completed or in the planning stage in the United States in the late 1950s. While Mies was supervising construction of the Seagram Building (1954–58) in Manhattan and Crown Hall (1950–56) on the campus of the Illinois Institute of Technology in Chicago, third-generation modernists including Eero Saarinen (Kresge Auditorium, MIT, 1954, Cambridge, Massachusetts; Yale Hockey Rink, 1953–58, New Haven, Connecticut), Paul Rudolph (Art and Architecture Building, Yale University, 1958–64), and Louis I. Kahn (Yale University Art Gallery, 1951–53; Richard Medical Research Laboratories, University of Pennsylvania, Philadelphia, 1957–65) were challenging the established leaders, who, in some cases, were also their former teachers. But nothing demonstrated that modern architecture had entered the mainstream like the success of the corporate giant Skidmore, Owings, and Merrill (SOM), with offices in major American commercial centers. The postwar building boom produced several landmarks for SOM: Lever House (1952) and Manufacturers Hanover Trust Bank Building (1954), both in New York City; Inland Steel Building (1957; Chicago); and the United States Air Force Academy (1958; Colorado Springs, Colorado).

If Wright took note of this activity—he was decidedly aware of SOM, whom he called "the three blind mice"—he made few references to it, except sarcastically. What was clear was that the

6.1 Frank Lloyd Wright on the balcony of the Guggenheim Museum, New York, 1959. Photo: William H. Short © SRGF, NY.

type of modern architecture he despised had begun to dominate America's city centers. Except for himself, there were no living architects he recognized as proponents of "Organic Architecture." So with the Guggenheim Museum in construction, more work in his office than he had had in his career previously, and almost universally regarded as America's greatest architect, Wright could look back over the past three decades and feel that if, indeed, he had not prevailed in changing the direction of American architecture, his self-reinvention had been an astounding success.

In fact, at times he even looked back nostalgically on the fierce debates with Johnson and Hitchcock. Although the three maintained contact, some of the old wounds never healed. In 1957, Johnson, then just over fifty years old, decided it was time to make candid remarks about Wright in public. Clearly smarting from Wright's witticisms about his Glass House—"a monkey cage for a monkey"—he gave a talk, "100 Years, Frank Lloyd Wright and Us," to the Washington State chapter of the American Institute of Architects in Seattle on the one hundredth anniversary of the institute's founding.[3] The lecture was conversational in tone, rather than formal, and consisted of critiques of Wright's rhetoric ("I'm annoyed by Mr. Wright's talking a good deal. He uses words in an unusual way"), contempt for history ("Was he born full-blown from the head of Zeus that he could be the only architect that ever lived or ever will?"), his use of structure ("Mr. Wright is very careless about how his buildings are held up once he has the way of looking at them settled"), and, perhaps most damning of all, his lack of regard for the Taliesin Fellows ("he treats them like slaves").[4]

By the end of Wright's life, Johnson clearly had ambivalent opinions about the elder architect, but his admiration had continued to grow after his surprising reassessment at the end of 1932. He ended his talk with a passionate two-page tribute to "the hieratic aspects of architecture, the processional aspects" that he had experienced at Taliesin West. Although Johnson is generally considered not to have been influenced by Wright, this is clearly not so. The "processional in architecture" became one of his fundamental tenets as he articulated it in his seminal 1965 article, "Whence and Whither," in *Perspecta, the Yale Architectural Journal*: "Architecture is surely *not* the design of space, certainly not the massing or organizing of volumes. These are auxiliary to the main point, which is the organization of procession. Architecture exists only in *time*."[5]

Only a few months later, Wright confronted Hitchcock, but on this occasion he softened his remarks. In the *New York Times Book Review*, Hitchcock made some keen observations in a review of Wright's *A Testament*. While he recommended it highly, Hitchcock nevertheless noted that it contained factual errors, but concluded "no one would look in such a text for precise historical fact but only for psychological atmosphere." Describing the text as "sermons" that were "studded with aphoristic sentences," the historian acutely discerned that: "These latest are somewhat clearer in their meaning than some of his earlier ones have been, and the vocabulary less private. They make the most sense—as interpretation of Wright's purpose, at least, if not as detailed guides for architectural conduct—if one can suspend one's sense of chronology and thus sense that they represent not his reaction to the immediate present of the Nineteen Fifties but to the entire seventy years during which he has been building."[6] Wright responded almost immediately by correcting Hitchcock on a point of fact, but devoted the majority of the letter to extending an olive branch. "The 'criticism' (*Times*) brings back to me the good old days 'in the making' when we were often together and yours was a hand 'up,' not 'out,'" Wright explained. "Couldn't you come out to Taliesin West sometime this winter—bring a friend—why not Philip?—for a friendly wrangle over consequences—and 'beyond modern architecture' at least?" Wright signed the letter: "Affection, Russell-Frank."[7] A turning point had been reached: a rapprochement between architect and historian.

With the superstructure of the Guggenheim now rising on Fifth Avenue, causing Wright to be frequently in New York to supervise construction, he evidently saw something of Johnson and Hitchcock periodically. In early 1958, when they were all to dine together, Wright became concerned when Hitchcock failed to appear.[8] Hitchcock's next, and probably his last, letter to Wright was addressed for the first time, "Dear Frank." He praised the museum building: "I think that you have created inside the most exciting sequence of spaces and a wholly new vocabulary of concrete forms."[9] Wright's last known letter to Hitchcock reiterated his credo that he cherished his enemies, yet he went on to declare, "we have been something to each other not easily discounted as life runs its course. I have hated internationalism in architecture with as lusty a hate as the enthusiasm with which you embraced it. And I've always felt you were not sure of what organic architecture meant. But the argument is still interesting and worth a man's good time? So next time I get to New York, . . . let's get together for a good drink and an even better dinner. Affection! Frank."[10]

One of the consequences of Wright's withdrawal from the Modern was the improvement in his relations with Johnson and Hitchcock, no longer subject to the strain of the public airing of their ideological differences. But after five years without official contact with the Museum of Modern Art, an invitation arrived. On March 24, 1958, Drexler wrote Wright a short businesslike letter, "We would like to organize an exhibition of your major buildings and projects since 1945. Such an exhibition might be scheduled for a year or two from now, and would occupy the Museum's third floor gallery."[11] Wright's reply was brief and to the point: "The answer is no." His explanation provides insight into his view of modern architecture at midcentury: "I am not much exhilarated by the thought of any exhibition of my work two years hence. Grandfather is not even now disposed to get out into the street to play with his grandchildren. The children, at any rate, might have profited by his example but most of them proved makeshift or have made a singularly unhonest [*sic*] denial of their grandparent. But many of them really knew no better and—so they say—'they had to live.' " He also revealed his current attitude about displaying his work after sixty-four years and over one hundred exhibitions. "Finally, I have lost any taste for 'exhibition' that any prospect of the sort does little more than raise boredom to positive distaste."[12] Apparently, Wright had other reasons for rejecting Drexler's invitation because he was considering organizing a small circulating exhibition himself around the same time.[13]

THE WORK OF FRANK LLOYD WRIGHT, DOW MEMORIAL LIBRARY, MIDLAND, MICHIGAN, JANUARY 1959 *FORM GIVERS AT MID-CENTURY*, CORCORAN GALLERY, WASHINGTON, DC, APRIL 1959 *FORM GIVERS AT MID-CENTURY*, METROPOLITAN MUSEUM OF ART, NEW YORK, JUNE 1959

In the last two years of his life, while Wright was distracted with major commissions and ambivalent about incorporating exhibiting back into his daily practice, he nevertheless produced shows of high quality. The last two major exhibitions organized during his lifetime reveal which of his later works he wished to present to the public and also how he was regarded in the mainstream architectural culture of the time. The first exhibition took place in a small Midwest city and the other was planned for the nation's capital and New York City. The first inquiry came from the Midland Art Association, Midland, Michigan, in November 1957, and the second came from *Time* Inc. in July 1958. While the Midland show opened first in January 1959, the *Time*-sponsored exhibition previewed at the Corcoran Gallery, Washington, DC, in April, two weeks after Wright's death.

The first request had a sympathetic reception because it came from an organization with a direct connection to a former Taliesin Fellow, Alden B. Dow. Midland is the location of Dow Chemical Company, which was founded in 1897 by Herbert Henry Dow, who died in 1930, but whose business grew to become one of the world's leaders in its field. His son, Alden B. Dow, graduated in architecture from Columbia University in 1931, joined the Taliesin Fellowship for the summer of 1933, and opened his practice in Midland in 1934. In 1953, Dow designed and built the local Grace A. Dow Memorial Library, which was named for his mother.

The association chose Wright as the subject for its major 1958 exhibition. It is unclear exactly how much influence Dow exerted from behind the scenes, but two of his employees, Phil Feddersen and Robert Gene Bell, were the co-organizers of the exhibition and correspondence was sent out on office letterhead. Feddersen wrote Wright's secretary, Gene Masselink, a friend he had known for some years, on November 7, 1957, to request a major exhibition of "drawings, photographs, models, etc." for spring 1958 to be held in the Dow Memorial Library gallery.[14] Masselink, who did not reply until January 13, 1958, reported that Wright "feels he has just about 'had it' " with exhibitions, but, held out some hope if the architect might be "persuaded against his better judgment."[15] On May 20, just two months after Wright had rejected the invitation from MoMA, Masselink added more encouragement when he reported that Wright was "considering putting together a small exhibition of the type you would want."[16] Motivated by this news, Feddersen and Bell proposed a definite date of February 1959 (later changed to January), and plans were made for a meeting with Wright at Taliesin.[17] The concept, as explained by Bell, was to show "a sequence of design development culminating in the work now in progress" drawing from "current and earlier years" by the use of "large photomurals, original drawings and renderings, and models" with emphasis on Michigan Usonian Houses. A brochure with a statement by Wright; an article by his Ann Arbor clients, William and Mary Palmer; and a checklist were planned.[18]

By the time a date was confirmed for the Michigan exhibition, planning had commenced on *Form Givers at Mid-Century*, which originated with the American Federation of the Arts (AFA) and *Time* magazine to commemorate the fiftieth anniversary of the AFA, an organization founded to bring art exhibitions to diverse regions of the nation. An impressive team of modernists was assembled to produce the show, inspired by the July 2, 1956, *Time* story, "The Twentieth Century Form Givers," which named six "masters" of modern architecture—Wright, Le Corbusier, Gropius, Mies, Breuer, and Neutra—and seven "significant" others: Johnson, Pei, R. Buckminster Fuller, Wallace K. Harrison, Gordon Bunshaft, Minoru Yamasaki, and Paul Rudolph.[19] *Time* associate editor, from 1945 to 1969, Cranston E. Jones (1918–1991), in consultation with Pietro Belluschi (1899–1994), dean of the Department of Architecture and Planning at MIT and an AFA trustee, acted as organizer. Belluschi, an Italian émigré who first made his reputation in Portland, Oregon, with the Equitable Building (1944–48), one of the first glass office towers ever built, had been dean since 1951. György Kepes (1906–2001), a Hungarian designer formerly of the New Bauhaus and Illinois Institute of Technology in Chicago, at the time a faculty member under Belluschi at MIT, was the installation designer. Jones also sought advice from former MoMA curators Kaufmann Jr., Johnson, and Peter Blake; the architects Breuer, Bunshaft, Edward D. Stone, and Eero Saarinen; and the staffs of *Time-Life* magazines: *Architectural Forum*, and *House and Home*.[20] The exhibition was planned to preview in Washington, DC, for the AFA convention in April 1959, travel to Manhattan for the summer season, and then tour for one or two years. *Time* Inc. was asked to produce a softcover catalog with a principal essay by Jones.[21]

The choice of Belluschi to shape the exhibition was a fortunate one for Wright because he had been one of his admirers for decades. Born in Italy, he settled in Portland, Oregon, in 1925, where he joined the office of A. E. Doyle.[22] Belluschi came to know two local figures in the late 1920s who influenced his thinking. One was the Prairie School architect William Gray Purcell (1880–1965), who had worked for Louis Sullivan in the early 1900s but is best known as a principal in the Minneapolis firm, Purcell and Elmslie. Through his lectures and book recommendations, Purcell introduced Belluschi to the Midwest origins of American modernism.[23] The other influence was W.R.B. Willcox of the University of Oregon, who introduced Wright to Portland with his exhibition and lecture in March 1931. Wright's visit coincided with an important event in Belluschi's career: tradition-bound members of the Portland Art Museum board were rejecting his modernist design for a new building. He sought to resolve the conflict by appealing directly to Wright for a letter of support. "You have sounded an intellectual awakening throughout the world, but our great public needs to have the trumpets blown into their ears," Belluschi declared.[24] Wright immediately responded with encouragement.[25] Even more revealing was the occasion in 1948 when Belluschi overcame opposition as one of the major supporters of Wright's nomination for the Gold Medal of the American Institute of Architects, which was awarded in 1949.[26]

In the first meeting to create the list of "form givers" in June 1958, Jones and Belluschi "took a leisurely three hours," which Jones later characterized as: "as much fun as picking the next Pope." First, they decided to select one important contemporary building at or nearing completion by each "genuinely creative man, rather than [focus] on movements, trends, water-down copies" and to exhibit scale models where possible. The tentative list consisted of three categories: the established leaders with Wright ranked as number one, followed by Le Corbusier and Mies; the second group consisted of Gropius and Breuer (considered together as one), Saarinen, Stone, and Aalto; and the last category consisted primarily of engineers: Pier Luigi Nervi and Fuller. Wright was ranked in first place without question, yet Belluschi had some reservations: "Certainly foremost. A free spirit forever inventing things, some of which are appropriate, some are not. Among those which are not are his Mile High Skyscraper. His Broadacres is a plan that was not meant for our society. He himself has invented the word 'mobocracy' for the desires and urges of our society. But he has great respect for the individual, and the emotional side of man." His reputation for being difficult had preceded him, but Kaufmann Jr. advised: "give the old man a booth to himself at the opening, and then forget about it."[27] The short list was finalized at twelve architects and one corporate firm: Wright, Mies, Le Corbusier, Gropius, Neutra, Aalto, Breuer, Harrison, Johnson, SOM, Eero Saarinen, Stone, and Fuller.[28]

By July 1958, the organizers of both exhibitions were ready to meet Wright to select material from his archives. Bell had an appointment with Wright for July 5 at Taliesin, but Wright was not there, so he met with Masselink and members of the Taliesin Fellowship. In a letter to Masselink several weeks later, Bell closed by stating, "Perhaps this might be the beginning of the travelling exhibit which Mr. Wright has hoped to assemble."[29]

Jones was more fortunate than Bell, he met with Wright the last week of July as an overnight guest at Taliesin. At this discussion the Guggenheim Museum was chosen as the featured building, and, at the as-yet-undetermined New York venue, Wright would be accorded a separate gallery of drawings of his earlier work that would provide context for the new museum design.[30] Although Masselink was brought in more than usual at the planning stage, probably due to the architect's increased architectural practice and more frequent travel to New York, Wright made the major decisions, such as choosing the drawings, which, ultimately, did not make it into the show.[31]

During the fall of 1958, details were being finalized on both exhibitions. Feddersen and Bell were at Taliesin in September to

6.2 Henry N. Cooper House, La Grange, Illinois (1887), 1890. Graphite pencil on off-white tracing paper, 15¼ × 25¼ in. (FLWFA, 8701.001). Wright inscribed at lower margin: "Drawing shown to Lieber Meister when applying for a job."

make the final selection, returning in November to transport the material to Michigan.[32] On November 9, Jones met with Wright at the Plaza Hotel. The architect initially chose the Larkin Building, Unity Temple, Robie House, Midway Gardens, SC Johnson Administration Building and Research Tower, Fallingwater, and the V. C. Morris Gift Shop, demonstrating the formal development of the Guggenheim. Wright also suggested two additional models: the Jester House (now Hennessey House for a new client) and the Marin County Civic Center.[33] A few days later, Jones met with James Rorimer, director of the Metropolitan Museum, who "became very enthusiastic" about securing the exhibition as "the big, summer long show," offering "two galleries in the new wing" in order to do something "pretty dazzling" as it was the first major architectural exhibition that the Metropolitan presented.[34] The museum schedule allowed for a preview opening on June 8, 1959, which was believed to be Wright's ninetieth birthday (in fact, his ninety-second). Jones telegraphed Wright on November 23 to tell him the good news.[35]

Exactly what happened next remains something of a mystery. Either Wright or Masselink or both were under the impression that the Midland exhibition, which had been largely selected by Wright, would be attached to *Form Givers*, thus fulfilling Wright's earlier wish for his own touring exhibition. In a December 12 letter from Feddersen to Masselink, he mentioned that the two had just had a "recent telephone call" where the "reception was poor." Feddersen remarked, "The news of the forthcoming exhibits of Mr. Wright's work at the Corcoran and Metropolitan was exciting to hear."[36] As a result of the telephone call, it appears, an announcement that the Midland show would be circulating "under the sponsorship of *Time* magazine" to Washington and New York was added to the Michigan exhibition invitation.[37] On January 11, the Midland exhibition opened; it continued until January 31.

On January 27, 1959, Jones arrived in Midland to review the material for possible additions to the Wright section of *Form Givers*, which to everyone's surprise set off a chain of events that put both exhibitions in jeopardy.[38] "[Jones] informed us that Mr. Wright's work will be but one among a dozen or more architects' work to be exhibited in their show," Bell wrote Gene, a few days later. "Therefore, he wants little (almost nothing) of what we have assembled. This is quite disappointing to us in many ways, as I am sure it is to Mr. Wright."[39] Wright reacted quickly. "A dozen or more other architects included I had not heard," Wright wrote, "and since I have never violated the determination made a half-century ago never to enter a competitive exhibition—please count me out."[40] Jones responded by spending the weekend of February 14–15 at Taliesin West, where Wright acquiesced, the schedule was set, and two new items were added to the checklist: the Price Tower model and a perspective of the Henry N. Cooper House (1887/1890; La Grange, Illinois), which Wright explained was the drawing that he had shown Sullivan when he was applying for the job as his draftsman (figure 6.2).[41]

On display at Midland were seven models, eight photo panels (8 feet by 8 feet) from the "Italian exhibition," thirteen large-format photographs, and thirty-one original drawings including the 22-foot-high original painting of the "Mile-High Illinois." The majority of the material was devoted to Michigan houses—built and unbuilt—including the Affleck House and Usonia I. In addition to landmark buildings, from Unity Temple to the Imperial Hotel to Taliesin West, projects of the last years of Wright's career such as Monona Terrace II, the Arizona State Capitol (1957; Phoenix), Baghdad Opera House and Cultural Center, Lenkurt Electric Company (1955–58; San Carlos, California), and the Marin County Civic Center and Fairgrounds (1957–62; San Rafael, California) were shown in a comprehensive exhibition for the first time (figures 6.3–5 and see figures B.55 and B.57). While the location was modest, the Michigan display stands as the last major exhibition primarily shaped by Wright himself and on view during his lifetime. At its closing, serious thought turned again to touring, either within the state or nationally, but attention was soon diverted to a more high-profile event.

After Jones's departure from Taliesin West in February 1959, Wright's enthusiasm grew: he had wanted a show at the Metropolitan Museum since 1953 when he unsuccessfully negotiated for *Sixty Years of Living Architecture*. "Since we have room enough at the Metropolitan," he queried Jones, "why not let us join your travelling show to one of our own, extending it on that occasion at our own expense? . . . Having so much hitherto unexhibited work in photographs, models, and drawings, it would be a pity not to see it together?" Wright also suggested that Taliesin could produce "an addenda" to slip into the exhibition catalog.[42] Wright's propensity to view exhibition planning as an extension of his architectural practice continued well past his eighties and stands in contrast to his disaffection for the Museum of Modern Art.

Jones was receptive to Wright's idea, but it took him two weeks to work out the arrangement with the museum. Wright may have been surprised when he heard that "the Metropolitan has an unbroken rule that no artist (architect) can have a one-man show while he is living." So Jones obtained permission to "extend the AFA show" into a generous gallery eighty and one-half feet by twenty-two feet ten inches for the additional Wright material

6.3 Monona Terrace II model, Madison, Wisconsin, 1954–57. Photograph by Richard Vesey. (FLWFA, 5632.0026-Vesey)

6.4 Marin County Civic Center, San Rafael, California, 1957–62. John H. Howe and A. Louis Wiehle with revision by Frank Lloyd Wright, delineators. Graphite pencil, color pencil, and sepia ink on white tracing paper, 34 × 83 in. (FLWFA, 5746.015)

6.5 Lenkurt Electric Company factory, San Mateo, California, 1955–58. Allen Davison, delineator. Watercolor, tempera, pastel, and color pencil on black illustration board mounted to plywood, 34 × 56 in. (FLWFA, 5320.015)

and a small introductory area devoted to Louis Sullivan and the Wainwright Building. Jones suggested new and unfamiliar material such as "fresh and original sketches," models (Marin County Civic Center), drawings (Arizona State Capitol), and examples of ornament.[43]

As spring approached, Jones was making last-minute preparations for the opening in Washington, DC, when Wright died on April 9, in Phoenix. After the April 23 opening at the Corcoran Gallery, arrangements continued with Masselink, who consulted with Olgivanna Wright over final details for the expanded exhibition in New York. When *Form Givers* opened on June 8, 1959, at the Metropolitan Museum, it occupied three galleries, one of which was devoted to Wright's work alone (figure 6.6). To insure that the exhibition design was uniform throughout, Kepes had dictated no original drawings for the group show. The centerpiece of the Wright section was the Guggenheim Museum model; next to "two, eight foot tall light columns (stainless steel, surrounded by translucent plastic) in which the color photographs are integrally a part." Of these, they included: Larkin Building, Robie House, Taliesin West, Price Tower, Marin County Civic Center, Fallingwater, and the SC Johnson Administration Building and Research Tower. The Ralph Jester model also was exhibited. After a sixty-five-year exhibition history, a breakthrough was reached when Jones exclaimed: "Of course, color tells the story as no black and white photograph can."[44] Wright's first posthumous exhibition was probably the first in which color photography, so crucial to understanding his built work, was used extensively.

Wright's private gallery was a contrast: in addition to photomurals, it contained original drawings, large models, three-dimensional objects, examples of building materials (custom bricks and concrete block), manuscripts, and books. Well-known masterworks such as Unity Temple and Midway Gardens were on display, but the Metropolitan exhibition is noteworthy because of the work that was added to bring the career retrospective current to the end of Wright's life. Buildings and projects added were a combination of selections by Jones and suggestions from Olgivanna Wright. Drawings displayed were of the Kalita Humphreys Theater; Annunciation Greek Orthodox Church; Helen Donahoe Triptych (1959; Phoenix, Arizona; figure 6.7); the Pilgrim Congregational Church (1958–63; Redding, California); and Wright's unbuilt gravesite, the Unity Temple and Cenotaph (1958; Spring Green, Wisconsin). Olgivanna Wright was reluctant to send this last design because she believed it was an unfinished work, but she relented. One of the most impressive exhibits was the model for the Master Plan of the Marin County Civic Center

6.6 Frank Lloyd Wright exhibition, *Form Givers at Mid-Century*, installation at the Metropolitan Museum of Art in New York, 1959. (American Federation of Arts, unknown photographer, American Federation of Arts records, 1895–1993, bulk 1909–69. Archives of American Art, Smithsonian Institution)

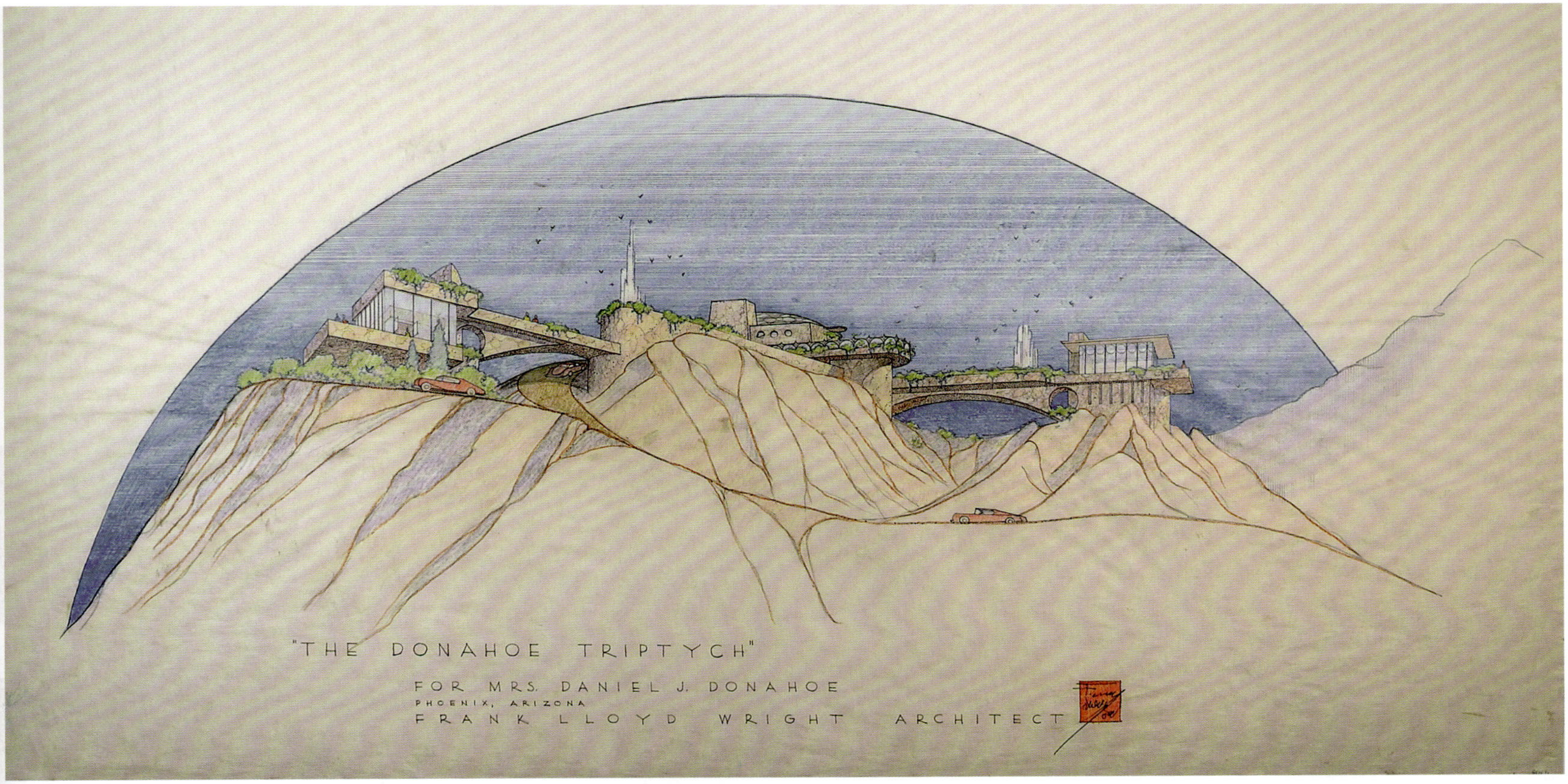

6.7 Donahoe Triptych, Helen Donahoe House, Paradise Valley, Arizona, 1959.
Graphite pencil and color pencil on white tracing paper, 55 × 58 in. (FLWFA, 5901.021)

and Fairgrounds, which was shipped from northern California by Wright's associate, Aaron Green.

The Metropolitan preview on June 8, which was attended by five hundred guests including Johnson, Breuer, Bunshaft, Gropius, and Stone, was regarded as a memorial tribute to Wright. Ironically, advance publicity—free and unplanned—was voluminous in the form of eulogies and obituaries that appeared in print media all over the world, especially in the United States, including all the trades (*Forum*, *Progressive Architecture*, *Architectural Record*, *Arts and Architecture*, *House and Home*, *House Beautiful*), and the art and mainstream magazines (*ARTNews*, *Arts*, *Atlantic*, *New Republic*, *Life*, and *Saturday Review*).[45]

Yet the April 27 review, "Art: The New Architecture," by the corporate sponsor, *Time*, exposed a shift in the architectural discourse that would become more pronounced by the mid-1960s. While declaring Mies the most influential exponent of modern architecture, the anonymous reviewer noted, "in the most advanced projects, it is equally clear that few architects now consider themselves blind Mies followers. . . . The reaction is recent, caused in part by the miles of glass facades that have resulted from Mies's approach in the hands of less talented practitioners." Johnson, in anticipation of another paradigm shift that would find elaboration in Robert Venturi's *Complexity and Contradiction in Architecture* (published by MoMA in 1966), was quoted as saying, "Mies is such a genius. But I grow old and bored." In contrast, among the form givers exhibited, *Time* concluded Wright stood out as "innovative" with "the sculptural form" of the Guggenheim Museum of reinforced concrete.[46] While *Form Givers* looked backward in its layout to Wright's first exhibitions with the Chicago Architectural Club fifty years before, it also presaged the intense architectural debates, some with Wright at the center, that would occur ten to twenty years into the future.

CHAPTER 7

Conclusion

A review of Frank Lloyd Wright's sixty-five-year exhibition history reveals that he was someone other than a self-promoter displaying his work in a search for clients, money, and fame; rather, he was an artist-architect projecting an avant-garde program, an innovator expanding the palette of installation design as technology evolved, and a social activist challenging architectural students and the public with his accompanying lectures and publications. Wright's motivations for staging his own exhibitions and cooperating with others to do so can be interpreted on many levels, and the rationale changed over time, but fundamentally his intentions can be directly traced to his formative years in Chicago in the 1890s and to his association with the Chicago Architectural Club, specifically. For the younger generation maturing in the decades after the destruction of the 1871 conflagration and the rebuilding of the central business district that followed, the new building types—office buildings, hotels, theaters, train stations, department stores—made possible by the mass production of the construction industry, proved that age-old European methods of architectural design were obsolete.

The image of a modern society rising on the shores of Lake Michigan rearticulated the earlier visions of Emerson, Whitman, and Horatio Greenough of an authentic American culture, a product of the unique conditions of its origins in the New World. Within professional organizations such as the Chicago Architectural Club and the Architectural League of America, architects were vigorously debating new roles for themselves in achieving these ends and how they would best serve the American people. The idealism of the era was captured most clearly in the writings of Sullivan from 1885 to 1900, years when Wright was decidedly under his Lieber Meister's influence.[1] In a series of essays, some originally delivered as lectures, some unpublished—"Characteristics and Tendencies of American Architecture," 1885; "May Not Architecture Again Become a Living Art?" 1897; "The Modern Phase of Architecture," 1899; and "The Young Man in Architecture," 1900—Sullivan called for nothing less than that American architects should be rooted to their particular time and place. Speaking to Wright's generation, if not to Wright himself, Sullivan invoked a moral argument when he stated, "you will realize at once and forever that you, by birth, and through the beneficence of the form of government under which you live—that you are called upon, not to betray, but to express the life of your own day and generation. That society will have just cause to hold you to account for your use of the liberty that it has given to you, and the confidence it has reposed in you."[2]

Wright came to believe that he was one of these, he became conscious of his destiny to employ his buildings symbolically to communicate ideas. His use of common words—nature, democracy, and organic—as Platonic ideals, which necessitated capitalization, gave them new meaning, which was not readily self-evident. Nature, Democracy, and Organic, while seemingly distinct, all shared one meaning in Wright's mind. Democracy was founded in America because it was conceived in pristine Nature, but by this Wright was not referring to flora and fauna. Rather, he meant "that inner harmony which penetrates the outward form ... and is its determining character; that quality in the thing that is its significance and its Life for us—what Plato called ... the 'eternal idea of the thing.'"[3] For instance, for him Democracy was an imaginary landscape or state of consciousness where the not-yet could be the now, eventually he called this Utopia, Broadacre City. Like neo-Platonists, Wright believed that concealed beneath the fractured and disordered surface of modern life lay a harmony and order—a latticework of logical and mathematical relations that demonstrated the natural laws of the universe and the power of the Divine, a Platonic notion of an ideal realm more real than his own perceived world. Geometry, proportion, and scale present in his design could elucidate the transcendental order of the universe, thus revealing the new truth. In this sense, the fabrication and display of the Broadacre City model as a representation of Democracy with its commanding physical form was a distraction from the more philosophical meaning found only in his writings.

Wright assumed the role of the nonconformist, who distrusted organized religion, education, and politics. He believed his inner conscience guided his actions and overrode institutions, it was his role to speak the truth even when it was offensive; in fact, the shock was meant to rouse people out of their passivity. Wright's unrelenting critique of American buildings and cities was just one side of a coin; on the reverse was his eternal optimism that reform was possible if the American people could rise up and overturn the status quo.

By showing in a museological setting, Wright sought to reach past the architectural profession to educate the public. To this end, he maintained his independence, for the most part, by financing his own exhibitions: he provided his own drawings and models, and to a lesser extent, photographs; he paid for shipping and the expenses of an apprentice to supervise the installation and act as a guide; and, in many instances, he funded self-generated publications that he intended to elucidate the shows. For instance, in the case of the 1932 MoMA exhibition, he financed the House on the Mesa model himself while other architects received a subsidy from the museum. By the 1950s when he began to see his self-funding as an unnecessary burden for the "Italian exhibition," which was supported by the corporate sponsor, Gimbel Brothers Department Store, he requested a $25,000 subsidy and accepted $5,000.

While representations of and writing about architecture through exhibitions were various means of communicating to the American people, realizing his vision in built form was of even greater consequence. While it is hard to quantify how many clients came to him as a result of exhibitions, there is no evidence that he had a strategic plan to meet the wealthy social elite or government officials at previews or other museum functions to realize projects for the purpose of obtaining income or social status.[4] In his decades-long association with the Modern, he never evinced any interest in courting, or even meeting, John D. Rockefeller Jr., or his son, Nelson; A. Conger Goodyear; or John Hay Whitney; and when Johnson proposed to introduce him to another MoMA trustee, Elizabeth Bliss Parkinson, the niece of Lillie P. Bliss—one of the three founders of the museum in 1929—as a guest at Taliesin West in 1948, Wright never pursued it. When Maloney insisted that the Broadacre City exhibition should be shown in Washington, DC, in 1935 to present Wright's planning ideas to the Roosevelt administration, the architect was reluctant to agree and had to be persuaded against his better judgment. Jensen was the one who conceived a plan to approach Rexford Tugwell and John Lansill of the Resettlement Administration; the architect remained at Taliesin.

Wright displayed his buildings and projects—symbolic representations of a higher order—as a means of communicating his expansive vision, what he came to call "In the Cause of Architecture." Since curators, historians, and critics rarely perceived their deeper meaning, he turned to the literary: lecturing, writing, and publishing. Yet again, his personal use of language led to miscomprehension. As European modern architecture was first introduced to the United States, then imported to the United States, and then assimilated into the United States, Wright's poetic vision for a new society appeared irrelevant. While his virtuosity combined with his abundance of formal ideas led to his masterworks of the 1950s and elevated his stature as a practicing architect, philosophically he was out of step with the times. Modern American architecture—a synthesis of European forms and American technology—that came to maturity in the 1950s was antithetical to his ideal. For Wright, being included in the 1950s surveys *Built in USA: Post-war Architecture* and *Form Givers* beside Gropius, Harrison, Johnson, and SOM was just as calamitous as his first exhibition in 1894 when he was hanging alongside adherents of the Beaux-Arts.

In fact, his fury at MoMA with the *Built in USA* show in early 1953 propelled him directly back sixty years to the 1893 Chicago World's Columbian Exposition, which was partially responsible for the resurgence of Classical Revival. In retrospect, Wright came to see the event as the signal moment when Sullivan's effort to realize an authentic American architecture was defeated by the importation of a European style, giving rise to the epithet, "the Lost Cause." "Owing to this first World's Fair," Wright declared, "recognition of organic American architecture would have to wait at least another half century."[5] The events of 1953: Wright's series of published articles in opposition to the "International Style" and his triumph with *Sixty Years of Living Architecture* at the site of the Guggenheim Museum in the fall was his demonstration that in his mind the "Cause" had not been lost.

While Wright's ideal of redeeming American society was impossible to realize, his exhibitions on other levels were successful, and in some cases, of historic importance. Over Wright's sixty-five-year exhibition history, technology evolved over the decades as various innovations were introduced. The importance of his formative years with the Chicago Architectural Club before World War I cannot be overemphasized. Since the original purpose of the club was to showcase draftsmanship, Wright's exhibitions featured drawings, which remained consistent elements of display throughout his career. Indeed, even after 1902 when he had a significant body of built work and the services of Fuermann and Sons, he strongly felt that showing drawings and photographs together destroyed the effect of the drawings, so he either placed the prints loosely on tabletops in 1907 and 1914 for casual perusal or mounted them separately in 1930–31.

This pattern was decisively interrupted during his first exhibitions at the Modern under the direction of Johnson (*Modern Architecture: International Exhibition*, 1932) and McAndrew (*Fallingwater*, 1938), both of whom had developed technical sophistication in Germany in 1929 by exposure to the consistent use of black-and-white photographs in architectural exhibitions and publications. Photographs of built work were a tangible demonstration of modernity, while Wright's delicate color renderings were reminders of the past. In fact, Wright's MoMA exhibitions were where continuous photographic experimentation was employed to overcome the limitations of simulacra: the curatorial goal was to replicate the experience of "the real thing" as closely as possible.

The one new development that was crucial for the exhibition of Wright's buildings was color photography, yet it was not until 1940 that he arranged for one of his apprentices, Larry Cuneo, to acquire equipment to shoot large-format color transparencies of Taliesin West for his career retrospective (*Frank Lloyd Wright: American Architect*, 1940–41). After World War II, the Modern mounted an entire show based on this technique showcasing Stoller's 8 by 10 color transparencies (*Taliesin and Taliesin West*, 1947), and Drexler carried it to the next logical step with stereo color slides (*Frank Lloyd Wright: Buildings for Johnson's Wax*, 1952). Scale came into play when photographic wall murals were introduced in the early 1950s (*Built in USA: Post-war Architecture*, 1953). Wright recognized that color photography and printing were critical to the visual understanding of his work.

It was not until 1951 at the "Italian exhibition" that all these techniques were employed simultaneously. Stonorov's modular installation utilized the four-foot grid to display photographic panels in a consistent format, but scale and color were shown to even greater advantage in a darkened room where Stoller's slides of Florida Southern College, the SC Johnson Administration Building and Research Tower, Taliesin, Taliesin West, and several Usonian Houses were projected on a 10-by-12-foot screen.[6] Finally, the major Wright room at *Form Givers* in 1959, designed by Kepes, a former faculty member at the New Bauhaus, Chicago, uniformly employed large-format color photographs to trace the evolution of Wright's built work. While Wright never wavered in his reliance on drawings for display, by the late 1950s, the advancement in color photography changed the way the public perceived Wright's architectural achievements.

Fundamental understanding of Wright's work is based on his skillful use of the figure-ground relationship, which separates him from other modernists. Wright did not create his buildings as objects isolated from their context. In his choice of materials—brick, stone, plaster, wood, concrete, copper—and in details such as art glass, textiles, and wall murals, color was critical. How these surfaces and architectural elements interacted with the materials of the site—foliage of trees and shrubs, landscape features such as hills, mountains, streams, waterfalls, or the ocean—was the essence of his design. It is astonishing to realize that for the first fifty years of his career, his built work was known only through black-and-white photographs, which certainly conveyed the forms but distorted their character.

While his use of scale models did not go through such a dramatic technological evolution, he continued to employ them for exhibition right up until his death. Materials changed over the decades from plaster to wood to plastic. While the size of the models was often consistent, on occasion he employed scale for specific effects. The most obvious case is the San Francisco high-rise for the The Call Building, first fabricated in plaster in 1914 at a height of 5 feet, 7¾ inches, and then remade in wood in 1940 at 7 feet, 8 inches; at each exhibition though, the model was paired with a tall base. The visitor saw the model from a worm's-eye view exaggerating its height: a dramatic representation of a skyscraper made imposing by scale. The other instance was House on the Mesa, which Wright made at a gargantuan size: 7 feet 8 inches by 3 feet 10 inches. Since he knew nothing of the other models or the installation plan, it is difficult to know if this was a conscious or unconscious decision on his part to command a spacious gallery to himself. Nevertheless, as it happened, the size of the model may have influenced where Wright's exhibit was placed in the museum galleries, thus ensuring him a commanding position over his rivals.

Models, even those that were designed with removable parts to reveal the interior, were insufficient to communicate moving through space in time (see figures 5.15 and 5.25). This was another reason why a full-scale exhibition house was of such paramount importance to Wright (see figures 5.34 and 5.36). His unrelenting resolve that extended over fourteen years and included five false starts demonstrates how fundamental Wright believed the exhibition house was to represent his architecture. In his planning discussions with Stonorov in 1950, he emphasized ideas over chronology, and the most important one was liberation of space. "New sense of a building as developing as Architecture, from within outward," Wright stated.

By 1900, Wright had eliminated the compartmentalization of the traditional house—boxes within boxes—allowing fluid movement where walls began to define, rather than enclose, space. This was the first revolutionary change in architectural space since the Renaissance. A building was no longer a massive enclosure punctuated with small openings to let in air and light; Wright had redefined the exterior walls as light screens, a composition of opaque and translucent panels—ribbons of glass over brick or plaster. The interior plan flowed around walls that acted more as free-standing partitions than as weight-bearing elements. Wright believed this was his fundamental contribution to architectural design, yet impossible to represent through simulacra.

While several of Wright's exhibitions stand out for their innovative installations designed by such talented modernists as Johnson (*Modern Architecture: International Exhibition*, 1932), Stonorov (the "Italian exhibition," 1951–54), and Kepes (*Form Givers*, 1959), Wright learned the nineteenth-century conventions of hanging with his first Chicago Architectural Club exhibition in 1894. But by the 1902 and 1907 Chicago Architectural Club shows, for instance, the gallery was arranged in a manner evoking his Oak Park Studio, where drawings were placed and models set out for viewing to impress clients. After the hiatus of 1915–29, there was a definite change in Wright's exhibition design. It was with the 1930–31 American/European tour that he began to show drawings only on a slanted surface, which mimicked an easel: he fabricated a doubled-sided panel system, each panel accommodating ten to twelve drawings, depending on size. For the next decade, this was Wright's preferred method, which he employed at least twice, in 1935 (*Broadacre City*) and 1940 (*Frank Lloyd Wright: American Architect*).

Since this technique was unique for architectural shows, it begs the questions: what was the source of Wright's idea and why was he using it? Wright was an art collector as well as an architect, and the heart of his collection was antique Japanese color woodcuts, printed with fugitive inks subject to fading, which lessen their aesthetic and financial value. At his house and studio, Taliesin, Wright designed slanted casework for displaying his matted prints, which he had amassed in the thousands after extended stays in Japan between 1913 and 1922.[7] He believed that the artwork was better viewed for brief intervals in natural light on a tilted surface. He also carried this approach over into his drafting studios at Taliesin and Taliesin West where slanted racks were built to review renderings. Wright felt so strongly about this method that he designed the Guggenheim Museum with outwardly slanted walls at a fifteen-degree angle for the ideal contemplation of abstract paintings on canvas. He did not back down when confronted by critics over his blatant disregard for the "rectilinear frame of reference"; however, in the end, the Guggenheim Museum curators ignored his wishes and employed alternate means of display.[8]

While Wright used didactics extensively in installations during the Depression (*Broadacre City*, 1935, and *Frank Lloyd Wright: American Architect*, 1940), his most effective means of communication was through publishing related to exhibitions. The synergy he established over a fifty-year period is remarkable in its achievements: the 1907 Chicago Architectural Club exhibition resulted in *Ausgeführte Bauten und Entwürfe* and the *sonderheft* of *XX. Jahrhunderts* (two of the most important architectural publications of the twentieth century); the 1930–31 tour and *Modern Architecture: International Exhibition* in 1932 involved preparation of material for a catalogue raisonné, which was used by Hitchcock for the 1942 *In the Nature of Materials*, the monograph that replaced the canceled 1940 MoMA exhibition catalog. McAndrew's *Fallingwater* exhibition was largely dependent on the 1938 *Architectural Forum* Wright issue. The sequence of 1907–11 was repeated again between 1951 and 1954 when Stonorov and Loeb ordered nine hundred photostats of drawings that were bound and then exhibited at the "Italian exhibition." The six volumes became the catalyst for reviving the discussion of publishing a "Magnum Opus," a proposal Kaufmann Jr. had initiated at the Modern in 1946. Despite Wright's involvement and the enthusiastic interest of Zevi and Stonorov, as well as Kaufmann Jr., this ambitious and costly enterprise was not realized as intended.

In one way, Wright's exhibition history is unique, as is evident by the fact that in the sixty-five years after his debut in 1894, only one independent exhibition catalog was produced of his monographic exhibitions: *Pictorial Record*, a product of Plaut in Boston in 1940.[9] Wright's aversion to objective critical attention remained a lifelong obstacle. Another important fact to consider is that aside from the illustrated booklet the Modern published for the 1938 *Fallingwater* show, which contained an excerpt of Wright's text from *Architectural Forum*, the only written material related to Wright exhibitions that the Modern issued were press releases. Press releases are rarely considered worth analysis due to their straightforward journalistic content, but the MoMA Publicity Department, and Sarah Newmeyer (MoMA, 1933–48) in particular, excelled in the new field of museum public relations.[10] Newmeyer's press releases, which were sent out through wire services beyond New York City to all parts of America, summarized exhibition descriptions provided by the curators, but promotional language was also used to increase interest in the event. MoMA's claim that Wright was America's "greatest living architect" was published in newspapers in major cities and small towns; it was one of the most effective ways MoMA popularized Wright.[11]

The majority of Wright's exhibitions were personal, which meant he avoided critical interpretation assiduously; in fact, his antipathy was so great that he habitually referred to historians and critics as the "enemy." Ironically, they were crucial to his reinvention beginning in 1929. Before the Wasmuth Verlag publications, Wright was primarily a regional figure, who was known in Chicago as one of the leaders of the "New School of the Middle West." During the 1920s, this perception began to change as modern architecture progressed in Germany and Holland. Without the architect's knowledge or cooperation, Walter Gropius included black-and-white photographs of the Larkin Building and the Robie House in the landmark show, *Ausstellung Internationaler Architekten* (Exhibition of International Architects), at the Weimar Bauhaus in 1923.[12] Equally important, the Austrian American architect, Frederick Kiesler, under the artistic direction of Mies, included one black-and-white photograph of the Alice Millard House (1923–24) (misidentified as Taliesin) at the *Internationale Plan-und Modell-Ausstellung neuer Baukunst* (Modern Architecture: Designs and Models Exhibition), which was part of the extremely well-attended *Werkbundausstellung Die Wohnung* (Werkbund exhibition, The Dwelling) at Stuttgart in 1927.[13]

As the postwar generation, the Europeans were seeking an architecture that rejected imperial dynasties, nationalism, and classical tradition in favor of social and political reform, Taylorism, and the abstract forms of De Stijl and Constructivism. As modern architecture coalesced in the 1920s, a canon was being codified in Dessau and Stuttgart. Part of the historicizing was the recognition of antecedents as foundation for the modern movement. Wright's Robie House and the Larkin Building were admired for their rejection of historical styles, use of industrial materials and structure, and as examples of a new modern society. With recognition by the Bauhaus and the Deutscher Werkbund, Wright had gone from a regional to an international figure, although he was regarded as a precursor. This was one of the aspects of the mythification of modern architecture that Wright seized on, but rather than rejecting this notion outright, he redefined his role as the "originator" of modern architecture. When he had the opportunity, he imposed this interpretation on the curators (McAndrew in 1940 and Stonorov in 1950) of career retrospectives. He held to this opinion until his death, even though he was continually disappointed that this was not widely recognized as fact.[14]

When presented in 1932, *Modern Architecture: International Exhibition* was an optimistic reflection of the decade before the Great Depression had begun to permeate all aspects of American society. The point of view of Barr, Hitchcock, and Johnson was free from the social and political concerns that came to preoccupy the nation during the Roosevelt administration; their pure formalist and European bias was more a product of the period before the 1929 American stock market crash than after. Within the context of the times, the reception of the museum's first architectural show was more complex than has generally been believed, as Philip L. Goodwin, a MoMA trustee and chairman of the 1944 Architecture Committee, revealed in his preface to *Built in USA: 1932–44*, "This ['International Style'] architecture was so new and surprising that hostile and ill-informed critics and architects still frequently assert that the Museum is trying to impose a foreign style on the United States. Such was not the Museum's intention in the first place, nor has it been the Museum's program since. First to proclaim the new European architecture here and constantly interested in its more recent developments, the Museum has also been first to show the growth of an authentic modern American style, its relationship to the American background and its debt to, as well as its reaction from, the 'International Style.'"[15]

This period of revisionism in the Department of Architecture at the Modern was carried out under the strong leadership of McAndrew, who was appointed in 1937, and was continued by Mock, who succeeded him in 1943. The decided shift to American architecture as subject matter, which had already begun in 1933 with the Chicago exhibition curated by Hitchcock and Johnson, increased under McAndrew and Mock, who explored themes such as regionalism; vernacular architecture, both rural and industrial; and social housing and community planning. Wright benefited from their less doctrinaire point of view; as a result, both McAndrew and Mock were his most sympathetic MoMA curators. McAndrew struck an appreciative tone when he wrote after the Fallingwater show in 1938, "His best recent work, like the Kaufmann House on Bear Run, Pennsylvania, and the Johnson Factory at Racine ... proclaim dramatically that his imaginative powers are undimmed and untarnished after the longest and most important career in American architecture."[16] For McAndrew, the canon was flexible. It was during this period between the two wars that the Modern consistently proclaimed Wright "America's greatest architect" in its press releases, and he became a fixture in the Department of Circulating Exhibitions helping to establish his reputation nationally for his revived practice and his emphasis on the Usonian House aimed at the American middle-class family.

While Wright continued to denigrate the European interpretation of modern architecture, its influence increased especially in the late 1930s after Gropius and Mies immigrated to the United States to take up positions at Harvard University and the Illinois Institute of Technology, respectively. He was judged against this standard, and he began to judge himself against this standard. While Wright always rejected the concept of "internationalism" in the history of modern architecture as Gropius, Barr, and Johnson espoused it, he seemingly was influenced by Hitchcock's rewriting of his career as it appeared in the MoMA catalog. With the exclusion of the book *The International Style: Architecture Since 1922*, which was not published by or under the sponsorship of MoMA, Johnson's installation and Hitchcock's essay (with some exceptions) had presented Wright as a modern architect in company with Le Corbusier and Mies. Although he always considered himself a modern architect dating from his years of exhibiting with the Chicago Architectural Club, he now realized that in order to compete in the new environment, he had to adapt to a new paradigm.

Without abandoning any of his own first principles, he began to design in a more "modern" style: he eliminated or reduced the use of ornament, he introduced system construction into his Usonian House program, and he interpreted traditional elements such as doors and windows in a more abstract vocabulary of flat roofs and alternating opaque and translucent planes. The Modern quietly abandoned its historical position of presenting Wright as the last surviving component of the triumvirate of Richardson-Sullivan-Wright; from 1953 to 1959, he was regarded as the most important modern American architect as he was presented at *Built in USA: Post-war Architecture* and *Form Givers*.

What was the impact of Wright's architectural exhibitions over the course of sixty-five years? Answering that question depends on under what circumstances and where and when the exhibition took place; each exhibition can be understood on many levels. Wright's shows were largely unique throughout his career when compared to his contemporaries because, for the most part, he originated them himself and controlled all aspects of their presentation, including the publications and lectures.[17] With the Chicago Architectural Club, Wright began by transforming the gallery into an extension of his studio, establishing direct communication with other architects and the public thereby eliminating the jury; from the very beginning, exhibition practice was integrated into his artistic production. During these formative years from the age of twenty-seven to forty-seven, exhibitions were not viewed as external events, they were complementary to his work like furniture or landscape design. Their popularity created a synergistic effect: high attendance led to greater coverage in the popular press, which itself increased attendance whether he was being recognized for his avant-garde design or his unconventional personal life. For Wright, the Chicago Architectural Club exhibitions became the standard by which all future exhibitions were compared: he returned automatically again and again to this model (to the shock of museum curators such as McAndrew and Barr in 1940). His last exhibition, *Form Givers*, in 1959 came full circle, repeating the formula he employed in 1902 and 1907 almost exactly: a group show where he demanded and received a separate gallery for a presentation of his own choosing.

Certainly, the club exhibitions were used as a means to attract local commissions, but the greatest impact during these years occurred outside the United States as a result of the landmark 1907 show. Wright clearly understood it contained his best work, and he was moved by Monroe's review to preserve its intent in his 1908 *Architectural Record* article, where he effectively used photography to communicate the breadth and depth of his executed buildings. There is little doubt that the *Record* article probably turned up in Berlin influencing one or more people at Ernst Wasmuth Verlag, who may have already been familiar with Wright's architecture, to choose him as a subject for a *XX. Jahrhunderts sonderheft*. The 1907 exhibition, thus, set off a chain of events that culminated in the two-volume Wasmuth Verlag portfolio, the most famous architectural publication of the twentieth century.

The Chicago Architectural Club paradigm expanded exponentially with the 1930–31 American-European tour and with it Wright's audience. With the American component, especially its showing in New York at the Architectural League, Wright sought to reestablish his reputation as the nation's most important architect as Mumford's assessment in *The Brown Decades* filtered down to such popular tastemakers as *Time* magazine. No exhibition had greater impact on that tour than the one shown at the Akademie der Kunst in the summer 1931; ostensibly, Wright's first and only monographic show in Berlin during his lifetime. While he had made the initial selection of material, the exhibition was shaped by Europeans: Wijdeveld, Mendelsohn, and Klumb (to exactly what degree each participated is unknown). But reviews indicate that the unofficial "curators" did not apply any theoretical or formalist criteria to communicate political or aesthetic issues, with the exception of prominently displaying redrawn perspectives of key buildings before 1910 to demonstrate Wright's level of abstraction predating Cubism. The survey revealed that the development of Wright's architecture had, in the estimation of the most vociferous German critics, retrogressed, relegating his significance to the past. Yet the confrontation in Berlin had lasting influence on second-generation German modern architects, Americans such as Philip Johnson, and, not least, on Wright himself. It is far more likely the Berlin exhibition that Mies and Gropius remembered later was the 1931 installation, an assumption that few commentators have taken into consideration.

Wright self-consciously entered the critical discourse regarding urbanism with a major visual statement, the 12-foot-square Broadacre City model, which sought to rewrite Le Corbusier's Radiant City. With the 1935 exhibitions, he took a bold stand, advocating social reform through community planning. His futurist projection of a nation redesigned from coast to coast fueled debate about the value of nineteenth-century city centers such as New York and Boston; at the same time, he admitted he was giving form to demographic changes that were already altering much of the topography of the western states. The creation and display of the model, which shifted attention away from Wright's more complex written theories, was the single most important factor in carrying the debate into the future.[18] For Zevi and Ragghianti in the aftermath of decades of Fascist oppression, the Broadacre City model was intended to become the centerpiece of an ambitious international conference on European postwar planning. Although this program was never realized, Broadacre City had significant representation in Florence and on the subsequent tour: a bird's-eye view of the model accompanied by a recorded explanation by Wright, and a major section (a dialogue between Wright and Stonorov) published in the catalogs. For the Wright partisans in Italy, the Broadacre City model captured their imaginations and became the architectural representation of individual liberty that had been absent from Italy during Mussolini's rule.

In the period before and after World War II, Wright benefited from the power and reach of the Museum of Modern Art. Despite his temperament, he had more exhibitions at MoMA's Manhattan venue and across the nation under the auspices of its well-organized Department of Circulating Exhibitions than any other artist. The museum curators—McAndrew, Drexler, and Johnson—immediately recognized the architectural importance of such disparate buildings as Fallingwater, SC Johnson Administration Building and Research Tower, and Taliesin and Taliesin West by selecting them for single building shows for presentation to the public. In the postwar period, the variety and complexity of Wright's monumental architecture as well as his humanist theoretical position challenged American modern architecture as it became increasingly institutionalized, lapsing into banality. Wright's Manhattan exhibitions were covered by the press, which led to even greater awareness by the architecture profession and the general public. With increased exposure through the new media of radio and television, he became the first "starchitect," perhaps the epitome of the term: an icon, a great hero of popular culture.

Wright's longevity made possible the immense impact of his exhibitions in the 1950s, he lived to within months of his ninety-second birthday and was an advocate and activist until the end. Life expectancy for an American man born in 1867 was approximately forty years, meaning Wright would have died not long after his 1907 Chicago Architectural Club exhibition; instead, he lived and produced for another fifty-two years. As a result, interest in his work and ideology spread globally, reaching beyond even western Europe to Asia. It is only possible to speculate on the reception his work would have received if *Sixty Years of Living Architecture* had been shown in Japan and India (a goal he had first articulated in 1933).

Wright's desire to bypass the architectural profession and direct his exhibitions to the public, especially the "young man in architecture," created a hybrid display that fits, with some reservations, the definition of a contemporary blockbuster. While even his most well-attended shows never attained the number of visitors recorded in the late twentieth and early twenty-first centuries at venues such as the Metropolitan Museum of Art, the Art Institute of Chicago, or the Tate Modern for artists such as Monet or Picasso, several share many of the traits of the genre as outlined by the art historian Emma Barker.[19] For instance, *Sixty Years of Living Architecture* (the "Italian exhibition") and *Form Givers* presented a career retrospective of a canonical modern artist, were planned as tours years in advance, museums competed to host the exhibition, and corporations provided the funding. While Wright was uncomfortable with the commercialism attached to the *Broadacre City* tour and *Sixty Years of Living*

Architecture when he was informed that they would be shown in department stores (in Pittsburgh and Philadelphia, respectively), this was the one perk the sponsors demanded. Advertising in the form of a corporate logo appearing in a prominent place in the display itself and on posters and invitations was never proposed; what the two Kaufmanns received, in addition to bringing potential customers into their stores, was the public esteem of being modern-day art patrons. However, *Time* Inc. not only funded *Form Givers*, it was also the organizer of the content. Wright's last exhibition was more commercial than any he had participated in up to that moment, begging the question: Why did he agree? Perhaps he was swayed by the prestigious venues.

One exhibition that certainly fits the genre is *Sixty Years of Living Architecture* at the site of the Guggenheim Museum in 1953; for its era, it was a genuine blockbuster.[20] It was a career survey of the "greatest living American architect" on an unprecedented scale (including a custom-designed fully furnished house constructed on site), which received advance publicity, primarily in the *New York Times*. The visitors, probably many of whom did not normally attend art exhibitions, stood in long lines motivated by what Barker describes as the major attraction of a blockbuster: a once-in-a-lifetime experience. The demand was so great the exhibition was open at night and was extended past its scheduled closing date.

While Wright had revised the material since the show had debuted in Philadelphia in early 1951, Stonorov's shaping remained intact. Stonorov did not concentrate exclusively on the formalist conventions of presenting Wright's buildings as individual works of art—comparable to modern paintings and sculpture—as was the method Johnson and Barr as connoisseurs employed at the Modern. Stonorov sought an exhibition of "atmosphere" as he described it: "FLW—The man, The landscape, His life, His looks/Poetry, Sentiment, Structure, Scale/creator-architect, inventor (gadget for living), engineer (steel, concrete). Universality (to remain), sentiment. Houses make love to trees and grow." Stonorov's creation of a blockbuster, which had drawn 100,000 people in one month in Philadelphia, is illustrated by his use of the two architectural photographers documenting Wright in the 1940s and 1950s: Pedro E. Guerrero and Ezra Stoller. Stonorov chose Guerrero's more personal images of Wright himself, his two studio-residences (Taliesin and Taliesin West), and Taliesin Fellows for the introduction, but he also featured the formalist interpretation: Stoller's photographs projected as large-scale images on a screen in a room arranged as a small theater. While Stonorov's approach was criticized by Zevi and Ragghianti for its lack of a historical or theoretical point of view and would have been rejected by Johnson and Drexler for its inclusion of biographical elements over strict formalist analysis, it struck just the right cord with Wright's preferred audience: the American people. While Wright's exhibitions from 1894 to 1959 were undoubtedly about buildings as art, what made them compelling for the public was the added factor of human interest: the artist and his work.

Frank Lloyd Wright Exhibitions, 1894–1959

Format: Curator, title, date, sponsor, organizer, venue, and notes to content.

Chicago Architectural Club exhibitions are documented here, but no attempt has been made to document exhibitions at other architectural clubs during the same time frame. It was not possible to be definitive as surviving evidence is imprecise.

Traveling exhibitions: All traveling exhibitions organized or coorganized by Frank Lloyd Wright are listed separately by venue.

Museum of Modern Art traveling exhibitions*: Modern Architecture: International Exhibition* (1932) is listed separately by venue. Other exhibitions organized by the Architecture [and Design] Department are listed once for the opening at MoMA, and only the number of venues is included. Exhibitions solely organized by the Department of Circulating Exhibitions (DCE) are listed once and the number of venues noted. For more details about these exhibitions see "Department of Circulating Exhibitions," in the Museum of Modern Art Archives.

Commercial displays of furniture and furnishings, which were presented in showrooms, are not included in this list.

Unconfirmed exhibitions: I have a file of approximately one hundred tentatively proposed exhibitions—primarily from colleges, universities, art museums, and art or architecture organizations—where no additional information could be documented. The correspondence falls into the following categories: (1) letters of request, no answer; (2) letters of request with marginal notes either by Wright or his secretary for possible material to lend, no further letters of confirmation; (3) letters of request, marginal note to contact MoMA to obtain either photographs or a circulating exhibition. This material is not included in this list.

1894
Frank Lloyd Wright
Untitled, Seventh Annual Exhibition
May 10–May 24 (extended to June 14), 1894
Chicago Architectural Sketch Club (later Chicago Architectural Club): W. W. Clay, chairman; Charles A. Coolidge, Irving K. Pond, W. G. Williamson, T. O. Fraenkel, Charles A. Kessell, jury
Art Institute of Chicago
Five watercolors by Ernest Albert and one pen and ink drawing by Wright for the Milwaukee Library and Museum competition

---

1895
Frank Lloyd Wright
Untitled, Eighth Annual Exhibition
May 23–June 10, 1895
Chicago Architectural Club: Irving K. Pond; Robert C. Spencer Jr.; T. O. Fraenkel, jury
Art Institute of Chicago
Study for Cheltenham Beach (delineated by Cecil Corwin and Hugh M. G. Garden)

1898
Frank Lloyd Wright
Untitled, Eleventh Annual Exhibition
March 22–April 11, 1898
Chicago Architectural Club: Louis J. Millett, J. K. Cady, Robert C. Spencer Jr., jury
Art Institute of Chicago
Examples of Electro Glazing, Luxfer Prism

1900
Frank Lloyd Wright
Untitled, Thirteenth Annual Exhibition
March 20–April 3, 1900
Chicago Architectural Club: Dwight Perkins, eight local members and two jurors from outside Chicago
Art Institute of Chicago
Oak Park Studio; Moore, McAfee, Eckhart, Waller, Devin Houses; All Souls Church (earlier version of Abraham Lincoln Center); and Husser fireplace
Ten-page illustrated section of the catalog

1902
Frank Lloyd Wright
The Work of Frank Lloyd Wright, Fifteenth Annual Exhibition
March 28–April 15, 1902
Chicago Architectural Club: George R. Dean, Richard E. Schmidt, Robert C. Spencer Jr., jury
Art Institute of Chicago
Sixty-four items, primarily from 1900–1902, including Hillside Home School, Oak Park Studio, *Ladies' Home Journal* Houses and Plan for a Prairie Town, Bradley, and Hickox Houses
The Work of Frank Lloyd Wright, fourteen-page illustrated section of the catalog

---

1907
Frank Lloyd Wright
Untitled, Twentieth Annual Exhibition, Including Exhibition of Frank Lloyd Wright
March 29–April 26, 1907
Chicago Architectural Club: Irving K. Pond, Alfred H. Granger, Howard Van Doren Shaw
Art Institute of Chicago
Thirty-eight items, primarily 1904–7, including Larkin Administration Building, Unity Temple, University of Wisconsin Boathouse (Yahara Boathouse), Dana, Darwin Martin, Cheney, and Coonley Houses
Checklist only

1910
Bruno Möhring
Untitled (Drawings displayed during lecture)
February 16, 1910
Union of Berlin Architects
Wilhelm Strasse, Berlin, Germany

Frank Lloyd Wright
Untitled, *First Annual New York Cement Show*
December 14–20, 1910
Universal Portland Cement Company; organizer unknown
Madison Square Garden, New York
Wright designed a concrete pavilion decorated with inlaid colored glass and tile, which served as one of the exhibits installed by the Cement Company

---

1913
Frank Lloyd Wright
Untitled (Non-competitive plan), Scheme of Development for a Quarter-Section of Land within the Limits of the City of Chicago, Illinois, Competition, as part of *Housing Exhibition*
April 15–June 15, 1913 (approximate)
City Club of Chicago: George E. Hooker, civic secretary
City Club of Chicago, 315 Plymouth Court, Chicago
Published in *City Residential Land Development: Studies in Planning; Competitive Plans for Subdividing a Typical Quarter Section of Land in the Outskirts of Chicago*, ed. Alfred B. Yeomans (Chicago: University of Chicago Press, 1916)

Frank Lloyd Wright
Untitled, Twenty-Sixth Annual Exhibition
May 6–June 11, 1913
Chicago Architectural Club: Andrew N. Rebori, chairman; R. S. Degolyer, Elmo C. Lowe
Art Institute of Chicago
Hotel Madison, Lake Geneva Hotel, Booth and Schroeder Houses
Checklist, two illustrations

1914
Frank Lloyd Wright
The Work of Frank Lloyd Wright: Work Done since the Spring of 1911, Only Is Included in This Exhibit, Twenty-Seventh Annual Exhibition
April 9–May 3, 1914
Chicago Architectural Club: Wright not juried
Art Institute of Chicago
Thirty-one exhibits including Midway Gardens, Imperial Hotel, Coonley Playhouse, and Taliesin
The Work of Frank Lloyd Wright: Work Done since the Spring of 1911, Only Is Included in This Exhibit, Wright designed checklist

---

1918
Curator unknown
Untitled, Thirty-First Annual Exhibition
Chicago Architectural Club
April 4–May 1, 1918
Some Wright work included as part of Illinois architects exhibit for the Illinois Centennial. Primary document unseen

1923
Walter Gropius
Ausstellung Internationaler Architekten (Exhibition of international architects)
August 8–September 30, 1923
Bauhaus: Walter Gropius, director
Weimar, Germany
Photographs of Larkin Administration Building, Robie House

1927
Friedrich [Frederick] Kiesler
Internationale Plan—Und Modellausstellung Neuer Baukunst (International Exhibition of Modern Architecture: Designs and Models), part of *Die Wohnung, Werkbund Ausstellung* (The Dwelling, Werkbund exhibition)
July 23–October 9, 1927
German Werkbund: Mies van der Rohe, artistic director
Stuttgart, Germany
Alice Millard House (misidentified as Taliesin)

1930
Pauline Schindler
Contemporary Creative Architecture
April 20–30, 1930
Western Association of Art Museum Directors: Thelma Spaeth, executive secretary
University of California, Los Angeles
Six photographs by Brett Weston of Wright's Los Angeles houses, 1920–24

Frank Lloyd Wright
The Work of Frank Lloyd Wright, 1893–1930
May 12–22, 1930
School of Architecture: E. Baldwin Smith, chairman
Princeton University, Princeton, New Jersey

Frank Lloyd Wright
The Work of Frank Lloyd Wright, 1893–1930
May 29–June 12, 1930
Architectural League of New York: Raymond Hood, president
115 East Fortieth Street, New York
"Approach and setting by Joseph Urban"

Frank Lloyd Wright
The Work of Frank Lloyd Wright, 1893–1930
September 25–October 12, 1930
Art Institute of Chicago: Robert B. Harshe, director
Art Institute of Chicago

Frank Lloyd Wright
The Work of Frank Lloyd Wright, 1893–1930
October 15–25, 1930
Madison Art Association: Walter Agard, president
State Historical Library, University of Wisconsin, Madison

Frank Lloyd Wright
The Work of Frank Lloyd Wright, 1893–1930
November 20–December 8, 1930
Layton Art Gallery: Charlotte Partridge, owner
Layton Art Gallery, Milwaukee

1931
Frank Lloyd Wright
The Work of Frank Lloyd Wright, 1893–1930
March 6–10, 1931
Department of Architecture: W.R.B. Willcox, head
Art Museum, University of Oregon, Eugene

Frank Lloyd Wright
The Work of Frank Lloyd Wright, 1893–1930
March 11–15, 1931
University of Washington, Seattle: Harlan Thomas, chairman
Henry Gallery, University of Washington, Seattle

Frank Lloyd Wright, H.Th. Wijdeveld, Heinrich Klumb
The Work of Frank Lloyd Wright, 1893–1930
May 9–31, 1931
Five-member Honorary Committee and five-member Exhibition Committee: H.Th. Wijdeveld
Stedelijk Museum, Amsterdam

Frank Lloyd Wright, H.Th. Wijdeveld, Heinrich Klumb, Erich Mendelsohn
The Work of Frank Lloyd Wright, 1893–1930
June 17–July 12, 1931
Preussische Akademie der Kunst: Max Liebermann, president
Preussische Akademie der Kunst, Berlin

Frank Lloyd Wright et al.
The Work of Frank Lloyd Wright, 1893–1930
July 22–August 16, 1931
Staaliche Beratungsstelle für das Baugewerbe: Organizer unknown
Staaliche Beratungsstelle für das Baugewerbe, Stuttgart

Frank Lloyd Wright et al.
The Work of Frank Lloyd Wright, 1893–1930
September 12–28, 1931
Koninklijke Maatschappij der Bouwmeesters: Organizer unknown
Kunst van Heden, Antwerp, Belgium

Frank Lloyd Wright et al.
The Work of Frank Lloyd Wright, 1893–1930
October 3–11, 1931
La Société Centrale d'Architecture et de l'Art Contemporain: Organizer unknown
Palais des Beaux-Arts, Brussels

Frank Lloyd Wright et al.
The Work of Frank Lloyd Wright, 1893–1930
Ca. December 1, 1931–January 1, 1932
Sponsor unknown, organizer unknown
Academie van Beeldende Kunsten en Technische Wetenschappen, Rotterdam

1932
Philip Johnson, Henry-Russell Hitchcock
Modern Architecture: International Exhibition
February 9–March 23, 1932
Museum of Modern Art, New York: Philip Johnson, Henry-Russell Hitchcock, Alfred H. Barr Jr.
Museum of Modern Art, New York
Roberts, Robie, Millard, Richard Lloyd Jones Houses; House on the Mesa; and Taliesin

Philip Johnson, Henry-Russell Hitchcock
Modern Architecture: International Exhibition
March 30–April 22, 1932
Museum of Modern Art, New York
Pennsylvania Museum of Art, Philadelphia

Philip Johnson, Henry-Russell Hitchcock
Modern Architecture: International Exhibition
May 2–28, 1932
Museum of Modern Art, New York
Wadsworth Atheneum, Hartford, Connecticut

Philip Johnson, Henry-Russell Hitchcock
Modern Architecture: International Exhibition
June 9–July 8, 1932
Museum of Modern Art, New York
Sears Roebuck, Chicago

Philip Johnson, Henry-Russell Hitchcock
Modern Architecture: International Exhibition
July 23–August 30, 1932
Museum of Modern Art, New York
Bullocks Wilshire, Los Angeles

Philip Johnson, Henry-Russell Hitchcock
Modern Architecture: International Exhibition
September 15–October 17, 1932
Museum of Modern Art, New York
Buffalo Fine Arts Academy, Buffalo, New York

Philip Johnson, Henry-Russell Hitchcock
Modern Architecture: International Exhibition
October 14–December 5, 1932
Museum of Modern Art, New York
Cleveland Museum of Art, Cleveland, Ohio

Frank Lloyd Wright
Architecture of Frank Lloyd Wright
November 14–December 5, 1932
Studio Committee: James Watrous, chairman
Memorial Union, University of Wisconsin, Madison

1933

Edwyn A. Hunt, Sheldon Cheney, Frank Lloyd Wright (for Wright section)
Title unknown (modern American architecture)
January 16–ca. January 26, 1933
Extension Division, University of California, Berkeley: Edwyn A. Hunt
UCB Extension Auditorium, 540 Powell Street, San Francisco
Photographs of Evans, Robie, Freeman Houses; Midway Gardens; plans and photographs of Conventional House (content unconfirmed)

Curator unknown
Title unknown
January 27–unknown 1933
San Francisco Forum
Beaux Arts Gallery, 116 Geary Street, San Francisco
Contents similar to above (unconfirmed)

Philip Johnson, Henry-Russell Hitchcock
Early Modern Architecture: Chicago, 1870–1910
January 18–February 23, 1933
Museum of Modern Art, New York
Museum of Modern Art, New York (six venues)
William H. Winslow House

Philip Johnson, Henry-Russell Hitchcock
Modern Architecture: International Exhibition
February 11–28, 1933
Museum of Modern Art, New York
Milwaukee Art Institute, Milwaukee

Philip Johnson, Henry-Russell Hitchcock
Modern Architecture: International Exhibition
March 17–April 19, 1933
Museum of Modern Art, New York
Cincinnati Art Museum, Cincinnati, Ohio

Philip Johnson, Henry-Russell Hitchcock
Modern Architecture: International Exhibition
April 29–May 25, 1933
Museum of Modern Art, New York
Rochester Memorial Art Gallery, Rochester, New York

Luigi Maria Caneva, Enrico Agostino Griffini
V Triennale: Fifth International Triennal of Modern Decorative and Industrial Arts and of Modern Architecture
Triennale: Giulio Barella, president
May 10–September 30, 1933
Palazzo dell'Arte, Parco Sempione, Milan
One of twelve galleries devoted to personal exhibitions of leading modern architects. Others were Auguste Perret, Konstantin Melnikov, André Lurçat, Josef Hoffmann, Willim Dudok, Walter Gropius, Mies van der Rohe, Erich Mendelsohn, Adolph Loos, Le Corbusier, Antonio Sant'Elia.

Philip Johnson, Henry-Russell Hitchcock
Modern Architecture: International Exhibition
June 5–July 8, 1933
Museum of Modern Art, New York
Worcester Art Museum, Worcester, Massachusetts

Philip Johnson, Henry-Russell Hitchcock
Modern Architecture: International Exhibition
July 22–August 20, 1933
Museum of Modern Art, New York
Currier Gallery of Art, Manchester, New Hampshire

Philip Johnson, Henry-Russell Hitchcock
Modern Architecture: International Exhibition
September 1–30, 1933
Museum of Modern Art, New York
Toledo Museum of Art, Toledo, Ohio

Philip Johnson, Henry-Russell Hitchcock
Modern Architecture: International Exhibition
October 11–November 11, 1933
Museum of Modern Art, New York
Fogg Museum of Art, Harvard University, Cambridge, Massachusetts

Philip Johnson, Henry-Russell Hitchcock
Modern Architecture: International Exhibition
November 17–December 15, 1933
Museum of Modern Art, New York
Dartmouth College, New Hampshire

1935

Frank Lloyd Wright
Broadacre City at the *Industrial Arts Exposition*
April 15–May 15, 1935
National Alliance of Art and Industry: Alon Bement, director
Rockefeller Center, New York; Thomas J. Maloney, manager, International Arts Exposition
Models including Broadacre City, House on the Mesa, St. Mark's Tower, San Marcos Water Gardens, Standardized Overhead Gas Station, New Theater, Colonial Equivalent, and Davidson Farm Unit. Drawings including Lake Tahoe Summer Colony, Emerald Bay, California.

Frank Lloyd Wright
Broadacre City
June 7–14, 1935
University of Wisconsin, Madison, organizer unknown
State Historical Library

Frank Lloyd Wright
Broadacre City, New Homes for Old
June 18–29, 1935
Kaufmann's Department Store and Federal Housing Administration: Edgar J. Kaufmann Sr., and William T. Schoyer, special assistant, FHA
Kaufmann's Department Store, Pittsburgh

Frank Lloyd Wright
Broadacre City
July 3–23, 1935
Corcoran Gallery, Washington, DC: Karl Jensen; Queene Ferry Coonley, and Susan E. Curran, financial sponsors; Emily P. Millard, manager of special exhibitions
Corcoran Gallery, Washington, DC

Frank Lloyd Wright
Broadacre City
August 1935
Southwestern Wisconsin Fair: N. S. Boardman, president
Iowa County, Wisconsin

Frank Lloyd Wright
Broadacre City
December 1–7, 1935
Abby Beecher Roberts (mother-in-law of John Lautner) arranged for a storefront
Marquette, Michigan

1936
Frank Lloyd Wright
Untitled
October 1936
Phillips Academy: Charles H. Sawyer, curator
Addison Gallery of American Art, Andover, Massachusetts
Twenty-eight drawings and photos including Robie, Millard, Coonley Houses; Larkin Building; Taliesin; San-Marcos-in-the-Desert; Hoult and Willey Houses

1937
Frank Lloyd Wright
Untitled
April 1937
Kalamazoo Institute of Arts: Mrs. William McKinley Robinson
Kalamazoo, Michigan
Drawings and photographs, unspecified

1938
John McAndrew
A New House on Bear Run, Pennsylvania by Frank Lloyd Wright
January 25–March 6, 1938
Museum of Modern Art, New York: John McAndrew
Museum of Modern Art, New York
Fallingwater: photographs by Hedrich-Blessing, Luke Swank, and John McAndrew

John McAndrew, Elizabeth Bauer Mock
Trois Siècles d'art aux États Unis
May 24–July 31, 1938
Museum of Modern Art, New York: A. Conger Goodyear, president
Galerie Nationale de Jeu de Paume, Paris

Leslie Cheek Jr., Frank Lloyd Wright
Title unknown
October 14–ca. October 24, 1938
Department of Fine Arts, College of William and Mary, Williamsburg, Virginia: Leslie Cheek Jr., head
Department of Fine Arts, College of William and Mary, Williamsburg, Virginia
Photographs from the college, MoMA, and Frank Lloyd Wright (Robie and Coonley Houses; Unity Temple, Taliesin, Imperial Hotel, Jacobs House I, SC Johnson) and eighteen to twenty drawings from Wright

1939
John McAndrew
Three Centuries of American Architecture
February 15–March 15, 1939
Museum of Modern Art, New York: John McAndrew
Museum of Modern Art, New York (twelve venues)
The architectural section shown in Paris reorganized by Elodie Courter as a traveling exhibition. Robie House model

Frank Lloyd Wright
Photographs and Drawings of Buildings by Mr. Frank Lloyd Wright
May 3–May 20, 1939
International Union of Architects: F. R. Yerbury, director
Building Center, 158 New Bond Street, London

Frank Lloyd Wright
Title unknown
Ca. May 26–June 9, 1939
Architectural Association: organizer unknown
36 Bedford Square, London
Transferred from the Building Center, see entry above

United States Housing Authority in collaboration with the Department of Architecture, Museum of Modern Art
Houses and Housing in *Art in Our Time: An Exhibition to Celebrate the Tenth Anniversary of the Museum of Modern Art*
May 10–September 20, 1939
Museum of Modern Art, New York
Museum of Modern Art, New York (six venues)
Robie House and Jacobs House I

1940
Henry-Russell Hitchcock, Frank Lloyd Wright
Buffalo Architecture, 1816–1940
January 12–February 12, 1940
Buffalo Fine Arts Academy: Gordon Washburn
Albright Art Gallery, Buffalo, New York
Drawings of Heath and Martin Houses, Larkin Administration Building

James S. Plaut, Nelson W. Aldrich Jr.
Frank Lloyd Wright: A Pictorial Record of Architectural Progress
January 24–March 3, 1940
Boston Architectural Club
Institute of Modern Art, Boston

John McAndrew, Elizabeth Bauer Mock, Frank Lloyd Wright
Frank Lloyd Wright: American Architect
November 13, 1940–January 5, 1941
Museum of Modern Art, New York: John McAndrew
Museum of Modern Art, New York

1941
Curator unknown
Title unknown
August 4, 1941
Chamber of Commerce: J. M. Moe, secretary
Mount Horeb, Wisconsin
Davidson Farm Unit model

Elizabeth Bauer Mock
The Wooden House in America
September 9–30, 1941
Museum of Modern Art, New York: Circulating Exhibitions Department
Museum of Modern Art (twenty-two venues)
James B. Christie House, Bernardsville, New Jersey

1943
Frederick B. Deknatel
Masters of the Four Arts: Wright, Maillol, Picasso, Strawinsky
May 4–29, 1943
Harvard University: Committee of Edward Waldo Forbes, Paul J. Sachs, Arthur Pope, W.R.W. Koehler, Priscilla B. Grace, A. Tillman Merritt, Frederick B. Deknatel
Fogg Museum of Art, Harvard University, Cambridge, Massachusetts
Models of Robie, Jacobs I, Lewis and Jester Houses; Usonia I. Drawings of Jester, Lewis, Pauson, Pope, Watkins, Wall, and Burlingham Houses; SC Johnson Administration Building, Taliesin West; Usonia I; and Cooperative Homesteads. Photographs of Little, Ennis, Jacobs, Pauson, and Wall Houses; Unity Temple, Taliesin, Fallingwater, Taliesin West. Drawings of decoration for Midway Gardens and Imperial Hotel

1944
Mrs. Otto Spaeth
Title unknown (religious buildings, unconfirmed)
March 15, 1944
Dayton Art Institute: Mrs. Otto Spaeth
Dayton Art Institute, Dayton, Ohio

Elizabeth Bauer Mock
Built in USA: 1932–1944 in *Art in Progress: A Survey Prepared for the Fifteenth Anniversary of the Museum of Modern Art*
May 24–October 22, 1944
Museum of Modern Art, New York: Elizabeth Bauer Mock
Museum of Modern Art, New York (sixteen venues)
Fallingwater, Taliesin West, Goetsch-Winckler House

1945
Elizabeth Bauer Mock
Tomorrow's Small House: Models and Plans
May 29–September 30, 1945
Ladies' Home Journal: Richard Pratt, editor
Museum of Modern Art, New York
"Opus 497 Glass House," built as Lowell Walter House (1948–50), was published in the June 1945 issue.

Frank Lloyd Wright
When Democracy Builds
November 9–December 9, 1945
Milwaukee Art Institute (after 1957, Milwaukee Art Museum): Mary Frances Coan (Frances "Polly" Nemtin), acting director
Milwaukee Art Institute

1946
Elizabeth Bauer Mock
If You Want to Build a House
January 8–30, 1946
Museum of Modern Art, New York
Museum of Modern Art, New York (fifty-one venues)
Reorganized by the DCE as *Modern American Houses* (twenty-four venues) and *Modern Houses in America* (twenty-four venues)

Elizabeth Bauer Mock
A New Country House by Frank Lloyd Wright: A Scale Model
June 18–September 3, 1946
Museum of Modern Art, New York
Museum of Modern Art, New York
Gerald Loeb House

Editors, *Life* and *Architectural Forum*
American Houses
November 18–December 7, 1946
Life and *Architectural Forum*
Architectural League, 115 East Fortieth Street, New York
Prepared for the State Department for circulation in South America

Edgar J. Kaufmann Jr.
Modern Rooms of the Last Fifty Years
November 26, 1946–January 16, 1947
Museum of Modern Art, New York (fifty venues)
Museum of Modern Art, New York

1947
Philip Johnson
Taliesin and Taliesin West
April 15–June 15, 1947
Museum of Modern Art, New York
Museum of Modern Art, New York
Color photographs by Ezra Stoller

Leon Kroll
(Exhibition of work of new inductees)
May 22, 1947
National Institute of Arts and Letters: Leon Kroll
633 West 155th Street, New York
Photographs borrowed from MoMA

Frank Lloyd Wright
Untitled
October 4–November 20, 1947
State Fair of Texas: John Rosenfield, *Dallas Morning News*
Dallas Museum of Fine Arts
Rogers Lacy Hotel, V. C. Morris House, Huntington Hartford Sports Club, Bell House, Unitarian Church at Madison

1948
Frank Lloyd Wright and Raymond Da Bell
Untitled
June 15–August 31, 1948
Art Committee, Cliff Dwellers Club: Raymond Da Bell
Cliff Dwellers Club, Chicago

Frank Lloyd Wright et al.
Organic Architecture by Frank Lloyd Wright
October 14–November 14, 1948
Gallery Committee, University of Wisconsin Memorial Union: Walter Prideaux, chairman
Memorial Union, University of Wisconsin, Madison

Leslie Cheek Jr.
The U.S. House—Then and Now
October 20–November 14, 1948
Virginia Museum of Fine Arts: Leslie Cheek Jr., director
Virginia Museum of Fine Arts, Richmond

1949
Paton Price
The Architectural Model, Plans, Renderings of A New Theatre
January 26–February 27, 1949
New Theatre Corporation: Paton Price, director
Wadsworth Atheneum, Hartford: C. C. Cunningham, director
Wadsworth Atheneum, Hartford, Connecticut
New Theatre

Paton Price
Frank Lloyd Wright: A New Theatre
April 5–17, 1949
New Theatre Corporation: Paton Price, director
Museum of Modern Art, New York: Philip Johnson
New Theatre

1951
Oscar Stonorov, Frank Lloyd Wright
Untitled
January 26–February 26, 1951
Gimbel Brothers Department Store, Philadelphia: Arthur C. Kaufmann, president
Gimbel Brothers Department Store, Philadelphia

Oscar Stonorov, Frank Lloyd Wright, Carlo Ludovico Ragghianti
Mostra dell'Opera di Frank Lloyd Wright (Work of Frank Lloyd Wright)
June 24–August 20, 1951 (exhibition cut short)
Studio Italiano di Storia dell'Arte, Florence: Carlo Ludovico Ragghianti, Italian and American Executive Committees (Mario Fabiani and Arthur C. Kaufmann, heads)
La Strozzina, Palazzo Strozzi, Florence

1952
Arthur Drexler
Frank Lloyd Wright: Buildings for Johnson's Wax
January 15–March 16, 1952
Museum of Modern Art, New York: Philip Johnson
Museum of Modern Art, New York
SC Johnson Administration Building and Research Tower

Oscar Stonorov, Frank Lloyd Wright
Frank Lloyd Wright: Sechzig Jahre lebendige Architektur; Sixty Years of Living Architecture
February 2–March 16, 1952
Kunsthaus, Zürich: Werner Moser
Kunsthaus, Zürich

J. J. Polivka
Untitled
February 19–March 2, 1952
Art Gallery, Stanford University
Art Gallery, Stanford University, Palo Alto, California
San Francisco Butterfly Bridge

Oscar Stonorov, Frank Lloyd Wright
Exposition de L'oeuvre de Frank Lloyd Wright
April 3–May 1, 1952
United States Information Agency and École Nationale Supérieure des Beaux-Arts, Paris: Darthea Speyer, USIA and G. Vedres
École Nationale Supérieure des Beaux-Arts, Paris

Karl Kamrath, Preston Bolton
New Directions in Domestic Architecture
April 20–May 11, 1952
Contemporary Arts Museum, Houston: Karl Kamrath, founder and board member
Contemporary Arts Museum, Houston

Oscar Stonorov, Frank Lloyd Wright
Frank Lloyd Wright: 60 Jahre Architektur
May 16–June 15, 1952
Haus der Kunst, Munich: Brigitte D'Ortschy, Otto Bartning
Haus der Kunst, Munich

Oscar Stonorov, Frank Lloyd Wright
Frank Lloyd Wright
July 2–August 10, 1952
Ahoy'gebouw, Rotterdam: B. P. Willebeek Le Mair, director; installation by J.J.P. Oud
Ahoy'gebouw, Rotterdam

Oscar Stonorov, Frank Lloyd Wright
Sixty Years of Living Architecture
October 19–26, 1952 (approximate)
Pan-American Congress of Architects: Carlos Lazo, president, Sociedad de Arquitectos Mexicanos
Colegio Nacional de Arquitectura, Ciudad Universitaria, Mexico City

1953
Henry-Russell Hitchcock, Arthur Drexler
Built in USA: Post-war Architecture
January 20–March 15, 1953
Museum of Modern Art, New York: Philip Johnson
Museum of Modern Art, New York (fifty venues)
V. C. Morris Gift Shop, Jacobs House II, SC Johnson Research Tower, Sol Friedman House

Frank Lloyd Wright
Untitled
May 1953
Frank Lloyd Wright office, San Francisco: Aaron Green
San Francisco Museum of Art
San Francisco Butterfly Bridge, also exhibited in May at Emporium Department Store, Joseph Magnin Store, and possibly other unconfirmed venues

Curator unknown
Untitled
May 14–23, 1953
H. C. Price Company
Oklahoma Building, International Petroleum Exposition, Tulsa
Price Tower model exhibited

Frank Lloyd Wright
Small Exhibition of Organic Architecture
May 27–June 28, 1953
American Academy of Arts and Letters: Leon Kroll
National Institute of Arts and Letters, New York

Frank Lloyd Wright
Small Exhibition of Organic Architecture
July 11–16, 1953
Fifth Annual Foreign Affairs Conference: John F. Fitchen III
Colgate University, Hamilton, New York

Frank Lloyd Wright, Oscar Stonorov
Sixty Years of Living Architecture: The Work of Frank Lloyd Wright
October 22–November 29, 1953 (extended to December 13)
Solomon R. Guggenheim Foundation, New York: Harry Guggenheim and Frank Lloyd Wright
Solomon R. Guggenheim Museum site, 1071 Fifth Avenue, New York

1954
Frank Lloyd Wright
Title unknown
March 8–21, 1954
Phoenix Fine Arts Association, Phoenix: Dorothy Johnson Bergamo, director
Phoenix Fine Arts Association, Phoenix, Arizona
Small exhibition of drawings and photographs of recent work

Frank Lloyd Wright, Oscar Stonorov
Sixty Years of Living Architecture: The Work of Frank Lloyd Wright
June 2–July 11, 1954 (extended to July 25)
Municipal Art Patrons of Los Angeles; Municipal Art Department, Recreation and Parks Department, City of Los Angeles: Kenneth Ross
Hollyhock House, Barnsdall Park, Los Angeles

Frank Lloyd Wright
Untitled
November 11–December ??, 1954
Stella Elkins Tyler School of Fine Arts: Boris Blai, dean
Temple University, Philadelphia
Work for Kaufmann family

1955
Frank Lloyd Wright
Untitled (Testimonial Banquet)
February 10, 1955
Frank Lloyd Wright Endowment: Cary Carraway, chairman
Great Hall, Memorial Union, University of Wisconsin, Madison
Monona Terrace II model

Frank Lloyd Wright
The Work of Frank Lloyd Wright
August 8–October 31, 1955
Memorial Library, University of Wisconsin, Madison: Louise Henning, reference librarian
Memorial Library, University of Wisconsin, Madison

Frank Lloyd Wright
Untitled
October 12–November 9, 1955
Memorial Union, University of Wisconsin, Madison: Elliott Starks, art director
Memorial Union, University of Wisconsin, Madison
Current drawings and models, 1932–55

1956
Frank Lloyd Wright
Sixty Years of Living Architecture: The Work of Frank Lloyd Wright
October 16–18, 1956
Frank Lloyd Wright Day Committee: Cary Carraway, president
Bal Tabarin, Hotel Sherman, Chicago

Frank Lloyd Wright
"The Mile High Building—The Illinois" and Architecture as He Sees It Today
October 19, 1956
A.R.H. Barker Presentation
Orchestra Hall, Chicago
Mile High Building

1957
Frank Lloyd Wright
Showcase for Better Living
May 4–12, 1957
U.S. Rubber Company: Unknown
International Home Building Exposition, New York Coliseum
Fiberthin Air House

Frederick Gutheim
Untitled
May 15–July 15, 1957
AIA Centennial Committee: Edward Purves, Leon Chatelain
National Gallery of Art, Washington, DC
Price Tower

Frank Lloyd Wright
Frank Lloyd Wright
May 1957
Institute of Contemporary Art, Washington, DC: Robert Richman, director
Corcoran Gallery of Art, Washington, DC
Extension of AIA Centennial exhibition due to need for more space showing Mile High Building; Beth Sholom Synagogue; Oasis, Phoenix Capitol

Frank Lloyd Wright
Untitled
June 29–30, 1957
Spring Green High School: Walter Koester
Spring Green High School, Spring Green, Wisconsin
Monona Terrace II

Frank Lloyd Wright
Recent Architecture
October 13–November 30, 1957
Institute of Contemporary Art, Washington, DC: Robert Richman, director
Corcoran Gallery of Art, Washington, DC

1958
Frank Lloyd Wright
Recent Architecture
February 14, 1958
School of Architecture, University of Oklahoma: J. Palmer Boggs
School of Architecture, University of Oklahoma
Traveling exhibition from Corcoran Gallery

Frank Lloyd Wright
Recent Architecture
March 16, 1958
University of Arkansas: John Williams
Fine Arts Center, Fayetteville, Arkansas
Traveling exhibition, which originated at the Corcoran Gallery

Frank Lloyd Wright
Untitled
May 2, 1958
Iraqi government: unknown organizer
Iraqi Consulate, 14 East Seventy-Ninth Street, New York
Baghdad Opera House and Cultural Center

Unknown curator
Marin's Finest Hour
August 27–September 7, 1958
Marin County: organizer unknown
California State Fair, Sacramento
Marin County Civic Center model

Frank Lloyd Wright
Untitled
September–October 1958
University of Kansas: Curtis Besinger
Museum of Art, Lawrence, Kansas

Frank Lloyd Wright
International Festival of Art
October 29–November 23, 1958
Women's Division of the Federation of Jewish Philanthropies: Mrs. Maurice Westheim, chairman
Seagram Building, 375 Park Avenue, New York

Frank Lloyd Wright
(Exhibition above traveled)
After November 19, 1958
International Festival of Art, Montreal, Canada: Roger Astous
Unknown

1959

Frank Lloyd Wright, Robert Gene Bell, Phil Feddersen
The Work of Frank Lloyd Wright
January 11–31 (extended to no later than February 7), 1959
Midland Art Association, Midland, Michigan: Robert Gene Bell, Phil Feddersen
Grace A. Dow Memorial Library, Midland, Michigan

Frank Lloyd Wright, Cranston E. Jones
Form Givers at Mid-Century
April 23–May 14, 1959
Time Inc. for American Federation of the Arts, Washington, DC: Cranston E. Jones, *Time* Inc.; Harris K. Prior, director, AFA
Corcoran Gallery of Art, Washington, DC
Preview of traveling show for AFA fiftieth anniversary convention

Frank Lloyd Wright, Cranston E. Jones, Olgivanna Lloyd Wright
Form Givers at Mid-Century
June 9–September 6, 1959
Time Inc. for American Federation of the Arts, Washington, DC: Cranston E. Jones, *Time* Inc.; James J. Rorimer, director, Metropolitan Museum of Art
Metropolitan Museum of Art, New York
Planned to travel to Museum of Fine Arts, Boston; Carnegie Institute; Minneapolis Institute of Arts; and Virginia Museum of Fine Arts

Frank Lloyd Wright Models, 1894–1959

Format: building title, date, and location; fabrication; present location

FLWFA Frank Lloyd Wright Foundation Archives (Museum of Modern Art/Avery Architectural and Fine Arts Library, Columbia University, New York)

MoMA Museum of Modern Art, New York

1. Abraham Lincoln Center (All Souls Building), 1898–1905
Chicago, Illinois
Fabricated by Albert Van den Berghen
FLWFA (Fragment)
(FLWFA)

2. Larkin Company Administration Building, 1902–6
Buffalo, New York
Fabricated by Albert Van den Berghen
FLWFA
(FLWFA)

3. Unknown Prairie House, ca. 1903–4
Unknown location
Whereabouts unknown, presumed destroyed
(From *Frank Lloyd Wright Newsletter*, vol. 4, 1981)

4. Unity Temple, 1905–8
Oak Park, Illinois
Fabricated by Albert Van den Berghen in 1906 for presentation to clients
Destroyed ca. 1913–14
(FLWFA, 0611.0004)

5. Unity Temple, 1905–8
Oak Park, Illinois
Replacement fabricated in Japan, ca. 1920
Kyoto University, Department of Architecture
(Private Collection)

6. Avery Coonley Playhouse, 1912
Riverside, Illinois
Fabricated by Albert Van den Berghen
Whereabouts unknown, presumed destroyed
(FLWFA, 1500.0007)

7. The Call Building model no. 1, 1912–13
San Francisco, California
FLWFA (Fragment)
(FLWFA, 1500.0004)

8. Midway Gardens, 1913–14
Chicago, Illinois
Whereabouts unknown, presumed destroyed
(FLWFA, 1500.0019)

9. Imperial Hotel, 1913–23
Tokyo, Japan
Fabricated in Japan
Kyoto University, Department of Architecture
(FLWFA, 1509.0421)

10. Aline Barnsdall Theater II, 1918
Los Angeles, California
Fabricated in Japan
FLWFA (Fragment top)
(Kathryn Smith Collection)

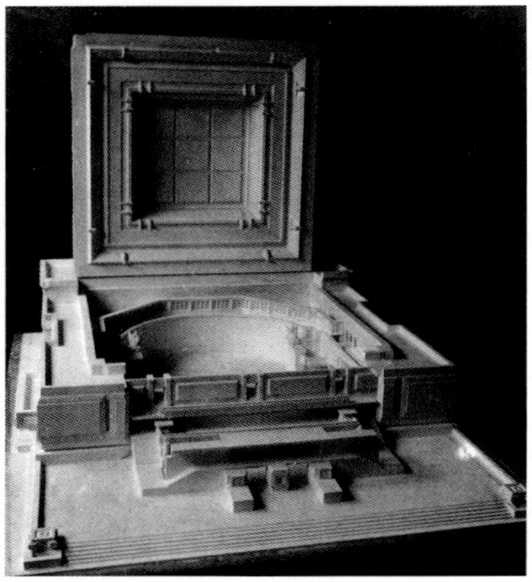

11. Tokyo Theater (also known as Ginza Movie Theater), ca. 1918
Tokyo, Japan
Fabricated in Japan
Kyoto University, Department of Architecture, Gift of the architect to Professor Goichi Takeda
(FLWFA, 1805.0001)

12. Tazaemon Yamamura House, 1918–24
Ashiya, Hyogo, Japan
Fabricated in Japan, ca. 1918
Whereabouts unknown, presumed destroyed
(Photo courtesy Koichi Mori)

13. Aline Barnsdall Theater III, 1919
Los Angeles, California
Fabricated in Japan
Whereabouts unknown, presumed destroyed
(Kathryn Smith Collection)

14. Aline Barnsdall Theater IV, 1920
Los Angeles, California
Fabricated in Japan
Whereabouts unknown, presumed destroyed
(FLWFA, 2005.0011 & 2005.0013)

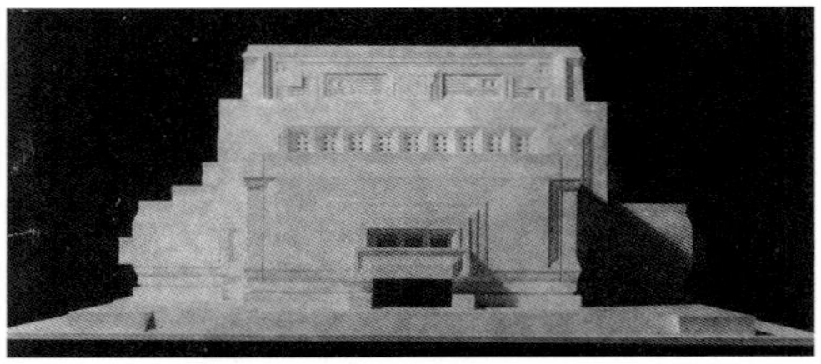

15. St. Mark's-in-the-Bouwerie Tower, 1927–31
New York, New York
Fabricated April 1930
FLWFA
(FLWFA, 3000.0011)

16. Standardized Overhead Gas Station, 1928
Buffalo, New York
Fabricated summer 1930
Whereabouts unknown, presumed destroyed
(FLWFA, 3206.0002)

17. Richard Lloyd Jones House, 1928–31
Tulsa, Oklahoma
Fabricated summer 1930
Whereabouts unknown, presumed destroyed
(FLWFA, 2902.0005)

18. Darwin D. Martin Blue Sky Mausoleum, 1925–29
Buffalo, New York
Fabricated in August–September 1930
Whereabouts unknown, presumed destroyed
(FLWFA, 3000.0001)

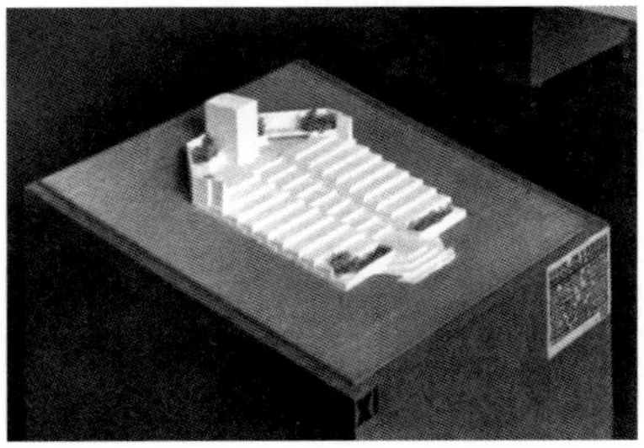

19. San Marcos Water Gardens cabins, 1929
Chandler, Arizona
Finished in February 1931
Whereabouts unknown, presumed destroyed
(FLWFA, 2705.0005)

20. New Theater, 1931
Woodstock, New York
Finished in November 1931
Whereabouts unknown, presumed destroyed
(FLWFA, 3106.0005)

21. House on the Mesa, 1931–32
Fabricated for the MoMA exhibition: *Modern Architecture, International Exhibition* and tour
Fabricated 1931–32
Destroyed
Sophia Wittenberg Mumford Papers, Ms. Collection 958, Kislak Center for Special Collections, Rare Books and Manuscripts, University of Pennsylvania. Photograph reproduced courtesy of the Estate of Lewis and Sophia Mumford.

22. San-Marcos-in-the-Desert Resort, 1928–29
Chandler, Arizona
Fabricated before February 1933
Not exhibited
Whereabouts unknown, presumed destroyed

23. Prefabricated Farm Unit for Walter V. Davidson, 1932
Buffalo, New York
Fabricated ca. 1932–33
FLWFA
(FLWFA, 3202.0001)

24. Malcolm Willey House I, 1932–33
Minneapolis, Minnesota
Fabricated before 1935
Whereabouts unknown, presumed destroyed
(FLWFA, 3204.0003)

25. Broadacre City, 1934–35
Designed for exhibition at the Industrial Arts Exposition, Rockefeller Center, New York, New York and tour
Fabricated in 1934–35
FLWFA
(FLWFA, 3402.0089)

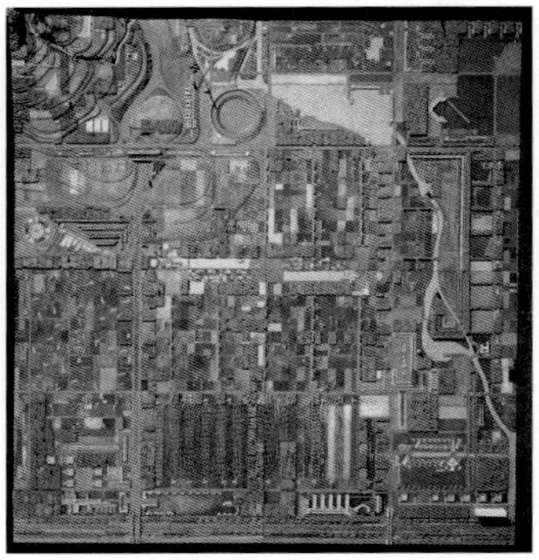

26. Top-Turn Intersection, 1934–35
Designed for exhibition at the Industrial Arts Exposition, Rockefeller Center, New York, New York and tour
Fabricated in 1934–35
FLWFA
(FLWFA, 3402.041)

27. Multi-Lane Bridge over Highway, 1934–35
Designed for exhibition at the Industrial Arts Exposition, Rockefeller Center, New York, New York and tour
Fabricated in 1934–35
Whereabouts unknown, presumed destroyed
(FLWFA, 3407.0001)

28. One-car House I and One-car House II (Minimum Houses), 1932
Fabricated for exhibition at the Industrial Arts Exposition, Rockefeller Center, New York, New York and tour
Fabricated in 1934–35
Whereabouts unknown, presumed destroyed
(Courtesy Wisconsin Historical Society, WHi-115574)

29. Two-car House (Medium House), 1934–35
Fabricated for exhibition at the Industrial Arts Exposition, Rockefeller Center, New York, New York and tour
Fabricated in 1934–35
Whereabouts unknown, presumed destroyed
(Reproduced with the kind permission of the Special Collections Library, Pennsylvania State University, University Park)

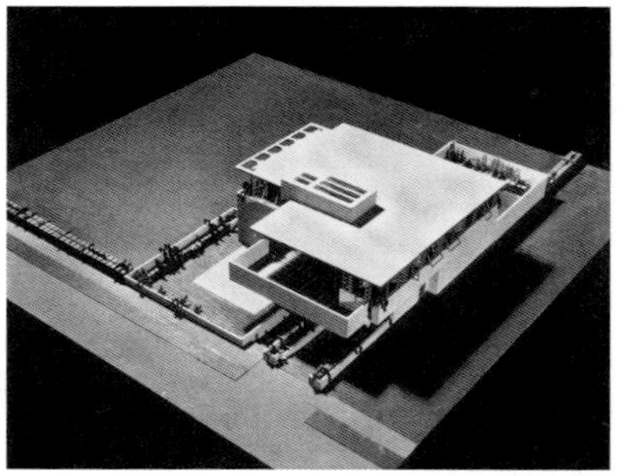

30. Colonial Equivalent (Two-car House), 1928
Fabricated before February 1933
Whereabouts unknown, presumed destroyed
(Reproduced with the kind permission of the Special Collections Library, Pennsylvania State University, University Park)

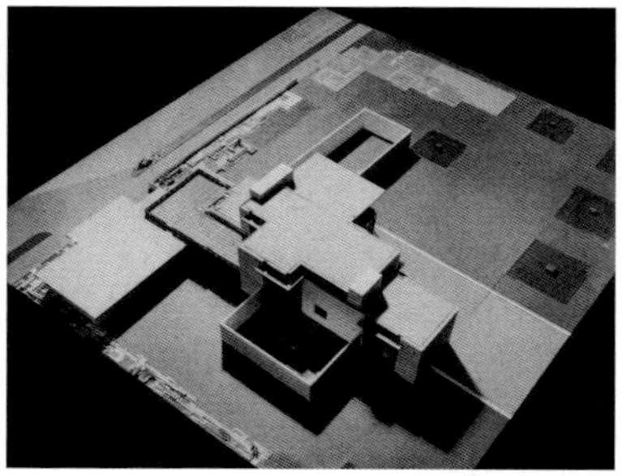

31. Garage concentration for minimum houses, 1934–35
Fabricated for exhibition at the Industrial Arts Exposition, Rockefeller Center, New York, New York and tour
Fabricated in 1934–35
Whereabouts unknown, presumed destroyed

32. Stanley Marcus House, 1934–36
Dallas, Texas
Fabricated before 1938
Whereabouts unknown, presumed destroyed
(DeGolyer Library, Southern Methodist University, Stanley Marcus Papers)

33. SC Johnson Administration Building, 1936–39
Racine, Wisconsin
Fabricated August 1936 by Blaine and Hulda Drake, Eugene Masselink
Whereabouts unknown, presumed destroyed
(Chicago History Museum)

34. Herbert Jacobs House I, 1936–37
Madison, Wisconsin
Fabricated November 1939 for Institute of Modern Art, Boston exhibition, 1940
Whereabouts unknown, presumed destroyed
(FLWFA, 3702.0001)

35. Charles Ross House, 1902
Lake Delavan, Wisconsin
Fabricated November 1939 for Institute of Modern Art, Boston exhibition, 1940
No information about the exhibition of this model or its whereabouts

36. Wingspread, Herbert F. Johnson House, 1937–39
Racine, Wisconsin
Fabricated 1939–40 for *Frank Lloyd Wright: American Architect*
FLWFA
(Courtesy SC Johnson [PD-18448-45.04 Object] Foundation)

37. Ralph Jester House, 1938–39
Palos Verdes, California
Fabricated 1939–40 for *Frank Lloyd Wright: American Architect*
Frank Lloyd Wright Foundation, Taliesin West, Scottsdale, Arizona
(Courtesy Don Kalec)

38. Sidney Bazett House, 1939–40
Hillsborough, California
Fabricated 1939–40 for *Frank Lloyd Wright: American Architect*
FLWFA
(FLWFA, 900034-Bazett)

39. Suntop Homes, 1938–39
Ardmore, Pennsylvania
Fabricated 1939–40 for *Frank Lloyd Wright: American Architect*
Whereabouts unknown, presumed destroyed
(FLWFA, 3906.0038)

40. Usonia I, 1939
Lansing, Michigan
Fabricated 1939–40 for *Frank Lloyd Wright: American Architect*
FLWFA
(FLWFA, 3912.0001)

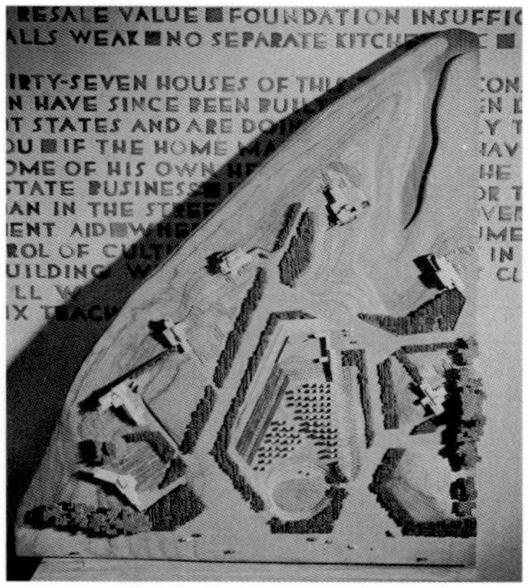

41. George Sturges House, 1939
Brentwood, California
Fabricated 1939–40 for *Frank Lloyd Wright: American Architect*
Whereabouts unknown, presumed destroyed
(FLWFA, 3905.018)

42. Lloyd Lewis House, 1939–41
Libertyville, Illinois
Fabricated 1939–40 for *Frank Lloyd Wright: American Architect*
FLWFA
(FLWFA, 4008.0020)

43. Gregor Affleck House, 1940
Bloomfield Hills, Michigan
Fabricated 1939–40 for *Frank Lloyd Wright: American Architect*
FLWFA
(FLWFA, 4111.0032)

44. Vigo Sundt House, 1940
Madison, Wisconsin
Fabricated between 1949 and 1951
FLWFA
(Courtesy Don Kalec)

45. The Call Building model no. 2, 1912–13
San Francisco, California
Fabricated in 1939–40 for *Frank Lloyd Wright: American Architect*
FLWFA
(Private Collection)

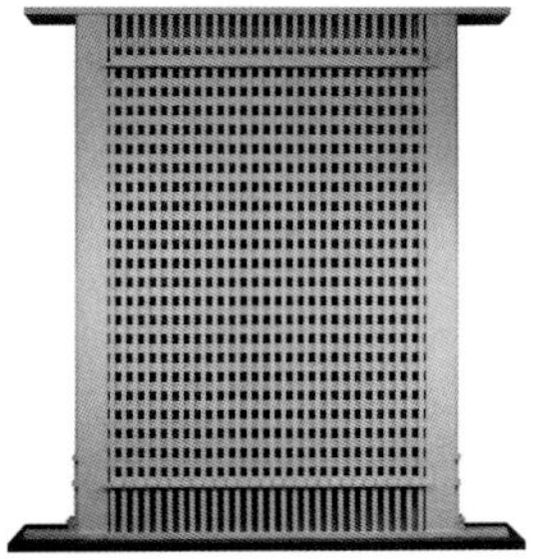

46. Roy E. Peterson House (original client: Edith Carlson, 1939), 1941
Racine, Wisconsin
Fabrication date before 1951
Whereabouts unknown, presumed destroyed

47. Solomon R. Guggenheim Museum, model no. 1, 1943–45
New York, New York
Displayed at press conference, July 9, 1945, at the Plaza Hotel; revised and displayed at press conference, September 20, 1945. Note on rear of model to right, unexecuted Annex.
Destroyed in shipping before March 18, 1947
(FLWFA, 4305.0632 and Courtesy Don Kalec)

48. Opus 497, The Glass House for *Ladies' Home Journal*, 1945
Commissioned by Richard Pratt, editor
Exterior fabricated by Raymond Barger Studios; interior fabricated by Devon Dennett
Exhibited *Tomorrow's Small House: Models and Plans*, MoMA, May 29–September 30, 1945
Whereabouts unknown, presumed destroyed
(From "Houses for the People," *Pencil Points*, September 1945, vol. 9, 65)

49. Pergola House, Gerald Loeb House, 1944
Redding, Connecticut
Fabricated for *A New Country House by Frank Lloyd Wright: A Scale Model*, MoMA, 1946
Destroyed at Wright's request
(Photograph by Ezra Stoller © Ezra Stoller/Esto)

50. Solomon R. Guggenheim Museum, model no. 2, 1947
New York, New York
Fabricated by September 23, 1947
FLWFA
(Courtesy Don Kalec)

51. New Theatre for Paton Price and Associates, 1948–49
Hartford, Connecticut
Fabricated 1948 for fund-raising by client
FLWFA
(FLWFA, 4922.0004)

52. Donald Schaberg House, 1950
Okemos, Wisconsin
Fabricated in 1950
Whereabouts unknown, presumed destroyed
(FLWFA, 1047.041)

53. Huntington Hartford Sports Club, 1946–48
Los Angeles, California
Unfinished model by Max Moffett, commissioned by Wright in 1950 for exhibition in Philadelphia and Florence, Italy, 1951
Never exhibited
Whereabouts unknown, presumed destroyed

54. San Francisco Butterfly Wing Bridge, 1949–53
Oakland-Southern Crossing, San Francisco Bay
Model made at Taliesin West, completed by J. J. Polivka, consulting engineer, and graduate students, Department of Architecture, Stanford University
The private collection of Tom Monaghan at Domino Farms in Ann Arbor, Michigan
(Courtesy Aaron Green FAIA Archive, Jan Novie, photographer)

55. Monona Terrace II, 1955
Madison, Wisconsin
Model fabricated December 1954 to January 1955 for presentation to city of Madison in February 1955, displayed at a Wright testimonial dinner on February 10, 1955, UW Memorial Union
Frank Lloyd Wright Foundation, Taliesin, Spring Green, Wisconsin
(FLWFA, 5632.0024 and Courtesy Don Kalec)

56. H. C. Price Company Tower, 1952–56
Bartlesville, Oklahoma
Fabricated for exhibition in May 1953 in Oklahoma
FLWFA
(Courtesy Eric M. O'Malley / OAD Archives)

57. Marin County Civic Center Master Plan, 1957–62
San Rafael, California
Fabricated in 1958
Marin County Civic Center Collection, San Rafael, California
(Anne T. Kent California Room, Marin County Free Library)
This is the original model made before 1959 showing the roof in gold leaf as Wright intended.

NOTES

Institutions are abbreviated in the notes as follows:

GRI/SC: Getty Research Institute for the History of Art and the Humanities, Los Angeles, Special Collections
FLWC/GRI: Frank Lloyd Wright Collection, Getty Research Institute
MoMA Archives: The Museum of Modern Art Archives, New York
HRH/AAA/SI: Henry-Russell Hitchcock papers, 1919–87. Archives of American Art, Smithsonian Institution, Washington, DC
AFA/AAA/SI: American Federation of Arts records, 1895–1993 (bulk 1909–69). Archives of American Art, Smithsonian Institution, Washington, DC
OS/AHC: Oscar Stonorov papers, American Heritage Center, University of Wyoming, Laramie
Letters are credited to a particular collection only if they are not in the Frank Lloyd Wright Archives. The archive correspondence is indexed in *Frank Lloyd Wright: An Index to the Taliesin Correspondence*, ed. Anthony Alofsin. The Wright Archives correspondence was accessed on microfiche at the GRI. The microfiche identification number is cited for each letter.
Letters in the Stonorov and Hitchcock papers are cited by box.

CHAPTER 1. CHICAGO ARCHITECTURAL CLUB, 1894–1914

1. Sherman Paul, *Louis Sullivan: An Architect in American Thought* (Englewood Cliffs, NJ: Prentice Hall, 1962), 26.
2. Louis Sullivan, "An Unaffected School of Modern Architecture: Will It Come?," in *Louis Sullivan: The Public Papers*, ed. Robert Twombley (Chicago: University of Chicago Press, 1988), 122.
3. Louis Sullivan, *Democracy, A Man-Search* (Detroit: Wayne State University, 1961), 65.
4. Louis Sullivan, "May Not Architecture Again Become a Living Art," *Public Papers*, 117.
5. Ibid., 118.
6. For the definitive study of the Chicago Architectural Club, see Wilbert R. Hasbrouck, *The Chicago Architectural Club: Prelude to the Modern* (New York: Monacelli Press, 2005).
7. Ibid., 208n16; 230n10; 244.
8. George R. Dean, "Progress before Precedent," *Brickbuilder* 9, no. 5 (1900): 91–97.
9. Hasbrouck, *Chicago Architectural Club*, 251–75.
10. Although there is no evidence that Wright ever joined the Chicago Architectural Club, in 1894, he served on the jury for the Clark competition. Hasbrouck, *Chicago Architectural Club*, 173.
11. A. N. Waterman, *Historical Review of Chicago and Cook County and Selected Biography*, 2 vols. (Chicago and New York: Lewis Publishing, 1908) 2: 913–14; H. Allen Brooks, "The Early Work of the Prairie Architects," *Journal of the Society of Architectural Historians* 19 (March 1960): 6; Hasbrouck, *Chicago Architectural Club*, 214.
12. H. Allen Brooks, *The Prairie School: Frank Lloyd Wright and His Midwest Contemporaries* (Toronto and Buffalo: University of Toronto Press, 1972), 28–31; Hasbrouck, *Chicago Architectural Club*, 210–16.
13. Chicago Architectural Club, *Catalogue Seventh Annual Exhibition, Chicago Architectural Sketch Club, Art Institute, Chicago, May MDCCCXCIV* (Chicago: Architectural Sketch Club, 1894), 4, 5, 8, 27, 36.
14. David Bernard Dearinger, ed., *Paintings and Sculpture in the Collection of the National Academy of Design* (New York: National Academy of Design; Manchester, VT: Hudson Hills Press, 2004), 309. Wendy Greenhouse, "Wright and the Landscape Painters," *Wright Angles*, 36, no. 1 (2010): 3–10.
15. This drawing is not at the Frank Lloyd Wright Archives.
16. For the Eighth Annual Exhibition in 1895, Wright exhibited "Study for a Pleasure Resort at Cheltenham," which could have been drawing 9903.015, a rendering. *Catalogue Eighth Annual Exhibition, Chicago Architectural Club, Art Institute, Chicago, May 23 to June 10, MDCCCXCV* (Chicago: Architectural Club, 1895), unpaginated. Hasbrouck, *Chicago Architectural Club*, 266. The checklist for the Eleventh Annual in 1898 lists one item: "Examples of Electro Glazing. Luxfer Prism Co.," *Catalogue Eleventh Annual Exhibition, Chicago Architectural Club, Art Institute, Chicago, March 23 to April 10, MDCCCXCVIII* (Chicago: Architectural Club, 1898), 51.
17. Robert C. Spencer Jr., "The Work of Frank Lloyd Wright," *Architectural Review* 7 (June 1900): 61–72.
18. Hasbrouck speculates that Wright's inclusion was probably "a last-minute endeavor," arranged by Spencer. Hasbrouck, *Chicago Architectural Club*, 265.
19. Chicago Architectural Club, *Annual of the Chicago Architectural Club, Being the Book of the Thirteenth Annual Exhibition 1900* (Chicago: Art Institute, 1900), 123–24; Hasbrouck, *Chicago Architectural Club*, 264.
20. The count of ninety-seven illustrations must be understood in the context of the unusual way the article was laid out. Almost every page was designed with thumbnail images forming a decorative motif. In some cases, decorative borders from the hand-printed version of *The House Beautiful* (1896), designed by Wright, were used as illustrations multiple times.
21. Spencer, "Work of Frank Lloyd Wright," 68.
22. Wright to Charles R. Ashbee, July 24, 1910, Frank Lloyd Wright Archive photocopy from the Papers of Charles Robert Ashbee, King's College Archive Centre, Cambridge, England.
23. Frank Lloyd Wright, "The Art and Craft of the Machine," Chicago Architectural Club, *Catalogue of the Fourteenth Annual Exhibition of the Chicago Architectural Club* (Chicago: Architectural Club, 1901), unpaginated.
24. Hasbrouck, *Chicago Architectural Club*, 297–98; Brooks, "Early Work of the Prairie Architects," 10.
25. Chicago Architectural Club, *Catalogue of Exhibits* (Chicago: Art Institute, 1902), 7–8. I am grateful to M. J. Hamilton, who shared this document with me; Hasbrouck had made it available to her. E-mail communication, M. J. Hamilton to author, March 8, 2007.
26. "The Work of Frank Lloyd Wright," in Chicago Architectural Club, *The Chicago Architectural Annual Published by the Chicago Architectural Club: A Selection of Works Exhibited at the Art Institute in March of the Year One Thousand Nine Hundred & Two* (Chicago: Architectural Club, 1902).
27. Wright credited Fuermann in the 1902 checklist: "414. Photographs Exterior. Glenlloyd. Photos made by Henry Fuerman [*sic*]. Enlarged by James Inglis," *Catalogue of Exhibits–1902*, 8; "Henry Fuermann Obituary," *Chicago Tribune*, April 7, 1949, 22; Crombie Taylor and Jeffrey Plank, *The Early Louis*

Sullivan Building Photographs (San Francisco: William Stout Publishers, 2001), 239–40.
28. "Success Greets Architectural Club," *Chicago Post*, April 5, 1902.
29. "Chicago," *American Architect* 76 (April 26, 1902): 29–30.
30. Ibid., 29.
31. Hasbrouck, *Chicago Architectural Club*, 308.
32. Ibid., 370.
33. Barry Bryne, review of Frank Lloyd Wright, *The Drawings of Frank Lloyd Wright Selected by Arthur Drexler* (New York: Horizon Press for the Museum of Modern Art, 1962), in *Journal of the Society of Architectural Historians* 22 (May 1963): 109.
34. Chicago Architectural Club, *Chicago Architectural Club Twentieth Annual* (Chicago: Chicago Architectural Club, 1907), frontmatter.
35. L. M. McCauley, "Exhibitions Next Week," *Chicago Evening Post*, April 6, 1907.
36. Frank Lloyd Wright's Teco ceramic vases are discussed in "The Chicago Architectural Club," in *Teco: Art Pottery of the Prairie School*, by Sharon Darling with a contribution by Richard Zakin (Erie, PA: Erie Art Museum, 1989), 25–29.
37. Paul Kruty, "Graphic Depictions: The Evolution of Marion Mahony's Architectural Renderings," in *Marion Mahony Reconsidered*, ed. David Van Zanten (Chicago: University of Chicago Press, 2011), 50–93; Janice Pregliasco, "The Life and Work of Marion Mahony Griffin," *Art Institute of Chicago Museum Studies* 21, no. 2, The Prairie School: Design Visions for the Midwest (1995): 166–70. For a detailed discussion of the operation of Wright's Oak Park Studio, see Kruty, "At Work in the Oak Park Studio," *Arris (Journal of the Southeast Chapter of the SAH)* 14 (2003): 17–31. Also see Fran Martone, *In Wright's Shadow: Artists and Architects at the Oak Park Studio* (Oak Park, IL: Frank Lloyd Wright Home and Studio Foundation, 1998).
38. Mary Jane Hamilton, "Albert Van den Berghen: An Elusive Figure in American Sculptural History," *Wright Angles, Publication of the Frank Lloyd Wright Preservation Trust* 32, no. 2 (2007): 3–7.
39. *Chicago Record Herald*, April 8, 1907.
40. L. M. McCauley, "Exhibitions Next Week," *Chicago Evening Post*, April 6, 1907.
41. Harriet Monroe, "An Interesting Experiment," *Chicago Examiner*, April 13, 1907.
42. Wright to Harriet Monroe, n.d. (ca. April 18, 1907). Harriet Monroe Papers, Special Collections Research Center, University of Chicago Library.
43. Wright to Monroe, ca. April 18, 1907.
44. Harriet Monroe to Wright, n.d., Special Collections, University of Chicago.
45. Wright to Monroe, April 22, 1907, Special Collections, University of Chicago.
46. Frank Lloyd Wright, "In the Cause of Architecture," *Architectural Record* 23 (March 1908): 155.
47. "Work of Frank Lloyd Wright, Its Influence," *Architectural Record* 17 (July 1905): 60–65. Herbert Croly, the editor, was probably the author of the anonymous article.
48. Wright, "In the Cause of Architecture," 167.
49. Eva Maria Froschauer, *"An Die Leser!": Baukunst darstellen und vermitteln—Berliner Architekturzeitschriften um 1900* (Tübingen: Ernst Wasmuth, 2009), 39, 44–46; "Zum 50 jährigen Bestehen des Verlagshauses Ernst Wasmuth in Berlin," *Deutsche Bauzeitung* 56, no. 35 (1922): 211–12. For corporate history by the firm itself, see Ernst Wasmuth A.-G., *Verlag in Berlin: Verlag Ernst Wasmuth A.-G., Markgrafenstrasse 31. Verlagskatalog 1872–1922 mit dem Beitrag "50 Jahre Verlag Ernst Wasmuth" von Günther Wasmuth* (Berlin: Wasmuth, 1922). Research on Wasmuth Verlag was conducted in cooperation with Filippo Fici, Florence, Italy. I am grateful for his valuable contributions.
50. Ernst Wasmuth Verlag, *Einhundert Jahre Wasmuth-Bücher* (Tübingen: Ernst Wasmuth Verlag, 1972), 1–4.
51. Froschauer, *An Die Leser!*, 39.
52. Günther Emil Ludolf Wasmuth (1888–1974), nephew of Ernst Carl Ludwig Wasmuth and son of Emil Eduard Bernhard Wasmuth, entered the firm in April 1913; Dorn left the following October to found Der Zirkel Verlag with Cornelius Gurlitt. *Einhundert Jahre*, 4–5; Froschauer, *An Die Leser!*, 45; Roland Jaeger, *Neue Werkkunst, Architektenmonographien der zwanziger Jahre mit einer Basis-Bibliographie deutschsprachiger Architekturpublikationen, 1918–1933* (Berlin: Gebr. Mann Verlag, 1998), 145.
53. The first of these was devoted to the graphic designer, Otto Eckmann (1865–1902). Frank Lloyd Wright, *Frank Lloyd Wright: Chicago 8. Sonderheft der Architektur des XX. Jahrhunderts* (Berlin: Ernst Wasmuth A.-G., 1911), advertisement on the back cover.
54. *Architektur des XX. Jahrhunderts* reproduced black-and-white photographs on oversize loose plates accompanied by separate bound sheets of text by Gustav Ebe—in German, French, and English—illustrated with plans. *Architektur des XX. Jahrhunderts, Zeitschrift für moderne Baukunst* (Berlin: Ernst Wasmuth, 1901–14).
55. Licht, born in Posen and died in Leipzig, studied architecture at the Berlin Bauakademie and served as the director of the municipal building administration in Leipzig from 1879 to 1906. Barbara Miller Lane, "Hugo Licht," *MacMillan Encyclopedia of Architects*, ed. Adolph Placzek, 4 vols. (New York: Free Press, ca. 1982), 2: 5–6.
56. "Architektur des XX. Jahrhunderts," advertisement in Max Creutz, *Martin Düfler 4. Sonderheft der Architektur des XX. Jahrhunderts* (Berlin: Ernst Wasmuth A.-G., 1910), inside back cover.
57. Creutz wrote the introductory text for eight of the thirteen issues. The first issue of this series appeared in 1908; see *F. v. Thiersch—München, Kurhaus in Wiesbaden 1. Sonderheft der Architektur des XX. Jahrhunderts* (Berlin: Ernst Wasmuth A.-G., 1908).
58. No correspondence between Wright and the Wasmuth firm has been located. Communication with Ernst J. Wasmuth of Wasmuth Verlag, Tübingen, Germany, August 2015.
59. Wright informed Charles R. Ashbee that he "surely would join him in England within a year." Wright to Ashbee, February 3, 1909, Frank Lloyd Wright Archive photocopy from the Papers of Charles Robert Ashbee, King's College Archive Centre, Cambridge, England.
60. Licht is listed as publisher and Dorn is listed as editor for Wright's *sonderheft* in *Börsenverein der Deutschen Buchhändler zu Leipzig (Germany). Deutsches Bücherverzeichnis: Eine Zusammenstellung Der Im Deutschen Buchhandel Erschienenen Bücher, Zeitschriften Und Landkarten Mit Einem Stich-Und Schlagwortregister*, 22 vols. (New York: Johnson Reprint, 1962), 1: 95. I am grateful to Filippo Fici, who called this citation to my attention. Some confusion exists in the Wright literature between the *sonderhefte* of *Architektur des XX. Jahrhunderts* and *Berliner Architekturwelt* due to the fact that the listings were combined in chronological order in the firm's advertisements, and thus were not separated as to the two distinct series.
61. Frank Lloyd Wright, *An Autobiography* (New York: Duell, Sloan, and Pearce, 1943), 161–62.
62. The primary source on the history of Wright's Wasmuth publications is Anthony Alofsin, *Frank Lloyd Wright—The Lost Years, 1910–1922: A Study of Influence* (Chicago: University of Chicago, 1993), to which my understanding is indebted. An abbreviated version of his seminal research was later published as Anthony Alofsin, preface to Frank Lloyd Wright, *Studies and Executed Buildings* (New York: Rizzoli International, 1998), 5–9.
63. Max Creutz, "Die 'Fine Arts' auf der Weltausstellung in St. Louis," *Die Kunst für Alle* 19 (1904): 568–74.
64. Wasmuth Verlag and Otto Dorn in particular had already been aware of Wright, at least, through F. Rudolf Vogel (1849–1926), an architect and reformer, living in Hanover. After traveling to the United States in the 1870s, Vogel returned home to write about American architecture for a German audience. By 1908, he was at work on *Das amerikanische Haus* (*The American House*), a well-illustrated volume that went to press while Wright was in Europe, appearing in 1910. Perhaps gaining information from periodicals and critics, Vogel reproduced five Wright residences: the exteriors of the Chauncey Williams, Joseph and Helen Husser, and Ward W. Willits Houses and interiors of the William Winslow and Harley Bradley Houses. In his preface, Vogel credits Dorn for encouraging him to complete his book. F. Rudolf Vogel, *Das amerikanische Haus: Entwicklung, Bedingungen, Anlage, Aufbau, Einrichtung, Innenraum und Umgebung* (Berlin: Ernst Wasmuth A.-G., 1910), 305, 306, 377, 379, 381.
65. Wright's folios followed this format almost exactly. Joseph Maria Olbrich, *Architektur von Olbrich*, 3 vols. (Berlin: Ernst Wasmuth A.-G., 1901–14); reprint: Joseph Maria Olbrich, *Architecture, Complete Reprint of the original plates of 1901–1914*, with texts by Peter Haiko and Bernd Krimmel, Catalogue of Works by Renate Ulmer (New York: Rizzoli International, 1988).
66. The only person at Wasmuth Verlag who Wright ever mentioned in print was

Dorn. Frank Lloyd Wright, *A Testament* (New York: Horizon Press, 1957), 84. Dorn is also mentioned contemporary to events in Wright to Taylor Woolley, July 20, 1910, University of Utah Library, Manuscripts Division, Special Collections Department, Taylor Woolley Papers, accession no. 152.

67. Wright to Ashbee, July 24, 1910, from Frank Lloyd Wright Archive photocopy from originals in Ashbee Papers, King's College.

68. Frank Lloyd Wright, *Ausgeführte Bauten und Entwürfe von Frank Lloyd Wright* (Chicago: Ralph Fletcher Seymour, ca. 1911), unpaginated. This version of events explains why Lloyd Wright Jr. was not asked to come to Europe to help with the redrawing until well after his father had arrived in Europe. Wright, with the knowledge of his family, had been planning his departure for Europe for many months in 1909. Certainly, the idea was well formed by the summer. If Wasmuth Verlag had initially proposed a one-hundred-plate portfolio of drawings while Wright was still in Chicago, he would have had sufficient time to inform his son before he started his college year. In other words, all these arrangements were initiated after the senior Wright made his proposal to Wasmuth Verlag in Berlin. Lloyd Wright to Linn Cowles, February 3, 1966. Photocopy provided to author by Bruce Brooks Pfeiffer, July 2010.

69. Otto Dorn's direct involvement with authors is verified by a file of his nineteen letters (1903–7) with the German artist, Melchior Lechter, regarding his *sonderheft*: M. Rapsilber, *Melchior Lechter Berliner Kunst 3* (Berlin: Ernst Wasmuth A.-G., 1904). *Melchoir Lechter Papers, 1879–1937*, Getty Research Institute, Research Library, accession no. 970039.

70. For the definitive history of Wright's studios during the preparation of the Wasmuth publications, see Filippo Fici, "Frank Lloyd Wright in Florence and Fiesole, 1909–1910," *Frank Lloyd Wright Quarterly* 22, no. 4 (2011): 4–17. I am indebted to Fici for sharing details of his original research with me and for providing a guided tour of these buildings in 2013. For additional history of Wright in Fiesole, see Giampaolo Fici and Filippo Fici, *Frank Lloyd Wright: Fiesole 1910* (Fiesole: Minello Sani, 1992).

71. H. Allen Brooks, "Frank Lloyd Wright and the Wasmuth Drawings," *Art Bulletin* 48, no. 2 (1966): 193–202.

72. The 1909 contract has not been located; however, it is referred to in the revised February 13, 1911, contract. Alofsin, *Frank Lloyd Wright—The Lost Years*, 317–18.

73. Wright to Ashbee, July 24, 1910.

74. The titles were: no. 4, Martin Düfler, Dresden (1910); no. 5, Bund Deutscher Architektur (1906); no. 6, Das Einfamilienhaus des Kunstgewerbevereins für Breslau (1905); no. 7, Carl Moritz, Cologne (1910); no. 8, Frank Lloyd Wright, Chicago (1911); no. 9, Carl Moritz, Cologne (1911); no. 10, Wilhelm Kreis, Elberfield (1912); no. 11, Friedrich Pützer, Darmstadt (1912); no. 12, Hans Erlwein, Dresden (1913); and no. 13, Edmund Körner, Essen (1914).

75. Wright to Ashbee, July 24, 1910.

76. Max Creutz, *Martin Düfler, 4. Sonderheft der Architektur des XX. Jahrhunderts* (Berlin: Ernst Wasmuth A.-G., 1910).

77. Bund Deutscher Architekten, *Bund Deutscher Architekten, Werke des Ortsgruppe Köln 5. Sonderheft der Architektur des XX. Jahrhunderts* (Berlin: Ernst Wasmuth A.-G., 1906); Karl Masner, *Das Einfamilienhaus des Kunstgewerbevereins für Breslau und die Provinz Schlesien auf der Ausstellung für Handwerk und Kunstgewerbe in Breslau 6. Sonderheft der Architektur des XX. Jahrhunderts* (Berlin: Ernst Wasmuth A.-G., 1905).

78. Alofsin, *Frank Lloyd Wright—The Lost Years*, 61–62, 73–78. Alofsin published the unexpurgated Ashbee text, highlighting Wright's deletions, in Appendix B, 312–15. Wright resorted to censorship again in 1940 when he read Walter Curt Behrendt's essay for the Museum of Modern Art catalog, *Frank Lloyd Wright: American Architect*. The unexpurgated text, noting Wright's deletions, is reprinted in *The Show to End All Shows: Frank Lloyd Wright and The Museum of Modern Art, 1940*, Studies in Modern Art 8, ed. Peter Reed and William Kaizen, with an essay by Kathryn Smith (New York: Museum of Modern Art, 2004), 116–24.

79. Robert L. Sweeney, *Frank Lloyd Wright: An Annotated Bibliography* (Los Angeles: Hennessey and Ingalls, 1978), plate 4 of *Berliner Architekturwelt* 14 (1911–12).

80. Ibid., 21. This is a curious fact as the 4,000 copies presumably had already been printed by Julius Sittenfeld, Hofbuchdrucker, Berlin, W, before this advertisement.

81. Walter Curt Behrendt, "*Frank Lloyd Wright, Chicago. Achtes Sonderheft der Architektur des zwanzigsten Jahrhunderts*. Ernst Wasmuth A.-G. Berlin 1911," *Kunst and Kunstler* 11, no. 9 (1913): 487.

82. Wright to D. D. Martin, December 27, 1910, University Archives, State University of New York at Buffalo.

83. Unsigned to George Burnett, January 15, 1913 (B001D02).

84. *Architectural Review* to Wright, October 13, 1912 (A001A05); *Western Architect* to Wright, October 14, 1912 (W033A01); *Architectural Record* to H. F. Robinson, December 17, 1912 (A001B02); *The Brickbuilder* to Wright, December 13, 1912 (C001C01).

85. The only known American review of the portfolios is Montgomery Schuyler, "An Architectural Pioneer: Review of the Portfolios Containing the Works of Frank Lloyd Wright," *Architectural Record* 31 (April 1912): 427–36.

86. "Frank Lloyd Wright Works in Two Port Folios recorded," n.d. (ca. 1912–13) (B001D04).

87. In 1946, Ludwig Mies van der Rohe published an essay on Wright in which he stated, "At this moment (1910) . . . there came to Berlin the exhibition of the work of Frank Lloyd Wright. This comprehensive display and the extensive publication of his works enabled us to become acquainted with . . . this architect." Ludwig Mies van der Rohe, "A Tribute to Frank Lloyd Wright," *College Art Journal* 6 (August 1946): 41–42. This article was originally written for the 1940 MoMA Wright catalog, *Frank Lloyd Wright: American Architect*. The idea was perpetuated in Reginald Isaacs, *Gropius: An Illustrated Biography of the Creator of the Bauhaus* (Boston: Bulfinch Press, 1991), 25. Gropius recalled attending a display of "one hundred drawings . . . at the Academy of Art" with his mother in 1910. Alofsin also rejects the notion that a formal exhibition took place; instead, offering evidence of a lecture by Bruno Möhring on February 16, 1910, to a professional group of architects where Wright drawings were shown. Alofsin, *Frank Lloyd Wright—The Lost Years*, 33–34.

88. In 1978, Robert L. Sweeney, in reference to the Wasmuth Verlag *sonderhefte*, wrote, "There is a third version of this book, similar to the other two, which was published as a catalogue to accompany the exhibition of Wright's work in Berlin in 1910." Sweeney attributes this information to a conversation with Hasbrouck in 1977. Sweeney further states that Mies's grandson, Dirk Lohan, and Howard Dearstyne, a former student of Mies, could not confirm this assertion. Sweeney, *Frank Lloyd Wright: An Annotated Bibliography*, xxiv. Between the years 1978 and 2003, the date of the next major Wright bibliography, this third publication had not surfaced. Donald Langmead, *Frank Lloyd Wright: A Bio-Bibliography*, Bio-Bibliographies in Art and Architecture 6 (Westport, CT: Praeger, 2003).

89. Chicago Architectural Club, *Book of Twenty Sixth Annual Exhibition of the Chicago Architectural Club in the Galleries of the Art Institute, Chicago. May 6 to June 11, 1913* (Chicago: Architectural Club, 1913), unpaginated.

90. Harriet Monroe, "Architectural Club Exhibit at Art Institute," *Chicago Daily Tribune*, May 7, 1913, 11.

91. Roy A. Lippincott, "The Chicago Architectural Club, Notes on the 26th Annual Exhibition," *Architectural Record* 33 (June 1913): 567–73.

92. Henry M. Hyde, "'Rebels' of West Shatter Styles of Architecture," *Chicago Daily Tribune*, September 12, 1913, 1, 8.

93. H. P. Berlage, "Neuere amerikanische Architektur," *Schweizerische Bauzeitung* 60 (September 14, 21, 28, 1912): 148–50, 165–67, 178.

94. Frank Lloyd Wright, "In the Cause of Architecture, Second Paper," *Architectural Record* 35 (May 1914): 405–13.

95. "Architects in Dispute over Wright Room," *Chicago Examiner*, April 10, 1914, 12.

96. Florence Patton, "Architects Quit Big Exhibit," *Chicago American*, April 9, 1914, 1.

97. *The Work of Frank Lloyd Wright: Work Done since the Spring of 1911, Only Is Included in This Exhibit* (Chicago: Art Institute, 1914).

98. For a history of the San Francisco tower, see Anthony Alofsin, "The *Call* Building: Frank Lloyd Wright's Skyscraper for San Francisco," in *Urban Dimension: Essays in Architectural History and Criticism* (Vienna: Bohlau Verlag, 1992), 17–27; Randolph Henning, "*Call* Building Project—1912 or 1913?" *OA+D, Journal of Organic Architecture + Design* 4, no. 1 (2016): 20–23.

99. Daniel Cahill, *Harriet Monroe* (New York: Twayne Publishers, 1973), 73.

100. Harriet Monroe, "The Orient an Influence on the Architecture of

Wright," *Chicago Daily Tribune*, April 12, 1914, G5.
101. Wright to Monroe, April 13, 1914. Special Collections, University of Chicago Library.
102. Wright to Monroe, April 20, 1914. Special Collections, University of Chicago Library.
103. Wright, *A Testament*, 132.
104. For scholarship on the relation of Whitman to Sullivan and Wright, see Kevin Murphy, "Walt Whitman and Louis Sullivan: The Aesthetics of Egalitarianism," *Walt Whitman Quarterly Review* 6 (Summer 1988): 1–15; John F. Roche, "Democratic Space: The Ecstatic Geography of Walt Whitman and Frank Lloyd Wright," *Walt Whitman Quarterly Review* 6 (Summer 1988): 16–32; Geoffrey M. Still and Roberta K. Tarbell, eds., *Walt Whitman and the Visual Arts* (New Brunswick, NJ: Rutgers University Press, 1992); Morton Schoolman, "Democratic Enlightenment: Whitman and Aesthetic Education," in *A Political Companion to Walt Whitman*, ed. John E. Seery (Lexington: University Press of Kentucky, 2011), 310–39.

CHAPTER 2. *THE WORK OF FRANK LLOYD WRIGHT, 1893–1930* AND *MODERN ARCHITECTURE: INTERNATIONAL EXHIBITION*, MUSEUM OF MODERN ART, 1932

1. Frank Lloyd Wright, *Frank Lloyd Wright: Collected Writings*, ed. Bruce Brooks Pfeiffer, 5 vols. (New York: Rizzoli, 1992), 1: 119.
2. Gilbert Herbert and Liliane Richter, *Through a Clouded Glass: Mendelsohn, Wijdeveld, and the Jewish Connection* (Berlin: Ernst Wasmuth Verlag, 2008), 22.
3. H. P. Berlage, "Frank Lloyd Wright," in *The Work of Frank Lloyd Wright: The Life-Work of the American Architect Frank Lloyd Wright* (New York: Horizon Press, 1965), 81, reprint of *The Life-Work of the American Architect Frank Lloyd Wright*, ed. H.Th. Wijdeveld (Santpoort, Holland: C. A. Mees, 1925).
4. Philip Johnson to Louise Johnson, August 18, 1929, Philip Johnson Papers, 1908–2002, bulk 1925–98, Getty Research Institute, Research Library, accession no. 980060.
5. Eric Mendelsohn, *Eric Mendelsohn: Letters of an Architect*, ed. Oskar Beyer (London: Abelard-Schuman, 1967), 74.
6. M. David Samson, "'Unser Newyorker Mitarbeiter,' Lewis Mumford, Walter Curt Behrendt, and the Modern Movement in Germany," *Journal of the Society of Architectural Historians* 55, no. 2 (1996): 128–29. For additional background on Behrendt and Mumford, see Miles David Samson, "German-American Dialogues and the Modern Movement before the 'Design Migration,' 1910–1933" (PhD diss., Harvard University, 1988).
7. Walter Curt Behrendt, "Frank Lloyd Wright, Chicago. Achtes Sonderheft der Architektur des zwanzigsten Jahrhunderts. Ernst Wasmuth A.-G. Berlin 1911," *Kunst und Kunstler* 11, no. 9 (1913): 487.
8. Samson, "Unser Newyorker," 128.
9. Lewis Mumford, *The Brown Decades: A Study of the Arts in America, 1865–1885* (New York: Harcourt, Brace, 1931), 165.
10. Untitled, n.d. (ca. November 1940) (M111D003).
11. Wright to H.Th. Wijdeveld, January 7, 1925 (W044A01).
12. Marguerite B. Williams, "Art to Have Place in Coming Skyscrapers," *Chicago Daily News*, February 5, 1925, in Hasbrouck, *Chicago Architectural Club*, 541.
13. Wright to Earl H. Reed, n.d. (ca. 1930) (P005E01).
14. Wright to Douglas Haskell, September 26, 1929 (A005B011).
15. A. Lawrence Kocher to Wright, September 27, 1929 (A005C01).
16. Robert A. M. Stern, *Raymond Hood* (New York: Institute for Architecture and Urban Studies and Rizzoli International Publications, 1982), 112.
17. Walter H. Kilham Jr., *Raymond Hood, Architect: Form through Function in the American Skyscraper* (New York: Architectural Book Publishing, 1973), 81; Robert A. M. Stern, Gregory F. Gilmartin, and Thomas Mellins, *New York 1930: Architecture and Urbanism between the Two World Wars* (New York: Rizzoli, 1994), 190.
18. "At Architectural League," *New York Times*, February 16, 1930.
19. Sue Goldblang for Joseph Urban to Wright, August 3, 1927 (U014B06); Sue Goldblang for Joseph Urban to Wright, September 30, 1929 (U014B07); Wright, *An Autobiography*, 344.
20. Names Nominated for Membership in Council (A003B08); AUDAC The officers and standing committees for the year 1928–1929, October 13, 1928 (A003B09).
21. Kilham, *Raymond Hood, Architect*, 79.
22. AUDAC announcement (A005D01).
23. Wright to Kocher, October 23, 1929 (A005D06); *Time*, October 7, 1929.
24. Wright to W.R.B. Willcox, October 17, 1930 (W051D07).
25. E. Baldwin Smith to Wright, February 3, 1930 (P004E01).
26. Wright to Smith, February 8, 1930 (P004E03).
27. Smith to Wright, February 10, 1930 (P004E04).
28. E-mail communication, Neil Levine to author, May 28, 2011.
29. Wright to Smith, May 1, 1930 (P005D04).
30. Ibid.
31. Telegram, Wright to Smith, n.d. (P005C02).
32. Henry Saylor, "The Editor's Diary, Thursday, May 15 and Friday, May 16," *Architecture* 62 (July 1930): 42, 44.
33. Wright to Donald Walker, May 22, 1930 (W051A10).
34. Frank Lloyd Wright, *Modern Architecture, Being the Kahn Lectures for 1930*, Princeton Monographs in Art and Archaeology 15 (Princeton, NJ: Princeton University Press for the Department of Art and Archaeology of Princeton University, 1931). For a penetrating analysis of Wright's essays, see Neil Levine, introduction to Frank Lloyd Wright, *Modern Architecture, Being the Kahn Lectures for 1930* (reprint; Princeton, NJ: Princeton University Press, 2008), ix–lxxi.
35. Henry Saylor, "Editor's Diary, Wednesday, May 28," *Architecture* 62 (August 1930): 105.
36. Wright to Raymond Hood, n.d. (ca. June 1930) (H009C03).
37. Wright to Lloyd Wright, n.d. (ca. June 3, 1930) (W052D01).
38. Wright to Mumford, n.d. (ca. June 1930), in Bruce Brooks Pfeiffer and Robert Wojtowicz, eds., *Frank Lloyd Wright + Lewis Mumford: Thirty Years of Correspondence* (New York: Princeton Architectural Press, 2001), 86.
39. Mumford to Wright, July 1, 1930, in *Wright + Mumford*, 88.
40. Alexander Woollcott, "The Prodigal Father," *New Yorker*, July 19, 1930, 25.
41. "Wright's Time," *Time*, June 9, 1930, 30.
42. H[enry] I[rving] Brock, "A Pioneer in Architecture That Is Called Modern," *New York Times Sunday Magazine*, June 29, 1930, 11, 19.
43. Douglas Haskell, "Frank L. Wright and the Chicago Fair," *Nation* 131 (December 3, 1930): 605; Lewis Mumford, "Two Chicago Fairs," *New Republic* 65 (January 21, 1931): 271–72.
44. Henry Saylor, "Thursday, February 26," *Architecture* 63 (April 1931): 238.
45. Kilham, *Raymond Hood, Architect*, 112.
46. Hood to Wright, June 10, 1930 (H009A01). There is no explanation why Hood suggested sending the exhibition back to Princeton University.
47. Wright to Earl Reed, n.d. (R004A06); Wright to Eric K. Hengerer, n.d. (H014D07).
48. Wright to Kameki Tsuchiura, April 21, 1931 (T002E010).
49. Frank Lloyd Wright, untitled, December 8, 1931, Registrar Exhibition Files (hereafter REG), Exh. #114 (Wright Chron.). The Museum of Modern Art Archives, New York.
50. Walter R. Agard to Wright, May 29, 1930 (A008A03).
51. Wright to Reed, n.d. (P005E01).
52. Wright to Katharine Atwater, n.d. (X001C08); Atwater to Wright, October 2, 1930 (X001C04); Wright to Darwin Martin, October 3, 1930.
53. Charles Morgan to Wright, n.d. (ca. June 19, 1930) (M015D02).
54. When the lectures were published, Wright changed the title "The New Architecture" to "To the Young Man in Architecture." Frank Lloyd Wright, *Two Lectures on Architecture* (Chicago: Art Institute, 1931).
55. *Art Institute of Chicago Newsletter*, October 11, 1930, 3.
56. *Chicago Daily Tribune*, September 21, September 24, September 28, October 2, 1930; *Chicago Daily News*, October 1, October 4, 1930.
57. Marguerite B. Williams, "Art Institute Draws Crowds with Exhibits," *Chicago Daily News*, October 4, 1930, 13.
58. Wright explained to Darwin Martin on October 5, "[The exhibition] is double the size of the New York show including model of gas station—your open-air mausoleum—the Jones House St. Mark's Tower—1000 drawings and 600 photographs—we got this together this summer. . . . The collection in its present form ought to be worth $50,000 when I am dead." Wright to Darwin Martin, October 5, 1930. MS 22.8, Frank Lloyd Wright—Darwin D. Martin Papers, 1888–1979, University Archives, State University of New York at Buffalo.
59. Wright to Gilman Lane, November 18, 1930 (L010A08).
60. Wright to Walter R. B. Willcox, October 17, 1930 (W051D07).

61. John H. Howe, "The Taliesin Drawings," oral history conducted by author, Phoenix, Arizona, March 7, 1987.
62. Atsuko Tanaka, in conversation with the author, May 6, 2015. For the definitive monograph on the architecture of Tsuchiura, see Atsuko Tanaka, *Tsuchiura Kameki To Shiroi Ie (Within White Boxes: The Architecture of Kameki Tsuchiura)* (Tokyo: Kajima Institute Publishing, 2014).
63. Howe, "Taliesin Drawings."
64. Henry Klumb in Edgar Tafel, *About Wright: An Album of Recollections by Those Who Knew Frank Lloyd Wright* (New York: John Wiley and Sons, 1993), 101.
65. Museum of Modern Art Meeting Notes, September 25, 1940. Museum of Modern Art Archives. Notes on these meetings were provided to me by Peter Reed, February 28, 2003, to whom I am grateful.
66. Wright to Guilio Barella, April 10, 1933 (B021B09).
67. "Glass Houses Become Things in Actual Use," *Christian Science Monitor*, September 25, 1930.
68. Wright to Charlotte Partridge, October 11, 1930 (L009E03).
69. "Wright Envisions Courthouse He Would Design," *Milwaukee Sentinel*, December 6, 1930; "Courthouse a Betrayal? Wright and Ross Differ," *Milwaukee Journal*, November 20, 1930.
70. Willcox to Wright, October 18, 1930 (W051A08).
71. For detailed description and illustrations of plans, see Donald Leslie Johnson, *Frank Lloyd Wright versus America: The 1930s* (Cambridge, MA: MIT Press, 1990), 154–69. Also see Donald Leslie Johnson, "Frank Lloyd Wright's Design for the 'Capital Journal,' Salem, Oregon (1932)," *Journal of the Society of Architectural Historians* 55, no. 1 (1996): 58–65.
72. Wright to Lloyd Wright, January 8, 1931. Collection of Eric Lloyd Wright.
73. Lloyd Wright contacted the Department of Art, Mills College, Oakland, California; Palace of the Legion of Honor, San Francisco, California; Los Angeles Museum; Department of Art, University of California, Berkeley, all to no avail.
74. When Okami returned to Japan, he published this material. Takehiro Okami, compiler, "List of Executed Buildings of Frank Lloyd Wright" and "List of Design and Unexecuted Buildings," *Kokusai-Kenchiku* 7 (August 1931): 277–81, 321–27. I am grateful to Karen Severns and Koichi Mori, Tokyo, who provided me with a copy of these articles. "Catalog of the Frank Lloyd Wright Exhibit—1931—," 1047.001. #2 Checklist—1931 show, 1047.013.
75. Wright to H.Th. Wijdeveld, n.d. (ca. September 25–October 12, 1930). Wijdeveld Collection, Netherlands Architecture Institute, copy provided to author by Pfeiffer.
76. The letter to de Fries is not extant. Wright to Eric Mendelsohn, November 27, 1930 (M018A04). For background on de Fries, see Roland Jaeger, *Heinrich de Fries und sein Beitrag zur Architekturpublizistik der Zwanziger Jahre* (Berlin: Gebr. Mann, 2001), 98–118.
77. Klumb to Wright, January 12, 1931 (K004B05).
78. de Fries to Wright, January 20, 1931 (D008A02); de Fries to Wright, January 24, 1931 (D008A06); Klumb to Wright, February 13, 1931 (K004C06).
79. Klumb to Wright, March 12, 1931 (K004D07). In 1924, de Fries revealed to Richard J. Neutra, one of Wright's draftsmen, his candid opinion of Mendelsohn: "If one meets occasionally Mendelsohn the human being, one is always irritated anew by his superficiality and the relative shallowness of his character which has no real depth. One is perplexed by the autocratic gesture of a conceited genius. There is no doubt that Mendelsohn is a great talent, but the holy spark of genius somehow passed him like lightning. All these considerations lead me to believe that his present quite substantial fame will soon be a transient phenomenon. However, despite all this he is nearly always interesting." Heinrich de Fries to Richard J. Neutra, n.d. ca. fall 1924, translation by Neutra family. Courtesy of Raymond Neutra.
80. *De Stijl* 1, no. 4 (1918): 39–41, in *Writings on Wright: Selected Comment on Frank Lloyd Wright*, ed. H. Allen Brooks (Cambridge, MA: MIT Press, 1981), 136.
81. J.J.P. Oud, "The Influence of Frank Lloyd Wright on the Architecture of Europe," *Wendingen* (reprint: 1965), 88. Oud's full statement as written was: "Whereas Wright proved to be an artist rather than a prophet, cubism paved the way for the more actual execution of that which was his theory too." The manuscript, which is in English, is typed on Oud's letterhead. "The Influence of Frank Lloyd Wright on the Architecture of Europe," ca. 1922. J.J.P. Oud Assorted Papers, Getty Research Institute, Getty Library, accession #840055. The essay was first published in 1925 in Wijdeveld, *Life-Work of the American Architect Frank Lloyd Wright*.
82. Karl Jensen to Lloyd Wright, February 14, 1931. Eric Lloyd Wright Collection.
83. Wijdeveld to Wright, January 3, 1931 (W054D02).
84. Wijdeveld to Wright, August 26, 1931 (W057A01).
85. Penny Fowler, *Frank Lloyd Wright: Graphic Designer* (San Francisco: Pomegranate, 2002), 114–15.
86. I have not seen the dummy, which Wright refers to in a letter to Wijdeveld on April 6, 1931, but a manuscript exists for the catalog. 1047.013—#2 Checklist—1931 show.
87. Wright to Wijdeveld, April 6, 1931 (W055B02).
88. Memorandum to Wijdeveld, n.d. (W058D07).
89. Wijdeveld to Wright, April 22, 1931 (W055B10); Wright to Wijdeveld, April 29, 1931 (W055C06).
90. Wijdeveld to Wright, August 26, 1931 (W057A01).
91. Klumb to Wright, May 28, 1931 (K005A05).
92. Michael [Kostanecki], George [Cronin], Karl [Jensen] to Klumb, n.d. (March–April 1931) (K004D03); Klumb to Wright, May 28, 1931 (K005A05).
93. Klumb to Wright, May 28, 1931 (K005A05).
94. H.Th. Wijdeveld, "Architect Frank Lloyd Wright naar Europa: Een tentoonstelling van zijn werk te Amsterdam," *Bouwkundig Weekblad* 52 (April 4, 1931): 117. Translation supplied to Wright by Wijdeveld contemporary with events.
95. W. Jos. De Gruyter, "Frank Lloyd Wright in het Stedelijk Museum Te Amsterdam," *Elsevier's Geïllustreerd Maandschrift* 82 (August 1931): 146.
96. Wijdeveld to Wright, June 10, 1931 (W056A01).
97. H. de Fries, ed., *Frank Lloyd Wright: Aus dem Lebenswerke eines Architekten* (Berlin: Verlag Ernst Pollak, 1926); H. de Fries, "Neue Pläne von Frank Lloyd Wright," *Die Form* 5 (July 1931): 342–43.
98. Siegfried Scharfe, "Theorie und Praxis bei Frank Lloyd Wright," *Wasmuths Monatshefte für Baukunst und Städtebau* 13 (August 1929): 331–32; Siegfried Scharfe, "Wright's Naturalismus," *Wasmuths Monatshefte für Baukunst und Städtebau* 14 (January 1930): 34–36; Frank Lloyd Wright, "Über das Blech in der Baukunst," *Wasmuths Monatshefte für Baukunst und Städtebau* 13 (August 1929): 333–41; Frank Lloyd Wright, "Beton," *Wasmuths Monatshefte für Baukunst und Städtebau* 14 (January 1930): 36–42; Frank Lloyd Wright, "Glas," *Wasmuths Monatshefte für Baukunst und Städtebau* 14 (March 1930): 135–38.
99. Erich Mendelsohn, "Frank Lloyd Wright," *Wasmuths Monatshefte für Baukunst und Städtebau* 10 (June 1926): 244.
100. Werner Hegemann, "Exotik und 'Amerikanismus,'" *Wasmuths Monatatshefte für Baukunst und Städtebau* 9 (March 1925): 119.
101. "Frank Lloyd Wright," n.d. (ca. June 17, 1931) (M128E07). English translation provided to Wright contemporary with events.
102. Philip Johnson, "In Berlin: Comment on Building Exposition," *New York Times*, August 9, 1931, 97.
103. Adolph Donath, "Der Amerikaner Wright," *Berliner Tageblatt und Handelszeitung*, June 22, 1931.
104. Paul F. Schmidt, "Gröse und Niedergang eines Bahnbrechers der modernen Architketur," *Baukunst* 7 (August 1931): 278–79.
105. Walter Curt Behrendt, "Frank Lloyd Wright Exhibition at the Academy of Art, Berlin," *Frankfurter Zeitung Handelsblatt*, June 30, 1931.
106. Wright's original text is dated July 23, 1931, and is not accompanied by a list of the German critics. Wijdeveld made a scrapbook of photographs, plans, and clippings, which he gave Wright, but due to internal evidence, it can be determined that it was not finished until much later in 1931. Frank Lloyd Wright, "To My Critics in the Land of the Danube and the Rhine," in *Frank Lloyd Wright: Collected Writings*, ed. Bruce Brooks Pfeiffer, 5 vols. (New York: Rizzoli, 1992–95), 3: 18–20.
107. Ibid.
108. Wilhelm Lotz, "Unter der Lupe: Frank Lloyd Wright und die Kritik," *Die Form* 6 (September 1931): 357–58.
109. It was the topic of Sigfried Giedion, "Les Problèmes Actuels de l'Architecture à l'occasion d'un manifeste de Frank Lloyd Wright aux Architectes et Critiques d'Europe," *Cahiers d'Art* (1932): 69–73. This essay also appeared as "Die architectonische Front," *De 8 en OPBOUW* 1 (1932): 177–84. In the same

Dutch issue were Wright's rebuttal and comments by the editor, Johannes Duiker. English translation appeared in *Forum* 22, no. 6 (1972): 136–37.
110. Johnson to Alfred H. Barr Jr., n.d. ca. July 11–30, 1931. REG, Exh. #15. The Museum of Modern Art Archives (Johnson-Barr-Blackburn Correspondence).
111. Johnson to Barr, July 11, 1931. REG, Exh. #15. MoMA Archives, NY (Johnson-Barr-Blackburn Correspondence).
112. Klumb to no name (Wright), July 16, 1931 (K005B09).
113. Wright to Klumb, July 20, 1931 (K005B10).
114. Klumb to Wright, July 25, 1931 (K005C01); Wright to Klumb, July 28, 1931 (K005C02); Klumb to Wright, August 25, 1931 (K005C01); Wright to Klumb, August 26, 1931 (K005E09).
115. "Sur Frank Lloyd Wright," *La Cité (Architecture, Urbanisme, Art, Public)* 10, no. 3 (1931): 39–42.
116. Wijdeveld arrived in New York on November 4. Wijdeveld to Wright, November 4, 1931 (W057D10); Wright to Olgivanna Wright, November 16, 1931 (W057E03).
117. Wijdeveld sailed from New York to Europe on December 9. Wijdeveld to Ellen Wijdeveld, December 5, 1931 (W058A02).
118. Henry-Russell Hitchcock, "Modern Architecture: A Memoir," *Journal of the Society of Architectural Historians* 27 (December 1968): 229.
119. Henry-Russell Hitchcock, *Modern Architecture: Romanticism and Reintegration* (New York: Payson and Clarke, 1929), 162.
120. Johnson to Louise Johnson, September 12, 1929, Philip Johnson Papers, 1908–2002, bulk 1925–98, Getty Research Institute, Getty Research Library, accession no. 980060.
121. Johnson to Louise Johnson, June 20, 1930, Johnson Papers.
122. Ibid.
123. Johnson to Louise Johnson, August 6, 1930, Johnson Papers.
124. Johnson to J.J.P. Oud, April 16, 1932 quoted in Terence Riley, *The International Style: Exhibition 15 and the Museum of Modern Art* (New York: Rizzoli and Columbia Books of Architecture, 1992), 41. Also see Terence Riley with Joshua Saks, "Philip Johnson: Act One, Scene One—The Museum of Modern Art," in *Philip Johnson: The Constancy of Change*, ed. Emmanuel Petit (New Haven, CT: Yale University Press, 2009), 60–63. For a theoretical interpretation, see Peter Eisenman, "Philip Johnson: Romanticism and Disintegration," in *Philip Johnson: The Constancy of Change*, 220–24.
125. For documentation of the apartments of Johnson and the Barrs, see David A. Hanks, "Laboratories for Modernism: The Barr and Johnson Apartments," in *Partners in Design: Alfred H. Barr Jr. and Philip Johnson*, ed. David A. Hanks (New York: Monacelli Press, 2015), 66–109.
126. In 1973, Johnson explained that after picking four "non-Americans," "out of misbegotten nationalism or, rather, a desire to encourage lagging American design, we (Johnson and Hitchcock) arbitrarily decided to include four Americans." Philip Johnson, "Beyond Monuments," *Architectural Forum* 138 (January–February 1973): 58.
127. Elizabeth Mock, "Built in U.S.A.: Since 1932," in *Built in USA, 1932–44* (New York: Museum of Modern Art, 1944), 12. Barry Bergdoll, curator of architecture and design at MoMA, who served as director of the department from 2007 to 2013, in 2015 confirmed Mock's assertion: "nine architects, [were] almost evenly divided between European and American practitioners, in part in response to a request by the trustees of the museum that Americans be given a significant representation." Barry Bergdoll, "Modern Architecture: International Exhibition," in *Partners in Design*, 141. Bergdoll did not cite his source. Robert A. M. Stern paraphrased directly from Mock in *George Howe: Toward a Modern American Architecture* (New Haven, CT: Yale University Press, 1975), 154n37. Stern did not cite his source. Richard Guy Wilson repeated the claim, "The museum trustees requested that American architects be accorded equal representation, and to circumvent this restriction, Johnson split the exhibit into three parts to mask the European predominance." Richard Guy Wilson, "International Style: The MoMA exhibition," *Progressive Architecture* (February 1982): 97. Wilson did not cite his source. Terence Riley wrote that he found no reference to any discussion of a requirement for American representation in the MoMA Board of Trustees minutes. Riley, *International Style: Exhibition 15*, 40–41n43.
128. Hitchcock, *Modern Architecture: Romanticism and Reintegration*, 102–18.
129. W. W. Norton also published the museum catalog as a trade book under a new title, *Modern Architects*, in 1932.
130. The final list of nine architects or firms is evident by the time of the publication of the pamphlet, *Built to Live In*, in March 1931. Riley, *International Style: Exhibition 15*, 43–44n6.
131. Johnson to Mumford, January 3, 1931, Letters of Lewis Mumford, Persons of Note File. I am grateful to Robert Wojtowicz, who made this letter available to me, May 8, 2004.
132. Ibid.
133. Itinerary of Exhibition, n.d., REG, Exh. #15. MoMA Archives, NY (Folder 8th, program, checklist, model information).
134. Mumford to Wright, March 29, 1931, in *Wright + Mumford*, 104.
135. Hitchcock, "Modern Architecture: A Memoir," 233.
136. Johnson to Wright, April 1, 1931 (J012B09).
137. Wright to Johnson, April 3, 1931 (J012B10).
138. Johnson to Wright, May 22, 1931 (M022E06).
139. Wright sailed to South America on the SS *American Legion* on September 19 and returned to New York on the SS *Western Prince*, arriving on the morning of November 6.
140. Johnson to Klumb, October 5, 1931 (J013D03).
141. Wright to Mumford, April 7, 1931, in *Wright + Mumford*, 105.
142. Johnson to Wright, October 26, 1931 (J013D10).
143. Johnson to Wright, December 16, 1931 (M026A07).
144. Johnson to Wright, December 4, 1931 (M025D07).
145. Lists of Executed Work, n.d. (M025C08).
146. Wright to Johnson, n.d. (ca. mid-December 1931) (M027C09).
147. Unsigned (Karl Jensen) to Johnson, January 5, 1932 (M027A07).
148. Wright to Johnson, January 5, 1932 (M027A05).
149. Philip Johnson, "Built to Live In," in Philip Johnson, *Writings*, commentary by Robert A. M. Stern (New York: Oxford University Press, 1979), 29.
150. "I find that it will not be practicable to use any project in the show. It is much better propaganda to exhibit buildings which have already been built." Johnson to Jensen, November 3, 1931 (J014A04).
151. "Possible procedure for publicizing and mounting exhibitions, 1929–31," http://www.moma.org/learn/resources/archives, accessed December 5, 2011.
152. John Cushman Fistere, "Poets in Steel," *Vanity Fair*, December 1931, 58.
153. Ibid.
154. *Raymond Hood*, foreword by Arthur Tappan North (New York: Whittlesey House, McGraw-Hill, 1931).
155. Wright, *Collected Writings*, 1: 31.
156. Telegram, Wright to Johnson, January 18, 1932 (M027C08).
157. "Models Assembled for Opening of Exhibit of Modern Architecture," press release, Museum of Modern Art, ca. January 16–17, 1932. MoMA Archives Press Releases, 1929–9, moma.org, accessed November 8, 2011.
158. Telegram, Wright to Johnson, January 18, 1932 (M027C07).
159. Wright to Johnson, January 19, 1932 (M027D01).
160. Telegram, Pauline Schindler to Wright, n.d. (before May 1930) (S016D01).
161. Telegram, Wright to Pauline Schindler, n.d. (before May 1930) (S016D02).
162. Wright to Mumford, January 19, 1932 (M027D01).
163. Telegram, Wright to Pauline Schindler, April 21, 1930 (S015D06). Wright's work appeared at UCLA but was removed before the show traveled to other venues.
164. Wright to Mumford, January 19, 1932 (M027D01). In anticipation of the return of the exhibition from Holland in January, Wright was generating plans for more venues. He pursued the idea of organizing a major survey of modern architecture to be shown in New York. Wright to Henry Churchill, February 12, 1932 (C016D02).
165. Telegram, Mumford to Wright, January 21, 1932 (M027D010).
166. Telegram, Wright to Mumford, January 21, 1932 (M027D09).
167. Telegram, Wright to Johnson, January 22, 1932 (M027E01).
168. Jensen to Johnson, January 23, 1932 (M027E08).
169. Mumford to Wright, January 23, 1932 in *Wright + Mumford*, 133.
170. Wright to Mumford, February 1, 1932 (M028B08). Mrs. Harry Payne (Gertrude Vanderbilt) Whitney was the founder of the Whitney Museum of American Art.

171. With the exclusion of group shows where one or more photographs were displayed, usually without Wright's knowledge.
172. Riley, *International Style: Exhibition 15*, 55.
173. Johnson to Jensen, November 3, 1931 (J014A05).
174. Henry-Russell Hitchcock, "Frank Lloyd Wright," in *Modern Architecture: International Exhibition* (New York: Museum of Modern Art, 1932), 33.
175. The model was shipped from Taliesin on January 23 and acknowledged by Johnson on February 4. Jensen to Johnson, January 24, 1932 (M027E08); transcription of telegram from Johnson, February 4, 1932 (M028C09).
176. In the catalog, Hitchcock made the same comparison: "Beside the classical formalism of the houses of Oud, Le Corbusier, and Mies van der Rohe this latest house of Wright's is a striking aesthetic statement of romantic expansiveness." Hitchcock, "Wright," *Modern Architecture*, 38.
177. For background and analysis of House on the Mesa, see Robert Wojtowicz, "A Model House and a House Model: Reexamining Frank Lloyd Wright's House on the Mesa Project," *Journal of the Society of Architectural Historians* 64, no. 4 (2005): 522–51; Terence Riley, *International Style: Exhibition 15*, 68; Robert L. Sweeney, *Wright in Hollywood: Visions of a New Architecture* (New York: Architectural History Foundation; Cambridge, MA: MIT Press, 1994), 195–200.
178. Wright, "House on the Mesa," *Collected Writings*, 3: 127.
179. Hitchcock, "Wright," *Modern Architecture*, 38.
180. Riley, *International Style: Exhibition 15*, 68–69.
181. Philip Johnson, interview by Mary Anne Staniszewski, in *The Power of Display: A History of Exhibition Installations at the Museum of Modern Art* (Cambridge, MA: MIT Press, 1998), 196.
182. While several commentators have noted that hanging artworks in a single row was first introduced at the Museum of Modern Art in the early 1930s, the art historian Kristina Wilson has proven otherwise. Kristina Wilson, *The Modern Eye: Stieglitz, MoMA, and the Art of the Exhibition, 1925–1934* (New Haven, CT: Yale University Press, 2009), 140.
183. Alfred H. Barr Jr., foreword to *Modern Architecture: International Exhibition* (New York: Museum of Modern Art, 1932), 15.
184. Henry-Russell Hitchcock Jr., "Modern Architecture, I: The Traditionalists and the New Tradition," *Architectural Record* 63 (April 1928): 337–49.
185. Wright to Hitchcock, n.d. (ca. January 1929) (H003B02).
186. Hitchcock, *Modern Architecture: Romanticism and Reintegration*, 118.
187. Haskell to Wright, November 26, 1929 (A006A07).
188. Frank Lloyd Wright, "Poor Little American Architecture," *Collected Writings*, 2: 17.
189. Ibid.
190. Hitchcock, "Wright," *Modern Architecture*, 31–33.
191. Hitchcock, "Modern Architecture: A Memoir," 230.
192. Hitchcock, "Wright," *Modern Architecture*, 34.
193. Ibid., 36.
194. Ibid., 38.
195. Wright to Johnson, n.d. (ca. February 19, 1932) (M029A05).
196. Wright to Hitchcock, February 26, 1932 (H015C02).
197. Wright to Johnson, February 11, 1932 (M028E03).
198. Johnson to Wright, February 16, 1932 (M028E09).
199. Wright to Johnson, February 19, 1932 (M029A057).
200. Frank Lloyd Wright, "Of Thee I Sing," *Shelter* 2 (April 1932): 10–12. Terence Riley, "Portrait of the Curator as a Young Man," in *Studies in Modern Art* 6, ed. John Elderfield (New York: Museum of Modern Art, 1998), 43–44; Riley, *International Style: Exhibition 15*, 83 and n. 34; Franz Schulze, *Philip Johnson: Life and Work* (New York: Alfred A. Knopf, 1994), 81–83.
201. Wright to Johnson, April 19, 1932 (M030A10).
202. Ibid.
203. Hitchcock to Wright, April 22, 1932 quoted in Schulze, *Philip Johnson: Life and Work*, 84. The original of the letter does not appear in the Wright Archives, suggesting that it may not have been sent. I am grateful to Robert Wojtowicz for pointing this out to me.
204. Johnson to Wright, April 25, 1932 (M030B10). Wright had been in New York at the invitation of his publisher, Longman Greens, for the release of *An Autobiography*.
205. Wright to Johnson, May 24, 1932 (M030C10).
206. Johnson to Blackburn, April 14, 1932. REG, Exh. #15. MoMA Archives, NY (Folder 5th Johnson/Blackburn/Barr correspondence).
207. Philip Johnson, "The Berlin Building Exposition of 1931," *T-Square* (January 1932): 17.
208. Johnson to Wright, n.d. (M031D02).
209. One building by Wright, the William Winslow House (1893), was included.
210. Johnson to Oud, n.d., 1930, quoted in Helen Searing, "International Style: The Crimson Connection," *Progressive Architecture* 2 (February 1982): 88 and n. 5. Searing wrote, "The letter is published in Dutch in *Americana* (catalog of the exhibition held in 1975 at the Kröller-Muller Museum, Otterlo)," 102. Presumably, it was originally written in English; translation from the Dutch is by Searing. Searing wrote: "At the time, 'international' immediately conjured up the organizations of the same name (the first two Internationals were socialist, the third, the Comintern of 1919, Bolshevik) and the anti-nationalist, anti-imperialist stance of leftists throughout the world." Searing, "International Style: The Crimson Connection," 90.
211. Wright, "Of Thee I Sing," *Collected Writings*, 3: 114.
212. Wright, *Collected Writings*, 3: 113. Wright cites no reference for this quote.
213. Ibid.
214. Mumford to Wright, July 10, 1928, in *Wright + Mumford*, 55.
215. Wright, *Collected Writings*, 3: 115.
216. Ibid.
217. Alice Garrett to Wright, October 27, 1932 (G013C02).
218. Agnolodomenico Pica, *V Triennale di Milano—Catalogo ufficiale* (Milan: Ceshina, 1933). *Architettura*, numero speciale 12, Roma, 1933. Also see Triennale di Milano, *La quinta triennale di Milano (5th, 1933)*: La Revista illustrata del "Popolo d'Italia," (August 1933), anno 11, numero speciale. The individual architects' exhibits were curated by Luigi Maria Caneva and Enrico Agostino Griffini except Sant'Elia, which was curated by Filippo Marinetti and Enrico Prampolini.
219. Johnson stated that the two most important factors in the development of modern architecture in the United States were Wright and American engineers. To prove the second claim, he chose to feature seventeen architects, firms, and engineers, including Howe and Lescaze, Raymond Hood, and Richard J. Neutra, but also O. H. Amman, Waddell and Hardesty, and Albert Kahn. Pica, *V Triennale di Milano—Catalogo ufficiale*, 163–67.
220. Johnson to Wright, December 3, 1932 (M033D01).
221. Philip Johnson, "Stati Uniti d'America," in Pica, *V Triennale di Milano—Catalogo ufficiale*, 163–64.
222. Carlo A. Felice, Giò Ponti, Mario Seroni, and Giulio Barella to Wright, n.d. (ca. November 14 to December 30, 1932) (B025B03). Barella to John W. Garrett, March 23, 1933. English translation provided to Wright contemporary with events (B021A01).
223. John W. Garrett to Wright, November 24, 1932 (G013D10).
224. Wright to Alice Garrett, November 29, 1932 (G013E04).
225. Wright to Giulio Barella, February 15, 1933 (B020A07).
226. "Exhibition of Mr. Wright's Work to Travel around the World," n.d. (B026A05).
227. Management Committee of Fifth Triennale di Milano to Wright, February 21, 1933 (B020B02).
228. Wright to Barella, April 10, 1933 (B021B09). Wright to Alice Garrett, 6 March 1933 (G015D03); cablegram, Wright to Barella, 6 March 1933 (B020C02). Wright took advantage of his contact with Ambassador Garrett to send a copy of *The Disappearing City* to be hand delivered to Benito Mussolini. John W. Garrett to Fulvio Suvich, Under-Secretary of Foreign Affairs, March 9, 1933 (G015D06).
229. The Commissione Ordinatrice consisted of Barella, Agnolodomenico Pica, Carlo Felice, Giò Ponti, Mario Sironi, Alberto Alpago-Novello, and Pietro Aschieri. Pica, *V Triennale di Milano—Catalogo ufficiale*, 282–84. An oblique view of the Wright exhibit in the *Catalogo* shows photographs of the Larkin Building, the Robie, and Evans Houses on display. Research into Wright's participation in the 1933 Triennale was conducted with Filippo Fici, Florence. His insights and generosity are gratefully acknowledged.
230. Ibid.
231. MSS. 1047.013-#2 Checklist.

CHAPTER 3. *BROADACRE CITY*, 1935

1. Le Corbusier, "A Noted Architect Dissects Our Cities," *New York Times Magazine*, January 3, 1932, 10–11, 19; Frank Lloyd Wright, "Broadacre City: An

Architect's Vision," *New York Times Magazine*, March 20, 1932, 8–9. Wright had earlier laid out ideas about urbanism in "The City," one of the Princeton Lectures.
2. For a comprehensive review, see Anthony Alofsin, "Broadacre City: The Reception of a Modernist Vision, 1932–1988," *Center: A Journal for Architecture in America, Modernist Visions and the Contemporary American City* 5 (1989): 8–43.
3. "Show to Feature Art in Industry," *New York Times*, April 14, 1935, N4.
4. Alon Bement to Wright, April 18, 1932 (N005D07); Jeffrey Meikle, *Twentieth Century Limited: Industrial Design in America, 1925–1939* (Philadelphia: Temple University Press, 2001), 181.
5. Harvey V. Fondiller, "Tom Maloney and U.S. Camera," *Camera Arts* 1, no. 4 (July–August 1981): 16, 19–23, 106–7; Gary Saretzky, "*U.S. Camera*: A Thomas J. Maloney Chronology," *Photo Review* 26, no. 4 and 27, no. 1 (double issue) (2004): 2–6, 26–28.
6. Karl Jensen of *Architectural Record* to Wright, June 27, 1930 (J010D07). Wright had initially expressed interest in employing Jensen to photograph some of his buildings.
7. Advertisement, "Industrial Arts Exposition," *New York Times*, April 14, 1935, 5.
8. *New York Times*, April 15, 1935; Maloney to Bement, April 10, 1935 (M052D01).
9. *Architectural Forum* 60 (May 1934): 331; "Arts in Industry Glorified in Show," *New York Times*, April 16, 1935, 23.
10. Maloney to Rodney Wilcox Jones, April 10, 1935 (M052B07).
11. Edgar J. Kaufmann Sr. to Wright, August 16, 1934 (K017D02).
12. Jensen to Wright, n.d. (before September 18, 1934) (J022D09).
13. Wright to Kaufmann Sr., September 28, 1934 (K018A08).
14. Jensen to Wright, n.d. (ca. September 21, 1934) (J025A04).
15. Wright to Jensen, October 5, 1934 (J022B08–10).
16. Maloney to Wright, October 12, 1934 (M049C05); Kaufmann to Wright, October 20, 1934 (K021B05).
17. Wright to Kaufmann Sr., November 3, 1934 (K021D06).
18. Jensen to Wright, November 8, 1934 (J022C06).
19. Jensen informed Wright that Kaufmann and Maloney had corresponded "before and after [Kaufmann's] visit to Taliesin. Furthermore, when Maloney went to see [Kaufmann] in Pittsburgh he had with him photostats prepared by me which he showed him to indicate what I was driving at." Jensen to Wright, n.d. (ca. November 26, 1934) (J022E08).
20. Maloney to Wright, November 9, 1934 (M050A03).
21. "From our previous discussion—in fact, at our first meeting when we discussed the Broad Acre model—the first exhibit will be yours." Maloney to Kaufmann Sr., November 26, 1934 (M050B04).
22. "Watch Wins Art Prize," *New York Times*, May 8, 1935, 17.
23. Wright to Maloney, n.d. (ca. November 10, 1934) (M041C02).
24. Neil Levine, *The Architecture of Frank Lloyd Wright* (Princeton, NJ: Princeton University Press, 1996), 257.
25. Edgar Tafel, *Apprentice to Genius: Years with Frank Lloyd Wright* (New York: McGraw-Hill, 1979), 2.
26. Telegrams, Jensen to Wright, n.d. (ca. November 21, 1934) (J022C08); Wright to Jensen, n.d. (ca. November 21, 1934) (J022D01).
27. Jensen to Wright, n.d. (ca. November 21, 1934) (J022E08).
28. Maloney to Kaufmann, November 26, 1934 (M050B04).
29. Masselink to Kaufmann Sr., December 3, 1934 (K018E10); Kaufmann Sr. to Wright, December 4, 1934 (K019A01); Wright to Kaufmann Sr., December 7, 1934 (K019A05).
30. Wright to Kaufmann Sr., December 7, 1934 (K019A060).
31. Wright to Jensen, December 7, 1934 (J022E05); Wright to Kaufmann Sr., December 7, 1934 (K019A06); Wright to Maloney, December 7, 1934 (M050C02).
32. Maloney to Wright, December 10, 1934 (M050C05).
33. Wright to Kaufmann Sr., December 26, 1934 (K019C01). Darwin D. Martin died December 18, 1935.
34. *"At Taliesin," Newspaper Columns by Frank Lloyd Wright and the Taliesin Fellowship, 1934–1937*, compiled and with commentary by Randolph C. Henning (Carbondale: Southern Illinois University Press, 1992), 121.
35. "Arts in Industry Glorified in Show," *New York Times*, April 16, 1935, 23; "Roosevelt to Open Exposition Tonight," *New York Times*, April 15, 1935, 17.
36. Tafel to Wright, April 18, 1935 (T009A05); Tafel to Wright, May 2, 1935 (T009B03); Wright to Tafel as written in margin of Tafel to Wright, April 29, 1935 (T009B02); "Radio Programs Scheduled for Broadcast This Week," *New York Times*, April 28, 1935, X2.
37. Maloney to Jones, April 10, 1935 (J035D10).
38. Stephen Alexander, "Frank Lloyd Wright's Utopia," *New Masses* 15 (June 18, 1935): 28.
39. Douglas Haskell, "Art: Industrial Art in Eclipse," *Nation* 140, no. 3644 (1935): 556.
40. Alofsin, "Broadacre City," 18.
41. Wright had thousands of hand-cut letters made for the 1940–41 exhibition. There are no photographs that record the text that he presented there.
42. No installation photographs survive that record this text. A drawing in the Wright Foundation Archives, which contains drafts for the text panels, provides a clue. The following text is not identified in either of the two photographs: A NEW ARCHITECTURE EMPLOYING STEEL IN TENSION/ GLASS AS A SUPERMATERIAL SLABS OF SYNTHETIC MA/TERIAL OR SHEET METALS OR CONCRETE BRICK TILE/ ALL IN FORMS OBJECTIVE— NATURAL TO MATERIAL AND PROCESS OF CONSTRUCTION. "Panel IV D" in 3406.003.
43. Wright used various terms to describe these houses. Sometimes he called the one-car house, the minimum house. He also called the two-car house, a medium house.
44. These houses are illustrated in *Truth against the World: Frank Lloyd Wright Speaks for an Organic Architecture*, ed. with introduction by Patrick Meehan (New York: John Wiley and Sons, 1987), 357.
45. Frank Lloyd Wright, "Broadacre City: Frank Lloyd Wright, Architect," *American Architect* 146 (May 1935): 60.
46. *Architectural Record* to Wright, February 7, 1935 (A034C01); *Architectural Forum* to Wright, February 10, 1935 (A034C02); *Architectural Record* to Wright, n.d. (ca. February 11, 1935) (A034C03).
47. *American Architect* published one month later. "Broadacre City: Frank Lloyd Wright, Architect," *American Architect* 146 (May 1935): 55–62. Wright devoted an issue of his self-published magazine, *Taliesin*, to Broadacre City, which appeared in October 1940, coincident with his retrospective at MoMA.
48. Frank Lloyd Wright, "Broadacre City: A New Community Plan," *Architectural Record* 78 (April 1935): 244–45.
49. Lewis Mumford, "The Sky Line: Mr. Wright's City—Downtown Dignity," *New Yorker*, April 27, 1935, 79–80.
50. Wright to Mumford, April 27, 1935, in *Wright + Mumford*, 164.
51. Mumford to Wright, June 25, 1935, in *Wright + Mumford*, 165.
52. Wright to Tafel, May 3, 1935 (J024B04).
53. Stephen Alexander, "Frank Lloyd Wright's Utopia," *New Masses* 15 (June 18, 1935): 28.
54. Frank Lloyd Wright, "Freedom Based on Form," *New Masses* 16 (July 23, 1935): 23–24.
55. Robert Wojtowicz, *Lewis Mumford and American Modernism: Eutopian Theories for Architecture and Urban Planning* (Cambridge: Cambridge University Press, 1996), 115–28.
56. Executive Order 7027, April 30, 1935, and Executive Order 7041, May 15, 1935, cited in *Public Papers and Addresses of Franklin D. Roosevelt*, ed. Samuel I. Rosenman, 4 vols. (New York: Random House, 1938–50), 4: 143.
57. Paul K. Conkin, *Tomorrow a New World: The New Deal Community Program* (Ithaca, NY: Cornell University Press, 1959), 263.
58. Tafel to Wright, April 26, 1935 (T009A10); Maloney to Wright, May 6, 1935 (M053A01).
59. Wright to Tafel, April 28, 1935 (Y009B01).
60. Tafel to Wright, May 15, 1935 (T009C01); Tafel to Wright, May 22, 1935 (T009C06); Tafel to Wright, n.d. (T010B05).
61. Masselink to Alden Dow, June 13, 1935 (D022E08).
62. "Frank Lloyd Wright Designs Ideal City for Students," *Daily Cardinal*, June 6, 1935.
63. Telegram, Kaufmann to Wright, May 28, 1935 (K017A07).
64. Frank Lloyd Wright scrapbooks, ca. 1920–ca. 1959. Getty Research Institute, Getty Library, accession no. 870496B (8003.40).
65. William T. Schoyer, FHA, to Wright, June 13, 1935 (F017C04).
66. Wright to Schoyer, June 15, 1935 (F017C06).
67. Schoyer to Wright, June 18, 1935 (F017C08).
68. Frank Lloyd Wright, "Broadacres to Pittsburgh," *Pittsburgh Sun-Telegraph*, June 24, 1935.
69. "M'Nair Scoffs at 'Model City,'" *Pittsburgh Post-Gazette*, June 20, 1935.
70. Schoyer to Wright, June 20, 1935 (F017D03).

71. James A. Baubie, "Flings Sneers at Pittsburgh," *Pittsburgh Sunday Sun-Telegraph*, June 30, 1935, Part I, 13.
72. Wright to Schoyer, June 24, 1935 (F017D07); "Designer of Future City Answers Mayor's Attack," *Pittsburgh Post-Gazette*, June 27, 1935, 7; "People," *Time*, July 15, 1935.
73. "Architect Hits 'Ugly Buildings,'" no title, n.d., Frank Lloyd Wright scrapbooks, ca. 1920–ca. 1959. Getty Research Institute, Getty Library, accession no. 870496B (8003.043).
74. James A. Baubie, "Flings Sneers at Pittsburgh," *Pittsburgh Sunday Sun-Telegraph*, June 30, 1935, 13.
75. Jensen to Wright, June 24, 1935 (J024E09); Jensen to Masselink, June 25, 1935 (J026A01).
76. Queene Coonley's first suggestion was the National Gallery. Jensen to Wright, June 20, 1935 (F017C09).
77. Jensen to Col. Lawrence Westbrook, June 24, 1935 (J024E03).
78. Wright to Jensen, June 17, 1935 (J024D09).
79. Wright to Alden Dow, July 17, 1935 (D023B07).
80. Jensen to Wright, June 10, 1935 (J024D06).
81. Frank Lloyd Wright, "A Note on the Models," *Taliesin* 1, no. 1 (1940): 23.
82. Ibid., 24.
83. *The Eleanor Roosevelt Encyclopedia*, ed. Maurine Hoffman Beasley, Holly Cowan Shulman, Henry R. Beasley (Westport, CT: Greenwood Press, 2001), 216.
84. Wright to Mendel Glickman, January 20, 1936 (G028A05).
85. Wright to Mrs. Franklin D. Roosevelt, July 12, 1935 (R014C04).
86. Thomas J. Doyle to Wright, July 17, 1935 (R014C07).
87. John Meunier, "A Model for the Decentralized City: An Interview with Cornelia Brierly," in *Frank Lloyd Wright—The Phoenix Papers: Broadacre City*, 2 vols. (Tucson: University of Arizona Press, 1995), 1: 40.
88. Interview, Joseph L. Arnold with John S. Lansill, February 8, 1965, quoted in Joseph L. Arnold, *The New Deal in the Suburbs: A History of the Greenbelt Town Program, 1935–1954* (Columbus: Ohio State University Press, 1971), 85–86.
89. J. S. Lansill to Leo Wolfsohn, December 28, 1935 (G027B03); Lansill to Glickman, January 8, 1936 (G028A01).
90. Wright to Glickman, January 20, 1936 (G028A05).
91. Wright to Lansill, January 20, 1936 (G028A06).
92. Arnold, *The New Deal*, 102–103; Arnold R. Alanen and Joseph A. Eden, *Main Street Ready-Made: The New Deal Community of Greendale, Wisconsin* (Madison, WI: State Historical Society, 1987), 38–40.
93. Frank Lloyd Wright, "A New Success Ideal," *Taliesin* 1, no. 1 (1940): 6.
94. For background on the development of the public relations industry, see Roger William Riis and Charles W. Bonner, *Publicity: A Study of the Development of Industrial News* (New York: J. H. Sears, 1926); Scott M. Cutlip, *The Unseen Power: Public Relations, A History* (Hillsdale, NJ: Lawrence Erlbaum, 1994).

CHAPTER 4. MUSEUM OF MODERN ART, 1933–53

1. Rene d'Harnoncourt, press release, Museum of Modern Art, New York, June 19, 1953, 1 (M230C06).
2. Memorandum, Porter McCray to Philip Johnson, "Re: Your Request for checklists of Circulating Exhibitions containing work by Frank Lloyd Wright," June 5, 1953. Department of Architecture and Design, "Frank Lloyd Wright" (file of correspondence with P. Johnson). MoMA Archives, NY.
3. Hitchcock, "Modern Architecture: A Memoir," 230.
4. Mumford to Catherine Bauer, February 9, 1931, Mumford Papers, folder 6345, as quoted in Wojtowicz, *Lewis Mumford and American Modernism*, 92, 180n83.
5. Terence Riley, "Portrait of the Curator as a Young Man," in *Philip Johnson and the Museum of Modern Art, Studies in Modern Art 6* (New York: Museum of Modern Art, 1998), 44–45. The Richardson book accompanied the exhibition, *The Architecture of Henry Hobson Richardson*, January 14–February 16, 1936. "Exhibitions of the Museum of Modern Art," in *Art in Progress: 15th Anniversary Exhibition* (New York: Museum of Modern Art, 1944), 242.
6. Hitchcock, "Modern Architecture: A Memoir," 230.
7. A. Conger Goodyear, *The Museum of Modern Art: The First Ten Years* (New York: A. Conger Goodyear, 1943), 41.
8. Holger Cahill and Alfred H. Barr, Jr., eds., *Art in America in Modern Times* (New York: Reynal and Hitchcock, 1934), 63, 66, and 69. Radio broadcasts were carried over Station WJZ and on a coast-to-coast network weekly from October 6, 1934, to January 26, 1935.
9. Press release, Museum of Modern Art, New York, September 21, 1935; Schulze, *Philip Johnson: Life and Work*, 172.
10. Hitchcock, "Modern Architecture: A Memoir," 230.
11. Jonathan Lipman, *Frank Lloyd Wright and the Johnson Wax Buildings* (New York: Rizzoli, 1986), 45.
12. Wright to Maloney, n.d. (ca. November 20, 1936) (M065C08); Wright to Kocher, December 7, 1936 (A043E04).
13. John E. Lautner Jr., "Letter to the Editor," *Architectural Review* 82 (November 1937): 221.
14. George Nelson to Masselink, May 11, 1937 (A046E02).
15. Howard Myers to Wright, August 6, 1937 (A048A06).
16. George Nelson, in *About Wright: An Album of Recollections by Those Who Knew Frank Lloyd Wright*, ed. Edgar Tafel (New York: Wiley, 1993), 228. Stanley Abercrombie, *George Nelson: The Design of Modern Design* (Cambridge, MA: MIT Press, 1995).
17. Myers to Wright, July 28, 1937 (A047D08).
18. Myers to Wright, October 4, 1937 (A049B05).
19. Nelson, *About Wright*, 225–26.
20. "To the Young Man in Architecture: A Challenge," manuscript (W106A04).
21. "Song of the Open Road" stanza 5 and "By Blue Ontario's Shore," stanza 4, Walt Whitman, *Leaves of Grass (1) & Democratic Vistas* (New York: E. P. Dutton, 1921), 125, 285.
22. Frank Lloyd Wright, "Frank Lloyd Wright," *Architectural Forum* 68 (January 1938): 37.
23. Philip Goodwin, chairman; Catherine Bauer, housing authority; John Coolidge, Vassar College; Hitchcock; Hudnut; Winslow Ames, Lyman Allyn Museum, New London; Nelson; Carl Feiss, Columbia University.
24. John McAndrew to Donald Hoffmann, December 15, 1975, cited in Donald Hoffmann, *Frank Lloyd Wright's Fallingwater: The House and Its History* (New York: Dover, 1978), 69–70n7.
25. Hoffmann, *Fallingwater*, 69 and n. 18.
26. Ingrid Schaffner and Lisa Jacobs, *Julien Levy: A Portrait of an Art Gallery* (Cambridge, MA: MIT, 1998), 90.
27. McAndrew to Swank, n.d. REG, Exh. #70. The Museum of Modern Art Archives, New York.
28. Swank to McAndrew, n.d. (ca. January 5, 1938) (M080E04).
29. "Frank Lloyd Wright Talks about Photography," *Photography* 34 (February 1954): 118.
30. Telegram, Tafel to Wright, n.d. (T013D03).
31. Franklin Toker, *Fallingwater Rising: Frank Lloyd Wright, E. J. Kaufmann, and America's Most Extraordinary House* (New York: Knopf, 2003), 262, and unnumbered note on 444.
32. McAndrew to Wright, n.d. (M079B05).
33. Wright to McAndrew, January 5, 1938 (M080E04).
34. McAndrew to Hedrich-Blessing, January 11, 1938. REG, Exh. #70. MoMA Archives, NY.
35. Howard Bossen, *Luke Swank: Modernist Photographer* (Pittsburgh: University of Pittsburgh Press, 2005); Clyde Hare, ed., *Luke Swank* (Pittsburgh: Museum of Art, Carnegie Institute, 1980).
36. Tony Hiss, "Seventy Years on the Higher Plane," in *Building Images: Seventy Years of Photography at Hedrich Blessing* (San Francisco: Chronicle Books, 2000), 36. See also Robert A. Sobieszek, ed., *The Architectural Photography of Hedrich-Blessing* (New York: Holt, Rinehart and Winston, 1984).
37. Masselink to Swank, March 29, 1938 (A052D08).
38. Wright to Swank, January 3, 1941 (S093A03).
39. For an analysis of McAndrew's exploration of regional identity, see Keith L. Eggener, "John McAndrew, the Museum of Modern Art, and the 'Naturalization' of Modern Architecture in America, ca 1940," in *Architecture and Identity*, ed. Peter Herrle and Erik Wegerhoff (Berlin: Lit, 2008), 235–42.
40. "Exhibition, A New House by Frank Lloyd Wright, Checklist," REG, Exh. #70. MoMA Archives, NY.
41. Ibid.
42. Ibid.
43. Press release, "House Built over Waterfall," Museum of Modern Art, New York, n.d., #38121 (MoMA Press Releases Archive, moma.org, accessed January 25, 2012). It is not possible to identify the author of the press release, but they were usually composites of text from the curator, edited and supplemented by Sarah Newmeyer.
44. *Time*, January 17, 1938, 29.
45. Lewis Mumford, "Skyline: At Home, Indoors and Out," *New Yorker*, February 12, 1938, 58.

46. John McAndrew, "Architecture in the United States," *Bulletin of the Museum of Modern Art* 6 (February 1939): 9.
47. Memorandum, Barr to Dorothy C. Miller, October 10, 1940, quoted in Kathryn Smith, "The Show to End All Shows: Frank Lloyd Wright and the Museum of Modern Art, 1940," in *The Show to End All Shows: Frank Lloyd Wright and The Museum of Modern Art*, Studies in Modern Art 8, ed. Peter Reed and William Kaizen with an essay by Kathryn Smith (New York: Museum of Modern Art, 2004), 62n77.
48. Trustee minutes, vol. 5, October 19, 1939, 4. MoMA Archives, NY. Notes provided by Peter Reed.
49. Architecture Committee minutes, November 19, 1937. MoMA Archives, NY. By February 9, 1939, the Wright show had been approved for the 1939–40 season. Trustee minutes, February 9, 1939, vol. 5, 5. MoMA Archives, NY. Notes provided by Peter Reed. In November 1939 McAndrew informed Wright that the exhibition was being rescheduled from summer to fall 1940. McAndrew to Wright, November 6, 1939. REG, Exh. #114. MoMA Archives, NY.
50. See also "The Boston Museum of Modern Art," *Bulletin of the Museum of Modern Art* 5 (March 1938): 3; Russell Lynes, *Good Old Modern: Intimate Portrait of the Museum of Modern Art* (New York: Atheneum, 1973), 166–67, 292–93; "James S. Plaut, 83, Museum Founder," *New York Times*, January 17, 1996, 17.
51. James S. Plaut to Wright, May 3, 1939 (I011A05).
52. Plaut to McAndrew, December 23, 1939. REG, Exh. #114. MoMA Archives, NY. The two institutions shared the costs of photography and fabrication of two new models: the Charles Ross House (1902; Lake Delavan, Wisconsin) and the Herbert Jacobs House I (1936–37; Madison, Wisconsin), and the repair of two existing models: the Stanley Marcus House (1935; Dallas), and the Suntop Homes (1938–39; Ardmore, Pennsylvania).
53. Plaut to Wright, July 14, 1939 (I011B09). The final exhibition dates were January 24 to March 3, 1940.
54. Plaut to Wright, September 26, 1939 (I013A04).
55. James S. Plaut, "Notes on the Exhibition," in *Frank Lloyd Wright: A Pictorial Record of Architectural Progress* (Boston: Institute of Modern Art, 1940), unpaginated.
56. Plaut to McAndrew, December 23, 1939. REG, Exh. #114 (Boston, correspondence). MoMA Archives, NY.
57. "Boston Photographs to be used in FLLW Show," n.d., "Photographs Made for the Frank Lloyd Wright Exhibition at the Boston Institute of Modern Art," "Photostats Made for the Exhibition of the Work of Frank Lloyd Wright at the Boston Institute of Modern Art," REG, Exh. #114. MoMA Archives, NY.
58. Plaut to Wright, December 7, 1939 (I013C04); telegram, Plaut to Wright, December 27, 1939 (I03D06). Wright ordered the House on the Mesa model exhibited, but there is no confirmation that it was sent, and if so, displayed. Wright to Robert Mosher, December 29, 1939 (M098E01); McAndrew to Plaut, January 10, 1940. REG, Exh. #114 (Boston Correspondence). MoMA Archives, NY.
59. Plaut to Wright, January 10, 1940 (I014C04).
60. Nelson W. Aldrich, oral history at Archives of American Art, http://www.aaa.si.edu/collections/interviews/oral-history-interview-nelson-w-aldrich-15643, accessed May 9, 2013.
61. McAndrew to Mumford, January 31, 1940. REG, Exh. #114. MoMA Archives, NY.
62. Plaut to Wright, January 8, 1940 (I014C02).
63. *Frank Lloyd Wright: A Pictorial Record of Architectural Progress* (Boston: Institute of Modern Art, 1940).
64. Wright inscribed a copy to Frederick Langhurst, a former apprentice, "Fred—the worst introduction I ever had. F.L.L.W." GRI/SC.
65. For background on Hudnut, see Jill Pearlman, *Inventing Modernism: Joseph Hudnut, Walter Gropius, and the Bauhaus Legacy at Harvard* (Charlottesville: University of Virginia Press, 2007); Anthony Alofsin, *The Struggle for Modernism: Architecture, Landscape Architecture, and City Planning at Harvard* (New York: W. W. Norton, 2002).
66. Joseph Hudnut, foreword to *Frank Lloyd Wright: A Pictorial Record*, unpaginated.
67. Wright to McAndrew, November 19, 1940 (M110A03).
68. Trustee minutes, vol. 5, October 19, 1939, 4. MoMA Archives, NY. Notes provided by Peter Reed.
69. See "Prospectus for Frank Lloyd Wright Show," October 20, 1939. REG, Exh. #114. MoMA Archives, NY.
70. McAndrew to Neutra, June 14, 1940. REG, Exh. #114. MoMA Archives, NY.
71. McAndrew to Wright, November 6, 1939 (M096E05).
72. Expense List, n.d. REG, Exh. #114. MoMA Archives, NY.
73. McAndrew to Neutra, June 14, 1940. REG, Exh. #114. MoMA Archives, NY.
74. McAndrew to Barr and Wheeler, December 1, 1939. Memorandum, Barr to McAndrew, December 2, 1939. REG, Exh. #114. MoMA Archives, NY.
75. For transcripts of the essays and critical analysis, see Peter Reed, "Original Manuscripts: Introduction," in *The Show to End All Shows*, 104–84.
76. McAndrew to Mumford, January 31, 1940. REG, Exh. #114. MoMA Archives, NY. See my essay, "Show to End All Shows," in *The Show to End All Shows*, 35, 62n99.
77. McAndrew to Behrendt, January 19, 1940; McAndrew to Mumford, January 31, 1940; Henrich to Behrendt, March 11, 1940. REG, Exh. #114. MoMA Archives, NY.
78. Mumford to McAndrew, March 10, 1940. REG, Exh. #114. MoMA Archives, NY.
79. Walter Curt Behrendt, *Modern Building: Its Nature, Problems, and Forms* (New York: Harcourt, Brace, 1937), 126–39, 143.
80. Ibid., 139.
81. Ibid., 130.
82. Ibid., 132–33.
83. Ibid., 143.
84. Architecture Committee minutes, April 11, 1940, 6. MoMA Archives, NY. Notes provided by Peter Reed.
85. Behrendt to Wright, May 27, 1940 (B075B02); Wright to Behrendt, June 6, 1940 (B075E02).
86. Wright to McAndrew, May 30, 1940 (M103B01).
87. Wright to Behrendt, June 6, 1940 (B075E02). In calling Boston's Institute of Modern Art the Museum of Modern Art, Wright is confusing the former and new name of the institution.
88. For additional background, see Smith, "Show to End All Shows," 62–63nn113, 114.
89. Wright to McAndrew, September 16, 1940 (M107A01).
90. Curtis Besinger, *Working with Mr. Wright: What It Was Like* (Cambridge: University of Cambridge Press, 1995), 97.
91. Telegram, Wright to McAndrew, December 17, 1939 (M098B06); telegram, Wright to McAndrew, December 21, 1939 (M098C06); telegram, Wright to McAndrew, January 5, 1940 (M099B01); telegram, McAndrew to Wright, January 10, 1940 (M099C01); Wright to McAndrew, January 12, 1940 (M099D01).
92. Besinger, *Working with Mr. Wright*, 97–100.
93. Memorandum, Barr to McAndrew, July 30, 1940; "Schedule for Catalogue and Exhibition," September 5, 1940. REG, Exh. #114 (Lists, memos, etc.). MoMA Archives, NY.
94. Telegram, Wright to McAndrew, September 10, 1940 (M106D09); telegram, Wright to McAndrew, September 10, 1940 (M106E06).
95. Leslie Cheek Jr. Papers, and Alfred H. Barr, Jr. Papers, 6.B.13.a–e. The Museum of Modern Art Archives, New York.
96. Memorandum, Alfred Barr to John E. Abbott, March 3, 1940. REG, Exh. #106, The Museum of Modern Art Archives, New York. Telegram, McAndrew to Barr, September 13, 1940. REG, Exh. #114. MoMA Archives, NY.
97. The other essay was Talbot Hamlin, "Frank Lloyd Wright: His Influence in America." For the complete text, see *Show to End All Shows*, 137–42.
98. Telegram, Wright to McAndrew, September 14, 1940 (M106E03).
99. Ibid.
100. Telegram, Wright to McAndrew, September 16, 1940 (M107A01).
101. Telegram, McAndrew to Wright, September 19, 1940 (M107B01).
102. For information about changes within the museum that affected the confrontation between the Modern and Wright, see Smith, "Show to End All Shows," 63n126.
103. Wright to McAndrew, September 16, 1940 (M107A01).
104. Postcard, Barr to McAndrew, n.d. (postmark September 17, 1940). REG, Exh. #114 (Memos, lists, etc.). MoMA Archives, NY.
105. Wright to McAndrew, November 19, 1940 (M107A09).
106. See Smith, "Show to End All Shows," 63n130.
107. Abby Aldrich Rockefeller, Nelson Rockefeller, Archibald MacLeish, Edward Stone, Beardsley Ruml, and Alfred H. Barr Jr., reviewed Exhibition X. The Executive Committee of the Board of Trustees rejected the exhibit on October 4, 1940. Leslie Cheek, Jr. Papers and Alfred H. Barr Jr. Papers, 6.B.13, a-e. MoMA Archives, NY.
108. McAndrew to Wright, September 18, 1940 (M107A08).
109. Telegram, Wright to McAndrew, September 19, 1940 (M107B01).

110. Wright to McAndrew, September 19, 1940 (M107A10).
111. Telegram, McAndrew to Wright, September 19, 1940 (M107B01).
112. Telegram, Wright to McAndrew, September 20, 1940 (M107B03).
113. For Behrendt's full text with Wright's editorial changes, see *Show to End All Shows*, 116–33.
114. Wright to Behrendt, September 19, 1940 (B078A02).
115. Walter Curt Behrendt, "Frank Lloyd Wright," manuscript, Version 2B, 14. FLWFA.
116. Ibid., 20–21.
117. Frank Lloyd Wright, "To My Critics in the Land of the Danube and the Rhine," July 23, 1931, revised September 14, 1940. FLWFA.
118. Wright to Behrendt, October 5, 1940 (B078B02).
119. Behrendt to Wright, October 17, 1940 (B078C02).
120. Behrendt to Mumford, n.d. (ca. September 19–22, 1940), Lewis Mumford Papers, Special Collections, University of Pennsylvania. I am grateful to Robert Wojtowicz for providing this letter.
121. Mumford to Behrendt, July 9, 1940, Lewis Mumford Papers, Special Collections, University of Pennsylvania.
122. Mumford to Behrendt, 23 September 23, 1940, Lewis Mumford Papers, Special Collections, University of Pennsylvania.
123. Meeting notes, September 25, 1940. REG, Exh. #114. MoMA Archives, NY.
124. The Walker Art Center, Minneapolis, was the first museum to construct a fully furnished modern house as part of their public programs. The first of these, Idea House I, opened to the public in June 1941; Idea House II opened in 1947. Arthur J. Pulos, *The American Design Adventure* (Cambridge, MA: MIT Press, 1988), 62; Alexandra Griffith Winton, "'A Man's House Is His Art': The Walker Art Center's Idea House Project and the Marketing of Domestic Design, 1941–7," in *The Modern Period Room: The Construction of the Exhibited Interior, 1870–1950*, ed. Penny Sparke, Brenda Martin, and Trevor Keeble (New York: Routledge, 2006), 87. David Hanks, "Spreading the Gospel of Modern Design," in *Partners in Design: Alfred H. Barr Jr. and Philip Johnson*, ed. David Hanks (New York: Monacelli Press, 2015), 186nn48–49. Hanks noted that Philip Goodwin wrote the Walker Art Center's director in 1948 for advice on a similar future MoMA program one year before Breuer's house was installed in the MoMA Garden. Goodwin, who had been the architect of record for Wright's aborted Usonian House in the Garden (1940), had direct experience with the idea of an exhibition house built by a museum. See also Helen Searing, "Case Study Houses: In the Grand Modern Tradition," in *Blueprints for Modern Living: History and Legacy of the Case Study Houses*, ed. Elizabeth A. T. Smith (Los Angeles: Museum of Contemporary Art; Cambridge, MA: MIT Press, 1989), 107–29. For history and analysis of the MoMA demonstration houses, see Mary Anne Staniszewski, "Houses in the Museum's Garden," *The Power of Display: A History of Exhibition Installations at the Museum of Modern Art* (Cambridge, MA: MIT Press, 1998), 199–202.
125. Wright to McAndrew, October 10, 1940 (M107E02).
126. Telegram, Wright to McAndrew, October 9, 1940 (M107D10); Wright to McAndrew, October 10, 1940 (M107E02); telegram, Wright to McAndrew, October 10, 1940 (M107E04); telegram, McAndrew to Wright, October 11, 1940 (M107E07).
127. John D. Rockefeller Jr. to John Abbott, October 29, 1940. Rockefeller Archive Center of the Rockefeller University.
128. Stephen C. Clark to Rockefeller Jr., November 16, 1940. Rockefeller Archive Center of the Rockefeller University.
129. McAndrew to Wright, December 2, 1940 (M110C01). For additional details about the dispute, see Smith, "Show to End All Shows," 63n156.
130. "Frank Lloyd Wright Talks about Photography," *Photography*, 118. The Frank Lloyd Wright Foundation fabricated a demonstration Usonian House based on the plans for the Gerald Sussman House (1955; Rye, New York) for the 1988–89 touring exhibition, *Frank Lloyd Wright: In the Realm of Ideas*. The exhibition was curated by Bruce Brooks Pfeiffer and Gerald Nordland and co-organized by the Scottsdale Arts Center Association. It traveled to Dallas; Washington, DC; Miami; Chicago; Scottsdale; and San Diego.
131. "Greatest Living Architect Exhibits Mass of Work," *Alameda* (California) *Times-Star*, n.d.; *Motion Picture Herald* (New York), August 24, 1940; Dimitri Tselos, "Frank Lloyd Wright," *Art in America* 29 (January 1941): 42.
132. Besinger, *Working with Wright*, 100.
133. McAndrew to Wright, October 24, 1940 (M108C05).
134. Victor Cusack, William Wesley Peters, and Robert Mosher, transcribed interview by Indira Berndtson and Greg Williams, Taliesin West, April 7, 1991, 22. FLWFA.
135. Alan Mather, "The Perennial Trailblazer," *Pencil Points* 21 supp. (December 1940): 16.
136. For McAndrew's outline, see appendix, *Show to End All Shows*, 210–12.
137. Wright to McAndrew, December 9, 1940 (M110C10).
138. Wright to McAndrew, November 19, 1940 (M110A03).
139. John H. Howe, "Taliesin Drawings," oral history conducted by the author, Phoenix, Arizona, March 9, 1987. For additional information on Wright's drawing techniques, see Bruce Brooks Pfeiffer, *Masterworks from the Frank Lloyd Wright Archives: Frank Lloyd Wright Drawings* (New York: Harry N. Abrams in association with the Frank Lloyd Wright Foundation and the Phoenix Art Museum, 1990), 6–9; "The Drawings," in *Frank Lloyd Wright Drawings: An Exhibition for the Benefit of the Frank Lloyd Wright Foundation* (Tokyo: GA Gallery, 1984), unpaginated.
140. Howe, "Taliesin Drawings," 1987.
141. Meeting notes, September 25, 1940. REG, Exh. #114. MoMA Archives, NY.
142. Wright to McAndrew, November 1, 1940 (M109B04).
143. Wright, in meeting notes, September 25, 1940, 2. REG, Exh. #114. MoMA Archives, NY.
144. *Grand Rapids Herald*, December 1, 1940.
145. McAndrew to Wright, October 14, 1940 (M108A03).
146. Frank Lloyd Wright quoted in Tselos, "Frank Lloyd Wright," 43.
147. Masselink quoted in *Grand Rapids Herald*, December 1, 1940.
148. Wright to McAndrew, November 19, 1940 (M110A03).
149. For additional details on the Bauhaus installation, see Staniszewski, "The Bauhaus Debacle," in *Power of Display*, 145; Lynes, *Good Old Modern*, 182.
150. E. (Edward) A. (Alden) J. (Jewell), "Museum of Modern Art: Two New Exhibitions Present the Careers of Frank Lloyd Wright, D. W. Griffith," *New York Times*, 17 November 1940.
151. Geoffrey Baker, "Wright as Iconoclast," *New York Times*, 24 November 1940.
152. Isabel Cooper, "The Art of a Master Builder," *New Masses* (New York), 17 December 1940.
153. Milton Brown, "Frank Lloyd Wright's First Fifty Years," *Parnassus* 12, no. 8 (December 1940): 37.
154. Tselos, "Frank Lloyd Wright," 42.
155. F. A. Gutheim, "First Reckon with His Future: Frank Lloyd Wright's Exhibit at the Modern Museum," *Magazine of Art* 34 (January 1941): 32.
156. Talbot Hamlin, "Frank Lloyd Wright," *The Nation* 151, no. 22 (1940): 541–42.
157. Brown, "Frank Lloyd Wright's First Fifty Years," 38.
158. Alofsin, "Broadacre City," 28. Robert L. Sweeney, *Frank Lloyd Wright: An Annotated Bibliography* (Los Angeles: Hennessey and Ingalls, 1978), no. 2040.
159. Barr, "Letter to the Editor," *Parnassus* 13 (January 1941): 3.
160. Jewell, "Modern Museum Opens Two Shows," *New York Times*, November 13, 1940.
161. Press release, Museum of Modern Art, New York, ca. November 10, 1940, #401108–67. MoMA Press Release Archives, moma.org, accessed May 3, 2002).
162. S. [Sarah] N. [Newmeyer] to Mumford, November 22, 1940. REG, Exh. #114. MoMA Archives, NY.
163. Behrendt to Mumford, January 5, 1941, Lewis Mumford Papers, University of Pennsylvania.
164. "'Bomb-Proof City' Shown as Model," *New York Times*, November 11, 1940.
165. "Frank Wright Here, Believes Cities Doomed," *New York Herald Tribune*, November 11, 1940.
166. Bruce Brooks Pfeiffer and Robert Wojtowicz, introduction to *Wright + Mumford*, 23.
167. Mumford to John Gould Fletcher, April 10, 1946, in *Wright + Mumford*, 189.
168. Lewis Mumford, *Sketches from Life: The Autobiography of Lewis Mumford, The Early Years* (New York: Dial Press, 1982), 435.
169. Lewis Mumford, untitled manuscript, Lewis Mumford Papers, University of Pennsylvania, folder 7343. Since the first page of the typed manuscript is missing, its association with MoMA's exhibition or the intended publisher cannot be determined. Internal evidence suggests, however, that the text was a review of the

exhibition. I am extremely grateful to Robert Wojtowicz for calling the manuscript to my attention and for providing a copy. Quotation from this unpublished manuscript is courtesy of the Estate of Lewis and Sophia Mumford.

170. Henry-Russell Hitchcock, "The Architectural Future in America," *Architectural Review* 82 (July 1937): 1–2.

171. John E. Lautner Jr. to Hitchcock, July 21, 1937 (H040E05); Masselink, "Letter to the Editor," *Architectural Review* 82 (September 1937): 114; "Correspondence: Professor Hitchcock and Mr. Frank Lloyd Wright," *Architectural Review* 82 (November 1937): 221–22.

172. Wright to Hitchcock, September 15, 1937 (H042B08).

173. Hitchcock to Wright, May 18, 1937 (H047C03).

174. Wright to Hitchcock, June 1, 1937 (H040C07); Hitchcock to Wright, June 8, 1938 (H047C09); Wright to Hitchcock, June 15, 1938 (H047B07).

175. Wright to Hitchcock, July 12, 1938 (H047D07).

176. Telegram, Hitchcock and Joseph Brewer to Wright, n.d. (H047C03); Hitchcock to Masselink, August 13, 1939 (B068B06); Hitchcock to Wright, September 20, 1940 (H047C04).

177. Hitchcock to Wright, November 20, 1940 (H057C04).

178. Wright to Hitchcock, November 23, 1940 (H057C08).

179. Hitchcock to Wright, November 27, 1940 (H057C08).

180. Hitchcock to McAndrew, n.d. (ca. June 15–30, 1940). REG, Exh. #114. MoMA Archives, NY.

181. Henry-Russell Hitchcock, *In the Nature of Materials: The Buildings of Frank Lloyd Wright, 1887–1941* (New York: Duell, Sloan and Pearce, 1942; reprint; Da Capo Press, 1973), xxxiii.

182. Duell sent Wright two reviews. On May 4, 1942, *Time* called the book "thorough" and Mumford in the *New Yorker* wrote "a superb job." Wright to Hitchcock, May 28, 1942 (H064E05).

183. Walter Curt Behrendt, "The Record of Frank Lloyd Wright," *Yale Review* 32, no. 1 (1942): 180.

184. Wright to Hitchcock, September 24, 1952 (H127D08). Hitchcock to Gutheim, May 17, 1959; Hitchcock to Charles Duell (Duell, Sloane and Pearce), October 18, 1959; Hitchcock to Duell, November 10, 1959; Duell to Hitchcock, November 18, 1959; Hitchcock to James Marston Fitch, December 6, 1959; Hitchcock to Leslie H. Fishel Jr., October 12, 1960, AAA/SI. I am grateful to Helen Searing, who called my attention to these letters and made copies of them available to me.

185. Sybil Gordon Kanter, *Alfred H. Barr, Jr., and the Intellectual Origins of the Museum of Modern Art* (Cambridge, MA: MIT Press, 2002); Bernice Kert, *Abby Aldrich Rockefeller: The Woman in the Family* (New York: Random House, 2003).

186. Margaret Scolari Barr, "Our Campaigns," *New Criterion* (September 1987): 62–63.

187. Janet Henrich and Alice Carson served in the interim, 1941–43.

188. Elizabeth B[auer] [Mock] Kassler, *The Taliesin Fellowship: A Directory of Members, 1932–1982* (Princeton, NJ: privately printed, 1981), unpaginated.

189. Her successor, Porter McCray, was the director during the tour of *New American Houses*, 1952–57.

190. Elodie Courter, "Circulating Exhibitions," *Bulletin of the Museum of Modern Art* 1, no. 7 (1934): 2–4; B. C., "Circulating Exhibitions," "Art for the Nation," *Bulletin of the Museum of Modern Art* 7, no. 5 (1940): 2–14. Prepared at the request of the Office of War Information were *Evolution of the Skyscraper* (seventeen venues, 1939–44) for showing in Great Britain, and *America Builds* (1944) for Stockholm, Sweden. "The Museum Goes Abroad," *Bulletin of the Museum of Modern Art* 12, no. 2 (1944): 2–6; Elodie Courter, "Circulating Exhibitions," in *Art in Progress: A Survey Prepared for the Fifteenth Anniversary of the Museum of Modern Art* (New York: Museum of Modern Art, 1944): 210–12, 246.

191. MoMA published 10,000 copies of a booklet, *What Is Modern Architecture?*, Introductory Series to the Modern Arts 1 (1942) based on the circulating show prepared by McAndrew and Mock. A second revised edition appeared in 1946.

192. Elizabeth Mock, *If You Want to Build a House* (New York: Museum of Modern Art, 1946), 96; "Circulating Exhibitions: 1931–1954," *Bulletin of the Museum of Modern Art*, 21, no. 3/4 (1954): 3–30; Museum of Modern Art Department of Circulating Exhibitions, *Department of Circulating Exhibitions Records: 1931–1990*, 2–6, 56–148. http://www.moma.org/research/archives/EAD/CEb.html, downloaded April 16, 2007.

193. Houses by Frank Lloyd Wright opens at [left blank] on [left blank]." Press release, Museum of Modern Art, New York, August 8, 1946 (Ryerson and Burnham Library, Art Institute of Chicago); checklist, dated July 29, 1946.

194. Edgar J. Kaufmann Jr., director of Industrial Design, MoMA, 1946–55, also popularized Wright through the Modern's Publications Department. He authored the classic booklet, *What Is Modern Interior Design?*, which featured Wright in the text and illustrated nine examples of his built work. Edgar J. Kaufmann Jr., *What Is Modern Interior Design?*, Introductory Series to the Modern Arts 4 (New York: Museum of Modern Art, 1953), color frontispiece, figures 2, 7, 16, 17, 21, 36, 55, 56.

195. Form letter, n.d. (M128C05).

196. "Museum of Modern Art Selects Forty-Seven Buildings of Best Modern Design Built in U.S.A. since 1932," Press release, Museum of Modern Art, New York, n.d. (1944), #44412-14 (Press Release Archives, moma.org); Philip Goodwin, preface to *Built in USA, 1932–1944*, ed. Elizabeth Mock (New York: Museum of Modern Art, 1944), 6–7.

197. Mock to Wright, May 24, 1943 (M128D05), and January 29, 1944 (M131B08).

198. Mock to Wright, March 29, 1944 (M132A07). The unnamed architect was George Howe, who was represented by the Philadelphia Savings Fund Society Building (Howe and Lescaze, 1932), Carver Court (Howe, Stonorov, and Kahn, 1944), and his independently designed Clara Fargo Thomas House (1939).

199. Wright to Mock, May 12, 1943 (M128C09); Wright to Mock, February 9, 1944 (M13105); Wright to Mock, March 15, 1944 (M131E06); telegram, Wright to MoMA, March 18, 1944 (M131E08).

200. "Built in USA, 1932–44," *Architectural Forum* 80 (May 1944): 81–82.

201. Mock, *Built in USA: 1932–1944*, 13.

202. In 1964, Mock was even more emphatic: "I am convinced that the International Style, as the dominant movement of the 1930s, produced no buildings of intrinsic value in this country. And I also now begin to question whether it really was very important in the development of [American] architecture." Elizabeth Mock Kassler, "Sunday Session," transcript of discussion at "Modern Architecture Symposium (MAS 1964): The Decade 1929–1939," *Journal of the Society of Architectural Historians* 24, no. 1 (1965): 92.

203. Loeb to Wright, July 7, 1941 (L064D04); Loeb to Wright, April 11, 1944 (L079E06); Loeb to Wright, June 19, 1944 (L079C07). Kenneth L. Fisher, "Gerald M. Loeb, The Father of Froth—He Knew the Lingo, Not the Logic," in *100 Minds That Made the Market* (New York: John Wiley and Sons, 2007), 104–7; Ralph G. Martin, *The Wizard of Wall Street: The Story of Gerald M. Loeb* (New York: William Morrow, 1965).

204. Loeb to Wright, dated September 32, 1944 by Loeb (L081D07). Loeb's eccentric dating.

205. Loeb to Wright, July 14, 1945 (L089D03).

206. Loeb to Wright, June 10, 1945 (L089A02); Mock to Loeb, December 10, 1945, quoted in Loeb to Wright, December 10, 1945 (L092E07); Loeb to Wright, February 21, 1946 (L094D04).

207. Loeb to Wright, December 6, 1945 (L092E03); Mock to Loeb, February 20, 1946 (L094D03).

208. Wright to Loeb, June 16, 1946 (L096E09).

209. Mary Roche, "New Home Design Has Odd Windows," *New York Times*, June 19, 1946; "Country House in Connecticut, USA designed by Frank Lloyd Wright," *Architect's Journal* 104 (September 19, 1946): 213–14; "Wright Makes It Right," *Time*, July 1946, 73; "House in Connecticut," *Architectural Forum* 84 (June 1946): 83–88.

210. "Letters," *Architectural Forum* 84 (August 1946): 34.

211. Loeb to Wright, August 5, 1946 (L098C055).

212. Wright to Rebay, August 27, 1946, in *Frank Lloyd Wright: The Guggenheim Correspondence*, selected and with commentary by Bruce Brooks Pfeiffer (Fresno: Press at California State University, Fresno; Carbondale: Southern Illinois University Press, 1986), 88.

213. Wright to Myers, September 19, 1946 (A091A06).

214. Wright to Hilla Rebay, August 27, 1946 (G078E07).

215. Johnson to Wright, October 23, 1946 (M155E07); Bruce Brooks Pfeiffer in conversation with the author, January 12, 2004.

216. Schulze, *Philip Johnson: Life and Work*, 167.

217. Mock to Wright, July 1, 1946 (L097A09); Schulze, *Philip Johnson: Life and Work*, 173–74.
218. Johnson to Wright, n.d. (L091E04). The date is confirmed by Loeb in his Loeb to Wright, August 28, 1945 (L091A03).
219. Johnson to Wright, September 25, 1945 (M142C08).
220. Johnson to Hitchcock, n.d. (ca. 1945 to 1946), Hitchcock collection, Box 3, 1947 "I-K." AAA/SI.
221. Wright to Johnson, September 6, 1948 (M180E04).
222. Wright to Johnson, September 7, 1946 (J115A06).
223. Loeb to Wright, January 10, 1947 (L103A10); Loeb to Wright, February 6, 1947 (L103D01); Loeb to Wright, August 29, 1947 (L107B05); Wright to Ezra Stoller, June 20, 1949 (S171B03).
224. Kaufmann Jr. to Wright, n.d. (K071E07); Wright to Kaufmann Jr., December 28, 1946 (K072C04).
225. Telegram, Kaufmann Jr. to Wright, May 5, 1947 (K075C03); Loeb to Kaufmann Jr., May 22, 1947 (K075C06); Loeb to Wright, August 29, 1947 (L107B05). Kaufmann Jr. applied to the Mellon-funded Bollingen Foundation for financial support, but the request was denied. Bollingen Foundation to Kaufmann Jr., February 18, 1948 (K079C04).
226. Kaufmann Jr. informed Wright that he was investigating a smaller format. Kaufmann Jr. to Wright, November 4, 1947 (K078B08). Loeb to Wright, August 3, 1949 (L122E06) and August 24, 1949 (L123D02); memorandum, Loeb gift, Kaufmann Jr., August 29, 1949 (L123D03); Wright to Loeb, September 15, 1949 (L123D05); Johnson to Loeb, quoted in Loeb to Kaufmann Jr., September 1, 1949 (L123E09).
227. Wright to Loeb, September 1, 1947 (L107B08).
228. Johnson to Wright, August 4, 1948 (M179C07).
229. Wright to Johnson, August 6, 1948 (M179D10).
230. Johnson to Wright, August 28, 1948 (M180B07).
231. Johnson to Wright, March 16, 1949 (J127B05).
232. Ibid.
233. Unsigned (Philip Johnson), "Interim Report: House in the Museum Garden, 1949," May 12, 1948. REG, Exh. #405. The Museum of Modern Art Archives, New York. Peter Blake, "The House in the Museum Garden," *Museum of Modern Art Bulletin* 16, no. 1 (1949): unpaginated.
234. Wright to Johnson, March 7, 1949 (M186B08).
235. Johnson to Wright, March 16, 1949 (J127B05).
236. Wright's ellipses. Wright to Johnson, April 23, 1949 (M187E03).
237. Blake, "House in the Museum Garden," unpaginated.
238. Peter Reed, "MoMA's Exhibition Houses," *a+u Architecture and Urbanism*, special issue (October 2000): 128.
239. Nelson to Wright, October 2, 1945 (N042A05).
240. Nelson to Wright, March 12, 1946 (N043B01).
241. George Nelson, "Wright's Houses," *Fortune* 34 (August 1946): 5, 116–25.
242. *Fortune* 34 (June 1946 and May 1946): 5, 7.
243. Nelson to Wright, August 6, 1946 (F068C01).
244. William S. Saunders, *Modern Architecture Photographs by Ezra Stoller* (New York: Abrams, 1990); *Ezra Stoller: Photographer* (New Haven, CT: Yale University Press, 2012).
245. Ezra Stoller, "Photography and the Language of Architecture," *Perspecta* 8 (1963): 44. For a penetrating analysis of Stoller's photographic vision, see Neil Levine, introduction to *Frank Lloyd Wright's Taliesin West Photographs by Ezra Stoller* (New York: Princeton Architectural Books, 1999), 1–13.
246. Stoller, "Photography and the Language of Architecture," 43.
247. Daniel Naegele, "An Interview with Ezra Stoller," *History of Photography* 22, no. 2 (1998): 115.
248. Mrs. Harriet S. Rosenberg, MoMA, to Brook Alexander, *Fortune*, February 7, 1947. REG, Exh. #348. The Museum of Modern Art Archives, New York. There is no record that the tour took place.
249. "Museum exhibited Model and 4 original color renderings by Frank Lloyd Wright of his Design for a New Theatre for Hartford," press release, Museum of Modern Art, New York, n.d., #490401–21 (M197A10); "Paton Price Dies in Los Angeles," *Pittsburgh Post-Gazette*, May 1, 1982, 7.
250. Lewis Mumford, "Skyline," *New Yorker*, October 1947, 94–96, 99.
251. Liane Lefaivre and Alexander Tzonis, "International Style versus Regionalism," in *Architecture of Regionalism in the Age of Globalization: Peaks and Valleys in the Flat World* (London: Routledge, 2012), 120–23.
252. Frank Lloyd Wright, *Genius and the Mobocracy* (New York: Duell, Sloan and Pearce, 1949). Frank Lloyd Wright, "Sullivan against the World," *Architectural Review* 105 (June 1949): 295–98.
253. Philip Johnson, "The Frontiersman," *Architectural Review* 106 (August 1949): 105–10.
254. Schulze, *Philip Johnson: Life and Work*, 194.
255. Ibid., 198.
256. Telegram, Wright to Johnson, n.d. (ca. 1949) (J152A04).
257. Johnson to Wright, December 1, 1949 (J130A08).
258. Wright to Johnson, January 2, 1950 (J131A01).
259. Johnson to Wright, January 6, 1950 (J131A03).
260. Wright to Johnson, January 13, 1950 (J131A08).
261. Johnson to Wright, April 3, 1952 (M220B09). Wright agreed, subject to his client's approval. Wright to Johnson, May 1, 1952 (J139D03); Johnson to Wright, May 6, 1952 (J139D04).
262. Bruce Brooks Pfeiffer, ed., *Frank Lloyd Wright: The Guggenheim Correspondence* (Carbondale: Southern Illinois University Press, 1986), 110–12, 118–19 and 130–31, 160–61; *The Guggenheim: Frank Lloyd Wright and the Making of the Modern Museum* (New York: Guggenheim Museum, 2009), 167–88.
263. "3-Dimensional Color Photographs of Buildings by Frank Lloyd Wright on Exhibition," press release, Museum of Modern Art, New York, n.d., #520109–2. Press Release Archives, moma.org, accessed May 19, 2009.
264. Untitled, n.d., REG, Exh. #498. The Museum of Modern Art, New York.
265. "Frank Lloyd Wright Talks about Photography," *Photography*, 118.
266. Wright to Johnson, April 3, 1951 (J136D09).
267. Johnson to Wright, April 16, 1951 (M212A02).
268. Wright to Johnson, April 21, 1951 (M212B01). Johnson to Wright, April 3, 1952 (M220B09); Wright to Johnson, May 1, 1952 (J139D03); Johnson to Wright, May 6, 1952 (J139D04).
269. Johnson to Wright, November 21, 1952 (J141B07). Wright's letter, if there was one, cannot be located.
270. Wallace K. Harrison to Wright, January 8, 1953 (M227C03); Wright to Harrison, January 12, 1953 (M227C10). Wright's spelling is eccentric. Balthazar was the last king of Babylon, who saw the handwriting on the wall predicting his kingdom would fall the next day (as reported in the book of Daniel of the Hebrew Bible).
271. Wright to Hitchcock, February 18, 1953, Henry-Russell Hitchcock Collection, Box 6 1953 "W." AAA/SI.
272. Frank Lloyd Wright, *In the Cause of Architecture: The "International Style"* (February 1953), self-published, 6.
273. Ibid., 2.
274. Ibid., 5.
275. Elizabeth Gordon, "The Threat to the Next America," *House Beautiful*, April 1953, 127.
276. Ibid., 129.
277. Ibid., 130.
278. Telegram, Wright to Gordon, March 24, 1953 (G135C06). This unconventional signature could refer to Wright's early association with the magazine circa 1896 when he was one of the intellectual founders.
279. Mumford, "Two Chicago Fairs." Wright to Gordon, March 25, 1953 (G135C10), (H132C05), and (H132C03); Wright to Gordon March 27, 1953 (G135D02).
280. Taliesin Fellow, John de Koven Hill, joined the staff of *House Beautiful* as editor several weeks later. Hill was with the magazine until 1963. I am grateful to Indira Berndston for this information. Joe Barry to Wright, July 9, 1953 (H135A08).
281. Wright to Gordon, May 9, 1953 (H133D04).
282. Frank Lloyd Wright, "Frank Lloyd Wright Speaks Up," *House Beautiful*, July 1953, 88.
283. Ibid., 90.
284. Frank Lloyd Wright, "Excerpts from 'The International Style,'" *Architectural Record* 113 (June 1953): 12, 332.
285. Rene d'Harnoncourt, "Letter," *Architectural Record* 114 (September 1953): 12.
286. Rene d'Harnoncourt, press release, Museum of Modern Art, New York, June 19, 1953, #530618–50. Press Release Archives, moma.org, accessed June 5, 2005. The total number of exhibitions is stated as fourteen. My total includes circulating and group shows.
287. Wright and d'Harnoncourt had both been delegates to the Pan-American Congress of Architects in Mexico City in October 1952, where they were photographed together on more than one occasion.
288. Henry-Russell Hitchcock, introduction to *Built in USA: Post-war*

Architecture, ed. Henry-Russell Hitchcock and Arthur Drexler (New York: Museum of Modern Art, 1953), 14. This author's underlining.
289. Philip Johnson, preface to *Built in USA: Post-war Architecture*, 9.
290. Arthur Drexler, "Post-War Architecture," in *Built in USA: Post-war Architecture*, 26.
291. Wright to Rene d'Harnoncourt, July 9, 1953 (D093A04).
292. Schulze, *Philip Johnson: Life and Work*, 225.
293. Kaufmann Jr. included Wright in his exhibition, *Modern Rooms of the Last Fifty Years*, November 26, 1946–January 26, 1947, held at MoMA and circulated to fifty venues.
294. Goodyear was the major force behind *Trois siècles d'art aux États Unis* in 1938, and Goodwin organized *Brazil Builds: Architecture New and Old*, in 1943.
295. For a wider discussion of this subject, see Mardges Bacon, "Modernism and the Vernacular at the Museum of Modern Art, New York," in *Vernacular Modernism: Heimat, Globalization, and the Built Environment*, ed. Maiken Umbach and Bernd Hüppauf (Palo Alto, CA: Stanford University Press, 2005), 25–52.
296. Johnson, preface to *Built in USA: Post-war Architecture*, 9.
297. Frank Lloyd Wright, *Organic Architecture: Language of an Organic Architecture* (May 20, 1953), self-published, 1.
298. Wright stated that his article, "Organic Architecture Looks at Modern Architecture," *Architectural Record* 111 (May 1952): 148–54, was a response to Hitchcock's article of August 1951.
299. Henry-Russell Hitchcock, "The International Style, Twenty Years After," *Architectural Record* 110 (August 1951): 91.
300. Ibid., 93.
301. Ibid., 91.
302. Wright was represented in a museum collection in a minor way before his death. In 1947, Wright donated five chairs to the Modern: four oak side chairs, 1904, and one pine side chair, ca. 1925. See 202.1947.1, 1–2, 2 and 203.1947. moma.org/collection.
303. Johnson stated that he did not feel his buildings were complete until they were "Stollerized." Robert A. M. Stern, Thomas Mellins, and David Fishman, *New York 1960: Architecture and Urbanism between the Second World War and the Bicentennial* (New York: Monacelli Press, 1997), 1170.

CHAPTER 5. THE ITALIAN EXHIBITION AND *SIXTY YEARS OF LIVING ARCHITECTURE*, 1948–56

1. Norman Kogan, *A Political History of Postwar Italy* (New York: Frederick A. Praeger, 1966); Muriel Grindrod, *The Rebuilding of Italy* (London: Royal Institute of International Affairs, 1955).
2. Gilles A. Tiberghien, "Carlo L. Ragghianti: Between Aesthetics and Criticism; The Cohesion of Art, the Diversity of Artistic Languages," in *Carlo Ludovico Ragghianti and the Cinematic Nature of Vision* (Milan: Charta, 2000), 51; Antonio Caleca, "A Biographical Profile of Carlo Ludovico Ragghianti," *Carlo Ludovico Ragghianti and the Cinematic Nature*, 52–59.
3. Maristella Casciato, "Wright and Italy: The Promise of Organic Architecture," in *Europe and Beyond*, ed. Anthony Alofsin (Berkeley: University of California Press, 1999), n. 48, 238; Cesare de Seta, "Carlo L. Ragghianti's Early Efforts as Architecture Critic and 'Casabella' Collaborator," *Carlo Ludovico Ragghianti and the Cinematic Nature*, 129.
4. Caleca, "Biographical Profile," 60.
5. De Seta, "Carlo L. Ragghianti's Early Efforts as Architecture Critic," 137, and Edoardo Detti, in "Critical Entries," in *Carlo Ludovico Ragghianti and the Cinematic Nature*, 320.
6. Carlo Ludovico Ragghianti to Bruno Zevi, October 28, 1948, in Ferruccio Canali, "La promozione della Modernità: La stagione della grandi Mostre internationali di architettura" a Firenze, 1951. "Frank Lloyd Wright: Sixty Years of Living Architecture." "Carissimo Bruno . . . Carissimo Carlo." "Il carteggio tra Carlo Ludovico Ragghianti e Bruno Zevi (1948–1951)," *Bollettino della Società di Studi Fiorentini* 18–19 (Florence: Società di Studi Fiorentini, 2010), 164. I wish to thank Filippo Fici, who kindly called this article to my attention and made it available to me. Canali published extensive excerpts from the correspondence archive at the Fondazione Ragghianti. This correspondence was unavailable to me due to restrictions imposed by the Ragghianti family at the time I conducted research at the Fondazione in Lucca in 2012. Ragghianti ultimately held two more modern architecture exhibitions at the Palazzo Strozzi after Wright: Le Corbusier in 1963 and Alvar Aalto in 1965. Carlo Cresti, "Ragghianti and Architecture," in *Carlo Ludovico Ragghianti and the Cinematic Nature*, 115. For background on these exhibitions, see Lisa Carotti, *I Maestri dell'architettura moderna in Mostra a Palazzo Strozzi: Wright, Le Corbusier, e Aalto*, Università degli Studi di Firenze, 2014. For additional background on Ragghianti, see Augusto Rossari, "Ragghianti e gli architetti," *LUK* no. 16 (21), Fondazione Centro Studi sull-arte Licia e Carlo Ludovico Ragghianti (gennaio–dicembre 2010): 113–36; "Album Ragghianti," *LUK* no. 2/3 (7/8), Fondazione Centro Studi sull-arte Licia e Carlo Ludovico Ragghianti (January–December 2003): 85–86. I wish to thank Valentina Del Frate at the Fondazione Ragghianti, Lucca, Italy, for calling my attention to *Carlo Ludovico Ragghianti and the Cinematic Nature of Vision* and these issues of *LUK* and making them available to me. One commentator suggested that Ragghianti hoped to use the Wright exhibition to stimulate ideas for the rebuilding of Florence after destruction by the retreating Nazi army. Raffaele Monti wrote that Ragghianti's aim in exhibiting Wright immediately after the war was "an intervention by Wright in recreating the city center of Florence." Raffaele Monti, "Reminiscences of an Unrepeatable Experience," *Carlo Ludovico Ragghianti and the Cinematic Nature*, 73.
7. Ragghianti to Zevi, February 1, 1950, in Canali, "Carissimo Bruno," 168. See also Ragghianti to Zevi, October 28, 1948 and January 4, 1949, in Canali, "Carissimo Bruno," 165; Ragghianti to Alberto Tarchiani, August 9, 1949, in Canali "Carissimo Bruno," 165.
8. Casciato, "Wright and Italy," 236n35. For Zevi's biography, see Andrea Oppenheimer Dean, *Bruno Zevi on Modern Architecture* (New York: Rizzoli, 1983), 23–25, 207.
9. Casciato, "Wright and Italy," 237–38n48; Zevi to Masselink, December 30, 1945 (X011A01). While on a trip to the United States in 1945, Zevi met Gutheim, Mumford, and Stonorov.
10. For the Italian perspective, see Augusto Rossari, "Sixty Years of Living Architecture: La mostra di Frank Lloyd Wright a Firenze nel 1951," *LUK* no. 4–5 (9/10), Fondazione Centro Studi sull-arte Licia e Carlo Ludovico Ragghianti (January–December 2004): 89–94.
11. Ragghianti to Zevi, October 28, 1948 in Canali, "Carissimo Bruno," 165.
12. Memorandum, Gutheim to Reid, February 21, 1949, OS/AHC, Box 43 (January–March 1949); Ferguson to Gutheim, March 7, 1949, OS/AHC, Box 43 (January–March 1949).
13. Press release, Museum of Modern Art, New York, June 20, 1938. Press Release Archives, moma.org, accessed June 10, 2007.
14. Mock, *Built in USA, 1932–44*, 122–23; Mardges Bacon, *Le Corbusier in America: Travels in the Land of the Timid* (Cambridge, MA: MIT Press, 2001), 22, 165, 170; Robert A. M. Stern, *George Howe: Toward a Modern American Architecture* (New Haven, CT: Yale University Press, 1975), 195–97; David B. Brownlee, "Adventures of Unexplored Places, Defining a Philosophy, 1901–51," in *Louis I. Kahn: In the Realm of Architecture*, by David B. Brownlee and David de Long (New York: Rizzoli; Los Angeles: Museum of Contemporary Art, Los Angeles, 1991), 29–37; "Oscar Stonorov, Architect Killed," *New York Times*, May 11, 1970; Doug Hassebroek, "Philadelphia's Postwar Moment," *Perspecta* 30 (1999): 84–91; "Philadelphia Plans Again," *Architectural Forum* 87 (December 1947): 65–88.
15. Lois Brunner, "What Makes Arthur Kaufmann Click . . . and Tick," *Philadelphia Magazine* 38 (January 1951): 14, 29–30.
16. Ragghianti to Stonorov, January 12, 1951, OS/AHC, Box 44 (January 1951).
17. Ragghianti to Stonorov, March 1, 1951, Stonorov office translation (E059E06). Ragghianti was particularly annoyed because he was assured that the State Department was fully informed of the exhibition and had given it "its blessing," yet official participation was denied. Stonorov held the opinion that "the State Department is afraid of the criticisms of certain Middle Western congressmen who might not think that our foreign ministry has any business in advertising the art and culture of the United States. . . . I should say that Gimbel Bros.—and very rightly so—had to refuse to assume responsibility for the international character of this show. Theirs ended at the pier of New York where the State Department's should have begun." Stonorov to Lawrence M. C. Smith, August 20, 1951, OS/AHC, Box 44 (August 1951).
18. Memorandum, Gutheim to Reid, February 21, 1949; Ferguson to Gutheim, March 7, 1949; Gutheim to

Stonorov, March 15, 1949, OS/AHC, Box 43 (January–March 1949). George V. Allen, assistant secretary of state, laid out policy in a letter to Lewis M. Stevens of the Foreign Policy Association, Philadelphia (the person chosen to address the State Department directly): "The Department is ready to give ... its moral support. ... In practice we find that this is perhaps as it should be since in many, many cases there is a heightening in the value of the activity if it is sponsored and executed by private initiative." Lewis M. Stevens, Foreign Policy Association to George V. Allen, Assistant Secretary, State Department, March 24, 1949; George V. Allen, Assistant Secretary, State Department to Lewis M. Stevens, Foreign Policy Association, April 6, 1949, OS/AHC, Box 43 (April–June, 1949).

19. Gutheim to Helen Reid, February 21, 1949, OS/AHC, Box 43, (January–March 1949).

20. Ibid.

21. Serge Guilbaut, *How New York Stole the Idea of Modern Art: Abstract Expressionism, Freedom, and the Cold War*, trans. Arthur Goldhammer (Chicago: University of Chicago Press, 1983), 150.

22. Louis Menand, "Unpopular Front: American Art and the Cold War," *New Yorker*, October 17, 2005, 174–79.

23. Frances Stonor Saunders, *The Cultural Cold War: The CIA and the World of Arts and Letters* (New York: New Press, 1999), 114. See also Eva Cockcroft, "Abstract Expressionism: Weapon of the Cold War," *Artforum* 12, no. 10 (1974): 39–41.

24. Other key anti-Fascist figures involved in the Wright exhibition were Count Carlo Sforza, minister of foreign affairs, and Alberto Tarchiani, Italian ambassador, both of whom exiled in the United States during the war years. John P. Diggins, "The Italo-American Anti-Fascist Opposition," *Journal of American History* 54, no. 3 (1967): 589–90; Grindrod, *Rebuilding of Italy*, 17.

25. Bruce Brooks Pfeiffer reported a conversation between Kaufmann and Clare Booth Luce, ambassador to Italy, in her office in 1949, focused on a concern for "the rising tide of Communism in Italy since the end of World War I"; as a result, out of this discussion came the idea for the Wright exhibition. "60 Years of Living Architecture," *Letters to Architects*, selected and with commentary by Bruce Brooks Pfeiffer (Fresno: California State University, 1984), 174. Pfeiffer explained to this author that Kaufmann himself provided this information in conversation at Taliesin West in 1982. E-mail communication, Bruce Brooks Pfeiffer, July 28, 2006. There is no other evidence of this connection. Luce did serve in government: two terms in the House of Representatives (1943–47) and as ambassador to Italy (1953–56). Luce was not ambassador at the time the exhibition was conceived. Both Casciato, "Wright and Italy," 84, and Rossari, "Sixty Years of Living Architecture," 89, cite Pfeiffer in explaining that the original idea for the exhibition was American. It was Italian in origin and anti-Fascist rather than anti-Communist. The president of La Strozzina, who supported Ragghianti in conceiving the Wright exhibition, was the Communist mayor of Florence, Mario Fabiani, an anti-Fascist leader and a partisan.

26. "Translation of Mr. Ragghianti's letter to Mr. Kaufmann: Florence, June 16, 1949," OS/AHC, Box 43 (April–June 1949).

27. "Per lo sviluppo delle relazioni italo-americane," *Il Globo*, May 24, 1949, in Marjorie Ferguson to Stonorov, n.d., OS/AHC, Box 43 (April–June 1949).

28. "Memorandum of meeting with Frank Lloyd Wright—26 May 1949," OS/AHC, Box 43 (April–June 1949).

29. Kaufmann to Ragghianti, August 2, 1949, OS/AHC, Box 43, (July–September 1949); Ragghianti to Ferguson, August 9, 1949, in Canali, "Carrisimo Bruno," 166.

30. Ragghianti to Zevi, August 19, 1949, in Canali, "Carissimo Bruno," 166.

31. Ragghianti to Stonorov, September 4, 1950, OS/AHC, Box 43 (September 1950), Stonorov office translation. Ragghianti repeated to Zevi the need for a "program of events ... such as congresses, conferences, meetings and others coinciding with the arrival of Wright, an event in itself ... [which] would constitute a great opportunity for modern Italian architects." Ragghianti to Zevi, September 8, 1950, in Canali, "Carissimo Bruno," 169. Ragghianti repeated the idea to Zevi, November 24, 1950, in Canali, "Carissimo Bruno," 170.

32. Zevi to Ragghianti, November 28, 1950, in Canali, "Carissimo Bruno," 170. Ragghianti to Roberto Papini, May 17, 1951; Papini to Ragghianti, May 25, 1951, and Ragghianti to Papini, May 26, 1951 in Canali, "Carissimo Bruno," 174–75. Wright was contacted privately by the Faculty of Architecture, Università degli Studi di Firenze, after his arrival in Florence. Attilio Arcangeli, Head of Faculty of Architecture, University of Florence, to Wright, June 19, 1951, and Bruno Borghi, President, University of Florence, to Wright, June 19, 1951, OS/AHC, Box 44 (June 1951). Wright asked to meet the students at the exhibition at the Palazzo Strozzi. Borghi refused.

33. *Frank Lloyd Wright: Works and Projects, 1887–1949*, OS/AHC, Box 25 (Exhibition Articles).

34. Stonorov to Ferguson, June 9, 1949, OS/AHC, Box 43 (April–June 1949).

35. Diary, OS/AHC, Box 33 (diary entry).

36. Stonorov to Mr. and Mrs. Frank Lloyd Wright, June 13, 1949, OS/AHC, Box 43 (April–June 1949).

37. Kaufmann to George V. Allen, Assistant Secretary of State, August 8, 1949, OS/AHC, Box 43 (July–September 1949).

38. Stonorov to Ragghianti, January 27, 1951; Stonorov to Wright, March 21, 1951, OS/AHC, Box 44 (March 1951). Kaufmann spent almost $50,000 on the exhibition.

39. Memorandum, n.d., OS/AHC, Box 25 (Exhibition Articles).

40. Memorandum, Stonorov to Dave Arons, n.d. (after October 26, 1949), OS/AHC, Box 43 (July–September 1949).

41. "Departure," OS/AHC, Box 25 (Exhibition Articles).

42. "A Frank Lloyd Wright 'Autobiography,'" American Heritage Center, University of Wyoming, Laramie, Frederick Albert Gutheim Papers, Box 105, Folder 5. Label on file, probably by Gutheim: "Holograph note by Wright, outlining his architectural career, for Oskar Stonorov to illustrate how it might be presented in the Wright exhibition at the Palazzo Strozzi (1951). A mixture of publicity, self-justification and favorite ideas and projects."

43. For further elaboration of these ideas, see Frank Lloyd Wright, *An American Architecture*, ed. Edgar Kaufmann (New York: Horizon Press, 1955), 76–81.

44. Zevi to Ragghianti, October 3, 1949, in Canali, "Carissimo Bruno," 167.

45. Ibid., 167–68.

46. Ibid., 168.

47. Ragghianti to Zevi, December 20, 1950 in Canali, "Carissimo Bruno," 171.

48. Stonorov to Ragghianti, November 28, 1950, OS/AHC, Box 44 (November–December 1950).

49. Ibid. Stonorov, a former resident of Florence, was referring to the "Explosion of the Cart," a festival held on Easter Sunday. A team of white oxen hauls an altar filled with fireworks to the Duomo, where it explodes.

50. Loeb to Stonorov, December 21, 1950, OS/AHC, Box 44 (November–December 1950).

51. Ibid.

52. Ibid.

53. Loeb to Wright, December 27, 1950 (L171A01) and January 9, 1951 (L172B03). Loeb explained to Stonorov, "If I had been approached by you and the proposition had been made to me that Mr. Wright wanted all his work photographed and wanted the photographs to remain without copies being made in the same buildings with the originals, I would have said no. It seems to me that the cultural purpose which I'm trying to serve fundamentally is that Mr. Wright's negatives are kept separate from his originals so that no fire or theft is possible. Aside from that, the 900 drawings represent Mr. Wright's work and are entirely his own and under his authority." Loeb to Stonorov, January 9, 1951, OS/AHC, Box 44 (January 1951).

54. Telegram, Wright to Loeb, December 30, 1950 (E057B02).

55. Telegram, Wright to Stonorov, December 30, 1950, OS/AHC, Box 44 (November–December 1950).

56. Loeb to Wright, January 4, 1951, OS/AHC, Box 44 (January 1951).

57. Wright to Kaufmann, January 8, 1951 (E058A07).

58. Telegram, Wright to Stonorov, January 4, 1950 (E058A06).

59. Telegram, Wright to Kaufmann, January 12, 1951 (E058B03).

60. Kaufmann to Stonorov, January 12, 1951, OS AHC, Box 44 (January 1951).

61. "Dinner in honor of Frank Lloyd Wright—Thursday, January 25, 1951—6:00 P.M. Frank Lloyd Wright Exhibition, Gimbel Brothers Banquet Hall, Philadelphia. Remarks by Arthur C. Kaufmann, Executive Head, Gimbel Brothers, Philadelphia 5, Pa. Wright Foundation Archives 1047.046.

62. Stonorov to Ragghianti, February 14, 1951, OS/AHC, Box 44 (February 1951).

63. Stonorov to Wright, February 22, 1951, OS/AHC, Box 44 (February 1951).

64. Wright to Stonorov, February 22, 1951, OS/AHC, Box 44 (February 1951).
65. Telegram, Wright to Kaufmann, February 22, 1951, OS/AHC, Box 44 (February 1951).
66. Kaufmann to Wright, February 23, 1951, OS/AHC, Box 44 (February 1951).
67. Kaufmann to Wright, February 23, 1951, OS/AHC, Box 44 (February 1951).
68. Stonorov raised $1,550 to be paid to the Frank Lloyd Wright Foundation. The foundation was to pay the insurance bill. The contributors were Otto Mallory (a former Wright client), $100; Donald D. Dodge, $500; American Federation of the Arts, $700; Alden B. Dow, $250. Stonorov to Wright, February 26, 1951, OS/AHC, Box 44 (February 1951); Stonorov to Wright, April 27, 1951 (E062A04). From this date forward as the exhibition toured Europe, Stonorov continued to handle all the financial transactions, charging each of the five venues for a share of the transportation costs and insurance. This effort made the European tour a reality.
69. Stonorov to Ragghianti, March 7, 1951, OS/AHC, Box 44 (March 1951).
70. A. Mazzoli to Kaufmann, March 13, 1951, OS/AHC, Box 44 (March 1951); telegram, Stonorov to Wright, April 13, 1951, OS/AHC, Box 44 (April 1951). Arrangements followed quickly after the Italian principals were informed that the French organizers were pressing to bypass Florence to be the first to hold the exhibition in Europe. Ragghianti to Fabiani, April 11, 1951, in Ferruccio Canali, "La Promozione della Modernità: La Stagione delle Grandi Mostre Internationali di Architettura" a Firenze, 1951: "Frank Lloyd Wright: Sixty Years of Living Architecture" . . . e il Contributo di Oskar Stonorov, di Carlo Ludovico Ragghianti e di Edoardo Detti," *Bollentino della Società di Studi Fiorentini* 20–21 (Florence: Società di Studi Fiorentini, 2011–12), 68.
71. Stonorov to Wright, April 27, 1951, OS/AHC, Box 44 (April 1951); Kaufmann in Paris to Stonorov in Florence, May 12, 1951, OS/AHC, Box 44 (May 1951).
72. It was planned that the Italian president, Luigi Einaudi, would formally open the exhibition. The election made this impossible, so the opening was postponed. Ragghianti to Zevi, May 18, 1951, in Canali, "Carissimo Bruno," 176; telegram, Stonorov to Wright, n.d. (ca. May 19, 1951), OS/AHC, Box 44 (May 1951); Stonorov to Wright, May 29, 1951 (E062C06); Mario Fabiani to Stonorov, May 23, 1951, OS/AHC, Box 44 (May 1951).
73. Addendum, *Mostra di Frank Lloyd Wright: Catalogo itinerario, Firenze, Palazzo Strozzi, 24 giugno–settembre 1951* (Florence: Palazzo, 1951).
74. Stonorov was in Florence by May 10 and departed for Paris on May 28. Stonorov to Wright, May 29, 1951 (E062C06).
75. Wright and his wife arrived Rome on June 16. Wright to Robert Furneaux Jordan, June 6, 1951 (J137A09). Wright arrived in Florence June 18 due to the second postponement of the exhibition. Ragghianti to Wright, June 16, 1951 (E062E08); cable, Stonorov to Ragghianti, June 13, 1951 in Canali, "Il Contributo di Oskar Stonorov," 70.
76. Wright to Zevi, n.d. (after February 25, 1951) (E059E08); Wright to Zevi, March 7, 1951 (E060A07); Wright to Stonorov, March 26, 1951 (E060D02–03).
77. For a rich account of the personal details of Wright's days in Italy, see Bruno Zevi, "Wright and Italy: A Recollection," in *Frank Lloyd Wright: Europe and Beyond*, ed. Anthony Alofsin (Berkeley: University of California Press, 1999), 70–71.
78. Stonorov to Wright, March 21, 1951, OS/AHC, Box 44 (March 1951).
79. Stonorov to Kaufmann, July 15, 1951, OS/AHC, Box 44 (July 1951).
80. Zevi, "Wright and Italy: A Recollection," 72.
81. Wright was also awarded the Star of Solidarity by the city of Venice on the same day. Casciato, "Wright in Italy," 85n49.
82. Stonorov to Lawrence M. C. Smith, American Federation of the Arts, August 20, 1951, OS/AHC, Box 44 (August 1951).
83. Wright to Kaufmann, July 15, 1951, OS/AHC, Box 44 (July 1951).
84. This publication captured the final intentions of the Italians as it bears the date of the June 24 opening, rather than the original date in May. Wright's statement printed within is dated June 10; thus, this document can be dated between June 10 and 24. Stonorov to Ragghianti, February 14, 1951, OS/AHC, Box 44 (February 1951).
85. Ragghianti to Zevi, June 2 1951, in Canali, "Carissimo Bruno," 177.
86. *Catalogo itinerario*, unpaginated.
87. Masselink to Stonorov, November 29, 1950 (E058E01).
88. On December 27, 1950, Moffett wrote to Wright that he was very far ahead in fabrication, but "the completion of the model in time for Philadelphia is impossible." He was down with influenza, and other family members were also ill. Max Moffett to Wright, December 27, 1950 (M208C01). Moffett again promised the model for May 1. Moffett to Wright, March 23, 1951 (M211C07).
89. "I also trust that Jack will have made a drawing for you of the living room and adjoining bedroom that we can use in a demountable way in the exhibition." Stonorov to Wright, August 24, 1950 (E055D02).
90. Oscar Stonorov, "Notes on the Frank Lloyd Wright Exhibitions," Wright Foundation Archives, 1047.050.
91. It was not until after the Philadelphia opening that Stonorov informed Ragghianti of the details of the exhibition. In this letter, he also listed what remained to be done in Florence: translation of captions and literary texts, lighting, flowers, and seating for the slide projection. He further mentioned that his plan was a suggestion and he volunteered that either Detti or Zevi might have other ideas. Stonorov to Ragghianti, February 14, 1951, OS/AHC, Box 44 (February 1951).
92. The Wordsworth quote is from *The Excursion*, Book Fourth, lines 332–50. Wright Foundation Archives 1047.054. This information was communicated to me by Margo Stipe, Frank Lloyd Wright Archives, February 2009.
93. Stonorov to Boston Insurance Company, December 17, 1952, OS/AHC, Box 45 (August–December 1952).
94. Stonorov to Ragghianti, February 14, 1951, OS/AHC, Box 44 (February 1951); *Catalogo itinerario*, unpaginated.
95. Stonorov to Gutheim, May 10, 1949, OS/AHC, Box 43 (April–June 1949).
96. Zevi to Stonorov, September 17, 1950, and January 10, 1951, OS/AHC, Box 44 (September 1950 and January 1951).
97. Zevi to Ragghianti, December 16, 1950, in Canali, "Carissimo Bruno," 170.
98. Ragghianti to Zevi, December 20, 1950, in Canali, "Carissimo Bruno," 171.
99. Werner M. Moser, *Frank Lloyd Wright: Sechzig Jahre lebendige Architektur* (Winterthur: Verlag Buchdruckerei Winterthur A.-G., 1952). It is highly likely that Wright suggested the title to Moser during the time they spent together in Italy and on a drive by automobile to Zurich in June 1951; however, there is no information in the correspondence to prove this.
100. "Frank Lloyd Wright," *Metron* 41–42 (May–August, 1951): 17–87; Carlo Ludovico Ragghianti, "Letture di Wright," *Edilizia Moderna*, no. 47, December 1951, 17–28; "Letture di Wright, I e II" (Readings of Wright 1 and 2) *Critica d'Arte* 1 (January 1954): 67–82, and 4 (July 1954): 355–83. Wright wrote Zevi that after reading the translated article (*Edilizia Moderna*), he came to the conclusion that Ragghianti "doesn't seem to know very well what Organic Architecture means." Wright to Zevi, March 18, 1953 (X024D06 and X023B05).
101. An English translation in a slightly shortened version was published in Frank Lloyd Wright, *Drawings for a Living Architecture* (New York: Published for the Bear Run Foundation Inc. and the Edgar J. Kaufmann Charitable Foundation by Horizon Press, 1959), 10–19. The original manuscript, "Man, Matter, and Space," was dedicated: "To the Master, in memory of the days in Venice, days which were heroic ones for us who knew the joy of living them with him" (E064A01–10, B01–10, C01–05).
102. Wright to Samonà, March 20, 1952 (S215B06); Wright to Gordon, March 25, 1953 (G135C10).
103. Samonà, in Wright, *Drawings for Living Architecture*, 15–16.
104. *Catalogo itinerario*, unpaginated.
105. The proposal to print 2,000 copies for Florence came at the end of the process, but Wright designed a special wrapper for Europe with translations in four languages: Italian, French, German, and Russian. Stonorov to Ragghianti, December 12, 1950, OS/AHC, Box 44 (November–December 1950).
106. (1) Wright self-published an English language version, *The Sovereignty of the Individual: In the Cause of Architecture*, and sent 1,250 copies to Italy. Wright to Zevi, May 6, 1951 (E062B07). (2) A variant edition of the above appeared in Italy in June with the following additions: a legend added to the cover, "Frank Lloyd Wright / allo / Studio Italiano di Storia dell'Arte / in Firenze / Giugno 1951" and an addenda titled "To Young Italy" dated Florence May 1951 tipped in as the last page. (3) Lastly, Wright instructed Zevi to translate the essay into Italian. Wright to Zevi, March 7, 1951 (E060A07). The Italian text was included as part of the contents of the special issue *Metron*

41–42, which appeared in July 1951. (4) Zevi issued 300 copies of an offprint of this version accompanied by Wright's salute, "To Young Italy," and Zevi's response, "To Frank Lloyd Wright."
107. Stonorov to Wright, September 20, 1951, OS/AHC, Box 44 (September 1951).
108. Zevi to Stonorov, September 14, 1951, OS/AHC, Box 44 (September 1951).
109. Wright to Kaufmann Jr., September 20, 1950 (K091B05); Kaufmann Jr. to Masselink, November 16, 1951 (K100B01); Masselink to Kaufmann Jr., November 20, 1951 (K100B06). Stonorov wrote Zevi on August 15, 1951, in reference to Kaufmann Jr.'s project: "I ran into Edgar Kaufmann at the airport in Pittsburgh 3 weeks ago and to my surprise saw the old master there. Edgar, Jr., made a face like the proverbial cat that swallowed the canary. (I asked him how the book went: 'very well' was his answer.) Should the old boy have put one over on us. Too bad for him. It is unfortunate that very frequently [Wright] does not see what really is good for him." Stonorov to Zevi, August 15, 1951, OS/AHC, Box 44 (August 1951).
110. Wright to Zevi, January 8, 1952 (X020A05); Zevi to Wright, March 5, 1952 (X020C08). The first Italian translation of *An Autobiography* was published as *F. L. Wright, Io e l'architettura*, trans. Bruno Oddera, 3 vols. (Milan: Arnoldo Mondadori, 1955).
111. Stonorov to Zevi, April 24, 1952, OS/AHC, Box 45 (April 1952). This idea could be the proposal discussed in Kaufmann Jr. to Wright, February 19, 1952 (K102B07); Wright to Kaufmann Jr., February 23, 1952 (K102B10). Additional correspondence refers to Kaufmann Jr.'s involvement in a book "setting forth the underlying concepts of Organic Architecture as practiced by Frank Lloyd Wright" that was terminated in 1953. Kaufmann Sr. to Masselink, June 23, 1953 (K108C07); Memorandum of Termination, 1953 (K108B01). Nevertheless, Kaufmann Jr. edited an anthology of writings by Wright from 1894 to 1954: Frank Lloyd Wright, *An American Architecture* (New York: Horizon Press, 1955).
112. Wright to Stonorov, March 31, 1956 (S253D10).
113. Giancarlo De Carlo, "Wright e l'Europa," *Sele Arte* 1 (September–October, 1952): 17–24.
114. Ibid., 24.
115. Giusta Nicco Fasola, "Wright a Firenze," *Panorami della Città Nuova* 5 (October 1951): 11–20. Giovanni Michelucci, "Wright: Un colloquio mancato," *Letteratura e Arti Contemporanee* 11 (September–October 1951): 7–19. I am grateful to Filippo Fici for calling these articles to my attention and making them available to me.
116. Philippe Duboy, "Edoardo Detti and Carlo L. Ragghianti: Rigorous Urbanism," *Carlo Ludovico Ragghianti and the Cinematic Nature*, 143.
117. Ermanno Migliorini, "Città di Wright," *Panorami della Città Nuova* 5 (October 1951): unpaginated, reprinted in *La nuova città*, a cura di Renato Risatti (Pistoia: Libreria Editrice Tellini, 1975), 590–92. I am grateful to Filippo Fici for calling my attention to these articles and making them available to me.
118. *Metron* 41–42 (May–August 1951): 20.
119. Piero Bottoni, "Alla direzione della rivista *Metron*, Roma," *Metron* 43 (September–December 1951): 6.
120. "La Polemica su Wright," *Metron* 43 (September–December 1951): 8, 10; Dean, *Zevi*, 23.
121. Ragghianti to Stonorov, August 29, 1951, office translation, OS/AHC, Box 44 (August 1951).
122. Ibid.
123. Stonorov to Smith, July 1, 1952, OS/AHC, Box 45 (July 1952).
124. Stonorov to Ragghianti, February 11, 1952, OS/AHC, Box 44 (February 1952). See Carlo Ludovico Ragghianti, "Letture di Wright," *Edilizia Moderna*, December 1951, 17–28; "Letture di Wright, I e II" (Readings of Wright 1 and 2), *Critica d'Arte*, January 1954, 67–82, and July 1954, 355–83.
125. Stonorov to Wright, February 28, 1952, OS/AHC, Box 45 (February 1952). There was no book published, but a dummy, *Truth aganist the World*, in the Edoardo Detti papers in the Archivio di Stato di Firenze, may be the aborted publication. Francesca Tondello, *L'architettura di Wright in mostra a Firenze: Le complesse vicende di un'esposizione. I progetti di Ragghianti, Zevi e Stonorov, 1948–1951*, Università degli Studi di Trieste, 2015, 88. I am grateful to Neil Levine, who brought this reference to my attention and who made a copy available to me.
126. Wright to Ragghianti, March 6, 1952 (X020C10).
127. Besinger, *Working with Mr. Wright*, 206–7.
128. Wright to Carlos Lazo, August 30, 1952 (E069E07); Lazo to Wright, September 10, 1952 (E070A08); Wright to Lazo, September 24, 1952 (E070B07).
129. Werner M. Moser, *Frank Lloyd Wright: Sechwig Jahre lebendige Architektur; Sixty Years of Living Architecture* (Winterthur: Verlag Buchdruckerei Winterthur A.-G.; Munich: Verlag Hermann Rinn, 1952). A softcover edition was issued by the German publisher only.
130. *Frank Lloyd Wright: 60 Jahre lebendige Architektur* (Zürich: Kunsthaus, 1952); *Exposition de L'oeuvre de Frank Lloyd Wright* (Paris: École Nationale Supérieure des Beaux-Arts, April 1952); *Frank Lloyd Wright: 60 Jahre Architektur* (Munich: Haus Der Kunst, 1952); *Frank Lloyd Wright: Rotterdam Ahoy'-gebouw* (Rotterdam: Academie van Beeldende Kunsten en Technische Wetenschappen, 1952). The following pamphlet, printed and available in Paris, also appeared in 1952: Frank Lloyd Wright, *L'Architecture Organique Regarde l'Architecture Moderne* (Organic Architecture Looks at Modern Architecture). The essay appeared in *Architectural Record* 111 (May 1952): 148–54.
131. "Frank Lloyd Wright," *Architecture Française* 13, nos. 123–24 (1952): 3–72, cover. Text by Wright, Noviant, and Jean Morey.
132. The breakdown was as follows: 25,000 visitors in Florence for a cost of $9,000; 23,000 in Zürich for a cost of $8,000; 35,000 in Paris for a cost of $11,000; 20,000 in Munich for a cost of $7,000; 23,000 in Rotterdam for a cost of $9,000. Stonorov to Smith, July 1, 1952, OS/AHC, Box 45 (July 1952).
133. Wright to Stonorov, June 13, 1952 (S217E05); Wright to Stonorov, December 17, 1952, OS/AHC, Box 45 (August–December 1952).
134. Wright to Gordon, May 5, 1953 (H133B10).
135. Wright to Francis H. Taylor, May 14, 1953; Taylor to Masselink, May 14, 1953; Masselink to Taylor, May 20, 1953; Wright to Taylor, June 4, 1953; Taylor to Wright, June 5, 1953. The Metropolitan Museum of Art Archives, New York. Taylor to Wright, May 27, 1953 (M230A07).
136. Wright to Gordon, May 5, 1953 (H133B10); Wright to James Johnson Sweeney, May 5, 1953 (G136D10); Wright to Stonorov, May 5, 1953 (S229C01); Untitled, Board of Trustees, Guggenheim Foundation, n.d., three pages (G140C03).
137. "Wright Makes New York!" *Architectural Record* 114 (October 1953): 20.
138. Aline B. Louchheim, "Wright Planning Edifice for His Art," *New York Times*, September 3, 1953, 23.
139. "Nautilus's Prune," *New Yorker*, July 12, 1952, 20.
140. "House of Wright Is Previewed Here," *New York Times*, October 21, 1953, 35; "Throngs Inspect Wright's Exhibit," *New York Times*, October 23, 1953, 34; Frank Lloyd Wright, *The Usonian House, A Souvenir of the Exhibition: 60 Years of Living Architecture, the Work of Frank Lloyd Wright* (New York: Solomon R. Guggenheim Museum, 1953); Besinger, *Working with Mr. Wright*, 253.
141. Jane King Hession and Debra Pickrel, *Frank Lloyd Wright in New York: The Plaza Years, 1954–1959* (Salt Lake City: Gibbs Smith, 2007), 85–88; "Television Programs This Week," *New York Times*, October 25, 1953, X12.
142. "Mr. Wright's Architecture," *New York Times*, September 5, 1953, 14.
143. Frank Lloyd Wright, *Sixty Years of Living Architecture* (New York: Solomon R. Guggenheim Museum, 1953); Wright, *Usonian House, A Souvenir.*
144. Lewis Mumford, *Sketches from Life: The Autobiography of Lewis Mumford, The Early Years* (New York: Dial Press, 1982), 437.
145. Lewis Mumford, "Sky Line: A Phoenix Too Infrequent," *New Yorker*, November 28, 1953, 85, and December 12, 1953, 102.
146. Mumford, "Sky Line: A Phoenix," (November), 80, 81.
147. Mumford, "Sky Line: A Phoenix," (December), 114.
148. Mumford to Wright, November 23, 1953 in *Wright + Mumford*, 240.
149. Wright to Mumford, n.d., in *Wright + Mumford*, 242.
150. Clinton N. Hunt, Solomon R. Guggenheim Museum, to Director of Internal Revenue Service, December 4, 1953 (G141B01).
151. Untitled press release, Solomon R. Guggenheim Foundation, October 20, 1953. guggenheim.org/library-archives.
152. "Expenditures by the Frank Lloyd Wright Foundation in connection with the Exhibition of the work of Frank Lloyd Wright: 'Sixty Years of Living

Architecture' at the Solomon R. Guggenheim Museum, New York City. October 22, 1953 to December 14th, 1953." Wright Foundation Archives 1047.052.

153. Quoted in Harry Guggenheim to Wright, November 19, 1953 (G140C01).

154. Ibid.

155. John Geiger to Wright, February 2, 1954 (E080A04); Geiger to Wright, February 9, 1954 (E080A08).

156. Wright to Guggenheim Trustees, February 15, 1954 (E080B04).

157. Hession and Pickrel, *Wright in New York*, 22.

158. Burton Cummings to Smith, July 8, 1952, OS/AHC, Box 45 (July 1952); Stonorov to Wright, August 19, 1952 (S345A01); Stonorov to Smith, October 8, 1952, OS/AHC, Box 45 (August–December 1952).

159. Jose M. Zaragoza to Wright, October 15, 1952 (E070C04–05).

160. Wright to Shigeru Ito, April 22, 1953 (E074C05); Kaufmann Jr., to Wright, April 28, 1953 (K107E10); Wright to Kei Ishii, Architectural Association of Japan, June 29, 1953 (E075B04); Wright to Zaragoza, Philippine Institute of Architects, July 22, 1953 (E075D04); J. B. Fernandes, Indian Institute of Architects, to Wright, July 27, 1953 (E075E05); Mansinhji Rana to Wright, July 27, 1953 (R083C04); Wright to Shri L. G. Selvam, International Housing Exhibition, August 8, 1953 (E076B02); Zaragoza to Wright, August 21, 1953 (E076C05); Wright to Selvam, September 23, 1953 (E076E09).

On July 23, 1953, Shri L. G. Selvam, director, International Housing Exhibition, Ministry of Works, Housing and Supply, Government of India, invited the exhibition to New Delhi as part of a larger housing exhibition. From that time on, Selvam became Wright's contact in India, although he received periodic inquiries from his former apprentice, Mansinhji Rana. Selvam to Wright, July 23, 1953 (E075D06); Wright to Zaragoza, July 22, 1953 (E075D04); Ishii to Masselink, August 10, 1953 (B076B09); Zaragoza to Wright, August 21, 1953 (E076C05).

161. Wright to Dean Acheson, September 30, 1952 (A134E06); Wright to Jessica Smith, *New World Review*, October 4, 1952 (N068C04).

162. Wright to Kaufmann Sr., August 2, 1954 (K114A05–07).

163. Kenneth Ross to Wright, November 23, 1953 (E077E01).

164. John Geiger, "My Last Summer at the Fellowship and the Los Angeles 60 Years of Living Architecture Pavilion," http://jgonwright.net/ep02Fellowship.html#top. Retrieved January 9, 2015.

165. Frank Lloyd Wright, *Sixty Years of Living Architecture* (Los Angeles: Municipal Art Patrons and the Art Commission of Los Angeles, 1954).

166. Frank Lloyd Wright, *Sixty Years of Living Architecture, Series Nine, Chicago: Early Chicago Buildings: Later Cantilever Structures Including Mile-High Illinois* (Chicago: n.p., 1956).

CHAPTER 6. CODA: 1957–59

1. Sweeney, *Frank Lloyd Wright: An Annotated Bibliography*, xxxix.

2. Hession and Pickrel, *Wright in New York*, 8.

3. Stern, in Philip Johnson, *Writings*, commentary by Robert A. M. Stern, 192–98.

4. Wright did not let the negative remarks pass without comment. He wrote a short note to Johnson and a three-page text, "Frank Lloyd Wright on Slavery," both of which may never have been sent. Wright to Johnson, n.d. (J152A07); "Frank Lloyd Wright on Slavery," n.d. (J152A08).

5. Stern, in Philip Johnson, *Writings*, commentary by Robert A. M. Stern, 151.

6. Henry-Russell Hitchcock, "Architecture and the Architect," *New York Times Book Review*, November 17, 1957, 7, part 1.

7. Wright to Hitchcock, November 19, 1957, HRH, AAA/SI, Box 8 (1957).

8. Wright to Hitchcock, February 28, 1958, HRH, AAA/SI, Box 9 (1958, W–Z).

9. Hitchcock to Wright, March 2, 1958 (H183B05).

10. Wright to Hitchcock, March 8, 1958, HRH, AAA/SI, Box 9 (1958, W-Z).

11. Drexler to Wright, March 24, 1958 (D115C04).

12. Wright to Drexler, April 2, 1958 (D115C06).

13. Masselink to Evelyn Busk, May 20, 1958 (M272B01).

14. Feddersen to Masselink, November 7, 1957 (M267A09).

15. Masselink to Feddersen, January 13, 1958 (M270C05).

16. Masselink to Mrs. Robert Busk, May 20, 1958 (M272B01).

17. Bell to Masselink, June 23, 1958 (M272E01).

18. Bell to Masselink, July 29, 1958 (M273B07).

19. "Art: The 20(th) Century Form Givers," *Time*, July 2, 1956, 51. The cover story was devoted to Eero Saarinen: "The Maturing Modern," 50–58.

20. "The Form Givers at Mid-Century," n.d., 2 pages, AFA/AAA/SI.

21. Memorandum, Frank Shea to Virginia Field, October 28, 1958, AFA/AAA/SI.

22. Meredith L. Clausen, *Pietro Belluschi: Modern American Architect* (Cambridge, MA: MIT Press, 1994), 22.

23. Clausen, *Pietro Belluschi*, 43.

24. Belluschi to Wright, July 3, 1931 (B011A06).

25. Wright to Belluschi, July 6, 1931 (B011B07).

26. Clausen, *Pietro Belluschi*, 190–91.

27. "The Form Givers—Confidential memo from Cranston Jones to James Linen and Harris K. Prior," June 28, 1958; Jones to Prior, July 2, 1958, AFA/AAA/SI.

28. "Form Givers—Confidential memo," AFA/AAA/SI.

29. Bell to Masselink, July 29, 1958 (M273B06).

30. Jones to Masselink, August 1, 1959 (J156C10); Memorandum, V. (Virginia) F. (Field) to Putney Westerfield, Roy Moyer, Anne Kobin, May 1, 1959, AFA/AAA/SI.

31. Masselink to Jones, December 9, 1958 (T087A09).

32. Expenses for Midland exhibition, n.d. (ca. January 1959) (M275D08).

33. Jones to Masselink, November 10, 1958, AFA/AAA/SI.

34. Memorandum, Jones to Prior and Frank Shea, November 14, 1958, AFA/AAA/SI, Box 37 (Exh. Files 59–15).

35. Telegram, Jones to Wright, n.d. (November 23, 1958, dated due to internal evidence), AFA/AAA/SI, Box 37 (Exh. Files 59–15).

36. Feddersen to Masselink, December 12, 1958 (M276D08).

37. "The major portion of this exhibition will proceed to the Corcoran Gallery in Washington D.C. under the sponsorship of Time Magazine, and then to the Metropolitan Museum of Art in New York City." Courtesy of Randolph Henning and Phil Feddersen.

38. Memorandum, Jones to Virginia Field and György Kepes, January 28, 1959, AFA/AAA/SI, Box 37 (Exh. Files 59–15).

39. Bell to Masselink, February 2, 1959 (M279B05).

40. Wright to Jones, February 4, 1959 (T089B01).

41. Masselink to Bell, February 20, 1959 (M279E08); Memorandum, Jones to Wright, February 15, 1959 (T089B08).

42. Wright to Jones, February 19, 1959 (T089D06).

43. Jones to Wright, March 3, 1959 (T090A04). Jones to Joseph V. Noble, March 17, 1959, Metropolitan Museum of Art Archives, New York. Jones wrote Wright on February 23; Wright responded with a note that may never have been sent offering photo blowups of Midway Gardens, Fallingwater, and Baghdad Post-Telegraph. Wright to Jones, n.d. (after February 23, 1959) (T090A02).

44. Jones to Masselink, April 22, 1959 (T090B01); memorandum, Jones to Masselink, *Frank Lloyd Wright section, Corcoran Gallery, April 23*, n.d. (T090B04).

45. Sweeney, *Frank Lloyd Wright: An Annotated Bibliography*, 155–64.

46. "Art: The New Architecture," *Time*, April 27, 1959, 21–22.

CHAPTER 7. CONCLUSION

1. Sullivan and Wright broke relations after Wright's departure from Adler and Sullivan in 1893, but Wright could not have been ignorant of Sullivan's lectures and publications in the late 1890s. Narciso G. Menocal, *Architecture as Nature: The Transcendentalist Idea of Louis Sullivan* (Madison: University of Wisconsin Press, 1981), 78–88.

2. Sullivan, "The Modern Phase of Architecture," in Twombley, *Louis Sullivan: The Public Papers*, 124. Twombley noted that Sullivan first delivered this lecture to the Chicago Architectural Club in May 1899. H. Webster Tomlinson subsequently read it in June at the convention of the Architectural League of America in Cleveland. Wright was in the audience.

3. Frank Lloyd Wright, *The Japanese Print: An Interpretation* (Chicago: Ralph Seymour Co., Fine Arts Building, 1912), 5.

4. There were confirmed instances of commissions related to exhibitions. In 1931 during the tour to Oregon, Wright met George Putnam, who commissioned him to design the unbuilt Capitol Journal Building in Salem, Oregon. After attending the 1931 Amsterdam exhibition, Mourad Hamil [*sic*] of the Egyptian legation in The Hague commissioned Beach Cabins (Wright Foundation Archives file number 2711), for a site at Ras el Bar, Damietta, Egypt.

In 1932, Wright's design of House on the Mesa was an attempt to secure George and Jean Cranmer as clients. During the activities surrounding the 1951 Florence exhibition, Wright met Angelo Masieri, a young architect associated with Carlo Scarpa. When Masieri was killed in an automobile accident in 1952, Wright was asked by his family to remodel an existing house on a canal in Venice as a memorial. It was never built.

5. Wright, *A Testament*, 33. For a historical analysis of the term, see Dimitri Tselos, "The Chicago Fair and the Myth of the 'Lost Cause,'" *Journal of the Society of Architectural Historians* 26, no. 4 (1967): 259–68.

6. Wright succeeded in using color in the offprint (planned as the catalog for Philadelphia and Florence) of the January 1951 *Architectural Forum* titled "A Four-Color Portfolio of the Recent Work of the Dean of Contemporary Architects, with His Own Commentary on Each Building." He also was successful in printing translations of the text in five languages (English, Italian, German, French, and Russian) in five colors, an effect he had proposed to Wijdeveld in 1931, but never realized.

7. For illustrations of the use of easels at Taliesin, see Julia Meech, *Frank Lloyd Wright and the Art of Japan: The Architect's Other Passion* (New York: Harry N. Abrams, 2001), 12–13, 24–25, 228–31. Wright also collected antique six-panel Japanese painted screens, which were created to be viewed folded in a zigzag configuration. Paradoxically, Wright, instead, hung them flat against the wall in the manner of conventional Western painting on canvas. See Meech, *Frank Lloyd Wright and the Art of Japan*, 155, 191, 231.

8. "First View of the Guggenheim," *Art News* 58 (November 1959): 46.

9. It could be argued that the double issue of the 1951 *Metron* produced by Zevi with the essay by Samonà is a second example, but technically it was not an exhibition catalog.

10. "Sarah Newmeyer," *Modern Women: A Partial History*, www.moma.org/explore/publications/modern women/history, accessed July 17, 2015.

11. "For Immediate Release: Greatest Living Architect Comes to Museum of Modern Art." Press release, Museum of Modern Art, New York, November 11, 1940, #401108-67. MoMA Press Release Archives, moma.org, accessed August 2, 2008. The last sentence of the four-page document stated: "the exhibition will do honor to a great and living prophet in his own time and country."

12. Barry Bergdoll, Leah Dickerman, Benjamin Buchlolh, and Brigit Doherty, *Bauhaus, 1919–33* (New York: Museum of Modern Art, 2009), 49; Walter Gropius, *Internationale Architektur*, 2nd ed. (Munich: Albert Langen, 1927).

13. *Internationale Architektur* (Stuttgart: Verlag J. Hoffmann, 1927); Ludwig Hilberseimer, *Internationale neue Baukunst* (Stuttgart: Verlag J. Hoffmann, 1928).

14. In 1941, the Frederick Robie House was threatened with imminent demolition until Wright successfully led a campaign to save it because it was "one of the cornerstones of modern architecture." In agreement with him were Mies, and his German colleagues at Illinois Institute of Technology, Ludwig Hilbersheimer and Walter Peterhans. During 1957 a second and more serious threat occurred that drew the same advocates, but this time they were joined by architects at SOM as well as supporters throughout the United States and western Europe. Kathryn Smith, "How the Robie House Was Saved," *Frank Lloyd Wright Quarterly* 19 (Fall 2008): 4–19.

15. Goodwin, preface to *Built in USA: 1932–1944*, ed. Mock, 5.

16. McAndrew, "Architecture in the United States," *Bulletin of the Museum of Modern Art* 6, nos. 1–2 (February 1939): 9. For the original essay before revision, see *Trois siècles d'art aux États-Unis*: Exposition organisée en collaboration avec le Museum of Modern Art, New York et Musée du Jeu de Paume. Paris. Mai–Juillet 1938. Editions des Musée Nationaux, 57–77. Fallingwater was reproduced in the French catalog as figure 83, "House on Bear Run."

17. The most pertinent comparisons of Wright's exhibitions with his contemporaries—Le Corbusier, Gropius, and Mies—are the career retrospectives held at MoMA, which were curated by MoMA staff, trustees, and associated historians, and, not the least, by the subjects themselves. *The Recent Work of Le Corbusier*, which was shown October 24–November 2, 1935, was organized by a committee (Goodwin, chair, with Hitchcock, Johnson, Barr, Hudnut, and George Howe), in consultation with the architect. Hitchcock wrote a short essay for the eight-page exhibition brochure. Mardges Bacon, *Le Corbusier in America: Travels in the Land of the Timid* (Cambridge, MA: MIT Press, 2001), 40–47. MoMA's recognition of Gropius came in the form of an exhibition, *The Bauhaus, 1919–1928*, held December 7, 1938, to January 30, 1939, devoted to his pedagogy, which, for various reasons, only covered the history of the school during his years as director. Based on Barr's long-standing admiration of the German school, he chose Gropius, Herbert Bayer, and, to a lesser extent, Marcel Breuer as shapers of the milestone show. While it opened to mixed reviews, MoMA's 224-page illustrated catalog/book of the same title, edited by Bayer, Gropius, and his wife, Ise, became a standard work on the subject. Mary Anne Staniszewski, "The Bauhaus Debacle," in *The Power of Display: A History of Exhibition Installation at the Museum of Modern Art* (Cambridge, MA: MIT Press, 1998), 143–52; Adrijana Sajic, "The Bauhaus as an Educational Model in the United States" (2013) CUNY Academic Works. http://academicworks.cuny.edu/cc_etds_theses/183, 12–13, accessed February 22, 2016. The most successful of the three retrospectives, both for the exhibition and the publication, was *Mies van der Rohe*, presented September 17 to November 23, 1947. It was a collaboration between Mies, who curated and designed the exhibition, and Johnson, the author of the authoritative monograph, which introduced the German architect's body of work, both historically and analytically, to an American audience. Terence Riley, "Making History: Mies van der Rohe and the Museum of Modern Art," in *Mies in Berlin*, ed. Terence Riley and Barry Bergdoll (New York: Museum of Modern Art, 2001), 10–23.

18. The Broadacre City model continued to serve as a catalyst for architectural discourse into the twenty-first century, as was evident with the MoMA exhibition, *Frank Lloyd Wright: Density vs. Dispersal*, February 1–June 1, 2014, curated by Barry Bergdoll.

19. For a summary and analysis, see Emma Barker, "Case Study 5: Exhibiting the Canon; The Blockbuster Show," in *Art and Its Histories: Contemporary Cultures of Display*, ed. Emma Barker (New Haven, CT: Yale University Press in association with the Open University, 1999), 127–46.

20. While most museums in the twentieth century welcomed blockbuster exhibitions, the trustees of the Guggenheim Foundation were reluctant to approve Wright's request to mount *Sixty Years of Living Architecture* in 1953. They only agreed on the proviso that he assume $15,000 of the estimated $25,000 cost. Their cautious stance could have been due to Wright's reputation for exceeding the budget, which proved to be the case.

INDEX